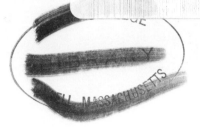

FOREIGN AFFAIRS

BIBLIOGRAPHY

1919-1932

FOREIGN AFFAIRS BIBLIOGRAPHY

A SELECTED AND ANNOTATED LIST OF
BOOKS ON INTERNATIONAL RELATIONS
1919-1932

WILLIAM L. LANGER
Associate Professor of History, Harvard University

HAMILTON FISH ARMSTRONG
Editor, "Foreign Affairs"

New York
RUSSELL & RUSSELL
1960

Printed in the United States of America

PREFACE

THE quarterly review *Foreign Affairs* was founded ten years ago by the Council on Foreign Relations. From the beginning, each issue has contained a selected list of recent books on international affairs. These bibliographies were at first compiled by Dr. Harry Elmer Barnes; but during the past seven years they have been prepared by one of the editors of the present volume. The bibliographies have been found of great value by students of foreign affairs, librarians, diplomats, and organizations of various kinds; so much so, in fact, that at the request of the League of Nations Institute of Intellectual Coöperation they are now printed separately each quarter and sent to many associations throughout the world. In view of the wide usefulness of these individual bibliographies, the Council on Foreign Relations has thought it desirable that they be made the basis for a much more complete and systematized bibliography, so that the student and librarian may have at hand a convenient guide to the vast number of volumes dealing with international relations published since the close of the World War.

It should be understood, however, that the present volume is not a mere rearrangement of the material already published in *Foreign Affairs*. That material goes back only to 1922, whereas the present bibliography includes books published since January 1919. Furthermore, items of minor importance in the quarterly lists have been dropped, while a very large number of titles have been added — especially of books on economic subjects, obscure but nevertheless important works, and books in languages like Russian. The classification is much more detailed, and the annotations have been entirely revised and in many cases expanded.

To present a complete list of all publications of interest to students of international affairs would of course be impracticable. It would fill many volumes. We have therefore been obliged to make a selection. We have on principle excluded all books which do not touch directly on the war and post-war periods. We have in most instances omitted documents of the League of Nations (which are already well listed elsewhere), as well as most governmental documents; in cases where a dearth of information exists, however, we have occasionally included handbooks like those published by the Department of Commerce. We have, generally speaking, excluded propaganda and pamphlet material, though exceptions have been made wherever it seemed advisable. We have included only economic material which seemed to have a distinct international bearing, though often it is impossible to draw a clear-cut line of demarcation. We have tried not to list books of merely local interest—that is, we have taken national and international significance as a criterion. We have omitted books in oriental languages. Travel books presented a special problem; we have omitted those chiefly geographical or anecdotal in character, and have tried to include only those giving a picture of conditions or a discussion of problems.

It is inevitable that in dealing with so large a number of books on so wide a variety of problems we should have made mistakes. No doubt books will still be found in the bibliography which appear to some readers rather insignificant, while other works of importance will be discovered to have been omitted. We expect this, and we regret it. But we hope that those who know something of the difficulties of current bibliography will make allowances.

This volume is designed principally for the use of the American public. We therefore give foreign books in English translation wherever translations exist; and we regularly list an American in preference to an English edition. The transliterations of names from alphabets other than our own as a rule follow the Library of Congress model. The annotations are in the main descriptive and analytical, and are meant to indicate the nature of the book and the competence of the author.

We have done our best to arrange titles according to a logical scheme, but without being arbitrary and with the reader's convenience principally in mind. The analytical table of contents and the cross references should guide the reader to the subject in which he is interested without serious difficulty. The index of authors will aid in locating a specific work.

In the tedious work of classification and checking of titles we have received invaluable aid from Miss Ruth Savord, the librarian of the Council on Foreign Relations, whose expert knowledge and untiring effort made lighter the burden of organizing so much material. We have also had valuable assistance from Mr. Walter H. Mallory and other members of the staff of the Council on Foreign Relations, and from Miss Elizabeth T. Platt, of the staff of the American Geographical Society. Mr. Alexander Kadison has assisted in checking the proofs, and Mr. Michael Karpovich has helped with the transliterations of Slavic names.

Work like that involved in preparing a bibliography can be carried out efficiently only in a great library. We have leaned heavily upon the Harvard College Library, which contains one of the world's finest collections of books on modern history and international relations, built up largely under the supervision of the late Archibald Cary Coolidge, the first editor of *Foreign Affairs*. We are in great debt to the officials of the Library, who have aided us in every possible way.

WILLIAM L. LANGER

HAMILTON FISH ARMSTRONG

September, 1932.

CONTENTS

FIRST PART:
GENERAL INTERNATIONAL RELATIONS

SECOND PART:
THE WORLD WAR

THIRD PART:

THE WORLD

FOURTH PART:

NORTH AND SOUTH AMERICA

FIFTH PART:
EUROPE

SIXTH PART:

ASIA

I. NEAR EAST

II. CENTRAL ASIA AND INDIA

SEVENTH PART:
THE PACIFIC AREA

EIGHTH PART:
POLAR REGIONS   498

NINTH PART:
AFRICA

FIRST PART:

GENERAL INTERNATIONAL RELATIONS

I. GENERAL TREATISES

See also (International Organization) Nationalism and Internationalism, p. 40; also (The World) General Post-War Conditions, p. 163.

ANGELL, SIR NORMAN. **The Public Mind.** New York: Dutton, 1927, 242 p.
A well-known publicist discusses public opinion, its formation and behavior, and possible methods of controlling it.

BARNES, HARRY ELMER. **World Politics and Modern Civilization.** New York: Knopf, 1930, 672 p.
An analysis of some fundamental characteristics of modern society, including nationalism, militarism and imperialism, and their reaction on international relations.

BARTLETT, VERNON. **The World—Our Neighbour.** London: Mathews and Marrot, 1930, 240 p.
A popular review of the conflict between nationalism and internationalism, economic problems, minorities, reparations, etc., by an ardent advocate of the new order.

BRAILSFORD, HENRY NOEL. **Olives of Endless Age.** New York: Harper, 1928, 431 p.
An eloquent plea, by an English radical, for adequate international organs to handle the complex international problems, especially economic, which are too frequently approached in a nationalist attitude.

BROWN, PHILIP MARSHALL. **International Society: Its Nature and Interests.** New York: Macmillan, 1923, 170 p.
A series of essays on many phases of international relations, including law, trade, diplomacy, disputes between nations, war and the League of Nations.

BRYCE, JAMES BRYCE, VISCOUNT. **International Relations.** New York: Macmillan, 1922, 275 p.
Mature reflective generalizations on the chief problems in international relations, such as war and its prevention, popular control of foreign policy, etc.

BUELL, RAYMOND LESLIE. **International Relations.** New York: Holt, rev. ed., 1929, 838 p.
A general textbook treatment.

BURNS, CECIL DELISLE. **International Politics.** London: Methuen, 1920, 189 p.
A brief introduction to problems of international law and organization, by an ardent internationalist.

BURNS, CECIL DELISLE. **Short History of International Intercourse.** New York: Oxford University Press, 1924, 159 p.
A useful primer, arguing for international peace from the utilitarian standpoint.

EDMUNDS, STERLING EDWIN. **The Lawless Law of Nations.** Washington: John Byrne, 1925, 449 p.
Thoughtful but destructive criticism of the present international system, which the author describes as "the last bulwark of absolutism against the political emancipation of man."

GIBBONS, HERBERT ADAMS. **An Introduction to World Politics.** New York: Century, 1922, 595 p.
A general historical introduction to the history of international relations during the 19th and 20th centuries, with much emphasis on colonial expansion and the evolution of world politics.

HARLEY, JOHN EUGENE. **International Understanding.** Stanford: Stanford University Press, 1931, 604 p.
A comprehensive if rather unbalanced survey of agencies which devote themselves to education in international affairs.

HARPER, HEBER REECE. **What European and American Students Think on International Problems.** New York: Teachers College, 1931, 268 p.
A digest of opinion.

HARTWIG, THEODOR. **Der Kosmopolitische Gedanke.** Ludwigsburg: Friede durch Recht, 1924, 216 p.
A good historical survey of the development of the cosmopolitan idea.

KRAUS, HERBERT. **Gedanken über Staatsethos im Internationalen Verkehr.** Berlin: Deutsche Verlagsgesellschaft für Politik und Geschichte, 1925, 206 p.
An original and stimulating lecture on the place of ethics in politics, by a German authority.

LAGARRIGUE, LUIS. **Politique Internationale.** Paris: Garnier, 1928, 281 p.
Another outline of the history of international relations, stressing the gradual improvement during the last centuries and emphasizing the sociological approach.

LION, FERDINAND. **Grosse Politik.** Stuttgart: Deutsche Verlagsanstalt, 1926, 221 p.
An analytical study of the general principles underlying politics, and a philosophical inquiry into the questions of power, agreement, hegemony, etc., as they affect international relations.

LOWELL, ABBOTT LAWRENCE. **Public Opinion in War and Peace.** Cambridge: Harvard University Press, 1923, 303 p.
A scholarly review of the nature and genesis of public opinion, with especial reference to the effect of the war upon political life and activities in England and the United States.

MOON, PARKER THOMAS. **Syllabus on International Relations.** New York: Macmillan, 1925, 280 p.
A manual for college courses.

MOWAT, ROBERT BALMAIN. **International Relations.** London: Rivington, 1931, 180 p.
A brief popular introduction.

POOLE, DEWITT CLINTON. **The Conduct of Foreign Relations under Modern Democratic Conditions.** New Haven: Yale University Press, 1924, 208 p.
Lectures dealing with the technique of foreign relations and the problems and difficulties of democratic control.

POTTER, PITMAN BENJAMIN. **An Introduction to the Study of International Organization.** New York: Century, 1928, 587 p.
The third, revised edition of a comprehensive history and analysis of the machinery and procedure in modern international relations, including diplomacy, treaties, arbitration, international administration, conferences, federations, and the League of Nations.

POTTER, PITMAN BENJAMIN. **This World of Nations.** New York: Macmillan, 1929, 385 p.
An introductory survey of the present international scene, the methods of international relations and the organization of the world for peace.

PRESCOTT, DANIEL ALFRED. **Education and International Relations.** Cambridge: Harvard University Press, 1930, 177 p.
A study of the social forces, institutions and educational influences that determine the popular attitude in international matters.

ROBINSON, JAMES HARVEY. **The Humanizing of Knowledge.** New York: Doran, 1923, 117 p.
A brilliant summary of the conditions and technique requisite for an intelligent study of modern problems, among them that of international relations.

STOKE, HAROLD WALTER. **Foreign Relations of the Federal State.** Baltimore: Johns Hopkins Press, 1931, 246 p.
A much needed examination of the limitations to which federal states are subject in the conduct of international relations, with special regard to the American experience.

STRATTON, GEORGE MALCOLM. **Social Psychology of International Conduct.** New York: Appleton, 1929, 387 p.
An interesting attempt, by a trained psychologist, to analyze the origin and nature of racial prejudices and the formation of national mentalities.

WALSH, EDMUND ALOYSIUS, *ed.* **The History and Nature of International Relations.** New York: Macmillan, 1922, 299 p.
A collection of admirable essays on special phases of international relations, by authorities like Duggan, Rostovtseff, Hayes, Scott, Moore and Rowe.

ZIMMERN, ALFRED ECKHARD. **Study of International Relations.** New York: Oxford University Press, 1931, 27 p.
An inaugural lecture, by a leading student of international problems.

II. GEOGRAPHICAL FACTORS

GENERAL POLITICAL GEOGRAPHY

DIX, ARTHUR. **Politische Geographie.** Munich: Oldenbourg, 1923, 615 p.
The second, revised edition of an excellent manual of world politics.

FAIRGRIEVE, JAMES. **Geography and World Power.** London: University of London Press, 1924, 373 p.
The latest edition of a general historical text.

HENNIG, RICHARD. **Geopolitik.** Leipzig: Teubner, 1928, 338 p.
The first systematic presentation of the new science which attempts to interpret political and international affairs in terms of geographic forces.

LANGHANS-RATZEBURG, MANFRED. **Die Grossen Mächte Geojuristisch Betrachtet.** Munich: Oldenbourg, 1931, 262 p.
The author examines the organization of the world's leading states and attempts to explain their peculiarities by geographical considerations.

MARCHI, LUIGI DE. **Fondamenti di Geografia Politica.** Padua: Milani, 1929, 208 p.
A general handbook of the new geopolitical type.

MAULL, OTTO. **Politische Geographie.** Berlin: Borntraeger, 1925, 743 p.
A standard work of modern anthropogeography.

CIVILIZATIONS AND RACE CONFLICTS
General

See also (League of Nations) Minorities, p. 60; also (United States) Immigration and Race Problems, p. 191; also (Far East) General, p. 460; also (Pacific Area) Australia and New Zealand, p. 492; also (Africa) General Treatises, Race Problems, Missions, p. 501; etc.

BIE, RICHARD. **Diagnose des Zeitalters.** Weimar: Duncker, 1928, 212 p.
A somewhat sensational essay forecasting the domination of the world by four great forces—Catholicism, Nationalism, Americanism and Russianism.

CORNÉJO, MARIANO H. **The Balance of the Continents.** London: Oxford University Press, 1932, 220 p.
World politics from a viewpoint far removed from that of Geneva. The conflict of races envisaged by a French sociologist.

DIXON, ROLAND BURRAGE. **The Racial History of Man.** New York: Scribner, 1923, 583 p.
A substantial descriptive work.

FLETCHER, JOHN GOULD. **Two Frontiers.** New York: Coward-McCann, 1930, 377 p.
A suggestive contrast and comparison of the course of development of American and Russian history and civilization.

GREGORY, JOHN WALTER. **The Menace of Colour.** London: Seeley, 1925, 264 p.
A dispassionate examination of the problem in all parts of the world, with constructive suggestions regarding white colonization of the tropics.

HADDON, ALFRED CORT. **The Races of Man and Their Distribution.** New York: Macmillan, 1925, 200 p.
A new and rewritten edition of a well-known treatise first published in 1909.

HANKINS, FRANK HAMILTON. **The Racial Basis of Civilization.** New York: Knopf, 1926, 394 p.
The Nordic doctrine subjected to critical and scholarly examination.

HERTZ, FRIEDRICH OTTO. **Race and Civilization.** New York: Macmillan, 1928, 340 p.
An Austrian sociologist examines and demolishes recent theories of race superiority. One of the noteworthy books on the subject.

HUNTINGTON, ELLSWORTH. **The Character of Races.** New York: Scribner, 1924, 393 p.
An original interpretation of the modern racial problem in its relation to the geographical environment.

HUNTINGTON, ELLSWORTH. **The Pulse of Progress.** New York: Scribner, 1926, 341 p.
A collection of essays dealing with the influence of environment and climate upon the development of civilization, as well as with racial theories, Jewish history, etc.

KOHN, HANS. **Orient und Okzident.** Berlin: Zentralverlag, 1931, 95 p.
A popular account of the impact of western culture upon the eastern nations, written by one of the foremost students of the problem.

LEGENDRE, AIMÉ FRANÇOIS. **Tour d'Horizon Mondiale.** Paris: Payot, 1920, 319 p.
The future of the white race threatened by the menace of Asia. A most interesting book, written by an eminent French Sinologue.

MARVIN, FRANCIS SYDNEY, *ed.* **Western Races and the World.** Oxford: Oxford University Press, 1922, 264 p.
A collection of valuable papers on the interaction of European and non-European civilizations from ancient to modern times.

MATHEWS, BASIL. **The Clash of Colour.** New York: Doran, 1924, 176 p.
Written from the missionary standpoint, but nevertheless a well-balanced introduction.

MILLER, HERBERT ADOLPHUS. **Races, Nations and Classes.** Philadelphia: Lippincott, 1924, 213 p.
Examining a large variety of group conflicts and racial problems, the author comes to the conclusion that such conflicts can never be settled by force, but only by the development of ideas and attitudes capable of correlation.

MUNTZ, ERAL EDWARD. **Race Contact.** New York: Century, 1927, 384 p.
A general sociological text, summarizing conditions and problems in the Americas, the Pacific area and Africa.

MURET, MAURICE. **The Twilight of the White Races.** New York: Scribner, 1926, 286 p.
A stimulating book reviewing the great cultural struggles of the past and foreshadowing the downfall of western civilization.

OLDHAM, JOSEPH HOULDSWORTH. **Christianity and the Race Problem.** New York: Doran, 1924, 300 p.
A sane discussion of the racial problem from the Christian standpoint, by the editor of the *International Review of Missions.*

PITT-RIVERS, GEORGE HENRY LANE FOX. **The Clash of Culture and the Contact of Races.** London: Routledge, 1927.
A scientific study centering chiefly on the problems of adaptability, depopulation and survival.

PITTARD, EUGÈNE. **Les Races et l'Histoire.** Paris: La Renaissance du Livre, 1924, 640 p.
A sound book, representing the moderate race theory and taking the stand that we are still in the investigating stage. One of the volumes in the Évolution de l'Humanité series.

SPENGLER, OSWALD. **The Decline of the West.** New York: Knopf, 1926-1928, 2 v.
The English translation of the most discussed and probably the most original of recent writings on the philosophy of history.

STODDARD, LOTHROP. **The Rising Tide of Color against World Supremacy.** New York: Scribner, 1920, 320 p.
One of the most provocative treatments of the world color problem, striking in presentation if not always sound on details.

TAYLOR, GRIFFITH. **Environment and Race.** New York: Oxford University Press, 1927, 370 p.
An exhaustive treatise on the evolution, migration, settlement and present status of the races of man, by an Australian professor.

Jewish Problem

See also (League of Nations) Minorities, p. 60; also (United States) Immigration and Race Problems, p. 191; also (Russia) Minorities, p. 396; also (Near East) Palestine, p. 433.

BROWNE, LEWIS. **The Story of the Jews.** London: Cape, 1926, 319 p.
A general survey of a popular nature.

DUBNOV, SEMEN MARKOVICH. **Die Neueste Geschichte des Jüdischen Volkes, 1789-1914.** Berlin: Jüdischer Verlag, 1920-1923, 3 v.
The standard history of the Jews in modern times.

FRIEDMAN, ELISHA MICHAEL. **Survival or Extinction.** New York: Seltzer, 1924, 297 p.
A collection of addresses and essays surveying various aspects of the Jewish question from the sociological angle, analyzing the Zionist movement, etc. A stimulating volume.

KALLEN, HORACE MEYER. **Frontiers of Hope.** New York: Liveright, 1929, 452 p.
Penetrating travel impressions, dealing primarily with the position of the Jews in
the Near East, in Poland and in Russia.

KREPPEL, JONAS. **Juden und Judentum von Heute.** Zurich: Amalthea, 1925, 891 p.
A ponderous statistical and demographic work dealing with the situation of the Jews
before, during and since the war, with special reference to Eastern Europe and Palestine. The author is a Zionist.

LAMBELIN, ROGER. **Le Péril Juif.** Paris: Grasset, 1924-1928, 3 v.
A rather sensational account of the Jews in England and the United States, their
"imperialism" and their victories.

LEWISOHN, LUDWIG. **Israel.** New York: Liveright, 1925, 294 p.
A thoughtful and beautifully written historical interpretation of the rôle and mission
of the Jew.

MARGOLIS, MAX LEOPOLD and MARX, ALEXANDER. **A History of the Jewish People.**
Philadelphia: Jewish Publication Society, 1927, 752 p.
A substantial general survey, covering the entire field.

SACHAR, ABRAM LEON. **A History of the Jews.** New York: Knopf, 1930, 408 p.
Probably the best one-volume introductory survey in English, commendable especially
for the effort made to put Jewish history in the larger setting and to stress social
and economic aspects.

TRAUB, MICHEL. **Jüdische Wanderbewegungen vor und nach dem Weltkriege.**
Berlin: Jüdischer Verlag, 1930, 142 p
Chiefly a discussion of the post-war migrations of Jews to the New World.

POPULATION PROBLEMS
General

CARR-SAUNDERS, ALEXANDER MORRIS. **Population.** New York: Oxford University
Press, 1925, 111 p.
An admirable popular introduction, stressing the connection of population problems
with international relations. The author is Professor of Social Science at Liverpool
University.

COX, HAROLD. **The Problem of Population.** London: Cape, 1923, 198 p.
The writer, who strongly favors controlling population, is here concerned primarily
with the question of social progress. He was formerly editor of the *Edinburgh Review*.

EAST, EDWARD MURRAY. **Mankind at the Crossroads.** New York: Scribner, 1923,
360 p.
A stimulating contribution to the relation between problems of population and world
politics, by a well-known American biologist.

GINI, CORRADO and others. **Population.** Chicago: Chicago University Press, 1930,
312 p.
Norman Wait Harris Lectures, touching upon some of the most vital questions of
politics and international relations.

KNIBBS, SIR GEORGE HANDLEY. **The Shadow of the World's Future.** London: Benn,
1928, 128 p.
An impressive essay on the world population problem by an eminent Australian
statistician whose outlook is gloomy.

MARÒI, LANFRANCO. **I Fattori Demografici del Conflitto Europeo.** Rome: Athenæum,
1919, 595 p.
A substantial study of the demographic factors in the pre-war international tension,
with special reference to France, Germany and Austria-Hungary.

PITT-RIVERS, GEORGE HENRY LANE FOX, *ed*. **Problems of Population.** London: Allen and Unwin, 1932, 369 p.
Papers read at the 1931 meeting of the International Union for the Scientific Investigation of Population Problems.

REUTER, EDWARD BYRON. **Population Problems.** Philadelphia: Lippincott, 1923, 338 p.
This manual includes sections on immigration and race mixture.

ROSS, EDWARD ALSWORTH. **Standing Room Only?** New York: Century, 1927, 368 p.
A general, rather popularized consideration of the population problem and of international migration, by an American sociologist.

THOMPSON, WARREN SIMPSON. **Danger Spots in World Population.** New York: Knopf, 1929, 364 p.
The author, director of the Scripps Foundation for Research in Population Problems, surveys urgent population questions in Japan, China, India, Italy, etc., and considers present tendencies and prospects. The Pacific area, Australia, South Africa and other sparsely settled regions are viewed from the standpoint of possible colonization.

VIRGILII, FILIPPO. **Il Problema della Popolazione.** Milan: Vallardi, 1924, 600 p.
A scholarly, documented history of the Malthusian controversy, with a survey of developments in the 19th and 20th centuries.

WRIGHT, HAROLD. **Population.** New York: Harcourt, 1923, 180 p.
One of the Cambridge Economic Handbooks; one of the most unbiased introductions to the subject in English.

International Migrations

See also (United States) Immigration and Race Problems, p. 191.

BROWN, JOHN WILLIAM. **World Migration and Labour.** Amsterdam: International Federation of Trade Unions, 1926, 398 p.
The general world situation surveyed by the secretary of the International Federation of Trade Unions, in preparation for the World Migration Congress of 1926.

BRYAS, MADELEINE DE. **Les Migrations Politiques et Économiques en Europe depuis la Guerre Mondiale.** Paris: Pedone, 1926, 224 p.
A useful general summary of post-war population shifts, including the Russian emigration, the Greek-Bulgar and Greek-Turk exchanges, the Armenian refugees, etc.

CAMPBELL, PERSIA CRAWFORD. **Chinese Coolie Emigration to Countries within the British Empire.** London: King, 1924, 240 p.
A scholarly account of one of the worst chapters in the history of international migrations.

GREGORY, JOHN WALTER. **Human Migration and the Future.** Philadelphia: Lippincott, 1928, 215 p.
A general treatment by a qualified and interesting writer.

International Migrations. New York: National Bureau of Economic Research, 1929, 1931, 2 v.
A very elaborate and exhaustive study sponsored by the National Bureau of Economic Research and compiled for the International Labor Office. This fundamental work brings together not only all available statistics, assembled with the aid of many governments, but also a large number of interpretative monographs based upon the statistics.

JEROME, HARRY. **Migration and Business Cycles.** New York: National Bureau of Economic Research, 1926, 256 p.
An exhaustive scientific examination of the interaction of business conditions and immigration and emigration.

MacLEAN, ANNIE MARION. **Modern Immigration.** Philadelphia: Lippincott, 1925, 405 p.
A first-rate examination of the immigration question in the United States, Latin America and the British Empire.

MacNAIR, HARLEY FARNSWORTH. **The Chinese Abroad.** Shanghai: Commercial Press, 1924, 340 p.
A juristic and social study of Chinese emigration and the relations of the Chinese government to its nationals abroad.

COLONIAL POLICIES

See also (Economic Factors) Imperialism, p. 11; also (Great Britain) Imperial Relations, p. 231; also (France) Colonial Questions, p. 270; also (Italy) Foreign and Colonial Policies, p. 283; also (Spain) Colonial Policy, p. 297; also (Germany) The Question of Colonies, p. 336; also (Africa) British Possessions, p. 508, French Possessions, p. 514, Italian Possessions, p. 525, Belgian Possessions, p. 526, Portuguese Possessions, p. 528.

ANGELO, VITO. **Introduzione allo Studio del Diritto Coloniale.** Milan: Dante Alighieri, 1930, 181 p.
A general survey of the international status of colonies and of their legal relationship to the motherland.

CESARI, CESARE. **Colonie e Possedimenti Coloniali.** Rome: Tipografia Regionale, 1930, 600 p.
The fifth, revised edition of a general survey of the colonial empires of the world.

HARRIS, JOHN H. **Slavery or "Sacred Trust"?** London: Williams and Norgate, 1926, 195 p.
A well-informed account of modern slavery, with a plea for a thoroughgoing revision of the colonial and native policies of the European Powers.

JOHNSTON, SIR HARRY HAMILTON. **The Backward Peoples and Our Relations with Them.** New York: Oxford University Press, 1920, 64 p.
An introduction, written by a famous British explorer and administrator, who till his death continued to stand by the theory of the "White Man's Burden."

KAT ANGELINO, ARNOLD DIRK ADRIAAN DE. **Colonial Policy.** Chicago: Chicago University Press, 1931, 2 v.
The first volume of this impressive work is concerned with the general principles of colonial administration, the second with the Dutch system in the East Indies.

KEY, HELMER. **The New Colonial Policy.** London: Methuen, 1927, 214 p.
The author, a thoughtful writer on population problems, sees in the development of colonies and the creation of new markets the only hope for a solution of Europe's economic ills.

LINDLEY, MARK FRANK. **The Acquisition and Government of Backward Territories in International Law.** New York: Longmans, 1926, 411 p.
An exhaustive, scholarly treatise.

NALDONI, NARDO. **La Politica Economico-Coloniale nell' Epoca Moderna.** Rome: Signorelli, 1930, 151 p.
A critical comparative study of the colonial economic policies of Powers like Spain, Holland, France, England, Russia and Germany.

SARRAUT, ALBERT. **Grandeur et Servitude Coloniales.** Paris: Éditions du Sagittaire, 1931.
An important book on general colonial policy, by a former French colonial minister, who calls upon Europe to protect her colonial heritage from assaults in the form of national movements.

SUCHER, ERNST. **Beseitigung der Kolonialmacht.** Wiesbaden: Friede durch Recht, 1927, 228 p.
A review of the colonial systems of modern times and a passionate plea for the liberation of the exploited "backward" races.

III. ECONOMIC FACTORS
ECONOMIC CONDITIONS AND TENDENCIES
General

BALLOD, KARL. **Der Bankerott der Freien Wirtschaft und die Notwendigen Finanz- und Wirtschaftsreformen.** Jena: Thüringer Verlagsanstalt, 1924.
A famous economist's bitter attack on the manœuvres of Big Business since the war, and suggestions as to how its influence may be broken.

BARKER, J. ELLIS. **Economic Statesmanship.** New York: Dutton, 1920, 624 p.
One of the best English analyses of the great economic problems of the world just after the war.

BOWLEY, ARTHUR LYON. **Some Economic Consequences of the Great War.** London: Butterworth, 1930, 252 p.
The author sets in high relief the destructive effects and general economic disruption resulting from the great conflict. A volume in the Home University Library Series.

CARVER, THOMAS NIXON and LESTER, HUGH WETZEL. **This Economic World and How It May Be Improved.** Chicago: Shaw, 1928, 438 p.
Two well-known economists discuss various current problems in a refreshing and original way.

CULBERTSON, WILLIAM SMITH. **International Economic Policies.** New York: Appleton, 1925, 593 p.
One of the best treatments of post-war policies, by a former member of the United States Tariff Commission.

DELAISI, FRANCIS. **Political Myths and Economic Realities.** New York: Viking, 1927, 463 p.
The author, a French economist, sets out to demolish the "myth" of nationalism by putting it in its proper setting. The modern world is based primarily on economic foundations, and the result of industrialism has been to make all parts of the world interdependent. Under the circumstances the "polytheism of sovereignties" has become a dangerous anomaly and no satisfactory solution of such problems as war can be expected without a readjustment of the world order.

DONALDSON, JOHN. **International Economic Relations.** New York: Longmans, 1928, 704 p.
An excellent and very inclusive text. The author, an expert on commercial problems, discusses geographic, political and legal aspects, as well as foreign trade, world trusts, raw materials, and problems of monopolies and control.

EINZIG, PAUL. **The World Economic Crisis, 1929-1931.** New York: Macmillan, 1931, 177 p.
An analysis by a facile writer on finance and economic problems.

GARVIN, JAMES LOUIS. **The Economic Foundations of Peace.** London: Macmillan, 1919, 574 p.
The editor of the *Observer* reviews the economic situation at the close of the war and shows the need for world partnership in the economic as in the political sphere.

HADLEY, ARTHUR TWINING. **The Economic Problems of Democracy.** New York: Macmillan, 1923, 162 p.
Suggestive essays on national and international problems, delivered as the Watson Lectures under the auspices of the Anglo-American Society.

HANSEN, ALVIN HARVEY. **Economic Stabilization in an Unbalanced World.** New York: Harcourt, 1932, 384 p.
The book is in four parts, dealing in turn with reparations, tariff, Russian dumping; unemployment; population stabilization; stabilized capitalism.

HANTOS, ELEMÉR. **L'Économie Mondiale et la Société des Nations.** Paris: Giard, 1930, 384 p.
Possibilities of the League as a factor in solving the economic problems of Europe.

HANTOS, ELEMÉR. **Die Weltwirtschaftskonferenz.** Leipzig: Gloeckner, 1928, 205 p.
A history of the Economic Conference of 1927 and an analysis of its results, by a protagonist of international coöperation. Contains a good bibliography.

HARMS, BERNHARD. **Vom Wirtschaftskrieg zur Weltwirtschaftskonferenz.** Jena: Fischer, 1927, 359 p.
A collection of addresses by a German economist, delivered between 1916 and 1927, dealing with the post-war crisis, the Dawes Plan and the Economic Conference of 1927.

JOFFE, A. A. **Genuesskaia Konferentsiia.** Moscow: Krasnaia Nov', 1922, 62 p.
The Genoa Conference, as viewed by a leading Bolshevik diplomat.

LYAUTEY, PIERRE. **La Bataille Économique.** Paris: Éditions Géographiques, 1929, 286 p.
An interesting and well-informed study of the post-war economic situation, with special reference to the problems of France.

MILLS, JOHN SAXON. **The Genoa Conference.** New York: Dutton, 1922, 436 p.
The policies and activities of Lloyd George at the Conference described in eulogistic fashion. The volume contains some valuable documents.

NEARING, SCOTT. **The Next Step.** Ridgewood: Author, 1922, 175 p.
A well-known American anti-imperialist puts forth a strong argument for world economic organization.

PAGE, KIRBY, ed. **A New Economic Order.** New York: Harcourt, 1930, 387 p.
A collection of essays dealing with questions like capitalism, Fascism, communism and socialism.

PAISH, SIR GEORGE. **The Road to Prosperity.** New York: Putnam, 1927, 179 p.
The author, a noted English financier, contrasts the international loans so popular after the war with the loans made for productive purposes in the pre-war period, and comes to the conclusion that future stability will depend in large part on the elimination of trade barriers and a return to a non-political basis of international finance.

PAISH, SIR GEORGE. **The Way to Recovery.** New York: Putnam, 1931, 169 p.
A searching analysis of the world crisis.

PATTERSON, ERNEST MINOR. **The World's Economic Dilemma.** New York: McGraw-Hill, 1930, 330 p.
A broad, competent study of the perennial problem presented by a competitive world organized on a national basis. The author discusses population pressure, larger-scale production, international finance, struggles for raw materials, etc. He concludes that action can perhaps best be taken through better commercial treaties, development of international trusts and consortiums, and more strenuous action by Chambers of Commerce.

A Picture of World Economic Conditions. New York: National Industrial Conference Board, 1928 ff.
A useful periodic publication surveying the situation in various parts of the world.

PRICE, MORGAN PHILIPS. **The Economic Problems of Europe, Pre-War and After.** New York: Macmillan, 1928, 218 p.
The writer analyzes the movement of capital during the last generation and discusses its effects on world economy.

RAYNAUD, BARTHÉLEMY. **La Vie Économique Internationale.** Paris: Sirey, 1926, 491 p.
An excellent survey by a French protagonist of coöperation.

RICHARDSON, JOHN HENRY. **Economic Disarmament.** London: Allen and Unwin, 1931, 224 p.
The author reëxamines the questions of tariffs, labor, large-scale industry and international finance from a thoroughgoing internationalist standpoint.

SALTER, SIR ARTHUR and others. **The Economic Consequences of the League.** London: Europa Publishing Co., 1928, 235 p.
A collection of articles, by experts, on the world situation in 1927 and the League's Economic Conference. The report of the Conference is printed in an appendix.

SALTER, SIR ARTHUR. **Recovery. The Second Effort.** New York: Century, 1932, 353 p.
This book, by the former economic and financial expert of the League, has been widely read and earnestly commented upon. It is characterized by thorough knowledge and breadth of view.

SOMARY, FELIX. **Changes in the Structure of World Economics since the War.** London: King, 1931, 221 p.
A stimulating series of essays by a European banker.

VIALLATE, ACHILLE. **Le Monde Économique, 1918-1927.** Paris: Rivière, 1928, 260 p.
One of the best general books on post-war economic developments, problems and possible solutions, by a professor at the École des Sciences Politiques.

WHELPLEY, JAMES DAVENPORT. **Reconstruction.** New York: Funk, 1925, 383 p.
A keen appraisal of conditions in the countries most affected by the war.

WILLIAMS, HERBERT GERAINT. **Politics and Economics.** London: Murray, 1926, 179 p.
A good exposition of the increasing importance of economic factors in shaping the destiny of society.

WRIGHT, QUINCY, ed. **Unemployment as a World-Problem.** Chicago: Chicago University Press, 1931, 261 p.
Three lectures under the Norman Wait Harris Foundation. Keynes gives an economic analysis of unemployment, Pribram surveys world unemployment, with emphasis on conditions in Germany, while Phelan discusses international machinery for coping with the problem.

Imperialism

See also (Geographical Factors) Colonial Policies, p. 8.

BRAILSFORD, HENRY NOEL. **After the Peace.** New York: Seltzer, 1922, 158 p.
Capitalistic imperialism arraigned by a leading English radical, who urges the adoption of thoroughgoing economic internationalism.

BUKHARIN, NIKOLAÏ IVANOVICH. **Imperialism and World Economy.** New York: International Publishers, 1929, 173 p.
A handy English translation of the classic Bolshevist indictment of imperialism.

EVOLA, GIULIO CESARE ANDREA. **Imperialismo Pagano.** Rome: Atanor, 1928, 160 p.
Europe must be freed from the democratic Christian tradition. Back to pagan imperialism and the *Machtstaat.*

HOVIKIAN, ARTAKI. **L'Impérialisme Économique d'après les Doctrines Socialistes Contemporaines.** Paris: Jouve, 1927, 139 p.
The author examines the theories of dumping, export of capital, foreign loans and other phenomena of economic imperialism and concludes that the entire theory of economic imperialism is part and parcel of socialist theory.

LA BRIÈRE, YVES DE. **Les Grands Impérialismes Contemporains.** Antwerp: 1925, 72 p.
Suggestive essays on English, German and American imperialism.

MOON, PARKER THOMAS. **Imperialism and World Politics.** New York: Macmillan, 1926, 583 p.
The best general account of imperialism and its recent expression, by a Professor of International Relations at Columbia University.

NEARING, SCOTT. **The Twilight of Empire.** New York: Vanguard, 1930, 350 p.
An economic interpretation of imperialist cycles, by a well-known radical.

PASHUKANIS, E. B. **Imperializm i Kolonial'naia Politika.** Moscow: Communist Academy, 1928, 118 p.
A series of lectures at Moscow University, dealing chiefly with the economics of imperialism.

PAVLOVICH, M. *pseud.* (MIKHAIL VEL'TMAN). **Sobranie Sochineniĭ. Imperializm i Mirovaia Politika Poslednikh Desiatiletiĭ.** Leningrad: Gosizdat, 1925.
Contains: Volume I. Imperialism (248 p.); II. Imperialism and the Struggle for Control of Railways and Waterways (256 p.); III. The Struggle for Asia and Africa (257 p.); V. The World War, 1914-1918. A course of lectures by the leading communist writer on the history of imperialism.

PAVLOVICH, M. *pseud.* (MIKHAIL VEL'TMAN). **The Foundations of Imperialist Policy.** London: Labour Publishing Company, 1922, 159 p.
A translation of Volume I of the preceding title.

PEFFER, NATHANIEL. **The White Man's Dilemma.** New York: Day, 1927, 312 p.
The economic side of imperialism discussed without recriminations. A well-informed and convincingly written volume.

ROSENTAL', P. A. **Za Kolonii i Mirovye Puti.** Moscow: Kniga, 1923, 252 p.
The first part of an extended study of the world struggle for colonies and communications.

SALZ, ARTHUR. **Das Wesen des Imperialismus.** Leipzig: Teubner, 1931, 201 p.
An interesting though rather inadequate attempt to establish the theory of imperialism and to derive it from ideas of power, nationalism, honor, etc.

STERNBERG, FRITZ. **Der Imperialismus.** Berlin: Malik, 1926, 614 p.
A full-length indictment of imperialism, by a vigorous Marxist.

VIALLATE, ACHILLE. **L'Impérialisme Économique.** Paris: Colin, 1923, 316 p.
An excellent summary of the international clash of economic interests in the pre-war and war periods.

WOOLF, LEONARD SIDNEY. **Economic Imperialism.** New York: Harcourt, 1920, 111 p.
A brilliant popular introduction to the subject, by a well-informed opponent of imperialism.

Woolf, Leonard Sidney. **Imperialism and Civilization.** New York: Harcourt, 1928, 182 p.

An excellent brief survey of the history of European imperialism in Asia and Africa. The author sees the only solution through the agency of the League, which alone can establish a synthesis of civilizations.

INTERNATIONAL TRADE; TARIFFS; CARTELS

General

See also (United States) Foreign Trade and Tariffs, p. 187; also (Europe) Pan-European Schemes, p. 229; also (Central Europe) Middle European Schemes, p. 299.

Angell, James Waterhouse. **The Theory of International Prices.** Cambridge: Harvard University Press, 1926, 571 p.

An exhaustive monograph dealing with the history of the theory and submitting a restatement. Probably the best single book on the subject.

Ashley, Percy Walter. **Modern Tariff History.** New York: Dutton, 1926, 365 p.

The latest edition of a well-known historical survey of the policies of Germany, the United States and France.

Beveridge, Sir William Henry, *ed.* **Tariffs: The Case Examined.** New York: Longmans, 1931, 301 p.

Essays by English economists reviewing the whole question of tariffs and free trade in language intelligible to the layman.

Boggs, Theodore Harding. **The International Trade Balance.** New York: Macmillan, 1923, 221 p.

A technical study of the nature and significance of the balance of trade in world commerce, based on the experience of the United States and the British Empire.

Bonhoeffer, Klaus. **Die Meistbegünstigung im Modernen Voelkerrecht.** Berlin: Springer, 1930, 64 p.

A scholarly study of the legal aspects of the most-favored-nation clause.

Cabiati, Attilio. **Principi di Politica Commerciale.** Genoa: Stabilimento Grafico Editoriale, 1924, 302 p.

This first volume of a large authoritative work deals with the general theory of foreign exchange.

Chiati, Mahmoud Badawi. **Les Ententes Industrielles Internationales.** Paris: Montparnasse, 1928, 199 p.

Not so much a descriptive study of international economic understandings as an examination of their objects, limits, effects, etc.

Daye, Pierre. **L'Europe en Morceaux.** Paris: Plon, 1932.

A brief treatment of the serious European tariff situation.

Dechesne, Laurent. **Économie Mondiale et Protectionnisme.** Paris: Sirey, 1927, 127 p.

A concise statement of the interrelationship of tariffs and problems of reconstruction.

Delle-Donne, Ottavio. **European Tariff Policies since the World War.** New York: Adelphi, 1928, 288 p.

After outlining the tariff situation as it existed in 1914, the author surveys the various war measures and the acute situation of the post-war period, closing with a discussion of the Economic Conference. A careful, scholarly work.

DENNIS, ALFRED PEARCE. **The Romance of World Trade.** New York: Holt, 1926, 493 p.
A general text covering all phases of foreign trade as they touch the United States, by a former vice-chairman of the Tariff Commission.

ESSLEN, JOSEPH BERGFRIED. **Die Politik des Auswärtigen Handels.** Stuttgart: Enke, 1925, 368 p.
A general text covering all phases of foreign trade, together with a history of tariff policies.

FEILER, ARTHUR. **Neue Weltwirtschaft.** Frankfurt: Societäts-Druckerei, 1927, 83 p.
A concise statement of the League policy with respect to tariffs and world trade, with the report of the Economic Conference of 1927.

FRASER, HERBERT FREEMAN. **Foreign Trade and World Politics.** New York: Knopf, 1926, 359 p.
An introduction to the principles and problems of foreign trade. A commendable effort to bind up the economic problems of the post-war period with the political factors lying behind them.

GEALE, ROBERT GEORGE. **International Commerce and Economic Theory.** London: King, 1925, 171 p.
An able presentation of the discrepancies between theory and practice in international commerce.

GENZMER, HANS. **Die Bestrebungen zur Schaffung eines International-Einheitlichen Zolltarifschemas.** Bigge: Josefs-Druckerei, 1929, 230 p.
A substantial dissertation, giving the pre-war and post-war history of efforts to establish a uniform tariff schedule and an analysis of the problem itself.

GRIFFIN, CLARE ELMER. **The Principles of Foreign Trade.** New York: Macmillan, 1924, 348 p.
A comprehensive economic analysis, stressing the principles and machinery involved.

GROTKOPP, WILHELM. **Breaking Down the Tariff Walls.** London: Benn, 1931, 130 p.
The translation of a stimulating book attacking the present high tariff systems.

GRUNTZEL, JOSEF. **System der Handelspolitik.** Vienna: Springer, 1928, 516 p.
The third edition of one of the best general treatments.

HAWTREY, RALPH GEORGE. **Trade Depression and the Way Out.** London: Longmans, 1931, 84 p.
A high Treasury official in London attempts to elucidate the character and causes of the slump in trade.

HELANDER, SVEN. **Die Internationale Schiffahrtskrise.** Jena: Fischer, 1928, 397 p.
The first adequate account of the development of the international carrying trade since the war. The author examines the effects of the shipping crisis on business and unemployment and puts the problem into the general setting of world economics.

HERMBERG, PAUL. **Der Kampf um den Weltmarkt.** Jena: Fischer, 1920, 135 p.
A purely statistical study of the development of German, British, American and French trade, to illustrate the changing position of these countries in world competition.

HIRST, FRANCIS WRIGLEY. **Safeguarding and Protection.** New York: Macmillan, 1927, 157 p.
A keen criticism of the conservative program in England and of the prohibitive tariff of the United States, by a persuasive English free-trader.

JENT, VIKTOR. **Die Handelspolitischen Bestrebungen des Völkerbundes.** Zurich: Gutzwiller, 1926, 109 p.
A systematic study of the efforts made by the League in the direction of tariff reduction, etc.

JÉRAMEC, JACQUES. **Le Monopole du Commerce Extérieur.** Paris: Librairie Générale de Droit, 1927, 183 p.
A valuable historical and analytical study of state monopolies of foreign trade. The larger part of the volume is devoted to the Russian experiment.

LADAS, STEPHEN PERICLES. **The International Protection of Industrial Property.** Cambridge: Harvard University Press, 1930, 987 p.
An indispensable volume for those interested in the legal aspects of foreign trade.

LEBÉE, EDMOND CHARLES ÉTIENNE. **Trusts et Cartels Internationaux.** Paris: Hachette, 1929, 104 p.
An admirable survey of the greatest international enterprises, which the author considers as valuable agents in reducing friction.

LEVY, HERMANN. **Der Weltmarkt 1913 und Heute.** Leipzig: Teubner, 1926, 116 p.
A good documented essay on the evolution of the world market as a result of the war and the post-war economic legislation.

LIEFMANN, ROBERT. **International Cartels, Combines and Trusts.** London: Europa Publishing Company, 1927, 152 p.
An illuminating survey of an urgent problem, based upon the discussions of the International Economic Conference.

MAGNIER, LÉON. **La Chambre de Commerce Internationale.** Paris: Rousseau, 1928, 138 p.
A convenient brief account of the organization and its work.

MANOÏLESCO, MIHAÏL. **Théorie du Protectionnisme et de l'Échange International.** Paris: Giard, 1929, 382 p.
An interesting contribution, by a former Rumanian Under-Secretary of Finance.

MELCHINGER, EUGEN. **Die Internationale Preisbildung.** Tübingen: Mohr, 1929, 125 p.
A well-documented technical essay to establish a theory of international prices within the larger frame of the theory of international trade.

PILAVACHI, ARISTOCLÈS C. **La Politique Douanière des Trois Principaux États Européens et Celle de la Société des Nations.** Paris: Guillon, 1928, 420 p.
A general review of the post-war tariff policies of France, Great Britain and Germany, followed by an account of the efforts made by the League to alleviate tariff difficulties.

RIEDL, RICHARD. **Die Meistbegünstigung in den Europäischen Handelsverträgen.** Vienna: International Chamber of Commerce, 1928, 115 p.
An admirable study of the most-favored-nation treatment in European tariff treaties, submitted to the Economic Committee of the League by the Austrian branch of the International Chamber of Commerce.

RÖPKE, WILHELM. **Weltwirtschaft und Aussenhandelspolitik.** Berlin: Spaeth und Linde, 1931, 105 p.
A very compact and concise introductory text, with much emphasis on the theoretical side.

SARTORIUS VON WALTERSHAUSEN, AUGUST, FREIHERR. **Die Weltwirtschaft.** Leipzig: Gloeckner, 1926, 416 p.
A thoroughly reliable handbook of world trade, by one of the foremost German authorities.

SHTEĬN, B. **Torgovaia Politika Zapadno-Evropeĭskikh Gosudarstv posle Voiny.** Moscow: Gosizdat, 239 p.
A careful study of the trade policies of the Western European states after the war.

STOLZMANN, RUDOLF. **Theoretische Grundfragen zum Problem Freihandel oder Schutzzoll?** Jena: Fischer, 1927, 109 p.
The question of free trade or protection considered in the broadest possible setting of economic theory, by a competent German authority.

TAUSSIG, FRANK WILLIAM. **International Trade.** New York: Macmillan, 1927, 425 p.
A general text, probably the best introduction available in English. The author, Professor of Political Economy at Harvard, was Chairman of the United States Tariff Commission, 1917-1919.

VINER, JACOB. **Dumping: A Problem in International Trade.** Chicago: University of Chicago Press, 1923, 343 p.
An important economic analysis, including a discussion of the bearing of the problem on international relations. Probably the best single treatment of an increasingly urgent question. By a Professor of Economics at the University of Chicago.

VLEESCHHOUWER, J. E. **Actieve Handelspolitiek.** Hague: Nijhoff, 1927, 251 p.
A thoroughly documented survey of the tariff policies of Switzerland, Czechoslovakia, France, Belgium, England and the United States, and their results, followed by a general argument for free trade.

Raw Materials Problem
General

FURNESS, JAMES W. and JONES, LEWIS M. **Mineral Raw Materials: Survey of Commerce and Sources in Major Industrial Countries.** Washington: Department of Commerce, 1929, 278 p.
A handbook, surveying by countries the sources of raw materials, with production statistics; prepared for the Bureau of Foreign and Domestic Commerce.

GLIWIC, HIPOLIT. **Podstawy Ekonomiki Światowej.** Warsaw: Naktadem Tygodnika Przemyst i Handel, 1928.
Volume I of a general treatise on world economics. The author here discusses the question of the supply of raw materials.

KILLOUGH, HUGH BAXTER and MRS. LUCY (WINSOR). **Raw Materials of Industrialism.** New York: Crowell, 1929, 426 p.
A good account of the world situation with regard to raw materials.

LIPPINCOTT, ISAAC. **Economic Resources and Industries of the World.** New York: Appleton, 1929, 656 p.
A general text and reference book surveying the world from the standpoint of raw material supply and industrial development.

REICHWEIN, ADOLF. **Die Rohstoffwirtschaft der Erde.** Jena: Fischer, 1928, 639 p.
An exhaustive handbook of the raw material production of the world.

WALLACE, BENJAMIN BRUCE and EDMINSTER, LYNN RAMSAY. **International Control of Raw Materials.** Washington: Brookings Institution, 1930, 479 p.
A standard account of the major efforts at government control.

Petroleum

APOSTOL, PAUL and MICHELSON, ALEKSANDR MIKHAĬLOVICH. **La Lutte pour le Pétrole et la Russie.** Paris: Payot, 1922, 217 p.
A most valuable and careful study of the Russian oil industry and its place in the larger world problem.

ARNOT, ROBERT PAGE. **The Politics of Oil.** London: Labour Publishing Company, 1924, 94 p.
A syllabus, crammed with statistics, setting forth the radical point of view.

AUDEMAR, JEAN. **Les Maîtres de la Mer, de la Houille et du Pétrole.** Paris: Nouvelle Librairie Nationale, 1923, 288 p.
A conventional study of the Anglo-American antagonism with emphasis on the oil and coal problems.

BRUNNER, CHRISTOPHER TATHAM. **The Problem of Oil.** London: Benn, 1930, 232 p.
An excellent discussion of the oil situation from the British angle, with particular reference to the present uses of oil and the system of distribution.

DAVENPORT, E. H. and COOKE, SIDNEY RUSSELL. **The Oil Trust and Anglo-American Relations.** New York: Macmillan, 1923, 272 p.
A strong argument for the open door policy in developing the world's resources.

DELAISI, FRANCIS. **Oil, Its Influence on Politics.** London: Labour Publishing Company, 1922, 94 p.
A brief but authoritative French account, tracing the British-American conflict and French participation to the San Remo Agreement.

DENNY, LUDWELL. **We Fight for Oil.** New York: Knopf, 1928, 297 p.
A well-documented though somewhat sensational account of the Anglo-American rivalry, with an interesting discussion of the situation in Colombia.

FILHOL, J. and BIHOREAU, CHARLES. **Le Pétrole.** Paris: Éditions Pittoresques, 1929, 207 p.
A competent monograph on the oil industry and its implications for international relations.

FISCHER, LOUIS. **Oil Imperialism.** New York: International Publishers, 1926, 256 p.
A well-informed radical interpretation of one phase of modern imperialism. The author deals in detail with the Russian aspects of the problem.

GARFIAS, VALENTINE RICHARD. **Petroleum Resources of the World.** New York: Wiley, 1923, 243 p.
A valuable handbook by an American engineer of the Bureau of Mines.

GIBBS, LEO VERNON. **Oil and Peace.** Los Angeles: Parker, Stone and Baird, 1930, 204 p.
An attack on the British oil interests.

HOFFMANN, KARL. **Oelpolitik und Angelsächsischer Imperialismus.** Berlin: Ring, 1927, 446 p.
A scientific study of the political aspects of the post-war petroleum situation. One of the most extensive and best treatments.

KRÜGER, KARL and POSCHARDT, G. R. **Die Erdölwirtschaft der Welt.** Stuttgart: Schweizerbart, 1926, 494 p.
An encyclopedic treatise.

L'ESPAGNOL DE LA TRAMERYE, PIERRE. **The World Struggle for Oil.** New York: Knopf, 1924, 259 p.
An analysis of the relation of the raw petroleum supply to diplomacy and international relations. The author reviews the struggle of the great countries, the effects of the war and the negotiations between governments.

LIDGETT, ALBERT. **Petroleum.** London: Pitman, 1928, 160 p.
The third edition of a general handbook.

LÓPEZ, PEDRO N. **Politica Petrolifera.** La Paz: Boliviana, 1929, 409 p.
An up-to-date and complete survey of the situation and the policies of the Powers, with particular reference to Latin America and especially Bolivia.

McBETH, REID SAYERS. **Oil, the New Monarch of Motion.** New York: Markets Publishing Corporation, 1919, 210 p.
A general introductory survey of the history and status of the industry, designed for the layman and investor.

MAUTNER, WILHELM. **Der Kampf um und gegen das Russische Erdöl.** Vienna: Manz, 1929, 261 p.
An important chapter in the story of the world struggle for oil, and at the same time a good account of the post-war petroleum situation in Russia.

MOHR, ANTON. **The Oil War.** New York: Harcourt, 1926, 267 p.
The translation of a somewhat dramatized study.

POMARET, CHARLES. **La Politique Française des Combustibles Liquides.** Paris: La Vie Universitaire, 1922, 418 p.
An exhaustive treatment of French policy in the international struggle as well as of the regulation of the industry within France.

ROSS, VICTOR. **The Evolution of the Oil Industry.** New York: Doubleday, 1920, 178 p.
A popular account of the oil revolution and its effects on industry, shipping and world politics.

SERDARU, VIRGILIU STEF. **Le Pétrole Roumain.** Paris: Jouve, 1921, 168 p.
A survey of the Rumanian industry since 1825, with a study of changing legislation and an analysis of the war and post-war situation.

THOM, WILLIAM TAYLOR, JR. **Petroleum and Coal.** Princeton: Princeton University Press, 1929, 223 p.
Largely a study of two key industries, with relatively little stress on political problems.

TRELLES, CAMILO BARCIA. **El Imperialismo del Petróleo y la Paz Mundial.** Valladolid: "Cuesta," 1925, 253 p.
A good general treatment of the much discussed "oil imperialism."

WOLFF, HELLMUTH. **Die Erdölwirtschaft, 1919-1924.** Leipzig: Hirzel, 1925, 802 p.
The sixth and last volume of an exhaustive study, covering the history of the industry since 1919.

Other Commodities

CAPRARA, UGO. **Il Commercio del Grano.** Milan: Istituto Editoriale Scientifico, 1928, 429 p.
The first volume of an extensive scholarly treatment of the grain trade. This part deals chiefly with the American and Argentine export trade.

JOHNSON, WILLIAM HENRY. **Cotton and Its Production.** London: Macmillan, 1926, 536 p.
An exhaustive authoritative study of the history and cultivation of cotton, with much stress on present conditions of world production.

LAWRENCE, JAMES COOPER. **The World's Struggle with Rubber, 1905-1931.** New York: Harper, 1931, 151 p.
The best general systematic study of the rubber problem and the evolution of international efforts to find a solution.

LEITH, CHARLES KENNETH. **World Minerals and World Politics.** New York: McGraw-Hill, 1931, 213 p.
A well-known geologist places the problem in its general setting in international relations. A valuable introductory study.

MOUTTÉ, FRÉDÉRIC. **La Question de l'Organisation Internationale de l'Industrie Charbonnière.** Paris: Jouve, 1929, 360 p.
A detailed statistical and economic study of the world coal problem and the solutions attempted in various countries, followed by an analysis of League efforts at regulation.

OLIVIER, M. **La Politique du Charbon, 1914-1921.** Paris: Alcan, 1922, 301 p.
A realistic study of the relations of the supply and consumption of coal to the political and diplomatic history of England and France since 1914.

SCHLENKER, MAX. **Die Eisenindustrie in der Welt.** Jena: Fischer, 1927, 34 p.
An instructive essay, discussing the conditions underlying the international iron syndicate.

SMITH, GEORGE OTIS. **The Strategy of Minerals.** New York: Appleton, 1919, 372 p.
An admirable picture of the mineral situation at the close of the war, by the former Director of the United States Geological Survey.

TODD, JOHN AITON. **The Cotton World.** London: Pitman, 1927, 236 p.
A general survey of the world cotton situation, with special reference to Liverpool and Lancashire.

VAN HISSENHOVEN, PAUL. **Le Commerce International des Grains.** Paris: Société d'Éditions Géographiques, 1923, 609 p.
An exhaustive study, with particular stress on the Antwerp grain market.

WARD, JOHN SEBASTIAN MARLOW. **Cotton and Wool.** London: Rider, 1921, 270 p.
A general treatment, covering both production and marketing, with particular emphasis on the British Empire.

WHITTLESEY, CHARLES RAYMOND. **Government Control of Crude Rubber.** Princeton: Princeton University Press, 1931, 235 p.
A criticism of the British experiment in controlling rubber production in the East Indies, by a competent American investigator.

WRIGHT, PHILIP GREEN. **Sugar in Relation to the Tariff.** New York: McGraw-Hill, 1924, 312 p.
The conclusions of an impartial investigator working with the staff of the Institute of Economics. Of value to everyone interested in the tariff, whether as an economic or a political question.

INTERNATIONAL COMMUNICATIONS

BECKMANN, FRITZ. **Die Organisationsformen des Weltfunkverkehrs.** Bonn: Marcus und Weber, 1925, 166 p.
An original discussion of radio as an international problem.

BÜHLER, HANS. **Der Weltpostverein.** Berlin: Dümmler, 1930, 197 p.
A careful monograph on the working of the International Postal Union.

CLARK, KEITH. **International Communications. The American Attitude.** New York: Columbia University Press, 1931, 261 p.
A study of the evolution of international posts, telegraphs and wireless, with an analysis of the American policy in the organization of these services.

GUÉRARD, ALBERT LÉON. **A Short History of the International Language Movement.** New York: Boni, 1922, 268 p.
An account of the efforts to establish an international language.

HARTE VAN TECKLENBURG, J. J. H. **International Transitrecht.** Hague: Mouton, 1925, 196 p.
The best general treatment of this important aspect of international communications.

PLANAS-SUÁREZ, SIMÓN. **La Sociedad de las Naciones y la Conferencia de Barcelona.** Lisbon: Centro Tipográfico Colonial, 1922, 149 p.
A reliable summary of the Barcelona Conference of 1921 on communications and transit.

RAJKOVIĆ, S. **Le Régime International des Voies Ferrées et la Société des Nations.** Paris: Sagot, 1925, 204 p.
A conventional account of more recent developments in European international railway traffic.

RISTOW, ALFRED. **Die Internationale Entwicklung und Bedeutung der Funken-telegraphie.** Königsberg: Ebering, 1926, 132 p.
A well-documented dissertation surveying the development and present international status of radio.

SALOM, GIULIO. **Le Radiocommunicazioni nel Diritto Internazionale.** Padua: Milani, 1927, 161 p.
A scholarly study dealing primarily with the projected Washington convention.

SCHWEDLER, W. **Die Nachricht im Weltverkehr.** Berlin: Deutsche Verlagsgesellschaft für Politik und Geschichte, 1922, 133 p.
An interesting account of the international news apparatus, with an appeal for a higher type of service free from propaganda.

SHENTON, HERBERT NEWHARD, SAPIR, EDWARD and JESPERSEN, OTTO. **International Communication.** London: Kegan Paul, 1931, 120 p.
A symposium on the problems of an international language.

TRIBOLET, LESLIE BENNETT. **The International Aspects of Electrical Communications in the Pacific Area.** Baltimore: Johns Hopkins Press, 1929, 282 p.
A valuable scholarly monograph which takes into account private as well as public enterprises.

VISSCHER, CHARLES DE. **Le Droit International des Communications.** Paris: Rousseau, 1924, 151 p.
The standard treatise on the subject.

INTERNATIONAL FINANCE
General

AFTALION, ALBERT. **Monnaie, Prix et Change.** Paris: Sirey, 1927, 353 p.
An admirable general account of post-war developments, together with an analysis of the new theories of money and exchange.

AFTALION, ALBERT. **L'Or et Sa Distribution Mondiale.** Paris: Dalloz, 1932, 235 p.
The author, a professor at the University of Paris, deals with the maldistribution of gold and points out the errors in the system as shown in the experience of the United States and France.

AUBIGNY, ALBERT, BARON D', CELIER, ALEXANDRE, COMTE and others. **Problèmes Financiers d'Après-Guerre.** Paris: Alcan, 1922, 244 p.
An important series of lectures delivered by distinguished authorities before L'École des Sciences Politiques.

BLAGOJEVIĆ, DRAGOSLAV O. **Le Problème d'une Monnaie Internationale.** Paris: Éditions et Publications Contemporaines, 1930, 185 p.
The author is concerned primarily with the history of the scheme for an international currency.

BONNET, GEORGES ÉTIENNE. **Les Expériences Monétaires Contemporaines.** Paris: Colin, 1926, 200 p.
A brief though competent survey of the events of the war and immediate post-war periods.

BORIS, GEORGES. **Problème de l'Or et Crise Mondiale.** Paris: Valois, 1931, 156 p.
A reconsideration of the question of gold and its effects on economic problems.

CAILLEZ, MAURICE. **L'Organisation du Crédit en Commerce Extérieur.** Paris: Librairie Générale de Droit, 1923, 364 p.
A descriptive study of the mechanism of commercial credit in France and other countries, including Germany, England and the United States.

CASSEL, GUSTAV. **The Crisis in the World's Monetary System.** Oxford: Clarendon Press, 1932, 98 p.
Rhodes Memorial Lectures by an eminent Swedish authority. He discusses the interaction of war debts, reparations, gold distribution, prices and tariffs, and calls for a radical reform.

CASSEL, GUSTAV and others. **Foreign Investments.** Chicago: University of Chicago Press, 1928, 240 p.
Harris Foundation Lectures dealing with the problem both theoretically and practically, by G. Cassel, T. E. Gregory, R. R. Kuczynski and H. K. Norton.

CASSEL, GUSTAV. **Money and Foreign Exchange after 1914.** New York: Macmillan, 1922, 287 p.
A technical summary, dealing especially with the problem of inflation and deflation, by a leading authority.

CASSEL, GUSTAV. **Post-War Monetary Stabilization.** New York: Columbia University Press, 1928, 109 p.
The Swedish economist reviews the monetary problem in its international aspects.

CASSEL, GUSTAV. **The World's Monetary Problems.** London: Constable, 1921, 154 p.
Two memoranda written at the invitation of the League in 1920-1921, discussing the financial disruption of the post-war world and making suggestions for a solution.

CLARE, GEORGE and CRUMP, NORMAN. **The A B C of the Foreign Exchanges.** London: Macmillan, 1927, 247 p.
The eighth edition of a practical guide to the purchase and sale of foreign exchange, with sections on the various national exchanges since the war.

COSTE, PIERRE. **La Lutte pour la Suprématie Financière.** Paris: Payot, 1932, 224 p.
A fascinating review of the triangular struggle for control between the London, Paris and New York money markets.

CROSS, IRA BROWN. **Domestic and Foreign Exchange.** New York: Macmillan, 1923, 572 p.
A theoretical and practical treatment, devoted largely to foreign exchange problems.

DIERSCHKE, KARL and MÜLLER, FRIEDRICH. **Die Notenbanken der Welt.** Berlin: Gürgens, 1926, 2 v.
A valuable systematic survey of the world's banks of issue, with special reference to changes since 1914 and to national legislation on the subject.

EDIE, LIONEL DANFORTH. **The Banks and Prosperity.** New York: Harper, 1931, 190 p.
The author discusses the rôle of the central banks of the United States, England, France and Germany, and calls for more progressive policies.

EDWARDS, GEORGE WILLIAM. **International Trade Finance.** New York: Holt, 1924, 495 p.
A general treatment of foreign exchange, credit and trade financing, designed to take full account of the profound changes wrought by the war.

EGNER, ERICH. **Der Lateinische Münzbund seit dem Weltkrieg.** Leipzig: Akademische Verlagsgesellschaft, 1925, 108 p.
Really a history of the Latin monetary union, with emphasis on the problems arising from the collapse of the franc.

EINZIG, PAUL. **Behind the Scenes of International Finance.** New York: Macmillan, 1931, 154 p.
The author, foreign editor of the *Financial News*, charges selfish misuse of money power by the French government.

EINZIG, PAUL. **The Fight for Financial Supremacy.** New York: Macmillan, 1931, 144 p.
The author is a well-informed if sometimes rather cocksure writer on post-war financial problems. In this volume he discusses the triangular struggle between New York, London and Paris, and gives his reasons for thinking the victory will eventually lie with London.

EINZIG, PAUL. **International Gold Movements.** New York: Macmillan, 1929, 114 p.
A useful monograph.

ESCHER, FRANKLIN. **Foreign Exchange Explained.** New York: Macmillan, 1920, 219 p.
A general handbook designed for the use of men of affairs.

FEILCHENFELD, ERNST HERMANN. **Public Debts and State Succession.** New York: Macmillan, 1931, 922 p.
A standard treatise. The author examines the theory and past history of the problem and discusses in detail the questions arising from the peace treaties of 1919-1920.

FEIS, HERBERT. **Europe: The World's Banker, 1870-1914.** New Haven: Yale University Press, 1930, 492 p.
The best general study of international loans and investments before 1914. Illuminating also for its light on pre-war international relationships. The author discusses in some detail the general policies of the governments and then reviews the most important financing operations. The volume is published for the Council on Foreign Relations.

FISHER, IRVING. **The Money Illusion.** New York: Adelphi, 1928, 245 p.
Based on a series of lectures at the Geneva School of International Studies in 1927. The author is the well-known Yale professor, whose weakness is a tendency to subjective interpretations.

FRIEDMAN, ELISHA MICHAEL. **International Finance and Its Reorganization.** New York: Dutton, 1922, 702 p.
A documented and detailed study of the effects of the war on public debts, currency and foreign exchange, especially in England, France and Germany.

FURNISS, EDGAR STEVENSON. **Foreign Exchange.** Boston: Houghton Mifflin, 1922, 409 p.
A general treatment, with particular attention given to the business and governmental aspects.

GAILLARD, ÉMILE. **Les Théories des Changes et Leur Évolution depuis 1914.** Paris: Presses Modernes, 1929, 316 p.
An analytical study of the theories of Keynes, Cassel, Nogaro and other specialists.

GOODLIFFE, WALTER. **Credit and Currency.** London: King, 1927, 178 p.
An inquiry into the fundamental problems of currency and credit, in the international as well as the national aspects, with numerous proposals for reform.

GREGORY, THEODOR EMANUEL. **The Gold Standard and Its Future.** New York: Dutton, 1932, 115 p.
An analysis of fundamentals, followed by a review of the situation resulting from the breakdown of the gold standard mechanism and a discussion of steps toward the reëstablishment of the standard.

GREUL, ROBERT. **Die Lateinische Münz-Union.** Berlin: Dümmler, 1926, 149 p.
A history and examination of the status and probable future of the Union.

HAWTREY, RALPH GEORGE. **Currency and Credit.** New York: Longmans, 1928, 477 p.
The third edition of a general treatise, giving also some consideration to the effect of the war, the gold standard and international indebtedness. The author is a high official of the British Treasury.

HAWTREY, RALPH GEORGE. **The Gold Standard in Theory and Practice.** New York: Longmans, 1927, 124 p.
An introductory study of a complex problem.

HAWTREY, RALPH GEORGE. **Monetary Reconstruction.** New York: Longmans, 1926, 175 p.
A second, enlarged edition of a collection of essays on post-war problems by an English authority.

HEYMANN, HANS. **Die Welt-Kredit und Finanzreform.** Berlin: Rowohlt, 1921, 141 p.
A vigorous plea for supernational action to solve supernational problems.

The International Gold Problem. New York: Oxford University Press, 1931, 240 p.
A most valuable collection of studies prepared between 1929 and 1931 under the auspices of the Royal Institute of International Affairs.

JACK, DANIEL THOMAS. **The Restoration of European Currencies.** London: King, 1927, 226 p.
A concise survey of developments in all countries to 1927.

JAMES, ÉMILE. **De l'Adoption d'une Monnaie de Compte Internationale.** Paris: La Vie Universitaire, 1922, 266 p.
An analytical treatment of projects for an international currency and an examination of the theories of Bendixen, Cassel, Nogaro, Lederer, Landesberger and others.

KEYNES, JOHN MAYNARD. **Monetary Reform.** New York: Harcourt, 1924, 227 p.
A suggestive work by an outstanding English economist. The volume includes an excellent chapter on foreign exchanges.

KISCH, CECIL HERMANN and ELKIN, W. A. **Central Banks.** London: Macmillan, 1928, 384 p.
A systematic study of banks of issue, their relations to the state, to commercial banks and to foreign exchange, and of coöperation between them.

LIPPERT, GUSTAV. **Handbuch des Internationalen Finanzrechts.** Vienna: Oesterreichische Staatsdruckerei, 1928, 1275 p.
The second edition of an exhaustive handbook and bibliography.

LUZZATTI, LUIGI. **La Paix Monétaire à la Conférence de Gênes.** Rome: Libreria di Scienze, 1922, 128 p.
A closely reasoned analysis of the monetary aspects of the Genoa Conference, by an eminent Italian financier and statesman.

MADDEN, JOHN THOMAS and NADLER, MARCUS. **Foreign Securities.** New York: Ronald Press, 1929, 452 p.
A general introduction, with due attention to political and legal aspects, written by the director and assistant director of the Institute of International Finance.

MARCONCINI, FEDERICO. **Vicende dell' Oro e dell' Argento.** Milan: Vita e Pensiero, 1929, 410 p.
A thorough study of the history of gold and silver in the 19th and 20th centuries, with special reference to the history of the Latin Monetary Union.

MARSHALL, ALFRED. **Money, Credit and Commerce.** New York: Macmillan, 1929, 369 p.
The latest printing of a general treatment of money, trade and exchange, by one of the world's leading theorists.

MARTIN, PAUL. **Les Déplacements du Pôle Monétaire et Ses Conséquences Économiques.** Paris: La Vie Universitaire, 1923, 276 p.
The author covers the period 1914 to 1923, showing what the war did to the London market and discussing the new problems raised by the competition of New York.

MASON, DAVID MARSHALL. **Monetary Policy, 1914-1928.** London: Hopkinson, 1928, 113 p.
Written by the chairman of the Sound Currency Association, this little book gives a good survey of the vicissitudes of the gold standard.

MEYNIAL, PIERRE. **Créances et Dettes Internationales.** Paris: Dalloz, 1926, 268 p.
Primarily a study of the balance of payments of England, France, the United States, Germany and Austria.

MILLER, HUGH FRANCIS RIDLEY. **The Foreign Exchange Market.** London: Arnold, 1925, 152 p.
An introductory account of post-war exchange.

MIROUX, HENRY. **Le Problème des Crédits Internationaux.** Lille: Sautai, 1922, 160 p.
The book is devoted largely to an analysis of different types of credit, though there is some discussion of the efforts of various conferences to solve the post-war problem.

NOGARO, BERTRAND. **Modern Monetary Systems.** London: King, 1927, 236 p.
An important treatment, by a French authority. The book takes up the monetary crisis since the war, and discusses the theory of currency and exchange.

PANDELE, C. A. **L'Assainissement des Monnaies Européennes et la Répartition de l'Or dans le Monde.** Paris: Librairie Générale de Droit, 1928, 326 p.
This book is taken up largely with a survey, country by country, though there is some discussion of broader movements and proposed solutions.

POMMERY, LOUIS. **Changes et Monnaies.** Paris: Giard, 1926, 592 p.
A useful survey of the monetary situation in the various countries.

RIST, CHARLES. **La Déflation en Pratique.** Paris: Giard, 1923.
A competent technical study of the situation in England, France, Czechoslovakia and the United States, by a leading French expert.

SACK, ALEXANDRE N. **Les Effets des Transformations des États sur Leurs Dettes Publiques et Autres Obligations Financières.** Paris: Sirey, 1927, 615 p.
Volume I of an authoritative study by a Russian jurist. An important contribution to the understanding of present-day financial problems.

SANCERY, JEAN. **Le Retour à l'Or dans les Régimes Monétaires après la Guerre.** Paris: Dalloz, 1925, 198 p.
A faithful if uninspired review of post-war monetary developments.

SCHWEIZER, ARTHUR. **Die Neue Goldwährung.** Basel: Helbing und Lichtenhahn, 1929, 215 p.
Brings out the need for international coöperation in the fixation of exchange.

SHAW, WILLIAM ARTHUR. **The Theory and Principles of Central Banking.** London: Pitman, 1930, 254 p.
A scholarly attempt to deduce the theory of central banking through an analysis of the structure and working of the Bank of England and the Federal Reserve System.

STAMP, SIR JOSIAH CHARLES. **The Financial Aftermath of War.** New York: Scribner, 1932, 149 p.
A well-known financial expert describes briefly and in non-technical language the fundamentals of inflation, reparations, debts and the gold standard.

STERN, SIEGFRIED. **Fourteen Years of European Investments, 1914-1928.** New York: Bankers Publishing Company, 1929, 293 p.
A detailed analysis of the course of securities in thirteen European countries, the United States and Canada, by an official of the Equitable Trust Company of New York.

SURUN, PHILIPPE. **La Distribution Internationale de l'Or.** Paris: Jouve, 1927, 164 p.
A general treatment of the theory of gold movements, followed by an account of some outstanding movements of the post-war period.

TODD, JOHN AITON. **The Mechanism of Exchange.** New York: Oxford University Press, 1927, 288 p.
The third edition of an introductory treatment.

WALTER, HUBERT CONRAD. **Foreign Exchange and Foreign Debts.** London: Methuen, 1926, 254 p.
An introduction to the subject, clear and concise, designed to take account of the changes wrought by the Dawes Plan, stabilization, return to gold and debt settlements, and to make accessible to the lay reader the new theories of Keynes and others.

WHITAKER, ALBERT CONSER. **Foreign Exchange.** New York: Appleton, 1929, 646 p.
An American college text on the financial aspects of international business.

WILLIS, HENRY PARKER and BECKHART, BENJAMIN HAGGOTT. **Foreign Banking Systems.** New York: Holt, 1929, 1311 p.
An encyclopedic survey.

Reparations and War Debts
General and Historical

See also (World War) Economic and Financial Aspects and War Costs, p. 153, and Peace Negotiations, p. 156; also (United States) Finance and Foreign Investments, p. 189; also (Germany) Financial and Economic Problems, p. 327.

ANGAS, LAWRENCE LEE BAZLEY. **Germany and Her Debts. A Critical Examination of the Reparations Problem.** London: Simmonds, 1923, 158 p.
The author urges the elimination of pensions from reparations and the reduction of the latter to £4,230,000,000, to be paid through forty-three years.

AUBOIN, MAX. **Les Prestations en Nature de l'Allemagne et le Problème des Réparations.** Paris: Stock, 1923, 210 p.
A fair study of the problem of deliveries in kind.

BARNICH, GEORGES. **Comment Faire Payer l'Allemagne.** Paris: Ferenczi, 1923, 231 p.
A moderate study of possible modes of enforcing the economic clauses of the Treaty of Versailles.

BASS, JOHN FOSTER and MOULTON, HAROLD GLENN. **America and the Balance Sheet of Europe.** New York: Ronald Press, 1922, 367 p.
An objective study of the facts of the economic situation in Europe, with particular emphasis on the reparations problem.

BATSELL, WALTER RUSSELL. **The Debt Settlements and the Future.** Paris: Lecram Press, 1927, 179 p.
A convenient handbook, buttressed with useful figures.

BERGMANN, KARL. **The History of Reparations.** Boston: Houghton Mifflin, 1927, 353 p.
One of the most important books on the question. The writer was one of the German financial experts throughout the entire negotiations, and his book may be taken as the authoritative presentation from the German point of view.

BONN, MORITZ JULIUS. **Befreiungspolitik oder Beleihungspolitik?** Berlin: Fischer, 1928, 141 p.
A brilliant discussion of the reparations problem by a German economist.

CALMETTE, GERMAIN. **Les Dettes Interalliées.** Paris: Costes, 1926, 254 p.
This publication of the Société de l'Histoire de la Guerre is probably the best survey of the question in French. The book is largely documentary, with running comment and interpretation.

CALMETTE, GERMAIN, ed. **Recueil de Documents sur l'Histoire de la Question des Réparations.** Paris: Costes, 1924, cvi+539 p.
One hundred pages reviewing the history of reparations to May 1921, followed by a valuable collection of pertinent documents bearing on inter-Allied debts as well as upon reparations during the same period.

CASSINELLI, RENÉ. **Les Dettes Interalliées.** Paris: La Vie Universitaire, 1923, 130 p.
Primarily a digest of arguments for and against cancellation, followed by a brief outline of the evolution of the problem from 1919 to 1923.

CHEW, OSWALD, ed. **The Stroke of the Moment.** Philadelphia: Lippincott, 1927, 551 p.
Articles by numerous writers tending to show that it would be either unjust or unprofitable to insist on the payment of the foreign debts.

COUVE DE MURVILLE, MAURICE. **Le Problème des Transferts.** Paris: Rousseau, 1929, 195 p.
A conventional review of the transfer problem, carrying the story down to the Young Plan.

DELATTRE, AUGUSTIN. **La Liquidation Financière de la Guerre.** Paris: Alcan, 1928, 200 p.
A serious scholarly treatment of the German and Allied debts.

DEXTER, PHILIP and SEDGWICK, JOHN HUNTER. **The War Debts: An American View.** New York: Macmillan, 1928, 180 p.
After rejecting the European arguments for cancellation, the writers advance arguments based upon considerations of American interest.

FICK, HARALD. **Transferproblem und Transfertheorie.** Jena: Fischer, 1929, 66 p.
The author examines the various theories of transfer and concludes that only a favorable balance of trade can make transfer possible.

FISK, HARVEY EDWARD. **The Inter-Ally Debts.** New York: Bankers Trust Company, 1924, 367 p.
An analysis of war and post-war public finance, with useful statistical tables based on official data.

FOSSATI, ERALDO. **Il Problema delle Riparazioni.** Pavia: Facoltà di Politica, 1926, 142 p.
A well-documented study of the reparations problem with particular stress on its reactions upon German economic life.

FRANÇOIS-MARSAL, FRÉDÉRIC. **Dettes Interalliées.** Paris: Renaissance du Livre, 1927, 176 p.
A forceful presentation of the debt problem, by a French statesman.

FRIEDRICH, JOHANNES. **Das Internationale Schuldenproblem.** Leipzig: Akademische Verlagsgesellschaft, 1928, 352 p.
One of the most thorough and dispassionate treatments of international debts. The book, which is heavily documented, gives the history of the problem and considers in detail its numerous implications.

FUDICKAR, KURT. **Deutsche Reparationen und Interalliierte Kriegsschulden-Abkommen.** Berlin: Reichsverband der Deutschen Industrie, 1926, 132 p.
A sound factual study of the twin problems as they stood after the Dawes Plan settlements.

FURST, GASTON A. **De Versailles aux Experts.** Paris: Berger-Levrault, 1927, 360 p.
The writer concludes, from his review of the reparations question, that the only possible solution lies in the cancellation of the debts owed to America.

GARRIGOU-LAGRANGE, ANDRÉ. **Le Problème des Réparations: La Technique des Règlements.** Paris: La Vie Universitaire, 1923, 254 p.
The author of this dissertation, while reviewing the whole problem of reparations and transfer, is chiefly concerned with the technique of payments in kind.

GEROULD, JAMES THAYER and TURNBULL, LAURA SHEARER, *comps.* **Selected Articles on Interallied Debts and Revision of the Debt Settlements.** New York: Wilson, 1928, 524 p.
Articles pro and con, with pertinent documents and a bibliography.

GIDEONSE, HARRY DAVID. **Transfert des Réparations et le Plan Dawes.** Paris: Payot, 1928, 124 p.
A careful examination of the various theories of transfer, followed by an analysis of the problem and its connection with inter-Allied debts.

GLASGOW, GEORGE. **The Dupe as Hero.** London: Cape, 1930, 223 p.
A witty but bitter attack on the war debt settlements as negotiated by the British government.

GNIAZDOWSKI, MICHEL. **Relations Économiques Internationales.** Paris: Presses Universitaires, 1928, 100 p.
An attempt to evolve a theory of balance of accounts between nations.

HAYS, ARTHUR GARFIELD. **Enemy Property in America.** Albany: Bender, 1923, 396 p.
A technical legal treatise.

HELFFERICH, KARL. **Die Politik der Erfüllung.** Munich: Schweitzer, 1922, 103 p.
A brilliant summary of the reparations question and the policy of fulfillment, of which the author was a vigorous opponent.

HILLS, RALPH WARREN. **The Unliquidated War.** Washington: Adams, 1928, 160 p.
From the Treaty to the Dawes Plan; scathing criticism of the reparations settlements and the methods of enforcing them.

HOMBERG, OCTAVE. **La Grande Injustice.** Paris: Grasset, 1926, 100 p.
A strong and cogent presentation of the French argument, written by an official of the French ministry of finance who acted as one of its agents in the United States during the war.

HOSCHILLER, MAX. **Une Enquête en Allemagne.** Paris: Alcan, 1923, 183 p.
An anthology of the views of German financial leaders on the reparations question.

KATZ, ÉMILE. **Les Prestations en Nature.** Paris: Morice, 1928, 159 p.
A doctoral dissertation containing a straightforward if uninspired account of the methods of payment in kind before and after the inauguration of the Dawes Plan.

KAUTSKY, BENEDIKT. **Reparationen und Rüstungen.** Vienna: Hess, 1931, 218 p.
The author attempts to set forth especially the connection between the questions of reparations and armaments and the domestic situation in Germany.

KEYNES, JOHN MAYNARD. **A Revision of the Treaty.** New York: Harcourt, 1922, 242 p.
A sequel to "The Economic Consequences of the Peace." It describes how events have vindicated the latter, and suggests a mode of solving the reparations problem. The author is a leading English economist, given to didactic statement.

KIESSELBACH, WILHELM. **Problems of the German-American Claims Commission.**
New York: Oxford University Press, 1930, 135 p.
The translation of the first part of an important German treatise. The decisions of
the commission may be found in the German edition, "Probleme und Entscheidungen
der Deutsch-Amerikanischen Schadens-Commission" (Mannheim: Bensheimer, 1927,
473 p.).

KRAUS, EMIL. **Von Versailles bis London.** Karlsruhe: Braun, 1921, 103 p.
A useful review of the difficult two years following the signature of the treaties, with
special reference to reparations and the development of German foreign policy.

LLOYD GEORGE, DAVID. **The Truth about Reparations and War Debts.** New York:
Doubleday, 1932, 150 p.
In unadorned language the British statesman, himself one of the "Big Three" at
Paris, gives his revised opinion of these vital questions. The book is a scathing indict-
ment of French politicians for what he considers to be their fantastic views regarding
German capacity to pay, and an equally unsparing criticism of the American attitude
on the matter of inter-Allied debts.

McFADYEAN, SIR ANDREW. **Reparation Reviewed.** London: Benn, 1930, 220 p.
One of the most useful books available in English. The author was intimately connected with the Reparations Commission and writes authoritatively as well as dispassionately of the whole evolution of the knotty reparations problem.

MAHLBERG, WALTER. **Reparations-Sabotage durch die Weltwirtschaft.** Leipzig:
Gloeckner, 1928, 122 p.
An analysis, by a German professor, of the reactions of world economics upon repara-
tions, which, in his opinion, make payments impossible.

MARTENS, HEINRICH. **Zur Transferierung der Deutschen Reparationsleistungen.**
Berlin: Hoffmann, 1927, 132 p.
A discussion of the transfer problem, by a competent writer.

MAUTNER, WILHELM. **Die Verschuldung Europas.** Frankfurt: Societäts-Druckerei,
1923, 215 p.
The inter-Allied debts problem and the efforts to solve it as viewed by a liberal German.
The book is a well-documented, systematic account.

MOULTON, HAROLD GLENN and McGUIRE, CONSTANTINE EDWARD. **Germany's Capacity to Pay: A Study of the Reparations Problem.** New York: McGraw-Hill,
1923, 384 p.
One of the first of a number of similar studies. A brief and yet thorough treatment of
the subject, buttressed with much statistical material.

MOULTON, HAROLD GLENN and PASVOLSKY, LEO. **War Debts and World Prosperity.**
Washington: Brookings Institution, 1932, 498 p.
A detailed examination of the debt problem, including both inter-Allied war debts
and reparations. The most complete and authoritative presentation of this complicated
and controversial subject.

MOULTON, HAROLD GLENN and PASVOLSKY, LEO. **World War Debt Settlements.** New
York: Macmillan, 1926, 460 p.
An indispensable handbook on reparations and inter-Allied debts, including many
important documents.

MÜHLENFELS, ALBERT VON. **Transfer.** Jena: Fischer, 1926, 101 p.
An excellent treatise on the technique and effects of transfers under the Dawes Plan,
with particular emphasis on the connection with the question of prices.

MÜHLENFELS, ALBERT VON. **Das Tributproblem und Seine Lösung.** Berlin: Junker und Dünnhaupt, 1931, 138 p.
A technical analysis of the reparations tangle, expounding the familiar German view of the Young Plan.

NOGARO, BERTRAND. **Réparations, Dettes Interalliées, Restauration Monétaire.** Paris: Presses Universitaires, 1922, 190 p.
A prominent French economist examines the problem of international indebtedness with special emphasis on its bearing upon the French currency situation.

NONU, JEAN MIRCEA. **Essai Critique sur la Thèse Officielle Américaine concernant les Dettes Interalliées.** Paris: Blanchard, 1929, 310 p.
A very detailed refutation of President Hoover's thesis, by a leading writer on inter-Allied debts. Contains a good bibliography.

NONU, JEAN MIRCEA. **Le Règlement des Dettes Interalliées et le Plan Dawes.** Paris: Blanchard, 1929, 630 p.
Volume I of a monumental, exhaustive treatise.

ORGIAS, M. and MARTINI, A. **Le Traité de Versailles devant le Droit.** Paris: Berger-Levrault, 1921.
Primarily a study of the status, organization and work of the Reparations Commission.

PEABODY, FREDERICK WILLIAM and COE, FREDERICK E. **"Honour" or Dollars.** London: Simpkin, 1927, 104 p.
Controversial writing in which an American and an Englishman present in strong terms the moral obligations of the United States.

PHILIPS, AUGUST. **Economic Aspects of Reparations and Interallied Debts.** Leyden: Van Doesburgh, 1930, 200 p.
By a Dutch scholar.

RATHENAU, WALTHER. **Cannes und Genua.** Berlin: Fischer, 1922, 78 p.
Four speeches on the reparations problem.

RECOULY, RAYMOND. **Où en Est l'Allemagne? Comment la Faire Payer.** Paris: Hachette, 1922, 224 p.
The German economic situation and the reparations tangle as viewed by a prolific French journalist.

REICHERT, JAKOB. **Rathenau's Reparationspolitik.** Berlin: Scherl, 1922, 301 p.
A critical study by a competent writer.

RÜPPEL, JULIUS and CUNTZE, ALBERT. **Die Reparationssachleistungen.** Berlin: Verlag für Politik und Wirtschaft, 1922, 116 p.
A commentary on the Wiesbaden and other agreements on deliveries in kind.

SALIN, EDGAR, *ed.* **Das Reparations-Problem.** Berlin: List-Gesellschaft, 1929, 2 v.
A fundamental work on the question, consisting of articles on all aspects of reparations by eighty-eight German scholars, statesmen and industrialists.

SCHACHT, HJALMAR. **The End of Reparations.** New York: Cape and Smith, 1931, 248 p.
The former president of the Reichsbank, one of the most familiar figures in reparations negotiations, sums up his arguments for the complete cancellation of payments.

SCHULTZE, ERNST. **Tributzahlung und Ausfuhrkraft.** Leipzig: Deutsche Wissenschaftliche Buchhandlung, 1929, 200 p.
The author examines the old problem of transfer, and concludes that payment in goods is alone possible.

SEYDOUX, JACQUES. **De Versailles au Plan Young.** Paris: Plon, 1932, 332 p.
These collected writings of one of the most competent French financial experts may well be read by way of refutation of much that is said in Lloyd George's book.

SIMON, HUGO FERDINAND. **Reparationen und Wiederaufbau.** Berlin: Heymann, 1925, 332 p.
A competent German study of the reparations problem in the larger setting of European reconstruction.

SPANGENBERG, BERNHARD. **Die Zukunft der Reparationen.** Berlin: Stilke, 1931, 127 p.
Regarding existing arrangements as impossible of fulfilment, the author dispassionately examines various solutions of the problem.

TERHALLE, FRITZ. **Die Reparationskontrolle.** Jena: Fischer, 1925, 112 p.
An examination of the technicalities of reparations collection, with reference to the methods of the Reparations Commission and of the system of transfer initiated by the Dawes Plan.

VILENCHUK, ABRAM M. **Meshdunarodnaia Zadolshennost' posle Voiny.** Moscow: Moskovskiĭ Rabochiĭ, 1929, 203 p.
A popular communist presentation of the problem of post-war indebtedness.

WEBER, KARL. **Die Einwirkungen der Reparationen auf die Weltwirtschaft.** Jena: Fischer, 1931, 98 p.
The author discusses, succinctly, different opinions regarding the effects of reparations on production, division of labor, etc.

WINGEN, OSCAR. **Fünf Jahre Reparationspolitik.** Berlin: Zentralverlag, 1925, 78 p.
A convenient summary of the development of the reparations question from the conclusion of the peace treaties through the Dawes settlements.

Dawes Plan

AULD, GEORGE PERCIVAL. **The Dawes Plan and the New Economics.** New York: Doubleday, 1927, 317 p.
This book, written by the former Accountant-General of the Reparations Commission, takes rank as one of the really noteworthy contributions to the literature of reparations. The point of view is diametrically opposed to that taken by Keynes and his school.

DAWES, RUFUS CUTLER. **The Dawes Plan in the Making.** Indianapolis: Bobbs-Merrill, 1925, 525 p.
The most authoritative account of the work of the Dawes Commission; a contemporary record, by one of the American staff of experts.

FEDER, G. **Der Dawespakt.** Munich: Eber, 1929, 141 p.
The text, with a detailed commentary.

LONG, ROBERT EDWARD CROZIER. **The Mythology of Reparations.** London: Duckworth, 1928, 200 p.
A substantial study, based upon eight years of investigation, with particular reference to the working of the Dawes Plan.

MOULTON, HAROLD GLENN. **The Reparation Plan.** New York: McGraw-Hill, 1924, 325 p.
A favorable analysis of the Dawes Plan, with a long documentary appendix.

PERREAU, PIERRE. **Le Plan Dawes.** Paris: Giard, 1928, 234 p.
A doctoral dissertation which gives in convenient form a general summary of the plan, the laws putting it into effect, and its more immediate results.

PREYER, WILHELM DIETRICH. **Die Dawesgesetze. Deutschlands Wirtschaftliche Versklavung.** Berlin: Stilke, 1925, 62 p.
An extremely hostile attack on the Dawes Plan.

RAAB, FRIEDRICH. **Handbuch der Londoner Vereinbarungen.** Berlin: Deutsche Verlagsgesellschaft für Politik und Geschichte, 1925, 379 p.
One of the most competent German writers on the subject reprints all the pertinent documents with illuminating commentaries.

SERING, MAX. **Germany under the Dawes Plan.** London: King, 1929, 251 p.
The English translation of one of the best single treatments, from the German side, of the whole reparations problem. The author gives an account of the origins, legal basis and economic effects of the plan, and makes numerous suggestions for a just solution of the reparations problem.

SORGE, J. K. **Das Dawes-Abkommen und Seine Auswirkungen.** Hamburg: Hoym, 1925, 120 p.
A controversial work on the effects of the Dawes Plan.

VARGA, EUGEN. **Plan Dauesa i Mirovoi Krizis 1924 goda.** Moscow: Moskovskiĭ Rabochiĭ, 1925, 126 p.
This little book, written, as would be expected, with strong antipathy to the capitalist system, gives a broad survey of the phases of the world economic crisis from which the Dawes Plan emerged.

Young Plan

BERGMANN, KARL. **Deutschland und der Young Plan.** Berlin: Christians, 1930, 168 p.
Apart from the introduction, which is the translation of an article published in *Foreign Affairs*, this little book is primarily an analysis, by Germany's leading expert, of the various agreements connected with the Young Plan.

BONN, MORITZ JULIUS. **Der Neue Plan als Grundlage der Deutschen Wirtschaftspolitik.** Munich: Duncker und Humblot, 1930, 266 p.
A well-known German economist reviews the development of the whole reparations problem, examines the Young Plan and discusses its implications for Germany's financial organization. One of the best books on the subject.

BROCKDORFF, ALEXANDER, GRAF. **Das Youngsystem und Seine Wirkung.** Langensalza: Beyer, 1930, 150 p.
A hostile review.

CABIATI, ATTILIO. **Da Versailles alla'Aja.** Turin: Bocca, 1930, 156 p.
A critique of the course of events from the Dawes Plan to the Young Plan, followed by a study of the Bank for International Settlements.

GESTRICH, HANS. **Der Youngplan.** Leipzig: Reclam, 1930, 135 p.
A satisfactory brief statement for popular consumption.

HEILFRON, EDUARD and NASSEN, PAUL. **Der Neue Plan.** Berlin: Heymann, 1931, 524 p.
A standard collection of documents, with elucidation, covering the Young Plan and the Hague agreements.

HORWITZ, LEO. **Endkampf um die Reparation.** Leipzig: Historisch-Politischer Verlag, 1931, 94 p.
An historical survey, with diagrams, stressing the economic effects of the Young Plan on Germany.

MYERS, DENYS PETER. **The Reparation Settlement.** Boston: World Peace Foundation, 1929, 249 p.
One of the Foundation's excellent manuals, containing the pertinent documents.

PEPY, ANDRÉ. **Le Plan Young.** Paris: Éditions Internationales, 1930, 186 p.
A legalistic analysis of the plan.

PFAFF, A. **Der Young Plan in 67 Fragen und Antworten.** Munich: Eher, 1930,
100 p.
A catechism for National Socialists.

PREYER, WILHELM DIETRICH. **Der Pariser Tributplan.** Berlin: Stilke, 1929, 114 p.
A violent denunciation of the new settlements.

RAAB, FRIEDRICH. **Der Neue Plan.** Berlin: Hobbing, 1930, 208 p.
The author stresses the political side of the question, and prints all the important
documents.

RAAB, FRIEDRICH. **Young Plan oder Dawes Plan?** Berlin: Hobbing, 1929, 246 p.
A careful analysis and comparison of the two plans, from the German viewpoint.
The author believes the Young Plan to be the lesser of the two evils.

REICHERT, J. W. **Young-Plan.** Berlin: Hobbing, 1930, 67 p.
A leading writer on reparations examines the financial and economic aspects of the
plan.

SALIN, EDGAR. **Die Deutschen Tribute.** Berlin: Hobbing, 1930, 248 p.
A series of addresses by an authority, dealing with the origin and content of the reparations provisions and attacking the Young Plan and its terms.

WHEELER-BENNETT, JOHN WHEELER and LATIMER, HUGH. **Information on the
Reparation Settlement.** London: Allen and Unwin, 1930, 254 p.
An admirable introduction to the study of the Young Plan and the Hague Conference
by means of the documents.

Bank for International Settlements

ARGOUD, JEAN. **La Banque des Règlements Internationaux dans le Cadre de
l'Économie Mondiale.** Paris: Chauny et Quinsac, 1931, 274 p.
A stimulating attempt to determine the probable influence of the bank on world
economic conditions.

DESCHIÉTÈRE, RAYMOND. **Les Réparations.** Paris: Presses Universitaires, 1931, 238 p.
Primarily a scientific analysis of the bank and its workings.

EINZIG, PAUL. **The Bank for International Settlements.** New York: Macmillan,
1930, 179 p.
A contribution to the discussion of the organization and function of the bank; one
of the most convenient treatments in English.

JAUDEL, PIERRE. **Les Paiements Internationaux.** Paris: Chauny et Quinsac, 1930,
312 p.
A competent examination of the organization and technique of international payments.

KARAMIKAS, CONSTANTIN. **La Banque des Règlements Internationaux.** Paris:
Domat-Montchrétien, 1931, 336 p.
One of the best historical and analytical studies of the bank.

KRUG, PAUL. **La Banque des Règlements Internationaux.** Paris: Rousseau, 1931,
298 p.
The author deals chiefly with the credit functions of the bank.

MENDÈS-FRANCE, PIERRE. **La Banque Internationale.** Paris: Valois, 1930, 293 p.
A competent study, approaching the subject as an aspect of the larger problem of a
United States of Europe.

MOITESSIER, ANDRÉ. **Le Rôle de la Banque des Règlements Internationaux.** Paris:
Presses Modernes, 1931, 179 p.
A good introductory study of the bank's functions.

OTLET, PAUL. **La Banque Internationale.** Paris: L'Églantine, 1929, 208 p.
A study by the secretary of the Union des Associations Internationales, who pleads for the establishment of the bank on a broad basis under League supervision.

SCHLÜTER, HANS L. **Die Bank für Internationalen Zahlungsausgleich.** Berlin: Rothschild, 1932, 423 p.
A scholarly study of the bank in all its aspects.

IV. INTERNATIONAL LAW
GENERAL TREATISES

BRIERLY, JAMES LESLIE. **The Law of Nations.** New York: Oxford University Press, 1928, 228 p.
A succinct and well-balanced introduction to the law of peace.

BUTLER, SIR GEOFFREY GILBERT and MACCOBY, SIMON. **The Development of International Law.** New York: Longmans, 1928, 566 p.
A detailed, authoritative account, by a leading British jurist.

DICKINSON, EDWIN DeWITT. **The Law of Nations.** New York: McGraw-Hill, 1929, 1133 p.
An elaborate general treatment.

DUPUIS, CHARLES. **Le Droit des Gens et les Rapports des Grandes Puissances avec les Autres États, avant le Pacte de la Société des Nations.** Paris: Plon, 1921, 544 p.
A leading French jurist reviews the problem of great powers and small states and analyzes the provisions of the Covenant designed to meet this situation.

FAUCHILLE, PAUL. **Traité de Droit International Public.** Paris: Rousseau, 1921-1926, 2 v.
The eighth edition of Bonfils' standard work, entirely recast and brought up to date. The best-known and most authoritative large-scale treatment in French.

FISCHER, EUGEN and WIDMANN, BERTHOLD. **Voelkerrecht im Weltkrieg.** Berlin: Deutsche Verlagsgesellschaft für Politik und Geschichte, 1927, 4 v.
Series III of the investigations of the Committee of the Reichstag, one of the most important collections of source material on the history of the war. The committee took testimony on all questions of violations of international law and now publishes all the very extensive evidence, the only problem of major importance that is omitted being that of the violation of Belgian neutrality, which is reserved for a later date.

GARNER, JAMES WILFORD. **International Law and the World War.** New York: Longmans, 1920, 2 v.
An elaborate standard treatment of international law problems as they arose in the Great War.

GARNER, JAMES WILFORD. **Recent Developments in International Law.** Calcutta: The University, 1925, 840 p.
An excellent handbook of international law as now practiced.

HALL, WILLIAM EDWARD. **A Treatise on International Law.** 8th ed., by A. Pearce Higgins. Oxford: Clarendon Press, 1925, 952 p.
The latest edition of a standard work, revised to include consideration of the peace treaties and developments since 1918.

HERSHEY, AMOS SHARTLE. **The Essentials of International Public Law and Organization.** New York: Macmillan, 1927, 806 p.
The revised edition of an excellent text-book.

HIGGINS, ALEXANDER PEARCE. **Studies in International Law and Relations.** New York: Macmillan, 1928, 322 p.
A series of essays by a competent writer, dealing with such questions as the Monroe Doctrine, the Locarno Treaties, the international position of the Papacy, etc., as well as with various aspects of international law during the war.

HUBER, MAX. **Die Soziologischen Grundlagen des Voelkerrechts.** Berlin: Rothschild, 1928, 101 p.
A competent and suggestive essay by the former president of the Hague Tribunal.

HYDE, CHARLES CHENEY. **International Law.** Boston: Little, Brown, 1922, 2 v.
A general treatment, designed to state the principles and practice of international law as understood and applied by the United States.

LUNDSTEDT, ANDERS VILHELM. **Superstition or Rationality in Action for Peace.** New York: Longmans, 1925, 239 p.
A very able attack on current theories of jurisprudence and international law.

MÉRIGNHAC, ALEXANDRE and LÉMONON, ERNEST. **Le Droit des Gens et la Guerre de 1914-1918.** Paris: Sirey, 1921, 2 v.
A systematic study presenting the French view of international law and German violations of it.

MOORE, JOHN BASSETT. **International Law and Some Current Illusions.** New York: Macmillan, 1924, 381 p.
Valuable essays by one of the world's foremost authorities on international law. Among the subjects treated are contraband, arbitration, the Permanent Court, the law of aircraft and radio.

NIPPOLD, OTFRIED. **The Development of International Law after the World War.** Oxford: Clarendon Press, 1923, 241 p.
A discussion not so much of the content of international law as of the means of enforcing it. Written in 1917, it looked forward to the formation of a League of Nations as the only means of realizing the victory of law over war.

OLIVART, RAMÓN DE DALMAU Y DE OLIVART, MARQUÉS DE. **El Derecho Internacional Público en los Últimos Veinticinco Años.** Madrid: Espasa-Calpe, 1927.
The first part of a competent study of the changes wrought by the war in international jurisprudence.

POLITIS, NICOLAS SOCRATE. **The New Aspects of International Law.** Washington: Carnegie Endowment for International Peace, 1928, 86 p.
A competent and interesting study of the changes wrought by the new world organization.

REDLICH, MARCELLUS DONALD DE. **International Law as a Substitute for Diplomacy.** Chicago: Independent Publishing Company, 1929, 208 p.
A capable survey of the history of international relations and the practice of diplomacy, as a background for the thesis that the abolition of war is dependent on the further development of international law.

REDSLOB, ROBERT. **Histoire des Grands Principes du Droit des Gens depuis l'Antiquité jusqu'à la Veille de la Grande Guerre.** Paris: Rousseau, 1923, 600 p.
An exhaustive historical treatment, by a competent French jurist.

Research in International Law. Draft Conventions on Nationality, Responsibility of States, Territorial Waters. Cambridge: Harvard Law School, 1929, 399 p.
These draft conventions were drawn up in anticipation of the First Conference on the Codification of International Law, held at The Hague in 1930.

ROEMER, WILLIAM FRANCIS. **The Ethical Basis of International Law.** Chicago: Loyola University Press, 1929, 203 p.
A study of the ethical principles embodied in international law, with special reference to the peace problem.

ROLIN, ALBÉRIC. **Le Droit Moderne de la Guerre.** Brussels: DeWit, 1920, 3 v.
An exhaustive standard treatment, by an eminent Belgian authority.

SIMONS, WALTER. **The Evolution of International Public Law in Europe since Grotius.** New Haven: Yale University Press, 1931, 146 p.
A brilliant essay by the former Chief Justice of the German Republic.

STOWELL, ELLERY CORY. **International Law.** New York: Holt, 1931, 855 p.
A fresh and original text, designed to emphasize actual theory and practice. Little is said of the laws of war, but much space is devoted to intervention, world organization, etc.

STRUPP, KARL. **Théorie und Praxis des Voelkerrechts.** Berlin: Liebmann, 1925, 206 p.
A splendid manual by a German scholar, stressing recent developments.

VOLLENHOVEN, CORNELIS VAN. **Du Droit de Paix.** Hague: Nijhoff, 1932, 251 p.
An able attempt to restate the principles of international law as the law of peace rather than the law of war.

WILLIAMS, SIR JOHN FISCHER. **Chapters on Current International Law and the League of Nations.** New York: Longmans, 1929, 514 p.
A collection of technical articles by a leading English jurist and legal representative on the Reparations Commission.

DIPLOMACY AND DIPLOMATIC PRACTICE

CLEMENS, SEVERUS. **Der Beruf des Diplomaten.** Berlin: Deutsche Verlagsgesellschaft für Politik und Geschichte, 1926, 107 p.
A pioneer essay on the psychology of the diplomat, by a former member of the German diplomatic service.

ESSEN, JAN LOUIS FREDERIK VAN. **Ontwikkeling en Codificatie van de Diplomatieke Voorrechten.** Arnhem: Gouda Quint, 1928, 227 p.
A scholarly monograph on the evolution and codification of diplomatic privileges.

MENDELSSOHN-BARTHOLDY, ALBRECHT. **Diplomatie.** Berlin: Rothschild, 1927, 115 p.
An address, with supplementary documents, in which a well-known German authority discusses the pros and cons of diplomatic methods, old and new.

REINSCH, PAUL SAMUEL. **Secret Diplomacy.** New York: Harcourt, 1922, 231 p.
An historical survey of the methods of diplomacy, followed by a stimulating discussion of the possibilities of eliminating secret diplomacy and establishing popular control.

SATOW, SIR ERNEST MASON. **A Guide to Diplomatic Practice.** London: Longmans, 1922, 2 v.
A reprinting, with some revision, of the standard manual in English.

STEWART, IRVIN. **Consular Privileges and Immunities.** New York: Columbia University Press, 1926, 216 p.
A thoroughly scholarly treatment of an important subject.

SZILASSY, GYULA, BÁRÓ. **Traité Pratique de Diplomatie Moderne.** Paris: Payot, 1928, 256 p.
The author, a former Austro-Hungarian diplomat, supplies an admirable guide to the practice of diplomacy, and in this field the book is almost unique.

YOUNG, GEORGE. **Diplomacy Old and New.** New York: Harcourt, 1921, 105 p.
Intended as a general introduction for the layman, this little book, written by a former English diplomat, is a telling critique of the accepted system.

SPECIAL TOPICS

Intervention and Recognition

See also (United States) Relations with Latin America, p. 179, and Relations with Europe, p. 184; also (China) International Relations and Status, p. 474.

ARANGUA RIVAS, CARLOS J. **La Intervención.** Santiago de Chile: Imprenta "La Sud-América," 1924, 247 p.
A general treatment of the principles of intervention, followed by an analysis of the doctrines of Monroe, Drago and Tobar and some discussion of Articles 10, 11 and 19 of the League Covenant.

HENRY, NOËL. **Les Gouvernements de Fait devant le Juge.** Paris: Guillon, 1927, 260 p.
The most exhaustive scholarly treatment of the numerous and frequently obscure problems connected with *de facto* governments.

HERVEY, JOHN G. **The Legal Effects of Recognition in International Law as Interpreted by the Courts of the United States.** Philadelphia: University of Pennsylvania Press, 1928, 184 p.
The author examines the effects of over 200 American and English decisions. His work is important in studying the possible implications of the recognition of Russia.

KUNZ, JOSEF LAURENZ. **Die Anerkennung von Staaten und Regierungen im Voelkerrecht.** Stuttgart: Kohlhammer, 1928, 218 p.
A scholarly analysis of the vexed problem of recognition.

SPIROPULOS, JEAN. **Die *de Facto* Regierung im Voelkerrecht.** Kiel: Verlag des Instituts für Internationales Recht, 1926, 188 p.
A thorough scholarly contribution.

STOWELL, ELLERY CORY. **Intervention in International Law.** Washington: Byrne, 1921, 558 p.
A standard, authoritative treatment.

STRUPP, KARL. **Intervention in Finanzfragen.** Leipzig: Noske, 1928, 110 p.
A well-known international jurist examines the right of intervention in financial matters and prints a draft agreement for the pacific settlement of disputes of this kind.

Freedom of the Seas

See also (Disarmament) Naval, p. 84; also (World War) Naval Operations, p. 140; also (United States) Relations with Europe, p. 184; also (Great Britain) Imperial Relations, p. 231.

ALESSANDRI, JEAN. **Contribution à l'Étude des Blocus Nouveaux.** Paris: Boccard, 1919.
A technical theoretical study of the law of blockade in the light of practice in the World War.

BUSTAMANTE Y SIRVÉN, ANTONIO SÁNCHEZ DE. **The Territorial Sea.** New York: Oxford University Press, 1930, 175 p.
A standard treatment of the subject, by an eminent Cuban jurist.

DUMAS, JACQUES. **Les Aspects Économiques du Droit de Prise.** Paris: Sirey, 1926, 2 v.
An exhaustive investigation of the conditions of commercial war, both before and after the Great War.

GARNER, JAMES WILFORD. **Prize Law during the World War.** New York: Macmillan, 1927, 712 p.
An exhaustive treatise by an American authority.

GIDEL, GILBERT. **Le Droit International Public de la Mer.** Paris: Sirey, 1932, 2 v.
The first two volumes of an exhaustive treatment, by an eminent authority.

GRISON, PHILIPPE. **La Liberté des Mers et la Rivalité Anglo-Américaine de 1920
à 1930.** Paris: Publications Contemporaines, 1930, 112 p.
The book is primarily an historical survey with analysis of the British and American
attitudes and policies.

JESSUP, PHILIP CARYL. **The Law of Territorial Waters and Maritime Jurisdiction.**
New York: Jennings, 1927, 548 p.
A scholarly treatment, with special reference to the problems raised by the attempt
to enforce American prohibition laws.

KENWORTHY, JOSEPH MONTAGUE and YOUNG, GEORGE. **Freedom of the Seas.** New
York: Liveright, 1929, 283 p.
A provocative study, hinging on the argument that the revolution of naval warfare
has made the old principles obsolete. The authors suggest a settlement of Anglo-
American tension by the introduction of compulsory arbitration, naval disarmament
except for police purposes, and exercise of police activity only by mutual understanding.

MASTERSON, WILLIAM EDWARD. **Jurisidction in Marginal Seas.** New York: Macmillan,
1929, 423 p.
A very thorough study, based in large part upon unpublished material. The author
is concerned chiefly with problems arising from smuggling, and analyzes in detail
recent developments

MORI, K. **The Submarine in War.** New York: Stechert, 1931, 185 p.
A reconsideration of this arm, with an analysis of the current law in respect to it.

PERCY, LORD EUSTACE. **Maritime Trade in War.** New Haven: Yale University Press,
1930, 114 p.
Williamstown lectures, in which the author discusses the freedom of the seas from
the practical standpoint and stresses the need for a complete revamping of international law to take account of the new conditions arising from the League Covenant
and the Kellogg Pact.

POHL, HEINRICH. **Der Deutsche Unterseebootkrieg.** Stuttgart: Enke, 1925, 54 p.
A lecture on submarine warfare from the point of view of international law, by a
German submarine commander.

POTTER, PITMAN BENJAMIN. **The Freedom of the Seas in History, Law, and Politics.**
New York: Longmans, 1924, 299 p.
An historical survey, followed by an analysis of the problem's legal aspects and an
extended discussion of the political side.

VERZIJL, JAN HENDRIK WILLEM. **Le Droit des Prises de la Grande Guerre.** Leyden:
Sijthoff, 1924, 1497 p.
An elaborate analysis of the law as it may be deduced from the decisions of the war
period.

Air Law

*See also (War, Peace, Security and Disarmament) Air Warfare, p. 70; also (World War) War
in the Air, p. 145; also Polar Regions, p. 498.*

COLEGROVE, KENNETH WALLACE. **International Control of Aviation.** Boston: World
Peace Foundation, 1930, 234 p.
One of the excellent handbooks published by the World Peace Foundation. The volume
considers the status of commercial and military aviation and the international law
of the air.

CONSTANTINOFF, JEAN. **Le Droit Aérien Français et Étranger.** Paris: Chauny et Quinsac, 1932, 342 p.
A competent review of the present status of air law.

HAMMARSKJÖLD, A. and others. **La Protection des Populations Civiles contre les Bombardements.** Geneva: Comité International de la Croix-Rouge, 1930, 253 p.
A collection of opinions by eminent jurists, setting forth the unsatisfactory nature of present laws on the subject.

HAUPT, G. **Der Luftraum.** Breslau: Schletter, 1931, 155 p.
A juristic study of the increasingly important questions of freedom of the air and the sovereign rights of states.

HENRY-COÜANNIER, ANDRÉ. **Légitimité de la Guerre Aérienne.** Paris: Per Orbem, 1925, 252 p.
A collection of opinions by statesmen, jurists and experts.

MEYER, ALEXANDER. **Das Neutralitätsrecht im Luftkriege.** Berlin: Heymann, 1931, 105 p.
Primarily a critical analysis of the proposals of the Hague commission of jurists in 1922-1923.

ROYSE, MORTON WILLIAM. **Aerial Bombardment and the International Regulation of Warfare.** New York: Harold Vinal, 1928, 241 p.
Discusses the extent to which air warfare is subject to restriction, and whether civilian populations have any inherent right to immunity.

SLOTEMAKER, L. H. **Freedom of Passage for International Air Services.** New York: Van Riemsdyck, 1932, 122 p.
A legal analysis of a subject of increasing importance.

SPAIGHT, JAMES MOLONY. **Air Power and War Rights.** New York: Longmans, 1924, 493 p.
The effect of air power on the future conduct of war, by an English specialist. The book emphasizes legal aspects and the problem of neutrality.

SPIROPULOS, JEAN. **Der Luftraum.** Leipzig: Rossberg, 1921, 130 p.
The author regards the air as an integral part of the national domain.

VOLKMANN, KURT. **Internationales Luftrecht.** Berlin: Dümmler, 1930, 218 p.
An authoritative statement of the international law of the air.

Miscellaneous

ADAMI, VITTORIO. **National Frontiers in Relation to International Law.** New York: Oxford University Press, 1927, 127 p.
The translation of an excellent Italian treatise on a vexed question.

BORCHARD, EDWIN MONTEFIORE. **The Diplomatic Protection of Citizens Abroad.** New York: Banks Law Publishing Co., 1928, 988 p.
An exhaustive authoritative treatment of the entire law of international claims.

BOURBOUSSON, ÉDOUARD. **Traité Général de la Nationalité dans les Cinq Parties du Monde.** Paris: Sirey, 1931, 613 p.
A detailed analysis of the divers nationality and citizenship laws prevalent throughout the world.

BUSTAMANTE Y SIRVÉN, ANTONIO SÁNCHEZ DE. **La Nacionalidad y el Domicilio.** Havana: República de Cuba, 1927, 77 p.
A famous jurist outlines the problem and criticizes various possible solutions.

DICKINSON, EDWIN DEWITT. **The Equality of States in International Law.** Cambridge: Harvard University Press, 1920, 424 p.
A scholarly study of the historical development and present status of the theory.

EAGLETON, CLYDE. **The Responsibility of States in International Law.** New York: New York University Press, 1928, 315 p.
A scholarly investigation of the responsibility of states for actions of agents and individuals, mobs and civil wars, with a discussion of the need of law codification.

EBRAY, ALCIDE. **Chiffons de Papier.** Paris: Delpeuch, 1926, 287 p.
Really a history of the violations of treaties from 1798 to the present, with much attention to the violation of Belgium, the Allied action in Greece, and above all the armistice agreements of 1918.

FLOURNOY, RICHARD W. and HUDSON, MANLEY OTTMER. **A Collection of Nationality Laws.** New York: Oxford University Press, 1929, 776 p.
An authoritative compilation, indispensable to the student of this vexed question.

GIROUD, J. **Le Plébiscite International.** Le Puy: Peyriller, Rouchon et Gamon, 1920, 210 p.
Very largely an historical survey which, the author believes, shows the urgent need of international supervision of plebiscites.

HAUSHOFER, KARL. **Grenzen in Ihrer Geographischen und Politischen Bedeutung.** Berlin: Vowinckel, 1927, 351 p.
An exhaustive treatise by one of the leaders of the "geopolitical" school.

HEYKING, AL'FONS AL'FONSOVICH, BARON. **L'Extraterritorialité.** Paris: Rousseau, 1926, 220 p.
A careful monograph by the former Russian Consul-General in London.

KUNZ, JOSEF LAURENZ. **Gaskrieg und Voelkerrecht.** Vienna: Springer, 1927, 83 p.
A keen discussion of the problem of regulating gas warfare, followed by a proposal for an international agreement.

KUNZ, JOSEF LAURENZ. **Die Voelkerrechtliche Option.** Volume I. Breslau: Hirt, 1925, 328 p.
The first volume of a monumental study, dealing with the principle of option as applied in the peace treaty.

LAPRADELLE, PAUL GEOUFFRE DE. **La Frontière.** Paris: Éditions Internationales, 1928, 368 p.
A doctoral dissertation analyzing the methods of delimitation and the law of established frontiers, as well as past arbitrations of frontier disputes.

LITTELL, CLAIR FRANCIS. **The Neutralization of States.** Meadville, Pa.: Author, 1920, 180 p.
A dissertation reviewing the neutralization of Switzerland, Belgium, Luxemburg and the Congo, with some consideration of legal principles.

LIU SHIH SHUN. **Extraterritoriality, Its Rise and Decline.** New York: Longmans, 1925, 235 p.
A well-documented historical account of the rise of the system and a discussion of the various methods by which the practice has been largely abolished.

MANNI, ERCOLE. **Il Problema della Nazionalità.** Modena: Società Tipografica Modenese, 1928, 153 p.
A competent technical study of post-war nationality problems.

MATTERN, JOHANNES. **The Employment of the Plebiscite in the Determination of Sovereignty.** Baltimore: Johns Hopkins Press, 1920, 214 p.
A keen and well-reasoned analysis, less full than Miss Wambaugh's study on the historical side, but somewhat fuller on the theoretical.

REALE, EGIDIO. **Le Régime des Passeports et la Société des Nations.** Paris: Rousseau, 1930, 226 p.
Not a theoretical work, but an admirable history of the passport system in national law and the international regulations adopted through the efforts of the League.

RODICK, BURLEIGH CUSHING. **The Doctrine of Necessity in International Law.** New York: Columbia University Press, 1928, 204 p.
A heavily documented monograph, concerned less with the political sides of the doctrine than with the examination of its legal validity.

STEINLEIN, WILHELM. **Der Begriff des Nicht-Herausgeforderten Angriffs.** Leipzig: Noske, 1927, 134 p.
The author attempts a definition of aggression and provocation, and discusses these concepts as they are found in the treaties from 1870 to the present.

WAMBAUGH, SARAH. **A Monograph on Plebiscites.** New York: Oxford University Press, 1920, 1088 p.
One of the publications of the Carnegie Endowment. The author gives a compact history of plebiscites from the French Revolution on. Most of the volume is devoted to a collection of the pertinent documents, in the original language and in English translation.

WITTMANN, ERNÖ. **Past and Future of the Right of National Self-Determination.** Amsterdam: Van Holkema and Warendorf, 1920, 208 p.
The English translation of a well-documented and stimulating book by a Hungarian lawyer.

YÜ TSUNE CHI. **The Interpretation of Treaties.** New York: Columbia University Press, 1927, 288 p.
A technical study of theory and practice in a most important aspect of international law.

ZIELENIEWSKI, LEON. **Plebiscyt u prawie narodów.** Warsaw: Hoesick, 1928, 106 p.
A study of the theoretical side of plebiscites.

V. INTERNATIONAL ORGANIZATION

NATIONALISM AND INTERNATIONALISM

See also (General International Relations) General Treatises, p. 1.

BARKER, ERNEST. **National Character and the Factors in Its Formation.** New York: Harper, 1927, 296 p.
The well-known English scholar and writer stresses the significance of education in molding the character of nations.

BIRKHILL, ROBERT, *pseud.* (DOUGLAS LOCKHART). **The Seeds of War.** London: Gandy, 1923, 164 p.
A study of nationalism in central and southeastern Europe, with an argument for confederation.

BLAGOJEVIĆ, VIDAN. **Le Principe des Nationalités et Son Application dans les Traités de Paix de Versailles et de Saint-Germain.** Paris: Vie Universitaire, 1922, 458 p.
A brief treatment of the theory of nationality and the Wilsonian doctrine, followed by a detailed survey of its application in the peace treaties with Germany and Austria.

BOEHM, MAX HILDEBERT. **Europa Irredenta.** Berlin: Hobbing, 1924, 334 p.
An unusually stimulating and well-informed book showing how the exaggerated notions of nationalism and the national state led to the disaster of 1914, the collapse of the "polynational" states and the creation of the post-war minorities problems.

BROĬDO, G. I. **Natsional'nyĭ i Kolonial'nyĭ Vopros.** Moscow: Moskovskiĭ Rabochiĭ, 1924, 128 p.
A brief exposition of the evolution of nationalism in imperialist countries and under the dictatorship of the proletariat.

BUCHER, J. **Volk ohne Politik.** Rostock: Verlag Nationale Revolution, 1926, 385 p.
A rather superficial examination of pre-war politics aiming to discredit the idea of Paneuropa and glc.ify the former *Machtstaat*.

CHARPENTIER, ARMAND. **La Guerre et la Patrie.** Paris: Delpeuch, 1926, 340 p.
A serious and well-documented examination of the theories and practice of war and of the nature of patriotism, by a convinced pacifist.

CLAPARÈDE, JEAN LOUIS. **L'Enseignement de l'Histoire et l'Esprit International.** Paris: Presses Universitaires, 1931, 105 p.
A stimulating essay on the important problem of instruction in history as the basis for the development of internationalism.

CURTIUS, ERNST ROBERT. **Maurice Barrès und die Geistigen Grundlagen des Französischen Nationalismus.** Bonn: Cohen, 1922, 255 p.
A telling dissection of the ultra-nationalism of Barrès and the League of Patriots, by one of the most competent German critics of things French.

DAȘCOVICI, NICOLAS. **Principiul Naționalităților și Societatea Națiunilor.** Bucharest: Cartea Românească, 1922, 177 p.
A general discussion of the effects of the war from the standpoint of the principle of nationality, with special reference to self-determination, plebiscites, protection of minorities, etc.

FELS, JOSEF. **Begriff und Wesen der Nation.** Münster: Aschendorff, 1927, 147 p.
An examination of various current theories and an evaluation of such factors as race, religion, and language.

FIERLINGER, Z. **Demokracie a Otazka Narodnostni.** Prague: Svaz Narodniko Osvobozeni, 1931, 338 p.
A thoughtful discussion of the relations between democracy and nationalism.

GENNEP, ARNOLD VAN. **Traité Comparatif des Nationalités.** Paris: Payot, 1922, 228 p.
The first volume of an extensive comparative study of nationality. The author here discusses external factors, notably language and frontiers. A valuable contribution.

HAYES, CARLTON JOSEPH HUNTLEY. **Essays on Nationalism.** New York: Macmillan, 1926, 279 p.
An excellent series of studies on nationalism, its historical development, and its relation to various aspects of modern life.

HAYES, CARLTON JOSEPH HUNTLEY. **The Historical Evolution of Modern Nationalism.** New York: R. R. Smith, 1931, 335 p.
An authoritative exposition of the development of nationalist doctrine and an interesting attempt at critical definition of types.

HEYKING, AL'FONS AL'FONSOVICH, BARON. **La Conception de l'État et l'Idée de la Cohésion Ethnique.** Paris: Rousseau, 1927, 156 p.
A suggestive essay, approaching the subject from the standpoint of international law.

HOLZMAN, JAMES MAYER. **Pacifist Imperialism.** London: Williams and Norgate, 1930, 96 p.
A penetrating critique of the nationalistic era, a forecast of the disasters to which it will lead, and a plea for a new supernationality.

INTERNATIONAL INSTITUTE OF INTELLECTUAL COÖPERATION. **La Révision des Manuels Scolaires.** Paris: Author, 1932, 224 p.
A report on the progress to date in all countries towards the elimination from textbooks of matter likely to impede the growth of international good will.

JOSEPH, BERNARD. **Nationality, Its Nature and Problems.** New Haven: Yale University Press, 1929, 380 p.
A discussion of the various attributes of nationality and its effects on the state and on international relations, by a writer who is convinced that nationality is "the only logical and reasonable division of mankind into groups."

JOSEY, CHARLES CONANT. **Race and National Solidarity.** New York: Scribner, 1923, 227 p.
A critique of internationalism and cosmopolitanism by a writer who is impressed with the ideas of race and national character.

KEYSERLING, HERMANN, GRAF VON. **Europe.** New York: Harcourt, 1928, 399 p.
A lengthy survey of the European nations leads the author to the conclusion that no good has come or ever will come from the idea of nationalism.

LAVERGNE, BERNARD. **Le Principe des Nationalités et les Guerres.** Paris: Alcan, 1921, 211 p.
A series of essays, by a French professor, who discusses the "active" and "passive" types of national movements, the compatibility of colonization with principles of nationality, and the need of a super-state to supplement the League.

LE FUR, LOUIS. **Races, Nationalités, États.** Paris: Alcan, 1923, 156 p.
The author analyzes the relation of the current theories of race, nationality, and the state to the problem of federalism, international law, and the League.

MADARIAGA, SALVADOR DE. **Englishmen, Frenchmen, Spaniards.** New York: Oxford University Press, 1928, 256 p.
A stimulating and really brilliant attempt at the definition of national characteristics— probably as successful as an attempt to capture such elusive ideas can be.

MANTIS, *pseud.* (HARTMUT PIPER). **Die Diktatur im Anmarsch.** Leipzig: Weicher, 1928, 103 p.
The author foresees a new age of enlightened imperialism, in which the national states, under dictators, are welded together for common cultural tasks by a supernational agency.

MARGUERITTE, VICTOR. **La Patrie Humaine.** Paris: Flammarion, 1931, 287 p.
A French writer and internationalist pleads for French leadership not in military power, but in the realm of ideas and service of humanity.

MICHELS, ROBERT. **Der Patriotismus.** Munich: Duncker und Humblot, 1929, 275 p.
The eminent German-Italian sociologist has collected a mass of interesting data for a study of national feeling, but the material is in raw form.

MIQUEL, PAUL. **De la Patrie et du Patriotisme.** Paris: Figuière, 1931, 300 p.
An honest effort to reconcile the ideas of patriotism and human brotherhood.

MITSCHERLICH, WALDEMAR. **Nationalismus.** Leipzig: Hirschfeld, 1929, 373 p.
The reprint of a work which appeared in 1920 under the title "Der Nationalismus Westeuropas." The author deals with nationalism in its philosophical and political aspect and gives a good historical account of nationalism and the modern state.

OAKESMITH, JOHN. **Race and Nationality.** New York: Stokes, 1919, 300 p.
An interesting analysis of the idea of nationality, written in a detached spirit before the war. The author rejects the popular race theory and puts in its place the principle of "organic continuity of common interest."

PILLSBURY, WALTER BOWERS. **The Psychology of Nationality and Internationalism.** New York: Appleton, 1919, 314 p.
An analysis of nationality by an American psychologist.

PRIVAT, EDMOND. **Le Choc des Patriotismes.** Paris: Alcan, 1931, 180 p.
A League expert discusses the conflict of separatist and federalist principles.

RANDALL, JOHN HERMAN. **A World Community: The Supreme Task of the Twentieth Century.** New York: Stokes, 1930, 311 p.
A semi-popular but competent discussion of the rise of internationalism in the modern world and the obstacles to the realization of the new ideal.

REDSLOB, ROBERT. **Le Principe des Nationalités.** Paris: Sirey, 1930, 275 p.
A scholarly review of the origins, psychological foundations and constituents of nationality, with a discussion of possible solutions for the problems raised by the principle's application, especially the possibility of cultural autonomy for minorities.

SCHNEE, HEINRICH. **Nationalismus und Imperialismus.** Berlin: Hobbing, 1928, 375 p.
Written by the former German governor of West Africa, this book serves well as a general introduction, though it adds little. In two concluding chapters the author criticizes the colonial and minorities settlements of the peace treaties.

STAWELL, FLORENCE MELIAN. **The Growth of International Thought.** New York: Holt, 1930, 248 p.
A stimulating introductory survey, in the Home University Library series.

STOCKS, JOHN LEOFRIC. **Patriotism and the Super-State.** New York: Harcourt, 1920, 105 p.
A popular analysis of patriotism and nationalism, their relations to the state and to any super-state international organization, such as the author favors.

WOOLF, LEONARD SIDNEY. **After the Deluge.** New York: Harcourt, 1931.
The first volume of a large-scale study of the evolution of political theory in the 19th and 20th centuries. Mr. Woolf deals here, in fascinating style, with the implications of democracy and nationalism.

INTERNATIONAL GOVERNMENT
General

HILL, NORMAN LLEWELLYN. **International Administration.** New York: McGraw-Hill, 1931, 292 p.
Using the term administration in a broad sense, the author examines the various types of international agency, their organization, personnel, functioning, etc.

HILL, NORMAN LLEWELLYN. **The Public International Conference.** Stanford: Stanford University Press, 1929, 267 p.
A scholarly examination of its history, organization and procedure.

HOBSON, ASHER. **The International Institute of Agriculture.** Berkeley: University of California Press, 1931, 356 p.
An exhaustive monograph on the history and accomplishments of the institute.

HUGHAN, JESSIE WALLACE. **A Study of International Government.** New York: Crowell, 1923, 401 p.
A careful analysis of what has been accomplished by international agreements in the past, of the difficulties of the present problem, and of the contributions of the League of Nations toward its solution.

MINOST, E. **Le Fédéralisme Économique et les Sociétés à Charte Internationale. Les Coopérations Interétatistes.** Paris: Sirey, 1929, 235 p.
The author traces the growing interdependence of politics and economics, and reviews such early expressions of the phenomenon as the Suez Canal Company, the Bank of Morocco and the Turkish Petroleum Company.

MOWER, EDMUND CURTIS. **International Government.** Boston: Heath, 1931, 735 p.
A clear and straightforward text, surveying the machinery of international government as established since the World War.

International Waterways

*See also (United States) Relations with Canada, p. 179, and Relations with Latin America,
p. 179; also (Turkey) The Straits Question, p. 431; also (Egypt) Suez Canal, p. 506.*

ADAMYA, SIMA. **Le Régime International de l'Escaut.** Paris: Éditions Domat-
Montchrétien, 1929, 146 p.
The most recent treatment of the Scheldt problem, carrying the story to 1925. Rather
thin.

ANTIPA, GREGOR. **Dunărea și Problemele ei Științifice, Economice și Politice.**
Bucharest: Cartea Românească, 1921, 191 p.
A leading Rumanian scientist deals with the Danube question.

CHAMBERLAIN, JOSEPH PERKINS. **The Régime of the International Rivers: Danube
and Rhine.** New York: Longmans, 1923, 317 p.
Based upon material collected for the use of the Peace Conference delegation, this
is one of the best scholarly treatments of the problem.

CORTHÉSY, FERNAND. **Étude de la Convention de Barcelone sur le Régime des
Voies Navigables d'Intérêt International.** Paris: Rousseau, 1927, 202 p.
An analytical study of the régime of international waterways as set up by the con-
ference of 1921.

HAJNAL, HENRY. **Le Droit du Danube International.** Hague: Nijhoff, 1929, 324 p.
One of the most important books on the international law of rivers, written by an
eminent jurist and based on unpublished material in the Vienna archives. Though
the author goes back to 1856 there is a detailed discussion of the post-war settlement.

HENNIG, RICHARD. **Freie Ströme!** Leipzig: Gloeckner, 1926, 104 p.
A substantial study of the history and present law of international rivers.

JAUMIN, A. and JOTTARD, M. **La Question de l'Escaut.** Paris: L'Églantine, 1927,
136 p.
An able review of the old question of the Scheldt, tracing the negotiations since 1839
and stressing the recent developments.

KASAMA, AKIO. **La Navigation Fluviale en Droit International.** Paris: Éditions
Internationales, 1928, 238 p.
An historical study, with special attention to the Danube and Scheldt, and some con-
sideration of the Barcelona Conference of 1921.

KRAUSE, GERHARD. **Die Internationalen Stromschiffahrtskommissionen.** Berlin:
Rothschild, 1931, 104 p.
A succinct technical study of the organization and working of the river commissions
since 1856.

OGILVIE, PAUL MORGAN. **International Waterways.** New York: Macmillan, 1920,
424 p.
A study of the evolution of international law in the matter of waterways, with an
extended collection of documents.

QUINT, ARENT WILLEM. **Internationaal Rivierenrecht.** Amsterdam: Paris, 1930, 147 p.
A dissertation introducing the important problems raised by the use of international
rivers for other than shipping purposes.

RADOVANOVITCH, VOYSLAV M. **Le Danube et l'Application du Principe de la Liberté de la Navigation Fluviale.** Geneva: Georg, 1925, 336 p.
A thorough if somewhat pedestrian review of the international administration of the Danube.

RAVARD, ROGER. **La Danube Maritime et le Port Galatz.** Paris: Sagot, 1929, 218 p.
A description of the commercial function of the Danube, and of the work of the international commission, including an account of the commission's disputes with the Rumanian Government.

ROSSETTO, CARLO, *ed.* **La Commission Européenne du Danube et Son Œuvre de 1856 à 1931.** Paris: Imprimerie Nationale, 1931, 526 p.
An exhaustive history of the Commission's work, based on its archives and on studies by technical experts, edited by the Italian member.

SAURE, WILHELM. **Die Voelkerrechtliche Stellung des Rheins.** Berlin: Rothschild, 1931, 81 p.
A history and study of the present status of the Rhine in international law.

SMITH, HERBERT ARTHUR. **The Economic Uses of International Rivers.** London: King, 1931, 224 p.
A pioneer study of an increasingly pressing set of problems arising from interferences with rivers for purposes of diverting water, hydro-electric power, etc.

STRUYCKEN, ARNOLDUS J. **Veranderingen in het Rijnregiem na den Wereldoorlog.** Hague: Langenhuysen, 1929, 125 p.
A convenient statement of the Rhine control as set up in the peace treaties.

The League of Nations

Theory and Origins

See also (World War) The Peace Conference and the Peace Treaties, p. 157.

BARTOLOTTI, DOMENICO. **L'Utopia della Società delle Nazioni.** Turin: Lattes, 1920, 112 p.
An Italian writer on colonial affairs reviews the progress of arbitration before the war and bitterly criticizes the League as an organ to enforce unjust peace settlements.

BOURGEOIS, LÉON. **Le Pacte de 1919 et la Société des Nations.** Paris: Fasquelle, 1919, 279 p.
A collection of speeches delivered between 1916 and 1919 by one of the foremost French exponents of the League idea.

COSENTINI, FRANCESCO. **Préliminaires à la Société des Nations.** Paris: Alcan, 1919, 236 p.
A well-known Latin American sociologist discusses the social and intellectual prerequisites for a sound League structure.

CROZIER, ALFRED OWEN. **League of Nations. Shall It Be an Alliance, or a Nation of Nations?** New York: Lecouver, 1919, 196 p.
Controversial writing, in which the author argues against any alliance or camouflaged alliance, but pleads strongly for a "nation of nations" which the United States can join.

DEMONT, HENRI. **Pour Supprimer Ce Crime: La Guerre.** Limoges: Thomas, 1921, 293 p.
A passionate French criticism of the League as an inadequate institution, together with most far-reaching proposals for a "real" League.

DOMBROWSKI-RAMSAY, NICOLAS. **La Morale Humaine et la Société des Nations.**
Paris: Alcan, 1930, 123 p.
A general discussion of ethics in international relations, passing ideas of sovereignty,
the new international solidarity, social justice and universal peace.

DUGGAN, STEPHEN PIERCE, *ed.* **The League of Nations, the Principle and the
Practice.** Boston: Atlantic Monthly, 1919, 357 p.
A valuable collection of essays on many aspects of the League idea, written by quali-
fied authors for the general enlightenment of the layman.

ERZBERGER, MATTHIAS. **The League of Nations.** New York: Holt, 1919, 328 p.
The German edition of this book was published before Germany's collapse. It is
really, therefore, an independent project put forward by the German Catholic leader
who took so prominent a part in seeing the Peace Resolution of July 1917 through
the Reichstag.

GUTHRIE, WILLIAM DAMERON. **The League of Nations and Miscellaneous Addresses.**
New York: Columbia University Press, 1923, 383 p.
Papers on various national and international problems by a New York lawyer who
is also a consistently conservative publicist.

HALECKI, OSKAR, RITTER VON. **Liga Narodów.** Poznań: no pub., 1920, 196 p.
A general account of the genesis and organization of the League.

HAMILTON, SIR IAN. **The Millennium?** London: Arnold, 1919, 156 p.
An English soldier sees no hope in the League or in any organization except the British
Empire in alliance with the United States.

HEERFORDT, CHRISTIAN FREDERIK. **A New Europe.** London: Allen and Unwin, 1925,
221 p.
A translation from the Danish of a constructive survey of various plans for international organization.

HODÉ, JACQUES. **L'Idée de Fédération Internationale dans l'Histoire.** Paris: **La**
Vie Universitaire, 1921, 294 p.
A systematic study of schemes for a League, from the time of the Greeks to the
present.

KALLEN, HORACE MEYER. **The League of Nations, Today and Tomorrow.** Boston:
Marshall Jones, 1919, 181 p.
Written before the end of the war, this book is a complete study of what a League
could and should be if its purposes are to be attained.

KAO LU. **Conception d'une Fédération Mondiale.** Paris: Sirey, 1930, 116 p.
The Chinese Minister to France enters the lists on behalf of international solidarity.

KEEN, FRANK NOEL. **Towards International Justice.** New York: Harcourt, 1923,
249 p.
A collection of well-reasoned papers in support of the League of Nations, written by
an active English proponent of organization for peace, in the years 1915-1923.

LAMMASCH, HEINRICH. **Voelkermord oder Voelkerbund?** Hague: Nijhoff, 1920,
128 p.
A strong plea for international organization, by one of the foremost Austrian advocates of arbitration and coöperation.

LANDBERG, GEORG. **Fredensorganisation och Maktpolitik.** Stockholm: Natur och
Kultur, 1931, 190 p.
A stimulating volume stressing the constant conflict between the new ideas and the
old.

LAWRENCE, THOMAS JOSEPH. **The Society of Nations, Its Past, Present and Possible Future.** New York: Oxford University Press, 1919, 194 p.
Lectures delivered in 1917 by a leading English jurist. He reviews the progress made in international organization prior to 1914, the disastrous effects of the war, and the conditions for reconstructing international law and society.

The League of Nations Starts. London: Macmillan, 1920, 282 p.
A series of essays, by men associated with the League, discussing its structure and machinery. A valuable picture of the League in its first year.

MAKAROV, ALEKSANDR NIKOLAEVICH. **Liga Natsiï.** Leningrad: Academiia, 1922, 77 p.
A brief account of the League as viewed from Moscow.

MATHIEU, MARIE HENRY. **Évolution de l'Idée de Société des Nations.** Nancy: Lorraine, Rigot, 1923, 268 p.
A well-documented general survey of the development of the League idea from ancient times to the present. With a very complete bibliography.

MORROW, DWIGHT WHITNEY. **The Society of Free States.** New York: Harper, 1919, 223 p.
A reprint of newspaper articles by the American banker and statesman. He outlines the evolution of the League idea and the efforts at international coöperation among the Allies during the war, at the same time stressing the force of nationalism and other obstacles to international organization.

NEWFANG, OSCAR. **The Road to World Peace; a Federation of Nations.** New York: Putnam, 1924, 372 p.
An analysis of the League and its machinery, together with a forceful argument for its development into a real federation of nations with much broader power.

NEWFANG, OSCAR. **The United States of the World.** New York: Putnam, 1930, 284 p.
An examination of the American federal system, with a view to its applicability to the international problem.

PERCY, LORD EUSTACE. **The Responsibilities of the League.** London: Hodder, 1919, 319 p.
An eminently sane essay on the situation at the close of the war, the arduous tasks of peace, and the responsibilities assumed by Great Britain in support of the League experiment.

POSADA, ADOLFO. **La Sociedad de las Naciones y el Derecho Político.** Madrid: Raggio, 1925, 212 p.
A semi-popular approach stressing the problems arising from the conflict of national law and interests and the efforts at international action.

PRAZERES, OTTO. **A Liga das Nações.** Rio de Janeiro: Impr. Nacional, 1922, 331 p.
This book, written by a Brazilian journalist at the Peace Conference, outlines the basic conceptions underlying the League and discusses, in a broad way, the realization of the League idea in 1919.

PRICE, BURR. **The World Talks It Over.** New York: Henkle, 1927, 308 p.
A survey of the development of the ideas of international peace during the last century and a half.

REDSLOB, ROBERT. **Théorie de la Société des Nations.** Paris: Rousseau, 1927, 349 p.
A most interesting treatise, written with great breadth of view. The author studies, among other things, the League as an experiment in federalism, and compares it to the Swiss Confederation and the British Commonwealth.

RIVERO GARCÍA, CARLOS. **La Sociedad de Naciones.** Madrid: Ratés, 1927, 116 p.
The author is concerned largely with the status of the League in international law and with its competence for its tasks.

RUFFIN, HENRY. **Croyez-vous à la Société des Nations?** Paris: Plon, 1925, 190 p.
What everyone should know about the League—a concise realistic view.

SCHANZER, CARLO. **Sulla Società delle Nazioni.** Rome: Anonima Romana Editoriale, 1925, 236 p.
Essays on the functions of the League by a former Italian Foreign Minister.

STALLYBRASS, WILLIAM TEULON SWAN. **A Society of States.** New York: Dutton, 1919, 243 p.
An examination of the problems of sovereignty and equality of states, the author arguing that these principles will not be materially affected by membership in the League.

TCHERNOFF, J. **Les Nations et la Société des Nations dans la Politique Moderne.** Paris: Alcan, 1919, 200 p.
A most interesting study of the evolution of the League idea in England, France and the United States, and its conflict with the ideas of a British Commonwealth, with the ideas of French nationalism and with the ideas of the Monroe Doctrine.

TORRIENTE Y PERAZA, COSME DE LA. **Labor Internacional.** Havana: Rambla, Bouza, 1924, 248 p.
Speeches on the League and on international coöperation, by the 1924 President of the Assembly.

WALKER, JAMES and PETRE, MAUDE D. **State Morality and a League of Nations.** London: T. Fisher Unwin, 1919, 121 p.
An essay on the perennial conflict between ideas of state sovereignty and international organization, by strong proponents of the latter.

WILLIAMS, BRUCE STOCKTON. **State Security and the League of Nations.** Baltimore: Johns Hopkins, 1927, 356 p.
Albert Shaw lectures, constituting a competent review of the subject.

WOERDEN, F. A. VAN. **La Société des Nations et le Rapprochement Économique International.** Hague: Nijhoff, 1932, 298 p.
The writer stresses the possibilities of the League as an agent for smoothing out economic antagonisms.

The Covenant

General Discussion

ALVAREZ, ALEJANDRO. **L'Organisation Internationale.** Paris: Éditions Internationales, 1931, 357 p.
An eminent Latin American jurist urges revision of the Covenant along continental and regional lines.

BARROS BORGOÑO, LUIS. **El Convenio de la Liga de las Naciones.** Santiago de Chile: Imprenta Universitaria, 1920, 134 p.
A conventional analysis of the pact, intended for the general public.

FREYTAGH-LORINGHOVEN, AXEL, FREIHERR VON. **Die Satzung des Voelkerbundes.** Berlin: Stilke, 1926, 379 p.
A good account of the constitution of the League and of the International Court.

GOELLNER, ALADAR. **L'Article 19 du Pacte de la Société des Nations.** Paris: Rousseau, 1925, 108 p.
A Hungarian jurist's criticism of Article 19 of the Covenant, and his argument against the use of force in efforts to revise the treaties.

GRASSI, CARMELO. **Il Patto della Società delle Nazioni di Fronte alla Scienza del Diritto Internazionale.** Catania: La Siciliana, 1925, 157 p.
The relation of the pact to international law and to the exigencies of international politics.

HARLEY, JOHN EUGENE. **The League of Nations and the New International Law.**
New York: Oxford University Press, 1921, 127 p.
An analysis of the relationship of the Covenant to international law, with special
emphasis on the provisions of the pact for the outlawry of war and the settlement of
disputes.

HOIJER, OLOF. **Le Pacte de la Société des Nations.** Paris: Spès, 1926, 520 p.
One of the most pretentious legal expositions of the pact.

KOMARNICKI, TITUS. **La Question de l'Intégrité Territoriale dans le Pacte de la
Société des Nations.** Paris: Presses Universitaires, 1924, 282 p.
A thorough juristic study of this important problem, and in particular an analysis
of Article 10 of the pact.

KORÉNITCH, FÉODOR. **L'Article 10 du Pacte de la Société des Nations.** Paris: Bossuet,
1931, 210 p.
A microscopic analysis of a crucial article of the Covenant, together with some discussion of its relationship to the Geneva Protocol, the Locarno Agreements and the
Kellogg Pact.

KUNZ, JOSEF LAURENZ. **Die Intrasystematische Stellung des Artikels XI des
Voelkerbundpaktes.** Leipzig: Noske, 1931, 143 p.
A keen analysis of Article 11 of the Covenant, which the author regards as crucial
for the prevention of war. One of the best monographic studies of the pact.

MANDEL'SHTAM, ANDREÏ NIKOLAEVICH. **La Conciliation Internationale d'après le
Pacte et la Jurisprudence du Conseil de la Société des Nations.** Paris: Hachette,
1928, 316 p.
Lectures by a Russian jurist and former diplomat.

MARIOTTE, PIERRE. **Les Limites Actuelles de la Compétence de la S. D. N.** Paris:
Pedone, 1926, 296 p.
A minute legal study of sections 7 and 9 of Article 15.

METTETAL, ROGER. **La Neutralité et la Société des Nations.** Paris: Sirey, 1920,
138 p.
The author is concerned chiefly with the possible effect of membership in the League
upon Swiss neutrality.

MILHAUD, EDGARD. **Plus Jamais! L'Organisation de la Paix.** Geneva: Sonor, 1919,
415 p.
An elaborate examination of the Covenant, with proposals for strengthening amendments.

MILLER, DAVID HUNTER. **The Drafting of the Covenant.** New York: Putnam, 1928,
2 v.
Probably the most important contribution to the history of the making of the Covenant. The author, a legal adviser of the American Commission, was in close touch with
the work. Using much unpublished material, he analyzes the various drafts submitted
and discusses at length the modifications made in the Wilson draft. Volume II is
devoted entirely to documents.

NIEMEYER, THEODOR, RÜHLAND, CURT and SPIROPULOS, JEAN. **Der Voelkerbund:
Verfassung und Funktion.** Kiel: Verlag des Instituts für Internationales Recht,
1926, 115 p.
One of the best brief accounts of the origin and the organization of the League.

RADOJKOVIĆ, MILOSH M. **La Révision des Traités et le Pacte de la Société des
Nations.** Paris: Pedone, 1930, 349 p.
A scholarly approach to the problem of treaty revision under the Covenant.

RAY, JEAN. **Commentaire du Pacte de la Société des Nations.** Paris: Sirey, 1930, 717 p.
A monumental treatise containing all the important decisions and resolutions (as well as extracts from the debates) of the Assembly and the Council as they bear on the terms of the Covenant and the methods of its application. The best commentary in French, and one of the best systematic analyses of the League's constitution.

ROUSSEAU, CHARLES. **La Compétence de la Société des Nations dans le Règlement des Conflits Internationaux.** Paris: Imprimerie Administrative, 1927, 320 p.
This is a careful, well-documented piece of work, perhaps the best study of the competence of the League. The author devotes special attention to the status of the British Dominions and to the problems raised by the Monroe Doctrine.

SCELLE, GEORGES. **Le Pacte des Nations et Sa Liaison avec le Traité de Paix.** Paris: Sirey, 1919, 459 p.
A very full exposition of the provisions of the pact, for readers unversed in international law.

SCHINDLER, DIETRICH. **Die Verbindlichkeit der Beschlüsse des Völkerbundes.** Zurich: Orell-Füssli, 1927, 90 p.
Written by a Swiss professor, this is a technical monograph on the nature and force of resolutions and recommendations made by the League.

SCHUBERT, WILHELM F. **Voelkerbund und Staatssouveränität.** Berlin: Heymann, 1929, 128 p.
A very capable and thoroughly documented study of the theory of sovereignty and its incompatibility with modern ideas of international organization, written by a member of the League secretariat.

SCHÜCKING, WALTHER and WEHBERG, HANS. **Die Satzung des Völkerbundes.** Berlin: Vahlen, 1924, 794 p.
The second, revised and enlarged edition of what is easily one of the most exhaustive and authoritative commentaries on the Covenant.

SEVENS, CONSTANTIN LOUIS. **Le Régime Nouveau des Traités Internationaux.** Ghent: Van Rysselberghe, 1925, 60 p.
Examines Article 18 of the League pact and the abolition of secret diplomacy.

STRUB, WILHELM. **Die Mitgliedschaft im Voelkerbund.** Basel: Helbing und Lichtenhahn, 1927, 108 p.
An examination of the principles governing the admission of new League members.

WEHBERG, HANS. **Die Voelkerbundsatzung Gemeinverständlich Erläutert.** Berlin: Heusel, 1929, 207 p.
The third edition of a popular introduction to the study of the Covenant, the Locarno Pacts and the Kellogg Pact, by an outstanding German jurist.

WIGNIOLLE, ALBERT. **La Société des Nations et la Révision des Traités.** Paris: Rousseau, 1932, 324 p.
A scholarly examination of the possibility of treaty revision under the Covenant.

WILSON, FLORENCE. **The Origins of the League Covenant.** London: Hogarth, 1928, 260 p.
This volume, by the former librarian of the League, consists primarily of a careful analysis of the text of the Covenant, article by article, in the light of the discussions at the Peace Conference. The work is based on contemporary notes.

Sanctions

BARDELEBEN, HERBERT VON. **Die Zwangsweise Durchsetzung im Voelkerrecht.** Leipzig: Noske, 1930, 90 p.
Largely an analysis of military sanctions as provided for in the Covenant.

CODSI GOUBRAN, ——. **Le Problème des Sanctions dans l'Évolution de l'Arbitrage International.** Paris: Sagot, 1923, 442 p.
The most extensive scholarly treatment of the methods of making League action effective.

COHN, GEORG. **Kriegsverhütung und Schuldfrage.** Leipzig: Noske, 1931, 200 p.
An analysis of the provisions of the Covenant and the Kellogg Pact, with special reference to Article 16 of the Covenant and the question of sanctions.

DAVIES, DAVID. **The Problem of the Twentieth Century.** New York: Putnam, 1931, 795 p.
One of the most exhaustive and impressive works on the problem of sanctions. The author urges the establishment of an international police, composed of contingents supplied by League members, and endowed with a monopoly of most modern weapons of warfare.

FRANKE, ROBERT. **Der Wirtschaftskampf.** Leipzig: Noske, 1931, 121 p.
An historical examination of the place of economic sanctions in international law, with a discussion of the provisions for such sanctions in the League Covenant.

GORGÉ, CAMILLE. **Une Nouvelle Sanction du Droit International.** Lausanne: Payot, 1926, 105 p.
A review of the whole problem, followed by a scheme for the use of economic sanctions.

MITRANY, DAVID. **The Problem of International Sanctions.** New York: Oxford University Press, 1925, 88 p.
An examination of military and economic sanctions as means of enforcing peace, with special reference to the provisions of the Covenant and to the question of American policy.

RESSEGUIER, GUY DE. **Les Sanctions Militaires de la Société des Nations.** Paris: Presses Universitaires, 1930, 141 p.
A philosophical disquisition, followed by a study of the League provisions.

WILLE, CONRAD A. **Der Versailler Vertrag und die Sanktionen.** Berlin: Stilke, 1925, 243 p.
The author discusses in some detail the problem of military sanctions under the League system.

Attitudes of Individual Powers

ADAMS, GEORGE BURTON. **The British Empire and a League of Peace.** New York: Putnam, 1919, 115 p.
Essays dealing chiefly with Anglo-Saxon solidarity and various phases of federal organization.

BRUNET, RENÉ. **La Société des Nations et la France.** Paris: Sirey, 1921, 286 p.
A thoughtful statement of French policy with respect to the League, by an authoritative writer on constitutional problems.

CANSACCHI, GIORGIO PROSPERO. **Il Papa e la Società delle Nazioni.** Turin: Bocca, 1929, 103 p.
A purely legal study of the anomalous position of the Papacy with regard to the League.

CARRASCO, JOSÉ. **Bolivia's Case for the League of Nations.** London: Selwyn, 1920, 156 p.
The author deals with the Tacna-Arica difficulty and inquires what Bolivia can hope to secure through League action.

CLARKE, JOHN HESSIN. **America and World Peace.** New York: Holt, 1925, 152 p.
Three lectures in which a former justice of the United States Supreme Court pleads for America's entry into the League and discusses the terms and meaning of the Geneva Protocol.

DEUTSCHE LIGA FÜR VÖLKERBUND, BERLIN. **Deutschland und der Voelkerbund.** Berlin: Hobbing, 1926, 216 p.
An important series of essays on the League by men like Stresemann, Löbe, Simons, Dernburg, Bernstorff, Kraus, Mendelssohn and Montgelas.

DICKINSON, THOMAS HERBERT. **The United States and the League.** New York: Dutton, 1923, 151 p.
An account of the "tragedy" of 1920 and a bitter criticism of the group of men who defeated what the author believes were the real desires of the American people.

ELLIS, A. D. **Australia and the League of Nations.** Melbourne: Macmillan, 2nd ed., 1926, 88 p.
A popular survey of Australia's position in the League and its contribution to the League's activities.

FERRI, CARLO EMILIO. **La Società delle Nazioni e l'Italia.** Milan: 1924, 126 p.
A good presentation of the possibilities of the League, by a competent writer on international affairs.

FEYLER, FERNAND. **La Ligue des Nations et la Neutralité de la Suisse.** Lausanne: Revue Militaire Suisse, 1919, 103 p.
A competent Swiss military man analyzes the possible reaction of League membership upon his country's neutrality.

FISHER, IRVING. **League or War.** New York: Harper, 1923, 268 p.
The author discusses the problem of war and its cost, and the accomplishments of the League as an agency for peace. He argues strongly for American participation.

FLEMING, DENNA FRANK. **The United States and the League of Nations.** New York: Putnam, 1932, 568 p.
A highly useful contribution to the study of American foreign policy. The author gives a complete documented account of the conflict between President Wilson and the Senate, and of the League issue as it was brought before the electorate in 1920.

FOLEY, HAMILTON, *comp.* **Woodrow Wilson's Case for the League of Nations.** Princeton: Princeton University Press, 1923, 271 p.
This little volume, written with Wilson's approval, is a digest of his opinions, based on speeches and on explanations to the Foreign Relations Committee.

GALEANO, VÉNANCIO B. **L'Amérique Latine, les États-Unis et la Société des Nations.** Paris: 1927, 234 p.
A doctoral dissertation analyzing, in rather conventional fashion, the difficulties of Latin America's position between the United States and the League.

GAY, FRANCISQUE. **L'Irlande et la Société des Nations.** Paris: Bloud et Gay, 1921, 164 p.
The author believes Ireland would be "assured her liberty" by adopting a policy of "pacific work" instead of following the catastrophic policy of the past.

HARRIMAN, EDWARD AVERY. **The Constitution at the Crossroads.** New York: Doran, 1925, 274 p.
A keen analysis of the legal aspects of the League, the Labor Office and the Court, designed to answer for the United States the question of what sacrifices membership would entail.

HEILE, WILHELM. **Nationalstaat und Voelkerbund.** Halberstadt: Meyer, 1926, 101 p.
The writer deprecates overemphasis on nationality and sees in coöperation with the League the possibility of an important mission for the new Germany.

KELCHNER, WARREN H. **Latin American Relations with the League of Nations.** Boston: World Peace Foundation, 1930, 207 p.
A detailed study of how and why the various states entered the League, what they contributed, and why several of them are no longer members. The book has chapters on the movement of Latin American opinion and is a useful contribution.

LODGE, HENRY CABOT. **The Senate and the League of Nations.** New York: Scribner, 1925, 424 p.
A work of importance, setting forth a Republican view of President Wilson's League policy in Paris and in Washington.

LUKAS, JOSEF. **Deutschland und die Idee des Völkerbundes.** Münster: Schultze, 1921, 127 p.
An inquiry into the fundamental ideas and possibilities of the League, with an ardent plea for German participation and support, despite the connection of the League with the Peace Treaty.

MACEDO-SOARES, JOSÉ CARLOS DE. **Brazil and the League of Nations.** Paris: Pedone, 1928, 270 p.
The English translation of a Brazilian statement regarding the establishment of the League and Brazil's considerable contribution, followed by a critical account of Brazil's withdrawal in 1926.

MANDERE, H. CH. G. J. VAN DER. **De Volkenbond en Zijn Belang voor Nederland.** Hague: n. d., 131 p.
The writer stresses the important part that Holland could and should play in the League, in accordance with past traditions.

MARIOTTE, PIERRE. **L'Europe et les États-Unis devant la Société des Nations.** Paris: Éditions Internationales, 1930, 300 p.
The author examines the elusive question of the relation of the United States to the League's work, and its obligations in that connection.

MATSUSHITA, MASATOSHI. **Japan in the League of Nations.** New York: Columbia University Press, 1929, 175 p.
A much-needed and thoroughly reliable discussion of the part played by Japan in the establishment of the League and of her interest in its activities.

MOREL, ALPHONSE. **La Neutralité de la Suisse et la Société des Nations.** Lausanne: Rouge, 1931, 177 p.
The author holds the League Covenant to be incompatible with the maintenance of Swiss neutrality.

MORIAUD, PAUL. **La Société des Nations et la Suisse.** Berne: Büchler, 1919, 100 p.
A book published under the auspices of the Société Suisse de la Paix and dealing with the vexed problem of Swiss neutrality.

MUNCH, PETER. **La Politique du Danemark dans la Société des Nations.** Geneva: Kundig, 1931, 43 p.
The Danish foreign minister gives an excellent survey not only of Danish policy but of Danish contributions.

NAGY, ELEK. **Magyarország és a Népszövetség.** Budapest: Franklin, 1925, 208 p.
A convenient study of Hungary's admission to the League and the treatment of Hungarian frontier, minorities and financial problems through the League.

NIPPOLD, OTFRIED. **Der Völkerbundsvertrag und die Frage des Beitritts der Schweiz.** Berne: Wyss, 1919, 102 p.
A veteran Swiss jurist and advocate of peace examines the peculiar problems raised for Switzerland by the League.

PAGE, KIRBY. **An American Peace Policy.** New York: Doran, 1925, 94 p.
A concise and convincing presentation of the internationalist view, stressing the urgent need for American participation in the League and the World Court to make effective the outlawry of war.

PLÁ CÁRCELES, JOSÉ. **La Misión Internacional de la Raza Hispánica.** Madrid: Morata, 1928, 136 p.
Primarily a study of Spain's opportunities for action through the League.

RAKOVSKIĬ, KHRISTIAN GEORGIEVICH. **Liga Natsiĭ i S. S. S. R.** Moscow: Communist Academy, 1926, 82 p.
A brief communist statement, including an essay by Chicherin on Soviet Russia and the League.

RAPPARD, WILLIAM EMMANUEL. **La Politique de la Suisse dans la Société des Nations, 1920-1925.** Geneva: Éditions Forum, 1925, 155 p.
One of the foremost protagonists of the League recalls the struggle to assure Swiss adherence and reviews the important part played by Switzerland during the League's first five years.

ROLIN, HENRI A. **La Politique de la Belgique dans la Société des Nations.** Geneva: Kundig, 1931, 87 p.
One of the useful series published by the Institut de Hautes Études Internationales.

SIVORI, JUAN B. **La Liga de las Naciones, Su Origen y la Obra Realizada en la República Argentina.** Buenos Aires: Roldán, 1928, 588 p.
An interesting record of the work carried on by proponents of the League in Argentina.

TAFT, WILLIAM HOWARD. **Papers on the League of Nations.** Edited by Theodore Marburg and Horace E. Flack. New York: Macmillan, 1926, 360 p.
A convenient compilation, well edited.

VALENTIN, VEIT. **Geschichte des Völkerbundgedankens in Deutschland.** Berlin: Engelmann, 1920, 170 p.
An excellent essay on the evolution of the League idea in the larger setting of German intellectual history.

WALDECKER, LUDWIG. **Die Stellung der Menschlichen Gesellschaft zum Voelkerbund.** Berlin: Heymann, 1931, 374 p.
This heavily documented book gives a comprehensive survey of the attitude of various social groups to the idea of international organization generally and to the League in particular. The bulk of the volume is devoted to examining the different nations as states, while other chapters take up such questions as Pan-America and Pan-Europe, and discuss the activities of parties, social classes, professions and religious groups.

WALLER, BOLTON C. **Ireland and the League.** Dublin: Talbot, 1925, 74 p.
A suggestive sketch, setting forth Ireland's obligations and opportunities.

WEHBERG, HANS. **Deutschland und der Genfer Voelkerbund.** Leipzig: Oldenburg, 1923, 116 p.
A popular presentation of League possibilities, by a leading German pacifist.

Activities

General

See also (France: Relations with Germany) Saar, p. 267; also (Central Europe) Austria, p. 305, and Hungary, p. 308; etc.

ALEXANDER, HORACE GUNDRY. **The Revival of Europe.** London: Allen and Unwin, 1924, 215 p.
An intelligent, moderate review of the League's work during the first five years, together with a constructive argument for increasing its power.

ARNSKOV, LAURITS THOMAS LAURSEN. **Folkeforbundet, dets Organisation og Virksomhed i Hovedtraek.** Copenhagen: Reitzel, 1925, 236 p.
A general treatment of the League machinery and its functioning.

AVILA LIMA, LOBO D'. **Da Sociedade das Nações.** Lisbon: Rodrigues, 1927, 191 p.
The history, constitutional structure and machinery of the League, surveyed by a Portuguese writer on economic and political problems.

BAKER, PHILIP JOHN NOEL. **The League of Nations at Work.** London: Nisbet, 1926, 151 p.
A competent popular presentation written for the layman.

BASSETT, JOHN SPENCER. **The League of Nations.** New York: Longmans, 1928, 415 p.
Detached and dispassionate chronological account of the work of the League during its first seven years, with an interesting chapter on the American attitude.

BEER, MAX. **Die Reise nach Genf.** Berlin: Fischer, 1932, 533 p.
The author, a German correspondent at Geneva, is disappointed by signs of the steady encroachments of the old diplomacy. An interesting book.

BOURGEOIS, LÉON. **L'Œuvre de la Société des Nations.** Paris: Payot, 1924, 456 p.
A survey by one of the most prominent participants in the League's work, covering the years 1920-1923, with emphasis on the French contribution.

BRADFIELD, B. **A Little Book of the League of Nations, 1920-1927.** New York: Stechert, 1927, 112 p.
A little survey for the general public, unusually well done.

BÜLOW, BERNHARD WILHELM VON. **Der Versailler Voelkerbund.** Berlin: Kohlhammer, 1923, 608 p.
An elaborate account of the League's organization and activity in early years, by a well-informed and sympathetic German.

BUTLER, SIR GEOFFREY GILBERT. **A Handbook to the League of Nations.** New York: Longmans, 1925, 255 p.
A well-known text, revised to include the fifth assembly and the Geneva Protocol. Half of the book is given over to a chronological table and to important documents.

CALOMFIRESCO, R. **L'Organisation et l'Œuvre Économique de la Société des Nations.** Paris: Presses Universitaires, 1929, 240 p.
A systematic review of the organization and work of the Economic Committee, the Conference of 1927 and the ensuing changes.

CONWELL-EVANS, THOMAS P. **The League Council in Action.** New York: Oxford University Press, 1929, 292 p.
A purely analytical scholarly study of the Council's action in the twenty-three disputes with which it had dealt.

DENMARK-UDENRIGSMINISTERIET. **Folkeforbundets Første Tiaar.** Copenhagen: Levin and Muncksgaard, 1930, 238 p.
A review of League activities in the first decade, published by the Danish Foreign Office and containing contributions by members of the Danish Government.

EPPSTEIN, JOHN, *comp.* **Ten Years' Life of the League of Nations.** London: Mayfair Press, 1930, 176 p.
One of the best of the many popular surveys of the history and activity of the League, the Labor Office and the World Court. Lavishly illustrated.

GONSIOROWSKI, MIROSLAS. **Société des Nations et Problème de la Paix.** Paris: Rousseau, 1927, 2 v., 1058 p.
A huge legal study of the mechanism of the League for preventing war.

GREAVES, HAROLD RICHARD GORING. **The League Committees and World Order.**
New York: Oxford University Press, 1931, 266 p.
The writer analyzes the system and working of the League technical and advisory committees, such as the economic, financial and health committees, the Committee on Intellectual Coöperation, and the mandates and disarmament committees. The book is well-informed and authoritative.

HARRIS, HENRY WILSON. **The League of Nations.** New York: Cape and Smith, 1930, 127 p.
A good brief survey along conventional lines.

HOWARD-ELLIS, CHARLES. **The Origin, Structure and Working of the League of Nations.** London: Allen and Unwin, 1928, 528 p.
On the whole the most complete and authoritative exposition in English. The author aims to go beyond mere popular surveys.

HUDSON, MANLEY OTTMER. **Current International Coöperation.** Calcutta: Calcutta University Press, 1927, 149 p.
The author outlines the growth of international coöperation before the war and gives an admirable brief summary of the work of the League and the international courts.

HUDSON, MANLEY OTTMER. **Progress in International Organization.** Stanford: Stanford University Press, 1932, 171 p.
A brief but authoritative statement of the evolution and present status of organs for international coöperation, with stress on American contributions and obligations.

JONES, ROBERT and SHERMAN, SIMON S. **The League of Nations: From Idea to Reality.** New York: Putnam, 1927, 229 p.
A survey of the whole development of the idea of world unity, with an account of the organization of the League and its activities.

LANGE, ROBERT. **Vers un Gouvernement International?** Paris: Commerce des Idées, 1928, 152 p.
The author, a protagonist of the League, examines the system of representation at Geneva and criticizes the organization of the Council.

LEAGUE OF NATIONS—SECRETARIAT. **Ten Years of World Co-operation.** Boston: World Peace Foundation, 1930, 467 p.
The distinguishing feature of this volume is that it is the work of the League Secretariat itself, brought out on the occasion of the tenth anniversary of the League. The writers are all of them thoroughly competent and speak with the authority of first-hand knowledge. The material is comprehensive and well integrated.

LEVERT, JOHAN ALEX. **De Economische en Financieele Organisatie van den Volkenbond.** Wageningen: Veenman, 1929, 197 p.
A monographic study of an important aspect of the League organization.

MENGELE, FERENC. **A Népszövetség Jogi és Politikai Rendszere.** Budapest: Franklin, 1927, 408 p.
A good Hungarian description and analysis of League activities.

MILIĆ, MILENKO. **Les Attributions Communes et les Rapports du Conseil et de l'Assemblée de la Société des Nations.** Paris: Derre, 1929, 316 p.
A doctoral dissertation setting forth the lack of system in the division of power and in the relations between the Council and the Assembly of the League.

MORLEY, FELIX. **The Society of Nations.** Washington: Brookings Institution, 1932, 700 p.
A valuable detailed study of the origin of the organization and the way it works. The author considers changes that have occurred, and weaknesses and limitations that have come to light.

MUNCH, PETER, *ed*. **Les Origines et l'Œuvre de la Société des Nations.** Copenhagen: Gyldendal, 1923, 2 v.
A large coöperative work.

MYERS, DENYS PETER. **Nine Years of the League of Nations.** Boston: World Peace Foundation, 1929, 220 p.
An excellent brief survey of the work of the League from 1920 to 1928, by a well-informed and careful writer.

ORÚE, JOSÉ RAMÓN DE. **La Sociedad de Naciones.** Madrid: Góngora, 1925, 244 p.
One of the best Spanish books on the League.

OTTLIK, GEORGES, *ed*. **Annuaire de la Société des Nations.** Geneva: Payot, 1927 ff.
An indispensable handbook of the organization and activities of the League, the Labor Office and the World Court. Annual since 1927; the first volume covers 1920-1927.

PHILIPSE, ADRIAAN HENDRIK. **Le Rôle du Conseil de la Société des Nations dans le Règlement des Différends Internationaux.** Hague: Nijhoff, 1929, 285 p.
A penetrating discussion of the part of the Council in the settlement of international disputes.

POLLOCK, SIR FREDERICK. **The League of Nations.** London: Stevens, 1922, 266 p.
A practical handbook, with an historical introduction.

QUIGLEY, HAROLD SCOTT. **From Versailles to Locarno.** Minneapolis: University of Minnesota, 1927, 170 p.
A convenient outline for popular use, discussing the organization of the League and the Court and reprinting the most important documents.

RAPPARD, WILLIAM EMMANUEL. **The Geneva Experiment.** New York: Oxford University Press, 1931, 115 p.
These lectures, by a man closely associated with the League, discuss the nature of the organization and its constitutional development, and its work in the cause of peace.

RAPPARD, WILLIAM EMMANUEL. **International Relations as Viewed from Geneva.** New Haven: Yale University Press, 1925, 238 p.
One of the best books on the League's work during the first lustrum.

RAPPARD, WILLIAM EMMANUEL. **Uniting Europe.** New Haven: Yale University Press, 1930, 334 p.
A review of the progress towards settlement of outstanding problems, with a concise summary of the League's work.

REDDIE, SAMUEL GEORGE. **The Great Delusion. The League of Nations.** London: Marshall, 1926, 54 p.
The League represented as the supreme disappointment.

RÉMOND, PIERRE. **Le Règlement Pacifique des Conflits Internationaux par la Société des Nations.** Paris: Revue Mondiale, 1927, 236 p.
A summary of the League's work in the cause of peace during the first six years of its existence.

ROTHBARTH, MARGARETE. **Geistige Zusammenarbeit im Rahmen des Voelkerbundes.** Münster: Aschendorff, 1931, 195 p.
The first monographic treatment of the League's work in the direction of intellectual coöperation, written by a woman closely associated with the League's activities.

SCELLE, GEORGES. **Une Crise de la Société des Nations.** Paris: Presses Universitaires, 1927, 256 p.
An excellent critical study of the difficult period from March to September 1926, with the reform of the Council and the admission of Germany.

SCHOU, PETER CHRISTIAN. **Nationernes Samfund.** Copenhagen: Martin, 1926, 253 p.
A record of the League's work, by a Danish protagonist.

SOFRONIE, GEORGE. **Contributii la Cunoasterea Sociețatei Natiunilor.** Bucharest:
Toroutiu, 1927, 165 p.
A general introduction.

SWEETSER, ARTHUR. **The League of Nations at Work.** New York: Macmillan, 1920,
215 p.
Primarily a survey of the organization and machinery of the League, written for
American enlightenment by an American closely connected with the Geneva organization.

VÖLLMAR, HENRI FRÉDÉRIC ARNOLD. **Les Finances de la Société des Nations.**
Hague: Nijhoff, 1924, 116 p.
An historical and analytical treatment of the financing of international organizations
and especially of the financial machinery of the League. The author is a Dutch judge.

WALP, PAUL K. **Constitutional Development of the League of Nations.** Lexington:
University of Kentucky, 1931, 190 p.
A documented analysis of the relations between the Council and the Assembly, as
originally worked out and as modified in practice.

WEHBERG, HANS. **Grundprobleme des Völkerbundes.** Berlin: Hensel, 1926, 108 p.
A valuable inquiry, by a leading German authority, into some of the fundamental
questions confronting the League after the first years of trial.

WILLIAMS, ROTH. **The League of Nations Today.** New York: Holt, 1923, 223 p.
A popular book on the machinery and history of the League, with a special section
on its value for Britain and its relationship to British problems.

ZIMMERMANN, M. A. **Společnost Národu.** Prague: Orbis, 1931, 387 p.
An historical and analytical treatment of the League of Nations, based on a wide
knowledge of the primary and secondary material.

ZIMMERN, MRS. LUCIE A. **Must the League Fail?** London: Hopkinson, 1932, 96 p.
An outspoken criticism of the development of the League in recent years and of the
efforts of some governments to appropriate it to purposes of the old diplomacy.

Mandates

*See also (Germany) The Question of Colonies, p. 336; also (Near East) General, p. 422, Pales-
tine, p. 433, Syria, p. 437, and Iraq, p. 441; also (Pacific Area) Pacific Islands, p. 494; also
(Africa: British Possessions) East Africa, p. 509; also (Africa: French Possessions) West
and Central Africa, p. 521.*

BENTWICH, NORMAN DE MATTOS. **The Mandates System.** New York: Longmans, 1930,
211 p.
The Attorney-General of Palestine reviews the working of the various mandates,
especially the A Mandates. One of the best books on the subject.

FEINBERG, NATHAN. **La Juridiction de la Cour Permanente de Justice Internationale dans le Système des Mandats.** Paris: Rousseau, 1930, 238 p.
A thorough and authoritative study of a neglected aspect of mandate control.

FERRI, CARLO EMILIO. **La Teoria dei Mandati Internazionali.** Turin: Bocca, 1927,
407 p.
An extensive study of the mandates system from the legal standpoint.

GERIG, BENJAMIN. **The Open Door and the Mandates System.** London: Allen and
Unwin, 1930, 236 p.
A pioneer study of the economic system under the old colonial régime as it has been
modified by the provisions of the mandates.

MAANEN-HELMER, ELIZABETH VAN. **The Mandates System in Relation to Africa and the Pacific Islands.** London: King, 1929, 332 p.
Primarily a study of the constitutional development of the mandates system and of the nature of the control of native populations, with special reference to B and C Mandates.

MARGALITH, AARON M. **The International Mandates.** Baltimore: Johns Hopkins Press, 1930, 251 p.
A general study of the origins and character of the mandates system, with much stress on the evolution of the principles involved and an extended discussion of the question of sovereignty.

PAHL, RUDOLF. **Das Völkerrechtliche Kolonial-Mandat.** Berlin: Stollberg, 1929, 222 p.
A careful and thoroughly documented study of the legal aspects of mandates.

REES, DANIEL FRANÇOIS WILLEM VAN. **Les Mandats Internationaux: Le Contrôle International de l'Administration Mandataire.** Paris: Rousseau, 1927, 145 p.
One of the most important books on the question of the organization and control of mandates, by the Vice President of the Permanent Mandates Commission of the League.

REES, DANIEL FRANÇOIS WILLEM VAN. **Les Mandats Internationaux: Les Principes Généraux du Régime des Mandats.** Paris: Rousseau, 1928, 259 p.
In this second book the author examines the theory of the system. His wide experience lends particular weight to his views.

RODRÍGUEZ DE GORTÁZAR, JOAQUÍN M. **Los Mandatos Internacionales en la Política Colonial.** Valencia: Rens, 1928, 305 p.
A good general work on the operation of the mandates.

ROTH, HEINZ. **Das Kontrollsystem der Voelkerbundsmandate.** Berlin: Dümmler, 1930, 124 p.
The author examines the general powers of the League and more especially the workings of the Mandates Commission as a fact-finding and supervisory organization.

SCHNEIDER, WOLFGANG. **Das Voelkerrechtliche Mandat in Historisch-Dogmatischer Darstellung.** Stuttgart: Ausland und Heimat, 1926, 103 p.
A technical study of the position of mandates in international law with particular stress on the problem of sovereignty in the B and C Mandates.

STOYANOVSKY, J. **La Théorie Générale des Mandats Internationaux.** Paris: Presses Universitaires, 1925, 254 p.
One of the best treatments of the general theory of mandates, questions of sovereignty, etc.

VALLINI, ALBERTO. **I Mandati Internazionali della Società delle Nazioni.** Milan: Hoepli, 1923, 282 p.
A competent technical study of the mandate system, with special emphasis on the responsibilities of mandatory powers to the League and to the mandated peoples.

WHITE, FREDA. **Mandates.** London: Cape, 1926, 196 p.
A popular, up-to-date presentation, published for the League of Nations Union. The book is largely a survey of the individual mandated territories.

WRIGHT, QUINCY. **Mandates under the League of Nations.** Chicago: Chicago University Press, 1930, 726 p.
The most inclusive and exhaustive treatment of the subject. The reader will find an authoritative account of the origin and organization of the mandate system, an extended analysis of the international law of mandates, their relation to accepted ideas of sovereignty and territorial rights, their bearing on problems of international administration and their achievements in furthering the political, economic and cultural development of the mandated peoples.

Minorities

See also (Italy) Dodecanese, p. 285, and South Tyrol Question, p. 289; also (Czechoslovakia) Minorities, p. 318; also (Germany) Minorities Abroad, p. 337; also (Poland) Minorities, p. 356; also (Russia) Minorities, p. 396; also (Rumania) Transylvania, p. 406; also (Jugoslavia) The Macedonian Problem, p. 411; etc.

ACI-MONFOSCA, ENRICO. **Le Minoranze Nazionali.** Rome: Vallecchi, 1929, 2 v.
One of the best books on the problem of minorities. Proceeding by nations, the author gives historical and statistical material and examines the working of the treaties. The first volume is devoted to the Baltic and Central European areas, the second to the Balkans and Turkey.

AUERHAN, JAN. **Die Sprachlichen Minderheiten in Europa.** Berlin: Hensel, 1926, 155 p.
A Czech writer reviews the situation of the minorities and the provisions for protection. Though tending to minimize grievances, the author admits the need for special protection.

BALOGH, ARTHUR VON. **Der Internationale Schutz der Minderheiten.** Munich: Dresler, 1928, 293 p.
This heavily documented study of the protection of minorities contains interesting chapters on the early phases of international action, the first constitutional safeguards in individual states, and the nationalities congresses during the Great War.

BANEKOVIĆ, ANTE. **Za Prava Čovjeka.** Zagreb: no pub., 1931, 96 p.
A series of speeches and essays published by the Institute for Minorities.

BOUFFAŁŁ, BRONISŁAW. **Ochrona Mniejszości w Prawie Narodów.** Warsaw: Towarzystwo Naukowe, 1928, 229 p.
A thorough, documented study of the treaties and the League procedure, written from a Polish nationalist viewpoint and rather critical of international interference.

BRUNS, KARL GEORG. **Grundlagen und Entwicklung des Internationalen Minderheitenrechtes.** Berlin: Deutsche Gesellschaft für Nationalitätenrecht, 1929, 48 p.
A concise legal study of the minorities clauses of the treaties, by the expert adviser of the German minorities organizations.

BUZA, LÁSZLÓ. **A Kisebbségek Jogi Helyzete.** Budapest: Magy. Tud. Akad., 1930, 432 p.
A scholarly but conventional study of the protection of minorities, with emphasis exclusively on the international machinery and its past workings.

ERLER, GEORG H. J. **Das Recht der Nationalen Minderheiten.** Münster: Aschendorff, 1931, 530 p.
Easily one of the best treatments of the history and actual status of European minorities, from the political as well as from the legal standpoint.

FEINBERG, NATHAN. **La Juridiction de la Cour Permanente de Justice dans le Système de la Protection Internationale des Minorités.** Paris: Rousseau, 1931, 215 p.
An exhaustive technical study of the provisions for the protection of minorities in the statute of the court.

FEINBERG, NATHAN. **La Question des Minorités à la Conférence de la Paix.** Paris: Rousseau, 1929, 167 p.
A Palestine judge reveals the action of Jewish interests at the Peace Conference in behalf of oppressed minorities and the efforts made to secure a system of cultural autonomy for the Jews.

FOUQUES-DUPARC, JACQUES. **La Protection des Minorités de Race, de Langue et de Religion.** Paris: Dalloz, 1922, 369 p.
The first scholarly post-war treatment. The author discusses principles and the historical evolution of the question, and analyzes the provisions for protection.

FRIEDMAN, SAMUEL. **Le Problème des Minorités Ethniques.** Paris: Librairie Générale de Droit et de Jurisprudence, 1927, 196 p.
A careful scholarly analysis, leading the author to advocate the introduction of a system of autonomy. The book contains a good discussion of the language problem in pre-war Austria.

GARGAS, SIGISMUND. **Die Minderheit.** Hague: Belinfonte, 1926, 104 p.
The problem of minorities attacked from the sociological standpoint by a purely descriptive method.

GRENTRUP, THEODOR. **Nationale Minderheiten und Katholische Kirche.** Breslau: Hirt, 1927, 174 p.
A scholarly monograph on an important aspect of the minorities question. The author examines provisions of ecclesiastical law as they touch persons and property, and then reviews the working of these regulations in European minority areas.

HAJN, ALOIS, *ed.* **Problém Ochrany Menšin.** Prague: Orbis, 1923, 300 p.
A collection of essays on aspects of the minorities problem, with special reference to provisions for protection by international agreement.

JAMES, EDWARD HOLTON. **Crossroads in Europe.** Geneva: Kundig, 1929, 201 p.
The minorities problem in easy doses. Articles reprinted from the New York *World*.

JUNGHANN, OTTO and BOEHM, MAX HILDEBERT. **Ethnopolitischer Almanach.** Vienna: Braumüller, 1930, 182 p.
A handy survey, by various authors, of some of the outstanding minorities problems of Europe, with an appendix containing the more important documents.

KRAUS, HERBERT. **Das Recht der Minderheiten.** Berlin: Stilke, 1927, 36 p.
A collection of the essential documents bearing on the problem of minorities, with valuable explanatory notes by a German expert. Probably the best and most useful collection of sources.

KRSTIĆ, DRAGOLJUB. **Les Minorités, l'État, et la Communauté Internationale.** Paris: Rousseau, 1924, 337 p.
The problem of the protection of minorities, from ancient times to the present.

LESSING, OTTO EDUARD, *ed.* **Minorities and Boundaries.** New York: Van Riemsdyck, 1931, 162 p.
A series of papers by various authors dealing with Alsace-Lorraine, the Germans in Czechoslovakia, the *Anschluss* problem, the Polish Corridor, and the general question of minorities.

LUCIEN-BRUN, JEAN. **Le Problème des Minorités devant le Droit International.** Paris: Spès, 1923, 230 p.
A well-informed treatment, historical, descriptive and largely legalistic, written with a pronounced Catholic bias.

MAIR, L. P. **The Protection of Minorities.** London: Christophers, 1928, 244 p.
A faithful account of the problem, reviewing in some detail the actual working of the minorities treaties in the various countries of Europe.

MANDEL'SHTAM, ANDREÏ NIKOLAEVICH. **La Protection Internationale des Minorités.** Paris: Sirey, 1931, 220 p.
One of the soundest treatments, written by a former Russian diplomat. The historical treatment of intervention by European powers in behalf of Christian minorities in the old Ottoman Empire is particularly good.

MINTZ, MORITZ. **Die Nationale Autonomie im System des Minderheitenrechts.** Riga: no pub., 1927, 142 p.
A theoretical treatment of the problems of national autonomy, together with an analysis of autonomy in practice in the Baltic States.

NOEL-BUXTON, EDWARD, BARON and CONWELL-EVANS, THOMAS P. **Oppressed Peoples and the League of Nations.** New York: Dutton, 1922, 230 p.
A keen critique of the territorial peace settlement, with a study of the post-war minorities problem and suggestions for a permanent minorities commission.

RAUCHBERG, HEINRICH. **Die Reform des Minderheitenschutzes.** Prague: Calve, 1930, 76 p.
Primarily a discussion of recommendations recently made by various international organizations and a critique of the League Council's stand.

ROUČEK, JOSEPH SLABEY. **The Working of the Minorities System under the League of Nations.** Prague: Orbis, 1929, 122 p.
A well-documented systematic study of the minorities problem at the Peace Conference, the minorities treaties, the procedure of the League and Court, and finally of certain selected cases as they have been dealt with in the last decade. One of the best general accounts in English.

RUYSSEN, THÉODORE. **Les Minorités Nationales d'Europe et la Guerre Mondiale.** Paris: Presses Universitaires, 1924, 422 p.
A valuable and competent study by a French professor. The book deals largely with the territorial changes wrought by the war, and not so much with the condition of minorities since the war.

SABELLI, LUCA DEI. **Nazionale Minoranze Etniche.** Bologna: Zanichelli, 1929, 2 v.
An elaborate work setting forth the Fascist view of the question.

STEPHENS, JOHN S. **Danger Zones of Europe.** London: Hogarth, 1929, 86 p.
A lucid exposition of the rise of the idea of nationality and its effects, followed by a review of the minorities questions of present-day Europe.

TRAMPLER, KURT. **Staaten und Nationale Gemeinschaften.** Munich: Oldenbourg, 1929, 141 p.
A more general treatment of the problem of minorities, including a keen criticism of the present system of protection and the action of the League, and a convincing plea for the extension of the system of cultural autonomy.

TRUHART, HERBERT VON. **Voelkerbund und Minderheitenpetitionen.** Vienna: Braumüller, 1931, 181 p.
The author enumerates the minority petitions that have been presented to the League and lays its failure to act effectively to its clumsy machinery.

VIDRASCO, ROMEO. **De la Réserve du Droit des Minorités et du Contrôle des Puissances.** Paris: Jouve, 1921, 193 p.
A dissertation reflecting the prevalent Rumanian hostility to the minorities régime and condemning efforts made to secure for minorities a "privileged" position.

WERTHEIMER, FRITZ. **Deutschland, die Minderheiten und der Voelkerbund.** Berlin: Heymann, 1926, 152 p.
A consideration of the minorities question and the possibilities of League action. The approach is from the German angle, but the book is eminently dispassionate and fair. A unique feature is the excellent account of the organization of the minorities movement since the war.

WINTGENS, HUGO. **Der Voelkerrechtliche Schutz der Nationalen Sprachlichen und Religiösen Minderheiten.** Stuttgart: Kohlhammer, 1930, 502 p.
A general treatise on the protection of minorities, with special reference to the problem of German minorities in Poland. The book is a reprint from the "Handbuch des Voelkerrechts," is heavily documented, and contains an extensive bibliography. On the whole the most exhaustive study of legal aspects of the question.

Opium

BUDISTEANU, RADU. **L'Aspect International de la Lutte contre l'Opium.** Paris: Pichon et Durand-Auzias, 1929, 106 p.
A concise review of the part played by the League in the control and regulation of the traffic.

DUNN, WIE TSAIN. **The Opium Traffic in Its International Aspects.** New York: Columbia University Press, 1920, 136 p.
A well-documented doctoral thesis reviewing the history of the problem in China, with further chapters on other countries and on the situation prior to 1920.

GASTINEL, JEAN. **Le Trafic des Stupéfiants.** Aix-en-Provence: Roubaud, 1927, 203 p.
A dissertation devoted largely to an analysis of the trade and efforts made before the war to control it.

GAVIT, JOHN PALMER. **Opium.** New York: Brentano, 1927, 308 p.
A general introduction for the layman, with emphasis on the work of the Geneva Conferences, by a competent American newspaperman.

HOIJER, OLOF. **Le Trafic de l'Opium et d'Autres Stupéfiants.** Paris: Spès, 1925, 300 p.
One of the ablest and most complete studies of the historical development of the problem from the early 19th century to the conferences of the post-war period.

KAKU, SAGATARO. **Opium Policy in Japan.** Geneva: Kundig, 1924, 56 p.
An account of the policy of gradual suppression followed by the Japanese in Formosa, by a former governor of the island.

LA MOTTE, ELLEN NEWBOLD. **The Ethics of Opium.** New York: Century, 1924, 205 p.
A description of the importance of the opium trade in modern diplomacy.

LA MOTTE, ELLEN NEWBOLD. **The Opium Monopoly.** New York: Macmillan, 1920, 84 p.
A convenient brief survey of the world market and trade.

LIAIS, MICHEL. **La Question des Stupéfiants Manufacturés et l'Œuvre de la Société des Nations.** Paris: Sirey, 1928, 208 p.
A conscientious review of the drug laws of the nations chiefly concerned, followed by a systematic account of international action for control and suppression.

PILA, J. JOSEPH. **Le Trafic des Stupéfiants et la Société des Nations.** Paris: Sirey, 1925, 398 p.
A review of all the stupefying drugs, followed by a detailed study of the work of the Geneva Conferences. The book, written by a druggist, contains an excellent bibliography.

SZE, SAO-KE ALFRED. **Geneva Opium Conferences.** Baltimore: Johns Hopkins Press, 1926, 163 p.
The statements of the Chinese delegation to the Conference, and a good general account of conditions as well as policies.

TERRY, CHARLES EDWARD and PELLENS, MILDRED. **The Opium Problem.** New York: Bureau of Social Hygiene, 1928, 1042 p.
An elaborate report drawn up for the Committee on Drug Addictions.

WILLOUGHBY, WESTEL WOODBURY. **Opium as an International Problem. The Geneva Conferences.** Baltimore: Johns Hopkins Press, 1925, 585 p.
An exhaustive scholarly examination of the subject by one who served as counsellor of the Chinese delegation. The book is the most complete analysis of the post-war problem and the efforts made to solve it.

WISSLER, ALBERT. **Die Opiumfrage.** Jena: Fischer, 1931, 274 p.
The history of the international effort to regulate the sale of opium. The most recent systematic treatment.

ZENDER, JUSTIN. **La Question de l'Opium.** Geneva: Jent, 1929, 283 p.
A good monographic study of the post-war conferences and agreements.

THE INTERNATIONAL LABOR OFFICE

ARGENTIER, CLÉMENT. **Les Résultats Acquis par l'Organisation Permanente du Travail.** Paris: Sirey, 1930, 592 p.
A conventional but unusually detailed review of the accomplishments of the International Labor Organization.

BARNES, GEORGE NICOLL. **History of the International Labour Office.** London: Williams and Norgate, 1926, 106 p.
A good brief survey by one of the officials of the Office.

BEHRENS, EDWARD BEDDINGTON. **The International Labour Office.** London: Parsons, 1924, 220 p.
The organization and work of the Labor Office. A good introductory account.

COURTIN, RENÉ. **L'Organisation Permanente Internationale du Travail.** Paris: Dalloz, 1923, 359 p.
A good, well-documented monograph. The author sketches the history of international regulation of labor, studies the legal status and competence of the new organization and discusses its work to 1923.

FABRA RIBAS, ANTONIO. **La Organización Internacional del Trabajo.** Madrid: Pedreño, n. d., 198 p.
A popular account, largely historical and covering the ground through the seventh conference of 1925. There is a good survey of the various commissions of the organization.

FEHLINGER, HANS. **Internationaler Arbeiterschutz.** Berlin: Heymann, 1926, 132 p.
A brief account of the organization and work of the International Labor Office, by one of the officials.

GODART, JUSTIN. **Les Clauses du Travail dans le Traité de Versailles.** Paris: Dunod, 1920, 230 p.
An historical study of the labor clauses, followed by an exposition of the new international organization provided for by the treaty.

GUERREAU, MAURICE. **L'Organisation Permanente Internationale du Travail.** Paris: Rousseau, 1923, 628 p.
Another competent and exhaustive historical and analytical monograph.

HETHERINGTON, HECTOR JAMES WRIGHT. **International Labour Legislation.** London: Methuen, 1920, 194 p.
A good introduction to the subject, with a detailed description of the Washington Conference and the organization of the Labor Office.

JOHNSTON, GEORGE ALEXANDER. **International Social Progress.** New York: Macmillan, 1924, 263 p.
An excellent documented study by a Scotch professor closely associated with the International Labor Organization. He describes in detail the machinery and its working during the first four years.

Labor as an International Problem. London: Macmillan, 1920, 345 p.
A valuable collection of papers on the subject indicated, including the Washington Conference and the International Labor Office. Among the authors are G. N. Barnes, J. T. Shotwell, E. Vandervelde and Albert Thomas.

LORWIN, LEWIS LEVITZKI. **Labor and Internationalism.** New York: Macmillan, 1929, 682 p.
This is probably the best general account in English of the development of international labor movements in the last century. The author deals in detail with the first "Internationales," the shock of the war, and post-war developments. The book contains an extensive bibliography.

MAHAIM, ERNEST. **L'Organisation Permanente du Travail.** Paris: Hachette, 1923, 155 p.
A useful survey, interesting especially for the analysis of fundamental problems confronting the organization.

MILLER, DAVID HUNTER. **International Relations of Labor.** New York: Knopf, 1921, 77 p.
Lectures on the history and present organization of international action in labor problems.

MONDAINI, GENNARO and CABRINI, ANGIOLO. **L'Evoluzione del Lavoro nelle Colonie e la Società delle Nazioni.** Padua: Studi Coloniali, 1931, 378 p.
The work of the League in dealing with labor questions in the colonies.

MÜNZENBERG, WILLI. **Solidarität.** Berlin: Neuer Deutscher Verlag, 1931, 527 p.
A competent survey of the work of the Labor Office during the last decade. One of the best books of its kind.

OLIVER, MRS. E. M. **The World's Industrial Parliament.** London: Allen and Unwin, 1925, 63 p.
One of the best short popular accounts of the International Labor Organization.

PÉRIGORD, PAUL. **The International Labor Organization.** New York: Appleton, 1926, 368 p.
A conventional detailed account of the history and organization of the Labor Office.

PŘIBRAM, KARL. **Die Probleme der Internationalen Sozialpolitik.** Leipzig: Hirschfeld, 1927, 196 p.
The author, an official of the Labor Office, reviews its organization and functioning and then analyzes some of the leading problems with which it has to deal.

RITZMANN, FRIEDRICH. **Internationale Sozialpolitik.** Mannheim: Bensheimer, 1925, 220 p.
An excellent historical study of international social legislation, with important documents in the appendix.

WORLD PEACE FOUNDATION. **The International Labour Organisation.** Boston: Author, 1931, 382 p.
This account of the organization and work of the Labor Office was written by officials with first-hand knowledge and experience. A companion volume to the ten-year survey of the League's work.

THE PERMANENT COURT OF INTERNATIONAL JUSTICE

BUSTAMANTE Y SIRVÉN, ANTONIO SÁNCHEZ DE. **The World Court.** New York: Macmillan, 1925, 404 p.
The English translation of a standard work by a justice of the Court. The author traces the idea of international justice from the time of the Greeks, recalls the activities of many organizations, reviews the work of the Hague Conferences and the Central American Court and then discusses in detail the establishment and work of the new Court.

DAUVERGNE, C. **La Fonction Consultative de la Cour Permanente de Justice Internationale.** Montpellier: 1925, 152 p.
A conscientious systematic study of the question of advisory opinions.

FACHIRI, ALEXANDER PANDELLI. **The Permanent Court of International Justice.** New York: Oxford University Press, 1925, 342 p.
A substantial account of the organization and working of the Court. The author gives a documented analysis of the first fourteen cases, discusses the connection between the Court and the League, and prints all the documents of importance in the history of the tribunal.

FARAG, WADIE M. **L'Intervention devant la Cour Permanente de Justice Internationale.** Paris: Librairie Générale de Droit, 1927, 144 p.
A technical study of Articles 62 and 63 of the Statute of the Court.

FRANCQUEVILLE, BERNARD DE. **L'Œuvre de la Cour Permanente de Justice Internationale.** Paris: Éditions Internationales, 1928, 2 v.
An exhaustive and authoritative study of the cases thus far submitted to the Court and the disposal made of them. The arrangement is in groups by subject.

GEÖCZE, BARTHOLOMAUS. **Nemzetközi Bíróságok Hatáskore.** Budapest: 1931, 335 p.
An important study of the jurisdiction of international tribunals in theory and practice, written by a man who has often represented Hungary in international litigation.

GIBLIN, JAMES VINCENT and BROWN, ARTHUR LEWIS. **The World Court Myth.** Boston: Wright and Potter, 1926, 457 p.
An examination of some of the problems connected with the Court.

HEYL, FRIEDRICH WILHELM. **Die Tätigkeit des Internationalen Gerichtshofs, 1922-1928.** Ochsenfurt: Fritz und Rappert, 1930, 110 p.
The author treats more especially the Court's handling of the question of German minorities in Poland.

HILL, DAVID JAYNE. **The Problem of a World Court.** New York: Longmans, 1927, 225 p.
A classic formulation of the argument against the "League Court," by a well-known American diplomat.

HUDSON, MANLEY OTTMER. **The Permanent Court of International Justice.** Cambridge: Harvard University Press, 1925, 389 p.
A reprint of valuable articles in which a leading American authority recounts the founding and early history of the Court and discusses, from many angles, the question of American participation. Many documents are printed in the appendices.

HUDSON, MANLEY OTTMER. **The World Court, 1921-1931.** Boston: World Peace Foundation, 1931, 245 p.
The third, revised edition of a general handbook of the Court. The author gives the essential facts of its history, composition and working. The bulk of the space is devoted to reviewing all the cases that have come before the tribunal, together with an analysis of the advisory opinions rendered. Thoroughly documented throughout.

JESSUP, PHILIP CARYL. **The United States and the World Court.** Boston: World Peace Foundation, 1929, 165 p.
A valuable and thoroughly detached record of the negotiations following the Senate resolution of January 1926, with much documentary material.

KELLOR, FRANCES ALICE and HATVANY, ANTONIA. **The United States Senate and the International Court.** New York: Seltzer, 1925, 372 p.
A detailed account of the Court and the attitude of the Senate.

LINDSEY, EDWARD. **The International Court.** New York: Crowell, 1931, 347 p.
An up-to-date manual of the Court's history, organization and activity.

MANDERE, H. CH. G. J. VAN DER. **Het Permanente Hof van Internationale Justicie s' Gravenhage.** Leyden: Sijthoff, 1922, 328 p.
A general introduction. The author reviews the work of the Hague Conferences and then discusses the organization of the new Court.

MULLER, HELEN MARIE, *comp.* **The World Court.** New York: Wilson, 1931, 252 p.
A good reference book, with an admirable bibliography.

PEPPER, GEORGE WHARTON. **In the Senate.** Philadelphia: Pennsylvania University Press, 1930, 148 p.
Reminiscences containing interesting chapters on the World Court and International Conferences, as they were dealt with in the Senate.

PEREIRA DA SILVA, FERNANDO CORREIA. **La Réforme de la Cour Permanente de Justice Internationale.** Paris: Sirey, 1931, 251 p.
The author discusses chiefly the protocol of 1929 and Cuba's veto.

SCOTT, JAMES BROWN. **The Project of a Permanent Court of International Justice and Resolutions of the Advisory Committee of Jurists.** Washington: Carnegie Endowment for International Peace, 1920, 235 p.
A valuable collection of source material for the history of the Court.

WHEELER-BENNETT, JOHN WHEELER. **Information on the Permanent Court of International Justice.** London: Association for International Understanding, 1925, 75 p.
A compact manual, containing all important documents.

WORLD PEACE FOUNDATION. **Ten Years of International Jurisdiction.** Boston: Author, 1932, 74 p.
A brief survey of the work of the Court, published on its tenth anniversary.

VI. WAR, PEACE, SECURITY AND DISARMAMENT

WAR

General

ALLEN, WILLIAM CHARLES. **War! Behind the Smoke Screen.** Philadelphia: Winston, 1929, 199 p.
War stripped of its glamour, with illustrations from the great conflict of 1914-1918.

ASTON, SIR GEORGE GREY, *ed.* **The Study of War for Statesmen and Citizens.** New York: Longmans, 1927, 213 p.
Lectures on various aspects of modern war, by authoritative writers.

CHARTIER, ÉMILE. **Mars, or the Truth about War.** New York: Cape and Smith, 1930, 318 p.
Essays by a French philosopher and pacifist who knows war at first hand.

COSTE, CHARLES. **La Psychologie Sociale de la Guerre.** Nancy: Berger-Levrault, 1928, 112 p.
An interesting doctoral thesis analyzing the methods of moral mobilization, the technique of propaganda, the value of psychological stimuli, etc.

COWAN, ANDREW REID. **War in World History.** New York: Longmans, 1929, 126 p.
The author sets forth the essentially destructive influence of war on the progress of civilization, but sees little prospect of man's rising above his fundamental malignity.

CUSTANCE, SIR REGINALD NEVILLE. **A Study of War.** Boston: Houghton Mifflin, 1925, 223 p.
A sound discussion of the political and military aspects, by a British admiral.

FULLER, JOHN FREDERIC CHARLES. **The Reformation of War.** New York: Dutton, 1923, 287 p.
A somewhat pompous but concise and pertinent discussion of the necessity of facing war as a permanent fact in human society, and of proceeding to reduce the brutality and carnage attendant upon the introduction of new methods of warfare based on contemporary applied science.

GINI, CORRADO. **Problemi Sociologici della Guerra.** Bologna: Zanichelli, 1921, 390 p.
A volume of important essays, explaining wars as due primarily to pressure of population.

HUBERT, RENÉ. **Les Interprétations de la Guerre.** Paris: Flammarion, 1919, 322 p.
A reappraisal of the arguments used to justify war, a consideration of war's less tangible results, and an evaluation of the peace problem.

MAUROIS, ANDRÉ. **The Next Chapter: The War against the Moon.** New York: Dutton, 1928, 46 p.
An effective take-off on the belligerent instincts of man. A book which will repay reading.

NEARING, SCOTT. **War: Organized Destruction and Mass Murder by Civilized Nations.** New York: Vanguard, 1931, 318 p.
An attack upon our present civilization, which makes war inevitable.

PALMER, JOHN MCAULEY. **Statesmanship or War.** New York: Doubleday, 1927, 232 p.
The author discusses the feasibility of a military system akin to the Swiss, in order to provide a "respectably defensive posture."

SAGERET, JULES. **Philosophie de la Guerre et de la Paix.** Paris: Alcan, 1919, 431 p.
One of the best general treatments of the biological and psychological factors in war, followed by an analysis of the peace problem.

SCHOMER, ABRAHAM SHAIKEWITZ. **War and Peace in the New Light of Intellectology.** Los Angeles: Provisional Committee for an Alliance for Control of War, 1929, 80 p.
An effort to get at the root causes of all wars through scientific study of thought.

STEINMETZ, SEBALD RUDOLF. **Soziologie des Krieges.** Leipzig: Barth, 1929, 704 p.
A new, rewritten and much enlarged edition of the author's "Philosophie des Krieges," published in 1907. The most pretentious post-war study of the nature and implications of war.

WINGFIELD-STRATFORD, ESMÉ CECIL. **They That Take the Sword.** New York: Morrow, 1932, 438 p.
An historical and philosophical critique of the use of force and a ruthless exposure of the ineptitude of the military mind.

Modern Warfare

General

AUSTIN, FREDERICK BRITTEN. **The War-God Walks Again.** New York: Doubleday, 1926, 274 p.
The war of the future, with stress on the new mechanisms and the new technique.

BERNHARDI, FRIEDRICH VON. **The War of the Future.** New York: Appleton, 1921, 310 p.
Starting with the lessons of the Great War, a famous German military writer discusses the changes that have come about in technique and tactics.

BOUVARD, H. **Les Leçons Militaires de la Guerre.** Paris: Masson, 1920, 320 p.
An analysis of the changes in various arms, with a discussion of their prospective use.

DOUHET, G. **Probabili Aspetti della Guerra Futura.** Palermo: Sandron, 1928, 67 p.
A short survey of the new technique in land, sea and air warfare.

GERMAINS, VICTOR WALLACE. **The Mechanization of War.** London: Sifton Praed, 1927, 269 p.
A solid study of the interdependence of services and the value of mechanical contrivances in modern warfare. The author has much to say of the use of tanks and takes issue with those who believe the future lies with mechanized armies.

GIBBS, SIR PHILIP. **The Day after Tomorrow.** New York: Doubleday, 1928, 240 p.
Not content with the evils of today, a well-known journalist engages in speculation on the future developments of science and paints a lugubrious picture of coming wars.

HALL, NORRIS FOLGER, CHAFEE, ZECHARIAH and HUDSON, MANLEY OTTMER. **The Next War.** Cambridge: Harvard Alumni Bulletin Press, 1925, 108 p.
An interesting little symposium by three Harvard professors.

IMMANUEL, FRIEDRICH. **Der Grosse Zukunftskrieg.** Berlin: Offene Worte, 1932, 164 p.
A realistic military view of the "impending" conflict, by a prolific German military writer.

INTER-PARLIAMENTARY UNION. **What Would Be the Character of a New War?** London: King, 1931, 411 p.
A report drawn up by experts for the Inter-Parliamentary Union. There are chapters on the mechanization of war and on the new weapons, on the adaptability of modern states for the needs of war, on the methods of defense against the new warfare, and a special section on chemical and bacteriological warfare. Other chapters take up the psychological, demographic, financial and general economic effects of war. Among the contributors are General Réquin, Major Lefebure, General Montgelas, Francis Delaisi, Paul Haensel, Sir Norman Angell and Nicolas Politis.

LIDDELL HART, BASIL HENRY. **The Remaking of Modern Armies.** Boston: Little, Brown, 1928, 327 p.
Taking as his keynote the mobility of armies, the author starts out by demonstrating that in the last war armies had mass without velocity, with the result that there was a general paralysis in the form of trench warfare. Military organization must adapt itself to the demands of mechanization and the only solution lies in the development of large numbers of small fast tanks to take the place of cavalry and in the extension of the use of non-lethal gases, which, for effectiveness and humaneness, are preferable to almost all other modes of warfare.

LUDENDORFF, ERICH. **The Coming War.** London: Faber, 1931, 176 p.
The famous German commander envisages a new and more technical war which will end in the complete ruin of Europe.

MANCEAU, ÉMILE. **La Guerre d'Hier et l'Armée de Demain.** Paris: Garnier, 1921, 214 p.
An analysis of various problems of material and personnel, with suggestions for general reorganization.

RITTER, HANS. **Der Zukunftskrieg und Seine Waffen.** Leipzig: Koehler, 1924, 102 p.
A most interesting discussion of the possible future development of death rays, bacteriological warfare, etc.

SOLDAN, GEORGE. **Der Mensch und die Schlacht der Zukunft.** Oldenburg: Stalling, 1925, 108 p.
The author believes that technical developments have sounded the end of conscripted armies, and that now small units, selected and fully equipped, are wanted.

Chemical Warfare

BLOCH, D. P. **La Guerre Chimique.** Paris: Berger-Levrault, 1927, 117 p.
　　One of the best general treatments of chemical warfare, with stress on the French and German potentialities in production.

FRADKIN, MRS. ELVIRA THEKLA (KUSH). **Chemical Warfare.** New York: Carnegie Endowment, 1929, 192 p.
　　A general treatment, historical and analytical, with consideration of the law of gas warfare and the difficulties involved in reduction or limitation of its use.

HANSLIAN, R. **Der Chemische Krieg.** Berlin: Mittler, 1927, 411 p.
　　The history of gas warfare, together with a detailed account of the principal gases, the modes of use and the methods of defense.

LEFEBURE, VICTOR. **The Riddle of the Rhine.** New York: Chemical Foundation, 1923, 282 p.
　　One of the best-informed English writers on the subject reviews the use of gas in the war, discusses its probable development and analyzes the problem in the larger setting of disarmament.

LEROUX, LUCIEN. **La Guerre Chimique.** Paris: Spès, 1932, 150 p.
　　A popular account of modern chemical warfare and its implications.

LE WITA, HENRI. **Autour de la Guerre Chimique.** Paris: Tallandier, 1928, 218 p.
　　An excellent survey of the present status of gas warfare and a keen analysis of future dangers.

MEYER, J. **Der Gaskampf und die Chemischen Kampfstoffe.** Leipzig: Hirzel, 1926, 470 p.
　　One of the most detailed technical studies of gas offense and defense, with an exhaustive catalogue of the principal gases and their handling.

WOKER, GERTRUD. **Der Kommende Giftgaskrieg.** Leipzig: Oldenburg, 1925, 134 p.
　　Reviewing the past history of gas warfare, the author stresses the inadequacy of defense methods and therefore the dangers involved in the future use of chemicals.

Air Warfare

See also (International Law) Air Law, p. 37; also (World War) War in the Air, p. 145.

ASHMORE, EDWARD BAILEY. **Air Defence.** New York: Longmans, 1929, 179 p.
　　A discussion of the attack and defense of cities, the author arguing that air defense is more necessary than offense. There is also a full description of the war-time raids on Britain.

BURNEY, SIR CHARLES DENNISTOUN. **The World, the Air, and the Future.** New York: Knopf, 1929, 356 p.
　　A criticism of the development of British Air forces since the war, a plea for pushing ahead with that branch of defense, and a suggestion for the international organization of civil flying.

DOUHET, G. **Il Dominio dell' Aria.** Rome: Stabilimento Poligrafico, 1921, 191 p.
　　A descriptive study of air warfare, with some consideration of its prospective development.

ENGBERDING, R. **Luftschiff und Luftschiffahrt in Vergangenheit, Gegenwart und Zukunft.** Berlin: Udi Verlag, 1928, 303 p.
　　One of the best books on dirigibles, with considerable attention to their military possibilities.

Jane's All the World's Aircraft. London: Sampson Low, 1930, 598 p.
　　The most recent edition of the standard English manual of aircraft. This publication lists the military as well as civil air forces of all countries.

MITCHELL, WILLIAM. **Winged Defense.** New York: Putnam, 1925, 261 p.
The former director of military aviation in the United States Army states his views regarding the development of modern air power and criticizes this branch of American national defense.

NEON, *pseud.* **The Great Delusion.** New York: Dial Press, 1927, 327 p.
The author presents a complete case against aircraft, for either military or commercial purposes, and collects an imposing number of testimonials to bolster up his case. The book is vigorously and brilliantly written, and though biased, serves as an antidote to excessive optimism. The introduction is by Arthur H. Pollen.

NIESSEL, HENRI ALBERT. **La Maîtrise de l'Air.** Paris: Perrin, 1928, 255 p.
An interesting study of the conditions of air power, followed by a discussion of air organization in France and other countries, and a consideration of the problem of coördinating air with land and sea operations.

ROYSE, MORTON WILLIAM. **Aerial Bombardment and the International Regulation of Warfare.** New York: Vinal, 1928, 356 p.
An impressive study showing the changes wrought in the position of non-combatant populations through the advance in technical aspects of warfare, and suggesting methods of meeting the new situation.

SHERMAN, WILLIAM CARRINGTON. **Air Warfare.** New York: Ronald Press, 1926, 307 p.
A discussion of the fundamental principles of aërial combat, with a description of the different forms of aircraft, their limitations and advantages. The author is an instructor in air tactics at Fort Leavenworth.

SPAIGHT, JAMES MOLONY. **Air Craft and Commerce in War.** New York: Longmans, 1926, 111 p.
A general examination of the problem of defending commerce from aërial attack, and a plea for the strengthening of British air forces with that end in view. The author is Director of Accounts in the British Air Ministry.

SPAIGHT, JAMES MOLONY. **The Beginnings of Organised Air Power.** New York: Longmans, 1927, 317 p.
A detailed and authoritative study of the organization and work of the British Air Ministry, with some consideration of the problems and policies of France, the United States and Germany.

SPAIGHT, JAMES MOLONY. **Air Power and the Cities.** New York: Longmans, 1930, 244 p.
One of the foremost writers on problems of air defense discusses the crucial question of the situation of cities under the new conditions of war and the security value of larger air forces.

SPAIGHT, JAMES MOLONY. **An International Air Force.** London: Gale and Polden, 1932, 115 p.
A realistic study of one of the newer phases of security discussions.

SUETER, MURRAY FRASER. **Airmen or Noahs?** London: Pitman, 1928, 441 p.
A loosely argued and rather ineffective reply to Neon's "The Great Delusion." The writer sees a great future for submarines, tanks and aircraft.

Taschenbuch der Luftflotten—Pocket Almanac of Aeronautics. Munich: Lehmann, 1931, 3 v.
One of the best surveys. Volume III deals with military aviation, the text being in German, English and French.

THOMSON, CHRISTOPHER BIRDWOOD THOMSON, BARON. **Air Facts and Problems.** London: Murray, 1927, 255 p.
The former British Secretary for Air discusses the importance of military aviation, especially for England.

VAUTHIER, ARSÈNE MARIE PAUL. **Le Danger Aérien et l'Avenir du Pays.** Paris: Berger-Levrault, 1930, 388 p.
A competent analysis of the nature of aërial warfare, followed by an original and thoughtful study of the fundamental principles of national defense.

WHALE, GEORGE. **British Airships.** London: Lane, 1919, 244 p.
The past, present and future of British dirigibles, with stress on their military accomplishments and possibilities.

Miscellaneous Phases

BAUER, HERMANN. **Das Unterseeboot.** Berlin: Mittler, 1931, 144 p.
The former German commander of the submarine service discusses the naval value, international status and probable future development of this weapon.

CASPARY, ADOLF. **Wirtschaftsstrategie und Kriegsführung.** Berlin: Mittler, 1932, 166 p.
Reviewing the history of wars since classic times, the author analyzes the economic aspects of the preparation, the conduct and the effects of international conflict.

DUMAS, SAMUEL and VEDEL-PETERSEN, KNUD OTTO. **Losses of Life Caused by War.** Oxford: Clarendon Press, 1923, 191 p.
A valuable statistical summary of the losses in war since 1756, with detailed information on the World War.

LEHMANN-RUSSBÜLDT, OTTO. **War for Profits.** New York: King, 1930, 175 p.
A valuable study of the international connections of the munitions industry.

MAURICE, SIR FREDERICK. **Governments and War.** London: Heinemann, 1926, 171 p.
A series of lectures dealing with the relationship of the civil to the military administration in times of war.

NORMAND, ROBERT. **Destructions et Dévastations au Cours des Guerres.** Paris: Berger-Levrault, 1927, 316 p.
A careful technical study of the basis of reparations.

ROMANET DU CAILLAUD, JACQUES. **L'Indemnité de Dommages de Guerre.** Paris: Sagot, 1925, 550 p.
An authoritative technical discussion of the problem of war damage in all its aspects.

WILSON, HERBERT WRIGLEY. **Battleships in Action.** Boston: Little, Brown, 2 v.
An exhaustive, standard history of the evolution of naval warfare since 1866.

PEACE

General

ALLEN, DEVERE. **The Fight for Peace.** New York: Macmillan, 1930, 751 p.
A broad history of the American peace movement during the last century, with abundant quotations from sources, followed by an analysis of the problem in our own day and the organizations working for its solution.

ALLEN, DEVERE, ed. **Pacifism in the Modern World.** New York: Doubleday, 1929, 296 p.
A series of essays by Tagore, J. H. Holmes, Kirby Page and others, in defense of the pacifist attitude.

ANGELL, SIR NORMAN. **The Fruits of Victory.** New York: Century, 1921, 338 p.
A sequel to "The Great Illusion." A brilliant analysis of the economic factors that go into the deep-seated instinct to dominate.

ANGELL, SIR NORMAN. **Human Nature and the Peace Problem. Foreign Policy and Our Daily Bread.** London: Collins, 1925, 171, 202 p.
Essays of a well-known pacifist writer.

ANGELL, SIR NORMAN. **The Unseen Assassins.** New York: Harper, 1932, 349 p.
The "Unseen Assassins" are the aims and policies followed by governments and peoples without full realization that they lead to war. Among these are doctrines of sovereignty, nationalism, etc., the implications of which are here fully revealed.

BAKELESS, JOHN EDWIN. **Economic Causes of Modern War.** New York: Moffat, 1921, 265 p.
An analysis of some twenty international conflicts between 1878 and 1918 with reference to the economic factors. An able and stimulating book.

BAKHMETEV, BORIS ALEKSANDROVICH. **The Legacy of War: Peace.** Boston: Houghton Mifflin, 1927, 53 p.
An eloquent defense of democratic ideas as the surest guarantees of domestic and international peace, by the former Russian Ambassador to the United States.

BAUER, LUDWIG. **War Again Tomorrow.** London: Faber, 1932, 314 p.
A pacifist's lugubrious view of the League, the Versailles settlement, Sovietism, Fascism, Americanism, and other matters. A critical work worth attention.

BEALES, ARTHUR CHARLES FREDERICK. **The History of Peace.** New York: Dial Press, 1931, 355 p.
A scholarly study of the history of the peace movement and peace organizations in the 19th century. Probably the best general historical approach.

BERGSTRÄSSER, ARNOLD. **Sinn und Grenzen der Verständigung zwischen Nationen.** Munich: Duncker und Humblot, 1930, 91 p.
A stimulating essay in which the author attempts to put "international understanding" on a realistic basis and to study it as a practicable and profitable policy.

BLACHEZ, RENÉ. **La Nation Armée et l'Idéologie des Nationalités.** Brussels: DeWit, 1921, 201 p.
A review of the development of European politics in the past century and a scathing indictment of ideas which have led to the massacre of ten million men.

BOECKEL, FLORENCE BREWER. **Between War and Peace.** New York: Macmillan, 1928, 601 p.
A valuable handbook for peace workers, reviewing what has been done and what can be done to promote international goodwill.

BOSANQUET, MRS. HELEN (DENDY). **Free Trade and Peace in the 19th Century.** London: Williams and Norgate, 1925, 155 p.
An interesting examination of the effects of commercial interests on peace.

BOWKER, RICHARD ROGERS. **Economic Peace.** New York: Putnam, 1923, 32 p.
A brief for the position that economic provisions for peace must precede political and diplomatic arrangements.

BRATT, KARL AXEL. **That Next War?** New York: Harcourt, 1931, 268 p.
A Swedish soldier and historian stresses the view that the danger of conflict is as great now as it ever was, and that some economic equivalent for war must be found.

Building International Goodwill. New York: Macmillan, 1927, 258 p.
A series of essays published under the auspices of the World Alliance for International Friendship, in which recognized authorities discuss obstacles to peace and examine methods for preserving it.

BULOC, E. **La Croisade et l'Esprit.** Paris: Alcan, 1927, 333 p.
A new doctrine of war and peace, and a keen critique of current international settlements and practices.

CARTER, JOHN. **Man Is War.** Indianapolis: Bobbs-Merrill, 1926, 398 p.
A skeptical survey of present-day conditions and the prospects for the future.

CECIL, ROBERT, VISCOUNT. **The Way of Peace.** New York: Day, 1928, 256 p.
Collected essays and addresses by one of the foremost English champions of the League.

COPPOLA, FRANCESCO. **La Pace Coatta.** Milan: Treves, 1929, 287 p.
The editor of *Politica* criticizes the peace work of the League since 1921.

COULET, R. P. **L'Église et le Problème International.** Paris: Spès, 1923, 248 p.
A capable Catholic critique of unreasonable nationalism and defective internationalism, with stress on the needed force of Christian morality.

DAWSON, WILLIAM HARBUTT. **The Future of Empire and the World Price of Peace.** London: Williams and Norgate, 1930, 286 p.
An examination of the fundamental causes of war, and a plea for British leadership in the movement for disarmament.

DEMARTIAL, GEORGES. **Le Mythe des Guerres de Légitime Défense.** Paris: Rivière, 1931, 164 p.
One of the most active French pacifists demonstrates the pitfalls of the term *défense*.

DICKINSON, GOLDSWORTHY LOWES. **War: Its Nature, Causes and Cure.** New York: Macmillan, 1923, 155 p.
An admirable presentation of the thesis that the future of civilization depends on the elimination of war and that general disarmament will further this end.

EDDY, SHERWOOD and PAGE, KIRBY. **The Abolition of War.** New York: Doran, 1924, 224 p.
The case against war, followed by an imposing array of questions and answers about war, its causes, results, etc.

FISHER, SIR JOHN F. **International Change and International Peace.** New York: Oxford University Press, 1932, 79 p.
An international lawyer frankly approaches the problem of how necessary changes can be brought about in the relations of nations without recourse to war.

FOX, HENRY WATSON, *ed*. **The Religious Basis of World Peace.** London: Williams and Norgate, 1929, 167 p.
A collection of articles, by Walter Simons, Edvard Beneš, Nicolas Politis, and others, stressing, among other things, the influence the Churches may exert in the work for peace and disarmament.

FÜSSENHAUSER, GOTTLOB. **Die Verfassung des Universalstaates.** Stuttgart: Füssenhauser, 1930, 625 p.
An elaborate draft constitution for the millennium.

GARBORG, ARNE. **Peace.** New York: American Scandinavian Foundation, 1930, 280 p.
The English translation of a very stimulating Norwegian essay.

GIMINEZ-VALDIVIESO, T. **La Suppression de la Guerre.** Paris: Rhea, 1925, 302 p.
A reconsideration of the arguments in favor of war, and of possible measures for suppressing it.

GULICK, SIDNEY LEWIS. **The Christian Crusade for a Warless World.** New York: Macmillan, 1922, 197 p.
A thoroughgoing program for the removal of causes for international friction and for the support of coöperation and peace, issued by the Federal Council of Churches of Christ in America.

HABICHT, MAX, *ed.* **Post-War Treaties for the Pacific Settlement of International Disputes.** Cambridge: Harvard University Press, 1931, 1109 p.
The larger part of this volume is devoted to the texts of all international treaties for the pacific settlement of international disputes concluded in the first decade since the war, one hundred and thirty in all. Its value is greatly enhanced by the second part of the volume, in which the author analyzes and compares the various types of agreement, discusses the different systems of settlement envisaged by the treaties, examines the reservations that have been made, and investigates the organization and working of the commissions and tribunals provided for. The volume contains an extended classified bibliography.

HAWTREY, RALPH GEORGE. **Economic Aspects of Sovereignty.** New York: Longmans, 1930, 162 p.
In these Lowell Lectures an English authority strikes at the fundamental problems of war and peace, with special reference to the economic aspects of international tension.

KENWORTHY, JOSEPH MONTAGUE. **Peace or War?** New York: Boni and Liveright, 1927, 338 p.
A British Laborite's disillusioning survey of the world scene and the numerous danger spots. The author considers the League ineffective and undependable and suggests combined economic pressure on offending states as the only reliable method of outlawing war.

KOBLER, FRANZ, *ed.* **Gewalt und Gewaltlosigkeit.** Zurich: Rotapfel, 1928, 388 p.
An extensive account of the movement of active pacifism from Penn to Tolstoi, Gandhi and the World War.

LABROSSE, EUGÈNE. **Quand On Veut la Paix.** Paris: Éditions de la Jeune Académie, 1931, 330 p.
"Paix humaine" can be attained only on the basis of present nations, free and strong.

LAPIERRE, MARCEL. **Le Cinéma et la Paix.** Paris: Valois, 1932, 128 p.
The author emphasizes the part played, for good or ill, by the motion picture.

LEHMANN-RUSSBÜLDT, OTTO. **Der Kampf der Deutschen Liga für Menschenrechte für den Weltfrieden.** Berlin: Hensel, 1927, 190 p.
A survey of the activities of the German peace league from 1914 to 1927, proving that at least some Germans were pacifically inclined.

LOBINGIER, MRS. ELIZABETH ERWIN and JOHN LESLIE. **Educating for Peace.** Boston: Pilgrim Press, 1930, 216 p.
World peace studied as an educational problem.

LOTHIAN, PHILIP HENRY KERR, MARQUIS OF and CURTIS, LIONEL. **The Prevention of War.** New Haven: Yale University Press, 1923, 169 p.
Williamstown Lectures, dealing with general problems and with such practical achievements in the prevention of international conflict as the establishment of the Union of South Africa and responsible government in India.

McDOUGALL, WILLIAM. **Janus: The Conquest of War.** New York: Dutton, 1927, 140 p.
A well-known psychologist tackles the question of war and its prevention in a brilliant but rather inconclusive essay.

MITCHELL, JONATHAN. **Goose Steps to Peace.** Boston: Little, Brown, 1931, 320 p.
The author, an American journalist, sets forth the aims and accomplishments of the various post-war conferences. He has little confidence in the diplomats and doubts that security against war can be attained by the signing of pacts, but sees a possible solution of the problem in a Great Power alliance, which would include Germany, Russia and Japan, as well as the United States, England and France.

Money, Sir Leo Chiozza. **Can War Be Averted?** London: Thornton Butterworth, 1931, 293 p.
A well-balanced survey of the great political and economic issues.

Morrison, Charles Clayton. **The Outlawry of War.** Chicago: Willett, Clark and Colby, 1927, 330 p.
The editor of the *Christian Century* advances a plan for the ending of international conflicts by outlawing war and strengthening the world organization for peace.

Murray, Gilbert. **The Ordeal of This Generation.** New York: Harper, 1929, 276 p.
A series of lectures by a famous scholar, dealing mainly with questions of peace and the League and the ways and means of ending the international anarchy.

Norton, Henry Kittredge. **Back of War.** New York: Doubleday, 1928, 371 p.
A rather conventional but well-informed review of the underlying causes of international conflict, social, economic and political.

Olphe-Galliard, G. **La Morale des Nations.** Paris: Giard, 1920, 306 p.
A documented history of the evolution of ideas of justice, international organization and peace from ancient times to the present.

Palmer, Frederick. **The Folly of Nations.** New York: Dodd, 1921, 408 p.
A diagnosis of the war disease, by a writer who has seen much of it and who is convinced of the possibility of its control.

Percin, Alexandre. **Guerre à la Guerre.** Paris: Montaigne, 1927.
A well-known French military man makes out a telling case against war.

Ponsonby, Arthur Ponsonby, Baron. **Now Is the Time.** London: Parsons, 1925, 192 p.
A ruthless exposure of war and an eloquent appeal for peace, by a British pacifist who knows international affairs from the inside.

Problems of Peace. New York: Oxford University Press, 1927 ff.
Since 1927 the Institute of International Relations at Geneva has published annually a series of lectures on important current problems delivered by outstanding authorities. They serve as an admirable periodical survey of world developments.

Problems of the International Settlement. New York: Macmillan, 1919, 205 p.
A convenient English selection from the voluminous reports of the "Central Organization for a Durable Peace." An international group of authorities discuss problems of nationality, arbitration, sanctions, disarmament, freedom of the seas, etc.

Rutherford, Vickerman Henzell. **War or Peace?** London: Williams and Norgate, 1930, 96 p.
This spirited attack on imperialism, high tariffs and armaments strikes at a number of fundamental causes for conflict.

Saint-Aulaire, Auguste Félix, Comte de. **La Mythologie de la Paix.** Paris: Éditions Prométhée, 1929, 320 p.
Peace where there is no peace, according to a noted French diplomat.

Schanzer, Carlo. **Il Mondo fra la Pace e la Guerra.** Milan: Treves, 1932, 398 p.
The author, a former Italian foreign minister, studies the evolution of the problem of war and peace, and adds a chapter on Italian policy regarding disarmament.

Scherer, Benedek. **Die Vorbedingungen des Internationalen Friedens.** Vienna: Amalthea, 1931, 162 p.
The book is concerned primarily with the international regulation of territorial difficulties, and makes proposals to this end.

Schoenaich, Paul Eugen, Freiherr von. **Vom Vorigen zum Nächsten Krieg.** Berlin: Verlag der Neuen Gesellschaft, 1925, 184 p.
An outspoken pacifistic review of present tendencies.

SIKORSKI, WŁADYSŁAW. **Le Problème de la Paix.** Paris: La Vie Latine, 1931.
The author deals primarily with the play of forces in eastern Europe and discusses at length the rôle of the Franco-Polish alliance.

SMITH, FRED BURTON. **Must We Have War?** New York: Harper, 1929, 339 p.
A thoughtful discussion of the peace problem by the chairman of the World Alliance for International Friendship through the Churches.

STURZO, LUIGI. **The International Community and the Right of War.** New York: R. R. Smith, 1930, 294 p.
In this book Don Sturzo, the famous Italian Populist leader, is not concerned with the possible ways and means of organizing the world for peace, but rather with the philosophical question whether war is a necessity. He finds no difficulty in disposing of the usual arguments advanced in favor of war as an instrument of justice, as a necessary attribute of state power, or as a purely biological factor, and comes to the conclusion that the idea of the necessity of war is a pure illusion.

TUTTLE, MRS. FLORENCE GUERTIN. **Alternatives to War.** New York: Harper, 1931, 282 p.
The author reviews the evolution of the post-war period in simple terms. Besides a discussion of the procedure of the League and the Court, the book treats the position of the United States, the Locarno and Kellogg Pacts, and disarmament.

VLIETINCK, EDWARD. **Le Problème de la Paix.** Antwerp: Van Tilborg and Kenens, 1927, 147 p.
Brushing aside pious hopes and well-intentioned generalities, the author lays stress on the fundamental cause of war, the struggle for existence.

WALLER, BOLTON C. **Paths to World Peace.** London: Allen and Unwin, 1926, 224 p.
A thoughtful essay urging the necessity of removing the causes of war before attempting to outlaw it.

Ways to Peace. New York: Scribner, 1924, 465 p.
Twenty representative plans submitted to the American Peace Award, with an introduction by Esther Everett Lape and a preface by Edward W. Bok.

WEHBERG, HANS. **The Outlawry of War.** Washington: Carnegie Endowment, 1931, 161 p.
A series of lectures by an eminent German pacifist, surveying in broad lines the evolution of the idea of outlawing war, and the efforts made towards that end both inside and outside the League.

WHITNEY, EDSON LEONE. **The American Peace Society.** Washington: American Peace Society, 1928, 360 p.
A centennial history of the activities of the Society.

Conciliation, Arbitration and Outlawry of War

See also (International Organization) The Permanent Court of International Justice, p. 65.

General

ARNOLD-FORSTER, W. **The Victory of Reason.** London: Hogarth, 1926, 88 p.
An excellent brief review of the history and problem of arbitration.

BRACHET, PAUL. **De l'Exécution des Sentences Arbitrales.** Paris: Rousseau, 1928, 233 p.
A scholarly study of the means for effecting the execution of arbitral decisions, and of the general problem of sanctions.

Brown, Philip Marshall. **La Conciliation Internationale.** Paris: Pedone, 1925, 95 p.
Six lectures, delivered in 1924 at the Académie de La Haye by an American authority, discussing the types of international differences and the various organs for settling them.

Clad, Clovis. **Wesen und Grenzen der Internationalen Schiedsgerichtsbarkeit.** Leipzig: Noske, 1928, 129 p.
A scholarly study devoted largely to considering possibilities of further development of arbitration.

Dotremont, Stanislas. **L'Arbitrage International et le Conseil de la Société des Nations.** Brussels: Lamertin, 1929, 464 p.
An authoritative monograph on the machinery of arbitration and how it works under the League system.

Hoijer, Olof. **La Solution Pacifique des Litiges Internationaux avant et depuis la Société des Nations.** Paris: Spès, 1925, 570 p.
An extended study of methods, from direct negotiation and good offices through mediation and arbitration. The second half of the book deals with methods of settling disputes through League action.

Kaufmann, Paul. **Die Fortbildung der Internationalen Schiedsgerichtsbarkeit seit dem Weltkrieg.** Leipzig: Noske, 1927, 77 p.
A technical study of post-war developments in arbitration, with special reference to the Locarno agreements.

Kraus, Herbert. **Internationale Schiedssprechung.** Berlin: De Gruyter, 1929, 348 p.
A German authority surveys the agreements binding upon Germany.

Politis, Nicolas Socrate. **La Justice Internationale.** Paris: Hachette, 1924, 325 p.
A series of admirable lectures, in which a leading authority reviews the history of arbitration, the work of the Hague Conferences and the organization of the World Court.

Ralston, Jackson Harvey. **International Arbitration from Athens to Locarno.** Stanford: Stanford University Press, 1929, 417 p.
The whole question of international justice, historically and topically considered. The author discusses principles and procedure, reviews ancient arbitration and the Hague Conferences, and finally analyzes the organization of the World Court. A standard scholarly treatment.

Saint-Seine, Arnold de. **La Conciliation Internationale.** Paris: Rousseau, 1930, 218 p.
A general survey of the principles and practice of conciliation in the post-war period.

Schücking, Walther. **Das Völkerrechtliche Institut der Vermittlung.** Oslo: Aschehoug, 1923, 346 p.
A technical study of the procedure of mediation in international law, by an outstanding German authority.

Scott, James Brown. **Sovereign States and Suits before Arbitral Tribunals and Courts of Justice.** New York: New York University Press, 1925, 370 p.
Lectures by a well-known American authority.

Urrutia, Francisco José. **La Evolución del Principio de Arbitraje en America.** Madrid: Editorial-America, 1920, 298 p.
Probably the best general study of the American contribution to arbitration.

Winiarski, Bohdan. **Bezpieczeństwo, Arbitraż, Rozbrojenie.** Poznań: Fiszer and Majewski, 1928, 256 p.
A Polish monograph on arbitration and disarmament.

Locarno Pacts

See also (France) Relations with Germany, p. 260.

BONNAMOUR, GEORGE. **Le Rapprochement Franco-Allemand.** Paris: Delpeuch, 1927, 386 p.
A review of the Locarno agreements and their origins, with some unpublished documents and correspondence.

FABRE-LUCE, ALFRED. **Locarno sans Rêves.** Paris: Grasset, 1927, 241 p.
A brilliant French writer attempts to penetrate the mist of sentiment shrouding the Franco-German reconciliation, and underlines the stark realities of the problem.

GLASGOW, GEORGE. **From Dawes to Locarno, 1924-1925.** London: Benn, 1925, 202 p.
The Labor view of the Locarno settlement, containing the more important documents on the negotiations.

SOUCHON, LUCIEN. **De Sedan à Locarno.** Paris: Fayard, 1931, 322 p.
Locarno pictured as the fatal step on the road to another Sedan.

STRUPP, KARL. **Das Werk von Locarno.** Berlin: De Gruyter, 1926, 179 p.
An essay on the origins, content and effects of the Locarno agreements, by an expert in the field of international law.

Kellogg-Briand Pact

See also (United States) Relations with Europe, p. 184.

BALBAREU, CÉCILE. **Le Pacte de Paris.** Paris: Gamber, 1929, 120 p.
A careful analysis of the agreement.

BUTLER, NICHOLAS MURRAY. **The Path to Peace.** New York: Scribner, 1930, 333 p.
A collection of essays and addresses dealing largely with the renunciation of war and the Pact of Paris.

CALOGEROPOULOS, STRATIS. **Le Pacte Général de Renonciation à la Guerre.** Paris: Rivière, 1931, 246 p.
A purely legal study.

GALLUS. **La Mise en Harmonie du Pacte de la Société des Nations avec le Pacte de Paris.** Paris: Éditions Internationales, 1930, 109 p.
A useful summary of the problems involved in the implementation of the pact.

HASSMANN, HUBERT. **Der Kellogg Pakt.** Würzburg: 1930, 95 p.
A doctoral dissertation, stressing the various reservations to the pact.

LE GALL, ROBERT. **Le Pacte de Paris.** Paris: Sirey, 1930, 160 p.
A clear presentation of the history of the negotiations, followed by an analysis of the text and of various interpretations put upon it.

MILLER, DAVID HUNTER. **The Peace Pact of Paris.** New York: Putnam, 1928, 283 p.
An account of the origins and purpose of the Kellogg-Briand Pact, with a careful examination of the American government's diplomatic correspondence with other signatory states, and a forecast of some of the consequences expected to flow from the treaty's adoption. The principal documents are included.

MYERS, DENYS PETER. **Origin and Conclusion of the Paris Pact.** Boston: World Peace Foundation, 1929, 235 p.
A convenient and well-informed review of the negotiations which led to the pact.

PENSA, HENRI. **De Locarno au Pacte Kellogg.** Paris: D'Artrey, 1929, 352 p.
The conspiracy for peace by the triumvirate Chamberlain-Briand-Stresemann.

SHOTWELL, JAMES THOMSON. **War as an Instrument of National Policy.** New York: Harcourt, 1929, 320 p.
One of the best analyses of the pact, written by an American authority who strives to see the agreement in the larger setting of the peace movement.

STRUPP, KARL. **Der Kellogg Pakt im Rahmen des Kriegsvorbeugungsrechts.** Leipzig: Noske, 1928, 83 p.
An illuminating lecture by a prominent German authority on international law.

WHEELER-BENNETT, JOHN WHEELER. **Information on the Renunciation of War, 1927-1928.** London: Allen and Unwin, 1928, 192 p.
The documents covering the negotiations for the pact, followed by an analysis of the text. A handy and competent manual.

SECURITY AND DISARMAMENT
Security
General

See also (Peace) Locarno Pacts, p. 79, and Kellogg-Briand Pact, p. 79.

See also (Peace) Locarno Pacts, p. 79, and Kellogg-Briand Pact, p. 79.

ALBANESE, T. **Sicurezza-Disarmo.** Rome: Anonima Romana Editoriale, 1930, 142 p.
The author argues that disarmament is a question of increasing military and economic security.

ALEXANDER, FREDERICK. **From Paris to Locarno.** London: Dent, 1928, 246 p.
The historical evolution of the security problem and its connection with the questions of arbitration and disarmament.

HEADLAM-MORLEY, SIR JAMES WYCLIFFE. **Studies in Diplomatic History.** New York: King, 1930, 312 p.
The late historical adviser of the Foreign Office reviews the problems of disarmament, arbitration and security in a series of well-balanced essays.

HOIJER, OLOF. **La Sécurité Internationale et Ses Modes de Réalisation.** Paris: Éditions Internationales, 1930, 4 v.
The author examines in detail the working of alliances and guarantees of neutrality, agreements like the Locarno agreements and the Kellogg Pact, the methods for the pacific solution of disputes and the problems of disarmament. A most exhaustive and scholarly analytical work.

JUDET, ERNEST. **La Politique de Sécurité.** Paris: Rivière, 1931, 406 p.
A French journalist outlines the evolution of the problem.

KELLOR, FRANCES ALICE and HATVANY, ANTONIA. **Security against War.** New York: Macmillan, 1924, 2 v.
An analysis of international disputes since 1918 and the manner of settling them.

LINNEBACH, KARL, *ed.* **Die Sicherheitsfrage.** Berlin: Hobbing, 1925, 265 p.
An excellent collection of documents on the security question from 1917 to June 1925.

MILENKOVIĆ, VELJKO. **Le Problème de la Sécurité Européenne d'après les Accords de Locarno.** Paris: Pedone, 1928, 240 p.
A substantial if uninspired chronicle of the evolution of the security problem, together with an analysis and appraisal of the Locarno Pacts.

RAAFAT, WAHEED. **Le Problème de la Sécurité Internationale.** Paris: Pedone, 1930, 684 p.
A substantial historical introduction followed by an analysis of the problem as it presented itself at the Peace Conference and during the post-war decade.

SPAIGHT, JAMES MOLONY. **Pseudo-Security.** New York: Longmans, 1928, 182 p.
 After analyzing the clauses of the Covenant and the various attempts to secure peace since 1918, the writer comes to the conclusion that only a pseudo-security can be arrived at by these methods.

WHEELER-BENNETT, JOHN WHEELER and LANGERMANN, FREDERIC EDWARD. **Information on the Problem of Security, 1917-1926.** London: Allen and Unwin, 1927, 272 p.
 An admirable handbook, giving the most important documents.

Geneva Protocol

BAKER, PHILIP JOHN NOEL. **The Geneva Protocol.** London: King, 1925, 228 p.
 A competent study by one long connected with the disarmament work of the League.

DJUROVIĆ, DJURA. **Le Protocole de Genève devant l'Opinion Anglaise.** Paris: Jouve, 1928, 246 p.
 This dissertation, based in part on English press comment, reviews the whole evolution of British policy towards the problem of French security after 1919.

KELLOR, FRANCES ALICE and HATVANY, ANTONIA. **Protocol for the Pacific Settlement of International Disputes.** New York: Authors, 1925, 183 p.
 A privately printed analysis of the Protocol, with arguments against American support of it.

MILLER, DAVID HUNTER. **The Geneva Protocol.** New York: Macmillan, 1925, 279 p.
 An authoritative examination of the Protocol's aspects by one of the advisers to the American Peace Commission.

WEHBERG, HANS. **Le Protocole de Genève.** Paris: Hachette, 1926, 150 p.
 A series of lectures by an eminent German jurist and proponent of disarmament.

WILLIAMS, ROTH. **The League, the Protocol and the Empire.** London: Allen and Unwin, 1925, 174 p.
 A useful examination of the Protocol as it affects the British dominions and America.

Disarmament

General

Armaments Year-Book. Geneva: League of Nations, 1924 ff.
 Annual survey of the armaments and military expenditures of thirty-seven countries, issued by the Secretariat of the League.

ARNOLD-FORSTER, W. **The Disarmament Conference.** London: National Peace Council, 1931, 91 p.
 A catechism of the facts and issues involved in the conference at Geneva.

BAKER, PHILIP JOHN NOEL. **Disarmament.** London: Hogarth, 1926, 366 p.
 An indispensable handbook, in which a well-known authority discusses the economic and political reasons for disarmament and analyzes methods by which this end may conceivably be attained.

BLUM, LÉON. **Peace and Disarmament.** London: Cape, 1932, 202 p.
 A vigorous plea by the leader of the French Socialist Party.

BÖHMERT, VICTOR. **Die Rechtsgrundlagen für Deutschlands Recht auf Abrüstung Seiner Vertragsgegner.** Berlin: Ebering, 1931, 59 p.
 Designed to prove Germany's claim that the Versailles Treaty obligates her former opponents to disarm.

CHARQUES, R. D. **The Soviets and the Next War.** London: Secker, 1932, 95 p.
 A strong plea for disarmament, emphasizing the apprehensions of Russia and the necessity for allaying them.

DENVIGNES, JOSEPH CYRILLE MAGDELAINE. **La Farce du Désarmement.** Paris: Tallandier, 1930, 260 p.
Like many Frenchmen, the author loves peace but distrusts the Germans, whose many ruses and surprises he carefully catalogues. He also stresses the impossibility of real disarmament in view of the ease with which the machinery of peace can be transformed into the machinery of war.

ENOCK, ARTHUR GUY. **The Problem of Armaments.** New York: Macmillan, 1923, 196 p.
A statistical condemnation of modern armaments as an economic burden and a leading cause of war. The author shows that organized disarmament will not increase unemployment.

FULLER, JOHN FREDERIC CHARLES. **The Dragon's Teeth.** London: Constable, 1932, 337 p.
An English soldier's thought-provoking argument and plea for disarmament.

GATTO, R. L. **Disarmo e Difesa.** Milan: Corbaccio, 1925, 535 p.
An excellent discussion of the problem as it affects Italy.

GLINBERG, ARON. **Le Problème du Désarmement devant la Société des Nations et en dehors d'Elle.** Paris: Presses Universitaires, 1930, 161 p.
A systematic study, devoted in large measure to the work of the Preparatory Commission.

GLODKOWSKI, ERICH. **Die Weltabrüstung und Deutschland.** Berlin: Junker und Dünnhaupt, 1932, 60 p.
Disarmament as viewed by a German military man.

JOHNSEN, JULIA EMILY, *comp.* **Disarmament.** New York: Wilson, 1930, 173 p.
Largely a collection of articles on various phases of disarmament, together with an admirable bibliography.

JOUHAUX, LÉON. **Le Désarmement.** Paris: Alcan, 1927, 215 p.
The author, one of the French delegates to Geneva, gives a succinct account of the progress made to 1925, and then outlines the main problems involved and the possible solutions. He advocates the substitution of a militia for the standing army and urges the reduction of all armaments. The question of controlling the manufacture of the instruments of warfare, and trade in them, is developed at considerable length.

KOROVIN, EVSEVIĬ ALEKSANDROVICH and EGOREV, V. V. **Razoruzhenie.** Moscow: Gosizdat, 1930, 431 p.
A discussion of the disarmament problem as a question of international relations, followed by an analytical review of the League's work, as seen by a communist writer.

LAVALLAZ, MAURICE DE. **Essai sur le Désarmement et le Pacte de la Société des Nations.** Paris: Rousseau, 1926, 506 p.
A thorough and conscientious investigation, covering the question as it presented itself to the Peace Conference and as it was dealt with in various drafts for a League Covenant.

LEFEBURE, VICTOR. **Common Sense about Disarmament.** London: Gollancz, 1932, 176 p.
Useful data on the problem, intended as a guide to the discussions at the Disarmament Conference.

LEFEBURE, VICTOR. **Scientific Disarmament.** New York: Macmillan, 1931, 318 p.
The author, an expert on chemical warfare, stresses the importance of controlling new inventions and weapons, more deadly than the old and more readily available.

LÉONTIN, L. **Les Armements de l'Europe.** Paris: Delagrave, 1932, 128 p.
A statistical work.

LYON, JACQUES. **Les Problèmes du Désarmement.** Paris: Boivin, 1931, 300 p.
A reasoned discussion of fundamental aspects of the question, including materials and their control, professional as against national armies, naval disarmament and its relation to questions of blockade and freedom of the seas.

MADARIAGA, SALVADOR DE. **Disarmament.** New York: Coward-McCann, 1929, 392 p.
One of the most outstanding books on the problem. The author, formerly chief of the disarmament section of the League, surveys the past and stresses the inadequacy of mere outlawry of war unless the actual causes of war are at the same time removed.

MARKOVIĆ, LAZAR. **Le Désarmement et la Politique de Belgrade.** Paris: Société Générale d'Imprimerie, 1931.
The Jugoslav view, expounded by a delegate to the preparatory conference.

MYERS, DENYS PETER. **World Disarmament.** Boston: World Peace Foundation, 1932, 370 p.
This is a reliable survey of the question in its historical evolution, together with a dispassionate discussion of the relation of disarmament to arbitration and security and an analysis of the main aspects of the problem discussed at the Geneva Conference. The appendices contain pertinent documents and statistical material.

NIEMEYER, THEODOR, ed. **Handbuch des Abrüstungsproblems.** Berlin: Rothschild, 1928, 3 v.
A truly monumental treatment of the disarmament problem. The first volume is systematic, written by an imposing array of experts; the others include all important papers on the subject between 1816 and 1925.

NOLLET, CHARLES MARIE ÉDOUARD. **Une Expérience de Désarmement.** Paris: Nouvelle Revue Française, 1932, 255 p.
The story of five years of military control in Germany, which led this well-known French officer to conclude that Germany was not disarmed.

OERTZEN, FRIEDRICH WILHELM VON. **Das Ist die Abrüstung!** Oldenburg: Stalling, 1931, 260 p.
The writer finds no difficulty in demonstrating that the disarmament provisions of the Versailles Treaty have thus far remained a farce.

OERTZEN, KARL LUDWIG VON. **Abrüstung oder Kriegsvorbereitung?** Berlin: Zentralverlag, 1931, 124 p.
The author reviews the disarmament, or lack of it, in various countries and gives his reasons for opposing the projected convention.

OLDING, HEINZ, ed. **Das Abrüstungsproblem.** Berlin: Zentralverlag, 1928, 100 p.
A convenient summary of the League's activity to 1928, together with a succinct analysis of the viewpoints of various governments.

PERILLIER, LOUIS. **De la Limitation des Armements par la Méthode Budgétaire.** Paris: Rousseau, 1932, 200 p.
The author has applied himself to a purely practical problem, namely, the ways and means of limiting expenditure on national defense, as envisaged by the preparatory commission on disarmament, and more particularly to the question of establishing the actual figures of expenditure.

REBOUL, JEAN MARIE PAUL. **Non, l'Allemagne n'a pas Désarmé.** Paris: Lavauzelle, 1932, 288 p.
A French officer, formerly attached to the military mission at Berlin, gives the facts of Germany's armaments as he saw them.

Rüstung und Abrüstung. Berlin: Mittler, 1931, 303 p.
A useful survey of the armies and military organization of all countries. This is the 45th volume of a periodic publication known as "Loebell's Jahresbericht über das Heer und Kriegswesen."

SCHWENDEMANN, KARL. **Abrüstung und Sicherheit.** Leipzig: Historisch-Politischer Verlag, 1932, 330 p.
This is one of the best German books on the question. It includes not only an historical account but also a collection of pertinent documents.

SMITH, RENNIE. **General Disarmament or War?** London: Allen and Unwin, 1927, 111 p.
A brief summary of the important facts concerning armaments, followed by a plea for general reduction along the lines laid down for Germany in 1919. Written by a former Labor M. P.

SPANNER, EDWARD FRANK. **Armaments and the Non-Combatant.** London: Williams and Norgate, 1927, 333 p.
The author suggests the substitution of airships for naval craft, and proposes that the decision in questions of policy and expenditure be left to the public rather than to the professional politicians.

TARGE, ANTOINE LOUIS. **La Garde des Frontières.** Paris: Lavauzelle, 1930, 140 p.
The author examines the whole question of frontier fortifications and forces, particularly as it confronts France.

WEHBERG, HANS. **Die Internationale Beschränkung der Rüstungen.** Berlin and Stuttgart: Deutsche Verlagsanstalt, 1919, 475 p.
A detailed study, by a German authority, of the efforts towards disarmament made before the war, followed by an analysis of the fundamental aspects of the problem.

WHEELER-BENNETT, JOHN WHEELER. **Disarmament and Security since Locarno.** New York: Macmillan, 1932, 383 p.
A complete review of the twin problems since 1925. An excellent background study.

WHEELER-BENNETT, JOHN WHEELER. **Information on the Reduction of Armaments.** London: Allen and Unwin, 1925, 216 p.
A useful handbook outlining the development of the problem since 1919 and supplying valuable documentary material.

WILLIAMS, BENJAMIN HARRISON. **The United States and Disarmament.** New York: McGraw-Hill, 1931, 361 p.
The author examines in turn the possibility of making American interests secure by means of further naval development, and the prospect of attaining the same end by international understanding for the limitation of armaments. He is convinced that theories of sea power are outworn, and that the future can be secured only through pacific methods.

Naval

See also (International Law) Freedom of the Seas, p. 36; also (United States) Relations with Europe, p. 184; also (Great Britain) Imperial Relations, p. 231; also (China) International Relations and Status, p. 474; also (Japan) Foreign Policy, p. 482; etc.

ACWORTH, BERNARD. **The Navies of Today and Tomorrow.** London: Eyre and Spottiswoode, 1930, 277 p.
Primarily a critical analysis of British naval policy since the war, but with some consideration of problems of disarmament.

ARCHIMBAUD, LÉON. **La Conférence de Washington.** Paris: Payot, 1923, 364 p.
The first important French analysis of the Washington Conference.

BOUY, RAYMOND. **Le Désarmement Naval.** Paris: Presses Universitaires, 1931, 288 p.
The best scholarly presentation of the work of the London Conference from the French viewpoint.

BUELL, RAYMOND LESLIE. **The Washington Conference.** New York: Appleton, 1922, 461 p.
One of the best general accounts of the Washington Conference. The author believes Chinese aspirations were defeated.

BULLARD, ARTHUR. **The A B C's of Disarmament and the Pacific Problems.** New York: Macmillan, 1921, 122 p.
The author deals largely with American interests and the disarmament question at the Washington Conference.

BYWATER, HECTOR CHARLES. **Navies and Nations.** Boston: Houghton Mifflin, 1927, 292 p.
A review of developments after 1921 by a well-known writer on naval affairs who concludes that the obstacles to naval disarmament are by no means insuperable.

DANIÉLOU, CHARLES. **L'Armée Navale.** Paris: Figuière, 1932, 228 p.
A clear statement of the French position on naval disarmament since the Washington Conference.

ENGELY, GIOVANNI. **The Politics of Naval Disarmament.** London: Williams and Norgate, 1932, 301 p.
This volume, written by the London correspondent of *La Tribuna*, is a good general study of the disarmament question as it touches sea power. The author goes over the whole ground from the Washington Conference to the present, not neglecting the political negotiations that went on between the interested Powers outside the regular conferences.

Les Flottes de Combat. Paris: Société d'Éditions Géographiques, 1931, 704 p.
The latest volume of a periodic survey of the naval forces of the world, classified by countries.

HARRIS, HENRY WILSON. **Naval Disarmament.** London: Allen and Unwin, 1930, 124 p.
A concise little handbook stressing the evolution of the problem since the Washington Conference and attempting to bring out the factors underlying the policy of the various Powers.

ICHIHASHI, YAMATO. **The Washington Conference and After.** Stanford: Stanford University Press, 1928, 455 p.
Professor Ichihashi's book belongs among the important original treatments of the Washington Conference. As Secretary to Viscount Kato he was in a position to follow closely the course of the negotiations. He draws a clear distinction between the work of the Conference in regard to the limitation of naval armaments and that concerned with the problems of China and the Pacific. Each phase of the discussions is taken up in detail and the obstacles in the way of agreement are discussed dispassionately.

Jane's Fighting Ships. London: Sampson Low, 1930, 510 p.
The latest volume of an important English annual survey of the naval strengths of the world.

LATIMER, HUGH. **Naval Disarmament.** London: Royal Institute of International Affairs, 1930, 112 p.
A succinct statement of developments from 1921 to 1929.

RÉVÉSZ, ANDRÉS. **La Conferencia de Washington y el Problema del Pacífico.** Madrid: Biblioteca Internacional, 1922, 158 p.
A realistic Spanish account of the Pacific problem with a succinct review of the Conference's work for naval limitation.

RICHMOND, SIR HERBERT WILLIAM. **Economy and Naval Security.** London: Benn, 1931, 227 p.
This volume, by the former Commandant of the Imperial Defense College and the

Naval War College, is one of the important books on disarmament. Admiral Richmond surveys the situation from a long sea experience and from a knowledge of naval history and politics second only, perhaps, to Mahan's. His opinion is that the essential function of a navy can be carried out at far less cost and with far less likelihood of international friction than is commonly admitted.

SULLIVAN, MARK. **The Great Adventure at Washington.** New York: Doubleday, 1922, 290 p.
A colorful chronicle, by a well-known American political writer.

TARBELL, IDA MINERVA. **Peacemakers—Blessed and Otherwise.** New York: Macmillan, 1922, 227 p.
The observations, reflections and "irritations" of a well-known American writer at the Conference; at the same time a reasonable and balanced view of its work.

Taschenbuch der Kriegsflotten. Munich: Lehmann, 1930.
The latest volume of the best German naval manual.

WILLOUGHBY, WESTEL WOODBURY. **China at the Conference.** Baltimore: Johns Hopkins Press, 1922, 419 p.
The most valuable and authoritative presentation of Chinese problems at the Washington Conference. The author was a technical adviser to the Chinese delegation.

SECOND PART:

THE WORLD WAR

I. DIPLOMATIC HISTORY

DOCUMENTS

Amtliche Aktenstücke zur Geschichte der Europäischen Politik, 1885-1914.
EDITED BY BERNHARD SCHWERTFEGER. Berlin: Deutsche Verlagsgesellschaft für Politik und Geschichte, 1925, 5 v., 2 supplementary v. and 2 v. of commentary.
The latest and most complete edition of the Belgian documents seized by the Germans in Brussels and first published under the title "Zur Europäischen Politik, 1897-1914" (Berlin: Hobbing, 1919, 5 v.).

Archives Secrètes de l'Empereur Nicolas II. Paris: Payot, 1928, 250 p.
A collection of material from Nicholas' private archives. These documents are a selection from the material published by V. P. Semennikov, "Monarkhiia pered Krusheniem" (Moscow: Gosizdat, 1927, 310 p.). It bears on many phases of Allied policy in the years 1914-1917.

Die Auswärtige Politik Serbiens, 1903-1914. EDITED BY MILOŠ BOGIĆEVIĆ. Berlin: Brückenverlag, 1928-1930, 3 v.
A collection of material by a former Serbian diplomat, throwing light on Serbian and general European (especially Russian) policy; but it cannot be described as complete or entirely reliable.

BENKENDORF, PAVEL KONSTANTINOVICH. Graf Benckendorffs Diplomatischer Schriftwechsel. EDITED BY B. DE SIEBERT. Berlin: De Gruyter, 1928, 3 v.
This is a new and more complete edition of a mass of Russian correspondence covering the years 1909-1914, which appeared in English, edited by B. de Siebert and G. A. Schreiner as "Entente Diplomacy and the World, 1909-1914" (New York: Putnam, 1922, 762 p.). The collection is of great value for the study of Anglo-Russian relations.

British Documents on the Origins of the War, 1898-1914. EDITED BY GEORGE P. GOOCH and HAROLD TEMPERLEY. London: H. M. Stationery Office, 1926 ff.
This great collection of British material forms one of the most important sources for the study of pre-war diplomacy. The material given is very full and is reliably as well as competently edited by two English historians. Thus far (1932) there have appeared volumes I-VII (1898-1911) and volume XI (July, 1914).

Diplomatische Aktenstücke zur Vorgeschichte des Krieges, 1914. Vienna: Staatsdruckerei, 1919, 3 v.
An important collection of Austrian documents on the 1914 crisis, supplementary to the "Red Book" of 1914.

Der Diplomatische Schriftwechsel Iswolskis, 1911-1914. EDITED BY FRIEDRICH STIEVE. Berlin: Deutsche Verlagsgesellschaft für Politik und Geschichte, 1924, 4 v.
An important collection of correspondence between Paris and St. Petersburg, containing some 500 unpublished documents. Much of this material is the same as that found in "Le Livre Noir," but it is better presented and better edited. There is a commentary on the volumes by the editor, of which an English edition has appeared: "Isvolsky and the World War" (New York: Knopf, 1926, 254 p.).

Documents Diplomatiques. Les Affaires Balkaniques, 1912-1914. Paris: Ministère des Affaires Étrangères, 1922, 3 v.
A valuable collection of material on the Balkan Wars and the aftermath. The material is not complete, but is nevertheless fuller than most collections of this kind.

Documents Diplomatiques Français Relatifs aux Origines de la Guerre de 1914. Paris: Costes, 1929 ff.
The great publication of French pre-war diplomatic correspondence threatens to become more voluminous even than the German. The work of publication has been entrusted to a large commission of French diplomats and historians, and has been divided into three series: I, 1870-1900; II, 1900-1911; III, 1911-1914. To date there have appeared series I, volumes 1-3 (May 1871-May 1881); series II, volumes 1-2 (January 1901-December 1902); series III, volumes 1-4 (November 1911-December 1912).

Les Documents Secrets des Archives du Ministère des Affaires Étrangères de Russie. EDITED BY ÉMILE LALOY. Paris: Bossard, 4th ed., 1920, 197 p.
A convenient French translation of a collection of miscellaneous Russian documents published by the Bolsheviks in 1917 and 1918.

Die Europäischen Mächte und die Türkei während des Weltkrieges. Konstantinopel und die Meerengen. EDITED BY E. A. ADAMOV. Dresden: Reissner, 1930-1932, 4 v.
The German translation of a valuable collection of Russian documents bearing on Constantinople and the Straits and first published in Russian as "Konstantinopl' i Prolivy" (Moscow: 1925-1926, 2 v.).

Evropeǐskie Derzhavy i Gretsiia. EDITED BY E. A. ADAMOV. Moscow: Kommissariat po Inostrannym Delam, 1922, 239 p.
Russian correspondence dealing with the Greek problem during the war.

Falsifications of the Russian Orange Book. EDITED BY G. VON ROMBERG. New York: Huebsch, 1923, 77 p.
English translation of a collection of telegrams of some importance in estimating the Franco-Russian attitude at the outbreak of the World War. These documents, originally published in German ("Die Fälschungen des Russischen Orangebuches," Berlin: Vereinigung Wissenschaftlicher Verleger, 1922), show how unreliable was the original Russian collection of 1914.

Das Französische Gelbbuch von 1914. Berlin: Deutsche Verlagsgesellschaft für Politik und Geschichte, 1926, 208 p.
The French Yellow Book revised to include important documents omitted or mutilated in the 1914 edition.

The German White Book Concerning the Responsibility of the Authors of the War. EDITED BY J. B. SCOTT. New York: Oxford University Press, 1924, 178 p.
A translation of the notes exchanged between the Allied and German Governments during the Paris Peace Conference relative to responsibility for the outbreak of the war. The German edition is entitled "Deutschland Schuldig? Deutsches Weissbuch über die Verantwortlichkeit der Urheber des Krieges" (Berlin: Heymann, 1919, 208 p.).

Die Grosse Politik der Europäischen Kabinette, 1871-1914. EDITED BY JOHANNES LEPSIUS, ALBRECHT MENDELSSOHN-BARTHOLDY and FRIEDRICH THIMME. Berlin: Verlagsgesellschaft für Politik und Geschichte, 1922-1927, 40 v.
This great German publication of correspondence still stands as the most important single source for the study of pre-war diplomacy. It is very full, especially for the period after 1890, and is admirably and honestly edited by competent historians. There is an abbreviated edition in four volumes under the title: "Die Auswärtige Politik des Deutschen Reiches, 1891-1914" (same place and publisher, 1928); a six-volume digest edited by Bernhard Schwertfeger: "Die Diplomatischen Akten des Auswärtigen

Amtes, 1871-1914" (same place and publisher, 1923-1928); a complete French translation in process of publication: "La Politique Extérieure de l'Allemagne, 1871-1914"
(Paris: Costes, 1927 ff., volumes 1-13, covering 1871-1898); and an English selection
and translation by E. T. S. Dugdale: "German Diplomatic Documents, 1871-1914"
(New York: Harper, 1928-1931, 4 v.).

How the War Began in 1914. London: Allen and Unwin, 1925, 122 p.
A most important contribution from the Russian side. This is the record of incoming
and outgoing correspondence and decisions of the Russian Foreign Office.

Die Internationalen Beziehungen im Zeitalter des Imperialismus. EDITED BY
M. N. POKROVSKIĬ. Berlin: Hobbing, 1931 ff.
The great Russian series of pre-war and war-time diplomatic correspondence. This
collection is being published simultaneously in German and Russian. To date there
have appeared two volumes (series I, volumes 1, 4), one covering the period January
to March 1914, and the other July 1914.

L'Intervento dell' Italia nei Documenti Segreti dell' Intesa. Rome: Casa Editrice
Rassegna Internazionale, 1923, 190 p.
A collection of first-rate importance consisting of the documents from the Russian
Foreign Office bearing on Italy's dickering with the Entente during the period before
Italy's entry into the World War.

Iswolski im Weltkriege. EDITED BY FRIEDRICH STIEVE. Berlin: Deutsche Verlagsgesellschaft für Politik und Geschichte, 1925, 265 p.
Important documents from the Russian archives dealing with Franco-Russian relations during the war and throwing much light on the war aims of these Powers.

**Un Livre Noir; Diplomatie d'avant Guerre d'après les Documents des Archives
Russes.** EDITED BY RENÉ MARCHAND. Paris: Librairie du Travail, 1922-1927, 3 v.
The first two volumes are based on the Russian "Materialy po Istorii Franko-Russkikh
Otnoshenii, 1910-1914" (Moscow: 1922), and consist largely of correspondence between
the Russian Foreign Office and the Paris Embassy. Volume III covers the period
from August 1914 to April 1915.

**Oesterreich-Ungarns Aussenpolitik von der Bosnischen Krise 1908 bis zum
Kriegsausbruch 1914.** EDITED BY LUDWIG BITTNER, ALFRED F. PŘIBRAM, etc.
Vienna: Oesterreichischer Bundesverlag, 1930, 8 v.
The most complete collection of diplomatic material for the immediate pre-war period.
These eight volumes, edited by a group of outstanding Austrian historians and ar-
chivists, contain more than eleven thousand documents dealing largely with Near
Eastern affairs. This publication supersedes all earlier ones from the Austrian side.

Official German Documents Relating to the World War. New York: Oxford University Press, 1923, 2 v.
Translations of the German documents dealing with the responsibility for the origins
and continuation of the World War, published by the Investigating Committee of the
German Reichstag.

The Outbreak of the World War. EDITED BY MAX MONTGELAS and WALTHER SCHÜCK-
ING. New York: Oxford University Press, 1924, 688 p.
The English translation of the so-called "Kautsky Documents" ("Die Deutschen
Dokumente zum Kriegsausbruch," Charlottenburg: Deutsche Verlagsgesellschaft für
Politik und Geschichte, 1919, 4 v.). A very important source for the history of the 1914
crisis. There is a French translation: "Documents Allemands Relatifs à l'Origine de
la Guerre" (Paris: Costes, 1922, 4 v.).

**Papers Relating to the Foreign Relations of the United States. Supplements.
The World War.** EDITED BY TYLER DENNETT and JOSEPH V. FULLER. Washington:
Government Printing Office, 1928 ff.

To date there have been published supplements for the years 1914-1916 inclusive, and supplements I and II for 1917, and supplements I, II and III for 1918, dealing with Russia. These supplements deal entirely with American negotiations relative to the war and form a most important body of material.

Razdel Aziatskoï Turtsii po Sekretnym Dokumentam b. Ministerstva Inostrannych Del. EDITED BY E. A. ADAMOV. Moscow: Commissariat for Foreign Affairs, 1924, 384 p.
An important collection of Russian documents bearing on the projected partition of the Ottoman Empire.

Das Russische Orangebuch über den Kriegsausbruch mit der Türkei. EDITED BY FRIEDRICH STIEVE. Berlin: Verlag für Kulturpolitik, 1926, 187 p.
New Russian documents tending to show that the Russian offer of territorial guarantee was mere camouflage.

The Secret Treaties of Austria-Hungary, 1879-1914. By A. F. PŘIBRAM (English edition by A. C. COOLIDGE). Cambridge: Harvard University Press, 1921-1922, 2 v.
A collection of importance, including the texts of all political agreements concluded by Austria-Hungary, and an extended critical study by A. F. Přibram of the formation and renewals of the Triple Alliance. The original edition is entitled: "Die Politischen Geheimverträge Oesterreich-Ungarns, 1879-1914" (Vienna: Braumüller, 1920, 327 p.).

Das Zaristische Russland im Weltkriege. EDITED BY ALFRED VON WEGERER. Berlin: Deutsche Verlagsgesellschaft für Politik und Geschichte, 1927, 337 p.
An excellent edition of the Russian documents dealing with the entrance of Turkey, Bulgaria, Italy and Rumania into the war.

DIPLOMATIC BACKGROUND; OUTBREAK OF WAR; WAR GUILT

ALMIRA, JOSÉ and STOYAN, GIV. Le Déclic de Sarajévo. Paris: Radot, 1928, 214 p.
A confused and rather flowery account of the Sarajevo plot, with considerable dramatic detail about Princip and his love affair. Evidently a book to be used with caution.

ANRICH, ERNST. Die Jugoslawische Frage und die Julikrise 1914. Stuttgart: Kohlhammer, 1931, 166 p.
A reëxamination of the South Slav question and its rôle in Austrian foreign policy before the war.

BACH, AUGUST. Poincaré und der Kriegsausbruch 1914. Stuttgart: Deutsche Verlagsanstalt, 1929, 112 p.
A scholarly presentation of the case against M. Poincaré in all its details.

BAERNREITHER, JOSEPH MARIA. Fragments of a Political Diary. New York: Macmillan, 1930, 322 p.
The notes of an outstanding politician of pre-war Austria, dealing with his country's policy toward its Slav subjects. This important book for the study of the question of war origins and Austrian policy in the Balkans is edited by Dr. Baernreither's friend Dr. Joseph Redlich.

BARBAGALLO, CORRADO. Come si Scatenò la Guerra Mondiale. Rome: Segati, 1923, 166 p.
An Italian account of the origins of the war, discussing Austrian, German and Russian policy.

BARNES, HARRY ELMER. The Genesis of the World War. New York: Knopf, 1926, 777 p.
The best presentation in English of the extreme revisionist viewpoint.

BARNES, HARRY ELMER. **In Quest of Truth and Justice.** Chicago: National Historical Society, 1928, 423 p.
Mainly a reprint of the author's numerous controversial articles, but also including a survey of the origins of the war in the light of recent revelations and particularly with reference to the writer's conversations with some of the surviving statesmen of 1914.

BAUSMAN, FREDERICK. **Let France Explain.** London: Allen and Unwin, 1922, 259 p.
An unusually keen review of pre-war international relations, hostile to French policy.

BISSOLATI, LEONIDA. **La Politica Estera dell' Italia dal 1897 al 1920.** Milan: Treves, 1923, 447 p.
A collection of the speeches and essays of an outstanding socialist and leader of Italian liberal thought.

BOGIĆEVIĆ, MILOŠ. **The Causes of the War.** Amsterdam: Van Langenhuysen, 1919, 135 p.
The author, Serbian *chargé* at Berlin in 1914, but later a fugitive from Serbia, criticizes his country's policy and publishes a number of documents.

BOGIĆEVIĆ, MILOŠ. **Le Colonel Dragoutine Dimitriévitch Apis.** Paris: Delpeuch, 1928, 168 p.
A volume bringing together all that is known of the famous leader of the Black Hand, by a hostile Serbian writer.

BORNHAK, CONRAD. **Die Kriegsschuld.** Berlin: Verlag Tradition, 1929, 590 p.
A German historian reviews German foreign policy from 1890 to 1914, relying almost entirely upon the German documents. He makes a conscious effort to set forth the innocence of the Emperor.

BOURGEOIS ÉMILE. **Manuel Historique de Politique Étrangère.** Paris: Belin, 1926, 836 p.
The fourth volume of a standard handbook, covering the period from 1878 to 1919. The account is conventional and does not get beyond the traditional French view.

BOURGEOIS, ÉMILE and PAGÈS, GEORGES. **Les Origines et les Responsabilités de la Grande Guerre.** Paris: Hachette, 1922, 500 p.
An authoritative conventional interpretation, by leading French scholars. Based on reports of a Senatorial commission and on unpublished documents.

BRANDENBURG, ERICH. **From Bismarck to the World War.** New York: Oxford University Press, 1927, 556 p.
Brandenburg's book is the accepted authoritative German account of German policy from the time of Bismarck's fall to the outbreak of the war, and for scholarly detachment outranks most books on war origins.

BÜLOW, BERNHARD WILHELM VON. **Die Krisis: Die Grundlinien der Diplomatischen Verhandlungen bei Kriegsausbruch.** Berlin: Deutsche Verlagsgesellschaft für Politik und Geschichte, 3rd enl. ed., 1922, 237 p.
A new edition bolstering up previous opinions opposed to those of Kautsky in regard to the diplomatic origins of the war.

The Cambridge History of British Foreign Policy. EDITED BY A. W. WARD and G. P. GOOCH. New York: Macmillan, 1922-1923, 3 v.
An exhaustive study by many authors, covering British policy since 1789. Like all such collaborative works it varies widely in quality.

CARROLL, EBER MALCOLM. **French Public Opinion and Foreign Affairs, 1870-1914.** New York: Century, 1931, 356 p.
A detailed study of public opinion and its currents, based on newspapers, documents and periodical literature. One of the few scholarly studies of its kind.

CHANG CHUNG FU. **The Anglo-Japanese Alliance.** Baltimore: Johns Hopkins Press, 1931, 315 p.
Easily the best scientific history of the alliance, with a special chapter on its relation to the United States.

CHÉRADAME, ANDRÉ. **La Cause Immédiate de la Guerre.** Évreux: Hérissé, 1927, 479 p.
Written by a strongly anti-German publicist, this book should be used with caution.

CHEROVIĆ, BOZHO. **Bosanski Omladinsci i Sarajewski Atentat.** Sarajevo: 1931, 272 p.
The author, a former Austrian official, revives the theory that the Bosnian youth were instigated to act by the provocations of the Austrian military.

CONVERSET, JEAN JOSEPH. **Les Trois Ans de Diplomatie Secrète Qui Nous Menèrent à la Guerre de 1914.** Paris: Levallois-Perret, 1924, 255 p.
A bitter critique of European diplomacy from 1911 to 1914.

DEMARTIAL, GEORGES. **L'Évangile du Quai d'Orsay.** Paris: Delpeuch, 1926, 189 p.
A brilliant French controversialist and radical turns his guns on the French Yellow Book in so far as it relates to the Russian mobilization.

DEMARTIAL, GEORGES. **Les Responsabilités de la Guerre.** Paris: Clarté, 1920.
One of the strongest indictments of the Poincaré policy, by a French radical.

DENNIS, ALFRED LEWIS PINNEO. **The Anglo-Japanese Alliance.** Berkeley: University of California Press, 1923, 111 p.
A scholarly monograph from a liberal and critical point of view, now largely superseded by Chang's book.

DICKINSON, GOLDSWORTHY LOWES. **The International Anarchy, 1904-1914.** New York: Century, 1926, 516 p.
A severe condemnation of the pre-war international system. One of the best reasonably brief accounts.

DOUMERGUE, ÉMILE. **Voici Pourquoi l'Allemagne Doit Payer.** Paris: Stock, 1922-1924, 2 v.
An elaborate restatement of the French grievances against Germany before, during and after the war.

DUPIN, GUSTAVE. **M. Poincaré et la Guerre de 1914.** Paris: Librairie du Travail, 1931, 160 p.
The well-known French pacifist attacks Poincaré's policy and reviews the whole problem of French responsibility. The latest word from this angle.

DURHAM, MARY EDITH. **The Serajevo Crime.** London: Allen and Unwin, 1925, 208 p.
An extreme indictment of the Serbs by a woman long versed in Balkan affairs. To be used with caution.

EARLE, EDWARD MEAD. **Turkey, the Great Powers, and the Bagdad Railway: A Study in Imperialism.** New York: Macmillan, 1923, 364 p.
By far the best single study of the Bagdad Railway problem, based in part upon unpublished materials.

EWART, JOHN SKIRVING. **The Roots and Causes of the Wars, 1914-1918.** New York: Doran, 1925, 2 v.
A reëxamination of the whole problem by a Canadian jurist. The work, which is characterized by its wide range and its common sense, is revisionist in its conclusions.

FABRE-LUCE, ALFRED. **The Limitations of Victory.** New York: Knopf, 1926, 367 p.
A translation of one of the most pointed French essays on the origins of the war, written from the revisionist standpoint.

FAY, SIDNEY BRADSHAW. **The Origins of the World War.** New York: Macmillan, 1928, 2 v.

This remains, and is likely to remain, a standard book on the causes of the war, both remote and immediate. It is scholarly, balanced, and well-informed. The first volume covers the period from 1870 to July 1914, the second the July crisis. The author's studies have led him to conclusions which are in general revisionist and favorable to the Central Powers.

FISCHER, EUGEN. **Kriegsschuldfrage und Aussenpolitik.** Berlin: Deutsche Verlagsgesellschaft für Politik und Geschichte, 1924, 59 p.

A brief but valuable discussion of the bearing of the question of war guilt on European international relations.

FISCHER, EUGEN. **Die Kritischen 39 Tage von Sarajewo bis zum Weltbrand.** Berlin: Ullstein, 1928, 278 p.

A somewhat dramatized account of the events of July 1914, designed for the interested layman.

FISHER, HERBERT WESTCOTT. **Alias Uncle Shylock.** New York: Boni, 1927, 214 p.

A penetrating review of the origins of the war, reminding one of Fabre-Luce's "The Limitations of Victory."

FLORENT-MATTER, EUGÈNE. **Les Vrais Criminels.** Paris: Berger-Levrault, 1926, 384 p.

A valiant attack upon the revisionist view of the origins of the war.

FRANTZ, GUNTHER. **Russlands Eintritt in den Weltkrieg.** Berlin: Deutsche Verlagsgesellschaft für Politik und Geschichte, 1924, 306 p.

While giving evidence of a German bias, this work is thorough.

FRIEDJUNG, HEINRICH. **Das Zeitalter des Imperialismus, 1884-1914.** Berlin: Neufeld und Henius, 1919-1922, 3 v.

The work of a well-known Austrian historian. The second and third volumes give an excellent account of the period from 1900 to 1914, especially so far as Near Eastern affairs are concerned.

GALSTER, KARL PAUL HANS. **England, Deutsche Flotte und Weltkrieg.** Kiel: Scheibel, 1925, 200 p.

A reconsideration of German naval policy as it affected relations with England.

GAUVAIN, AUGUSTE. **L'Europe au Jour le Jour.** Paris: Bossard, 1921-1924, 14 v.

A valuable collection of the articles published by this distinguished French publicist in the *Journal des Débats* since 1908.

GERIN, RENÉ. **Comment Fût Provoquée la Guerre de 1914.** Paris: Rivière, 1931, 216 p.

An outgrowth of a questionnaire submitted to M. Poincaré by a pacifist and revisionist.

GESHOV, IVAN EVSTRATIEV. **La Genèse de la Guerre Mondiale.** Berne: Haupt, 1919, 165 p.

Written by the former Premier of Bulgaria, this book is in many ways a continuation of the author's book on the Balkan League.

GOOCH, GEORGE PEABODY. **Recent Revelations of European Diplomacy.** New York: Longmans, 1930, 218 + ccxi p.

A masterly discussion of the literature dealing with the Great War, indispensable for students of recent history. This is the fourth impression, containing supplementary chapters on the new books of 1927-1929.

GOOSS, RODERICH. **Das Wiener Kabinett und die Entstehung des Weltkrieges.** Vienna: Seidel, 1919, 312 p.

Based upon research in the Austrian archives, this is still the best single account of Austrian policy during the crisis.

GORIČAR, JOSEF and STOWE, LYMAN BEECHER. **The Inside Story of the Austro-German Intrigue.** New York: Doubleday, 1920, 301 p.
How the war was brought about by the intrigues and expansionist designs of the Austrians in the Balkans.

GOUTTENOIRE DE TOURY, FERNAND. **Jaurès et le Parti de la Guerre.** Paris: Éditions des Cahiers Internationaux, 1922, 234 p.
A lucid account of Jaurès' struggle against French militarism and imperialism and the Franco-Russian Alliance, by a leading French radical.

GRAHAM, STEPHEN. **St. Vitus Day.** New York: Appleton, 1931, 349 p.
A romanticized but vivid account of the character and actions of the men and boys who planned the murder of the Archduke.

GRELLING, RICHARD. **La Campagne "Innocentiste" en Allemagne et le Traité de Versailles.** Paris: Costes, 1925, 319 p.
A hostile account of Germany's efforts at revision of Article 231 of the Treaty, by the renowned author of "J'Accuse."

GRELLING, RICHARD. **Comment la Wilhelmstrasse Écrivait l'Histoire Pendant la Guerre.** Paris: Costes, 1928, 276 p.
The story of the deletions and alterations contained in the German White Book, taking its place beside the often-told stories of similar manipulations in the French and Russian books.

GREY, EDWARD GREY, VISCOUNT. **Speeches on Foreign Affairs, 1904-1914.** Edited by Paul Knaplund. Cambridge: Harvard University Press, 1932, 327 p.
A convenient collection.

HAKE, FRITZ VON. **Am Brandherd des Weltkrieges.** Erfurt: Bodung, 1929, 342 p.
A scholarly monograph dealing with the July days in St. Petersburg.

HAMMANN, OTTO. **Bilder aus der Letzten Kaiserzeit.** Berlin: Hobbing, 1923, 163 p.
The last book of reminiscences by the former chief of the publicity department of the German Foreign Office, including interesting character studies of the leading German figures of the immediate pre-war period.

HAMMANN, OTTO. **The World Policy of Germany, 1890-1912.** New York: Knopf, 1927, 269 p.
This outline, by the former chief of the press division of the German Foreign Office, is noteworthy for the breadth of view of the author. One of the most readable and instructive books on the origins of the war.

HAUSER, HENRI, *ed.* **Histoire Diplomatique de l'Europe, 1871-1914.** Paris: Presses Universitaires, 1929, 2 v.
The most recent general survey of the period, written by a large number of leading French historians. The work lacks unity of viewpoint and many chapters are conventional in treatment.

HERRE, PAUL, *ed.* **Weltgeschichte der Neuesten Zeit.** Berlin: Ullstein, 1925, 851 p.
The supplementary volume of a well-known world history and the most pretentious treatment of the period from 1890 to 1925.

HERZFELD, HANS. **Die Deutsche Rüstungspolitik vor dem Weltkriege.** Leipzig: Schroeder, 1923, 162 p.
A detailed analysis of the last army bills, between 1911 and 1914, with some keen criticism of the divided responsibility in the German system so far as military preparation was concerned.

HEYROWSKY, ADOLF. **Neue Wege zur Klärung der Kriegsschuld.** Berlin: Buchkunst, 1932, 218 p.
A former Austrian officer deals chiefly with the Sarajevo crime and the Austro-Serbian crisis, adducing some new material.

HOENIGER, ROBERT. **Russlands Vorbereitung zum Weltkrieg.** Berlin: Mittler, 1919, 139 p.
A valuable study of the preparation and mobilization of the Russian forces.

HORVÁTH, JENÖ. **A Balkáni Kérdés Utolsó Fázisa.** Budapest: Pfeifer, 1921, 227 p.
A general history of the Balkan question from 1895 to 1920, by a leading Hungarian historian.

HORVÁTH, JENÖ. **So Starb der Friede.** Berlin: Brückenverlag, 1930, 86 p.
A Hungarian review of Austro-Serbian relations before the war, coming to the conclusion that the Sarajevo murder was the logical outcome of Serbian policy.

HOYOS, ALEXANDER. **Der Deutsche-Englische Gegensatz und Sein Einfluss auf die Balkanpolitik Österreich-Ungarns.** Berlin: De Gruyter, 1922, 105 p.
An important essay on the general pre-war situation by a high official of the Austrian foreign office. He strongly condemns the German estrangement from England, which, he believes, was the decisive factor in the international crisis.

HUMBERT, CHARLES. **Chacun Son Tour.** Paris: Île de France, 1925, 442 p.
A bitter attack on Poincaré, who is accused of having neglected to prepare sufficiently for war.

IBBEKEN, RUDOLF. **Das Aussenpolitische Problem Staat und Wirtschaft in der Deutschen Reichspolitik, 1880-1914.** Schleswig: Ibbeken, 1928, 285 p.
Traces the influence of economic problems upon German foreign policy and discusses such matters as colonial activity, international finance, commercial treaties and the Bagdad Railway.

JEVTIĆ, BORIVOJE. **Sarajevski Atentat.** Sarajevo: Gakovič, 1924, 77 p.
An account of the assassination, by one of the plotters. Of primary importance.

JUX, ANTON. **Der Kriegsschrecken des Frühjahres 1914.** Berlin: Hendriok, 1929, 248 p.
A microscopic study of the German-Russian press war of March 1914.

KANNER, HEINRICH. **Kaiserliche Katastrophen-Politik.** Leipzig: Tal, 1922, 468 p.
The author attributes to Austria the major responsibility for bringing on the war of 1914, especially condemning Austrian militarists and chauvinists.

KANNER, HEINRICH. **Der Schlüssel zur Kriegsschuldfrage.** Munich: Südbayerische Verlagsgesellschaft, 1926, 89 p.
A well-known Austrian publicist's interpretation of the Moltke-Conrad military conversations of January 1909, which he declares to have been a military convention obliging Germany to support Austria.

KANTOROWICZ, HERMANN. **The Spirit of British Policy and the Myth of the Encirclement of Germany.** New York: Oxford University Press, 1932, 541 p.
A more than sympathetic study of British political psychology and the encirclement theory. A well-informed book, worth reading, but not well balanced.

KAUTSKY, KARL. **Guilt of William Hohenzollern.** London: Skeffington, 1920, 272 p.
A leading German socialist uses the German documents to make out a strong case against the Emperor and his ministers.

KIERSCH, H. J. P. A. **Le Kaiser et la Responsabilité de la Guerre.** Paris: Argo, 1931, 116 p.
A reassessment of the Emperor's responsibility, by a neutral writer.

KORFF, SERGIEĬ ALEKSANDROVICH, BARON. **Russia's Foreign Relations during the Last Half Century.** New York: Macmillan, 1922, 227 p.
Scholarly but conventional.

LANGER, WILLIAM LEONARD. **European Alliances and Alignments.** New York: Knopf, 1931, 509 p.
The first volume of an extended study of the pre-war alliance systems.

LOREBURN, ROBERT THRESHIE REID, EARL. **How the War Came.** London: Methuen, 1919, 340 p.
The author reviews British policy 1905-1914, and criticizes the Liberal imperialist views of Grey and especially the obligations to France.

LUDWIG, EMIL. **July 1914.** New York: Putnam, 1929, 378 p.
This book, for all its brilliant writing, can hardly be taken seriously as history. It has quite evidently been written without reference to some of the most important source material, and its conclusions will not stand up under the criticism of well-informed students. In attributing the responsibility to a few dozen incapable and misled statesmen and in whitewashing the general population the author facilitates his own task and satisfies the self-righteousness of the proverbial man in the street.

LUMBROSO, ALBERTO, BARONE. **Le Origine Economiche e Diplomatiche della Guerra Mondiale.** Milan: Mondadori, 1927, 544 p.
The first volume of an imposing history of the causes of the war, dealing largely with the economic factors. The author sees the ultimate reason for the catastrophe in the imperialism of the Anglo-Saxon race, and holds England chiefly responsible.

LUTZ, HERMANN. **Lord Grey and the World War.** New York: Knopf, 1928, 346 p.
An exhaustive study of Grey's policy, scholarly in form and generous in tone, by an outstanding German critic.

MAGRINI, LUCIANO. **Il Dramma di Seraievo.** Milan: Athena, 1930, 250 p.
This book is concerned chiefly with the political situation in the Hapsburg Monarchy and the plans of Francis Ferdinand for a constitutional reorganization.

MARGUERITTE, VICTOR. **Les Criminels.** Paris: Flammarion, 1925, 356 p.
A review of European developments from 1870 to 1914, by an ardent French pacifist, director of *Évolution*, the French revisionist periodical.

MARIE, PRINCESS OF BATTENBERG. **Reminiscences.** London: Allen and Unwin, 1925, 395 p.
Interesting recollections of personalities and events in the old Europe.

MARRIOTT, SIR JOHN ARTHUR RANSOME. **Europe and Beyond.** New York: Dutton, 1922, 335 p.
A brief survey of world politics since 1870, by a leading English publicist. Like many excellent early post-war books, this volume is now out of date.

MAURRAS, CHARLES. **Kiel et Tanger, et la République Française devant l'Europe.** Paris: Nouvelle Librairie Nationale, 1921, 401 p.
French diplomatic policy during the past half century interpreted to support royalist theories of government.

MICHON, GEORGES. **The Franco-Russian Alliance, 1891-1917.** London: Allen and Unwin, 1929, 340 p.
The only systematic study of the history of the famous combination from its beginning in 1891 to the collapse of one of its members in 1917. Somewhat journalistic in style but soundly critical.

MONTGELAS, MAXIMILIAN, GRAF VON. **British Foreign Policy under Sir Edward Grey.**
New York: Knopf, 1928, 159 p.
A searching criticism of Grey's apology by a well-known German writer on war guilt.

MONTGELAS, MAXIMILIAN, GRAF VON. **The Case for the Central Powers.** New York:
Knopf, 1925, 255 p.
A translation of the best German account of the immediate origins and outbreak of
the war.

MORAES SARMENTO, JOSÉ ESTEVÃO DE. **Causes Déterminantes de la Guerre Mondiale.**
Paris: Ferin, Torres, 1930, 391 p.
An unfriendly account of German *Machtpolitik*, notable chiefly for the extensive dis-
cussion of the problem of the Portuguese colonies.

MORHARDT, MATHIAS. **Les Preuves. Le Crime de Droit Commun. Le Crime Diplomatique.** Paris: Librairie du Travail, 1924, 380 p.
An unmeasured attack on Poincaré, by one of the *Évolution* group.

MOUSSET, ALBERT. **L'Attentat de Sarajévo.** Paris: Payot, 1929, 656 p.
A French translation of the entire court record of the trial of the Sarajevo assassins.
A most valuable documentary record.

MOWAT, ROBERT BALMAIN. **The Concert of Europe.** New York: Macmillan, 1931, 379 p.
A general review of the development of international relations in the period from 1870
to 1914, with special reference to the functioning of the concert in the solution of important questions.

MOWAT, ROBERT BALMAIN. **The European States System.** London: Milford, 1924, 96 p.
A brief history of European international relations since the Treaty of Westphalia,
by a prolific English writer.

MÜHLMANN, KARL. **Deutschland und die Türkei, 1913-1914.** Berlin: Rothschild, 1929,
104 p.
An important contribution to a key problem of pre-war politics written by the adjutant
of Liman von Sanders and based on unpublished material.

OMAN, SIR CHARLES WILLIAM CHADWICK. **The Outbreak of the War of 1914-1918.**
London: H. M. Stationery Office, 1919, 146 p.
A careful presentation of the classic English view.

OWEN, ROBERT LATHAM. **The Russian Imperial Conspiracy, 1892-1914.** New York:
Boni, 1927, 224 p.
A former senator from Oklahoma proves to his own satisfaction that Russia and France
had for many years prior to 1914 been plotting against the peace of the world. The
book makes up in violence of statement what it lacks in sound scholarship.

OXFORD AND ASQUITH, HERBERT HENRY ASQUITH, EARL OF. **The Genesis of the War.**
New York: Doran, 1922, 405 p.
A defense of British policy before the war by one of the men most responsible for it.
The volume does not contain much that is new.

POKROVSKIĬ, MIKHAIL NIKOLAEVICH. **Diplomatiia i Voiny Tsarskoĭ Rossii v XIX
Stoletii.** Moscow: Krasnaia Nov', 1924, 391 p.
Written by an able Bolshevik historian, this book may be taken as the classical formu-
lation of the communist view of Russian imperial policy.

POKROVSKIĬ, MIKHAIL NIKOLAEVICH. **Drei Konferenzen.** Berlin (?): Russische Korres-
pondenz, 1920, 72 p.
An important study of the conferences of 1913 and 1914, based on unpublished material.

POKROVSKIĬ, MIKHAIL NIKOLAEVICH. **Vneshniaia Politika Rossii v XX Veke.** Moscow: Sverdlov University, 1926, 95 p.
A popular sketch of Russian world policy in the 20th century, by a leading communist historian.

POLETIKA, N. P. **Saraevskoe Ubiĭstvo.** Leningrad: Krasnaia Gazeta, 1930, 443 p.
The most extensive Russian treatment of the Austro-Serbian problem from 1903 to 1914, with emphasis on the events leading up to the assassination. The book is full of condemnation of the Serbian government and its policy, but deals harshly with the other governments as well.

PONIANKOWSKI, JOSEPH. **Der Zusammenbruch des Ottomanischen Reiches.** Vienna: Amalthea, 1928, 444 p.
The writer was Austro-Hungarian military attaché at Constantinople from 1909 to 1918 and his reports on the situation were largely relied upon by the Austrian government. The part played by the clash of Russian, German and English interests in the Near East in bringing about the war is ably analyzed and emphasized.

PONS, AMILDA A. **The Holocaust.** London: Murray, 1919, 329 p.
Italy's struggle with the Hapsburg, from the out-and-out Italian standpoint.

PRELLER, HUGO. **Die Weltpolitik des 19. Jahrhunderts.** Berlin: Mittler, 1923, 217 p.
A survey of world politics by an independent German scholar.

PŘIBRAM, ALFRED FRANCIS. **Austrian Foreign Policy, 1908-1918.** London: Allen and Unwin, 1923, 128 p.
A series of lectures by a distinguished Austrian authority. Well-informed and dispassionate.

PŘIBRAM, ALFRED FRANCIS. **England and the International Policy of the European Great Powers, 1871-1914.** New York: Oxford University Press, 1931, 156 p.
A series of lectures by the foremost Austrian authority on pre-war diplomacy. They give in succinct form all the essentials of British continental policy in the period between the two great wars, as this policy appears from recent documentary publications.

RADOSLAVOV, VASIL'. **Bulgarien und die Weltkrise.** Berlin: Ullstein, 1923, 312 p.
The pro-German Premier of Bulgaria who came into power in 1913 describes his country's rôle in the World War and interprets the diplomatic background, beginning with the Congress of Berlin.

RECOULY, RAYMOND. **Les Heures Tragiques d'avant Guerre.** Paris: Renaissance du Livre, 1923, 341 p.
A series of articles on events in the various capitals. Noteworthy chiefly for the accounts given the author by Paul and Jules Cambon and General Messimy.

RENOUVIN, PIERRE. **The Immediate Origins of the War.** New Haven: Yale University Press, 1928, 409 p.
The translation of a well-known French work. Perhaps the best single book on the events of July 1914 as viewed from the French side. Scholarly and moderate.

REVENTLOW, ERNST, GRAF ZU. **Kriegsschuldlüge und Kriegsschuldlügner.** Munich: Lehmann, 1929, 258 p.
An extreme statement of the German thesis, by a well-known controversialist.

REVENTLOW, ERNST, GRAF ZU. **Politische Vorgeschichte des Grossen Krieges.** Berlin: Mittler, 1919, 354 p.
The author, dealing primarily with the period from Agadir to Sarajevo, shows a strongly nationalist viewpoint and an anti-English bias.

SALVEMINI, GAETANO. **Dal Patto di Londra alla Pace di Roma.** Turin: Gobetti, 1925, 360 p.
The most important history yet published of Italian foreign policy during the war.

SCHAER, WILHELM. **Katechismus zur Kriegsschuldfrage.** Berlin: Verlag des Arbeiter-ausschusses Deutscher Verbände, 1926, 160 p.
A collection of abstracts from Allied writers purporting to set forth the pre-war policies of England, France and Russia.

SCHEFER, CHRISTIAN. **D'une Guerre à l'Autre: Essai sur la Politique Extérieure de la Troisième République.** Paris: Alcan, 1920, 371 p.
One of the best surveys of the foreign policy of the Third Republic. The author stresses the colonial aspects.

SCHMITT, BERNADOTTE EVERLY. **The Coming of the War: 1914.** New York: Scribner, 1930, 2 v.
This is the most exhaustive scholarly study of the events of July 1914 and the entrance of the various Powers into the war. It shows the results of painstaking labor to unearth all the evidence. The author's conclusions are in general "anti-revisionist" and favorable to the Allies. For a reply see "Germany Not Guilty in 1914," by Michael Hermond Cochran (Boston: Stratford, 1931, 244 p.).

SCHNEE, HEINRICH. **Weltpolitik.** Leipzig: Quelle und Meyer, 1924, 465 p.
Written by the former German Governor of East Africa. A survey of world politics before and during the war and of the imperialistic peace settlements.

SCHÜSSLER, WILHELM. **Oesterreich und das Deutsche Schicksal.** Leipzig: Quelle und Meyer, 1925, 215 p.
A keen analytical treatment of the whole problem of German relations with Austria and the implications of the alliance.

SCOTT, JONATHAN FRENCH. **Five Weeks.** New York: Day, 1927, 313 p.
An examination of the European press in July 1914. A real contribution.

SEELHOFF, PAUL. **Die Europäischen Bilder.** Berlin: Hobbing, 1928, 275 p.
A fascinating series of dramatic essays, reviewing the development of the European situation from 1870 to 1914.

SETON-WATSON, ROBERT WILLIAM. **Sarajevo. A Study in the Origins of the Great War.** London: Hutchinson, 1926, 303 p.
A scholarly and interestingly written study of the Southern Slav movement and the Sarajevo assassination, by a leading authority who has long been friendly to the Slav peoples formerly under Hapsburg rule.

SHAPOSHNIKOV, B. **Mozg Armii.** Moscow: Gosizdat, 1929, 3 v.
A Russian staff officer's detailed and well-informed study of the work and influences of the general staffs of the various countries during the past century. The third volume contains a detailed account of the period preceding the World War, in which the Russian staff and government are given merciless condemnation.

SNIJDERS, C. J. and DUFOUR, R. **De Mobilisatiën bij de Groote Europeesche Mogend-heden in 1914.** Leyden: Sijthoff, 1927, 336 p.
A systematic study of the critical question of mobilizations in 1914, with a sound appreciation of the influence of the general staffs upon the outbreak of the war.

STANOJEVIĆ, STANOJE. **Die Ermordung des Erzherzogs Franz Ferdinand.** Frankfurt: Frankfurter Societätsdruckerei, 1923, 66 p.
The author ascribes the planning of the murder of Franz Ferdinand to Dragutin Dimitriević, chief of the Intelligence Bureau of the Serbian General Staff. The earliest revelation of the subterranean activities that led to the assassination.

STEED, HENRY WICKHAM. **Through Thirty Years.** New York: Doubleday, 1924, 2 v.
The reminiscences of an active life spent in Paris, Berlin, Rome, Vienna and London in the service of the London *Times*. The author knew the old Austria well and has much to say of Austrian pre-war diplomacy, but his judgments often are colored by his likes and dislikes.

STIEVE, FRIEDRICH. **Deutschland und Europa, 1890-1914.** Berlin: Verlag für Kultur-politik, 1926, 247 p.
A brief account of German policy, based largely on the documents published by the German government.

STIEVE, FRIEDRICH and MONTGELAS, MAXIMILIAN, GRAF VON. **Russland und der Welt-konflikt.** Berlin: Verlag für Kulturpolitik, 1927, 177 p.
Two German experts demolish the apology published by Sazonov, and quote exten-sively from the available documentary material to refute the late Russian Foreign Minister's account statement by statement.

STIEVE, FRIEDRICH. **Die Tragödie der Bundesgenossen.** Munich: Bruckmann, 1930, 200 p.
A careful study of Austro-German relations from 1908 to 1914, based on the Austrian as well as the German documents.

STUART, GRAHAM HENRY. **French Foreign Policy from Fashoda to Serajevo, 1898-1914.** New York: Century, 1921, 392 p.
A documented study, abreast of the literature to 1921, but requiring revision in view of subsequent revelations.

SZÁNTÓ, ALEXANDER. **Apis, der Führer der "Schwarzen Hand."** Berlin: Neue Gesell-schaft, 1928, 77 p.
A convenient digest of material on the career and activity of the notorious Serbian conspirator.

TAUBE, MIKHAIL ALEKSANDROVICH, BARON. **La Politique Russe d'Avant-Guerre.** Paris: Leroux, 1928, 412 p.
Written by a former official of the Russian Foreign Office. The best systematic treat-ment of Russian policy from 1904 to 1917.

TÖNNIES, FERDINAND. **Der Tsarismus und Seine Bundesgenossen.** Berlin: Deutsche Verlagsgesellschaft für Politik und Geschichte, 1922, 188 p.
A German critique of Russian imperialism and militarism in 1914.

TOSCANO, MARIO. **Il Patto di Londra.** Pavia: Treves, 1931, 133 p.
A scholarly monograph. The best treatment of the most important "secret treaty."

TRAMOND, JOANNÈS and REUSSNER, ANDRÉ. **Éléments d'Histoire Maritime et Colo-niale Contemporaine, 1815-1914.** Paris: Société d'Éditions Géographiques, 1924, 728 p.
One of the few books on pre-war international relations taking into account the varying balance of sea power.

UPLEGGER, FRITZ. **Die Englische Flottenpolitik vor dem Weltkriege, 1904-1909.** Stuttgart: Kohlhammer, 1930, 129 p.
A scholarly treatment of British naval policy from 1900 to 1910, based upon the German documents.

VALENTIN, VEIT. **Deutschlands Aussenpolitik von Bismarcks Abgang bis zum Ende des Weltkrieges.** Berlin: Deutsche Verlagsgesellschaft für Politik und Ge-schichte, 1921, 418 p.
The work of an able German historian. Though now somewhat outmoded, it still is one of the substantial accounts.

WEGERER, ALFRED VON, *ed.* **Das Ausland Urteilt.** Berlin: Stilke, 1929, 156 p.
A collection of quotations from statesmen and writers of many nations, directed against the war-guilt clause of the Treaty of Versailles, prepared by the editor of the German revisionist periodical, *Berliner Monatshefte.*

WEGERER, ALFRED VON. **Der Entscheidende Schritt in den Weltkrieg.** Berlin: Quader, 1931, 85 p.

The author, a persistent exponent of the German thesis regarding the war-guilt question, makes a fresh examination of the Austro-Serbian crisis.

WEGERER, ALFRED VON. **A Refutation of the Versailles War Guilt Thesis.** New York: Knopf, 1930, 415 p.
This is perhaps the best recent presentation of the German view of war origins. The author investigates the material used by the commission set up by the Peace Conference to investigate the question of responsibility, and then dissects its report.

WENDEL, HERMANN. **Die Habsburger und die Südslawenfrage.** Leipzig: Geza Kohn, 1924, 112 p.
An anti-Hapsburg recapitulation of Austria's pre-war policy in the Balkans, by a moderate German publicist thoroughly conversant with Balkan affairs.

Das Werk des Untersuchungsausschusses des Deutschen Reichstages, 1919-1930. Berlin: Deutsche Verlagsgesellschaft für Politik und Geschichte, 1930, 2 v.
Volumes 10 and 11 of series I of the reports of the German Investigating Committee contain extended treatments of the Austro-Serbian problem by Roderich Gooss and Hermann Wendel, and by Hermann Lutz on the crisis of July 1914.

WERTHEIMER, MILDRED SALZ. **The Pan-German League, 1890-1914.** New York: Columbia University Press, 1924, 256 p.
A scholarly investigation of the organization, membership and influence of the famous nationalist league.

WILHELM II, EX-EMPEROR OF GERMANY. **Comparative History, 1878-1914.** London: Hutchinson, 1922, 190 p.
An apologia by means of a revival of the historical methods of Eusebius' "Chronicle."

WILLSON, BECKLES. **The Paris Embassy.** New York: Stokes, 1927, 368 p.
Sketches of Anglo-French relations from 1814 to 1920, based in part on unpublished English correspondence.

WILSON, HERBERT WRIGLEY. **The War Guilt.** London: Sampson Low, 1928, 366 p.
A survey of the diplomatic background of the war, beginning in 1871. The author salvages what he can of the Entente thesis.

ZIMMERMANN, WALTER. **Die Englische Presse zum Ausbruch des Weltkrieges.** Charlottenburg: Hochschule und Ausland, 1928, 269 p.
A minute study not only of the metropolitan press but of the more important provincial papers.

BIOGRAPHIES OF WARTIME STATESMEN AND DIPLOMATS

See also Biographies under individual countries; also (World War) Military Memoirs and Biographies, p. 117; also (Europe) Biographies, p. 228.

ANDRASSY, GYULA, GRÓF. **Diplomacy and War.** London: Bale and Danielson, 1921, 323 p.
These important memoirs by an eminent Hungarian statesman constitute a defense of the policies of the central European Powers and a denunciation of democratic tendencies.

BEAVERBROOK, WILLIAM MAXWELL AITKEN, BARON. **Politicians and the War.** New York: Doubleday, 1928, 264 p.
Primarily an account of the first coalition government. The writer makes some use of Bonar Law's papers, and attempts, rather unsuccessfully, to glorify the former Premier.

BERNSTORFF, JOHANN HEINRICH, GRAF VON. **My Three Years in America.** New York: Scribner, 1920, 428 p.
The former German Ambassador at Washington explains his difficult task.

BERTIE, FRANCIS LEVESON BERTIE, VISCOUNT. **The Diary of Lord Bertie.** New York: Doran, 1924, 2 v.
The diary of the former British Ambassador at Paris; an important contribution to the sources of the war.

BETHMANN-HOLLWEG, THEOBALD VON. **Reflections on the World War.** London: Butterworth, 1920, 2 v.
The apologia of the German Chancellor.

BEYENS, NAPOLÉON EUGÈNE LOUIS, BARON. **Deux Années à Berlin.** Paris: Plon, 1931, 2 v.
The memoirs of the Belgian statesman, covering the period when he was Minister to Germany, from May 1912 to the outbreak of war. One of the best and most detached outside studies of the course of events in Berlin.

BILIŃSKI, LEON. **Wspomnienia i Dokumenty.** Warsaw: Hoesick, 1924-1925, 2 v.
These memoirs of the Austrian Finance Minister are important for the contribution they make to the history of Austrian policy in Bosnia-Herzegovina and for the evolution of the Polish problem during the war.

BOSDARI, ALESSANDRO DE. **Delle Guerre Balcaniche, della Grande Guerra et di Alcuni Fatti Precedenti ad Esse.** Milan: Mondadori, 1928, 225 p.
A record of an Italian diplomat, who takes care not to lift the veil very high. Contains an account of the Greek problem during the war.

BUCHANAN, SIR GEORGE. **My Mission to Russia.** Boston: Little, Brown, 1923, 2 v.
The memoirs of the British Ambassador to Russia. Important for Russian conditions and policies from 1914 to 1917 and as a defense of the author's own activities. Contains no revelations.

BÜLOW, BERNHARD, FÜRST VON. **Memoirs.** Boston: Little, Brown, 1931-1932, 4 v.
The reminiscences of the well-known German Chancellor who preceded Bethmann-Hollweg. The whole work is interestingly written, strongly colored, outspokenly apologetic. There have been a number of criticisms and replies, including: Friedrich Thimme, "Front wider Bülow" (Munich: Bruckmann, 1931, 408 p.); Paul Herre, "Fürst Bülow und Seine Denkwürdigkeiten" (Berlin: Quaderverlag, 1931, 55 p.); Edgar von Schmidt-Pauli, "Fürst Bülows Denk-Unwürdigkeiten" (Berlin: Schlieffen, 1931, 216 p.).

BURIAN VON RAJECZ, STEPHAN, GRAF. **Austria in Dissolution.** New York: Doran, 1925, 455 p.
The Austro-Hungarian Foreign Minister from 1915 to 1918 describes his conduct of foreign policy when the empire was at its last gasp. He also throws interesting light on the nationalities problem.

CAILLAUX, JOSEPH. **Mes Prisons.** Paris: Éditions de la Sirène, 1921, 351 p.
The defense and apology of the French radical statesman for his course in the war.

CHARLES-ROUX, FRANÇOIS. **Trois Ambassades Françaises à la Veille de la Guerre.** Paris: Plon, 1928, 228 p.
An appreciative account of the remarkable work of the Cambon brothers at London and Berlin, and of Barrère at Rome.

CHARYKOV, NIKOLAÏ VALERIEVICH. **Glimpses of High Politics.** New York: Macmillan, 1931, 330 p.
The author was one of the leading diplomats of pre-war Russia, but in these memoirs he does not reveal much about the mainsprings and inner workings of Russian policy.

CHESTER, SAMUEL BEACH. **Life of Venizelos.** London: Constable, 1921, 321 p.
A full-length biography by a well-informed and sympathetic Englishman.

CHIROL, SIR VALENTINE. **Fifty Years in a Changing World.** New York: Harcourt,
1927, 351 p.
The interesting reminiscences and reflections of the former foreign editor of the London
Times. There are no indiscretions, but the book abounds in shrewd observations and
well-balanced appreciations. The character sketches of men like Cromer, Kitchener,
Alexander of Battenberg, Ferdinand of Coburg, Curzon and Holstein are particularly noteworthy.

CLEMENCEAU, GEORGES. **France Facing Germany.** New York: Dutton, 1922, 200 p.
Important speeches from the time of the Morocco crisis to the World War.

CLEMENCEAU, GEORGES. **Grandeur and Misery of Victory.** New York: Harcourt, 1930,
432 p.
An angry book, by an old man. The Tiger, like Bismarck, spent the last years of his
life in bemoaning the destruction of his work, and this volume may well be compared
to the third volume of Bismarck's memoirs. The importance of the present volume lies
chiefly in the discussion of Clemenceau's attitude toward the peace settlement and the
demands raised by Foch and Poincaré.

CREEL, GEORGE. **The War, the World and Wilson.** New York: Harper, 1920, 367 p.
The President in the war years, as seen by the Director of Public Information.

CZERNIN, OTTOKAR, GRAF. **In the World War.** New York: Harper, 1920, 387 p.
The apologia of the Austrian Foreign Minister during the latter part of the war. Over-
drawn in places, but a source of great importance.

DAUDET, LÉON A. **Raymond Poincaré.** Paris: Capitole, 1930, 208 p.
Daudet never wrote a dull book, and this scornful attack on Poincaré is in his best
vein.

DEVILLE, GABRIEL. **L'Entente, la Grèce et la Bulgarie.** Paris: Figuière, 1920, 355 p.
Recollections of the former French minister at Athens. Important for its light on the
development of the Greek problem in the first years of the war.

DJUVARA, TRANDAFIR G. **Mes Missions Diplomatiques.** Paris: Alcan, 1930, 180 p.
These recollections of one of Rumania's leading diplomats are a valuable contribution
to the literature of diplomacy in the last forty years and especially to the study of
Near Eastern affairs.

DUBLY, HENRY LOUIS. **La Vie Ardente de Georges Clemenceau.** Lille: Mercure de
Flandre, 1930, 2 v.
A full-length biography, with detailed treatment of Clemenceau's earlier career.
Journalistic in style.

DUMAINE, ALFRED. **La Dernière Ambassade de France en Autriche.** Paris: Plon,
1921, 244 p.
Attractively written recollections of the French Ambassador at Vienna, but of secondary historical importance.

DUMBA, KONSTANTIN. **Memories of a Diplomat.** Boston: Little, Brown, 1932, 354 p.
Dumba was Austrian minister to the United States during the war. He here reviews
his whole career and defends his activities in Washington.

EPPSTEIN, GEORG, FREIHERR VON and FRANÇOIS, HERMANN VON. **Der Deutsche Kron-
prinz.** Leipzig: Koch, 1926, 428, 247 p.
The first part a conventional eulogy, the second part a valuable contribution to the
history of German operations on the west front.

FRANCIS, DAVID ROWLAND. **Russia from the American Embassy.** New York: Scribner, 1921, 361 p.
These memoirs of the American Ambassador cover the crowded period from April 1916 to November 1918. Rather thin.

GEFFROY, GUSTAVE. **Georges Clemenceau.** Paris: Larousse, 1929, 192 p.
On the whole a good review of Clemenceau's career and accomplishments in the larger setting of French history. Lavishly illustrated, with a detailed bibliography of Clemenceau's writings.

GIBBONS, HERBERT ADAMS. **Venizelos.** Boston: Houghton Mifflin, 2nd ed., 1923, 418 p.
A good appreciative biography, by an American correspondent who treats fully the war period and the Peace Conference.

GIESL VON GIESLINGEN, WLADIMIR, FREIHERR. **Zwei Jahrzehnte im Nahen Orient.** Berlin: Verlag für Kulturpolitik, 1927, 331 p.
The reminiscences of the former Austrian diplomat, who spent fully twenty years at the various Balkan courts. The author takes up all the important crises from the Turkish-Greek War of 1897 to the days of Sarajevo.

GIOLITTI, GIOVANNI. **Memoirs of My Life.** London: Chapman and Dodd, 1923, 472 p.
Important memoirs of the former Italian Premier, especially valuable for the period since 1900.

GREGORY, JOHN DUNCAN. **On the Edge of Diplomacy.** London: Hutchinson, 1929, 286 p.
The former Under-Secretary of the Foreign Office carefully avoids indiscretions, but throws sidelights on the events and personalities of the period from 1902 to 1928.

GREY, EDWARD GREY, VISCOUNT. **Twenty-five Years.** New York: Stokes, 1925, 2 v.
An honest but unimpressive account of his policy, by the former British Foreign Minister. These volumes are attractively written and have been very widely read. One should consult, with them, Lutz' "Lord Grey and the World War," and Montgelas' "British Foreign Policy under Sir Edward Grey."

HALDANE, RICHARD BURDON HALDANE, VISCOUNT. **Before the War.** New York: Funk, 1920, 233 p.
A balanced book by the former Secretary for War who was sent to Berlin in 1912. The author surveys the Anglo-German problem with special reference to the writings of Bethmann and Tirpitz.

HALDANE, RICHARD BURDON HALDANE, VISCOUNT. **Richard Burdon Haldane. An Autobiography.** New York: Doubleday, 1929, 391 p.
The interesting autobiography of an unusual man.

HARDINGE, SIR ARTHUR HENRY. **A Diplomatist in Europe.** London: Cape, 1927, 272 p.
The reminiscences of an English diplomat who served at many courts but is careful not to say too much of the inner workings of British diplomacy.

HENDRICK, BURTON JESSE. **Life and Letters of Walter H. Page.** New York: Doubleday, 1922, 2 v.
An important part of the first-hand history of the war. We get interesting light not only on Page's Anglophile outlook but on the information which reached the administration at Washington.

HERTLING, KARL, GRAF VON. **Ein Jahr in der Reichskanzlei.** Freiburg: Herder, 1919, 192 p.
A study of the brief chancellorship of von Hertling, by his son.

HIBBEN, PAXTON. **Constantine I and the Greek People.** New York: Century, 1920, 592 p.

An able presentation of the King's side in the argument with the Allies and Venizelos, by an American journalist who was on the spot.

HOUSE, EDWARD MANDELL. **The Intimate Papers of Colonel House.** Arranged by Charles Seymour. Boston: Houghton Mifflin, 1926-1928, 4 v.
The highly important papers of President Wilson's confidential adviser, covering the period from House's mission to Europe on the eve of the war through the Peace Conference of 1919.

HUDDLESTON, SISLEY. **Poincaré: A Biographical Portrait.** Boston: Little, Brown, 1924, 192 p.
A biography of the former French Premier by the Paris correspondent of the London *Times*. One of the best-balanced books in English.

HULDERMAN, BERNHARD. **Albert Ballin.** London: Cassell, 1922, 326 p.
The life of the Chairman of the Hamburg-American Line, who had a hand in many important wartime negotiations and decisions.

IONESCU, TAKE. **Some Personal Impressions.** New York: Stokes, 1920, 292 p.
A Rumanian Prime Minister draws pen portraits of his contemporaries—Berchtold, Czernin, Tisza, King Charles of Rumania, Talaat Pasha, etc.—as a way of giving his story of events in which he participated.

JAGOW, GÜNTHER GOTTLIEB VON. **England und der Kriegsausbruch.** Berlin: Verlag für Kulturpolitik, 1925, 82 p.
A reply to Grey's memoirs, by a former German Foreign Minister.

JAGOW, GÜNTHER GOTTLIEB VON. **Ursachen und Ausbruch des Weltkrieges.** Berlin: Hobbing, 1919, 195 p.
The author, Secretary for Foreign Affairs in 1914, reviews pre-war developments and the crisis of 1914. An inadequate account.

JUDET, ERNEST. **Le Véritable Clemenceau.** Berne: Wyss, 1920, 362 p.
Scenes from Clemenceau's life, stressing the oppositional and negative sides of his character, by a French journalist whose relations with the Tiger were anything but pleasant.

KOROSTOVETS, VLADIMIR KONSTANTINOVICH. **Lenin im Hause der Väter.** Berlin: Verlag für Kulturpolitik, 1928, 444 p.
Interesting memoirs of a former official of the Russian Foreign Office, covering the period from 1911 to 1919.

LANCKEN-WAKENITZ, OSCAR, FREIHERR VON DER. **Meine Dreissig Dienstjahre.** Berlin: Verlag für Kulturpolitik, 1931, 326 p.
Lancken played quite a part in the Moroccan crisis of 1911, and during the war served with the German administration in Belgium. His memoirs are a valuable contribution to the story of pre-war diplomacy and of the German administration in Belgium.

LAUZANNE, STÉPHANE. **Great Men and Great Days.** New York: Appleton, 1921, 263 p.
Impressions and character sketches by the editor of *Le Matin*, including Joffre, Poincaré, Wilson, House, Lloyd George, Clemenceau and Millerand.

LICHNOWSKY, KARL MAX, FÜRST VON. **Auf dem Wege zum Abgrund.** Dresden: Reissner, 1927, 2 v.
The writings and papers of the former German Ambassador in London. The larger part is made up of his correspondence with the German Foreign Office, already published.

LOUIS, GEORGES. **Carnets de Georges Louis, 1908-1917.** Paris: Rieder, 1926, 2 v.
The diaries and notes of the French Ambassador to Russia, replaced in 1913 by Delcassé. They are of interest in connection with the study of Poincaré's influence.

McAdoo, William Gibbs. **Crowded Years.** Boston: Houghton Mifflin, 1931, 552 p.
Recollections of the former Secretary of the Treasury; an important contribution to the history of the United States in the World War period.

Macchio, Karl, Freiherr von. **Wahrheit. Fürst Bülow und Ich in Rom, 1914, 1915.** Vienna: Jung Oesterreich Verlag, 1931, 137 p.
The apologia of the Austrian Ambassador at Rome. A dispassionate rejoinder to Bülow's accusations, forming an important contribution to the history of Austrian policy in Italy before the latter's entry into the war.

Malcolm, Sir Ian. **Lord Balfour.** London: Macmillan, 1930, 124 p.
A warmly sympathetic sketch devoted largely to the war period, by Balfour's secretary.

Malvy, Louis Jean. **Mon Crime.** Paris: Flammarion, 1921, 286 p.
The recollections and defense of the French Minister of the Interior who, during the war, was accused of defeatist connections.

Martin, William. **Statesmen of the War in Retrospect.** New York: Minton, Balch, 1928, 329 p.
Brilliant pen portraits of the leading statesmen of the war period, written by the foreign editor of the *Journal de Genève*.

Maximilian, Prince of Baden. **Memoirs.** New York: Scribner, 1928, 2 v.
The English translation of the last imperial chancellor's memoirs, which throw a flood of light upon the closing days of the Empire and the beginnings of the Revolution.

Mélas, George. **Ex-King Constantine and the War.** London: Hutchinson, 1920, 290 p.
Random recollections and impressions by Constantine's secretary, who was strongly Ententist in sympathies.

Michon, Georges. **Clemenceau.** Paris: Rivière, 1931, 300 p.
A critical biographical study.

Mordacq, Jean Jules Henri. **Le Ministère Clemenceau.** Paris: Plon, 1930, 2 v.
The day-by-day journal of General Mordacq, one of Clemenceau's closest associates, covering the period from November 1917 to November 1918.

Mott, Thomas Bentley. **Myron T. Herrick.** New York: Doubleday, 1929, 409 p.
A good picture of Herrick the man, but lacking breadth of view and understanding of the background of his diplomatic work.

Mowat, Robert Balmain. **The Life of Lord Pauncefote.** Boston: Houghton Mifflin, 1929, 322 p.
An account of the diplomatic questions that Pauncefote had to deal with rather than a conventional biography. Contains important chapters on Egypt and the Suez Canal and especially on Anglo-American Isthmian diplomacy.

Münz, Sigmund. **Fürst Bülow, der Staatsmann und Mensch.** Berlin: Verlag für Kulturpolitik, 1930, 317 p.
A sympathetic study by an Austrian journalist who was in close touch with him.

Musulin von Gomirje, Alexander, Freiherr. **Das Haus am Ballplatz.** Munich: Verlag für Kulturpolitik, 1924, 310 p.
These recollections of a high official in the Austrian Foreign Office throw light on the crisis of 1914 and Austrian diplomacy during the war.

Naumann, Victor. **Profile.** Munich: Duncker und Humblot, 1925, 374 p.
A German journalist's impressions of German and Austrian princes, statesmen and soldiers. One of the best books of its kind.

NEKLIUDOV, ANATOLIĬ VASIL'EVICH. **Diplomatic Reminiscences.** London: Murray, 1920, 541 p.
These recollections of the Russian minister to Bulgaria and Sweden are of interest in connection with attempted peace negotiations during the war.

NEVINS, ALLAN. **Henry White.** New York: Harper, 1930, 530 p.
An attractively written biography, based on unpublished papers, of an experienced American diplomat who served as one of the American Plenipotentiaries at the Peace Conference in 1919.

NEWTON, THOMAS WODEHOUSE LEGH, BARON. **Lord Lansdowne.** New York: Macmillan, 1929, 536 p.
The authoritative life, but it does not add very much to what we know about Lansdowne's policy from the British documents.

NICHOLAS, PRINCE OF GREECE. **Political Memoirs, 1914-1917.** London: Hutchinson, 1928, 320 p.
A war diary full of valuable material and shedding much light on the incredible Allied policy and on the deposition of Constantine.

NICOLSON, HAROLD GEORGE. **Portrait of a Diplomatist; Being the Life of Sir Arthur Nicolson, First Lord Carnock, and a Study of the Origins of the Great War.** Boston: Houghton Mifflin, 1930, 337 p.
A beautifully written account of the career of an important English diplomat, and of his times, by his son. The author is very critical of the pre-war system of international relations.

NOEL-BUXTON, EDWARD, BARON. **Travels and Reflections.** Boston: Houghton Mifflin, 1929, 224 p.
These reminiscences deal with travels all the way from Japan to Africa, but are of particular importance for the pre-war history of the Balkans, for Buxton is a Bulgarophile of long standing and he and the Balkan Committee were powerful influences in shaping English opinion and policies.

ORLANDO, VITTORIO EMANUELE. **I Discorsi per la Guerra e per la Pace.** Foligno: Campitelli, 1924, 442 p.
The former Premier's speeches delivered during the war and post-war periods.

OXFORD AND ASQUITH, HERBERT HENRY ASQUITH, EARL OF. **Memories and Reflections, 1852-1927.** Boston: Little, Brown, 1928, 2 v.
Amiable and sometimes interesting reminiscences of an eminent statesman. Volume II adds to our knowledge of British affairs during the war, but on the whole these volumes are disappointing.

PALÉOLOGUE, MAURICE. **An Ambassador's Memoirs.** New York: Doran, 1924-1925, 3 v.
Among the most interesting of all war memoirs, by the French Ambassador at St. Petersburg to 1917.

PALMER, FREDERICK. **Newton D. Baker.** New York: Dodd, 1931, 2 v.
An excellent biography of Wilson's Secretary of War, and a most important addition to the literature of America's rôle in the World War.

POINCARÉ, RAYMOND. **The Origins of the War.** London: Cassell, 1922, 275 p.
A series of lectures by the outstanding French statesman of recent times. The account here given of the origins of the war is the traditional French account, one which M. Poincaré himself does not maintain *in toto*, in view of subsequent revelations.

POINCARÉ, RAYMOND. **Au Service de la France.** Paris: Plon, 1926, 8 v.
These well-prepared and very detailed memoirs set forth the full story of events as seen by the French statesman, beginning with his first premiership in 1912. The eight volumes thus far published go as far as 1916. They are of unequal interest to the general reader, those covering the period after M. Poincaré became President often dealing with formal and routine matters. But the work as a whole is of course of the first importance. An abridged English translation by Sir George Arthur is in process of publication: "The Memoirs of Raymond Poincaré" (New York: Doubleday, 1926, 2 v., covering volumes 1-4 of the original).

POURTALÈS, FRIEDRICH, GRAF VON. **Meine Letzten Verhandlungen in St. Petersburg.** Berlin: Deutsche Verlagsgesellschaft für Politik und Geschichte, 1927, 198 p.
A new edition of the memoirs of the former German Ambassador at St. Petersburg, supplemented by the texts of his correspondence with his government in the critical days of July 1914. The earlier edition was called "Am Scheideweg zwischen Krieg und Frieden" (Charlottenburg, 1919).

RANDI, OSCAR. **Nicola P. Pasic.** Rome: Istituto per l'Europa Orientale, 1927, 96 p.
A commemorative essay, surveying the career of the Serbian statesman, by a well-informed Italian writer on Balkan affairs.

RIBOT, ALEXANDRE. **Lettres à un Ami.** Paris: Bossard, 1924, 354 p.
The war-time recollections of an eminent French statesman. An important source for the history of French politics in that stormy period.

ROBERTS, CARL ERIC BECHHOFER. **Winston Churchill.** New York: McBride, 1928, 272 p.
A clever and telling critique of the man and his policy as revealed in his writings.

ROCH, WALTER FRANCIS. **Mr. Lloyd George and the War.** London: Chatto and Windus, 1920, 222 p.
A study of the War Minister's activities before as well as during the conflict.

RODD, SIR JAMES RENNELL. **Social and Diplomatic Memories.** Series III. New York: Longmans, 1925, 413 p.
An English diplomat's reminiscences covering the period from 1902 to 1919, important for the story of Italy's entrance into the war and indeed for the whole war period.

ROSEN, ROMAN ROMANOVICH, BARON. **Forty Years of Diplomacy.** New York: Knopf, 1922, 2 v.
One of the most readable and interesting accounts of Russian policy before and during the war.

SALANDRA, ANTONIO. **La Neutralità Italiana. L'Intervento.** Milan: Mondadori, 1928-1931, 2 v.
These volumes, by the former Italian Prime Minister, are carefully written and evidently leave much unsaid. Still they are the fullest and best account of Italian policy in 1914-1915.

SAVINSKIĬ, ALEKSANDR ALEKSANDROVICH. **Recollections of a Russian Diplomat.** London: Hutchinson, 1927, 316 p.
The writer was an official in the Russian Foreign Office from 1901 to 1910 and was minister at Sofia in 1914-1915. His book fills in some gaps in the history of Russian foreign policy, particularly in the Near East.

SAZONOV, SERGEĬ DMITRIEVICH. **Fateful Years.** New York: Stokes, 1928, 328 p.
The apologia of the Russian Foreign Minister, interestingly written but presenting only the oft-stated defense of Russian policy. One should read with it the replies of Austrian and German statesmen published in an interesting volume edited by Eduard von Steinitz: "Rings um Sasonow" (Berlin: Verlag für Kulturpolitik, 1928, 186 p.).

SCHOEN, WILHELM EDUARD, FREIHERR VON. **The Memoirs of an Ambassador.** London: Allen and Unwin, 1922, 254 p.
The interesting reflections of a former German Minister for Foreign Affairs and Ambassador at Paris in 1914.

SEYMOUR, CHARLES. **Woodrow Wilson and the World War.** New Haven: Yale University Press, 1922, 383 p.
An important volume in the "Chronicles of America" series. The most authoritative statement of the conventional view.

SONNINO, SIDNEY. **Discorsi per la Guerra.** Foligno: Campitelli, 1922, 153 p.
Speeches by the late Italian Minister for Foreign Affairs during the World War.

SPENDER, HAROLD. **The Prime Minister, David Lloyd George.** New York: Doran, 1920, 388 p.
Probably still the best and most understanding biography of the Liberal leader.

SPENDER, JOHN ALFRED and ASQUITH, CYRIL. **Life of Lord Oxford and Asquith.** London: Hutchinson, 1932, 2 v.
The standard biography.

SPRING-RICE, SIR CECIL ARTHUR. **The Letters and Friendships of Sir Cecil Spring-Rice.** Edited by Stephen Gwynn. Boston: Houghton Mifflin, 1929, 2 v.
Of the greatest importance, naturally, are the sections dealing with Spring-Rice's ambassadorship to the United States from 1913 to 1917, which are based upon the extensive use of unpublished material. These years covered the critical period of American neutrality and were filled with the tension resulting from British interference with American trade. There can be no doubt that the moderating influence of the British Ambassador in Washington was quite as important as the influence of Page in preventing a conflict.

SUAREZ, GEORGES. **La Vie Orgueilleuse de Georges Clemenceau.** Paris: Éditions de France, 1930, 700 p.
The most complete and on the whole probably the best biography, written in a vein of strong human sympathy.

TISZA, ISTVÁN, GRÓF. **Briefe.** Edited by Oskar von Wertheimer. Berlin: Hobbing, 1928, 272 p.
An important collection of correspondence, covering the period from July 1914 to July 1915. The letters show how great was the Magyar influence in the foreign affairs of the Dual Monarchy, and supply invaluable material on the negotiations of the Central Powers with Italy in the spring of 1915. A character study of Tisza is also included.

VIVIANI, RENÉ. **As We See It.** New York: Harper, 1923, 314 p.
A brilliant defense of French foreign policy from 1870 to the present.

VIVIANI, RENÉ. **Réponse au Kaiser.** Paris: Ferenczi, 1924, 300 p.
A rebuttal to the Kaiser's memoirs.

WILHELM, EX-CROWN PRINCE OF GERMANY. **I Seek the Truth.** New York: Sears, 1926, 352 p.
The English translation of the former Crown Prince's book on the origins of the war. An honest if not an impressive attempt at moderate statement.

WITTE, SERGIEĬ IUL'EVICH, COUNT. **The Memoirs of Count Witte.** Translated and edited by Abraham Yarmolinsky. New York: Doubleday, 1921, 445 p.
An abridgment of the Russian edition of the apologia of an outstanding Russian statesman. It must be used with caution.

WOLFF, THEODOR. **Das Vorspiel.** Munich: Verlag für Kulturpolitik, 1925, 304 p.
Reminiscences of the editor of the *Berliner Tageblatt*. A moderate, sympathetic criticism of German pre-war policy, with interesting sidelights on Bülow, Holstein and Tirpitz.

II. HISTORY

OFFICIAL HISTORIES

Les Armées Françaises dans la Grande Guerre. Paris: Imprimerie Nationale, 1922 ff.
The French official history, published by the historical section of the General Staff and based on unpublished material. To date there have appeared tomes 1, 3, 7, 8 and 10, several in two volumes, with a number of volumes of annexes.

CHACK, PAUL. **La Guerre des Croiseurs.** Paris: Challamel, 1922-1923, 2 v.
A well-documented study of cruiser operations, through the Battle of the Falklands. Based on material in the French Ministry of Marine and published under the direction of the historical department of the ministry.

L'Esercito Italiano nella Grande Guerra, 1915-1918. Rome: Provveditorato Generale dello Stato, 1927 ff.
The Italian official history. To date there have appeared two volumes in several parts, covering the campaigns of 1915.

FROTHINGHAM, THOMAS GODDARD. **The Naval History of the World War.** Cambridge: Harvard University Press, 1924-1926, 3 v.
A careful work, based on data provided by the historical section of the United States Navy.

History of the Great War. Military Operations. London: Macmillan, 1922 ff.
The great official British history, based on official documents and published by direction of the historical section of the Committee of Imperial Defense. To date there have appeared: four volumes of text and four volumes of maps on the campaigns in France and Belgium to July 1916, compiled by Brigadier-General J. E. Edmonds; four volumes, completing the history of the Mesopotamian campaign, compiled by Brigadier-General F. J. Moberly; three volumes of text and two volumes of maps, completing the history of the Egyptian and Palestine campaigns, compiled by Lieutenant-General Sir George MacMunn and Captain Cyril Falls; one volume on the Gallipoli operations, compiled by C. F. Aspinall-Oglander; one volume on Togoland and the Cameroons, 1914-1916, by Brigadier-General F. J. Moberly.

History of the Great War. Naval Operations. New York: Longmans, 1920-1931, 5 v.
The British official history, based on unpublished material and published by the historical section of the Committee of Imperial Defense. There have appeared five volumes, with additional volumes of maps, by Sir Julian Corbett and Henry Newbolt. These cover all phases of naval operations in which British forces participated. There have also been published in the official history three volumes and maps on Seaborne Trade, by C. Ernest Fayle (London: Murray, 1920-1924), and three volumes on the Merchant Navy, by Archibald Hurd (London: Murray, 1921-1929).

History of the Great War. The War in the Air. New York: Oxford University Press, 1922 ff.
These three volumes, by Walter Raleigh and H. A. Jones, part of the British official history of the war, carry the story of the Royal Air Force to 1917.

The Italian Navy in the World War, 1915-1918. Rome: Provveditorato Generale dello Stato, 1927, 58 p.

A collection of facts, figures and pictures published by the historical section of the Italian Naval Staff.

Der Krieg zur See. Under the direction of E. von Mantey. Berlin: Mittler, 1920 ff.
The German official history of naval operations. There have appeared to date "Der Krieg in der Nordsee," by O. Gross, five volumes, going to June 1916; "Der Krieg in der Ostsee," by Rudolph Firle and Heinrich Rollmann, two volumes, going through 1915; "Der Krieg in den Türkischen Gewässern," by Hermann Lorey, covering the work of the Mediterranean Division; "Die Überwasserstreitkräfte und Ihre Technik," by Paul Köppen; "Der Kreuzerkrieg," by E. Raeder, two volumes, covering the Coronel and Falklands engagements and the sea raids; "Der Handelskrieg mit U-Booten," by Arno Spindler.

Oesterreich-Ungarns Letzter Krieg. Under the direction of Edmund Glaise von Horstenau. Vienna: Verlag der Militärwissenschaftlichen Mitteilungen, 1929 ff.
The Austrian official history. To date there have appeared two volumes and two supplements, carrying the story through the campaigns of the summer of 1915.

Oesterreich-Ungarns Seekrieg, 1914-1918. Vienna: Amalthea, 1930 ff.
The Austrian official history, written by Hans Sokol and published by the War Office. The work is to be complete in four parts, of which three have appeared.

Official History of Australia in the War of 1914-18. Sydney: Angus and Robertson, 1921 ff.
A detailed narrative and statistical compilation, by various authors, surveying the organization and operation of the Australian forces.

Official History of New Zealand's Effort in the Great War. Auckland: Whitcombe and Tombs, 1921-22.
Three volumes of this detailed account have been published, covering the operations at Gallipoli, in France, and in Palestine and Egypt.

Der Weltkrieg, 1914-1918. Berlin: Mittler, 1925 ff.
The German official history, based in large part on unpublished material. To date there have appeared seven volumes covering operations to the spring of 1915, one on military railroads, and two on preparations and economic measures.

UNOFFICIAL HISTORIES AND GENERAL DISCUSSIONS

See also (International Law) General Treatises, p. 33; also (World War) Military Efforts of Participants, p. 146, and Neutrals and the War, p. 152, and Peace Negotiations, p. 156; also (Central Europe) Collapse of the Hapsburg Empire, p. 301; also (Czechoslovakia) Establishment of the State, p. 313; also (Germany) Old Régime and Revolution, p. 318; also (Poland) Resurrection of the State, p. 347; also (Russia) The War and the Revolution, p. 360.

Alvin, G. and Tuffran, P. **La Grande Guerre.** Paris: Gauthier-Villars, 1930, 312 p.
One of the better French texts.

Aston, Sir George Grey. **The Great War of 1914-1918.** London: Butterworth, 1930, 252 p.
An excellent brief introductory survey.

Bourget, Jean Marie. **Les Origines de la Victoire.** Paris: Renaissance du Livre, 1924, 582 p.
An important critical history of the war, showing the interrelationship of military and political events, written by an officer close to the Ministry of War and the high command.

BUCHAN, JOHN. **A History of the Great War.** New York: Nelson, 1921-22, 4 v.
An abridgment and revision of Nelson's "History of the War" (24 v., 1915-19).

CAREY, GORDON VERO and SCOTT, HUGH SUMNER, *comps.* **An Outline History of the Great War.** New York: Macmillan, 1928, 279 p.
A brief and strictly military narrative confined almost entirely to British campaigns.

CHERFILS, PIERRE JOSEPH MAXIME. **La Guerre de la Délivrance.** Paris: Gigord, 1920-1922, 3 v.
A critical military history of considerable value.

CHURCHILL, WINSTON SPENCER. **The World Crisis, 1911-1918.** New York: Scribner, 1923-1927, 4 v.
Brilliantly written, often indiscreet, sometimes obviously "special pleading," these four volumes form one of the most important sources for the study of British policy before and during the war. Most of the material has subsequently been rearranged and concentrated in one bulky volume, "The World Crisis" (New York: Scribner, 1931, 866 p.). A number of criticisms have been collected in a volume by Lord Sydenham of Combe and others: "Winston Churchill: The World Crisis. A Criticism" (London: Hutchinson, 1927, 192 p.).

CONSETT, MONTAGU WILLIAM WARCOP PETER and DANIEL, OCTAVIUS HAROLD. **The Triumph of Unarmed Forces, 1914-1918.** New York: Brentano, 1923, 344 p.
Admiral Consett, who was British Naval Attaché in Scandinavia throughout the war, throws light on the reasons for certain loopholes in the British blockade of Germany.

CORDA, HENRY. **La Guerre Mondiale.** Paris: Chapelot, 1922, 418 p.
An excellent military study, concise and well documented.

DOMANEVSKIĬ, V. N. **Mirovaia Voĭna.** Paris: Rosty, 1929, 83 p.
The first part of a general survey of the war, dealing with the campaigns of 1914.

DOMMES, WILHELM VON, HOSSE, KARL and others. **Der Deutsche Landkrieg.** Leipzig: Finking, 1927, 3 v.
A large-scale history of the war, written by experts and well supplied with charts.

FRAUENHOLZ, EUGEN. **Ueberblick über die Geschichte des Weltkrieges.** Munich: Oldenbourg, 1926, 115 p.
One of the best brief sketches, commendable especially for the skillful interweaving of military, political and economic factors.

FROTHINGHAM, THOMAS GODDARD. **A Guide to the Military History of the World War.** Boston: Little, Brown, 1920, 367 p.
A convenient synopsis with useful maps, by an American army officer.

GIRAUD, VICTOR. **Histoire de la Grande Guerre.** Paris: Hachette, 1919, 775 p.
One of the best general French accounts, chiefly military.

GUIXÉ, JUAN. **La Moral de la Paz y la Guerra Futura.** Madrid: Imprenta Latina, 1923, 330 p.
A psychological interpretation of the World War and its consequences by a pacifically inclined Spaniard.

HALÉVY, ÉLIE. **The World Crisis, 1914-1918.** New York: Oxford University Press, 1930, 57 p.
Discounting the Ludwigian thesis of the responsibility of individual statesmen, a brilliant French historian seeks to uncover the great movements which brought on the storm.

HAYES, CARLTON JOSEPH HUNTLEY. **A Brief History of the Great War.** New York: Macmillan, 1920, 461 p.
This is still one of the best brief general accounts of the war.

HELFFERICH, KARL THEODOR. **Der Weltkrieg.** Berlin: Ullstein, 1919, 3 v.
An apologia for the German government, written by a former minister. A good formulation of the "stab in the back" theory of Germany's collapse.

JOHNSON, DOUGLAS WILSON. **Battlefields of the World War: A Study in Military Geography.** New York: American Geographical Society, 1921, 648 p.
A valuable study, illustrated with photographs and sixty maps and diagrams, by one of the geographical experts of the American delegation at the Peace Conference.

KUHL, HERMANN VON. **Der Weltkrieg.** Berlin: Kolk, 1929, 2 v.
One of the latest and beyond dispute one of the best histories of the war in reasonable scope. General von Kuhl, chief of staff of the First German Army, is one of the outstanding writers on strategy.

KUHL, HERMANN VON. **Der Weltkrieg im Urteil Unserer Feinde.** Berlin: Mittler, 1922, 134 p.
A systematic review of operations, with critical analyses in the light of the chief Allied revelations.

LIDDELL HART, BASIL HENRY. **The Real War.** Boston: Little, Brown, 1930, 508 p.
A somewhat racy but withal excellent and very readable short history of the war.

McPHERSON, WILLIAM LENHART. **A Short History of the Great War.** New York: Putnam, 1920, 410 p.
A military and diplomatic study, with emphasis on the part played by the United States, by the military critic of the *New York Tribune*.

MARCH, FRANCIS ANDREW. **History of the World War.** Philadelphia: Winston, 1919, 800 p.
A straightforward compendium of facts, with little interpretation.

MOSER, OTTO VON. **Kurzer Strategischer Ueberblick über den Weltkrieg, 1914-1918.** Berlin: Mittler, 1923.
A splendid but purely military history of the war in brief scope, by a leading German authority.

MOSER, OTTO VON. **Die Obersten Gewalten im Weltkriege.** Stuttgart: Belser, 1931.
A critical study of the relations of the staff to the command, with special reference to the difficulties of German leadership in the last years of the war.

NORMAN, C. H. **A Searchlight on the European War.** London: Labour Publishing Company, 1924, 178 p.
Largely a radical's indictment of British policy, and of militarism, imperialism and the existing social and governmental system.

O'NEILL, HERBERT CHARLES. **A History of the War.** London: Jack, 1920, 1064 p.
A digest of material, carefully done.

POLLARD, ALBERT FREDERICK. **A Short History of the Great War.** London: Methuen, 1928, 411 p.
The third edition of one of the best brief English histories.

RÜDT VON COLLENBERG, LUDWIG KARL, FREIHERR. **Die Deutsche Armee von 1871 bis 1914.** Berlin: Mittler, 1922.
Really a careful comparative study of European armaments, the Austrian, Italian, Russian, French and English being considered with the German.

Schlachten des Weltkrieges. Berlin: Stalling, 1921-1930, 36 v.
A series of valuable technical monographs by various writers, published under the auspices of the German archive administration and based in part on unpublished material.

SCHNITLER, GUDMUND. **Der Weltkrieg, 1914-1918.** Berlin: Verlag für Kulturpolitik, 1926.
The German translation of a well-balanced study by a teacher at the Norwegian war college.

SCHWARTE, MAX, *ed.* **Der Grosse Krieg, 1914-1918.** Leipzig: Barth, 1923, 10 v.
The most important coöperative history of the war in German, written by high officers and other authorities. The volumes cover Austria-Hungary's war, the German campaigns, the war at sea, and in detail the military organization.

SCHWARTE, MAX, *ed.* **Die Militärischen Lehren des Grossen Krieges.** Berlin: Mittler, 1920, 489 p.
A series of technical studies, by experts, of various arms and services.

SEESELBERG, FRIEDRICH. **Der Stellungskrieg, 1914-1918.** Berlin: Mittler, 1926, 488 p.
An exhaustive standard study of the war of position.

SIMONDS, FRANK HERBERT. **A History of the World War.** New York: Doubleday, 1917-1920, 5 v.
Clear and straightforward, and not over-technical.

STEGEMANN, HERMANN. **Geschichte des Krieges.** Stuttgart: Deutsche Verlags-Anstalt, 1918-1921, 4 v.
A Swiss writer gives a sober account of the principal operations.

THÉVENET, CLAUDE MARIE FRÉDÉRIC. **La Grande Guerre.** Paris: Colin, 1924, 200 p.
A clear, concise, impartial summary.

THOMPSON, PETER ANTHONY. **Lions Led by Donkeys.** London: Laurie, 1927, 317 p.
This outline of the war is better informed and better balanced than the facetious title indicates.

VAN DEN BELT, J. C. **Die Ersten Wochen des Grossen Krieges. Der Zweite Abschnitt des Grossen Krieges. Von Gorlice bis zur Russischen Revolution. Das Ende des Ringens.** Berlin: Mittler, 1922-1926.
Four parts of a well-informed and eminently fair treatment of the war by a Dutch officer.

VILLATE, ROBERT HENRI JEAN. **Les Conditions Géographiques de la Guerre.** Paris: Payot, 1925, 350 p.
The best study of geographic and meteorological factors. Unfortunately it deals only with the western front.

WOODS, WILLIAM SEAVER. **Colossal Blunders of the War.** New York: Macmillan, 1930, 282 p.
Admitting that mistakes in war are inevitable, the editor of the *Literary Digest* reviews the great blunders on all sides that cost hundreds of thousands of lives.

ZURLINDEN, ÉMILE AUGUSTE FRANÇOIS THOMAS. **La Guerre de Libération, 1914-1918.** Paris: Hachette, 1919, 2 v.
An excellent compact history of operations, by a former Belgian war minister.

CONDUCT OF THE WAR; STRATEGY

BALCK, WILLIAM. **Entwickelung der Taktik im Weltkriege.** Berlin: Eisenschmidt, 1922, 410 p.
The second, enlarged edition of an excellent German survey, by a high officer.

BECKER, GEORGES. **Trois Conférences sur Ludendorff**. Paris: Berger-Levrault, 1920, 106 p.
Three technical studies of Ludendorff's strategy and tactics.

BOURGET, JEAN MARIE. **Gouvernement et Commandement**. Paris: Payot, 1930, 318 p.
A most valuable, documented study of the relations of civil and military powers during the war, with special reference to France and Germany.

BOURGET, JEAN MARIE. **Si Napoléon en 1914**. Paris: La Nouvelle Revue, 1930, 222 p.
A semi-humorous but enlightening dialogue between Foch and a resurrected Napoleon.

BUAT, EDMOND ALPHONSE LÉON. **Hindenburg et Ludendorff Stratèges**. Paris: Berger-Levrault, 1923, 252 p.
A competent French critique, based primarily on the writings of Falkenhayn, Hindenburg and Ludendorff, and equipped with numerous excellent maps and plans.

La Crise du Commandement Unique. By GENERAL * * * . Paris: Bossard, 1931.
An important supplement to the treatment of the Clemenceau-Foch-Haig-Pétain conflict as found in Foch's memoirs.

DEWAR, GEORGE ALBEMARLE BERTIE. **Sir Douglas Haig's Command**. Boston: Houghton Mifflin, 1923, 2 v.
A detailed study of British strategy from December 1915 to November 1918, in the larger setting of Allied operations.

DOMÈGE, NOËL. **En Marge de Plutarque**. Paris: Renaissance du Livre, 1924, 227 p.
An able indictment of the offensive tactics of Messimy and Joffre.

FALKENHAYN, ERICH GEORG ANTON SEBASTIAN VON. **The German General Staff and Its Decisions, 1914-1916**. New York: Dodd, 1920, 332 p.
A fundamental study, reviewing all German operations during the author's service on the general staff.

FOERSTER, WOLFGANG. **Aus der Gedankenwerkstatt des Deutschen Generalstabes**. Berlin: Mittler, 1931, 151 p.
A series of essays on the German, French and Russian plans of campaign, by one of the foremost German authorities.

FOERSTER, WOLFGANG. **Graf Schlieffen und der Weltkrieg**. Berlin: Mittler, 1925, 305 p.
A competent, sympathetic study of the German chief of staff and the German plans of campaign prior to 1914, and of the first operations up to and including the defeat at the Marne.

FRANÇOIS, HERMANN VON. **Marneschlacht und Tannenberg**. Berlin: Scherl, 1920, 296 p.
A study of German strategy during the first six weeks, by a German general who contrasts the final debacle in the west with the victory in the east, thereby contrasting the leadership of Moltke and of Hindenburg.

FREYTAG-LORINGHOVEN, HUGO FRIEDRICH, FREIHERR VON. **Heerführung im Weltkriege**. Berlin: Mittler, 1920, 206 p.
A German general and historian makes a comparison of procedure in the past and in the World War in matters of concentration, envelopment and frontal attack.

GASCOUIN, FIRMIN ÉMILE. **Le Triomphe de l'Idée**. Paris: Berger-Levrault, 1931, 264 p.
A critique, from the military standpoint, of the factors which decided the course of events in 1914.

GROENER, WILHELM. **Der Feldherr wider Willen**. Berlin: Mittler, 1931, 250 p.
A continuation of the following title. Gen. Groener here studies the Marne campaign in the light of our present knowledge.

GROENER, WILHELM. **Das Testament des Grafen Schlieffen.** Berlin: Mittler, 1927, 244 p.
One of the best monographic studies of the famous Schlieffen plan, its modifications and its working in 1914.

HOFFMANN, MAX. **The War of Lost Opportunities.** New York: International Publishers, 1925, 246 p.
The reflections of a high German staff officer on the strategy and politics of the war, with special reference to the eastern front. An impressive book.

KABISCH, ERNST. **Streitfragen des Weltkrieges.** Stuttgart: Literarisches Büro, 1924, 400 p.
A competent review of the more important problems of leadership, with a presentation of evidence and arguments on both sides.

KUHL, HERMANN VON. **Der Deutsche Generalstab in Vorbereitung und Durchführung des Weltkrieges.** Berlin: Mittler, 2nd ed., 1920, 218 p.
One of the best comparative studies of plans of campaign as worked out by the various staffs. The author, chief of staff of the First German Army under von Kluck, defends the German plan.

LUDENDORFF, ERICH. **Kriegführung und Politik.** Berlin: Mittler, 2nd ed., 1922, 342 p.
A book of prime importance, in which the famous German general reviews the whole problem of civil and military control over economic matters, foreign policy, etc.

McPHERSON, WILLIAM LENHART. **The Strategy of the Great War.** New York: Putnam, 1919, 417 p.
Primarily an analysis of major operations, by an American military critic.

MARCHAND, A. **Plans de Concentration de 1871 à 1914.** Paris: Berger-Levrault, 1926, 220 p.
An important contribution to the history of the war, by the French Inspector-General of State Railways.

MAURICE, SIR FREDERICK. **British Strategy.** London: Constable, 1929, 243 p.
Lectures on the fundamentals of strategy, with copious examples drawn from the World War, by the Director of Military Operations of the British General Staff, 1915-1918.

MERMEIX, *pseud.* (GABRIEL TERRAIL). **Fragments d'Histoire.** Paris: Ollendorff, 1919-1920, 4 v.
Revelations of the inner workings of the French high command—Joffre and the crisis of November 1915-December 1916, and the Nivelle-Painlevé interlude of December 1916-May 1917. The last two volumes are devoted to Foch and to Sarrail's command in the Near East.

MIQUEL, LIEUTENANT-COLONEL. **Enseignements Stratégiques et Tactiques de la Guerre de 1914-1918.** Paris: Lavauzelle, 1926, 360 p.
One of the best French treatments.

MORDACQ, JEAN JULES HENRI. **Le Commandement Unique. Comment Il Fut Réalisé.** Paris: Tallandier, 1929, 176 p.
A valuable account of the negotiations which led to the establishment of the supreme command, written by the chief of Clemenceau's military cabinet.

MÜLLER-BRANDENBURG, HERMANN. **Von Schlieffen bis Ludendorff.** Leipzig: Oldenburg, 1925, 170 p.
A terse but restrained criticism of German staff leadership.

NIEMANN, ALFRED. **Kaiser und Heer.** Berlin: Verlag für Kulturpolitik, 1929, 416 p.
An analysis of the Emperor's constitutional relation to the military machine. The author tends to exonerate William from responsibility for military disaster.

OENMICHEN, COLONEL. **Essai sur la Doctrine de Guerre des Coalitions.** Paris: Berger-Levrault, 1927, 161 p.
Three studies of the inter-Allied command—the campaign of 1916, the Dardanelles-Near Eastern campaign, and the debacle of 1917.

PERCIN, ALEXANDRE. **1914. Les Erreurs du Haut Commandement.** Paris: Michel, 1920, 284 p.
Scathing criticism of French army organization before the war, and of Russian interference, followed by bitter reflections on Joffre and the Marne campaign.

PERREAU, JOSEPH. **La Grande Guerre et la Vérité.** Paris: Catin, 1924, 452 p.
A very critical history of the war, by a professor of military history and tactics at the School of Saint-Cyr.

PIERREFEU, JEAN DE. **G. Q. G.—Secteur I.** Paris: Édition Française Illustrée, 1920, 2 v.
An unvarnished account of what went on at French Headquarters during three years of the war. An indispensable book.

PIERREFEU, JEAN DE. **Plutarch Lied.** New York: Knopf, 1924, 307 p.
Translation of the French "Plutarque a Menti" (Paris: Grasset, 1923). A brilliant critique of the strategy of the military leaders in the World War and of the alleged stupidity of the professional soldier.

PIERREFEU, JEAN DE. **Nouveaux Mensonges de Plutarque.** Paris: Rieder, 1931, 280 p.
A later volume of criticism of the official account of the war.

Plutarque n'a pas Menti. By GENERAL * * * . Paris: Renaissance du Livre, 1923.
An effective reply to Pierrefeu's "Plutarch Lied."

RITTER, HANS. **Kritik des Weltkrieges.** Leipzig: Koehler, 1921.
The author, a staff officer, condemns the stormy advance of 1914 as the root of Germany's later disaster.

ROBERTSON, SIR WILLIAM. **Soldiers and Statesmen, 1914-1918.** New York: Scribner, 1926, 2 v.
This work by the British Field Marshal is easily one of the most important contributions to the history of the conduct of the war.

SARGENT, HERBERT HOWLAND. **Strategy on the Western Front, 1914-1918.** Chicago: McClurg, 1920, 259 p.
By an American expert, who argues that a decision should have been sought on the Balkan front.

La Vérité sur la Guerre, 1914-1918. Paris: Michel, 1930, 2 v.
A detailed study of French strategy from Joffre to Foch, by one evidently close to the generalissimo, whom he glorifies.

MILITARY MEMOIRS AND BIOGRAPHIES

See also Naval Operations and Naval Memoirs, p. 140.

ALEXANDER, ROBERT. **Memories of the World War.** New York: Macmillan, 1931, 317 p.
The reminiscences of the general who commanded the American 77th Division, particularly interesting in connection with the Argonne battle.

ARTHUR, SIR GEORGE COMPTON ARCHIBALD. **The Life of Lord Kitchener.** New York: Macmillan, 1920, 3 v.
The standard biography of the great soldier.

ARTHUR, SIR GEORGE COMPTON ARCHIBALD. **Lord Haig.** London: Heinemann, 1929, 164 p.
A good brief sketch.

ARZ, ARTUR. **Zur Geschichte des Grossen Krieges.** Vienna: Rikola, 1924, 398 p.
Recollections and impressions of the last Austrian chief of staff, valuable especially for the years 1917-1918 and for domestic as well as military affairs.

ASTON, SIR GEORGE GREY. **The Biography of the Late Marshal Foch.** New York: Macmillan, 1929, 509 p.
On the whole the best biography of Foch, well-informed and understanding.

AUFFENBERG-KOMARÓW, MORITZ, FREIHERR VON. **Aus Oesterreichs Höhe und Niedergang.** Munich: Drei Masken Verlag, 1921, 524 p.
The autobiography of the Austrian war minister. One of the most important sources for the history of the Austro-Russian campaign.

BALDINI, ALBERTO. **Diaz.** Florence: Case Editrice Barbèra, 1928, 263 p.
Diaz glorified in a competent study of the campaign after Caporetto, by the editor of *Esercito e Nazione.*

BALLARD, COLIN ROBERT. **Kitchener.** New York: Dodd, 1930, 341 p.
A competent one-volume study for the general reader.

BALLARD, COLIN ROBERT. **Smith-Dorrien.** London: Constable, 1931, 345 p.
Based on Smith-Dorrien's papers, this is a valuable contribution to the history of the earlier campaigns in the west.

BERNHARDI, FRIEDRICH VON. **Denkwürdigkeiten aus Meinem Leben.** Berlin: Mittler, 1927, 541 p.
The well-known German general gives a valuable picture of the old army and the old system.

BRUN, ALF HARALD. **Troublous Times.** London: Constable, 1931, 243 p.
The thrilling experiences of a Danish officer sent to Central Asia to investigate the condition of over a million Austrian war prisoners.

BUAT, EDMOND ALPHONSE LÉON. **Hindenburg.** Paris: Chapelot, 1921, 241 p.
Written by an eminent French general and based on Hindenburg's and Ludendorff's memoirs. The author finds Hindenburg much the more attractive.

BUAT, EDMOND ALPHONSE LÉON. **Ludendorff.** Paris: Payot, 1920, 285 p.
An extended analysis of Ludendorff's policies and tactics, by a competent critic.

BUGNET, CHARLES. **Foch Speaks.** New York: Dial Press, 1929, 308 p.
A revealing character sketch by Foch's aid-de-camp. One of the best of many books on the Marshal.

BULLARD, ROBERT LEE. **Personalities and Reminiscences of the War.** New York: Doubleday, 1925, 375 p.
An important source for the history of American participation in the war, written by the commanding general of the Second American Army.

CADORNA, LUIGI, CONTE. **La Guerra alla Fronte Italiana.** Milan: Treves, 1921, 2 v.
A most important account, by the Italian commander-in-chief until Caporetto. There is a French translation entitled: "Mémoires du Général Cadorna" (Paris: Lavauzelle, 1924, 442 p.).

CALLWELL, SIR CHARLES EDWARD. **Experiences of a Dug-Out.** London: Constable, 1920, 339 p.
Varied experiences of a British general. Interesting chapters on Kitchener, the Dardanelles, the War Office and Russia.

CALLWELL, SIR CHARLES EDWARD. **Field Marshal Sir Henry Wilson.** New York: Scribner, 1927, 2 v.
A work based to a large extent upon the general's diaries, revealing him as an out-and-out military man of great ability and determination, with a highly realistic outlook on things political. Wilson had no use whatsoever for the sentimental approach, and this unusually frank and honest account of his life and career is a valuable addition to recent world history.

CALLWELL, SIR CHARLES EDWARD. **The Life of Sir Stanley Maude.** London: Constable, 1920, 360 p.
The biography of a British general active in the Dardanelles and Mesopotamian campaigns.

CAPELLO, LUIGI. **Note di Guerra.** Milan: Treves, 1920, 2 v.
An apology for Caporetto, with much important documentary material, by one of the principal Italian commanders on the eastern front.

CHAPMAN-HUSTON, DESMOND and RUTTER, OWEN. **General Sir John Cowans.** London: Hutchinson, 1924, 2 v.
A full-length biography of the British Quartermaster-General.

CHARTERIS, JOHN. **Field Marshal Earl Haig.** New York: Scribner, 1929, 407 p.
The most competent and authoritative biography of Haig published to date, written by one closely associated with him. The book throws much light on Allied strategy as well as on the problem of the high command.

CONRAD VON HÖTZENDORF, FRANZ, GRAF. **Aus Meiner Dienstzeit, 1906-1918.** Vienna: Rikola, 1921-1925, 5 v. and atlas.
Extremely frank and very valuable memoirs, letters and despatches of the Austrian Field Marshal. They reveal admirably the aggressive anti-Italian and anti-Serbian policy of the army group in Austria previous to the World War.

CRAMON, AUGUST VON. **Unser Oesterreich-Ungarischer Bundesgenosse im Weltkriege.** Berlin: Mittler, 1920, 205 p.
The interesting recollections of a high German officer attached to Austrian headquarters. Throws valuable light on Austro-German relations during the war. French edition, "Quatre Ans au G. Q. G. Austro-Hongrois" (Paris: Payot, 1922, 330 p.).

DANILOV, IURIĬ NIKIFOROVICH. **Grossfürst Nikolai Nikolajewitsch.** Berlin: Schröder, 1930, 321 p.
A panegyric of the Russian commander, by the former Quartermaster-General of the Russian armies.

DAWES, CHARLES GATES. **A Journal of the Great War.** Boston: Houghton Mifflin, 1921, 2 v.
Some interesting side-lights on the conduct of the campaign on the American side.

DICKMAN, JOSEPH THEODORE. **The Great Crusade.** New York: Appleton, 1927, 313 p.
War recollections by the commander of the Third American Army.

DICKSON, WILLIAM EDMUND RITCHIE. **East Persia.** London: Arnold, 1924, 279 p.
An account by the British commander in East Persia—the story of a remote phase of activities.

DUNSTERVILLE, LIONEL CHARLES. **The Adventures of Dunsterforce.** London: Arnold, 1920, 323 p.
The story of the "Hush-Hush" force in Armenia and Transcaucasia, by the commander. Not a technical study, but a narrative for the layman.

ESHER, REGINALD BALIOL BRETT, VISCOUNT. **The Tragedy of Lord Kitchener.** London: Murray, 1921, 219 p.

Kitchener in the World War, from the diaries of one who was in close contact with him.

FABRY, JEAN JOSEPH. **Joffre et Son Destin.** Paris: Charles-Lavauzelle, 1931, 374 p.
A defense of the French commander, by an officer who for two years was his *chef de cabinet*. A useful if somewhat incoherent account.

FOCH, FERDINAND. **Memoirs.** New York: Doubleday, 1931, 580 p.
The memoirs of the Allied generalissimo. An interesting and at time highly important addition to the controversial literature of the World War, though rather irregular and spotty.

FRENCH, GERALD. **The Life of Field Marshal Sir John French.** London: Cassell, 1931, 454 p.
The first part of this volume consists of French's unfinished autobiography. The section dealing with the war, though based upon his diaries, does not add materially to our knowledge.

FREYTAG-LORINGHOVEN, HUGO FRIEDRICH, FREIHERR VON. **Menschen und Dinge.** Berlin: Mittler, 1923, 338 p.
The autobiography of a soldier who for a time during the war was Quartermaster-General of the German army.

GALET, ÉMILE JOSEPH. **Albert, King of the Belgians, in the Great War.** New York: Putnam, 1931, 341 p.
The military adviser of the King reviews the first three months of the war. A contribution to the story of the Belgian accomplishment and the relations of Belgium with France and England.

GALLIENI, JOSEPH SIMON. **Mémoires.** Paris: Payot, 1920, 256 p.
The famous marshal's memoirs, important for the history of the battle of the Marne and the defense of Paris.

GALLWITZ, MAX VON. **Meine Führertätigkeit im Weltkriege.** Berlin: Mittler, 1929, 528 p.
The first volume of the reminiscences of the famous leader, based on diaries and material in the archives and dealing with the campaigns in Belgium, Russia and the Balkans, 1914-1916.

GALLWITZ, MAX VON. **Erleben im Westen, 1916-1918.** Berlin: Mittler, 1932, 531 p.
The second volume of the general's reminiscences.

GEBSATTEL, LUDWIG, FREIHERR VON. **Generalfeldmarschall Karl von Bülow.** Munich: Lehmann, 1929, 172 p.
This biography, dealing chiefly with Bülow's command at the Marne, is an important contribution to the story of German strategy.

GERMAINS, VICTOR WALLACE. **The Truth about Kitchener.** London: Lane, 1925, 344 p.
A rather successful attempt to rehabilitate Kitchener.

GHEUSI, PIERRE BARTHÉLEMY. **Gallieni.** Paris: Charpentier, 1922, 248 p.
The best general biography of the savior of Paris.

GLEICH, GEROLD VON. **Vom Balkan nach Bagdad.** Berlin: Scherl, 1921, 185 p.
The impressions and reflections of a high German officer on mission during the Balkan Wars and the Mesopotamian campaign.

GOLTZ, COLMAR, FREIHERR VON DER. **Denkwürdigkeiten.** Berlin: Mittler, 1929, 468 p.
The important reminiscences of the famous organizer of the modern Turkish armies.

GORGES, EDMUND HOWARD. **The Great War in West Africa.** London: Hutchinson, 1930, 284 p.

This account, written by the commanding officer, fills a gap in the history of the World War. It is detailed and well illustrated.

GRASSET, ALPHONSE LOUIS. **Le Maréchal Foch.** Paris: Berger-Levrault, 1919, 96 p.
A keen study of Foch in the war, by a French military historian.

GRASSET, ALPHONSE LOUIS. **Le Maréchal Franchet d'Espérey.** Paris: Crès, 1920, 136 p.
A competent and sympathetic biographical sketch of the Commander of the Armée d'Orient.

GRAVES, WILLIAM SIDNEY. **America's Siberian Adventure.** New York: Cape and Smith, 1931, 363 p.
The most important account of the Siberian enterprise, by the American general in command.

HANOTAUX, GABRIEL and FABRY, JEAN JOSEPH. **Joffre, le Vainqueur de la Marne.** Paris: Plon, 1929, 102 p.
A brief sketch, with some facsimile letters.

HARBORD, JAMES GUTHRIE. **Leaves from a War Diary.** New York: Dodd, 1925, 407 p.
A valuable contribution, based on the diary of the commander of the American service of supply.

HERBILLON, ÉMILE EMMANUEL. **Du Général en Chef au Gouvernement.** Paris: Tallandier, 1930, 2 v.
The day-by-day notes of a liaison officer. A valuable addition to the material on the Joffre period.

HINDENBURG, PAUL VON. **Out of My Life.** New York: Harper, 1921, 2 v.
A simple, straightforward narrative, in which the German leader surveys his entire military career.

HOFFMANN, MAX. **War Diaries and Other Papers.** London: Secker, 1929, 2 v.
A most valuable collection of writings, by a man supposed by some to have been the brain behind German operations in the East.

JOFFRE, JOSEPH JACQUES CÉSAIRE. **Personal Memoirs.** New York: Harper, 1932, 2 v.
The Field Marshal's recollections were eagerly awaited. Volume I opens with his appointment to the War Board in 1910, and carries the story through the autumn of 1914. Volume II is an account of the "war of stabilization" (in contrast to the earlier "war of movement"), down to Joffre's resignation in 1916. The work, which is of particular importance for the study of the Marne campaign, should of course be read in connection with Foch's reminiscences.

KIESLING, HANS VON. **Mit Feldmarschall von der Goltz Pascha in Mesopotamien und Persien.** Leipzig: Dietrich, 1922, 192 p.
A valuable account of the Mesopotamian-Persian campaigns from the Turkish-German side, by Goltz' general staff officer.

KLUCK, ALEXANDER VON. **Wanderjahre—Kriege—Gestalten.** Berlin: Eisenschmidt, 1929, 232 p.
A dispassionate autobiography, revealing von Kluck not only as a great commander but as a fine personality. Relatively little is said of the war period.

LEBLOND, MARIUS. **Gallieni Parle.** Paris: Michel, 1920, 2 v.
Conversations of the general with his secretaries on many phases of World War history.

LEGRAS, JULES. **Mémoires de Russie.** Paris: Payot, 1921, 449 p.
The reminiscences and experiences of a Frenchman who for years served on the staff of the Russian armies.

LEMKE, MIKHAIL KONSTANTINOVICH. **250 Dneĭ v Tsarskoĭ Stavke.** Petrograd: Gosizdat, 1920, 859 p.

A most detailed day-by-day record of doings in the Russian staff, covering the period from September 1915 to July 1916.

LETTOW-VORBECK, PAUL EMIL VON. **My Reminiscences of East Africa.** London: Hurst and Blackett, 1920, 335 p.
An important and interesting record, by the German commander.

LIDDELL HART, BASIL HENRY. **Foch: The Man of Orleans.** Boston: Little, Brown, 480 p.
A facile British military writer reconsiders the career of the generalissimo, bringing his work into a new perspective.

LIDDELL HART, BASIL HENRY. **Reputations Ten Years After.** Boston: Little, Brown, 1928, 316 p.
A fascinating book reviewing the careers and accomplishments of famous World War generals as seen at a distance of ten years. Joffre, Falkenhayn, Gallieni, Haig, Foch, Ludendorff, Pétain, Allenby, Liggett and Pershing are passed in review and their actions put under the spotlight of present-day knowledge. The author gives some play to personal prejudices.

LIGGETT, HUNTER. **Commanding an American Army.** Boston: Houghton Mifflin, 1925, 208 p.
The recollections of the commander of the First American Army.

LIMAN VON SANDERS, OTTO. **Five Years in Turkey.** Annapolis: U. S. Naval Institute, 1927, 325 p.
The memoirs of the chief of the German mission before and during the war, and a source of the first magnitude for the study of the Turkish campaigns.

LUDENDORFF, ERICH. **The General Staff and Its Problems.** New York: Dutton, 1920, 2 v.
Primarily a collection of documents to illustrate the author's arguments as presented in his reminiscences.

LUDENDORFF, ERICH. **Ludendorff's Own Story, August 1914-November 1918.** New York: Harper, 1920, 2 v.
A very important account, illuminating in the political as well as the military field.

MacMUNN, SIR GEORGE FLETCHER. **Behind the Scenes in Many Wars.** London: Murray, 1930, 370 p.
These reminiscences of a British general are of importance for the history of the Dardanelles expedition and especially for the later phases of the Mesopotamian campaign.

MACPHAIL, SIR ANDREW. **Three Persons.** New York: Carrier, 1929, 346 p.
A study of Sir Henry Wilson, Colonel Lawrence and Colonel House, as revealed in their writings.

MADELIN, LOUIS. **Foch.** Paris: Plon, 1929, 269 p.
This volume, written by an eminent French historian, has something of the authorized biography about it, since most of it was read and annotated by the Marshal before his death.

MANCEAU, ÉMILE. **Nos Chefs de 1914.** Paris: Stock, 1930, 320 p.
Personal recollections of Joffre, Foch, Lanrezac, and others.

MANCEAU, ÉMILE. **Trois Maréchaux—Joffre, Gallieni, Foch.** Paris: Gallimard, 1928, 229 p.
Brilliant character sketches and estimates, based on personal acquaintance.

MARCH, PEYTON CONWAY. **The Nation at War.** New York: Doubleday, 1932, 407 p.
General March's report on his work as Chief of Staff in the culminating phase of America's war effort, with illuminating comment on Pershing, Baker, Foch and other associates, whose papers and biographies should also be consulted.

MARSHALL, SIR WILLIAM. **Memories of Four Fronts.** London: Benn, 1929, 340 p.
Three of the four fronts on which General Marshall served were Gallipoli, Mesopotamia and Persia.

MAURICE, SIR FREDERICK, *ed.* **Life of General Lord Rawlinson of Trent.** London:
Cassell, 1928, 394 p.
The journals and letters of one of the commanders on the Western Front. Important
also for the history of the Russian expedition of 1918-1919.

MORGEN, CURT VON. **Meiner Truppen Heldenkämpfe.** Berlin: Mittler, 1920, 182 p.
The war record of a German general, of interest for what he says about Tannenberg
and the Rumanian campaign.

MÜLLER, LOUIS ÉDOUARD. **Joffre et la Marne.** Paris: Crès, 1931, 139 p.
The record of one of Joffre's closest associates. One of the most important contributions
to the study of the Marne campaign.

MURRAY, SIR ARCHIBALD JAMES. **Sir Archibald Murray's Despatches.** New York:
Dutton, 1920, 229 p.
Four important despatches of the commander in Egypt, covering the period from
June 1916 to June 1917, with other material. Important as a background for the
campaigns of Allenby.

NIEMANN, ALFRED. **Hindenburg.** Berlin: Koehler, 1926, 229 p.
A well-informed popular biography, carrying the story down to the collapse of Germany in 1918.

NOGALES, RAFAEL DE. **Four Years beneath the Crescent.** New York: Scribner, 1926,
416 p.
An interesting report on the Turkish campaigns by a neutral general attached to the
Turkish forces. Important especially for events in Armenia.

PAINLEVÉ, PAUL. **Comment J'Ai Nommé Foch et Pétain.** Paris: Alcan, 1924, 424 p.
The story of the author's tenure of office as Minister of War and as Prime Minister.

PALAT, BARTHÉLEMY EDMOND. **La Part de Foch dans la Victoire.** Paris: Charles-
Lavauzelle, 1931, 280 p.
Written by one of the leading French military historians, this is perhaps the best
study of the famous soldier's contribution.

PERSHING, JOHN JOSEPH. **My Experiences in the World War.** New York: Stokes, 1931,
2 v.
These volumes by the Commander-in-Chief of the American Expeditionary Forces are
of course among the most important first-hand sources for the history of the American
participation. The papers of March and Baker are the other volumes of comparable
importance. The papers of Tasker H. Bliss, Chief of Staff before March, and member of
the Supreme War Council, have not yet been announced for publication.

PILANT, PAUL. **Le Rôle du Général Gallieni.** Paris: Renaissance du Livre, n. d., 129 p.
A detailed, heavily documented study of Gallieni's activities down to the battle of
the Marne.

RAWLINSON, SIR ALFRED. **Adventures in the Near East, 1918-1922.** New York: Dodd,
1924, 353 p.
Dramatic and illuminating adventures of a British officer in Mesopotamia, Armenia,
Persia and Anatolia in the stormy years 1918-1922.

RECOULY, RAYMOND. **Foch: My Conversations with the Marshal.** New York:
Appleton, 1929, 332 p.
Recouly seems to have been an unexcelled listener, and the reader will find here much
that is interesting about the Rhine policy advocated by Foch and about his conflict
with Clemenceau.

RECOULY, RAYMOND. **Joffre.** New York: Appleton, 1931, 369 p.
A well-known journalist's popular but well-informed study of Joffre's war services.

REPINGTON, CHARLES À COURT. **The First World War, 1914-1918.** Boston: Houghton Mifflin, 1920, 2 v.
The personal impressions of a British staff officer. An enlightening, gossipy book on the methods and personalities of the war era.

ROBERTSON, SIR WILLIAM. **From Private to Field-Marshal.** Boston: Houghton Mifflin, 1921, 396 p.
The interesting memoirs of a remarkable man who served as British Chief of Staff during the war.

RUPPRECHT, CROWN PRINCE OF BAVARIA. **Mein Kriegstagebuch.** Berlin: Mittler, 1929, 3 v.
This selection from the extensive diary material left by the Crown Prince forms an almost unique record of operations on the western front.

SAVAGE, RAYMOND. **Allenby of Armageddon.** Indianapolis: Bobbs, 1926, 353 p.
Not an authorized biography, but a good general account of Allenby's achievements.

SIMONDS, FRANK HERBERT. **They Won the War.** New York: Harper, 1931, 120 p.
A well-known political writer evaluates the work of war leaders.

STÜRGKH, JOSEF, GRAF VON. **Im Deutschen Grossen Hauptquartier.** Leipzig: List, 1921, 160 p.
The recollections of the Austrian military plenipotentiary at German headquarters. The counterpart of Gen. Cramon's book.

SUKHOMLINOV, VLADIMIR ALEKSANDROVICH. **Erinnerungen.** Berlin: Hobbing, 1924, 526 p.
The very interesting, if not wholly reliable, memoirs of the Russian Minister of War in 1914. Important for the story of Russian army reform and the military conventions with France.

TOWNSHEND, SIR CHARLES VERE FERRERS. **My Campaign in Mesopotamia.** New York: James A. McCann Co., 1920, 400 p.
A valuable detailed account of the operations by the British commander during the first phase. Based on the general's diaries.

TSCHUPPIK, KARL. **Ludendorff.** Vienna: Epstein, 1931, 429 p.
One of the best character studies of Ludendorff, setting forth his military ability and his utter lack of intelligent leadership in politics.

VINOGRADSKI, ALEKSANDR NICOLAEVICH. **La Guerre sur le Front Oriental.** Paris: Charles-Lavauzelle, 1926, 380 p.
These recollections are important chiefly for what is said about the campaign in East Prussia and the war on the Rumanian front.

WILHELM, EX-CROWN PRINCE OF GERMANY. **Meine Erinnerungen an Deutschlands Heldenkampf.** Berlin: Mittler, 1923, 371 p.
The recollections of the Crown Prince throw some light on his relations to his father and make interesting contributions to the story of the great struggle for Verdun.

WILSON, SIR ARNOLD TALBOT. **Loyalties. Mesopotamia.** New York: Oxford University Press, 1930-1931, 2 v.
These volumes, by a high officer in the service of supply and administration, form one of the most important records of Mesopotamian affairs in the years 1914-1920.

WRISBERG, ERNST VON. **Erinnerungen an die Kriegsjahre.** Leipzig: Koehler, 1921-1922, 3 v.

The reminiscences of a general directing the war department. A valuable contribution to the history of the supply service and to the story of political developments at home.

ZWEHL, HANS VON. **Erich von Falkenhayn.** Berlin: Mittler, 1925.
A penetrating study of the German commander, containing some unpublished material from his diaries.

MILITARY OPERATIONS
Western Front
Belgium

BERTRAND, LOUIS. **L'Occupation Allemande en Belgique.** Brussels: Dechenne, 1919, 2 v.
A systematic study of the German administration, by a Belgian deputy.

BREDT, JOHANNES VICTOR. **Die Belgische Neutralität und der Schlieffensche Feldzugsplan.** Berlin: Stilke, 1929, 216 p.
Easily one of the most illuminating and important books on the whole Belgian question. The author, a German deputy and professor at Marburg, not only reviews the problem of Belgian neutrality before and during the war, but shows that Schlieffen intended to concentrate on the Belgian frontier in case of war, though without executing a *coup de main* against Liège. His hope evidently was that the French would become so nervous that they would violate Belgian neutrality first.

La Défense de la Position Fortifiée de Namur en Août 1914. Brussels: Institut Cartographique, 1930, 788 p.
An exhaustive analysis of a much disputed operation. Published by the Belgian General Staff and based on much new material.

DEGUISE, GENERAL. **La Défense de la Position Fortifiée d'Anvers en 1914.** Paris: Berger-Levrault, 1921, 291 p.
A detailed military study, by the Belgian commander who surrendered Antwerp.

DELVAUX, GASTON. **L'Invasion de la Belgique devant la Science Allemande du Droit des Gens.** Liège: Demarteau, 1930, 150 p.
The author reviews, only to reject, the various legal arguments advanced by German scholars to explain the invasion of Belgium.

GAY, GEORGE INNESS. **Public Relations of the Commission for Relief in Belgium.** Stanford: Stanford University Press, 1929, 2 v.
A collection of documents bearing on the great enterprise.

GOTTSCHALK, EGON. **Frankreich und das Neutralisierte Belgien.** Stuttgart: Enke, 1926, 149 p.
A reconsideration of the problem of Belgian neutrality and of French policy with respect to it.

HENNING, E. **Les Déportations de Civils Belges en Allemagne et dans le Nord de la France.** Brussels: Vromant, 1919.
An early study of the deportations.

HENRY, ALBERT. **Études sur l'Occupation Allemande en Belgique.** Brussels: Lebègue, 1920, 465 p.
Studies of the Activist movement, the deportations, and the work of the Comité National, written by the general secretary of the Comité National de Secours.

HEUZÉ, PAUL, ed. **L'Épopée Belge dans la Grande Guerre.** Paris: Quillet, 1923, 351 p.
A beautifully illustrated coöperative work, by authoritative writers.

Hosse, Karl. **Die Englisch-Belgischen Aufmarschpläne gegen Deutschland vor dem Weltkrieg.** Vienna: Amalthea, 1930, 65 p.
The author, a former major of the imperial general staff, reëxamines the vexed question of Belgian neutrality and the relations of England and Belgium in the period 1906-14, making use of the British documents and the Belgian documents seized by the Germans in 1914 and returned to the Belgian Government in 1919. The political parts of these papers have already been published.

Köhler, Ludwig von. **Die Staatsverwaltung der Besetzten Gebiete. I. Belgien.** New Haven: Yale University Press, 1927, 239 p.
A volume in the Carnegie series. A thorough study of the German occupation of Belgium, going a long way towards explaining the difficulties faced by the German administration.

Kurth, Godefroid. **Le Guet-Apens Prussien en Belgique.** Paris: Champion, 1919, 226 p.
Belgium's case against Germany, strongly presented by a Belgian historian.

Menzel, E. **Le Déblocus d'Anvers.** Paris: Berger-Levrault, 1928, 100 p.
An important contribution by the former director of the Belgian General Staff, who stresses the failure of the Allies to plot any definite course of common action.

Normand, Robert. **Défense de Liège, Namur, Anvers.** Paris: Fournier, 1923, 183 p.
One of the best military studies of the first operations.

Oszwald, Robert P. **Der Streit um den Belgischen Franktireurkrieg.** Cologne: Gilde, 1931, 284 p.
This book on the vexed question of civilian warfare in Belgium may be taken as the most competent presentation of the German view, and at the same time a complete digest of the extensive literature on the subject.

Passelecq, Fernand. **Déportation et Travail Forcé des Ouvriers et de la Population Civile de la Belgique Occupée, 1916-1918.** New Haven: Yale University Press, 1928, 491 p.
A scholarly treatment of the deportation system, published in the Carnegie series.

Pirenne, Jacques and Vauthier, Maurice. **La Législation et l'Administration Allemandes en Belgique.** New Haven: Yale University Press, 1926, 284 p.
One of the outstanding volumes in the Carnegie series, equipped with valuable documentary material.

Rapports et Documents d'Enquête. Brussels: De Wit, 1922-1924, 4 v.
A huge mass of material collected by the Commission d'Enquête sur les Violations des Règles du Droit des Gens, etc.

Ridder, Alfred de. **La Belgique et la Guerre. Histoire Diplomatique.** Brussels: Bertels, 1928, 390 p.
An authoritative study of Belgium's position during the war, and of Belgian policy.

Ridder, Alfred de. **Histoire Diplomatique du Traité de 1839.** Brussels: Vromant, 1920, 399 p.
One of the ablest Belgian presentations of the neutrality problem.

Ridder, Alfred de. **La Violation de la Neutralité Belge et Ses Avocats.** Brussels: De Wit, 1926, 324 p.
A well-balanced and dispassionate examination of the history of Belgian neutrality, the interpretations given to it, the nature of Belgium's military preparations, etc.

Schmitz, Jean and Nieuwland, Norbert. **L'Invasion Allemande dans les Provinces de Namur et de Luxembourg.** Brussels: Van Oest, 1919-1925, 8 v.
An elaborately illustrated collection of testimony and documents.

SCHRYVER, A. DE. **La Bataille de Liège.** Liège: Vaillant-Carmanne, 1922, 258 p.
A technical study of the operations around Liège, by a Belgian staff officer.

SCHWERTFEGER, BERNHARD. **Der Geistige Kampf um die Verletzung der Belgischen Neutralität.** Berlin: Engelmann, 1919, 191 p.
One of the ablest presentations of the German view. Chiefly a study of the Anglo-Belgian pre-war conversations.

SELLIERS DE MORANVILLE, ANTONIN, CHEVALIER DE. **Du Haut de la Tour de Babel.** Paris: Berger-Levrault, 1924, 238 p.
A commentary on the French and German plans of campaign, and the strategic position of Belgium in 1914, by the former generalissimo of the Belgian army.

VERDEYEN, R. **België in Nederland, 1914-19.** The Hague: Nijhoff, 1920, 268 p.
The story of the Belgian refugees in Holland.

VERHULST, RAFAEL. **The Question of the Belgian Franc-Tireurs.** Bruges: Geerardijn, 1930, 89 p.
An attack on the accepted Belgian version, written by a fugitive Flemish leader.

WHITLOCK, BRAND. **Belgium.** New York: Appleton, 1919, 2 v.
One of the best-known books on Belgium during the war, by the American Minister at Brussels.

France

See also (France: Relations with Germany) Alsace-Lorraine, p. 261.

BAUMGARTEN-CRUSIUS, ARTHUR. **Die Marneschlacht 1914.** Leipzig: Lippold, 8th ed., 1919, 192 p.
A vigorous documented defense of the direction and operation of the Third German Army.

BAZAREVSKIĬ, A. **Mirovaia Voĭna, 1914-1918. Kampaniia 1918 g. vo Frantsii i Bel'gii.** Moscow: Gosizdat, 1927, 267 p.
Volume one of a detailed study of the great offensive of 1918.

BIRCHER, EUGEN. **Die Krisis in der Marneschlacht.** Bern: Huber, 1928, 304 p.
A thorough contribution, dealing with the operations of the Second and Third German Armies.

BÜLOW, KARL PAUL WILHELM VON. **Mein Bericht zur Marneschlacht.** Berlin: Scherl, 1919, 85 p.
A terse factual statement, by the commander of the Second German Army.

CHARBONNEAU, JEAN. **La Bataille des Frontières et la Bataille de la Marne.** Paris: Charles-Lavauzelle, 1928, 165 p.
The first six weeks of the war, as seen by a French staff officer.

CLERGERIE, JEAN BAPTISTE and DELAHAYE D'ANGLEMONT, LUCIEN. **La Bataille de la Marne. Le Rôle du Gouvernement Militaire de Paris.** Paris: Berger-Levrault, 1920, 136 p.
A brief outline of Gallieni's action from September 1 to 12, 1914, with many important documents.

GASIOROWSKI, WACLAW. **Historja Armji Polskiej we Francji.** Warsaw: Dom Książki Polskiej, 1931, 405 p.
The first volume of a history of the Polish forces in France, down to 1915.

GOUGH, SIR HUBERT. **The Fifth Army.** London: Hodder and Stoughton, 1931, 355 p.
The commander of the army rectifies a number of misapprehensions respecting the great battle of March 1918.

GROMAIRE, GEORGES. **L'Occupation Allemande en France, 1914-1918.** Paris: Payot, 1925, 512 p.
An account of the occupation of northern France, based largely on personal investigation, but also on French and German documents.

GROUARD, AUGUSTE ANTOINE. **La Conduite de la Guerre.** Paris: Chapelot, 1922, 214 p.
A careful study of the Marne campaign by a French military historian.

HAUSEN, HEINRICH, FREIHERR VON. **Erinnerungen an den Marnefeldzug 1914.** Leipzig: Koehler, 2nd ed., 1922, 248 p.
The memoirs and apologia of the commander of the Third German Army, who was commonly made the scapegoat in Germany.

HUGUET, CHARLES JULIEN. **Britain and the War.** London: Cassell, 1928, 244 p.
A more than critical account of Britain's military effort during the first year and a half, by the chief of the French military mission.

KANN, RÉGINALD. **Le Plan de Campagne Allemand de 1914.** Paris: Payot, 1923, 311 p.
A monographic study of the Schlieffen Plan, its modifications and its operation in the Marne campaign.

KLUCK, ALEXANDER VON. **The March on Paris and the Battle of the Marne, 1914.** New York: Longmans, 1920, 175 p.
A technical study based on Kluck's papers, with notes by the Historical Section of the British Committee of Imperial Defence.

KOELTZ, LOUIS. **L'Armée von Kluck à la Bataille de la Marne.** Paris: Charles-Lavauzelle, 1931, 240 p.
A French military historian retells an exciting story, using the voluminous recent material from the German side.

KOELTZ, LOUIS. **Le G. Q. G. Allemand et la Bataille de la Marne.** Paris: Payot, 1931, 410 p.
The latest and probably the best study of the German command, written by a competent authority, based on German material, and taking account not only of the German right wing, but of the other armies as well.

LANREZAC, CHARLES LOUIS MARIE. **Le Plan de Campagne Français.** Paris: Payot, 1920, 284 p.
An important and much disputed account of the Marne campaign.

LE GROS, HENRI. **La Genèse de la Bataille de la Marne.** Paris: Payot, 1919, 216 p.
A critical account of the early weeks, and an indictment of French plans and activities.

MADELIN, LOUIS. **La Bataille de France.** Paris: Plon, 1920, 379 p.
A detailed account of operations on the Western Front from March to November 1918, by an eminent French historian.

MANGIN, JOSEPH ÉMILE. **Comment Finit la Guerre.** Paris: Plon, 1920, 330 p.
A direct, clear and well informed study of the last years of the war, by an eminent French general.

MARCHAND, A. **Plans de Concentration de 1871 à 1914.** Paris: Berger-Levrault, 1926, 219 p.
A valuable study of the seventeen plans of campaign.

MAURICE, SIR FREDERICK. **Forty Days in 1914.** New York: Doran, 1919, 212 p.
A detailed study of the Mons and Marne campaigns, by the Director of Military Operations of the British General Staff.

MAURICE, SIR FREDERICK. **The Last Four Months.** New York: Cassell, 1919, 259 p.
A splendid, straightforward account of the Foch campaign of 1918 and the winning of the war.

MELIKOV, V. **Marna, 1914 goda; Visla, 1920 goda; Smirna, 1922 goda.** Moscow: Gosizdat, 1928, 468 p.
The Marne, Vistula and Smyrna episodes as turning points in history.

MERLOT, A. **L'Armée Polonaise; Constitution en France et Organisation.** Paris: Imprimerie Levé, 1919, 104 p.
An account of the Polish legions, now superseded by later Polish works.

MONTGOMERY, SIR ARCHIBALD ARMAR. **The Story of the Fourth Army in the Battles of the Hundred Days.** London: Hodder, 1920, 370 p.
An exhaustive technical study of the operations from August to November 1918, by a high staff officer.

NOVITSKIĬ, VASILIĬ FEDOROVICH. **Mirovaia Voĭna 1914-1918 goda. Kampaniia 1914 goda v Bel'gii i Frantsii.** Moscow: Gosudarstvennoe Voennoe Izdatel'stvo, 1926-1928, 2 v.
A most detailed Russian study of the year 1914, based on foreign as well as Russian material and published by the Russian War Academy.

PAGE, ARTHUR WILSON. **Our 110 Days Fighting.** New York: Doubleday, 1920, 283 p.
A straightforward popular account of the American campaigns.

PALAT, BARTHÉLEMY EDMOND. **La Grande Guerre sur le Front Occidental.** Paris: Chapelot, 1917-29, 13 v.
A voluminous work, covering the period to the end of 1916. A detailed and critical account of operations by an authoritative writer.

PALMER, FREDERICK. **Our Greatest Battle.** New York: Dodd, 1919, 629 p.
Probably the best general account of the Meuse-Argonne battle, by an American military correspondent.

PAQUET, CHARLES. **La Défaite Militaire de l'Allemagne en 1918.** Paris: Berger-Levrault, 1926, 290 p.
Very largely a study of the disposition and use of the German troops, prepared in 1918 for the French General Staff.

PERRIS, GEORGE HERBERT. **The Battle of the Marne.** Boston: Luce, 1920, 274 p.
The author discusses chiefly the Allied side and analyzes in detail the operations of the eight armies.

PÉTAIN, HENRI PHILIPPE. **Verdun.** New York: Dial, 1930, 235 p.
The English translation of a classic. Pétain attributes the failure of the Germans to their error in not attacking on both sides of the Meuse.

POIRIER, JULES. **La Bataille de Verdun.** Paris: Chiron, 1922, 304 p.
A detailed, exclusively military study of operations from February to December 1916.

ROUQUEROL, JEAN JOSEPH. **Le Drame de Douaumont.** Paris: Payot, 1931, 152 p.
A detailed French study of a noteworthy phase of the military operations.

SNIJDERS, WILLEM GEORGE FREDERICK. **De Wereldoorlog op het Duitsche Westfront.** Amsterdam: Maatschappij voor Goede Lectuur, 1922, 390 p.
An excellent account of the Marne campaign, written for the layman by a high Dutch officer.

SPEARS, EDWARD LOUIS. **Liaison, 1914.** New York: Doubleday, 1931, 598 p.
An important contribution to the history of the early days of the war, with special reference to the relations between Generals French and Lanrezac.

WENDT, HERMANN. **Verdun, 1916.** Berlin: Mittler, 1931, 257 p.
A sound study and criticism from the strategic viewpoint. The best scholarly account in German.

WILHELM, EX-CROWN PRINCE OF GERMANY. **Der Marne Feldzug, 1914.** Berlin: Dob-Verlag, 1927, 100 p.
An able but hardly impartial commentary on the German official history of the war.

WISE, JENNINGS CROPPER. **Turn of the Tide.** New York: Holt, 1920, 255 p.
A competent study of the crucial campaigns in the summer of 1918.

YPRES, JOHN DENTON PINKSTONE FRENCH, EARL OF. **1914.** Boston: Houghton Mifflin, 1919, 386 p.
An unusually frank account of the first stage of English operations, with outspoken criticism of Kitchener, Asquith and others.

Russian Front

See also (Central Europe) Collapse of the Hapsburg Empire, p. 301; also (Russia) The War and the Revolution, p. 360, and Counter-Revolution and Intervention, p. 367.

APUSHKIN, V. A. **General ot Porazhenii V. A. Sukhomlinov.** Leningrad: Byloe, 1925, 132 p.
The general of defeat; a study of Suchomlinov's career of command.

BELOÏ, A. **Galitsiĭskaia Bitva.** Moscow: Gosizdat, 1929, 371 p.
An authoritative Russian account of the great battle in Galicia in 1914.

BRUSILOV, ALEXEÏ ALEXEIEVICH. **A Soldier's Notebook.** London: Macmillan, 1930, 340 p.
An important contribution by the Russian commander on the Austrian front.

CAMON, HUBERT. **Ludendorff sur le Front Russe, 1914-1915.** Paris: Berger-Levrault, 1925, 121 p.
A French military writer attempts to establish the principles of Ludendorff's strategy, at the same time giving a critical review of Ludendorff's own account.

CHURCHILL, WINSTON SPENCER. **The Unknown War.** New York: Scribner, 1931, 411 p.
Written with Churchill's usual brilliance, both of grasp and style, this is the best general narrative in English of the war on the Eastern Front.

DANILOV, IURIĬ NIKIFOROVICH. **La Russie dans la Guerre Mondiale.** Paris: Payot, 1927, 558 p.
The French translation of a most important account, written by the former Russian quartermaster-general. The author gives much attention to non-military as well as military problems.

DEZSÖ, LAJOS. **Az 1914-1917 évi Osztrák-Magyar-Orosz Háború.** Debrecen: M. nemzeti könyv-és lapkiadó, 1925, 181 p.
A good survey of the Austro-Russian war in its broader aspects, with special emphasis on the operations of Hungarian units.

ELZE, WALTER. **Tannenberg.** Breslau: Hirt, 1928, 370 p.
A detailed study of the battle, followed by an extended selection of the most important sources, published and unpublished. An essential book.

FRANÇOIS, HERMANN VON. **Gorlice, 1915.** Leipzig: Koehler, 1922, 254 p.
An excellent monographic study of the Austrian victory in Galicia, by a high German officer.

FRANÇOIS, HERMANN VON. **Tannenberg.** Berlin: Deutscher Jägerbund, 1926, 72 p.
Tannenberg as the Cannae of the World War—an excellent brief study by one of the German commanding generals.

FRANTZ, GUNTHER. **Russlands Eintritt in den Weltkrieg**. Berlin: Deutsche Verlagsgesellschaft für Politik und Geschichte, 1924, 306 p.
A very valuable study, based in part on unpublished material, of the Russian army organization, Russia's preparation for war, the mobilization, plans of campaign, etc.

GAUSE, FRITZ. **Die Russen in Ostpreussen, 1914-1915**. Königsberg: Gräfe und Unzer, 1931, 425 p.
An official publication dealing with one of the lesser-known chapters of the war.

GOLOVIN, NIKOLAĬ NIKOLAEVICH. **Iz Istorii Kampanii 1914 goda**. Prague: Plamia, 1926-1930, 3 v.
The best Russian account of the first campaigns, based on complete command of the literature and well documented. The first two volumes deal with East Prussia, the third with Galicia.

GRONDIJS, LUDOVIC H. **La Guerre en Russie et en Sibérie**. Paris: Bossard, 1922, 586 p.
The observations and experiences of a Dutch correspondent covering the period from 1915 to the death of Kolchak in Siberia.

HADTÖRTÉNELMI, LEVÉLTÁR, *ed*. **A Világ Háború 1914-1918**. Budapest: Stadium, 1928 ff.
The standard Hungarian history of the war, with special reference to Hungary's part. To date volumes I, II and IV have appeared, dealing extensively with the background and with the Serbian and Galician operations of 1914.

HOFFMANN, MAX. **Tannenberg wie Es Wirklich War**. Berlin: Verlag für Kulturpolitik, 1926, 94 p.
A critical account by a famous staff officer who tends to deflate the exaggerated stories of Ludendorff's accomplishment and gives much credit to subordinates like von François and von Morgen.

IRONSIDE, SIR EDMUND. **Tannenberg. The First Thirty Days in East Prussia**. London: Blackwood, 1925, 316 p.
An exhaustive military study, based on both German and Russian sources. The best account in English.

JOSEPH, ARCHDUKE OF AUSTRIA. **A Világ Háború a Milyennek én Láttam**. Budapest: Hungarian Academy of Sciences, 1926, 678 p.
An important contribution to the history of the campaigns on the Serbian and Galician fronts in 1914 and 1915.

KNOX, SIR ALFRED WILLIAM FORTESCUE. **With the Russian Army, 1914-1917**. New York: Dutton, 1921, 2 v.
Extracts from a military attaché's diary, and a most important outsider's commentary on the development of the Russian situation. The account goes as far as the Bolshevik Revolution of November 1917.

NOWAK, KARL FRIEDRICH. **Der Weg zur Katastrophe**. Berlin: Reiss, 1919, 299 p.
An apology for Conrad's policy, written by one of his journalist friends.

PITREICH, ANTON. **Der Oesterreich-Ungarische Bundesgenosse im Sperrfeuer**. Klagenfurt: Kolitsch, 1930, 400 p.
The author concludes that Austria-Hungary did all that the Germans could reasonably expect of her during the war.

SAINT-PIERRE, EUGENIO BOLLATI DI. **Le Grandi Operazioni Militari della Russia**. Rome: Ausonia, 1919, 152 p.
A systematic study of the Russian campaigns to the end of 1917, by a high Italian officer with the Russian armies.

Austro-Italian Front

See also (Central Europe) Collapse of the Hapsburg Empire, p. 301.

BARONE, ENRICO. **La Storia Militare della Nostra Guerra.** Bari: Laterza, 1919, 222 p.
Very largely an account of events leading to the Caporetto disaster, with a discussion of responsibilities.

Battle of the Piave. London: Hodder, 1920, 82 p.
The translation of the official Italian account published by the supreme command, with many excellent maps.

BENCIVENGA, R. **Saggio Critico sulla Nostra Guerra.** Rome: Agostiniana, 1930, 345 p.
The first volume of a careful study of the war from the Italian side.

CARACCIOLO, MARIO. **L'Italia e i Suoi Alleati nella Grande Guerra.** Milan: Mondadori, 1932, 329 p.
An analysis of Italian and Allied policies and operations during the war.

CAVIGLIA, ENRICO. **Vittorio Veneto.** Milan: Edizione del' Eroica, 1920, 121 p.
A popular narrative, by an Italian general.

CHAURAND DE SAINT EUSTACHE, FELICE DE. **Come l'Esercito Italiano Entrò in Guerra.** Milan: Mondadori, 1929, 368 p.
A serious study of the earlier days of the war.

DUPONT, AMELIO. **La Battaglia del Piave.** Rome: Littorio, 1929, 214 p.
The best general account of this important engagement.

DUPONT, AMELIO. **Vittorio Veneto.** Rome: Littorio, 1930, 324 p.
Another good and readable volume in the same series as the preceding.

GOLDSMID, CYRIL H. **Diary of a Liaison Officer in Italy, 1918.** London: Williams, 1920, 178 p.
The author throws interesting side-lights on events after Caporetto and the offensives of 1918.

KERCHNAWE, HUGO. **Der Zusammenbruch der Oesterreichisch-Ungarischen Wehrmacht im Herbst 1918.** Munich: Lehmann, 1921, 205 p.
Papers of the Austrian high command and other official material, with running commentary.

MARAVIGNA, PIETRO. **Come Abbiamo Vinto.** Turin: Unione Tipografico Tormese, 1919, 254 p.
A general illustrated history of the last year of the war and especially of the Italian victory.

ODDONE, ALBERTO. **Storia della Guerra d'Italia.** Brescia: Apollonio, 1926, 521 p.
One of the best general histories of the Italian war, prefaced by an outline of Italian history in the nineteenth and twentieth centuries.

PAGE, THOMAS NELSON. **Italy and the World War.** New York: Scribner, 1920, 422 p.
An admiring account of Italy's war effort, by the former American Ambassador at Rome.

SARDAGNA, FILIBERTO. **Il Disegno di Guerra Italiano.** Turin: Gobetti, 1925, 281 p.
A critical study of the campaign plans of 1914-1915 and the reasons why they ended in disaster.

SCHIARINI, POMPILIO. **L'Armata del Trentino.** Milan: Mondadori, 1926, 417 p.
A detailed chronicle of operations in the Trentino, by an Italian general.

SCIPIONE, PIETRO. **L'Italia nella Guerra Mondiale.** Florence: Vallecchi, 1930, 320 p.
Written by an officer of the Italian General Staff. One of the best brief accounts, aiming to put the Italian war in the larger European setting.

SEGATO, LUIGI. **L'Italia nella Guerra Mondiale.** Milan: Vallardi, 1927, 2 v.
Two impressive volumes setting forth the history of Italy's participation in the conflict. Naval and aëronautic matters are dealt with in the appendices.

TREVELYAN, GEORGE MACAULAY. **Scenes from Italy's War.** Boston: Houghton Mifflin, 1919, 240 p.
The noted writer served as head of the British Red Cross in Italy and gives a vivid account of the Italian campaigns.

VALORI, ALDO. **La Guerra Italo-Austriaca.** Bologna: Zanichelli, 1925, 602 p.
The second revised edition of a detailed critical history of Italian campaigns.

VILLARI, LUIGI. **The War on the Italian Front.** London: Cobden-Sanderson, 1932, 308 p.
A comprehensive narrative of operations in the whole Italian theatre of war, as seen by a patriotic Italian.

Balkan Front

General

See also Russian Front, p. 130; also (Balkan Area) General, p. 399.

ANCEL, JACQUES. **Les Travaux et les Jours de l'Armée d'Orient, 1915-1918.** Paris: Bossard, 1921, 233 p.
A general political and military survey, with some discussion of economic and social problems. Written by a French historian and based in part on unpublished material and conversations with Venizelos and other leaders.

ASCHAUER, GENERAL. **Auf Schicksalswegen gen Osten.** Münster: Helios, 1931, 378 p.
The general throws considerable light on the extraordinary campaign of the Germans in Rumania, the Crimea and the Caucasus.

BREIT, JÓZSEF. **Az 1914 évi Osztrák-Magyar Szerb-Montenegrói Hadjárat.** Budapest: Grill, 1929, 226 p.
An expert and unbiassed account of the Austrian campaign against Serbia and Montenegro in the autumn of 1914, by a participant.

CAZEILLES, COMMANDANT. **La Rupture du Front Bulgare.** Paris: Lavauzelle, 1929, 107 p.
A technical account of the work of the French 17th Colonial Division in the critical battle of Dobropolje, September 15, 1918, revealing the general plan of the battle and the causes of victory.

COBLENTZ, PAUL. **The Silence of Sarrail.** London: Hutchinson, 1930, 288 p.
Reviewing the Sarrail controversy and adding a few new documents.

CORDONNIER, ÉMILIEN LOUIS VICTOR. **Ai-Je Trahi Sarrail?** Paris: Les Étincelles, 1930, 352 p.
An elaborate defense against the charges brought against him in Coblentz' book, by one of the commanding officers of the French Armée d'Orient. An unedifying picture of intrigue.

DAVID, ROBERT. **Le Drame Ignoré de l'Armée d'Orient.** Paris: Plon, 1927, 369 p.
A general account of the Dardanelles and Balkan campaigns, by a French deputy who was one of the early exponents of the Eastern orientation.

DESMAZES, MARIE ALPHONSE THÉODORE and NAUMOVIĆ, COMMANDANT. **Les Victoires Serbes en 1914**. Paris: Berger-Levrault, 1928, 124 p.
An excellent account of the Serb campaign in 1914, by a professor at the French War College and an officer of the Serbian General Staff.

DEYGAS, F. J. **L'Armée d'Orient dans la Guerre Mondiale**. Paris: Payot, 1932, 320 p.
A detailed account of campaigns and of the Eastern policy of the Allies.

DJUVARA, MIRCEA. **La Guerre Roumaine, 1916-1918**. Paris: Berger-Levrault, 1919, 335 p.
A general political and military history, by a Rumanian diplomat of note.

DUNAN, MARCEL. **L'Automne Serbe**. Paris: Berger-Levrault, 1932, 272 p.
The Vienna correspondent of the *Temps* gives an eyewitness's account of the Serbian drama of 1915.

FALKENHAYN, ERICH GEORG ANTON SEBASTIAN VON. **Der Feldzug der Neunten Armee gegen die Rumänen und Russen, 1916-1917**. Berlin: Mittler, 1920-1921, 2 v.
The most important single account of the campaigns in Transylvania and Rumania, by the former chief of staff and commander of the Ninth Army.

FEYLER, FERNAND. **La Campagne de Macédoine, 1916-18**. Geneva: Boissonnas, 1921, 122 p.
A detailed account, based upon personal observation, by a Swiss officer and historian. One of the best monographic treatments.

FEYLER, FERNAND. **Les Campagnes de Serbie, 1914-1915**. Paris: Boissonnas, 1926, 133 p.
A military monograph, by a Swiss officer who took part in the campaign; well-balanced and reliable.

FRAPPA, JEAN JOSÉ. **Makédonia**. Paris: Flammarion, 1921, 279 p.
The notes of an officer on the staff of Sarrail. Entertaining pen pictures, with some revelations thrown in.

GIRELLI, A. G. **L'Italia nei Balcani**. Turin: Libreria Italiana, 1923, 106 p.
The diary of the leader of the Italian forces, and a valuable contribution to the history of Italian policy in Albania.

GORDON-SMITH, GORDON. **From Serbia to Jugoslavia**. New York: Putnam, 1920, 360 p.
An English correspondent's account of Serbian military fortunes, from the Battle of the Morava and the retreat through Albania to the reorganization of the army at Saloniki and the final victory.

GOUIN, GUSTAVE. **L'Armée d'Orient**. Marseille: Detaille, 1931, 300 p.
Notes and correspondence written in the course of various operations, illustrated by photographs.

HELSEY, ÉDOUARD. **Les Aventures de l'Armée d'Orient**. Paris: Renaissance du Livre, 1920, 249 p.
A political and military study of the campaigns from 1915 to 1918.

KIRCH, PAUL. **Krieg und Verwaltung in Serbien und Mazedonien**. Stuttgart: Kohlhammer, 1928, 179 p.
An important contribution to the war-time history of the Balkans.

LARCHER, MAURICE. **La Grande Guerre dans les Balkans**. Paris: Payot, 1929, 320 p.
On the whole the best single account of the Balkan campaigns—well-documented and dispassionate.

MÉLOT, HENRY. **La Mission du Général Pau**. Paris: Payot, 1931, 208 p.
This volume throws light on the French policy towards the Balkan countries and Russia in the spring of 1915.

NEDEV, N. **La Bulgarie et la Guerre Mondiale.** Sofia: Librairie Française, 1925, 168 p.
A strictly military study.

NEDEV, N. **Les Opérations en Macédoine.** Sofia: Carasso, 1927, 299 p.
The years 1915-1918, described by an officer of the Bulgarian staff.

PAVLOVIĆ, ZHIVKO G. **Bitka na Jadru.** Belgrade: Makarije, 1924, 623 p.
A detailed day-by-day study of the Austro-Serbian fighting in August, 1914, with excellent maps.

PÉTIN, GENERAL. **Le Drame Roumain.** Paris: Payot, 1932, 160 p.
The best general study of the Rumanian débâcle, by a French corps commander.

PHOTIADÈS, CONSTANTIN. **La Victoire des Alliés en Orient.** Paris: Plon, 1920, 247 p.
A detailed account of operations from mid-September of 1918 to the Armistice.

REISS, RODOLPHE ARCHIBALD. **Lettres du Front Macédono-Serbe.** Geneva: Éditions d'Art Boissonnas, 1921, 173 p.
Vignettes of 1916-1918, by a Swiss observer.

REVOL, JOSEPH FORTUNÉ. **La Victoire de Macédoine.** Paris: Charles-Lavauzelle, 1931, 136 p.
A succinct military study of the campaign.

RIPERT D'ALAUZIER, LOUIS MARIE JOSEPH DE. **Un Drame Historique.** Paris: Payot, 1923, 240 p.
A valuable account of the retreat and resurrection of the Serbian Army in 1915 and 1916, written by a member of the French mission attached to Serbian headquarters.

SARRAIL, MAURICE PAUL EMMANUEL. **Mon Commandement en Orient.** Paris: Flammarion, 1920, 424 p.
The French Commander-in-Chief of the Armée d'Orient tells his side of the story about the 1916 defense of Saloniki, the Allied offensive in the autumn of 1916, and the situation on the Macedonian front in 1917.

SAVADJIAN, LÉON, *ed.* **L'Armée d'Orient Vue à 15 Ans de Distance.** Paris: Revue des Balkans, 1932.
A collection of essays by distinguished French commanders and statesmen, among them Briand, Painlevé, Franchet d'Esperey and Guillaumat.

TORAU-BAYLE, XAVIER. **Salonique, Monastir, et Athènes.** Paris: Chiron, 1922, 136 p.
A vigorous criticism of British policy as being responsible for the Allied débâcle in the Near East.

VELBURG, GERHARD. **Rumänische Etappe.** Minden: Köhler, 1930, 324 p.
The experiences of a German soldier in the Rumanian campaign.

VILLARI, LUIGI. **The Macedonian Campaign.** London: Unwin, 1922, 285 p.
A general account of the campaign by an Italian historian who served as liaison officer and had some opportunity to use unpublished material.

Dardanelles

ASHMEAD-BARTLETT, ELLIS. **The Uncensored Dardanelles.** London Hutchinson, n. d., 286 p.
An important volume of memoirs by an experienced English war correspondent.

CALLWELL, SIR CHARLES EDWARD. **The Dardanelles.** Boston: Houghton Mifflin, 1919, 361 p.
A technical study of the campaign with reference to the peculiar strategical problems.

CHARLES-ROUX, FRANÇOIS. **L'Expédition des Dardanelles.** Paris: Colin, 1920, 353 p.
The interesting diary of a French historian who took part in the expedition.

DELAGE, EDMOND. **The Tragedy of the Dardanelles.** London: Lane, 1932, 268 p.
A good systematic account, which does not, however, add to our knowledge.

ELLISON, SIR GERALD FRANCIS. **The Perils of Amateur Strategy.** New York: Longmans, 1926, 177 p.
An able indictment of civilian interference with questions of strategy, especially as exemplified by the history of the Dardanelles campaign.

HAMILTON, SIR IAN. **Gallipoli Diary.** London: Arnold, 1920, 2 v.
The diary of the British commander; one of the most complete and important sources for the history of the campaign.

HEAD, CHARLES OCTAVIUS. **A Glance at Gallipoli.** London: Eyre, 1931, 203 p.
An outline of the operation, but especially a critique of British leadership, by a British army officer.

KANNENGIESSER, HANS. **The Campaign in Gallipoli.** London: Hutchinson, 1927, 280 p.
One of the most important books on the subject, and one of the few detailed statements from the Turkish-German side.

MACKENZIE, COMPTON. **Gallipoli Memories.** New York: Doubleday, 1930, 387 p.
The recollections of an English novelist who served as an intelligence officer during the campaign.

MÜHLMANN, KARL. **Der Kampf um die Dardanellen.** Oldenburg: Stalling, 1927, 195 p.
A good substantial account of the Gallipoli campaign, by one of the German generals who participated.

PULESTON, WILLIAM DILWORTH. **The Dardanelles Expedition.** Annapolis: U. S. Naval Institute, 1926, 154 p.
An excellent brief study from the naval viewpoint.

TORAU-BAYLE, XAVIER. **La Campagne des Dardanelles.** Paris: Chiron, 1920, 170 p.
A brief narrative of the operation, together with some revelations on diplomatic activity in Greece, Bulgaria and Rumania.

WESTER-WEMYSS, ROSSLYN ERSKINE WEMYSS, BARON. **The Navy in the Dardanelles Campaign.** London: Hodder, n. d., 288 p.
The naval side of the operation as it appeared to the British admiral.

Greek Problem

See also (Greece) General, p. 418; also (Turkey) The War with Greece and the Lausanne Treaty, p. 430.

ABBOTT, GEORGE FREDERICK. **Greece and the Allies, 1914-1922.** London: Methuen, 1922, 242 p.
A critical analysis of the nationalistic aspirations of Venizelos. A valuable corrective to the conventional view of Greek politics since 1914.

ADAMOV, E. A., *ed.* **Evropeïskie Derzhavy i Gretsiia v Epochu Mirovoï Voïny.** Moscow: Commissariat for Foreign Affairs, 1922, 240 p.
The important collection of documents from the Russian archives. A contribution of prime value.

CARACCIOLO, MARIO. **L'Intervento della Grecia nella Guerra Mondiale e l'Opera della Diplomazia Alleata.** Rome: Maglione, 1925, 254 p.
A valuable and thoroughly documented contribution to the history of Allied diplomacy during the war, by a former Italian military attaché at Athens.

COMBOTHECRA, XÉNOCRATE SPIRIDON. **La Grèce Loyale.** Geneva: Kundig, 1919, 186 p.
An able exposition of the royalist view, with stress on the King's rights as against parliament and Greece's rights as against the Entente.

COSMIN, S., *pseud.* (S. P. PHOCAS-COSMETATOS). **Diplomatie et Presse dans l'Affaire Grecque, 1914-1916.** Paris: Société Mutuelle d'Édition, 1921, 313 p.
The story of events in Greece during the war, expounded by a partisan of King Constantine.

COSMIN, S., *pseud.* (S. P. PHOCAS-COSMETATOS). **L'Entente et la Grèce pendant la Grande Guerre.** Paris: Société Mutuelle d'Édition, 1926, 2 v.
A fundamental study, based upon French, German, Russian and Greek documents, aiming to justify Greek neutrality and Constantine's policy.

COSMIN, S., *pseud.* (S. P. PHOCAS-COSMETATOS). **The Tragedy of Greece.** New York: Brentano, 1928, 327 p.
An indictment of the Allies' policy toward Greece, and in particular of their support of Venizelos and their slander of King Constantine. An abridged translation of the author's "L'Entente et la Grèce pendant la Grande Guerre," with some added material.

MACKENZIE, COMPTON. **First Athenian Memories.** London: Cassell, 1931, 402 p.
The writer was on mission in Athens in the autumn of 1915 and draws a vivid picture of the chaotic nature of Allied policy towards Greece. This is the first of several volumes of memoirs.

PHRANGOULES, A. P. **La Grèce et la Crise Mondiale.** Paris: Félix Alcan, 1926, 2 v.
A former Greek diplomat's juridical study of the problem of Greek neutrality, based in part on unpublished documents, with an account of wartime negotiations with Serbia, Bulgaria and the Great Powers. The viewpoint is interventionist.

REGNAULT, CHARLES LOUIS JACQUES. **La Conquête d'Athènes.** Paris: Fournier, 1920, 262 p.
The account of the taking of Athens in 1917, by the commander of the landing force.

ROCHE, R. **Légitimité de l'Occupation Militaire Française en Territoire Hellénique au Cours de la Guerre.** Toulouse: 1923, 126 p.
A purely legal study of the basis and justification of Allied intervention.

SELIGMAN, VINCENT J. **The Victory of Venizelos.** London: Allen and Unwin, 1920, 185 p.
A survey of Greek politics from 1910 to 1918, ending on a strong Venizelist note.

Near and Middle Eastern Front

See also (Turkey) Armenia, p. 432.

BOWMAN-MANIFOLD, SIR MICHAEL GRAHAM EGERTON. **An Outline of the Egyptian and Palestine Campaigns, 1914 to 1918.** Chatham: MacKay, 1922, 100 p.
An excellent brief account, by a high British officer. The book is an outgrowth of lectures at the Staff College.

BRÉMOND, ÉDOUARD. **Le Hedjaz dans la Guerre Mondiale.** Paris: Payot, 1931, 352 p.
The Arab campaign viewed by a French officer who participated in it.

CANDLER, EDMUND. **Long Road to Baghdad.** Boston: Houghton Mifflin, 1919, 2 v.
A detailed history of the Mesopotamian campaigns, by a British official observer, valuable for its flavor of contemporary reality.

DANE, EDMUND. **British Campaigns in the Nearer East, 1914-1918.** New York: Hodder, 1917-1919, 2 v.

One of the best general accounts, with due consideration for political as well as military matters.

Douin, Georges. **L'Attaque du Canal de Suez.** Paris: Delagrave, 1922, 114 p.
A documented monograph on the attack of February 1915. The author considers diplomatic and political as well as military factors.

Emel'ianov, A. G. **Persidskiĭ Front.** Berlin: Gamaiun, 1923, 200 p.
The experiences of a Russian officer on the Persian front, 1915-1918.

Essad Bey. **Blood and Oil in the Orient.** New York: Simon and Schuster, 1932, 317 p.
The sensational and in parts incredible story of the British occupation of Baku and what followed in Transcaucasia. A book to be used with great caution.

Evans, Roger. **A Brief Outline of the Campaign in Mesopotamia.** London: Sifton Praed, 1926, 143 p.
A very readable account by one of the participants.

Graves, Robert. **Lawrence and the Arabian Adventure.** New York: Doubleday, 1928, 400 p.
The writer gives the substance of "Seven Pillars of Wisdom" and "Revolt in the Desert" and has added many new facts concerning the earlier career of the hero. What comes out particularly is the independent initiative taken by Lawrence and the failure of the government officials fully to appreciate the situation and support the arrangements which had been made with the Arabs.

Korganoff, G. **La Participation des Arméniens à la Guerre Mondiale sur le Front Caucase.** Paris: Geuthner, 1932, 210 p.
This monograph, on a little-known aspect of military operations, is particularly interesting for the account of events in the period after the withdrawal of the Russians.

Larcher, Maurice. **La Guerre Turque dans la Guerre Mondiale.** Paris: Berger-Levrault, 1926, 682 p.
The most detailed and on the whole the best single account of the campaigns in the Near East. The book, by a well-known military historian, takes account of political as well as military problems, is well documented, and has an excellent bibliography.

Lawrence, Thomas Edward. **Revolt in the Desert.** New York: Doran, 1927, 351 p.
A classic narrative of one of the most astonishing adventures of the World War.

Lock, Henry Osmond. **With the British Army in the Holy Land.** London: Scott, 1919, 149 p.
A good brief contemporary account, by an officer who took part.

Massey, William Thomas. **Allenby's Final Triumph.** London: Constable, 1920, 347 p.
Concludes the author's "How Jerusalem Was Won."

Massey, William Thomas. **How Jerusalem Was Won.** New York: Scribner, 1920, 295 p.
An unusually illuminating account, by an English correspondent. The best contemporary treatment.

Murphy, Charles Cecil Rowe. **Soldiers of the Prophet.** London: Hogg, 1921, 233 p.
A collection of articles, by a British officer, covering various operations in Turkey from 1910 on, including the Mesopotamian campaign.

Niedermayer, Oskar von. **Unter der Glutsonne Irans.** Munich: Einhorn, 1925, 331 p.
Reminiscences of the war-time German expedition to Persia and Afghanistan.

Thomas, Lowell. **With Lawrence in Arabia.** New York: Century, 1924, 408 p.
An enthusiastic description of British exploits among the Arabs, for popular consumption.

VARANDIAN, MIKAEL. **Le Conflit Arméno-Géorgien et la Guerre du Caucase.** Paris: Flinikowski, 1919, 152 p.
The story of the conflict in Transcaucasia, from the Armenian side.

WAVELL, ARCHIBALD PERCIVAL. **The Palestine Campaigns.** London: Constable, 1928, 275 p.
The best brief general account in English.

Siberia

See also (Russia) The War and the Revolution, p. 360, and Counter-Revolution and Intervention, p. 367; also (Far East) Siberia, p. 485.

ACKERMAN, CARL WILLIAM. **Trailing the Bolsheviki.** New York: Scribner, 1919, 308 p.
An important contribution to the history of Far Eastern developments, by the correspondent of the *New York Times.*

BAERLEIN, HENRY. **The March of the Seventy Thousand.** London: Leonard Parsons, 1926, 287 p.
The first adequate account in English of the exploits of the Czech legions in Siberia.

ČERVINKA, VINCENT. **Naši na Sibiři.** Prague: 1920, 338 p.
A collection of essays by various authors on different aspects of Czech organization and activity in Siberia.

CHANNING, C. G. FAIRFAX. **Siberia's Untouched Treasure.** New York: Putnam, 1923, 475 p.
A lieutenant in the A. E. F. tells the story of the Siberian campaign of the American forces. He also devotes a section to the natural resources of the country.

GAJDA, R. **Moje Paměti.** Prague: 1921, 179 p.
The anabasis of the Czech legions described by one of their generals.

HODGES, PHELPS. **Britmis.** London: Cape, 1931, 364 p.
The extraordinary story of a British officer on mission with Kolchak's forces, and a valuable contribution to the history of the counter-revolutionary debacle.

JANIN, MAURICE. **Moje Účast na Československem Boji za Svobodu.** Prague: Otto, 1930, 384 p.
The book deals very largely with the career and activities of Štefanik, and the Odyssey of the Czech troops in Siberia.

KLANTE, MARGARETE. **Von der Wolga zum Amur.** Berlin: Ost-europa Verlag, 1931, 346 p.
A doctoral dissertation which is of value in bringing some sort of order out of the chaos of conflicting accounts regarding the Czech legions in Siberia. The book contains a very full bibliography.

PARFENOV, P. S. **Bor'ba za Dal'nii Vostok, 1920-1922.** Leningrad: Priboi, 1928, 368 p.
A detailed account of the war in the Far East.

SAKHAROV, KONSTANTIN V. **Die Tschechischen Legionen in Sibirien.** Berlin: Hendriock, 1930, 100 p.
This bitter attack upon the conduct of the Czech legions, written by a commander of the Kolchak forces, should be read in connection with the Czech rhapsodies.

ŠTEIDLER, FRANT. VL. **Československé Hnutí na Rusi.** Prague: Památníku Odboje, 1922, 115 p.
A detailed narrative of the vicissitudes of the Czech legions.

VERGÉ, COLONEL. **Avec les Tchécoslovaques.** Paris: Guillon, 1926, 208 p.
A colorful picture of the Czech adventure in Siberia.

ZEMAN, ADOLF. **Československá Odyssea.** Prague: Otto, 1920, 308 p.
An interesting contemporary account of Czech activities in the Far East.

Africa

BUCHANAN, ANGUS. **Three Years of War in East Africa.** London: Murray, 1919, 247 p.
The operations of one of the British columns, by an officer in command.

BUHRER, J. **L'Afrique Orientale Allemande et la Guerre de 1914-1918.** Paris: Fournier, 1922, 427 p.
A study of the operations in German East Africa by a Belgian officer. Very complete, well-balanced and scholarly.

DANE, EDMUND. **British Campaigns in Africa and the Pacific, 1914-1918.** New York: Hodder, 1919, 215 p.
A general account of operations, marked by anti-German feeling.

DEPPE, LUDWIG. **Mit Lettow-Vorbeck durch Afrika.** Berlin: Scherl, 1919, 505 p.
Not a systematic history, but a collection of pictures and impressions which make interesting reading.

FERRANDI, JEAN. **Conquête du Cameroun-Nord, 1914-1915.** Paris: Charles-Lavauzelle, 1928, 293 p.
A detailed account of the operations, by a French officer.

HENNIG, RICHARD. **Deutsch-Südwest im Weltkriege.** Berlin: Süsserott, 1920, 313 p.
An authoritative account of the war in Southwest Africa, detailed and conscientious.

O'NEILL, HERBERT CHARLES. **The War in Africa and in the Far East.** London: Longmans, 1919, 114 p.
A useful introductory survey, with excellent maps.

SCHNEE, HEINRICH. **Deutsch-Ostafrika im Weltkriege.** Leipzig: Quelle, 1919, 439 p.
A general history of East Africa during the war, with due consideration of military events, by the former German governor.

NAVAL OPERATIONS; NAVAL MEMOIRS

See also (Military Operations) Dardanelles, p. 135; also (World War) Economic and Financial Aspects, p. 153.

ARDOIN, PAUL. **L'Escadre Allemande du Pacifique.** Paris: Challamel, 1920, 161 p.
The spectacular career of von Spee's squadron, described by an author who draws heavily on German accounts.

BACON, SIR REGINALD HUGH SPENCER. **The Dover Patrol.** London: Hutchinson, n. d., 2 v.
A detailed account of the very active and important patrol, by the commander.

BACON, SIR REGINALD HUGH SPENCER. **The Jutland Scandal.** London: Hutchinson, 4th ed., n. d., 152 p.
A reconsideration and summing up, by a British admiral, and at the same time a strong criticism of the Admiralty report and the relevant volume of the "Official History."

BACON, SIR REGINALD HUGH SPENCER. **The Life of Lord Fisher of Kilverstone.** New York: Doubleday, 1929, 2 v.
The authoritative biography of Fisher, based upon his correspondence, but written in a highly eulogistic and polemical vein.

BELLAIRS, CARLYON WILFROY. **The Battle of Jutland.** London: Hodder, 1919, 312 p.
A critical study of the battle and Jellicoe's strategy.

BIENAIMÉ, AMÉDÉE PIERRE LÉONARD. **La Guerre Navale de 1914-1915.** Paris: Tallandier, 1920, 307 p.
A very critical account of French naval operations in the Mediterranean by an admiral who was former chief of the naval general staff.

BINGHAM, BARRY. **Falklands, Jutland and the Bight.** London: Murray, 1919, 155 p.
A dramatic and lively account of the battles, by a British officer whose ship was sunk at Jutland and who was taken prisoner to Germany.

CARR, WILLIAM GUY. **By Guess and by God.** New York: Doubleday, 1930, 310 p.
A vivid story of the life and exploits of the submarines.

CATO, CONRAD. **The Navy Everywhere.** London: Constable, 1919, 297 p.
A popular account of activities and operations off Africa, on the Danube, in the Persian Gulf and in the Red Sea.

CHATTERTON, EDWARD KEBLE. **Sea-Raiders.** London: Hurst, n. d., 285 p.
A well-written narrative of the German raiders (with the exception of the *Emden*), based in part on British admiralty material.

CLARK, WILLIAM BELL. **When the U-Boats Came to America.** Boston: Little, Brown, 1929, 371 p.
The surprising story of German submarine activities on the American coast, dispassionately told.

DANIELS, JOSEPHUS. **Our Navy at War.** New York: Doran, 1922, 390 p.
An account by the Secretary of the Navy of the organization and activity of the American fleet.

DARTIGE DU FOURNET, ADMIRAL. **Souvenirs de Guerre d'un Amiral.** Paris: Plon, 1920, 320 p.
The recollections of the French commander-in-chief of the fleet in the east. They also throw light on the Greek problem.

DAVELUY, RENÉ. **L'Action Maritime pendant la Guerre Anti-Germanique.** Paris: Challamel, 1920, 2 v.
An authoritative, systematic and documented history, covering naval operations all over the world.

DAVELUY, RENÉ. **Les Enseignements Maritimes de la Guerre Anti-Germanique.** Paris: Challamel, 1919, 167 p.
A French admiral considers problems of cruiser warfare, submarine activity, coast defense, mine-laying, aviation, etc.

DELAGE, EDMOND. **Le Drame de Jutland.** Paris: Grasset, 1929, 233 p.
A clear, brief, popular account by a competent French naval writer. On the whole the author accepts the English view.

DOHNA-SCHLODIEN, NIKOLAUS, GRAF ZU. **Der Möwe Fahrten und Abenteuer.** Stuttgart: Perthes, 1927, 223 p.
The spectacular and almost incredible career of the famous German commerce destroyer, told by her commander.

DORLING, HENRY TAPRELL. **Endless Story.** London: Hodder, 1931, 451 p.
An account of the work of the British destroyer squadrons.

FARNAISE, MICHEL. **L'Aventure du Goeben.** Paris: Renaissance du Livre, n. d.,
263 p.
An attempt to get at the truth of the *Goeben-Breslau* episode. The author carefully
analyzes all the French and British controversial writings.

FAWCETT, HAROLD WILLIAM and HOOPER, GEOFFREY WILLIAM WINSMORE, *eds.* **The
Fighting at Jutland.** London: Hutchinson, 1929, 256 p.
The personal experiences of forty-five officers and men of the British fleet, as told in
their letters.

FISHER, JOHN ARBUTHNOT FISHER, BARON. **Memories and Records.** New York: Doran,
1920, 2 v.
Somewhat scrappy but often illuminating notes of the First Lord of the Admiralty.

FROTHINGHAM, THOMAS GODDARD. **A True Account of the Battle of Jutland.** Cambridge: Bacon, 1920, 54 p.
An American attempt to give both sides of the battle in brief scope for the layman.

GILL, CHARLES CLIFFORD. **What Happened at Jutland.** New York: Doran, 1921, 187 p.
A detailed, tactical study by an American officer.

GINOCCHETTI, A. **La Guerra sul Mare.** Rome: Libreria del Littorio, 1930, 321 p.
A general account of Italian operations, classed by services.

GLEAVES, ALBERT. **A History of the Transport Service.** New York: Doran, 1921, 284 p.
A review of the convoy service, by the American admiral in command.

GRAF, H. **La Marine Russe dans la Guerre et dans la Révolution.** Paris: Payot,
1928, 426 p.
A mixture of personal reminiscences and pure historical writing. The best general
account of the Russian navy available, especially strong on the revolutionary period.

HANDEL-MAZZETTI, PETER ANTON GEORG WILHELM ERNST, FREIHERR VON. **Die Oester-
reichisch-Ungarische Kriegsmarine vor und im Weltkriege.** Klagenfurt: Rosch-
nar, 1925, 127 p.
A satisfactory brief sketch of the Austrian navy.

HARPER, JOHN ERNEST TROYTE. **The Record of the Battle of Jutland.** London: H. M.
Stationery Office, 1927.
The famous record prepared for the Admiralty by Admiral Harper and others in 1919-
1920.

HARPER, JOHN ERNEST TROYTE. **The Truth about Jutland.** London: Murray, 1927,
200 p.
Utilizing the record, Admiral Harper reviews the evidence, largely exonerates Jellicoe,
but by no means whitewashes the British Fleet. This is one of the most important
studies yet made.

HASE, GEORG VON. **Kiel and Jutland.** London: Skeffington, n. d., 233 p.
One of the best German accounts of the battle, by the first gunnery officer of the powerful *Derfflinger*.

HASHAGEN, ERNST. **The Log of a U-Boat Commander.** New York: Putnam, 1931,
277 p.
The experiences of a German submarine commander covering the years 1914-1918.
One of the best German accounts of the sort.

HURD, ARCHIBALD. **A Merchant Fleet at War.** London: Cassell, 1920, 139 p.
The best brief popular account of the war services of the merchantmen.

HURD, ARCHIBALD and BASHFORD, HENRY HOWARTH. **Sons of Admiralty.** London:
Constable, 1919, 294 p.
A general non-technical history of British naval operations, by competent writers.

IRVING, JOHN. **Coronel and the Falkland Islands.** London: Philpot, 1927, 247 p.
The cruiser warfare admirably described.

JELLICOE, JOHN RUSHWORTH JELLICOE, VISCOUNT. **The Crisis of the Naval War.** New York: Doran, 1920, 331 p.
The author is concerned primarily with the anti-submarine operations of 1917-1918.

JELLICOE, JOHN RUSHWORTH JELLICOE, VISCOUNT. **The Grand Fleet, 1914-1916.** New York: Doran, 1919, 510 p.
An account of the organization and activity of the Grand Fleet, by its commander. The volume contains Jellicoe's account of Jutland and his reflections on that engagement.

KERR, MARK. **Land, Sea and Air.** New York: Longmans, 1927, 416 p.
Recollections of an experienced British seaman, who for two years commanded the Greek navy, commanded the British Adriatic Squadron 1916-1917, and helped organize the Royal Air Force.

LAURENS, ADOLPHE. **Le Commandement Naval en Méditerranée.** Paris: Payot, 1931, 356 p.
A French military historian studies the vicissitudes and rivalries of the high command in the Mediterranean.

LAURENS, ADOLPHE. **Histoire de la Guerre Sous-Marine Allemande.** Paris: Société d'Éditions Géographiques, 1930, 462 p.
The best single-volume treatment of the submarine war in its naval, political and economic aspects. Written by the chief of the historical section of the French Ministry of Marine, based on wide knowledge of published material and upon unpublished documents.

LAURENS, ADOLPHE. **Précis d'Histoire de la Guerre Navale.** Paris: Payot, 1929, 305 p.
An excellent, concise survey of the naval war, by the chief of the historical section of the French naval staff.

LUCKNER, FELIX, GRAF VON. **Seeteufel.** Leipzig: Koehler, 1921, 344 p.
The thrilling memoirs of the famous commander of the *Seeadler.*

LÜTZOW, FRIEDRICH. **Der Nordseekrieg.** Oldenburg: Stalling, 1931, 202 p.
An authoritative study of the Doggerbank and Skagerrak operations, based upon the German naval archives.

MANFRONI, CAMILLO. **Storia della Marina Italiana durante la Guerra Mondiale.** Bologna: Zanichelli, 1923, 397 p.
The standard Italian account, based in large measure on unpublished material.

MICHELSEN, ANDREAS HEINRICH. **Der U-Bootskrieg.** Leipzig: Koehler, 1925, 207 p.
An authoritative account of the submarine campaign by the officer in command.

MILNE, SIR ARCHIBALD BERKELEY. **The Flight of the "Goeben" and the "Breslau."** London: Nash, 1921, 160 p.
An explanation of the escape of the German ships, written in reply to the "Official History" by the former British commander in the Mediterranean.

MONASTEREV, N. **Vom Untergang der Tsarenflotte.** Berlin: Mittler, 1930, 184 p.
Reminiscences of a Russian submarine officer with the Black Sea Fleet, adding much to our knowledge of the story of the revolution in the navy.

MÜCKE, HELLMUTH VON. **The "Ayesha."** London: Allan, 1930, 218 p.
The story of the *Emden* raids and von Mücke's own account of the adventures and escape of the landing party.

MUNRO, DONALD JOHN. **Scapa Flow. A Naval Retrospect.** London: Low, 1932, 264 p.
The sinking of the German fleet reconsidered in the light of present knowledge.

NEWBOLT, SIR HENRY. **A Naval History of the War, 1914-1918.** London: Hodder, n. d., 350 p.
Written by an eminent British expert, this is probably the best one-volume account in English of the operations in which the British were engaged.

PARRATT, GEOFFREY. **The Royal Navy.** New York: Macmillan, 1930, 249 p.
A warm appreciation of the history of the navy, with special reference to its work for England during the war.

POCHHAMMER, HANS. **Before Jutland; Admiral von Spee's Last Voyage.** London: Jarrolds, 1931, 255 p.
An important German account of the cruiser warfare, the engagements at Coronel and the Falkland Islands.

POHL, HUGO VON. **Aus Aufzeichnungen und Briefen.** Berlin: Siegismund, 1920, 150 p.
Papers of the chief of the German naval staff, published in order to refute charges made in Tirpitz's memoirs.

RAWSON, GEOFFREY. **Earl Beatty, Admiral of the Fleet.** London: Jarrolds, 1930, 256 p.
A straightforward narrative of one of the most remarkable careers in British naval history.

REUTER, LUDWIG VON. **Scapa Flow.** Leipzig: Koehler, 1921, 107 p.
The story of how the German fleet was sunk, by the admiral who was in command.

RIVOYRE, CAMILLE LOUIS MARIE DE. **Histoire de la Guerre Navale.** Paris: Fournier, 1921, 426 p.
A teacher at the French Naval Academy surveys the course of operations, analyzes the work of the various arms and discusses at length the problems of submarine warfare.

SCHEER, REINHARDT. **Vom Segelschiff zum U-Boot.** Leipzig: Quelle und Meyer, 1925, 390 p.
The reminiscences of the famous German admiral. One of the most important accounts of the Battle of Jutland.

SCHOULTZ, GUSTAV VON. **With the British Battle Fleet.** London: Hutchinson, n. d., 360 p.
The recollections of a Russian officer serving with the Grand Fleet. The author gives a detailed account of Jutland.

SIMS, WILLIAM SOWDEN and HENDRICK, BURTON JESSE. **The Victory at Sea.** New York: Doubleday, 1920, 410 p.
A valuable contribution to the story of anti-submarine operations, convoys and mine-laying, by the chief of American naval operations.

SPARRE, CHRISTIAN. **Verdenskrigen Tilsjos.** Oslo: Aschehoug, 1925, 382 p.
One of the most impartial histories of the naval operations of the war. An account written for the layman by a Norwegian admiral.

SPENCER-COOPER, HENRY EDMUND HARVEY. **The Battle of the Falkland Islands.** London: Cassell, 1919, 224 p.
An early but reliable account of the operations leading up to the battle and the battle itself, by a British officer.

THOMAS, LOWELL. **Count Luckner, the Sea Devil.** New York: Doubleday, 1927, 308 p.
A popular narrative of Luckner's astounding raiding activities, based on his own account.

THOMAS, LOWELL. **Raiders of the Deep.** New York: Doubleday, 1928, 363 p.
An account of the work of the submarines during the war, containing some new and interesting information.

THOMAZI, AUGUSTE ANTOINE. **La Marine Française dans la Grande Guerre.** Paris:
Payot, 1925-1927, 2 v.
A French naval officer's detached and analytic study of the North Sea and Adriatic
operations.

TIRPITZ, ALFRED VON. **My Memoirs.** New York: Dodd, 1919, 2 v.
An important volume which not only deals with the author's part in constructing the
German navy, but throws light on the political views and influence of the naval staff.

TIRPITZ, ALFRED VON. **Politische Dokumente.** Berlin: J. G. Cotta, 1924-1926, 2 v.
Important documents from among the papers of the former Grand Admiral of the
German Fleet.

TSCHISCHWITZ, E. VON. **Armee und Marine bei der Eroberung der Baltischen Inseln.**
Berlin: Eisenschmidt, 1931, 187 p.
A study of army and navy coöperation in the taking of the Baltic Islands in 1917.

VASCHALDE, JOSEPH. **Marine et Guerre Navale.** Paris: Masson, 1920, 327 p.
A semi-popular review of the doctrines of naval war, the actual operations of the
war, and the lessons to be learned, with stress on submarine war.

VERNER, RUDOLF HENRY COLE. **The Battle Cruisers at the Falklands.** London: Bale,
1920, 85 p.
An account of the action by the commander of one of the two battle cruisers which had
hurried from Europe.

VOLLERTHUN, WALDEMAR. **Der Kampf um Tsingtau.** Leipzig: Hirzel, 1920, 200 p.
A good account of the taking of Tsingtau, based on the diaries of a German admiral.

WALDEYER-HARTZ, HUGO VON. **Der Kreuzerkrieg, 1914-1918.** Oldenburg: Stalling,
1931, 211 p.
A complete survey of German cruiser operations, but with special emphasis on Coronel
and the Falklands, and upon the exploits of the *Emden, Königsberg* and *Karlsruhe*.

WEGENER, WOLFGANG. **Die Seestrategie des Weltkrieges.** Berlin: Mittler, 1929, 86 p.
In spite of its brevity, this is a most stimulating and pregnant essay on naval strategy,
approaching the problem from the German side.

THE WAR IN THE AIR

See also (War, Peace, Security and Disarmament) Air Warfare, p. 70.

BOMPIANI, GIORGIO and PREPOSITI, CLEMENTE. **Le Ali della Guerra.** Milan: Mondadori,
1931, 433 p.
General Bompiani writes on the aviation of the Allies and the Central Empires, while
his collaborator discusses Italian wartime aviation in detail.

GAMBLE, C. F. SNOWDEN. **The Story of a North Sea Air Station.** New York: Oxford
University Press, 1928, 446 p.
The story of the Great Yarmouth Station. But the book is more than the title implies
and comes nearer being a history of the struggle for air supremacy in the North Sea.

HOEPPNER, ERNST WILHELM ARNOLD VON. **L'Allemagne et la Guerre de l'Air.** Paris:
Payot, 1923, 264 p.
A competent and reasonably impartial history of the German air campaign by the
commander of the German air forces.

LEHMANN, ERNST A. and MINGOS, HOWARD. **The Zeppelins.** New York: Putnam, 1928,
329 p.
A general history of the airships and their development, with special reference to the
raids over England during the war. Lehmann was director of these raids.

MORRIS, JOSEPH. **The German Air Raids on Great Britain.** London: Sampson Low, 1925, 306 p.
A very detailed study, based upon official records.

NEUMANN, GEORG PAUL. **Die Deutschen Luftstreitkräfte im Weltkriege.** Berlin: Mittler, 1920, 600 p.
An exhaustive coöperative work by experts. Based on official material and easily the most important German account.

PATRICK, MASON MATHEWS. **The United States in the Air.** New York: Doubleday, 1928, 191 p.
A former chief of the Air Service of the American Expeditionary Force describes American air operations at the front and activities behind the lines and at home, and also discusses post-war developments in aviation, both military and commercial.

POIRIER, JULES. **Les Bombardements de Paris, 1914-1918.** Paris: Payot, 1930, 274 p.
The author goes into all the phases of the attacks, by airplane, dirigible and "Big Bertha," and describes the military and civilian measures for protection. A statistical time-table of all bombardments is included for the period March 23-August 9, 1918.

RALEIGH, SIR WALTER ALEXANDER and JONES, H. A. **War in the Air.** New York: Oxford University Press, 1922, 1928, 1931, 3 v.
A history of the rôle of the British air forces in the war, based largely on the records of the Air Ministry.

RAWLINSON, SIR ALFRED. **The Defence of London, 1915-1918.** New York: Melrose, 1923, 267 p.
A detailed account of how some sort of defense against air raids was worked out. The author is very critical of post-war provisions.

SWEETSER, ARTHUR. **American Air Service.** New York: Appleton, 1919, 384 p.
A record of the problems and final achievements of this branch of the American forces, by a former officer of the aviation section of the United States Army.

THENAULT, GEORGES. **The Story of the Lafayette Escadrille.** Boston: Small, 1921, 172 p.
A narrative, by the commander, of life and activity in the famous squadron.

TREUSCH VON BUTTLAR-BRANDENFELS, HORST, FREIHERR. **Zeppelins over England.** New York: Harcourt, 1932, 320 p.
The dramatic story of the air raids, by a German commander.

TURNER, CHARLES CYRIL. **The Struggle in the Air, 1914-1918.** London: Arnold, 1919, 288 p.
A general non-technical account of the work of the British air forces.

MILITARY EFFORTS OF PARTICIPANTS

See also (World War) Unofficial Histories and General Discussions, p. 111, and Conduct of the War, p. 114, and Military Memoirs and Biographies, p. 117, and Economic and Financial Aspects, p. 153.

United States

BASSETT, JOHN SPENCER. **Our War with Germany.** New York: Knopf, 1919, 386 p.
The best brief general account of America's part in the great conflict.

BEAMISH, RICHARD JOSEPH and MARCH, FRANCIS ANDREW. **America's Part in the World War.** Philadelphia: Winston, 1919, 608 p.
An exuberant detailed chronicle of the American achievement.

FROTHINGHAM, THOMAS GODDARD. **The American Reinforcement in the World War.**
New York: Doubleday, 1927, 427 p.
The larger part of the book is taken up with a review of conditions when the United
States entered the conflict, and the story of the recruiting, equipping and transporting
of the forces. The author has been supplied with a goodly amount of material by Mr.
Newton D. Baker, so that in a sense the book may be regarded as the first presentation
of the subject from the viewpoint of the War Department and the officials directly
responsible.

HAGOOD, JOHNSON. **The Services of Supply.** Boston: Houghton Mifflin, 1927, 420 p.
An important and authoritative contribution to the history of the war by an American
general.

HURLEY, EDWARD NASH. **The Bridge to France.** Philadelphia: Lippincott, 1927, 338 p.
The former Chairman of the Shipping Board tells the inside story of the transportation
problem.

JOHNSON, THOMAS M. **Without Censor.** Indianapolis: Bobbs-Merrill, 1928, 411 p.
A history of the American engagements, by the former correspondent of the *New
York Sun*. Based not only on contemporary notes and records, but on information
from many officers.

LONERGAN, THOMAS CLEMENT. **It Might Have Been Lost.** New York: Putnam, 1929,
340 p.
An account of the efforts made by the French and English to incorporate the A. E. F.
with the other forces, by an officer of the American general staff.

McCORMICK, ROBERT RUTHERFORD. **The Army of 1918.** New York: Harcourt, 1920,
276 p.
A general narrative of the organization and operation of the A. E. F. with reflections
on problems of national defense.

McMASTER, JOHN BACH. **The United States in the World War.** New York: Appleton,
1918-20, 2 v.
Probably the best general contemporary history, making extensive use of newspapers
and other unofficial material.

RÉQUIN, ÉDOUARD JEAN. **America's Race to Victory.** New York: Stokes, 1919, 211 p.
By an officer of the French military mission. An able account of the mobilization of
America's military and economic resources.

THOMAS, SHIPLEY. **History of the A. E. F.** New York: Doran, 1920, 540 p.
A competent and attractively written survey of American operations.

VIERECK, GEORGE SYLVESTER, *ed.* **As They Saw Us.** New York: Doubleday, 1929, 392 p.
In this collection a number of Allied and German generals discuss the work of the American reinforcements in the war. By far the most important chapters are those by Foch
and Ludendorff. Among the other contributions special mention may be made of the
discussion of the Meuse-Argonne operations by General Savatier, French assistant
chief of staff, and General von Gallwitz, the German commander.

VILLENEUVE-TRANS, ROMÉE DE. **À l'Ambassade de Washington, Octobre, 1917-
Avril, 1919. Les Heures Décisives de l'Intervention Américaine.** Paris: Bossard,
1921, 287 p.
Some sidelights on America's participation in the World War, particularly as regards
Russia and the Far East.

WILGUS, WILLIAM JOHN. **Transporting the A. E. F. in Western Europe.** New York:
Columbia University Press, 1931, 612 p.
An exhaustive technical study by the director of military railways of the A. E. F.

Other Powers

AUFFENBERG-KOMARÓW, MORITZ, FREIHERR VON. **Aus Oesterreich-Ungarns Teilnahme am Weltkriege.** Berlin: Ullstein, 1920, 391 p.
Perhaps the best study of the Austrian army, by a former war minister.

BERNARD, AUGUSTIN. **L'Afrique du Nord pendant la Guerre.** New Haven: Yale University Press, 1927, 162 p.
A thorough monograph, covering an important chapter of war history and throwing light especially on the recruiting of colonial troops by the French Government.

BUAT, EDMOND ALPHONSE LÉON. **L'Armée Allemande pendant la Guerre de 1914-1918; Grandeur et Décadence.** Paris: Chapelot, 1920, 69 p.
A French military expert comes to the conclusion that Germany was much less prepared in 1914 than France, and that she should have sent more than half a million additional men into the field.

Canada in the Great World War. Toronto: United Publishers, 1917-1921, 6 v.
A great coöperative survey of the organization and operations of the Canadian troops.

GERMAINS, VICTOR WALLACE. **The Kitchener Armies.** London: Davies, 1930, 306 p.
A careful scholarly study of the organization and achievement of the first British armies.

GOLOVIN, NIKOLAÏ NIKOLAEVICH. **The Russian Army in the World War.** New Haven: Yale University Press, 1931, 306 p.
This volume in the Carnegie Series discusses the composition of the army, and the munitions supply, food supply, and transport.

Histoire des Troupes Coloniales pendant la Guerre, 1914-1918. Paris: Lavauzelle, 1923, 304 p.
An historical and statistical analysis of the French colonials in the World War.

HOPKINS, JOHN CASTELL. **Canada at War.** New York: Doran, 1919, 448 p.
A detailed, unofficial general account, with much factual material and many illustrations.

HORVÁTH, JENÖ. **Ungarn und der Weltkrieg.** Budapest: Drachen, 1931, 162 p.
An attempt to survey and appraise the sources. Written by a leading Hungarian historian.

KEITH, ARTHUR BERRIEDALE. **The War Government of the British Dominions.** New York: Oxford University Press, 1921, 353 p.
An authoritative treatment by a leading historian of imperial relations. In the Carnegie Series.

KIRITESCU, CONSTANTIN. **Histoire de la Guerre Roumaine.** Paris: Berger-Levrault, 1925, 2 v.
A full history of Rumania's part in the war, moderate in tone.

LUCAS, SIR CHARLES PRESTWOOD, *ed.* **The Empire at War.** Oxford: Oxford University Press, 1921-26, 5 v.
An account of the contribution made by Britain's oversea possessions to British wars down to 1918. Written by a group of experts drawn from the dominions and colonies.

PIRENNE, HENRI. **La Belgique et la Guerre Mondiale.** New Haven: Yale University Press, 1929, 296 p.
A volume of the Carnegie Series, in which the great Belgian historian reviews the trials and tribulations of his native land during the German occupation.

STEELE, HARWOOD ELMES ROBERT. **The Canadians in France, 1915-1918.** London: Unwin, 1920, 364 p.

A general and somewhat fulsome account of the Canadian part in the campaigns of the West.

SUPKA, GÉZA. **A "Nagy Dráma."** Miskolcz: Miskolci Reggeli Hirlap, 1925, 489 p.
A general, semi-popular account of Hungary's part in the war.

PUBLIC OPINION AND PROPAGANDA

BARRÈS, MAURICE. **De la Sympathie à la Fraternité d'Armes; les États-Unis dans la Guerre.** Paris: Alcan, 1919, 96 p.
A warm tribute to America, by the great French nationalist writer. A series of war letters and essays.

BORNECQUE, HENRI and DROUILLY, JOSÉ GERMAIN. **La France et la Guerre; Formation de l'Opinion Publique pendant la Guerre.** Paris: Payot, 1921, 159 p.
A study of the efforts made to enlighten the French people as to their own ideals and mission, the crimes of Germany, the virtue of France's Allies and the purity of French war aims.

CREEL, GEORGE. **How We Advertised America.** New York: Harper, 1920, 466 p.
An astonishing story of successful propaganda; the history of the Committee on Public Information, written by its Chairman.

DEMARTIAL, GEORGES. **La Guerre de 1914. Comment on Mobilisa les Consciences.** Paris: Éditions des Cahiers Internationaux, 1922, 325 p.
A frank analysis of war-time propaganda and censorship in France.

DROUILLY, JOSÉ GERMAIN and GUÉRINON, E. **Les Chefs-d'Œuvre de la Propagande Allemande.** Paris: Berger-Levrault, 1919, 277 p.
An examination and analysis of the leading German propagandist writings. A valuable contribution.

FALCKE, HORST P. **Vor dem Eintritt Amerikas in den Weltkrieg.** Dresden: Reissner, 1928, 304 p.
An important book, in which the former German Consul-General in New York gives an unvarnished account of German propaganda and activities.

FOERSTER, FRIEDRICH WILHELM. **Mes Combats à l'Assaut du Militarisme et de l'Impérialisme Allemands.** Paris: Librairie Istra, 1923, 310 p.
A critique of militaristic Germany, with a hopeful note for the future, by a distinguished German pacifist.

GAFFNEY, THOMAS ST. JOHN. **Breaking the Silence.** New York: Liveright, 1930, 367 p.
A former American consul at Munich tells the story of his conflict with the State Department and his ultimate recall at the instigation of the British Government. The book contains much on the activity of British propaganda agencies and their effective work.

HALLAYS, ANDRÉ. **L'Opinion Allemande pendant la Guerre, 1914-1918.** Paris: Perrin, 1919, 268 p.
A study of the main currents and phases of German opinion, based on newspapers, memoirs and other evidence.

HAPGOOD, NORMAN, *ed.* **Professional Patriots.** New York: Boni, 1927, 219 p.
A collection of studies setting forth the personalities and methods of those who made a business of arousing the national impulses during the war.

HOVELAQUE, ÉMILE. **Les États-Unis et la Guerre.** Paris: Alcan, 1919, 467 p.
Primarily a study of the evolution of American opinion from neutrality to the crusading spirit.

HUBER, GEORG. **Die Französische Propaganda im Weltkrieg gegen Deutschland.**
Munich: Pfeiffer, 1928, 314 p.
A serious and valuable study in journalism and organized propaganda.

JUSSERAND, JEAN JULES. **Le Sentiment Américain pendant la Guerre.** Paris: Payot,
1931, 176 p.
Written by the former French Ambassador in Washington, this is a concise and
brilliant little study of American public opinion and its evolution towards war.

LASSWELL, HAROLD DWIGHT. **Propaganda Technique in the World War.** New York:
Knopf, 1927, 233 p.
An examination of the methods of systematic propaganda. One of the best books on
the subject.

LECHARTIER, GEORGES. **Intrigues et Diplomaties à Washington, 1914-1917.** Paris:
Plon, 1919, 302 p.
An indictment of German activity in the United States.

MARCHAND, LOUIS. **L'Offensive Morale.** Paris: Renaissance du Livre, 1920, 338 p.
A study of the *Gazette des Ardennes* and the *Bonnet Rouge* to show how the German
general staff attempted to undermine French morale.

MAXE, JEAN, *pseud.* **L'Anthologie des Défaitistes.** Paris: Bossard, 1925, 2 v.
A highly interesting collection of extracts to illustrate the defeatist propaganda, especially the red propaganda in France.

MICHEL, HENRI. **Ma Mentalité avant, pendant, après la Guerre.** Paris: Ged, 1931,
436 p.
A remarkable psychological self-analysis, by a former French senator.

PLAYNE, CAROLINE ELISABETH. **The Neuroses of Nations. The Neuroses of Germany
and France.** London: Allen and Unwin, 1925, 468 p.
A study in the national psychology of pre-war Europe and a valuable contribution
to the study of war origins.

PLAYNE, CAROLINE ELISABETH. **The Pre-War Mind in Britain.** London: Allen and
Unwin, 1928, 445 p.
An admirable analysis of British opinion on foreign affairs.

PLAYNE, CAROLINE ELISABETH. **Society at War, 1914-1916.** Boston: Houghton Mifflin,
1931, 380 p.
Another one of the author's interesting studies of national psychology, dealing here
with British opinion in the first years.

PONSONBY, ARTHUR PONSONBY, BARON. **Falsehood in Wartime.** New York: Dutton,
1928, 192 p.
A devastating criticism, by an English radical, of the garbling of colored books in
1914, the exaggerations about atrocities, and related topics.

RECKTENWALD, FRIEDERIKE. **Kriegsziele und Öffentliche Meinung Englands, 1914-
1916.** Stuttgart: Kohlhammer, 1929, 147 p.
A study of the way in which the ideas of 1918 evolved during the first war years.

STUART, SIR CAMPBELL. **Secrets of Crewe House.** New York: Hodder, 1920, 256 p.
The frank story of the extraordinarily efficient British propaganda organization, by
one of its chiefs, subsequently a director of the London *Times*.

TOSTI, AMEDEO. **Come ci Vide l'Austria Imperiale.** Milan: Mondadori, 1930, 312 p.
A very detailed study of Austrian opinion of Italy during the war, based on examination of the Vienna archives, parliamentary debates, newspapers and memoirs.

TROMMER, HARRY. **Urkundenfälschung und Betrug im Weltkriege.** Leipzig: Wiegandt, 1928, 190 p.
The subject is the same as that of Ponsonby's book, but the author attacks it rather as a problem in criminology.

VIERECK, GEORGE SYLVESTER. **Spreading Germs of Hate.** New York: Liveright, 1930, 327 p.
An astonishingly frank account of propaganda activities in the United States during the war, by one who has much to tell.

WALTZ, JEAN JACQUES and TONNELAT, ERNEST. **À Travers les Lignes Ennemies.** Paris: Payot, 1922, 191 p.
The story of the French "paper" war against Germany and the whole effective campaign of demoralization.

WILLIS, IRENE COOPER. **England's Holy War.** New York: Knopf, 1928, 399 p.
The author traces the evolution of English liberalism from confirmed pacifism to the crusading spirit of the World War, and scathingly exposes the contradictions which she discovers. The evidence is taken primarily from the files of the leading liberal newspaper, the *Daily News*, and the story covers the period through the peace settlements.

SECRET SERVICE AND ESPIONAGE

ADAM, GEORGE. **Treason and Tragedy.** London: Cape, 1929, 254 p.
The thrilling story of the French treason trials, from Bolo through the Caillaux case.

ASTON, SIR GEORGE GREY. **Secret Service.** New York: Cosmopolitan Book Corporation, 1930, 348 p.
This is not a technical study of modern secret services but primarily a volume of recollections by an English officer closely connected with naval intelligence.

BERNDORFF, HANS RUDOLF. **Espionage!** New York: Appleton, 1930, 268 p.
Better reading than any detective novel.

BOUCARD, ROBERT. **Les Dessous de l'Espionnage Allemand.** Paris: Hachette, 1931, 256 p.
Another sensational book on espionage. One wonders if things were really like that.

BYWATER, HECTOR CHARLES and FERRABY, H. C. **Strange Intelligence.** New York: Long and Smith, 1931, 308 p.
An account of the working of the British naval intelligence before and during the war, by former members of the staff.

CROZIER, JOSEPH. **In the Enemy's Country.** New York: Knopf, 1931, 235 p.
The translation of one of the most astounding French accounts of espionage.

EVERITT, NICHOLAS. **British Secret Service during the Great War.** London: Hutchinson, 1920, 320 p.
A valuable account, based largely on personal experience.

MAXE, JEAN, *pseud.* **De Zimmerwald au Bolchévisme, ou le Triomphe du Marxisme Pangermaniste. Essai sur les Menées Internationalistes pendant la Guerre.** Paris: Bossard, 1920, 236 p.
A somewhat wild denunciation of socialism and defeatist activity, which is regarded as just one part of the Pan-German machinery.

NICOLAI, WALTER. **The German Secret Service.** London: Paul, 1924, 299 p.
A systematic account of the organization and activity of the German secret service, by the chief of the intelligence service of the German General Staff.

NICOLAI, WALTER. **Nachrichtendienst, Presse und Volkstimmung im Weltkrieg.**
Berlin: Mittler, 1920, 226 p.
An important study of intelligence and propaganda.

RONGE, MAXIMILIAN. **Kriegs- und Industrie-Espionage.** Vienna: Amalthea, 1930, 424 p.
The revealing account of the Austrian chief of intelligence. One of the most important
books on military intelligence.

SEELIGER, EMIL, *comp.* **Spione und Verräter.** Berlin: Verlag für Kulturpolitik, 1930,
271 p.
One of the best of the espionage revelations that have appeared recently in Germany.

SILBER, J. C. **Die Anderen Waffen.** Breslau: Korn, 1932, 303 p.
Tales by a German who had the extraordinary experience of serving as an Assistant
Censor in the Censor Department of the British post office from November 1914 to
June 1919.

THOMSON, SIR BASIL. **The Allied Secret Service in Greece.** London: Hutchinson, 1931,
288 p.
A thrilling and almost incredible story of Allied activity. An important addition to the
literature on the Greek affair.

THOMSON, SIR BASIL. **Queer People.** London: Hodder, 1922, 320 p.
Experiences and reflections of a noted British intelligence officer.

NEUTRALS AND THE WAR

*See also (Western Europe) Switzerland, p. 250; also (Northern Europe) Scandinavian States,
p. 339.*

BORDEAUX, PAUL ÉMILE. **La Suisse et Son Armée dans la Guerre Mondiale.** Paris:
Payot, 1931, 192 p.
This competent study of Switzerland's military position during the war fills an im-
portant gap.

HECKSCHER, ELI FILIP, BERGENDAL, KURT and others. **Sweden, Norway, Denmark,
and Iceland in the World War.** New Haven: Yale University Press, 1930, 593 p.
This volume in the Carnegie Series is the most authoritative study of the important
Scandinavian neutrals during the world conflict.

JAPIKSE, NICOLAAS. **Die Stellung Hollands im Weltkriege.** Gotha: Perthes, 1921, 383 p.
A discussion, by a competent Dutch historian, of the difficulties presented by Holland's
neutrality.

NYGH, WILLEM JOHANNIS CORNELIS ANTHONY. **La Politique Financière des Pays-
Bas pendant la Guerre.** The Hague: Nijhoff, 1923, 129 p.
A doctoral dissertation analyzing the peculiar financial problems confronting the
Netherlands.

ROCUANT Y FIGUEROA, ENRIQUE. **La Neutralité du Chili.** Santiago: Imprenta Universitaria, 1919, 316 p.
An apology for the policy of neutrality.

VANDENBOSCH, AMRY. **The Neutrality of the Netherlands during the World War.**
Grand Rapids: Eerdmans Publishing Company, 1927, 349 p.
An exhaustive scholarly study of the legal aspects of Dutch neutrality.

VIGNESS, PAUL G. **The Neutrality of Norway in the World War.** Stanford: Stanford
University Press, 1932, 188 p.
A study of the blockade and the rôle of the neutral Powers.

VISSERING, GERARD, HOLSTIJN, JAN WESTERMAN and BORDEWIJK, HUGO WILLEM CON-
STANTIJN. **The Netherlands and the World War.** New Haven: Yale University
Press, 1923, 1928, 4 v.
A collaborative study, in the Carnegie Series, of various aspects of the war as it affected
the Netherlands.

III. ECONOMIC AND FINANCIAL ASPECTS; WAR COSTS

*See also (International Finance) Reparations and War Debts, p. 25; also (Peace ʿNegotia-
tions) Criticism and Proposals for Revision, p. 160.*

BAKER, CHARLES WHITING. **Government Control and Operation of Industry in
Great Britain and the United States during the World War.** New York: Oxford,
1921, 138 p.
An important scholarly monograph in the Carnegie Series. The author examines all
the fundamental aspects of war organization—railways, shipping, labor and capital,
food, fuel, etc.

BARRON, CLARENCE WALKER. **War Finance as Viewed from the Roof of the World in
Switzerland.** Boston: Houghton Mifflin, 1919, 368 p.
Observations and material collected by an American financial expert. The book is keen
but disjointed and contains much that has no direct bearing on finance.

BERINDEY, A. **La Situation Économique et Financière de la Roumanie sous
l'Occupation Allemande.** Paris: Duchemin, 1921, 216 p.
A faithful analysis of the more obvious factors in the German administration.

BEVERIDGE, SIR WILLIAM HENRY. **British Food Control.** New Haven: Yale University
Press, 1928, 447 p.
A volume of the Carnegie Series dealing with the all-important question of England's
food supply during the war.

BOGART, ERNEST LUDLOW. **Direct and Indirect Costs of the Great World War.** New
York: Oxford, 1919, 338 p.
This volume, in the Carnegie Series, surveys most of the important countries of the
world. Still one of the best treatments.

BRUNEAU, PIERRE. **Le Rôle du Haut Commandement au Point de Vue Économique de 1914 à 1921.** Paris: Berger-Levrault, 1924, 90 p.
An original study of the unique economic problems of modern warfare and of the non-
political aspects of French war plans and strategy.

BUKSHPAN, M. **Voenno-Khoziaĭstvennaia Politika.** Moscow: Gosizdat, 1929, 544 p.
A detailed monograph on the forms and organs of economic regulation during the war.

CHARBONNET, GERMAIN. **La Politique Financière de la France pendant la Guerre.**
Bordeaux: Cadoret, 1922, 360 p.
A systematic but conventional study of French war finance.

CLARK, JOHN MAURICE. **The Costs of the World War to the American People.**
New Haven: Yale University Press, 1931, 328 p.
The author does not confine himself to a study of finance, but examines such problems
as displacement of man-power, death and disability, effects on agriculture and shipping,
population problems, etc. A volume in the Carnegie Series.

CLARKSON, GROSVENOR B. **Industrial America in the World War.** Boston: Houghton
Mifflin, 1923, 573 p.
A eulogy of the part played in the World War by American business, as directed and
controlled by the War Industries Board.

COCHIN, DENYS. **Les Organisations du Blocus en France pendant la Guerre.** Paris:
Plon, 1926, 292 p.
An authoritative collaborative work with stress on international law aspects.

COLLINET, PAUL and STAHL, PAUL. **Le Ravitaillement de la France Occupée.** New
Haven: Yale University Press, 1928, 183 p.
The author deals almost exclusively with the organization and work of the Comité
d'Alimentation du Nord de la France. A study in the Carnegie Series.

CROWELL, BENEDICT and WILSON, ROBERT FORREST. **How America Went to War.**
New Haven: Yale University Press, 1921, 6 v.
A large compilation of official material and figures, dealing chiefly with the mobilization
of industry, the organization, transport and supply of the army, munitions, etc.

CROWELL, JOHN FRANKLIN. **Government War Contracts.** New York: Oxford, 1920,
357 p.
The author deals with the principles and mechanism of contracts, with special reference to the experience of the United States. Published by the Carnegie Endowment.

DELBRÜCK, CLEMENS VON. **Die Wirtschaftliche Mobilmachung in Deutschland.**
Munich: Verlag für Kulturpolitik, 1924, 322 p.
The posthumous papers of the German Minister of the Interior, who realized more
clearly than most people the urgency of economic preparation and control.

ELIASHEV, BORIS. **Les Finances de Guerre de la Russie.** Paris: Giard, 1919, 274 p.
A systematic doctoral dissertation.

FAIRLIE, JOHN ARCHIBALD. **British War Administration.** New York: Oxford, 1919,
302 p.
A volume published by the Carnegie Endowment. The author studies the changes
wrought by the war in the cabinet, the military and naval departments, trade and
food control, finance, etc.

FAYLE, CHARLES ERNEST. **The War and the Shipping Industry.** New Haven: Yale
University Press, 1927, 472 p.
A splendid study, in the Carnegie Series, of one of the most crucial problems of the war,
dealing chiefly with the economic and administrative questions presented by the
shipping industry.

FOLKS, HOMER. **The Human Costs of the War.** New York: Harper, 1920, 326 p.
An impressive survey of the misery in Serbia, Belgium, France and Italy, by an American Red Cross commissioner.

GIDE, CHARLES and OUALID, WILLIAM. **Le Bilan de la Guerre pour la France.** New
Haven: Yale University Press, 1931, 370 p.
This volume, in the Carnegie Series, surveys the whole cost of the war, moral as well
as material, so far as it affected France.

GIDE, CHARLES, *ed.* **Effects of the War upon French Economic Life.** New York:
Oxford, 1923, 197 p.
A series of five monographs written by experts and published in the Carnegie Series.
The contributions deal with French shipping, textile industry, finance, commercial
policy, and labor.

GRADY, HENRY FRANCIS. **British War Finance.** New York: Columbia, 1927, 316 p.
A scholarly treatment, based on all available material.

GRÁTZ, GUSZTÁV and SCHÜLLER, RICHARD. **The Economic Policy of Austria-Hungary during the War.** New Haven: Yale University Press, 1928, 286 p.
An authoritative monographic study, one of the volumes in the Carnegie Series. The authors, both high government officials, deal in detail with economic arrangements with Germany, the Brest-Litovsk Treaties, the Bucharest Treaty and the Polish question.

GRENIER, GEORGES. **La Mobilisation Financière de la France en 1914.** Paris: Sirey, 1928, 182 p.
A valuable contribution, equipped with numerous official documents.

GUICHARD, LOUIS. **The Naval Blockade.** New York: Appleton, 1930, 321 p.
A scholarly, detached account not only of the blockade of Germany, but of the commercial war in general and its effects. Based in part on unpublished French material.

HIRST, FRANCIS WRIGLEY and ALLEN, JOHN ERNEST. **British War Budgets.** New Haven: Yale University Press, 1926, 495 p.
This volume, one of the Carnegie Series, consists of a minute analysis of the twelve war budgets from 1914 to 1924.

JÈZE, GASTON and TRUCHY, HENRI. **The War Finance of France: The War Expenditure of France; How France Met Her War Expenditure.** New Haven: Yale University Press, 1927, 344 p.
An expert account. Part of the Carnegie Series.

JOFFE, I. **Blokada i Narodnoe Khoziaïstvo v Mirovuiu Voïnu.** Moscow: Gosizdat, 1929, 224 p.
A study of the blockade and its effects.

LANDWEHR, OTTOKAR. **Hunger. Die Erschöpfungsjahre der Mittelmächte, 1917-1918.** Zurich: Amalthea, 1931, 325 p.
An important contribution to the history of the war on the domestic side, written by the Austrian food administrator.

LAURENS, ADOLPHE. **Le Blocus et la Guerre Sous-Marine.** Paris: Colin, 1924, 215 p.
A concise work on the Allied blockade and the German submarine campaign. Written by an expert for the layman.

LENZ, FRIEDRICH and SCHMIDT, EBERHARD, eds. **Die Deutschen Vergeltungsmassnahmen im Wirtschaftskrieg.** Bonn and Leipzig: Kurt Schroeder, 1924, 368 p.
A study of the commercial war from 1914 to 1919.

LORIA, ACHILLE. **Aspetti Sociali ed Economici della Guerra Mondiale.** Milan: Vallardi, 1921, 458 p.
A suggestive book by a well-known exponent of economic determinism, who reviews the cost of the war and its effects on production, distribution, finance, etc.

MICHEL, EDMOND. **Les Dommages de Guerre de la France et Leur Réparation.** Paris: Berger-Levrault, 1932, 656 p.
An imposing study of war costs and reparations, by a French expert.

MICHELSON, ALEKSANDR MIKHAÏLOVICH and others. **Russian Public Finance during the War.** New Haven: Yale University Press, 1928, 484 p.
One of the most welcome volumes in the Carnegie Series, for it contains a much-needed history of Russian war finance and monetary policy, as well as an excellent account of the pre-war and war credit operations of the government.

OLPHE-GALLIARD, G. **Histoire Économique et Financière de la Guerre.** Paris: Rivière, 1925, 502 p.
A general treatment of the problem, with emphasis on the French side.

PARASCHIVESCO, C. C. **Les Finances de Guerre de la Roumanie.** Paris: Bailet, 1920.
 A doctoral dissertation, which does not get far beyond fundamentals.

PARMELEE, MAURICE FARR. **Blockade and Sea Power.** New York: Crowell, 1924, 449 p.
 A survey of blockade policies and the regulation of sea trade from 1914 to 1919,
 with their bearing on the problems of a world state.

PETIT, LUCIEN CHARLES. **Histoire des Finances Extérieures de la France.** Paris:
 Payot, 1929, 816 p.
 An exhaustive account of French financial operations during the war, based on the
 archives of the Ministry of Finance.

RIST, CHARLES. **Les Finances de Guerre de l'Allemagne.** Paris: Payot, 1921, 294 p.
 An expert account of the financing of the war on the German side.

SALTER, SIR ARTHUR. **Allied Shipping Control: An Experiment in International
 Administration.** New York: Oxford, 1921, 372 p.
 A volume in the Carnegie Series, by an expert in international economic problems.

SHIGALIN, G. **Podgotovka Promyshlennosti k Voĭne.** Moscow: Gosizdat, 1928, 228 p.
 A study of the war-time mobilization of industry, with special reference to Russia.

SHOTWELL, JAMES THOMSON, *ed.* **Economic and Social History of the World War.**
 New Haven: Yale University Press, 1924- .
 The great series of monographs published by the Carnegie Endowment is the most
 ambitious project of World War history yet undertaken. The various volumes are
 written by experts, frequently by officials, and cover most conceivable phases of the
 subject. Many of them are separately listed in this bibliography.

SMITH, JOSEPH RUSSELL. **Influence of the Great War upon Shipping.** New York:
 Oxford, 1919, 357 p.
 The author gives detailed treatment especially of rates, insurance, government aid and
 control, and shipbuilding. A volume published by the Carnegie Endowment.

SURFACE, FRANK MACY. **The Grain Trade during the World War.** New York: Macmillan, 1928, 707 p.
 An exhaustive treatment of the work of the Food Administration Grain Corporation
 during the war, with valuable statistics on this phase of the food situation.

WRISBERG, ERNST VON, FOST, HANS and others. **Die Organisationen der Kriegführung.**
 Leipzig: Finking, 1927, 3 v.
 An important contribution to the study of supply, organization of education for the
 armies, etc.

ZIESE, MAXIM and ZIESE-BERINGER, HERMANN. **Generäle, Händler und Soldaten.**
 Berlin: Frundsberg Verlag, 1930, 261 p.
 These German authors get considerable satisfaction from exposing the unsavory trade
 relations which existed between England on the one hand and Germany and the
 neutrals on the other in spite of the war.

IV. THE PEACE NEGOTIATIONS

PRELIMINARY DISCUSSIONS; ARMISTICE NEGOTIATIONS

See also (Central Europe) Collapse of the Hapsburg Empire, p. 301.

DEMBLIN, AUGUST. **Czernin und die Sixtus-Affäre.** Munich: Drei Masken, 1920, 101 p.
 A defense of Czernin by one of his close collaborators.

ERDÖDY, TAMÁS, GRAF VON. **Memoiren.** Vienna: Amalthea, 1931, 312 p.
 A volume throwing light on the Austrian negotiations for a separate peace.

FESTER, RICHARD. **Die Politik Kaiser Karls und der Wendepunkt des Weltkrieges.**
Munich: Lehmann, 1925, 310 p.
A careful historical study of the stormy reign of the last Hapsburg, with special emphasis on the famous peace negotiations carried on through Prince Sixtus of Bourbon.

MORDACQ, JEAN JULES HENRI. **Pouvait-On Signer l'Armistice à Berlin?** Paris:
Grasset, 1930, 239 p.
The chief of Clemenceau's military cabinet tells of the projected offensive in Lorraine in 1918, shelved because of the armistice. He takes the view that the armistice terms made the acceptance of any peace terms by the Germans inevitable. There was therefore no need for going to Berlin.

MORDACQ, JEAN JULES HENRI. **La Vérité sur l'Armistice.** Paris: Tallandier, 1929,
125 p.
A detailed study of the events from November 8 to 11, 1918, by the chief of Clemenceau's military cabinet.

SCOTT, JAMES BROWN. **Official Statements of War Aims and Peace Proposals,
December 1916 to November 1918.** Washington: Carnegie Endowment, 1921, 515 p.
An exhaustive compilation, of use for reference.

SCOTT, JAMES BROWN, *ed*. **Preliminary History of the Armistice.** New York: Oxford
University Press, 1924, 163 p.
Contains a translation of German documents of the pre-armistice and armistice periods. An important collection.

SEMENNIKOV, VLADIMIR PETROVICH. **Politika Romanovykh nakanune Revoliutsii.**
Moscow: Gosizdat, 1926, 246 p.
A study of Russian foreign policy on the eve of the Revolution, with special reference to negotiations with Germany. Based on new documentary material.

SEMENNIKOV, VLADIMIR PETROVICH. **Romanovy i Germanskie Vliianiia.** Leningrad:
Krasnaia Gazeta, 1929, 152 p.
A documented study of the relations between the Russian Court and the German Government during the war and the efforts to arrange a separate peace.

SIXTE, PRINCE OF BOURBON-PARMA. **Austria's Peace Offer, 1916-1917.** Edited by E. DE
MANTEYER. London: Constable, 1921, 360 p.
An account of the Prince's negotiations on behalf of France with his brother-in-law, the Emperor Charles. An essential part of the history of Austrian efforts to make peace.

WERKMANN VON HOHENSALZBURG, KARL MARTIN, FREIHERR. **Deutschland als Verbün-
deter.** Berlin: Verlag für Kulturpolitik, 1931, 350 p.
This volume adds to and corrects our knowledge of the policy of the Emperor Charles, and throws some new light on the question of separate peace negotiations.

THE PEACE CONFERENCE AND THE PEACE TREATIES

*See also (League of Nations) Theory and Origins, p. 45; also (World War) Biographies of
Wartime Statesmen and Diplomats, p. 101.*

BAKER, RAY STANNARD. **What Wilson Did at Paris.** New York: Doubleday, 1919, 113 p.
Practically an official statement of President Wilson's views, and a vindication of his policies.

BAKER, RAY STANNARD. **Woodrow Wilson and the World Settlement.** New York:
Doubleday, 1922, 3 v.

The most complete account of the peace negotiations yet published in any language. While sympathetic with Mr. Wilson's policies, the work is primarily expository. The manuscript and the *New York Times* articles have been edited by technically equipped scholars prior to reprinting in this edition. The third volume contains a very complete collection of documentary material.

BARTHOU, LOUIS. **Le Traité de Paix.** Paris: Fasquelle, 1919, 249 p.
An analysis of the peace terms by a French statesman.

BARUCH, BERNARD MANNES. **The Making of the Reparation and Economic Sections of the Treaty.** New York: Harper, 1920, 352 p.
An important contribution, by one of the American advisers.

BEER, GEORGE LOUIS. **African Questions at the Paris Peace Conference.** New York: Macmillan, 1923, 628 p.
A series of papers prepared for "The Inquiry" by the late Professor G. L. Beer, the highest authority in America on colonial questions. His views reflect the hostility to German colonial methods prevalent in 1919.

BÉRARD, VICTOR. **La Paix Française. Les Principes de la Paix.** Paris: Colin, 1919.
An able exposition of the French viewpoint by one of the keenest French political writers.

BOURGEOIS, LÉON. **Le Traité de Paix de Versailles.** Paris: Alcan, 1919, 328 p.
An analysis of the peace settlements by a French exponent of the League idea who regards the treaties merely as a beginning toward peace. The volume contains a number of Bourgeois' speeches.

BRIGGS, MITCHELL PIRIE. **George P. Herron and the European Settlement.** Stanford: Stanford University Press, 1932, 178 p.
This study of the activities of one of President Wilson's agents in Europe is based upon unpublished papers and constitutes an interesting addition to the history of World War diplomacy.

DILLON, EMILE JOSEPH. **The Inside Story of the Peace Conference.** New York: Harper, 1920, 512 p.
Violent criticism of the work of the Conference, and especially of the Big Three, by a well-known British correspondent and critic of international affairs.

HANOTAUX, GABRIEL. **Le Traité de Versailles.** Paris: Plon, 1919, 366 p.
A collection of writings, some previously unpublished, written by an eminent French historian on various aspects of the settlement.

HARRIS, HENRY WILSON. **Peace in the Making.** London: Swarthmore Press, 1919, 246 p.
By the special correspondent of the *Daily News*. Well-balanced and well-informed.

HASKINS, CHARLES HOMER and LORD, ROBERT HOWARD. **Some Problems of the Peace Conference.** Cambridge: Harvard University Press, 1920, 307 p.
The authors deal chiefly with territorial and boundary problems. Their volume is still the best exposition of certain problems confronting the Conference as seen by American historical experts.

HOFMANNSTHAL, EMIL VON. **Der Deutsche und Oesterreichische Friedensvertrag.** Vienna: Strache, 1920, 442 p.
A guide to the Treaties of Versailles and St. Germain.

HOUSE, EDWARD MANDELL and SEYMOUR, CHARLES, *eds.* **What Really Happened at Paris.** New York: Scribner, 1921, 528 p.
A series of lectures by American plenipotentiaries and experts at the Conference. An illuminating and important book.

KLOTZ, LOUIS LUCIEN. **De la Guerre à la Paix.** Paris: Payot, 1924, 254 p.
Recollections of the Peace Conference, by a French Finance Minister, with some documents.

KOZICKI, STANISŁAW. **Sprawa Granic Polski.** Warsaw: Perzyński, Niklewicz, 1921, 177 p.
A good brief account of the drawing of the Polish frontiers, by the secretary-general of the Polish delegation.

KUTRZEBA, STANISŁAW. **Kongres, Traktat i Polska.** Warsaw: Gebethner and Wolff, 1919, 198 p.
The story of the Peace Conference, with special reference to the organization of the Polish delegation, by a professor who acted as expert on territorial questions.

LANSING, ROBERT. **The Big Four and Others of the Peace Conference.** Boston: Houghton Mifflin, 1921, 212 p.
The former Secretary of State and member of the American delegation describes the leading personalities.

LANSING, ROBERT. **The Peace Negotiations, a Personal Narrative.** Boston: Houghton Mifflin, 1921, 328 p.
The apology of the former Secretary of State. One of the important books from the American side, to be read with Baker's "Woodrow Wilson and the World Settlement."

LAPRADELLE, ALBERT GEOUFFRE DE, *ed.* **La Documentation Internationale. La Paix de Versailles.** Paris: Éditions Internationales, 1931- .
An important collection of minutes of peace conference commissions together with other documents. The work is expected to be completed in twelve volumes. Thus far the minutes of the following commissions have been published: League of Nations; Responsibility of the Authors of the War and Sanctions; Reparations; International Régime of Ports, Waterways and Railroads; New States.

LIPPMANN, WALTER. **The Political Scene: An Essay on the Victory of 1918.** New York: Holt, 1919, 124 p.
Largely a reprint of editorial articles in the *New Republic* by one of the most discerning American writers on international affairs.

MARIN, LOUIS. **Le Traité de Paix.** Paris: Floury, 1920.
A thorough-going nationalist commentary on the Treaty.

MERMEIX, *pseud.* (GABRIEL TERRAIL). **Les Négociations Secrètes et les Quatres Armistices, 1914-1919.** Paris: Ollendorff, 1921, 355 p.
A defense of Clemenceau, containing valuable correspondence of the Supreme War Council, the Council of Ten and the Council of Four.

MILLER, DAVID HUNTER. **My Diary at the Conference of Paris.** Privately printed, 1928, 20 v.
An immense and exceedingly valuable collection of documentary material, by a legal adviser of the American delegation. The forty sets printed have been distributed among the important libraries of America and Europe.

NOWAK, KARL FRIEDRICH. **Versailles.** New York: Payson and Clarke, 1929, 287 p.
A counterblast to the Wilsonian stories of the Conference. Based upon information from the German delegation, it adds materially to our knowledge of the other side of the peace negotiations, though revealing at points an absence of familiarity with American political and constitutional facts.

Peace Handbooks. Issued by the Historical Section of the Foreign Office. Edited by SIR G. W. PROTHERO. London: H. M. Stationery Office, 1920, 161 nos. in 25 v.

These are the competent surveys prepared for the use of the British peace delegation. They are still of value for the ethnic, geographical and other statistical information which they contain, and also as a guide to understanding how world problems confronted statesmen in 1919.

SCHIFF, VICTOR. **The Germans at Versailles.** London: Williams and Norgate, 1930, 208 p.
The English translation of an interesting account of the German deputation and its activities, by the official press representative. There are chapters by Landsberg and Müller on the cabinet meeting which decided upon signature.

SCHÜCKING, WALTHER, *ed.* **Kommentar zum Friedens-Vertrage.** Berlin: Engelmann, 1920-1922, 5 v.
The standard German analysis and critique of the Treaty of Versailles.

SCOTT, ARTHUR PEARSON. **Introduction to the Peace Treaties.** Chicago: University of Chicago Press, 1920, 292 p.
A good guide, reviewing the negotiations and analyzing the terms.

STOSCH, ALBRECHT VON. **Die Kriegsbeschuldigtenfrage.** Hannover: Letsch, 1924, 261 p.
A detailed study of the Allied demands for the surrender of those accused of misdeeds during the war.

TARDIEU, ANDRÉ. **The Truth about the Treaty.** Indianapolis: Bobbs, 1921, 473 p.
An able and spirited defense of Clemenceau's policy, by one of his closest collaborators. An important contribution. The French edition, "La Paix" (Paris, 1921), differs materially from the English.

TEMPERLEY, HAROLD WILLIAM VAZIELLE, *ed.* **A History of the Peace Conference of Paris.** London: Frowde, 1920-24, 6 v.
An indispensable work written by English and American experts and published under the auspices of the Royal Institute of International Affairs. It is still the standard account of the Conference, how it was organized, and how it carried out its duties.

THOMSON, CHRISTOPHER BIRDWOOD THOMSON, BARON. **Old Europe's Suicide.** New York: Seltzer, 1922, 192 p.
A well-written work on secret diplomacy and the Paris settlement. The author predicts a general uprising against Europe's present régime, which he considers reactionary and reprehensible.

CRITICISM AND PROPOSALS FOR REVISION

See also (International Finance) Reparations and War Debts, p. 25; also (World War) War Guilt, p. 90; also (Europe) Post-War History and Conditions, p. 221; also (Italy) South Tyrol Question, p. 289; also (Central Europe) The Anschluss Problem, p. 307, and Hungary, p. 308; also (Germany) Post-War Germany, p. 321, and The Question of Colonies, p. 336; also (Poland) The Corridor and Danzig, p. 354; etc.

ANGELL, SIR NORMAN. **The Peace Treaty and the Economic Chaos of Europe.** London: Swarthmore, 1919, 143 p.
An able criticism of the economic clauses.

BASS, JOHN FOSTER. **The Peace Tangle.** New York: Macmillan, 1920, 345 p.
A critical survey of the settlements, both territorial and economic.

BITTER, FRIEDRICH and ZELLE, ARNOLD. **Die Krankheit Europas.** Freiburg: Kampmann, 1932, 316 p.
A restatement of the arguments for the revision of the treaties.

CIMBALI, EDUARDO. **La Guerra degli Stati dell'Intesa.** Catania: Giannotta, 1931, 107 p.
The Fourteen Points as a possible basis for the revision of the mandates and of the peace treaties in general.

EBRAY, ALCIDE. **A Frenchman Looks at the Peace.** New York: Knopf, 1927, 281 p.
The English translation of a much-discussed French indictment of the peace treaty and the post-war diplomacy. The author is a confirmed revisionist.

FRANCIS, FRANCIS. **Our Ruling Class.** London: Humphreys, 1923, 289 p.
An arraignment of the Treaty of Versailles and of democratic trends in contemporary Europe from the standpoint of a "bitter-ender" and believer in autocratic ideals.

JUGE, LÉONCE. **Notre Abdication Politique. Essai d'Introduction à l'Étude des Origines de l'Europe Nouvelle.** Paris: Bossard, 1920, 236 p.
A criticism of the peace settlements because of their inadequacy for French needs.

KEYNES, JOHN MAYNARD. **The Economic Consequences of the Peace.** New York: Harcourt, 1920, 298 p.
Probably the best-known and most widely read indictment of the economic phases of the peace settlements. Written by a prominent English economist and controversialist. Still of much interest.

LEMERY, H. **De la Guerre Totale à la Paix Mutilée.** Paris: Alcan, 1930, 368 p.
A lament for the lost fruits of victory.

LÉVY, RAPHAEL GEORGES. **La Juste Paix, ou, La Vérité sur le Traité de Versailles.** Paris: Plon, 1920, 243 p.
A warm rejoinder to Keynes' "Economic Consequences of the Peace," followed by an analysis of the economic clauses of the Treaty and of German capacity to pay. Parts of this volume have appeared in English: "The Peace of Justice" (New York: Doran, 1921, 96 p.).

LUKÁCS, GÉZA. **Die Revision der Friedensverträge.** Berlin: Stilke, 1928, 119 p.
A Hungarian statesman attempts to show the impracticability of the treaties, with special reference to the minorities, the war guilt clause and the social, economic and moral results of existing settlements.

MAITROT, CHARLES ARTHUR ÉDOUARD XAVIER. **La Paix qu'il Faut à la France.** Paris: Berger-Levrault, 1919, 144 p.
A demand not only for reparations, but for adequate guarantees and punishment, by a French general.

NITTI, FRANCESCO SAVERIO. **The Wreck of Europe.** Indianapolis: Bobbs-Merrill, 1922, 294 p.
The American édition of the former Italian Prime Minister's attack on the peace settlement which, he thinks, placed cultured German peoples on a plane of mere equality with what he considers inferior barbarians such as Poles, Czechs and Serbians.

PERREAU, JOSEPH. **Victoire Chère et Paix de Dupes.** Paris: Catin, 1921-1923, 2 v.
Representative of the current dissatisfaction of French military circles with a peace and no security.

RADEK, KARL. **Die Liquidation des Versailler Friedens.** Moscow: Verlag der Kommunistischen Internationale, 1922, 72 p.
A noted Bolshevik journalist argues brilliantly that Russia can wait while the Peace of Versailles is torn up and a new grouping of powers is constructed.

ROUX, GEORGES. **Réviser les Traités?** Paris: Éditions de la Revue Plans, 1931, 186 p.
In the interests of an "organization of peace" the author reëxamines the treaty settlements, stresses the harshness of the terms imposed on the vanquished and makes suggestions for remedial steps.

SEMBAT, MARCEL ÉTIENNE. **Defeated Victory.** London: Labour Publishing Company, 1925, 128 p.
A stimulating essay by a prominent French socialist.

SZÁDECKY, LAJOS. **Revision of the Peace.** Budapest: Hornyánszky, 1926, 132 p.
A collection of utterances, by foreign statesmen and writers, condemning the Treaty of Trianon as an injustice to Hungary.

ZIMMERN, ALFRED ECKHARD. **Europe in Convalescence.** New York: Putnam, 1922, 237 p.
Stimulating critical essays embodying a severe indictment of British policy, especially in the making of the peace.

THIRD PART:
THE WORLD

GENERAL POST-WAR CONDITIONS

See also (General International Relations) General Treatises, p. 1, and Civilizations and Race Conflicts, p. 4; etc.

BOWMAN, ISAIAH. **The New World.** New York: World Book Company, 1928, 803 p.
The fourth edition, entirely revised, of an excellent handbook by a leading American geographer. A comprehensive and useful work of reference.

BRASOL, BORIS LEO. **The World at the Cross-Roads.** Boston: Small, 1921, 409 p.
The author deals largely with the Russian overturn and the dangers of world revolution. Rather wordy and prejudiced.

BURNS, CECIL DELISLE. **1918-1928. A Short History of the World.** New York: Payson and Clarke, 1928, 473 p.
A useful short survey text, touching economic and social as well as political events and problems. The viewpoint is that of the hopeful internationalist.

BUXTON, CHARLES RODEN and MRS. DOROTHY FRANCES (JEBB). **The World after the War.** London: Allen and Unwin, 1920, 155 p.
Brief sketches of national problems and the "Balkanization" of Europe, questions of international organization, socialism, economic collapse, etc.

COOLIDGE, ARCHIBALD CARY. **Ten Years of War and Peace.** Cambridge: Harvard University Press, 1927, 280 p.
Essays by the late editor of *Foreign Affairs*, dealing dispassionately and in a spirit of broad understanding with some of the main problems of international relations.

DAVIS, JEROME. **Contemporary Social Movements.** New York: Century, 1930, 901 p.
A general text, treating of such subjects as socialism, communism, fascism, and the peace movement.

FERRERO, GUGLIELMO. **The Unity of the World.** New York: Boni, 1930, 196 p.
An essay surveying the world order; characterized by the author's usual human sympathy and vigor of expression.

GIBBONS, HERBERT ADAMS. **Wider Horizons.** New York: Century, 1930, 402 p.
The sub-title of this book is "The New Map of the World." In it a well-known American writer discusses chiefly non-political currents—cultural changes, labor, youth movements, church history, international organization, etc.

KJELLÉN, RUDOLF. **Die Grossmächte vor und nach dem Weltkriege.** Leipzig: Teubner, 1930, 348 p.
The twenty-second edition of a geopolitical guide of the post-war world. Easily one of the best works of its kind.

LE BON, GUSTAVE. **Le Déséquilibre du Monde.** Paris: Flammarion, 1924, 291 p.
An analysis of current world problems by the French social psychologist and publicist. The author dilates on such diverse subjects as security, race conflict, economic chaos.

ORTEGA Y GASSET, JOSÉ. **The Revolt of the Masses.** New York: Norton, 1932, 204 p.
A loosely-hung series of essays in which the professor of philosophy at the University
of Madrid dissects modern changes in popular institutions and behavior. A highly
suggestive work.

A Political Handbook of the World. Edited by WALTER H. MALLORY. New Haven:
Yale University Press, 1927-1930; New York: Harper, 1931 ff.
This handbook, published annually for the Council on Foreign Relations, gives all
the essential information of a political nature regarding every country of the world.
Most valuable is the enumeration of the various parties represented in the parliaments,
the programs of these parties, and the survey of the press in the various countries.

RIVIÈRE, PAUL LOUIS. **L'Après-Guerre.** Paris: Charles-Lavauzelle, 1930, 389 p.
One of the few systematic histories in French of the post-war world. The book is well
proportioned and well done, but gives a French coloring to many matters.

Statesman's Yearbook. New York: Macmillan. Annual.
The most useful single statistical reference work for political affairs.

TOYNBEE, ARNOLD JOSEPH. **Survey of International Affairs.** New York: Oxford University Press, 1925 ff.
The most extensive current review of world affairs, scholarly and brilliant in presentation, published by the Royal Institute of International Affairs. In 1925 appeared
the volume covering the years 1920-1923. Since then volumes have been published
for all years, including 1931.

TOYNBEE, ARNOLD JOSEPH. **The World after the Peace Conference.** New York:
Oxford University Press, 1925, 91 p.
A successful attempt by a highly competent scholar to compare the world of 1920
with that of 1914, and to look forward from the detailed problems of today to the
problems of the future.

WHEELER-BENNETT, JOHN WHEELER, *ed.* **Documents on International Affairs.** New
York: Oxford University Press, 1929 ff.
A useful collection of important documents and utterances on foreign affairs, published
annually as a supplementary volume to the "Survey of International Affairs."

WIDMAN, S. **Weltgeschichte der Neuesten Zeit, 1914-1930.** Münster: Theissing, 1930,
266 p.
A good German text for the war and post-war period. A remarkable amount of information in brief scope.

FOURTH PART:
NORTH AND SOUTH AMERICA

I. CANADA

See also (United States) Relations with Canada, p. 179; also (Great Britain) Imperial Relations, p. 231; also Polar Regions, p. 498.

AIKIN, JAMES ALEXANDER. **Economic Power for Canada.** New York: Macmillan, 1930, 265 p.
A competent study of the trade and industrial problems of Canada.

BORDEN, SIR ROBERT LAIRD. **Canada in the Commonwealth.** New York: Oxford University Press, 1929, 160 p.
In the first series of Rhodes Memorial Lectures the Canadian statesman surveys the evolution of the Dominion in its imperial setting. The book contains an extended discussion of the war and post-war situation.

BORDEN, SIR ROBERT LAIRD. **Canadian Constitutional Problems.** Toronto: University of Toronto Press, 1922, 163 p.
A series of lectures on the historical evolution of the Canadian constitution, by the former Prime Minister.

BOYD, JOHN. **The Future of Canada.** Montreal: Beauchemin, 1919, 106 p.
An address stressing and explaining the national ideals of Canadians, in reply to projects put forward by apostles of greater imperial solidarity.

BRACQ, JEAN CHARLEMAGNE. **The Evolution of French Canada.** New York: Macmillan, 1924, 476 p.
An historical and descriptive study, by a French Protestant writer. Sympathetic and understanding. One of the best books on the subject.

Canada: Natural Resources and Commerce. Ottawa: Natural Resources Intelligence Service, 1924, 221 p.
A comprehensive official compilation.

CORBETT, PERCY ELLWOOD and SMITH, HERBERT ARTHUR. **Canada and World Politics.** London: Faber and Gwyer, 1928, 244 p.
The authors deal primarily with the constitutional position of the Dominion and its place in the international relations of the empire, with special attention to Canada's relations to the League and her rôle at the Imperial Conference of 1926.

CORY, HARPER. **Modern Canada.** London: Heinemann, 1930, 289 p.
The best survey of post-war Canada and Canadian activities, based largely on official publications.

DAFOE, JOHN WESLEY. **Laurier: A Study in Canadian Politics.** Toronto: Allen, 1923, 182 p.
Four essays by an able Canadian writer. One deals with Laurier and Imperial relations.

DAVID, LAURENT OLIVIER. **Laurier, Sa Vie, Ses Œuvres.** Beauceville: L'Éclaireur, 1919, 268 p.
A general biographical sketch and appreciation, by one of Laurier's great admirers.

DE CELLES, ALFRED DUCLOS. **Laurier et Son Temps.** Montreal: Beauchemin, 1920, 228 p.
A well-informed biographical sketch.

FISK, HARVEY EDWARD. **The Dominion of Canada.** New York: Bankers Trust Company, 1920, 174 p.
A compact handbook covering history, government, financial system and particularly economic resources and activities.

GROULX, LIONEL. **Le Français au Canada.** Paris: Delagrave, 1932, 234 p.
A useful survey of the French elements in Canada, from the time of settlement to the present, by a leading French-Canadian writer.

HARRIS, W. ERIC. **Stand to Your Work.** Toronto: Musson, 1927, 269 p.
A survey of pressing Canadian problems, domestic, imperial and foreign.

KENNEDY, WILLIAM PAUL MCCLURE. **The Constitution of Canada.** New York: Oxford University Press, 1922, 519 p.
A scholarly documented historical study. The standard work on the subject.

KING, WILLIAM LYON MACKENZIE. **The Message of the Carillon.** New York: Macmillan, 1927, 284 p.
A collection of addresses, in which the former Prime Minister deals with domestic affairs, Canada's position in the Empire and with relations with the United States.

LAUT, AGNES CHRISTINA. **Canada at the Cross Roads.** Toronto: Macmillan, 1921, 279 p.
A discussion of Canada's economic problems, the reasons for the unsatisfactory development of her resources, and the ways and means of more extensive exploitation.

LÉVESQUE, ALBERT. **Les Canadiens Français et la Confédération Canadienne.** Montreal: Action Française, 1927, 145 p.
An evaluation of the influence and activity of the French element since the confederation.

McARTHUR, PETER. **Sir Wilfrid Laurier.** London: Dent, 1919, 182 p.
A well-written journalistic sketch of the eminent statesman.

McINNES, TOM. **Oriental Occupation of British Columbia.** Vancouver: Vancouver Sun, 1927, 170 p.
The writer raises the hue and cry and points out the danger threatening the whites. Restriction of immigration is not enough; the author demands restrictions on occupation, land holding, etc.

MACKAY, ROBERT ALEXANDER. **The Unreformed Senate of Canada.** New York: Oxford University Press, 1926, 284 p.
An exemplary study of Canadian constitutional history.

MARTIN, CHESTER. **Empire and Commonwealth.** New York: Oxford University Press, 1929, 408 p.
A scholarly study of the development of Canada from the old colonial system to membership in the Commonwealth, with particular emphasis on the evolution of responsible government.

MASSEY, VINCENT. **Good Neighbourhood.** New York: Macmillan, 1930, 362 p.
This volume of addresses by a former Canadian Minister to the United States contains several bearing on the inter-relationship of the English-speaking nations.

MORLEY, PERCIVAL FELLMAN. **Bridging the Chasm.** Toronto: Dent, 1919, 182 p.
A reconsideration of the difficulties between Ontario and Quebec, and a plea for a more tolerant attitude and policy.

MUNRO, WILLIAM BENNETT. **American Influences on Canadian Government.** Toronto: Macmillan, 1929, 153 p.
A series of lectures by an American authority, dealing not only with the constitution, but with the party system and municipal government.

NELSON, JOHN. **The Canadian Provinces; Their Problems and Policies.** Toronto: Musson, 1924, 219 p.
A survey of the chief domestic problems of Canada, province by province. The emphasis, naturally, is on economic questions.

PRESTON, W. T. R. **My Generation of Politics and Politicians.** Toronto: Rose, 1927, 462 p.
The reminiscences of a Liberal statesman, giving a vivid picture of Canadian public life from 1860 on.

RAY, JOSEPH EDWARD. **The New Canada.** London: Hutchinson, 1926, 156 p.
A competent, closely-packed, descriptive account, with stress on post-war changes, especially in the economic sphere.

RIDDELL, WILLIAM RENWICK. **The Canadian Constitution in Form and in Fact.** New York: Columbia University Press, 1923, 77 p.
Lectures delivered at Columbia University by a prominent Canadian jurist; the author stresses the fundamentally democratic working of the monarchical constitution.

SKELTON, OSCAR DOUGLAS. **The Life and Letters of Sir Wilfrid Laurier.** New York: Century, 1922, 2 v.
The authorized biography, based upon the Laurier papers.

SMALLWOOD, JOSEPH ROBERTS. **The New Newfoundland.** New York: Macmillan, 1931, 276 p.
A popular account of its recent progress and economic transformation.

SMITH, WILLIAM GEORGE. **A Study in Canadian Immigration.** Toronto: Ryerson, 1920, 406 p.
The best general survey of the history of Canadian immigration and the problems to which immigration has given rise.

STOWELL, OLIVER. **If I Were King of Canada.** Toronto: Dent, 1931, 173 p.
A lively and interesting program for the solution of Canada's economic and cultural problems.

VATTIER, GEORGES. **Essai sur la Mentalité Canadienne Française.** Paris: Champion, 1928, 381 p.
A heavily documented dissertation, and an interesting study in national psychology.

WALLACE, WILLIAM STEWART. **The Growth of Canadian National Feeling.** Toronto: Macmillan, 1927, 85 p.
A well-written essay, tracing the effect of the constitutional development on the growth of a national consciousness.

WARD, N. LASCELLES. **Oriental Missions in British Columbia.** Westminster: Society for the Propagation of the Gospel, 1925, 128 p.
This volume, by the superintendent of Chinese missions in British Columbia, gives a good picture of conditions among the immigrants.

WITTKE, CARL. **A History of Canada.** New York: Crofts, 1931, 439 p.
An excellent general text on Canadian history, in which the political, diplomatic and economic problems are all adequately treated.

II. UNITED STATES

GENERAL TREATISES

See also (World War: Military Efforts of Participants) United States, p. 146.

ADAMS, JAMES TRUSLOW. **The Epic of America.** Boston: Little, Brown, 1931, 433 p.
One of the most wide-read general surveys of American development. Well-written, critical and somewhat deeply colored by disillusionment.

ARAQUISTAIN, LUIS. **El Peligro Yanqui.** Madrid: Publicaciones España, 1921, 204 p.
Observations made in the United States in the autumn of 1919 by a leading Spanish liberal writer, later Spanish Ambassador in Berlin. The writer deals largely with economic and social problems, the press, the attitude towards Spain, and especially with America's international position.

ARON, ROBERT and DANDIEU, ARNAUD. **Le Cancer Américain.** Paris: Rieder, 1931, 240 p.
The authors regard the Yankee mentality, with all it implies, as the root factor of the world crisis.

BACON, GASPAR GRISWOLD. **The Constitution of the United States.** Cambridge: Harvard University Press, 1928, 201 p.
A series of lectures on some of the fundamental aspects of the American constitutional system.

BAKER, NEWTON DIEHL. **Progress and the Constitution.** New York: Scribner, 1925, 94 p.
Three lectures by the former Secretary of War, one of them dealing with the Constitution and Foreign Relations.

BATES, ERNEST SUTHERLAND. **This Land of Liberty.** New York: Harper, 1930, 383 p.
A collection of material to show how far the attack on personal liberty has gone in the United States and how little is left of the old ideal.

BEARD, CHARLES AUSTIN. **The Navy: Defense or Portent?** New York: Harper, 1932, 198 p.
An effective exposure of conditions and policies.

BEARD, CHARLES AUSTIN and MRS. MARY (RITTER). **The Rise of American Civilization.** New York: Macmillan, 1927, 2 v.
The best general history of the United States in its social and cultural aspects.

BEARD, CHARLES AUSTIN and WILLIAM. **The American Leviathan.** New York: Macmillan, 1930, 824 p.
This stimulating analysis of our governmental system contains interesting chapters on the conduct of foreign policy, imperial problems and the military system.

BECK, JAMES MONTGOMERY. **The Constitution of the United States.** New York: Doran, 1924, 352 p.
Written by a former Solicitor-General; an historical and analytical study.

BELLOC, HILAIRE. **The Contrast.** London: Arrowsmith, 1923, 302 p.
A brilliant English Catholic's impressions of the United States, its social order, political system, religious outlook, etc.

BENT, SILAS. **Machine Made Man.** New York: Farrar and Rinehart, 1930, 341 p.
An amusing and at the same time saddening critique of the American scene and the exaggerations of the American machine civilization.

BIRKENHEAD, FREDERICK EDWIN SMITH, EARL OF. **America Revisited.** New York: Cassell, 1924, 216 p.
A collection of addresses delivered in the United States and Canada.

BONN, MORITZ JULIUS. **Geld und Geist.** Berlin: Fischer, 1927, 190 p.
A noteworthy survey of American tendencies and problems, by a German well-acquainted with the country.

BONN, MORITZ JULIUS. **Prosperity; Myth and Reality in American Economic Life.** London: Hopkinson, 1931, 188 p.
A German economist reviews the post-war development of the United States and the economic and psychological effects of the depression.

BRAUNSCHVIG, MARCEL. **La Vie Américaine et Ses Leçons.** Paris: Colin, 1931, 384 p.
A serious attempt to interpret American life—literary and artistic as well as economic—to the French people.

CHINARD, GILBERT. **La Doctrine de l'Américanisme.** Paris: Hachette, 1919, 90 p.
This brilliant survey of the historical evolution of the American tradition contains an interesting discussion of American nationalism and internationalism.

CIARLANTINI, FRANCO. **Incontro col Nord America.** Milan: Alpes, 1929, 298 p.
The United States as it appears to an intelligent observer from across the Atlantic. A stimulating volume of travel impressions.

COLYER, W. T. **Americanism, a World Menace.** London: Labour Publishing Company, 1922, 178 p.
A severe indictment of American chauvinism and present political and economic systems in the United States.

DENISON, JOHN HOPKINS. **Emotional Currents in American History.** New York: Scribner, 1932, 420 p.
An interesting attempt to show how ideas and emotions have swept the American people along in certain channels.

DUHAMEL, GEORGES. **America: The Menace.** Boston: Houghton Mifflin, 1931, 230 p.
An exceptionally frank and thought-provoking exposure of the American mentality and social order—somewhat overdrawn at times, but always stimulating.

FAULKNER, HAROLD UNDERWOOD. **American Economic History.** New York: Harper, 1924, 721 p.
A reliable general text.

FAŸ, BERNARD and CLAFLIN, AVERY. **The American Experiment.** New York: Harcourt, 1929, 264 p.
One of the French writers who knows the United States best joins in surveying its historical development, present institutions, and outlook, social and international.

FEILER, ARTHUR. **Amerika-Europa.** Frankfurt: Frankfurter Societäts-Druckerei, 1926, 338 p.
An exceptionally keen study of American conditions as compared with European, by the editor of the *Frankfurter Zeitung*.

GAUBA, KANHAYA LAL. **Uncle Sham.** Lahore: Times Publishing Company, 1929, 213 p.
An Indian reply to Miss Mayo's "Mother India," by an Indian journalist. Relying on the books of Judge Lindsey and other American writers he draws a lurid and what will seem to Americans a grotesque picture of American sexual degeneracy.

GIBBS, SIR PHILIP. **People of Destiny.** New York: Harper, 1920, 198 p.
An estimate of America and Americans by a well-known English journalist. Among other things he discusses the nation's new place in the world.

GRATTAN, CLINTON HARTLEY. **Why We Fought.** New York: Vanguard, 1929, 468 p.
Though somewhat biassed, this is a substantial book, a useful antidote to the wartime ideology and a contribution to the study of American intervention.

HAMMOND, JOHN HAYS and JENKS, JEREMIAH WHIPPLE. **Great American Issues.** New York: Scribner, 1921, 274 p.
A competent concise survey. Among the issues discussed are the tariff, foreign trade and exchange, and immigration.

HAUSER, HENRI. **L'Amérique Vivante.** Paris: Plon, 1923, 157 p.
These impressions of a French economist and historian turn chiefly on economic problems and the evolution of American public opinion on foreign affairs.

HOLCOMBE, ARTHUR NORMAN. **The Political Parties of To-day.** New York: Harper, 2nd ed., 1925, 427 p.
A good historical survey of the American party system, with extended discussion of the bases of national politics and the meaning of modern alignments.

HUDDLESTON, SISLEY. **What's Right with America.** Philadelphia: Lippincott, 1930, 251 p.
A noted English journalist surveys the American scene from the political, social and cultural standpoints, in an amiable and sympathetic volume.

Initiation à la Vie aux États-Unis. Paris: Delagrave, 1931, 313 p.
A valuable coöperative survey of American life published under the auspices of the Comité France-Amérique. It is written by a number of well-known French scholars, including Siegfried, Viallate, Cestre, Roz and others, and is intended to give the Frenchman going to the United States all the information he needs in order to observe intelligently and understand the life about him. The book is extraordinarily well done, and is not over-weighted in the direction of politics. There are excellent chapters on artistic and social life, as well as on all economic aspects of American civilization.

KENT, FRANK RICHARDSON. **The Democratic Party.** New York: Century, 1928, 568 p.
An interesting journalistic survey of Democratic Party history to 1928, with considerable emphasis on the later period.

LEHMAN, LUCIEN. **The American Illusion.** New York: Century, 1931, 263 p.
The translation of a disillusioning French study. The author discusses, among other problems, the political system, the negro question, the press, etc.

LOBO, HELIO. **A Passo de Gigante.** Rio de Janeiro: Imprensa Nacional, 1925, 380 p.
A Brazilian journalist, reviewing the outstanding problems of the United States, pays special attention to disarmament, the Pan-American Conference, and the election of 1924.

LYON, LAURANCE. **Where Freedom Falters.** New York: Scribner, 1927, 391 p.
Discursive and sensational essays by the author of "The Pomp of Power." Among other topics, he treats of American foreign policy, the United States and Canada, Colonel House, the United States as creditor and debtor, etc.

McBAIN, HOWARD LEE. **The Living Constitution.** New York: Workers Education Bureau, 1927, 284 p.
An excellent popular account of the American system and its implications, by a leading authority.

McDOUGALL, WILLIAM. **The Indestructible Union.** Boston: Little, Brown, 1925, 249 p.
The psychological approach to problems of American nationhood, by a well-known psychologist and sociologist.

McDOUGALL, WILLIAM. **Is America Safe for Democracy?** New York: Scribner, 1921, 218 p.
Lowell Lectures, in which an English psychologist analyzes the American mentality.

MADARIAGA, SALVADOR DE. **I. Americans.** New York: Oxford University Press, 1931, 148 p.
Really a collection of essays and addresses dealing with international coöperation. Like all the author's writings they are full of discernment and originality.

MAGRUDER, THOMAS PICKETT. **The United States Navy.** Philadelphia: Dorrance, 1928, 179 p.
A timely exposition of Admiral Magruder's well-known views, with a general survey of the present state of the navy.

MERRIAM, CHARLES EDWARD. **American Political Ideas.** New York: Macmillan, 1926, 481 p.

The best general account of the development of American political theory since the Civil War.

MUIR, RAMSAY. **America the Golden.** London: Williams and Norgate, 1927, 151 p.
An English Liberal's impressions of America. The emphasis on American business methods, the wide distribution of ownership in industrials, etc., is quite conventional.

MYERS, WILLIAM STARR. **The Republican Party.** New York: Century, 1928, 487 p.
A scholarly historical account.

NORTON, THOMAS JAMES. **The Constitution of the United States.** Boston: Little, Brown, 1922, 298 p.
An introductory account of the Constitution and the amendments.

ODEGARD, PETER H. **The American Public Mind.** New York: Columbia University Press, 1930, 317 p.
An able sociological study of American behavior. The author treats of the family, church and school, of political parties, propaganda, censorship, etc.

ORSINI RATTO, MARIO. **Gli Stati Uniti di Domani.** Milan: Treves, 1930, 232 p.
Travel impressions, bringing in stimulating discussions of the United States and world peace, dollar diplomacy, nationalism, relations with Latin America, and the part of Italians in American life.

PAGE, KIRBY, *ed.* **Recent Gains in American Civilization.** New York: Harcourt, 1928, 357 p.
A collection of essays by American radicals and critics. There are chapters by Beard on government, Thomas on peace, Johnson on race relations, Villard on the press, and Dewey on American civilization. A stimulating if frankly one-sided volume.

PAULLIN, CHARLES O. **Atlas of the Historical Geography of the United States.** New York: American Geographical Society, 1932, 145 p., 166 plates.
A notable piece of work, overshadowing anything of the kind heretofore attempted. There are 166 beautiful plates and 145 pages of descriptive text. Among the headings are: The Natural Environment; Population; Boundaries; Political Parties and Opinion; Industries and Transportation; Foreign Commerce; Distribution of Wealth; Military History; and Possessions and Territorial Claims. As may be seen, both economic and political aspects are given full treatment.

PHELPS, PHELPS. **Our Defenses Within and Without.** New York: Powers, 1932, 320 p.
A handy survey of the various branches of American defense.

PIERCE, BESSIE LOUISE. **Civic Attitudes in American School Textbooks.** Chicago: Chicago University Press, 1930, 297 p.
This capable analysis of American school books deals in large measure with the formation of the American attitude towards foreign countries, and is therefore of much interest to students of international affairs.

PIERSON, CHARLES WHEELER. **Our Changing Constitution.** New York: Doubleday, 1922, 181 p.
A series of essays on the gradual fading out of the powers of the individual states, and the effects of this change.

PUAUX, RENÉ. **Découverte des Américains.** Paris: Fasquelle, 1930, 199 p.
This appreciation of the American scene, by a French journalist, was awarded a prize as the best French work of the year on the United States.

ROBINSON, EDGAR EUGENE. **The Evolution of American Political Parties.** New York: Harcourt, 1924, 382 p.
A reliable general survey, with considerable emphasis on party formation.

ROMIER, LUCIEN. **Qui Sera le Maître? Europe ou Amérique?** Paris: Hachette, 1927, 243 p.

One of the best of many analyses of the American mentality and the American scene. The author studies American mass civilization and stresses the fact that the ultimate decision between Europe and America will depend, not on economic superiority, but on spiritual forces.

Roz, Firmin. **L'Amérique Nouvelle.** Paris: Flammarion, 1923, 282 p.
A lively and well-informed account of American policy and opinion in the war and post-war years, with special reference to international relations.

Roz, Firmin. **Les États-Unis d'Amérique.** Paris: Alcan, 1927, 280 p.
A general economic and political survey, of the type recently become popular.

Siegfried, André. **America Comes of Age.** New York: Harcourt, 1927, 353 p.
Easily one of the most brilliant and penetrating books written on America in recent years, emphasizing the fundamental character of the racio-religious problem.

Slosson, Preston William. **The Great Crusade and After, 1914-1928.** New York: Macmillan, 1930, 486 p.
The concluding volume of the admirable "History of American Life" series.

Spender, Harold. **A Briton in America.** London: Heinemann, 1921, 323 p.
Travel impressions of an English author and journalist. The book contains interesting discussions of such matters as American naval policy, relations with Japan, attitude on the Irish question, and the color problem.

Spender, John Alfred. **The America of To-day.** London: Benn, 1928, 269 p.
The larger part of this volume, by a well-known British journalist, deals with American institutions and problems and with American foreign and naval policy.

Stearns, Harold Edmund, *ed.* **Civilization in the United States.** New York: Harcourt, 1922, 577 p.
A collection of essays by thirty American writers and critics, surveying almost all important aspects of American political and social life.

Stoddard, Lothrop. **Reforging America.** New York: Scribner, 1927, 389 p.
A rather lurid picture of present day America, with a suggested solution for our race problem.

Tessan, François de. **Le Président Hoover et la Politique Américaine.** Paris: Baudinière, 1931.
A fair and friendly estimate of American life and policies.

Thomas, Louis. **Les États-Unis Inconnus.** Paris: Perrin, 1920, 288 p.
These observations and reflections of a French visitor contain much that is of interest on American relations to France, on America's financial position, foreign trade, attitude towards the League, etc.

Turner, John Kenneth. **Shall It Be Again?** New York: Huebsch, 1922, 448 p.
A striking challenge to conventional views regarding the motives of the United States in entering the World War. It ascribes American intervention chiefly to pressure from Wall Street.

Viallate, Achille. **Les États-Unis d'Amérique et le Conflit Européen.** Paris: Alcan, 1919.
A French study of America's entrance into the war, with emphasis on the question of world power.

BIOGRAPHIES, PAPERS AND ADDRESSES

See also (World War) Biographies of Wartime Statesmen and Diplomats, p. 101, and Military Memoirs and Biographies, p. 117, and Naval Memoirs, p. 140.

Archer, William. **The Peace-President.** New York: Holt, 1919, 123 p.
A biographical study and appreciation, by a man who puts Wilson on a par with

Washington and Lincoln and stresses his "wisdom of patience" as well as his "wisdom of courage."

BAKER, RAY STANNARD. **Woodrow Wilson. Life and Letters.** New York: Doubleday, 1927-1931, 4 v.
The first volumes of the authorized life, based on the voluminous unpublished correspondence. These volumes cover the story of Wilson's career to 1914.

BAKER, RAY STANNARD and DODD, WILLIAM EDWARD, *eds*. **The Public Papers of Woodrow Wilson.** New York: Harper, 1925-1927, 6 v.
The authorized edition.

BISHOP, JOSEPH BUCKLIN. **Theodore Roosevelt and His Time.** New York: Scribner, 1920, 2 v.
One of the best biographies of Roosevelt, not critical, but containing much valuable material.

BORAH, WILLIAM EDGAR. **American Problems.** New York: Duffield, 1924, 329 p.
A selection from the Senator's speeches, including those on immigration, the League, disarmament, militarism, Russia, etc.

CHAPPLE, JOE MITCHELL. **Life and Times of Warren G. Harding.** Boston: Chapple, 1924, 386 p.
An uncritical popular survey of his career.

COOLIDGE, CALVIN. **Autobiography.** New York: Cosmopolitan, 1929, 247 p.
First published serially in the magazines; hardly a great document.

COOLIDGE, HAROLD JEFFERSON and LORD, ROBERT HOWARD. **Archibald Cary Coolidge.** Boston: Houghton Mifflin, 1932, 368 p.
The life and letters of an American historian who played an influential rôle in international affairs as exchange professor at Paris and Berlin, head of the American mission in Central Europe during the Peace Conference, diplomatic member of the American Relief Commission in Russia in 1921-22, editor of *Foreign Affairs*, and adviser to many men in public office. An interesting and important addition to American biography.

DANIELS, JOSEPHUS. **The Life of Woodrow Wilson.** Chicago: Winston, 1924, 381 p.
Written by the Secretary of the Navy in the Wilson Cabinet, this biography does not pretend to be more than an intimate, warmly admiring study of a great leader.

DAUGHERTY, HARRY MICAJAH and DIXON, THOMAS. **The Inside Story of the Harding Tragedy.** New York: Churchill, 1932, 323 p.
Based on the papers of Harding's Attorney-General and designed to discredit and controvert a number of hostile writings.

DODD, WILLIAM EDWARD. **Woodrow Wilson and His Work.** New York: Doubleday, 1927, 454 p.
The new edition of a biographical study first published in 1920. One of the best informed and soundest of the sympathetic studies of the President.

GREEN, HORACE. **The Life of Calvin Coolidge.** New York: Duffield, 1924, 263 p.
The usual type of general, uncritical biography.

HAGEDORN, HERMANN. **Leonard Wood.** New York: Harper, 1931, 2 v.
A full-length biography, with many sidelights on General Wood's relations with Roosevelt and on his position during the World War.

HALÉVY, DANIEL. **President Wilson.** New York: Lane, 1919, 283 p.
The translation of a popular, uncritical French biography.

HOUSTON, DAVID FRANKLIN. **Eight Years with Wilson's Cabinet, 1913-1920.** New York: Doubleday, 1926, 2 v.
A valuable contribution to the history of the Wilson administration, by the former Secretary of the Treasury and of Agriculture.

HOWLAND, HEWITT HANSON. **Dwight Whitney Morrow.** New York: Century, 1930, 91 p.
The briefest kind of appreciative biographical sketch of the late Ambassador to Mexico.

HUNTLEY, THEODORE A. **The Life of John W. Davis.** New York: Duffield, 1924, 290 p.
A popular biographical sketch of the former Ambassador to England and Democratic candidate for the presidency, together with a selection of speeches.

JOHNSON, WILLIS FLETCHER. **George Harvey.** Boston: Houghton Mifflin, 1929, 446 p.
An over-enthusiastic but well-written biography of the American editor and Ambassador to England.

JOHNSON, WILLIS FLETCHER. **The Life of Warren G. Harding.** New York: Johnston, 1923, 288 p.
An illustrated biography of no great value.

KERNEY, JAMES. **The Political Education of Woodrow Wilson.** New York: Century, 1926, 524 p.
A revealing and unsentimental study of Wilson's political career, by the editor of the *Trenton Evening Times*.

KOETZSCHKE, RICHARD. **Thomas Woodrow Wilson.** Dresden: Jess, 1931, 274 p.
An impartial review of the career and work of Wilson, based upon the leading American sources.

LANE, MRS. ANNE (WINTERMUTE) and WALL, LOUISE HERRICK, *eds.* **The Letters of Franklin K. Lane.** Boston: Houghton Mifflin, 1922, 473 p.
The correspondence of the Secretary of the Interior in the Wilson Cabinet, important for the history of the war years.

LAWRENCE, DAVID. **The True Story of Woodrow Wilson.** New York: Doran, 1924, 368 p.
A study of the President from his Princeton days onward, by a newspaperman closely associated with him.

LEACH, PAUL R. **That Man Dawes.** Chicago: Reilly and Lee, 1930, 349 p.
A biographical sketch, by the political writer of the *Chicago Daily News*.

LIPPMANN, WALTER. **Men of Destiny.** New York: Macmillan, 1927, 244 p.
Discerning studies of leading American personalities, among them Smith, Coolidge, Bryan, Wilson, House and Borah.

The Mirrors of Washington. New York: Putnam, 1921, 256 p.
Amusing, clever and sometimes brutally frank studies of Harding, Wilson, Hughes, House, Hoover, Lodge, Root, Lansing and others.

PRINGLE, HENRY FOWLES. **Theodore Roosevelt.** New York: Harcourt, 1931, 637 p.
Based upon unpublished Roosevelt papers, this is perhaps the most important biography of the former President now available.

ROOSEVELT, THEODORE and LODGE, HENRY CABOT. **Selections from the Correspondence of Theodore Roosevelt and Henry Cabot Lodge.** New York: Scribner, 1925, 2 v.
An important source in studying American foreign policy.

ROOT, ELIHU. **Men and Policies.** Cambridge: Harvard University Press, 1924, 509 p.
Papers and addresses, many on international topics, before, during and after the war, by the former Secretary of State.

SLEMP, CAMPBELL BASCOM. **The Mind of the President.** New York: Doubleday, 1926, 357 p.
The opinions and policies of President Coolidge in domestic and foreign affairs, as deduced from his speeches by his secretary.

STIMSON, FREDERIC JESUP. **My United States.** New York: Scribner, 1931, 478 p.
An interesting volume of reminiscences and reflections on American life, together with an account of the author's ambassadorship to Argentina.

STRAUS, OSCAR SOLOMON. **Under Four Administrations.** Boston: Houghton Mifflin, 1922, 456 p.
The interesting memoirs of a public-spirited American, containing much valuable material on the political and diplomatic problems of Eastern Europe and Turkey.

SYNON, MARY. **McAdoo.** Indianapolis: Bobbs-Merrill, 1924, 355 p.
A general biography of Wilson's Secretary of the Treasury, carrying the story of his career to 1918.

UNDERWOOD, OSCAR WILDER. **Drifting Sands of Party Politics.** New York: Century, 1931, 411 p.
The reminiscences and reflections of the late Senator from Alabama. The volume contains interesting discussions of the tariff and international relations.

VILLARD, OSWALD GARRISON. **Prophets True and False.** New York: Knopf, 1928, 355 p.
The editor of *The Nation* evaluates the work of men like Smith, Hoover, Hughes, Borah, Dawes, Wilson, House, Bryan and Lansing.

WELLS, WELLS, *pseud.* **Wilson the Unknown.** New York: Scribner, 1931, 365 p.
A not very convincing attempt to solve the Wilsonian enigma.

WHITE, WILLIAM ALLEN. **Calvin Coolidge.** New York: Macmillan, 1925, 252 p.
A critical journalistic biography, as good as any available.

WHITE, WILLIAM ALLEN. **Woodrow Wilson.** Boston: Houghton Mifflin, 1924, 527 p.
Written by a well-known American newspaperman—an unemotional though appreciative study of the man and the problems he had to face.

FOREIGN POLICY

General

See also (League of Nations) Attitudes of Individual Powers, p. 51; also (Peace) Kellogg-Briand Pact, p. 79; also Polar Regions, p. 498.

ADAMS, RANDOLPH GREENFIELD. **A History of the Foreign Policy of the United States.** New York: Macmillan, 1924, 490 p.
A reliable documented text.

American Foreign Policy: Based upon Statements of Presidents and Secretaries of State of the United States and of Publicists of the American Republics. With an introduction by NICHOLAS MURRAY BUTLER. Washington: Carnegie Endowment for International Peace, 1920, 132 p.
A convenient collection of fundamental documents and declarations forming the basic principles of American foreign policy.

BELMONT, PERRY. **National Isolation an Illusion.** New York: Putnam, 1925, 631 p.
A reply to the arguments of isolationists. The approach is historical and topical.

BEMIS, SAMUEL FLAGG, *ed.* **The American Secretaries of State and Their Diplomacy.** New York: Knopf, 1927-1929, 10 v.
A series of biographical studies of all American Secretaries of State from Livingston to Hughes. Written by many American authorities, they form a good survey of the evolution of American foreign policy.

BLAKESLEE, GEORGE HUBBARD. **The Recent Foreign Policy of the United States.**
New York: Abingdon Press, 1925, 361 p.
Lectures on various aspects of American foreign policy by a competent scholar, Professor of International Relations at Clark University.

BULLARD, ARTHUR. **American Diplomacy in the Modern World.** Philadelphia: University of Pennsylvania Press, 1928, 133 p.
Three stimulating lectures by a well-known writer and correspondent, surveying the American position in regard to problems of peace and disarmament.

CARTER, JOHN. **Conquest; America's Painless Imperialism.** New York: Harcourt, 1928, 358 p.
A journalistic account of American imperialism and the methods of dollar diplomacy.

COLE, TAYLOR. **The Recognition Policy of the United States since 1901.** Baton Rouge: Louisiana State University, 1928, 104 p.
The author concludes that we have been consistent in recognizing governments or states that are stable and willing to fulfil their international obligations. A heavily documented, scholarly monograph.

DEALEY, JAMES QUAYLE. **Foreign Policies of the United States.** Boston: Ginn, 1926, 402 p.
The author stresses the fundamental and broader aspects.

FISH, CARL RUSSELL. **American Diplomacy.** New York: Holt, 4th ed., 1923, 551 p.
The latest revised edition of one of the best-known texts, now out-dated.

FLEMING, DENNA FRANK. **The Treaty Veto of the American Senate.** New York: Putnam, 1930, 334 p.
A thorough investigation of an important aspect of the conduct of American diplomacy. The author shows how great a factor the Senate's veto power has been, especially as an obstacle to American coöperation in world affairs.

GACHON, JEAN. **La Politique Étrangère des États-Unis.** Paris: Alcan, 1928, 252 p.
A brief review of American policies as seen from across the Atlantic, with much emphasis on American imperialism.

GARNER, JAMES WILFORD. **American Foreign Policies.** New York: New York University Press, 1928, 272 p.
Lectures by an American professor of international law, who once more explodes the idea of American isolation and stresses the American contribution to peace.

GHIRALDO, ALBERTO. **La Lucha contra el Imperialismo.** Madrid: Edición Historia Nueva, 1929, 214 p.
Another volume in the growing number of foreign attacks upon the imperialistic policies of the United States.

GIBBONS, HERBERT ADAMS. **America's Place in the World.** New York: Century, 1924, 227 p.
A breezy discussion of the more important phases of America's foreign policy.

HOWLAND, CHARLES PRENTICE, *ed.* **Survey of American Foreign Relations.** New Haven: Yale University Press, 1928-1931, 4 v.
A series of volumes published for the Council on Foreign Relations, forming an invaluable guide for the study of contemporary American policies. The first is devoted largely to a treatment of fundamental factors and principles, with sections on foreign policy, the United States as an economic power, relations with the League, reparations and debts, and arms limitation. The second deals with Caribbean affairs, with an additional section on immigration policies. The third covers Pacific problems, with

additional sections on arms limitation, post-war financial relations, and alien enemy property. The fourth is devoted mainly to Mexico, with a section entitled "World Order and Coördination," and one on the Bank for International Settlements.

HUGHES, CHARLES EVANS. **The Pathway of Peace.** New York: Harper, 1925, 338 p.
Addresses on foreign affairs delivered between 1920 and 1924 by the former Secretary of State.

JÄCKH, ERNST. **Amerika und Wir. Amerikanisch-Deutsches Ideenbündnis.** Stuttgart: Deutsche Verlagsanstalt, 1929, 139 p.
Six radio talks setting forth the continuity of American foreign policy, by the director of the Hochschule für Politik.

LATANÉ, JOHN HOLLADAY. **From Isolation to Leadership.** New York: Doubleday, rev. ed., 1922, 296 p.
A brilliant survey of the principal American policies, in their historical setting.

LATANÉ, JOHN HOLLADAY. **A History of American Foreign Policy.** New York: Doubleday, 1927, 725 p.
An advanced text, considered by many to be the best general survey of the evolution of American diplomacy.

LAY, TRACY HOLLINGSWORTH. **The Foreign Service of the United States.** New York: Prentice-Hall, 1925, 438 p.
The standard work on the subject, by a man with wide experience in consular posts.

LIPPMANN, WALTER and SCROGGS, WILLIAM OSCAR. **The United States in World Affairs, 1931.** New York: Harper, 1932, 390 p.
The first volume of a series published for the Council on Foreign Relations, correlating the main events in foreign policy during the year, and showing the way the current is moving. A thoughtful book, fundamental to any study of the international contacts of the United States.

MATHEWS, JOHN MABRY. **American Foreign Relations.** New York: Century, 1928, 713 p.
A general text, stressing the later period.

MATHEWS, JOHN MABRY. **The Conduct of American Foreign Relations.** New York: Century, 1922, 353 p.
A thorough, scholarly analysis of the legislative and administrative organs involved in our relations with other states.

MOORE, FREDERICK. **America's Naval Challenge.** New York: Macmillan, 1929, 166 p.
A survey of the Anglo-American naval problem, and of American opinion on naval armaments. The author discusses also the situation in the Pacific, and adduces evidence to disprove the arguments for a larger navy.

MOTHERWELL, HIRAM. **The Imperial Dollar.** New York: Brentano, 1929, 310 p.
A well-informed and readable study of American imperialism, viewed as the natural result of American growth and the post-war world situation.

MOWRER, PAUL SCOTT. **Our Foreign Affairs.** New York: Dutton, 1924, 348 p.
An appraisal of the problems and responsibilities involved in the position of the United States as a world power, by one of the most competent American foreign correspondents.

NEARING, SCOTT. **The American Empire.** New York: Rand School, 1921, 266 p.
A succinct historical survey of the evolution of American plutocracy and imperialism, by one of the ablest anti-imperialist writers, lecturer at the Rand School of Social Science.

NEARING, SCOTT and FREEMAN, JOSEPH. **Dollar Diplomacy.** New York: Huebsch, 1925, 353 p.
A well-informed and well-documented study of American economic interests and activities abroad. A book that should be read with more conventional accounts of American diplomacy.

OFFUTT, MILTON. **The Protection of Citizens Abroad by the Armed Forces of the United States.** Baltimore: Johns Hopkins Press, 1928, 170 p.
A doctoral dissertation, giving a well-documented review of cases from 1813 to 1927.

PAGE, KIRBY. **Dollars and World Peace.** New York: Doran, 1927, 214 p.
A well-known pacifist writer presents once more the dangers arising from nationalism, industrialism and imperialism, lays bare the shortcomings of our own policy, and calls for more constructive action in our colonial policy, our trade policy and questions arising from international debts.

REDFIELD, WILLIAM COX. **Dependent America.** Boston: Houghton Mifflin, 1926, 278 p.
An exposition of the economic bases of our foreign relations, aiming to demonstrate the absurdity of a policy of isolation.

SAVORD, RUTH, *comp.* **Directory of American Agencies Concerned with the Study of International Affairs.** New York: Council on Foreign Relations, 1931, 138 p.
A comprehensive and well-balanced handbook.

SEARS, LOUIS MARTIN. **A History of American Foreign Relations.** New York: Crowell, 1927, 648 p.
A good general survey of the international relations of the United States, conventional in presentation, but straightforward and generally up-to-date.

TANIN, M. **Amerika na Mirovoï Arene.** Moscow: Gosizdat, 1927, 216 p.
How Moscow pictures the United States as a world power.

TRELLES, CAMILO BARCIA. **La Política Exterior Norteamericana de la Postguerra.** Valladolid: Cuesta, 1924, 199 p.
An impartial exposition of American foreign policy since 1914 by an eminent Spanish international lawyer.

TRITONJ, ROMOLO. **La Politica Estera degli Stati Uniti.** Rome: Nuova Europa, 1932, 310 p.
This volume by the former Italian Consul-General in New York, while not particularly novel, is written with fairness and understanding. It gives the Italian public a well-balanced account of fundamental American policies, particularly as they operate in the Caribbean, Latin America and the Far East.

VANDENBERG, ARTHUR HENDRICK. **The Trail of a Tradition.** New York: Putnam, 1926, 428 p.
A plea for the continuance of a national policy as against internationalism.

VITETTI, LEONARDO. **La Politica del Presidente Harding.** Rome: Politica, 1921, 84 p.
A series of keen and well-informed reports on American foreign policy published in *Politica* on the eve of the Washington Conference. The author subsequently became an official in the Italian Foreign Office.

WRIGHT, QUINCY. **The Control of American Foreign Relations.** New York: Macmillan, 1922, 412 p.
A critical comparison of the powers and duties of governmental organs in foreign relations under international and constitutional law. A valuable supplement to Mathews' "The Conduct of American Foreign Relations."

WRIGHT, QUINCY, *ed.* **Interpretations of American Foreign Policy.** Chicago: Chicago University Press, 1930, 269 p.

Harris Lectures, in which G. H. Blakeslee, George Young, Yusuke Tsurumi and others survey various aspects of American policy.

WRISTON, HENRY MERRITT. **Executive Agents in American Foreign Relations.** Baltimore: Johns Hopkins Press, 1929, 886 p.
A scholarly study of the constitutional position of executive agents, followed by a survey of different types of diplomatic agents, their status and activities. A valuable contribution.

Relations with Canada

See also Canada, p. 165.

CHACKO, CHIRAKAIKARAN JOSEPH. **The International Joint Commission between the United States of America and the Dominion of Canada.** New York: Columbia University Press, 1932, 431 p.
A scholarly monograph on the organization and functioning of the commission which has handled boundary questions so efficiently during the past twenty years.

FALCONER, SIR ROBERT ALEXANDER. **The United States as a Neighbor.** London: Cambridge University Press, 1925, 277 p.
A series of lectures by the President of the University of Toronto, discussing past boundary and fisheries problems, trade and commerce, education, and Canada's position as interpreter of America to Britain.

KEENLEYSIDE, HUGH LLEWELLYN. **Canada and the United States.** New York: Knopf, 1929, 396 p.
This is a careful and well-documented history of Canadian relations with the United States that should be in the hands of every student of American foreign relations.

MOULTON, HAROLD GLENN, MORGAN, CHARLES STILLMAN and LEE, ADAH L. **The St. Lawrence Navigation and Power Project.** Washington: Brookings Institution, 1929, 675 p.
An exhaustive scientific study of all phases of the problem. Much of the volume is taken up with statistics and documents.

STEPHENS, GEORGE WASHINGTON. **The St. Lawrence Waterway Project.** New York: Carrier, 1930, 460 p.
A general treatment, historical and analytical, written from the Canadian standpoint.

WRONG, GEORGE MACKINNON. **The United States and Canada.** New York: Abingdon, 1921, 191 p.
A series of lectures by a Canadian historian, dealing chiefly with constitutional and political problems of the United States and Canada.

Relations with Latin America

See also (International Law) Intervention and Recognition, p. 36; also (Latin America) General, p. 195, and Pan-Americanism, p. 198, and West Indies, p. 200, and Mexico, p. 205, and Central America, p. 210.

General

BLANCO FOMBONA, HORACIO. **Crímenes del Imperialismo Norteamericano.** Mexico: Churubusco, 1929, 144 p.
The title adequately describes this indictment of Yankee imperialism.

BURNS, JUAN T. **El Pulpo.** Madrid: Reus, 1921, 392 p.
A bitter attack on the policy of the United States in Mexico, by the former Mexican Consul-General in New York, who accuses the government of having encouraged disorders in Mexico.

CALLAHAN, JAMES MORTON. **American Foreign Policy in Mexican Relations.** New York: Macmillan, 1932, 644 p.
Based largely on the unpublished correspondence in the State Department.

CARDENAS Y ECHARTE, RAÚL DE. **La Política de los Estados Unidos en el Continente Americano.** Havana: Sociedad Editorial Cuba Contemporánea, 1921, 284 p.
A remarkably charitable and sympathetic exposition of the growth of the United States as a world power.

CESTERO, TULIO MANUEL. **Estados Unidos y las Antillas.** Madrid: Compañía General de Artes Gráficas, 1931, 232 p.
A Dominican's systematic study of the Caribbean policy of the United States.

DENNY, HAROLD NORMAN. **Dollars for Bullets.** New York: Dial Press, 1929, 411 p.
A well-informed journalist's account of American policy and the recent happenings in Nicaragua. The author stresses the importance of the canal project and the pressure of Wall Street interests.

ESQUIVEL OBREGÓN, TORIBIO. **México y los Estados Unidos ante el Derecho Internacional.** Mexico: Herrero, 1926, 191 p.
An historical study of the Monroe Doctrine and the recognition policy of the United States as they have affected Mexico.

EVANS, HENRY CLAY, JR. **Chile and Its Relations with the United States.** Durham: Duke University, 1927, 253 p.
An excellent book, based in large part upon the unpublished material in the Department of State.

FABELA, ISIDRO. **Los Estados Unidos contra la Libertad.** Barcelona: Talleres Gráficos Lux, 1921, 312 p.
A Mexican publicist's vigorous indictment of the policies of the United States towards Latin America.

GHIRALDO, ALBERTO. **Yanquilandia Bárbara.** Madrid: Historia Nueva, 1929, 214 p.
An attack upon the imperialism of the United States as it appears from a review of recent happenings in Mexico, Santo Domingo, Haiti and Nicaragua, and from a reconsideration of American policy in Cuba, Porto Rico and the Philippines.

GOLDSCHMIDT, ALFONS. **Die Dritte Eroberung Amerikas.** Berlin: Rowohlt, 1929, 259 p.
The old imperialistic theme, with some new variations.

GUILAINE, LOUIS. **L'Amérique Latine et l'Impérialisme Américain.** Paris: Colin, 1928, 274 p.
A French publication, issued evidently in anticipation of the Havana Conference. The argument is a stock one: The Monroe Doctrine is merely an instrument of dollar diplomacy, Latin idealism is fast losing ground before Anglo-Saxon materialism, and Latin America is rapidly becoming a preserve for American syndicates. Withal a substantial, well-informed book.

HARING, CLARENCE HENRY. **South America Looks at the United States.** New York: Macmillan, 1928, 243 p.
A good discussion of the relations of the United States with South America just prior to the revolutions precipitated by the economic crisis. The author, a Harvard professor, not only discusses the various reasons for the distrust felt by Latin American countries, but also outlines the Pan-Hispanic movement and its aims. The book is written with sound knowledge and freedom from bias.

HOPKINS, JOHN APPLETON HAVEN and ALEXANDER, MELINDA. **Machine-Gun Diplomacy.** New York: Lewis Copeland, 1928, 216 p.
The Central-American situation viewed from the radical angle.

HUGHES, CHARLES EVANS. **Our Relations to the Nations of the Western Hemisphere.** Princeton: Princeton University Press, 1928, 123 p.
A series of lectures by the former Secretary of State, dealing with relations with Canada and the various Latin American states. The book may be taken almost as an official presentation of the American policy.

JONES, CHESTER LLOYD, NORTON, HENRY KITTREDGE and MOON, PARKER THOMAS. **The United States and the Caribbean.** Chicago: Chicago University Press, 1929, 240 p.
A competent review of the Caribbean problem, with both sides set forth. Harris Lectures at the University of Chicago.

KIMPEN, EMIL. **Die Ausbreitungspolitik der Vereinigten Staaten von Amerika.** Stuttgart: Deutsche Verlags-Anstalt, 1923, 404 p.
A general survey of American westward expansion and the history of American policy in the Caribbean and in Mexico; a scholarly though undocumented book.

LATANÉ, JOHN HOLLADAY. **The United States and Latin America.** New York: Doubleday, 1920, 346 p.
A competent study, dealing primarily with diplomatic relations in the period since the establishment of the Latin American Republics.

LOBO, HELIO. **Brasilianos y Yankees.** Rio de Janeiro: Pimenta de Mello, 1926, 198 p.
About half the book is devoted to a discussion of various American domestic and foreign problems. The other half takes up relations with Brazil, with special reference to the coffee problem.

MUÑOZ, IGNACIO. **La Verdad sobre los Gringos.** Mexico: Ediciones Populares, 1927, 131 p.
The havoc wrought in Mexico during twenty years by dollar diplomacy and American "tramps." Not serious.

NOGALES, RAFAEL DE. **The Looting of Nicaragua.** New York: McBride, 1928, 304 p.
The writer, a famous Venezuelan general, gives the history of the exploitation of Nicaragua as he sees it and as no doubt many other Latin Americans do. He then proceeds to an account of his own observations and experiences during a recent journey through the country. He finds almost nothing to say for the American policy and regards the whole incident as a classic example of ruthless and indefensible imperialism to be taken to heart by all Latin Americans.

PÉREZ Y SOTO, JUAN BAUTISTA. **Causas y Consecuencias, Antecedentes Diplomáticos y Efectos de la Guerra Hispano-americana.** San Juan: La Correspondencia de Puerto Rico, 1922, 295 p.
A careful, unprejudiced account of the Spanish-American War and American rule in Cuba, the Philippines, and Porto Rico, written by a native of the latter country.

QUIJANO, CARLOS. **Nicaragua.** Paris: Agencia Mundial, 1928, 148 p.
An historical survey and criticism of American policy in Nicaragua.

RIPPY, JAMES FRED. **The United States and Mexico.** New York: Crofts, 1931, 423 p.
The revised edition of an excellent general historical survey.

ROBERTSON, WILLIAM SPENCE. **Hispanic-American Relations with the United States.** New York: Oxford University Press, 1923, 470 p.
A comprehensive review of American international relations, with particular emphasis on the influence of the United States in Latin America.

ROLLIN, LÉON. **Sous le Signe de Monroe.** Paris: Alcan, 1930, 213 p.
The American empire in Mexico, Cuba, Panama and Colombia, as a Frenchman sees it.

RÖMER, HANS GUSTAV. **Amerikanische Interessen- und Prinzipienpolitik in Mexiko, 1910-1914.** Hamburg: Friedrichsen, de Gruyter, 1929, 149 p.

A systematic study of American policy in Mexico from 1910 to 1914, in connection with American relations with England.

SÁENZ, VICENTE. **Norteamericanización de Centro América.** San José: La Opinión, 1925-1926, 312 p.
A collection of articles on the policy of the United States during the last generation, by one of its ablest opponents.

SHERMAN, WILLIAM RODERICK. **The Diplomatic and Commercial Relations of the United States and Chile, 1820-1914.** Boston: Badger, 1926, 224 p.
A pioneer monographic study in a neglected field.

SMITH, LAUNA M. **American Relations with Mexico.** Oklahoma City: Harlow Publishing Company, 1924, 249 p.
A conscientious, documented historical study.

STIMSON, HENRY LEWIS. **American Policy in Nicaragua.** New York: Scribner, 1927, 129 p.
This may be taken as the government view in the Nicaraguan question. The author, who went to Nicaragua in March 1927 as the President's special representative, and who was responsible for the agreement with the warring factions, here gives a sketch of the historical background of the problem, stressing the importance of Nicaragua in the foreign policy of the United States, and recounting in some detail his negotiations with the rival parties. The book is written in a dispassionate way, and throws light on some obscure phases of the crisis.

STUART, GRAHAM HENRY. **Latin America and the United States.** New York: Century, 2nd ed., 1928, 465 p.
A survey of the commercial and diplomatic factors involved in the recent relations of the United States with Latin America. A well-documented text.

TANSILL, CHARLES CALLAN. **The Purchase of the Danish West Indies.** Baltimore: Johns Hopkins Press, 1932, 548 p.
The author reviews the whole story of the Danish West Indies as it touches the policy of the United States, adding considerably to our knowledge of Caribbean affairs.

UGARTE, MANUEL. **The Destiny of a Continent.** New York: Knopf, 1925, 317 p.
A translation from the Spanish of a collection of essays published in 1923.

WILSON, HENRY LANE. **Diplomatic Episodes in Mexico, Belgium and Chile.** New York: Doubleday, 1927, 416 p.
An important contribution to the history of American policy during the Madero and Huerta periods, in which the former American Ambassador defends his record in Mexico.

WINKLER, MAX. **Investments of United States Capital in Latin America.** Boston: World Peace Foundation, 1929, 297 p.
Surveying American investments in each Latin American country, the writer of this valuable monograph shows how far-reaching the American economic interest in the countries to the south has become.

Monroe Doctrine

ALVAREZ, ALEJANDRO. **The Monroe Doctrine: Its Importance in the International Life of the States of the New World.** New York: Oxford University Press, 1924, 582 p.
A well-documented analysis by a leading South American publicist. One of the most important books on the subject.

ARANGUA RIVAS, CARLOS J. **La Intervención; Doctrinas de Monroe, Drago y Tobar.**
Santiago de Chile: Imprenta La Sud-América, 1924, 247 p.
A scholarly study of the theory of intervention in international law, with special refer-
ence to Latin America and the policy of the United States.

CLARK, JOSHUA REUBEN. **Memorandum on the Monroe Doctrine.** Washington:
Govt. Print. Off., 1928, 238 p.
The official position of the United States Government as it was in 1928, described by
a former Under-Secretary of State and in quotations from state documents and official
pronouncements. The most important contemporary account.

CLELAND, ROBERT GLASS. **One Hundred Years of the Monroe Doctrine.** Los Angeles:
Times-Mirror Press, 1923, 127 p.
A general historical review, stressing the evolution of the doctrine.

IZAGA, LUIS. **La Doctrina de Monroe.** Madrid: Razón y Fe, 1929, 288 p.
A general documented account of the origin and chief phases in the evolution of the
doctrine, interesting for the viewpoint disclosed rather than for any contribution of
fact.

THOMAS, DAVID YANCEY. **One Hundred Years of the Monroe Doctrine.** New York:
Macmillan, 1923, 580 p.
An excellent and thorough study, written to mark the centenary of the doctrine.

TRELLES, CAMILO BARCIA. **Doctrina de Monroe y Cooperación Internacional.**
Madrid: Compañía General de Artes Gráficas, 1931, 741 p.
The work of a Spanish jurist. The book reviews the making and evolution of the doctrine, but concentrates on a discussion of the problem as it arose in 1919 and of the
part played by the doctrine in determining the American attitude towards the League
and other post-war efforts towards peace.

Canal Problems

See also Central America, p. 210.

BUNAU-VARILLA, PHILIPPE. **The Great Adventure of Panama.** New York: Doubleday,
1920, 267 p.
A French engineer closely connected with the Panama Canal project exposes the
machinations of the "Boche" to frustrate the scheme and secure control of the situation.

HOWARD, HARRY N. **Military Government in the Panama Canal Zone.** Norman:
University of Oklahoma Press, 1931, 62 p.
A much-condensed summary, beginning with the treaty basis for American jurisdiction
in Panama and ending with the development of American rights there since the war.

IMBERG, KURT EDUARD. **Der Nikaragua-Kanal.** Berlin: Lissner, 1920, 112 p.
A well-documented diplomatic study of the history of the Nicaragua project.

MILLER, HUGH GORDON. **The Isthmian Highway.** New York: Macmillan, 1929, 327 p.
A reconsideration of the problems of the Panama Canal and American policy in Central
America in their international aspects and in the setting of American Caribbean
policy. A sane, well-balanced study by a former assistant United States Attorney.

SMITH, DARRELL HEVENOR. **The Panama Canal.** Baltimore: Johns Hopkins Press, 1927,
430 p.
A detailed account of the history, organization and working of the canal, published
as one of the service monographs of the United States Government.

Relations with Europe

See also (Economic Factors) International Trade, Tariffs, Cartels, p. 13, and International Finance, p. 20; also (International Law) Freedom of the Seas, p. 36; also (War, Peace, Security and Disarmament) Kellogg-Briand Pact, p. 79.

BAUSMAN, FREDERICK. **Facing Europe.** New York: Century, 1926, 330 p.
A rather emotional and over-drawn exposition of America's isolation, with much criticism and denunciation of British policy.

BROOKE-CUNNINGHAM, C. A. **Anglo-Saxon Unity.** London: Selwyn and Blount, 1925, 306 p.
Four essays by a race purist, of which one deals with the conditions of Anglo-American unity while another is an apology for American neutrality in 1914.

BROOKS, SIDNEY. **America and Germany, 1918-1925.** New York: Macmillan, 1925, 209 p.
A sympathetic narrative of the gradual restoration of friendship and good-will.

CAPPER JOHNSON, KARLIN MENZIES and FRANKLAND, JOHN MIDDLETON. **Aspects of Anglo-American Relations.** New Haven: Yale University Press, 1928, 126 p.
The first Oxford-Yale prize essays, dealing respectively with the significance of the American Revolution in the development of the British Commonwealth and the influence of international trade upon British-American relations.

COHEN, KADMI. **L'Abomination Américaine.** Paris: Flammarion, 1930, 282 p.
Well described in the title. A vitriolic attack upon the perfidious and insidious plan for American domination of Europe.

COOK, J. G. **Anglophobia.** Boston: Four Seas, 1919, 138 p.
An English analysis of the anti-British prejudices current in the United States.

FAIRBURN, WILLIAM ARMSTRONG. **America's Attitude to Soviet Russia.** New York: Nation Press, 1931, 92 p.
The hundred-percenter's view with regard to the encouragement of Bolshevism, cancellation of just debts, etc.

FISCHER, LOUIS. **Why Recognize Russia?** New York: Cape and Smith, 1931, 298 p.
A review of the problem by a warm sympathizer with the Bolsheviks. The author argues that sooner or later recognition must come, that Bolshevik principles are not involved, and that the propaganda of the Third International is a mere bogey. Recognition, he maintains, will lead to improvement of trade and advancement of peace.

FISH, CARL RUSSELL, ANGELL, SIR NORMAN and HUSSEY, CHARLES LINCOLN. **The United States and Great Britain.** Chicago: Chicago University Press, 1932, 235 p.
Brief and to the point, these essays form a convenient symposium.

FISHER, HAROLD HENRY. **America and the New Poland.** New York: Macmillan, 1928, 428 p.
An exhaustive account of American aid in the restoration of Poland.

FOGDALL, SOREN JACOB MARIUS PETERSON. **Danish-American Diplomacy, 1776-1920.** Iowa City: University of Iowa Press, 1922, 171 p.
The first scholarly review of this subject available in the English language. A systematic doctoral dissertation.

GARDINER, ALFRED GEORGE. **The Anglo-American Future.** New York: Seltzer, 1921, 111 p.
An English historian's analysis of the causes for estrangement, together with an earnest exhortation to understand and be friends.

GORDON, LELAND JAMES. **American Relations with Turkey, 1830-1930.** Philadelphia: University of Pennsylvania Press, 1932, 402 p.
Based in part upon unpublished material, this monograph deals not only with diplomatic relations but stresses the economic and philanthropic aspects of American activities in Turkey. An excellent piece of work.

GRAHAM, JOHN WILLIAM. **Britain and America.** London: Hogarth, 1930, 134 p.
This Merttens Lecture supplies in brief scope one of the best general accounts of Anglo-American relations, with special reference to the war and post-war periods.

GRISON, PHILIPPE. **La Liberté des Mers et la Rivalité Anglo-Américaine de 1920 à 1930.** Paris: Bossuet, 1930, 102 p.
A concise review of American-British post-war relations, with special reference to the naval problem. Adds little.

HODGSON, JAMES GOODWIN, *comp.* **Recognition of Soviet Russia.** New York: H. W. Wilson, 1925, 111 p.
A useful reprint of the best articles *pro* and *con.*

JEFFERSON, CHARLES EDWARD. **The Friendship Indispensable.** New York: Macmillan, 1923, 88 p.
An attempt to interpret Britain to America, and a churchman's argument for close friendship and coöperation.

MILLER, FRANCIS and HILL, HELEN. **The Giant of the Western World.** New York: Morrow, 1930, 318 p.
A study of the political, economic and social activities of Americans in Europe, their effects, and some conditions for the satisfactory development of "North Atlantic" civilization.

MOYER, GEORGE SAMUEL. **Attitude of the United States towards the Recognition of Soviet Russia.** Philadelphia: University of Pennsylvania Press, 1926, 293 p.
A carefully documented doctoral thesis, analyzing the American recognition policy, the attitude of the Government, Congress and public opinion towards Soviet Russia, the experiences of England and France, etc. The author's conclusions are adverse to recognition.

PENFOLD, SAXBY VOULER. **The Marriage of Two Nations.** New York: American English Literature Society, 1924, 106 p.
A fantastic mystical argument for the marriage of "masculine" Britain and "feminine" America.

ROOSEVELT, NICHOLAS. **America and England.** New York: Cape and Smith, 1930, 264 p.
A well-informed and realistic survey of the position of the two Powers in the post-war world. The author discounts lugubrious prophecies of England's decline, examines the fundamental factors of Anglo-American relationship and discusses the naval problem at length.

SCHIEBER, CLARA EVE. **The Transformation of American Sentiment toward Germany, 1870-1914.** Boston: Cornhill, 1923, 294 p.
A study of the changes in the attitude of the United States towards Germany since the Franco-German War as reflected in newspaper comments.

SCHUMAN, FREDERICK LEWIS. **American Policy toward Russia since 1917.** New York: International Publishers, 1928, 399 p.
A scholarly study of Russian-American relations since March 1917, with an extended analysis of the reasons advanced for withholding recognition, such as propaganda, financial claims, etc.

TARDIEU, ANDRÉ. **France and America.** Boston: Houghton Mifflin, 1927, 312 p.
A prominent French statesman contrasts French mentality and institutions with those of America and presents an unvarnished account of Franco-American relations during the war and reconstruction periods.

WAKEFIELD, CHARLES CHEERS WAKEFIELD, BARON. **America To-day and To-morrow.** London: Hodder, 2nd ed., 1924, 304 p.
An appreciation of America, of Wilson and of Page, by the former Lord Mayor of London.

WHELPLEY, JAMES DAVENPORT. **British-American Relations,** Boston: Little, Brown, 1924, 325 p.
British and American characters and institutions compared and contrasted, together with an analysis of British-American relations as they are affected by the ideas and conceptions of each nation regarding the other.

WHITE, ELIZABETH BRETT. **American Opinion of France from Lafayette to Poincaré.** New York: Knopf, 1927, 362 p.
This conscientious and scholarly work is the first systematic study of the evolution of American opinion of France and deals a blow to the prevalent idea that France has always been sympathetically regarded by the people of the United States.

WILLSON, BECKLES. **America's Ambassadors to France, 1777-1927.** New York: Stokes, 1928, 433 p.
The author of "The Paris Embassy" draws a series of illuminating pictures of American representatives, using the embassy archives to some extent. Readable if not profound.

WILLSON, BECKLES. **America's Ambassadors to England, 1785-1929.** New York: Stokes, 1929, 497 p.
A survey of Anglo-American relations along the line marked out by the author's earlier books.

WISTER, OWEN. **A Straight Deal; or, The Ancient Grudge.** New York: Macmillan, 1920, 287 p.
An American novelist reëxamines the bases of the "ancient grudge" against England and pleads for deeper friendship.

Far Eastern Policy

See also (Disarmament) Naval, p. 84; also (World War) Siberia, p. 139; also (United States) Immigration and Race Problems, p. 191; also (Pacific Area) General Pacific Problems, p. 491, and The Philippines, p. 494, and Hawaii, p. 495.

American Relations with China. Baltimore: Johns Hopkins Press, 1925, 198 p.
Lectures on various aspects of the Chinese problem, by leading authorities.

CARTER, EDWARD CLARK, *ed.* **China and Japan in Our University Curricula.** New York: American Council, Institute of Pacific Relations, 1929, 183 p.
A survey of Far Eastern studies in American institutions.

CHUNG, HENRY. **The Oriental Policy of the United States.** New York: Revell, 1919, 306 p.
A review of the Far Eastern situation at the end of the war, of Japan's policy in China, and of American relations with Japan. The book reprints many pertinent documents.

CROLY, HERBERT DAVID. **Willard Straight.** New York: Macmillan, 1924, 569 p.
A biography, valuable for its light on American relations with the Far East.

DULLES, FOSTER RHEA. **America in the Pacific.** Boston: Houghton Mifflin, 1932, 299 p.
A readable historical narrative of American enterprise and interests in the Pacific area.

FIELD, FREDERICK VANDERBILT. **American Participation in the China Consortiums.**
Chicago: Chicago University Press, 1931, 198 p.
This monograph, published for the Institute of Pacific Relations, shows how, in actual
practice, the difficulties of international coöperation present themselves in the economic
sphere.

FUGLSANG, WALTER. **Der Amerikanisch-Holländische Streit um die Insel Palmas.**
Berlin: Stilke, 1931, 148 p.
A technical work on the Palmas Island dispute.

GALKOVICH, M. G. S. **Shtaty Dal'nevostochnaia Problema.** Moscow: Gosizdat, 1928,
208 p.
American policy in the Far East, as viewed from Moscow.

KAWAKAMI, KIYOSHI KARL. **The Real Japanese Question.** New York: Macmillan,
1921, 269 p.
A moderate, well-informed discussion of the Japanese immigration problem and the
"orgy" of American anti-Japanese legislation. The author, a Japanese newspaperman long stationed in Washington, stresses Japan's inescapable need for land and
resources as well as for population outlets.

PITKIN, WALTER BOUGHTON. **Must We Fight Japan?** New York: Century, 1921, 536 p.
An able discussion of American-Japanese problems in their broader aspects, such as
immigration, food supply, racial conflict in California and Hawaii, etc.

SHERRILL, CHARLES HITCHCOCK. **Have We a Far Eastern Policy?** New York: Scribner,
1920, 307 p.
Travel impressions of an American diplomat in the Pacific area, with an urgent plea
for closer Japanese-American relations. Not profound.

TOKUTOMI, IICHIRO. **Japanese-American Relations.** New York: Macmillan, 1922, 207 p.
The translation of a work by an eminent Japanese politician and writer. A sane and
dispassionate examination of the problem from the Japanese standpoint.

TREAT, PAYSON JACKSON. **Japan and the United States, 1853-1921.** Stanford: Stan-
ford University Press, 1928, 307 p.
The revised edition of a standard treatment covering the period from 1853 to 1928.
The best historical account of Japanese-American relations.

YOSHITOMI, MACAOMI. **Les Conflits Nippo-Américains et le Problème Pacifique.**
Paris: Pedone, 1926, 388 p.
A substantial scholarly study of the history of Japanese-American relations, followed
by a critical analysis of the sociological, economic, political and legal considerations
underlying the existing tension.

FOREIGN TRADE AND TARIFFS

See also (General International Relations) International Trade, Tariffs, Cartels, p. 13.

BISHOP, AVARD LONGLEY. **Outlines of American Foreign Commerce.** Boston: Ginn,
1923, 321 p.
A good manual for the layman.

BOTT, ERNESTO J. J. **El Comercio entre los Estados Unidos y la América Latina
durante la Gran Guerra.** Buenos Aires: Menéndez, 1919, 359 p.
An exhaustive study of trade relations with Latin America during the war, with much
statistical material.

CROMPTON, GEORGE. **The Tariff.** New York: Macmillan, 1927, 226 p.
A reconsideration of the history and theory of protection and the arguments advanced to support the system.

CULBERTSON, WILLIAM SMITH. **Commercial Policy in War Time and After.** New York: Appleton, 1919, 479 p.
An able analysis of the deeper changes wrought by the war and of the new problems presented in the post-war world; by a former member of the United States Tariff Commission.

DENNY, LUDWELL. **America Conquers Britain.** New York: Knopf, 1930, 456 p.
A somewhat sensational but nevertheless well-informed study of the economic relationship between Britain and America, the struggle for raw materials, competition for markets, etc.

FORD, MRS. LILLIAN COPE and THOMAS FRANCIS. **The Foreign Trade of the United States.** New York: Scribner, 1920, 325 p.
A general survey text, descriptive and analytical.

GROTKOPP, WILHELM. **Amerikas Schutzzollpolitik und Europa.** Berlin: Rothschild, 1929, 318 p.
A timely book, in which the author, after setting forth the essentials of the American tariff, proceeds to discuss the deleterious effects of that system upon the world economic system.

KAHN, OTTO HERMANN. **Our Economic and Other Problems.** New York: Doran, 1920, 420 p.
A collection of essays by a prominent banker. Among the topics treated are various aspects of American economic relations during the war.

KAHN, OTTO HERMANN. **Of Many Things.** New York: Boni, 1926, 437 p.
A large part of this second volume of essays is devoted to the discussion of international problems and the European situation.

KLEIN, JULIUS. **Frontiers of Trade.** New York: Century, 1929, 328 p.
An Assistant Secretary of Commerce gives the salient facts about American foreign trade in understandable form, discusses our policies and problems, and reviews the policies of our customers and competitors.

LAHEE, ARNOLD WARBURTON. **Our Competitors and Markets.** New York: Holt, 1924, 496 p.
A competent review of our trade relations, country by country, by an American trade expert.

LAURENT, JOSEPH PIERRE. **Nationalisme et Impérialisme Économique Américain.** Paris: Sirey, 1931, 252 p.
A vigorous indictment of our particular brand of imperialism.

MAZUR, PAUL MYER. **America Looks Abroad.** New York: Viking, 1930, 314 p.
A stock-taking of America's position in the world as it has developed since the war, with special attention to economic problems.

MAZUR, PAUL MYER. **American Prosperity.** New York: Viking, 1928, 283 p.
An important book by a New York banker. The chapter entitled "Money and the Shadows of Europe" is particularly revealing.

NOTZ, WILLIAM FREDERICK and HARVEY, RICHARD SELDEN. **American Foreign Trade.** Indianapolis: Bobbs-Merrill, 1921, 593 p.
A general manual for those planning to enter the field of foreign commerce or the government service.

NOURSE, EDWIN GRISWOLD. **American Agriculture and the European Market.** New York: McGraw-Hill, 1924, 333 p.
Special attention is given to the effect of the World War, and to the present purchasing power of European countries. A useful work by a competent authority.

SOUTHARD, FRANK ALLAN, JR. **American Industry in Europe.** Boston: Houghton
Mifflin, 1931, 264 p.
The story of the export of capital, with examples of control through branch factories
and subsidiaries.

TAUSSIG, FRANK WILLIAM. **The Tariff History of the United States.** New York: Putnam, 8th ed., 1931, 453 p.
The standard treatment, carrying the story through the tariff of 1922.

THOMAS, JAMES A. **Trailing Trade a Million Miles.** Durham: Duke University Press,
1931, 314 p.
Observations of a successful American merchant in the Orient, a document of value
for the student of American interests abroad.

Trends in the Foreign Trade of the United States. New York: National Industrial
Conference Board, 1930, 329 p.
A well-documented factual survey.

WILLIAMS, BENJAMIN HARRISON. **Economic Foreign Policy of the United States.**
New York: McGraw-Hill, 1929, 426 p.
The evolution of American foreign policy under the influence of growing economic
interests and commitments, discussed in a scholarly way.

WRIGHT, PHILIP GREEN. **The American Tariff and Oriental Trade.** Chicago: Chicago
University Press, 1931, 177 p.
A scholarly monograph prepared for the Institute of Pacific Relations, valuable as
showing scientifically the effects of the tariff in a concrete instance.

FINANCE AND FOREIGN INVESTMENTS

See also (General International Relations) International Finance, p. 20.

BOGART, ERNEST LUDLOW. **War Costs and Their Financing.** New York: Appleton,
1921, 510 p.
One of the best general treatments of American financial operations, war loans and
post-war loans, and the currency and taxation problems to which they gave rise.

BONNEFON-CRAPONNE, JEAN. **La Pénétration Économique et Financière des Capitaux Américains en Europe.** Paris: Labor, 1930, 233 p.
A doctoral dissertation summarizing American investments in Europe.

CHÉRADAME, ANDRÉ. **Sam, à Votre Tour, Payez.** Paris: Victorion, 1931.
The well-known French publicist, using American arguments, proves to his own satisfaction that the United States owes France a larger sum than that advanced to France
during the war.

DUNN, ROBERT WILLIAMS. **American Foreign Investments.** New York: Huebsch,
1926, 432 p.
A valuable treatise on the foreign investments, contracts and concessions of American
firms at the present time.

GLASS, CARTER. **An Adventure in Constructive Finance.** New York: Doubleday,
1927, 423 p.
A fascinating story of the making of the Federal Reserve Act, in which the author
claims paternity as against the claims put forward for House, Warburg and others.

HARDY, CHARLES OSCAR. **Credit Policies of the Federal Reserve System.** Washington:
Brookings Institution, 1932, 374 p.
How the central banking system of the United States stood the strains of the war,
with a detailed account of post-war changes in American banking and credit operations, gold movements, coöperation of central banks, etc.

KEMMERER, EDWIN WALTER. **The A B C of the Federal Reserve System.** Princeton: Princeton University Press, 2nd ed., 1919, 192 p.
Perhaps the best brief exposition of the subject.

KUCZYNSKI, ROBERT RENÉ. **American Loans to Germany.** New York: Macmillan, 1927, 378 p.
An excellent monograph published by the Institute of Economics. The author, a well-known German economist and statistician, examines the nature and terms of the loans made to Germany, and the uses to which they have been put.

NOYES, ALEXANDER DANA. **The War Period of American Finance, 1908-1925.** New York: Putnam, 1926, 459 p.
An account by the financial editor of the *New York Times*.

PHELPS, CLYDE WILLIAM. **The Foreign Expansion of American Banks.** New York: Ronald, 1927, 233 p.
A study of the development of the American branch banking system.

POMARET, CHARLES. **L'Amérique à la Conquête de l'Europe.** Paris: Colin, 1931, 296 p.
The author takes up the familiar problems of inter-Allied debts, transfer of capital and goods, American investments, etc., and attempts to draw up a program of European defense.

REED, HAROLD LYLE. **Federal Reserve Policy, 1921-1930.** New York: McGraw-Hill, 1930, 207 p.
A convenient survey.

REIBNITZ, KURT GUSTAV HANS OTTO WILHELM, FREIHERR VON. **Amerikas Internationale Kapitalwanderungen.** Berlin: De Gruyter, 1926, 123 p.
A brief but scholarly study of the foreign investments of the United States.

ROGERS, JAMES HARVEY. **America Weighs Her Gold.** New Haven: Yale University Press, 1931, 258 p.
This study, written by a well-known economist, Professor of Political Economy at Yale, goes beyond the mere question of the distribution of gold and touches on the general financial and trade relations of the United States. The volume is not profound.

STODDARD, LOTHROP. **Europe and Our Money.** New York: Macmillan, 1932, 266 p.
An attack upon the uncritical investment of American money in Europe, and of the methods by which the American public was "educated" to the export of capital. Like most of the author's books, this volume is stimulating, readable and one-sided.

WARBURG, PAUL MORITZ. **The Federal Reserve System.** New York: Macmillan, 1930, 2 v.
The first volume is devoted to this leading banker's account of the making of the Federal Reserve Act and to documents bearing on it. The second consists of a collection of papers and addresses.

WILLIS, HENRY PARKER and STEINER, WILLIAM HOWARD. **Federal Reserve Banking Practice.** New York: Appleton, 1926, 1016 p.
A standard handbook of Federal Reserve operations, domestic and foreign.

WILLIS, HENRY PARKER. **The Federal Reserve System.** New York: Ronald, 1923, 1765 p.
An authoritative account of the origin, organization and operation of the system, by an economist closely connected with it in its early years.

WILLOUGHBY, WILLIAM FRANKLIN. **Financial Condition and Operations of the National Government, 1921-1930.** Washington: Brookings Institution, 1931, 234 p.
One of the excellent "Studies in Administration" published by the Institute for Government Research.

YOUNG, RALPH A. **The International Financial Position of the United States.**
New York: National Industrial Conference Board, 1929, 276 p.
A doctoral dissertation reviewing the position of the United States historically, with
full treatment of post-war developments and problems, such as the effects of foreign
investments on trade relations, banking conditions, etc.

ZEELAND REULEUX, MARCEL VAN. **Les États-Unis d'Amérique, Banquiers du Monde.**
Brussels: De Wit, 1928, 357 p.
A substantial monograph on the post-war evolution of America as a creditor nation.

IMMIGRATION AND RACE PROBLEMS

*See also (Population Problems) International Migrations, p. 7; also (United States) Far
Eastern Policy, p. 186.*

ABBOTT, EDITH. **Historical Aspects of the Immigration Problem.** Chicago: Chicago
University Press, 1926, 881 p.
This supplements the author's earlier collection of materials.

ABBOTT, EDITH. **Immigration: Select Documents and Case Records.** Chicago:
Chicago University Press, 1924, 809 p.
A useful and very extensive collection of documents, statements and opinions. Invalu-
able as a source book.

BLOCH, CHAJIM. **Das Jüdische Amerika.** Vienna: Das Leben, 1926, 120 p.
An interesting and well-balanced survey of the conditions and accomplishments of
American Jews.

BONN, MORITZ JULIUS. **Amerika und Sein Problem.** Munich: Meyer und Jessen, 1925,
176 p.
A penetrating reëxamination of the "melting-pot" theory and problems of immigration and Americanization, by one of the best-informed German writers on America.

BREWER, DANIEL CHAUNCEY. **The Peril of the Republic.** New York: Putnam, 2nd ed.,
1922, 354 p.
The dangers and dire results of unrestricted immigration—the tendency towards
radicalism and revolution.

BURR, CLINTON STODDARD. **America's Race Heritage.** New York: National Historical
Society, 1924, 337 p.
An historical survey and critique of the old sentimentalism, by an advocate of rigid
restriction.

ČAPEK, THOMAS. **The Čechs in America.** Boston: Houghton Mifflin, 1920, 294 p.
The best book on the subject, covering the history and social, economic and cultural
aspects.

CAVANAUGH, FRANCIS PATRICK. **Immigration Restriction at Work Today.** Washington: Catholic University, 1928, 116 p.
A doctoral dissertation which examines the administrative machinery for enforcing
the present laws, and its actual operation.

COX, EARNEST SEVIER. **White America.** Richmond: White America Society, 1923, 389 p.
How past civilizations have been ruined by contact with colored races. The writer
puts forward a strong argument for repatriation of the negro.

DAS, RAJANI KANTA. **Hindustani Workers on the Pacific Coast.** Berlin: De Gruyter,
1923, 126 p.
A study of the problem of the Indian laborers on the Pacific coast in the United States
and Canada.

DAVIS, JAMES JOHN. **Selective Immigration.** St. Paul: Scott-Mitchell, 1925, 227 p.
A strong plea for restriction, by the former Secretary of Labor.

DAVIS, JEROME. **The Russian Immigrant.** New York: Macmillan, 1922, 219 p.
A scholarly historical and sociological survey.

DAVIS, JEROME. **The Russians and Ruthenians in America.** New York: Doran, 1922, 155 p.
A volume in the "New American" series, primarily a sociological survey and a program of needs. Scholarly, and with an extensive bibliography.

DOWD, JEROME. **The Negro in American Life.** New York: Century, 1926, 611 p.
The most extensive scholarly survey of the negro since the Civil War both in the North and South, his part in the World War, recent migrations, his place in literature and art, and finally an extended discussion of possible solutions of the color problem.

L'Évolution de la Race Française en Amérique. Montreal: Beauchemin, 1921, 277 p.
Primarily a newspaper survey of the French Canadian settlements in New England.

FAIRCHILD, HENRY PRATT. **Immigration: A World Movement and Its American Significance.** New York: Macmillan, rev. ed., 1928, 520 p.
A revised edition of a standard treatise approaching the problem historically and analytically. See also volume two of Howland's "Survey of American Foreign Relations" (New Haven: Yale Press, 1929).

FAIRCHILD, HENRY PRATT. **The Melting-Pot Mistake.** Boston: Little, Brown, 1926, 266 p.
A well-known sociologist attacks the idea of assimilation and stresses the fundamental problems raised by racial and group contacts.

FAUST, ALBERT BERNHARDT. **The German Element in the United States.** New York: Steuben Society, 1927, 2 v.
The latest edition of an excellent historical study which gives much prominence to the political and cultural influence of the Germans.

GAMIO, MANUEL. **Mexican Immigration to the United States.** Chicago: Chicago University Press, 1930, 280 p.
An exemplary study by a high Mexican official. Far from limiting himself to a purely statistical study of migrations, the author has approached the problem rather from the angle of cultural relations. The writer feels that migration of a temporary nature is not to be deprecated, but insists that some effort should be made to restrict permanent immigration, for the good of both countries.

GARIS, ROY LAWRENCE. **Immigration Restriction.** New York: Macmillan, 1927, 376 p.
A substantial scholarly study of the history of opposition to immigration and the legislation passed to restrict the influx of foreigners.

GRANT, MADISON and DAVISON, CHARLES STEWART, *eds.* **The Alien in Our Midst.** New York: Galton, 1930, 238 p.
A collection of statements, from the "Founding Fathers" and from present-day leaders in various walks of life, stressing the dangers from alien elements in the body politic.

HENDRICK, BURTON JESSE. **The Jews in America.** New York: Doubleday, 1923, 171 p.
A review of the Jewish immigration and an examination of the position, especially financial and political, of American Jewry. The author stresses the problems raised in the effort to assimilate the Polish Jew.

HITTI, PHILIP KHURI. **The Syrians in America.** New York: Doran, 1924, 139 p.
An excellent scholarly survey of the background of Syrian immigration and of the social and religious situation in the United States.

HUNTINGTON, ELLSWORTH and WHITNEY, LEON FRADLEY. **The Builders of America.**
New York: Morrow, 1927, 382 p.
An interesting contribution, investigating the problems arising from the birth-rates
of various nationalities comprising the American population.

INUI, KIYO SUE. **The Unsolved Problem of the Pacific.** Tokyo: Japan Times, 1926,
619 p.
A competent discussion of the immigration question and the situation in California,
together with an extended analytical study of the Johnson Report.

IYENAGA, TOYOKICHI and SATO, KENOSKE. **Japan and the California Problem.** New
York: Putnam, 1921, 249 p.
One of the best scholarly treatments from the Japanese side, with a reprint of crucial
documents.

JENKS, JEREMIAH WHIPPLE, LAUCK, WILLIAM JETT and SMITH, RUFUS DANIEL. **The
Immigration Problem.** New York: Funk and Wagnalls, 6th ed., 1926, 717 p.
The latest revised edition of a competent survey of the question in all its many aspects.

JOHNSEN, JULIA EMILY, *comp.* **Japanese Exclusion.** New York: Wilson, 1925, 134 p.
A useful collection of material on the question, with a good bibliography.

JOHNSON, CHARLES SPURGEON. **The Negro in American Civilization.** New York: Holt,
1930, 538 p.
An extended sociological report prepared for the executive committee of the National
Interracial Conference, together with a report of discussions of the conference.

KANSAS, SIDNEY. **United States Immigration, Exclusion and Deportation.** Washington: Holland, 1928, 247 p.
Primarily a digest of the most important court cases and decisions.

LASKER, BRUNO. **Filipino Immigration to Continental United States and to
Hawaii.** Chicago: Chicago University Press, 1931, 467 p.
An excellent and exhaustive treatment of a problem, published under the auspices of
the Institute of Pacific Relations.

LEWIS, EDWARD RIEMAN. **America: Nation or Confusion?** New York: Harper, 1928,
424 p.
A moderate, clear examination of the immigration question and the melting pot
fallacy. The author favors the continuation of the system of national quotas.

LINFIELD, HARRY SEBEE. **The Jews in the United States, 1927.** New York: American
Jewish Committee, 1929, 107 p.
A thorough statistical survey.

MCKENZIE, RODERICK DUNCAN. **Oriental Exclusion.** Chicago: Chicago University
Press, 1928, 200 p.
How the restrictive measures work and their effect upon Orientals on the Pacific coast;
a paper prepared for the Institute of Pacific Relations.

MALCOM, M. VARTAN. **The Armenians in America.** Boston: Pilgrim, 1919, 142 p.
An historical sketch followed by a survey of the distribution, activities and conditions
of the Armenians.

MEARS, ELIOT GRINNELL. **Resident Orientals on the American Pacific Coast.**
Chicago: Chicago University Press, 1928, 561 p.
A valuable contribution to the subject. The author examines the legal background
and the present status of the Oriental population, based upon all available printed
material and upon wide personal investigation.

NORLIE, OLAF MORGAN. **History of the Norwegian People in America.** Minneapolis: Augsburg, 1925, 510 p.
A detailed illustrated history, with much statistical material.

PAN NAI WEI. **L'Immigration Asiatique aux États-Unis d'Amérique.** Lyon: Bosc, 1926, 164 p.
A doctoral dissertation. The author reviews the history of Oriental immigration and the law of 1924, and then examines the economic and international sides of the problem.

PANUNZIO, CONSTANTINE MARIA. **Immigration Crossroads.** New York: Macmillan, 1927, 307 p.
A sympathetic reconsideration of the immigration problem, written from the immigrant's viewpoint by one who has made a close study of the situation as it has developed and as it is now handled. He exposes certain weaknesses of the present system and urges the necessity of a broader international viewpoint in the matter of restriction.

REUTER, EDWARD BYRON. **The American Race Problem.** New York: Crowell, 1927, 448 p.
A competent, up-to-date sociological survey of the American negro.

SANTIBÁÑEZ, ENRIQUE. **Ensayo acerca de la Inmigración Mexicana en los Estados Unidos.** San Antonio: Clegg, 1930, 105 p.
A collection of articles by a Mexican journalist, dealing with the causes and development of Mexican immigration, conditions among the immigrants, and the problems raised by American restrictive measures.

SAVOY, PREW. **La Question Japonaise aux États-Unis.** Paris: Boccard, 1924, 253 p.
A doctoral thesis, concerned chiefly with the Alien Land Laws and the socio-economic aspects of the problem.

SCOTT, EMMETT JAY. **Negro Migration during the War.** New York: Oxford, 1920, 189 p.
A scientific study of one of the most important phases in the development of the negro problem. Published by the Carnegie Endowment.

SPERANZA, GINO CHARLES. **Race or Nation.** Indianapolis: Bobbs-Merrill, 1925, 278 p.
An able discussion of the problem of unassimilated foreigners in America.

STELLA, ANTONIO. **Some Aspects of Italian Immigration to the United States.** New York: Putnam, 1924, 124 p.
An analytical study of types and conditions of Italian immigrants, with special reference to mentality, disease, criminality, etc.

STEPHENSON, GEORGE MALCOLM. **A History of American Immigration.** Boston: Ginn, 1926, 316 p.
Primarily a discussion of the political effects of immigration since 1824. One of the best scholarly studies of the immigration problem.

STODDARD, LOTHROP. **Re-Forging America.** New York: Scribner, 1927, 389 p.
How the bright promise of early nationhood was clouded by the influx of alien elements and how the closing of the gates promises a better future. The book discusses also the negro problem and possible solutions.

STOWELL, JAY SAMUEL. **The Near Side of the Mexican Question.** New York: Doran, 1921, 123 p.
A sympathetic review of the Mexican and Spanish-American immigration, and the religion, education and contribution of the immigrants.

SZAWLESKI, MIECZYSŁAW. **Wychodźtwo Polskie w Stanach Zjednoczonych Ameryki.** Warsaw: Ossolińskich, 1924, 472 p.
A scholarly study of the history and present position of the Polish immigration, by the Polish vice-consul in New York.

Tow, Julius Su. **The Real Chinese in America.** New York: Academy Press, 1923, 168 p.
Chiefly a picture of the social conditions of the Chinese, by a member of the consulate-general in New York.

Woodson, Carter Godwin. **The Negro in Our History.** Washington: Associated Publishers, 5th ed., 1928, 628 p.
An extensive illustrated account, by the editor of the *Journal of Negro History;* about the best one-volume history of the negro and his contribution.

Wurtz, Pierre. **La Question de l'Immigration aux États-Unis.** Paris: Dreux, 1925, 334 p.
A French dissertation devoted chiefly to an analysis of legislation between 1915 and 1925 and its effects. There is a separate treatment of the problem of Oriental immigration.

Young, Donald Ramsey. **American Minority Peoples.** New York: Harper, 1932, 636 p.
Studies of the American minorities and of possible means of reconciliation and co-operation.

III. LATIN AMERICA

GENERAL

See also (United States) Relations with Latin America, p. 179.

Bayo, Ciro. **Historia Moderna de la América Española.** Madrid: Caro Raggio, 1930, 266 p.
A general introductory history, covering the period from the attainment of independence.

Blakeslee, George Hubbard, *ed.* **Mexico and the Caribbean.** New York: Stechert, 1920.
More than twenty articles by different authorities, presenting in a popular way various Latin American problems, domestic and foreign.

Capdevila, Arturo. **América.** Buenos Aires: Gleizer, 1926, 165 p.
A patriotic Argentine poet and writer discusses the position of Latin America facing the encroaching power of the United States.

Carrancá y Trujillo, Raúl. **La Evolución Política de Iberoamérica.** Madrid: Pérez, 1925, 304 p.
An excellent brief exposition of the political history of Latin America, both domestic and foreign.

Carrión, Benjamin. **Los Creadores de la Nueva América.** Madrid: Sociedad General Española de Librería, 1928, 217 p.
Biographical studies of Vasconcelos, Ugarte, Calderon and Arguedas.

Cleven, Nels Andrew Nelson. **Readings in Hispanic-American History.** Boston: Ginn, 1927, 791 p.
A much-needed selection of representative documents and readings.

Colmo, Alfredo. **Política Cultural en los Países Latinoamericanos.** Buenos Aires: Nosotros, 1925, 256 p.
A collection of essays and addresses on various aspects of Latin American problems centering more or less on the Congreso Científico Panamericano, at Lima.

COOPER, CLAYTON SEDGWICK. **Latin America: Men and Markets.** Boston: Ginn, 1927, 475 p.
A general descriptive and reference work, stressing the economic side.

DELATORRE, VICTOR RAÚL HAYA. **Por la Emancipación de América Latina.** Buenos Aires: Gleizer, 1927, 213 p.
A collection of articles, proclamations, appeals, etc., from the pen of a Peruvian leader of the intelligentsia and vigorous opponent of imperialism.

EDWARDS BELLO, JOAQUÍN. **El Nacionalismo Continental.** Madrid: Hernández, 1927, 174 p.
A plea for a return to realities and for the self-development of Latin America.

ENOCK, CHARLES REGINALD. **Spanish America.** London: Fisher Unwin, 1920, 2 v.
A descriptive work, with perhaps too much emphasis on the scenic and romantic.

FRANK, WALDO. **America Hispana.** New York: Scribner, 1931, 388 p.
A stimulating if somewhat mystical study of Latin American types and psychology, beautifully written in lyric prose.

GONZÁLEZ-ARRILI, BERNARDO. **El Futuro de América.** Barcelona: Araluce, 1928, 255 p.
Essays touching on many aspects of Latin American problems and Latin American relations to Spain and the United States.

GONZÁLEZ-RUANO, CÉSAR. **El Terror en América de Gómez a Leguía Pasando por Machado.** Madrid: Compañ a Iberoamericana, 1930, 245 p.
The author emphasizes the Cuban situation, but reviews the general conditions in South America during the recent revolutionary period.

GRAHAM, STEPHEN. **In Quest of El Dorado.** New York: Appleton, 1923, 334 p.
A vivid description of travels in Spain, the West Indies, Central America, Mexico, and the Southern United States.

GUIÑAZÚ, ENRIQUE RUIZ. **La Tradición de América.** Buenos Aires: El Ateneo, 1930, 202 p.
An interpretative study of Latin America by a leading Argentine publicist. The author discusses racial and social factors, expansionism, educational forces, etc.

JAMES, HERMAN GERLACH and MARTIN, PERCY ALVIN. **The Republics of Latin America.** New York: Harper, 1923, 533 p.
A convenient summary of the political history and international relations of the South American states.

JANE, CECIL. **Liberty and Despotism in Spanish America.** New York: Oxford University Press, 1929, 190 p.
A stimulating volume, based on keen and objective analysis. The author examines the causes for Latin American unrest and seeks the explanation in the inadequate development of these countries rather than in native political incapacity.

JORDAN, WILLIAM F. **Glimpses of Indian America.** New York: Revell, 1923, 279 p.
An interesting sketch of the native life in Mexico, Central and South America.

LAFOND, GEORGES. **La France en Amérique Latine.** Paris: Plon, 1922, 181 p.
An historical description of French influence, followed by a survey of French culture, propaganda, economic activity, etc.

LEE, THOMAS FITZHUGH. **Latin American Problems.** New York: Brewer, 1932, 339 p.
The author, a banker who has had a long experience in Latin America, seeks especially to interpret the economic and investment problems.

LUFFT, HERMANN A. L. **Lateinamerika.** Leipzig: Bibliographisches Institut, 1930, 484 p.
A beautifully illustrated general survey of the Latin American world, the chief emphasis being placed on social and economic aspects.

MAITROT, CHARLES ARTHUR ÉDOUARD XAVIER. **La France et les Républiques Sud-Américaines.** Paris: Berger-Levrault, 1920, 382 p.
A review of Latin America in the World War, followed by a survey of Argentina, Brazil, Uruguay, Chile, Bolivia and Peru, with emphasis on economic and military resources.

MANN, W. **Volk und Kultur Lateinamerikas.** Hamburg: Broschek, 1927, 301 p.
One of the best general surveys, by a former Chilean professor.

MARTIN, PERCY ALVIN. **Latin America and the War.** Baltimore: Johns Hopkins Press, 1925, 594 p.
A series of illuminating lectures, by a competent writer.

MIRKIN-GETSEVICH, BORIS SERGIEEVICH. **Les Constitutions des Nations Américaines.** Paris: Delagrave, 1932, 486 p.
The texts of all American constitutions, with an introduction.

NORTON, HENRY KITTREDGE. **The Coming of South America.** New York: Day, 1932, 300 p.
The result of an inquiry in Latin America by a well-known journalist and publicist.

PECK, ANNIE SMITH. **Industrial and Commercial South America.** New York: Crowell, 1927, 489 p.
A revised edition of a useful survey of economic possibilities, by the well-known mountain climber.

PEREYRA, CARLOS. **Historia de América Española.** Madrid: Saturnino Calleja, 1920-1926, 8 v.
A large scale popular history, country by country, with much illustrative material.

RIPPY, JAMES FRED. **Latin America in World Politics.** New York: Knopf, 1928, 286 p.
A good historical introduction to the study of Latin America in its international setting. The author reviews the relations of the South American states to the various Powers. The chapters dealing with the attitude of France and Germany respectively are illuminating, and the Pan-Hispanic movement and immigration problems are successfully handled.

ROBERTSON, WILLIAM SPENCE. **History of the Latin-American Nations.** New York: Appleton, 2nd ed., 1932, 821 p.
The revised edition of a standard text.

ROUMA, GEORGES. **Les Ressources Économiques de l'Amérique Latine.** Brussels: Renaissance du Livre, 1923, 414 p.
A thorough, comprehensive reference book.

SHEPHERD, WILLIAM ROBERT. **Hispanic Nations of the New World.** New Haven: Yale University Press, 1919, 251 p.
An interpretative study, in the "Chronicles of America" series.

South American Handbook. London: South American Publications. Annual since 1924.
A volume containing brief summaries of each country in Central and South America, giving information on agriculture, governments, trade, and geographical features.

THOMPSON, WALLACE. **Greater America.** New York: Dutton, 1932, 275 p.
An introduction to the conditions and problems of Latin America, again with special stress on economic aspects.

UGARTE, MANUEL. **La Patria Grande.** Madrid: Editor Internacional, 1924, 286 p.
A collection of essays and articles touching on many aspects of Latin America's international position, by one of the most stimulating Latin American publicists.

VASCONCELOS, JOSÉ. **Indología.** Paris: Agencia Mundial de Librería, 1930, 231 p.
An interpretation of Latin American culture and thought, by a gifted Mexican educator.

VENTURINO, AGUSTÍN. **Sociología General Americana.** Barcelona: Cervantes, 1931, 360 p.
A most interesting essay on the forces that entered into the formation and evolution of Latin America.

WARSHAW, JACOB. **The New Latin America.** New York: Crowell, 1922, 415 p.
A survey of contemporary Latin American civilization and problems, with emphasis on the economic side.

WILLIAMS, MARY WILHELMINE. **The People and Politics of Latin America.** Boston: Ginn, 1930, 852 p.
Though primarily intended as a college text, this volume will serve as an introductory history of the Latin American world.

PAN-AMERICANISM

See also (United States) Relations with Latin America, p. 179.

BRUM, BALTASAR. **The Peace of America.** Montevideo: Imprenta Nacional, 1924, 80 p.
A brief but lucid Uruguayan plea for a league of American states based on principles of equality.

BUSTAMANTE Y SIRVÉN, ANTONIO SÁNCHEZ DE. **Le Code de Droit International Privé et la Sixième Conférence Panaméricaine.** Paris: Sirey, 1929, 226 p.
The translation of an important book by the prominent Cuban jurist; the larger part is taken up by the record of the proceedings of the conference.

CARBONELL, NÉSTOR. **Las Conferencias Internacionales Americanas.** Havana: Montalvo y Cárdenas, 1928, 606 p.
A thorough historical review of the conferences, with a digest of their work, by the director of the Cuban Pan-American Office.

EYMA, JEAN. **La Cour de Justice Centre-Américaine.** Paris: Sagot, 1929, 200 p.
A scholarly legal study of an interesting organization.

FERRARA, ORESTES. **El Panamericanismo y la Opinión Europea.** Paris: Le Livre Libre, 1930, 302 p.
An excellent survey of the evolution of European opinion on Pan-Americanism, with special reference to the Santiago and Havana Conferences and their work; written by the Cuban delegate to the League of Nations.

HERNÁNDEZ-USÉRA, RAFAEL. **De América y de España, Problemas y Orientaciones.** Madrid: Rivadeneyra, 1922, 197 p.
The author, a Porto Rican, assumes a friendly attitude towards the United States and seeks to reconcile Pan-Americanism and Pan-Hispanism.

HERNÁNDEZ-USÉRA, RAFAEL. **Semillas a Voleo.** Madrid: Editorial Puerto Rico, 1925, 352 p.
A series of essays dealing with Spanish influence in Latin America, the policy of the United States in Puerto Rico and Cuba, and miscellaneous articles on Mexican affairs.

HUGHES, CHARLES EVANS. **Pan American Peace Plans.** New Haven: Yale University Press, 1929, 68 p.
The former Secretary of State reviews the accomplishments of the Pan-American Conference at Havana.

INMAN, SAMUEL GUY. **Hacia la Solidaridad Americana.** Madrid: Jorro, 1924, 448 p.
An able study of the Santiago Conference of 1923, its aims and achievements, and the further problems of Pan-Americanism.

INMAN, SAMUEL GUY. **Problems in Pan Americanism.** New York: Doran, 1925, 439 p.
A well-informed historical survey of the fluctuations of Latin American sentiment towards the United States, and a discussion of fundamental problems of Pan-Americanism, written by a liberal American teacher with a religious background.

JOHANNESSON, FREDRIK. **Det Panamerikanska Problemet, 1826-1920.** Norrköping: Norrköpings Tidningars, 1922, 266 p.
A scholarly dissertation giving a reliable review of the historical evolution of Pan-Americanism.

MORENO QUINTANA, LUCIO M. **El Sistema Internacional Americano.** Buenos Aires: Facultad de Derecho, 1925-1926, 2 v.
An exhaustive scholarly study of the Pan-American conferences and the machinery for peace set up in the western hemisphere.

SCOTT, JAMES BROWN, *ed.* **The International Conferences of American States, 1889-1928.** New York: Oxford University Press, 1931, 551 p.
An important collection of source material, published by the Carnegie Foundation.

SENILLOSA, JUAN ANTONIO. **Panamericanismo Cultural.** Buenos Aires: Pedemonte, 1924, 123 p.
A series of essays on university extension and other aspects of Latin American cultural coöperation.

URRUTIA, FRANCISCO JOSÉ. **Les Conférences Pan-Américaines.** Paris: Rousseau, 1924, 92 p.
A concise survey of Pan-American conferences, including the Santiago Conference of 1923. Lectures by an eminent Colombian jurist delivered at the Institut des Hautes Études Internationales.

URRUTIA, FRANCISCO JOSÉ. **Le Continent Américain et le Droit International.** Paris: Rousseau, 1928, 404 p.
The organization of Latin America for peace; an excellent history of arbitration, the Pan-American Union and the work of codifying international law.

YEPES, JESÚS MARÍA. **El Panamericanismo y el Derecho Internacional.** Bogotá: National Printing Office, 1930, 447 p.
A review of the history of Pan-Americanism, with special reference to the work of the various conferences.

PAN-HISPANISM

ALTAMIRA Y CREVEA, RAFAEL. **La Política de España en América.** Valencia: Edeta, 1921, 230 p.
A stimulating volume, in which an eminent Spanish historian discusses the competition of Italy with Spain for influence in Latin America, and what can be done by Spain to counteract it.

ARAGONÉS, EUTIQUIO. **Los Temas Fundamentales de Hispanoamérica.** Madrid: Pueyo, 1927, 194 p.
A restatement of the program of the movement.

EDNESOR, SUIL. **Apuntes para el Hispano-Americanismo.** Montevideo: 1925, 123 p.
Another attempt to set forth the advantages of Hispanic Americanism.

GARCÍA CAMINERO. **El Problema Ibero-Americano.** Cádiz: Renacimiento, 1926, 216 p.
Another plea for the strengthening of the ties between Spain and Latin America. The author stresses economic and cultural ties and the methods of strengthening them.

MICHEL, PAUL HENRI. **L'Hispanisme dans les Républiques Espagnoles d'Amérique pendant la Guerre.** Paris: Costes, 1931, 111 p.
An interesting essay on the movement of opinion in Latin America during the war, with stress on Spanish influence, Pan-Americanism and German propaganda.

SUÁREZ, CONSTANTINO. **La Des-Unión Hispano-Americana.** Barcelona: Bauzá, 1919, 312 p.
A collection of articles published in the Cuban press, dealing chiefly with Spanish influence and immigration in Latin America.

SUÁREZ, CONSTANTINO. **La Verdad Desnuda.** Madrid: Rivadeneyra, 1924, 185 p.
Further writings on Hispano-Americanism, with emphasis on the removal of past misunderstandings between Spain and Latin America, and the possibility of cultural contacts.

UGARTE, MANUEL. **Mi Campaña Hispanoamericana.** Barcelona: Cervantes, 1922, 233 p.
A collection of essays on Latin American solidarity and resistance to northern imperialism, by a leading publicist.

VASCONCELOS, JOSÉ. **La Raza Cósmica.** Paris: Agencia Mundial de Librería, n. d., 296 p.
Notes and impressions of post-war travels in Latin America, by a leading exponent of Hispanism.

VERGARA, MÁXIMO. **La Unidad de la Raza Hispana.** Madrid: Reus, 1925, 250 p.
An anthropological proof for the Pan-Hispanic argument.

ZURANO MUÑOZ, EMILIO. **Alianza Hispano-Americana.** Madrid: Pueyo, 1926, 320 p.
An extreme statement of the idea of Spanish-American solidarity; a project for an international alliance of Spanish-American nations, with headquarters in Spain.

WEST INDIES

See also (United States) Relations with Latin America, p. 179.

General

ARAQUISTAÍN, LUIS. **La Agonía Antillana.** Madrid: Espa-Calpe, 1928, 296 p.
A brilliant but restrained indictment of Yankee imperialism in the Caribbean. The travel observations of an able Spanish journalist, who sees the chief danger in the crowding out and impoverishment of the white population by the sugar interests and the system of absentee landlordism.

CROKAERT, JACQUES. **La Méditerranée Américaine.** Paris: Payot, 1927, 288 p.
A former Belgian diplomat in Central America gives an account of his travels in Central America and the West Indies, and an unflattering description of designs of the United States in that region, emphasizing perhaps unduly the uncompromising struggle between the United States and England.

FOSTER, HARRY LA TOURETTE. **Combing the Caribbees.** New York: Dodd, Mead, 1929, 302 p.
Delightful travel notes interspersed with keen observations.

JONES, CHESTER LLOYD. **Caribbean Backgrounds and Prospects.** New York: Appleton, 1931, 362 p.

A scholarly study of the social and economic factors in the Caribbean countries, with considerable discussion of American investments and interests. See also the second volume of Howland's "Survey of American Foreign Relations" (New Haven: Yale Press, 1929).

KEY, HELMER. **Kaffee, Zucker und Bananen.** Munich: Drei Masken Verlag, 1929, 360 p.
The well-known Swedish publicist and writer on colonial affairs surveys the workings of economic imperialism in the Caribbean.

MACMILLAN, ALLISTER, *ed.* **The Red Book of the West Indies.** London: Collingridge, 1922, 424 p.
A compilation dealing with economic activities and resources.

MANINGTON, GEORGE. **The West Indies.** London: Nash, 1930, 304 p.
The latest edition of a convenient descriptive handbook.

VAN DYKE, JOHN CHARLES. **In the West Indies.** New York: Scribner, 1932, 211 p.
Travel impressions, with some interesting sidelights on political conditions.

VASSEUR, CARLOS A. **El Derecho de Soberanía sobre la Isla de Pinos.** Panamá: Star and Herald, 1925, 43 p.
A good outline of the Isle of Pines question, now at last settled, by the Cuban envoy in Panama.

WRONG, HUME. **The Government of the West Indies.** Oxford: Clarendon Press, 1923, 190 p.
The first serious analysis of the political system of the British West Indies, historical and analytical, with emphasis on problems of representative government and federation.

Cuba

ALVAREZ, LUIS SOLANO. **Mi Actuación Militar.** Havana: Cervantes, 1920, 356 p.
The story of the February revolution of 1917, by the former commander of the army.

CABRERA, RAIMUNDO. **Mis Malos Tiempos.** Havana: El Siglo xx, 2nd ed., 1920, 416 p.
A Cuban literary man's reminiscences of the revolution of 1917; a well-documented and important source.

Carlos Mendieta, Personalidad, Vida y Hechos. Havana: Magazine de la Raza, 1923, 166 p.
A biographical sketch and appreciation of one of the foremost Cuban Liberal politicians.

CHAPMAN, CHARLES EDWARD. **A History of the Cuban Republic.** New York: Macmillan, 1927, 697 p.
An outspoken and scholarly account of Cuban history since independence, by an American authority. Little account is taken of economic factors.

CORTINA, JOSÉ MANUEL. **Por la Nación Cubana.** Havana: El Siglo xx, 1926, 311 p.
The first volume of the speeches of a Cuban Liberal leader, several dealing with Cuba's international position and policy.

FERNÁNDEZ VEGA, WIFREDO. **Alma y Tierra.** Havana: Rambla, 1928, 240 p.
A collection of articles by an influential Cuban newspaperman.

JENKS, LELAND HAMILTON. **Our Cuban Colony.** New York: Vanguard, 1928, 341 p.
The best study of American business interests in Cuba before and since the establishment of independence. A scholarly monograph on one phase of American imperialism and its effects.

Johnson, Willis Fletcher. **History of Cuba.** New York: B. F. Buck, 1920, 5 v.
A detailed, semi-popular account of Cuba's checkered history from the time of discovery to the present; weak on the republican period. Volume V is a useful survey of Cuban resources.

López Hidalgo, Ambrosio Valentín. **Cuba y la Enmienda Platt.** Havana: El Siglo xx, 1921, 171 p.
One of the better Cuban studies of the Platt Amendment; the author objects to it because it was "imposed" on Cuba and leaves the door open to American intervention.

Lugo-Viña, Ruy de. **Un Internacionalista Representativo.** Paris: Cervantes, 1924, 273 p.
A general study of the diplomatic career of the eminent Cuban statesman Cosme de la Torriente, with emphasis on Cuba's part in the League and the securing of independence.

Machado y Ortega, Luis. **La Enmienda Platt.** Havana: El Siglo xx, 1922, 150 p.
Perhaps the keenest Cuban analysis of the Platt Amendment and permanent treaty, raising many objections to the terms of the settlement.

Ortiz, Fernando. **En la Tribuna.** Havana: El Siglo xx, 1923, 2 v.
The parliamentary addresses of an influential Cuban historian and publicist. Several deal with the war and international relations.

Pardo Suárez, Vicente. **La Elección Presidencial en Cuba.** Havana: Rambla, Bouza, 1923, 298 p.
The author maintains that political peace and administrative efficiency in Cuba demand that reëlection to the presidency be prohibited.

Torriente y Peraza, Cosme de la. **La Enmienda Platt y el Tratado Permanente.** Havana: Rambla, Bouza, 1930, 78 p.
An amplification of the interesting article on Cuba and the United States written for *Foreign Affairs* by the former Cuban Ambassador at Washington.

Varona, Franco. **El Presidente Zayas.** Havana: Martin, 1923, 215 p.
A popular biographical sketch of the Cuban statesman.

Verrill, Alpheus Hyatt. **Cuba, Past and Present.** New York: Dodd, rev. ed., 1920, 240 p.
The latest edition of a popular descriptive handbook.

Whitmarsh, Calixto. **Algo sobre Cuba.** Santiago de Chile: Imprenta Universitaria, 1923, 241 p.
A useful survey of Cuba's constitutional position, population, intellectual life, etc., by a Cuban diplomat.

Wright, Philip Green. **The Cuban Situation and Our Treaty Relations.** Washington: The Brookings Institution, 1931, 207 p.
A review of the intervention of the United States and the subsequent treaties, with special reference to their effects upon Cuba's economic life.

Dominican Republic

Franco-Franco, Tulio. **La Situation Internationale de la République Dominicaine à Partir du 8 Février, 1907.** Paris: Presses Universitaires, 1923, 285 p.
A well-informed doctoral dissertation examining the legal justification for American intervention, and reviewing American and Spanish public opinion on the subject.

Henríquez Ureña, Max. **Los Estados Unidos y la República Dominicana.** Havana: El Siglo xx, 1919, 206 p.

An important account based on Dominican documents, by the former secretary of the Dominican president.

HENRÍQUEZ UREÑA, MAX. **Los Yanquis en Santo Domingo.** Madrid: Aguilar, 1929, 285 p.
The Caribbean exploits of the United States supply endless food for criticism in this second book by a Dominican publicist.

INMAN, SAMUEL GUY. **Through Santo Domingo and Haiti.** New York: Committee on Coöperation in Latin America, 1920, 96 p.
A general survey of conditions in 1919, with suggestions for educational and social reforms.

KNIGHT, MELVIN MOSES. **The Americans in Santo Domingo.** New York: Vanguard, 1928, 208 p.
This, the first of a series of studies in American imperialism, represents perhaps the first attempt to treat both the intangible and the material relations of the United States with Santo Domingo. The viewpoint is anti-imperialistic. The book is a scholarly and conscientious attempt to give a true picture of the gradual entrenchment of American business interests and a succinct discussion of the problems arising therefrom.

WELLES, SUMNER. **Naboth's Vineyard.** New York: Payson and Clarke, 1928, 2 v.
An extensive and painstaking work, sympathetically treating the political history of the Dominican Republic from 1844 to 1924, by the former chief of the Latin American Division of the Department of State and former American Commissioner to the Dominican Republic.

Haiti

BALCH, EMILY GREENE. **Occupied Haiti.** New York: Writers Publishing Company, 1927, 186 p.
The report of an unofficial committee of six sent to Haiti under the auspices of the Woman's International League for Peace and Freedom, giving an excellent survey of the circumstances leading to the occupation and a dispassionate picture of conditions as they have been under American control. The members recommend the evacuation of the American forces and the return to a normal constitutional régime, and offer suggestions as to ways and means.

BEAUVOIR, VILFORT. **Le Contrôle Financier du Gouvernement des États-Unis d'Amérique sur la République d'Haïti.** Paris: Sirey, 1930, 268 p.
A doctoral dissertation by a Haitian lawyer and diplomat, analyzing the treaty rights of the United States and giving a critical account of the way in which they have been exercised.

DAVIS, H. P. **Black Democracy.** New York: Dial, 1928, 383 p.
A history of Haiti by one long resident in the island. Fair in tone, though critical of the policy of the United States.

MILLSPAUGH, ARTHUR CHESTER. **Haiti under American Control.** Boston: World Peace Foundation, 1931, 266 p.
A well-documented study of the evolution of the Haitian situation between 1915 and 1930, written by the former Financial Adviser-General of Haiti.

NILES, MRS. BLAIR (RICE). **Black Haiti.** New York: Putnam, 1926, 325 p.
An amiable historical and descriptive account.

VORBE, CHARLES. **Économie et Finances Haïtiennes: Comment les Restaurer?** Port-au-Prince: Chenet, 1921, 188 p.
A survey by a patriotic Haitian.

Puerto Rico

CLARK, VICTOR SELDEN, *ed.* **Porto Rico and Its Problems.** Washington: Brookings
Institution, 1930, 707 p.
An elaborate survey of economic and social conditions in the island, with extensive
recommendations for ameliorating the situation, by a group headed by the former
editor of *The Living Age*, who served as Commissioner of Education under the military
governorship. An indispensable source.

CUESTA, J. ENAMORADO. **Porto Rico, Past and Present.** New York: Eureka Printing
Company, n. d., 170 p.
The history of the past thirty years, and a description of conditions as they now are,
by a native Puerto Rican who paints an unlovely picture of American rule.

DANA, ARNOLD GUYOT. **Porto Rico's Case.** New Haven: Tuttle, Morehouse and Taylor,
2nd ed., 1928, 64 p.
The writer, after extensive investigation, has arrived at the conclusion that the
American achievement in the island is largely superficial.

DIFFIE, BAILEY W. and MRS. JUSTINE (WHITFIELD). **Porto Rico: A Broken Pledge.**
New York: Vanguard, 1931, 287 p.
Political, social and economic conditions in the island after thirty years of American
rule. A good book.

FERNÁNDEZ GARCÍA, E., *ed.* **The Book of Porto Rico.** San Juan: El Libro Azul, 1923,
1188 p.
An immense illustrated descriptive work, with contributions by many writers, and text
in Spanish and English.

MIXER, KNOWLTON. **Porto Rico, History and Conditions.** New York: Macmillan,
1926, 329 p.
One of the best general historical and descriptive works, with much emphasis on
economic life and social conditions.

Other Islands

CORBIN, PIERRE and others. **Les Colonies Françaises d'Amérique.** Paris: Notre
Domaine Colonial, 1924, 126 p.
Saint-Pierre and Miquelon; Guadeloupe; Martinique; Guiana.

LE PAGE, ADRIEN, DEVEZ, DR. and BAUDE, THÉODORE. **Guadeloupe, Guyane, Mar-
tinique, Saint-Pierre et Miquelon.** Paris: Société d'Éditions Géographiques, 1931.
An excellent descriptive survey of the French possessions, prepared for the Colonial
Exposition of 1931.

MAZIN, THÉRÈSE EREMBERT. **Les Antilles Françaises.** Toulouse: Languedocienne, 1921,
157 p.
A doctoral thesis giving a brief and superficial study of the governmental system,
with some discussion of finance and trade.

SKUTSCH, ILSE. **Die Inseln Trinidad und Tobago.** Leipzig: Vogel, 1929, 198 p.
A German dissertation, one of the best geographical, descriptive and statistical surveys
of the islands and their trade.

MEXICO

See also (United States) Relations with Latin America, p. 179, and Immigration and Race Problems, p. 191.

ALVARADO, SALVADOR. **La Reconstrucción de México.** Mexico: Ballesca, 1919, 3 v.
A Mexican general makes a long and rambling survey of Mexican problems and policy, domestic and foreign, political, social and economic.

ARAQUISTAIN, LUIS. **La Revolución Mejicana, Sus Orígenes, Sus Hombres, Su Obra.** Madrid: Renacimiento, 1929, 356 p.
A very sympathetic account of the revolution. The author, a foremost Spanish political writer, stresses its agrarian aspects and the fight against the exploitation of the Indian, against privilege and against the Church.

BALDERRAMA, LUIS C. **El Clero y el Gobierno de México.** Mexico: Cuauhtemoc, 1927, 2 v.
An exhaustive statement from the governmental viewpoint.

BEALS, CARLETON. **Mexican Maze.** Philadelphia: Lippincott, 1931, 369 p.
Highly interesting and instructive pictures of Mexican life and problems, by a well-known writer and lecturer.

BEALS, CARLETON. **Mexico: An Interpretation.** New York: Huebsch, 1923, 280 p.
The first penetrating study, in English, of the Mexican revolution. It is favorable to the Obregón régime.

BLASCO IBÁÑEZ, VICENTE. **Mexico in Revolution.** New York: Dutton, 1920, 245 p.
A collection of articles published in American newspapers by the famous Spanish novelist. A scathing exposure of Mexican politics and conditions. For a detailed reply to the author's assertions see Rosas y Reyes: "Las Imposturas de Vicente Blasco Ibáñez" (Barcelona: Librería Sintes, 1923, 434 p.).

BROWN, JOHN WILLIAM. **Modern Mexico and Its Problems.** London: Labour Publishing Company, 1927, 128 p.
Essentially an account of the Mexican labor movement, with chapters dealing also with the Church, the oil interests and the relations of Mexico and the United States.

La Caída de Carranza. Mexico: no publisher, 1920, 248 p.
A valuable collection of proclamations, orders, articles, speeches, etc., by Obregón and his followers, throwing much light on the movement against Carranza.

CALLCOTT, WILFRID HARDY. **Liberalism in Mexico.** Stanford: Stanford University Press, 1931, 410 p.
A documented history of Mexico from 1857 to the present time. Not very original.

CALLES, PLUTARCO ELÍAS. **Mexico before the World.** New York: Academy Press, 1927, 244 p.
A selection from the former President's state papers and addresses, designed to explain his aims in domestic and foreign policy.

CAPETILLO, ALONSO. **La Rebelión sin Cabeza.** Mexico: Botas, 1925, 318 p.
An insider's history of the De la Huerta rebellion of 1923.

CHASE, STUART. **Mexico.** New York: Macmillan, 1931, 338 p.
Mexican life and culture as seen by a well-known interpreter of the advantages of pre-machine civilization and believer in the superiority of the Mexican Indian. A readable and interesting book.

CREEL, GEORGE. **The People Next Door.** New York: Day, 1926, 418 p.
A survey of Mexican history, showing many evidences of bias. The author was sent to Mexico in 1920 as an unofficial agent of President Wilson.

CUADROS CALDAS, JULIO. **México-Soviet.** Puebla: Santiago Loyo, 1926, 606 p.
A revolutionist's detailed study of the growing social radicalism of the Mexican revolutionary governments since Diaz' time.

La Deuda Exterior de México. Mexico: Editorial Cultura, 1926, 341 p.
An official publication of importance, dealing especially with the Lamont-De la Huerta Agreement and the Pani Amendment.

DILLON, EMILE JOSEPH. **Mexico on the Verge.** New York: Doran, 1921, 296 p.
An outspoken survey of Mexican domestic and international problems, with much emphasis on the oil question, foreign investments and the blindness of American imperialism.

DILLON, EMILE JOSEPH. **President Obregón—A World Reformer.** Boston Small, Maynard, 1923, 350 p.
An effort to present the President of Mexico as a statesman of a new moral order. A well-informed book by a well-known English political writer. Both this and the preceding title give an impression of having been written to order.

DIVINIE, LOUIS LA. **Les Phases de la Persécution au Mexique.** Paris: Bloud et Gay, 1929, 200 p.
A review of the religious problem in Mexico from colonial times, from a standpoint favorable to the church.

Ensayo sobre la Reconstrucción de México. New York: De Laisne, n. d., 118 p.
A series of articles on Mexican domestic and foreign problems, published by a group of Mexican exiles during the last months of the Carranza régime.

EVANS, MRS. ROSALIE (CADEN). **Letters from Mexico.** Indianapolis: Bobbs-Merrill, 1926, 472 p.
Letters which throw much light on the agrarian problem and on the problem of the security of property held by foreigners. The author was murdered and these letters were published posthumously by her sister.

GALARZA, ERNEST. **The Roman Catholic Church as a Factor in the Political and Social History of Mexico.** Sacramento: Capital Press, 1928, 188 p.
An indictment.

GALINDO, HERMILA. **La Doctrina Carranza y el Acercamiento Indo-Latino.** Mexico: no publisher, 1919, 200 p.
The author, editor of the journal *Mujer Moderna*, gives a most sympathetic discussion of Carranza's foreign policy, of his championship of weak states and of the transformation in Latin American relations.

GIBBON, THOMAS EDWARD. **Mexico under Carranza.** New York: Doubleday, 1919, 270 p.
A lawyer's indictment of the crowning infamy of four hundred years of misrule.

GONZÁLEZ ROA, FERNANDO. **El Aspecto Agrario de la Revolución Mexicana.** Mexico: 1919, 330 p.
An excellent historical and analytical study of the agrarian problem.

GONZÁLEZ ROA, FERNANDO. **Las Cuestiones Fundamentales de Actualidad en México.** Mexico: Secretaría de Relaciones Exteriores, 1927, 251 p.
A useful semi-official statement of policy on crucial problems.

GRUENING, ERNEST. **Mexico and Its Heritage.** New York: Century, 1928, 747 p.
A careful and original study of Mexico's history, revolutions, church struggles and present situation. One of the best general works, written in a frank vein. See also the fourth volume of Howland's "Survey of American Foreign Relations" (New Haven: Yale Press, 1931), for an extensive background treatment of Mexican problems.

GUZMÁN, MARTÍN LUIS. **The Eagle and the Serpent.** New York: Knopf, 1930, 360 p.
A translation of highly impressionistic reminiscences of the revolutionary period. Valuable for its light on the morals and motives of the revolutionary leaders.

HERRING, HUBERT CLINTON and TERRILL, KATHARINE, *eds.* **The Genius of Mexico.** New York: Committee on Cultural Relations with Latin America, 1931, 343 p.
This collection of lectures, delivered at a seminar in Mexico City in 1930, covers the most diverse aspects of Mexican life and Mexico's relations to the rest of the world.

INMAN, SAMUEL GUY. **Intervention in Mexico.** New York: Association Press, 1919, 248 p.
A careful study of the intervention policy, by a recognized authority on Latin America, long Secretary of the Commission on Coöperation in Latin America, a body representing missionary interests. Hostile to intervention.

An Inquiry on Mexico. Mexico: Rivadeneyra, 1926, 295 p.
Chiefly a defense of the Mexican government policy in the petroleum problem, evidently written by a Frenchman.

JONES, CHESTER LLOYD. **Mexico and Its Reconstruction.** New York: Appleton, 1922, 330 p.
A cool and dispassionate analysis of the Mexican problem at the end of the first decade of revolution. Based on much study and personal investigation.

LILL, THOMAS RUSSELL. **National Debt of Mexico.** New York: Searle, 1919, 115 p.
A concise study by a trained accountant who for some months directed the Commission on Financial and Administrative Reorganization set up by Carranza.

LONG, WILLIAM RODNEY. **Railways in Mexico.** Washington: Department of Commerce, 1925, 220 p.
One of the excellent handbooks prepared by the Bureau of Foreign and Domestic Commerce.

McBRIDE, GEORGE McCUTCHEN. **The Land Systems of Mexico.** New York: American Geographical Society, 1923, 204 p.
An accurate and valuable picture of the agrarian influences in Mexico and their part in the revolution.

McCALEB, WALTER FLAVIUS. **Present and Past Banking in Mexico.** New York: Harper, 1920, 269 p.
A documented study, dealing chiefly with the period 1884 to 1919.

McCALEB, WALTER FLAVIUS. **The Public Finances of Mexico.** New York: Harper, 1922, 268 p.
One of the best historical accounts in English, though since superseded in part by Turlington's volume. Written by an experienced banker, it covers the whole period of Mexican independence down to the date of publication.

McCULLAGH, FRANCIS. **Red Mexico.** New York: Carrier, 1928, 415 p.
A lurid philippic by a well-known British correspondent who excoriates the Calles régime for its persecution of the church and of political opponents, its confiscatory land policy, etc., all of which, says the author, has delivered Mexico yet further into the hands of the United States.

MÉNDEZ DE CUENCA, LAURA. **Alvaro Obregón.** Hermosillo: Sisniega, n. d., 122 p.
A general biography, by an admiring supporter.

Mexican Petroleum. New York: Pan American Petroleum and Transport Company, 1922, 300 p.
A history and survey of the oil industry, with descriptions of the properties of the large foreign countries.

MIDDLETON, PHILIP HARVEY. **Industrial Mexico.** New York: Dodd, 1919, 270 p.
A systematic survey of Mexico's economic life as it was in 1919.

MONROY DURAN, LUIS. **El Ultimo Caudillo.** Mexico: Rodríguez, 1924, 155 p.
A useful collection of material bearing on the military rising of 1923 and surveying the course of events in the separate states.

ORTEGA, A. N. **Noticia Histórica de las Relaciones Políticas y Comerciales entre México y el Japón.** Mexico City: Ministry of Foreign Affairs, 1923.
A semi-official account of Japanese-Mexican relations in recent times.

PANI, ALBERTO J. **La Política Hacendaria y la Revolución.** Mexico: Cultura, 1926, 738 p.
An exhaustive review of Mexican public finance in the years 1923 to 1926, by the Minister of Finance.

PÉREZ LUGO, J., *comp*. **La Cuestión Religiosa en México.** Mexico: Cuauhtemoc, 1927, 428 p.
A collection of Mexican laws and other documents bearing on the church, from earliest Spanish times, designed to support the government's position.

PRIESTLEY, HERBERT INGRAM. **The Mexican Nation, a History.** New York: Macmillan, 1923, 507 p.
The first comprehensive one-volume history of Mexico produced in this country. It is chiefly narrative and descriptive, and its emphasis is political rather than economic.

PUIG CASAURANC, JOSÉ MANUEL. **De Nuestro México.** Mexico: no publisher, 1926, 193 p.
A series of articles and addresses on social problems and their political aspects, by a former cabinet minister.

PUIG CASAURANC, JOSÉ MANUEL. **La Cosecha y la Siembra.** Mexico: no publisher, 1928, 388 p.
Further essays and addresses.

RABASA, EMILIO. **L'Évolution Historique du Mexique.** Paris: Alcan, 1924, 344 p.
An excellent synthesis and interpretation of movements and problems, by a Mexican lawyer identified with the old régime.

REICHWEIN, ADOLF. **Mexiko Erwacht.** Leipzig: Bibliographisches Institut, 1930, 274 p.
An admirably illustrated socio-geographical work, by a recognized authority.

RIPPY, JAMES FRED, VASCONCELOS, JOSÉ and STEVENS, GUY. **Mexico.** Chicago: Chicago University Press, 1929, 264 p.
Three good little essays—by an American historian, a Mexican patriot and a representative of American oil interests.

ROSS, EDWARD ALSWORTH. **The Social Revolution in Mexico.** New York: Century, 1923, 176 p.
An analysis by a talented observer, affording one of the first glimpses in English of the revolution.

SAENZ, MOISES and PRIESTLEY, HERBERT INGRAM. **Some Mexican Problems.** Chicago: Chicago University Press, 1926, 183 p.
An authoritative discussion of some of the great questions of the present.

SCHNITZLER, HERMANN, *comp*. **The Republic of Mexico.** New York: Nicholas L. Brown, 1924, 637 p.
The first volume of the Library of Latin American Information. An exhaustive statistical handbook.

SHERWELL, GUILLERMO BUTLER. **Mexico's Capacity to Pay.** Washington: Author, 1929, 119 p.
A documented study comparing Mexico's economic situation in 1910 and 1927; the author's conclusions point to the great potentialities of Mexico and her ability to pay her creditors.

STELZMANN, ALEXANDER. **Mexico.** Lübeck: Quitzow, 1927, 296 p.
A thoroughly scientific picture of present-day Mexico, with stress on economic matters.

STERRETT, JOSEPH EDMUND and DAVIS, JOSEPH STANCLIFFE. **The Fiscal and Economic Condition of Mexico.** New York: 1928, 255 p.
An extensive report submitted to the International Committee of Bankers on Mexico. The best thing of its kind at the time it was published.

TANNENBAUM, FRANK. **The Mexican Agrarian Revolution.** New York: Macmillan, 1929, 543 p.
This volume, based in part upon unpublished material, deals with the land problem as it presented itself to the revolutionary leaders, the process of distribution of land, foreign ownership and the effects of recent legislation upon this important aspect of international relations. A publication of the Institute of Economics.

THOMPSON, WALLACE. **The Mexican Mind.** Boston: Little, Brown, 1922, 303 p.
An interesting, non-technical study of Mexican psychology, by a firm believer in the superiority of the white man.

TORO, ALFONSO. **La Iglesia y el Estado en México.** Mexico: Talleres de la Nación, 1927, 500 p.
Practically an official history of the conflict between clergy and government since the attainment of independence. Published under the auspices of the Archivo General de la Nación.

TURLINGTON, EDGAR WILLIS. **Mexico and Her Foreign Creditors.** New York: Columbia University Press, 1930, 449 p.
The first volume of a series on "Mexico in International Finance and Diplomacy." The author, who has had experience in the State Department, gives a detailed study of the financial and political sides of Mexican indebtedness. The book is fully documented and prints many of the important contracts and agreements.

VAGTS, ALFRED. **Mexico, Europa und Amerika.** Berlin: Rothschild, 1928, 415 p.
An excellent book on Mexico, published under the auspices of the Hochschule für Politik and the Institut für Auswärtige Politik. The author is conversant with the whole literature bearing upon his problem and has made extensive investigations in the United States and Mexico. He begins with an admirable account of the development of Mexico since she secured independence, stressing the international aspects of her position and analyzing the changing interests of Great Britain and the United States. He works out in detail the emergence of the oil question and its reaction upon the general situation.

VALENZUELA, CLODOVEO and MATAMOROS, AMADO CHAVERRI. **Sonora y Carranza.** Mexico: Sisniega, 1921, 522 p.
A huge collection of proclamations, letters, telegrams, pictures, etc., dealing with the Obregón movement and Carranza's fall.

VASCONCELOS, JOSÉ and GAMIO, MANUEL. **Aspects of Mexican Civilization.** Chicago: Chicago University Press, 1926, 202 p.
Stimulating and suggestive lectures delivered at the Norman Wait Harris Institute.

VERA ESTAÑOL, JORGE. **Carranza and His Bolshevik Régime.** Los Angeles: Wayside Press, 1920, 247 p.
A series of articles by a former Mexican Minister of the Interior, in which he criticizes the constitution of 1917 and the whole Carranza régime.

WALLING, WILLIAM ENGLISH. **The Mexican Question.** New York: Robins, 1927, 205 p.
A review of Mexican-American relations during the administrations of Obregón and Calles, with a sympathetic discussion of the Labor movement, by a writer close to the American Federation of Labor.

WINTER, NEVIN OTTO. **Mexico and Her People.** Boston: Page, new rev. ed., 1923, 548 p.
A new and revised edition of a comprehensive popular work.

WINTON, GEORGE BEVERLY. **Mexico, Past and Present.** Nashville: Cokesbury, 1928, 296 p.
An historical and interpretative study of Mexico, with the chief emphasis on the revolutionary period.

CENTRAL AMERICA

See also (United States) Relations with Latin America, p. 179.

BAYLE, LÉON DE. **Les Emprunts Extérieurs et la Réforme Monétaire de la République de Nicaragua.** Paris: Librairie Générale de Droit, 1927, 146 p.
A scholarly investigation of the monetary aspects of the Nicaraguan situation since the establishment of American control. A French doctoral thesis.

BEALS, CARLETON. **Banana Gold.** Philadelphia: Lippincott, 1932, 367 p.
Vivid travel impressions of Central America.

BONES QUIÑÓNEZ, ANTONIO. **Geografía é Historia de Honduras.** Choluteca: Portillo, 1927, 212 p.
A good general book.

CERNA, JOSÉ RODRÍGUEZ. **Un Pueblo en Marcha.** Madrid: Compañía General de Artes, 1931, 250 p.
The geography, history, economic life and artistic activity of Guatemala.

CRAMER, FLOYD. **Our Neighbor Nicaragua.** New York: Stokes, 1929, 243 p.
An outline of Nicaraguan history and discussion of recent happenings, by a defender of the policy of the United States.

CROWTHER, SAMUEL. **The Romance and Rise of the American Tropics.** New York: Doubleday, 1929, 390 p.
A readable and well-informed introductory sketch of the history of Central America.

CUMBERLAND, WILLIAM WILSON. **Nicaragua, an Economic and Financial Survey.** Washington: Government Printing Office, 1928, 178 p.
The report of an investigation conducted under the auspices of the State Department at the request of the Nicaraguan Government.

HALL, MÁXIMO SOTO. **Nicaragua y el Imperialismo Norteamericano.** Buenos Aires: Artes y Letras, 1928, 163 p.
An able journalistic review of the evolution of the Nicaraguan situation, marked throughout by violent hostility to the policy of the United States.

LANDINI, PIERO. **Guatemala.** Rome: Treves, n. d., 164 p.
A scientific descriptive work, with an excellent bibliography. One of the publications of the Istituto Cristoforo Colombo.

MORENO, LAUDELINO. **Historia de las Relaciones Interestatuales de Centro-América.** Madrid: Compañía Ibero-Americana, 1928, 507 p.
An exhaustive scholarly treatment, covering the period since the attainment of independence. Easily the best treatment of the subject.

OTERO, LUIS ALFREDO. **Panamá.** Bogotá: Imprenta Nacional, 1926, 148 p.
An historical review of the Panama question in United States-Colombian relations, by a Colombian diplomat.

PLAYTER, HAROLD. **Nicaragua: Commercial and Economic Survey.** Washington: Department of Commerce, 1927, 158 p.
A handbook covering resources and industries of Nicaragua, its transportation and banking facilities, and trade, prepared for the Bureau of Foreign and Domestic Commerce.

QUARTA, ORONZO. **Costa Rica.** Rome: Treves, 1925, 189 p.
One of the excellent descriptive works published by the Istituto Cristoforo Colombo.

RUHL, ARTHUR. **The Central Americans.** New York: Scribner, 1928, 284 p.
A sane and well-balanced travel book.

SEQUEIRA, DIEGO MANUEL. **Émission et Amortissement des Emprunts Extérieurs de la République du Nicaragua.** Paris: Librairie Générale de Droit, 1931, 114 p.
Another doctoral dissertation reviewing the loans and the American control in the period between 1900 and 1920.

THOMPSON, WALLACE. **Rainbow Countries of Central America.** New York: Dutton, 1926, 284 p.
A good descriptive volume treating historical backgrounds and present social and economic problems.

VANNI, MANFREDO. **Salvador.** Rome: Treves, n. d., 159 p.
A scientific descriptive study in the same series as Landini's "Guatemala" and Quarta's "Costa Rica."

VERRILL, ALPHEUS HYATT. **Panama, Past and Present.** New York: Dodd, 1921, 262 p.
A popular historical and descriptive outline.

YOUNG, JOHN PARKE. **Central American Currency and Finance.** Princeton: Princeton University Press, 1925, 258 p.
An exhaustive monograph on Central American financial policy.

SOUTH AMERICA

General

DOMVILLE-FIFE, CHARLES WILLIAM. **Modern South America.** London: Seeley, 1931, 320 p.
A comprehensive, illustrated survey.

EDSCHMID, KASIMIR. **Glanz und Elend Süd-Amerikas.** Frankfurt: Societäts-Verlag, 1932, 479 p.
Observations and reflections on extensive travels in South America. An illuminating book.

GIBBONS, HERBERT ADAMS. **The New Map of South America.** New York: Century, 1928, 400 p.
A general survey of the present situation, written in the style of this prolific author's well-known earlier volumes on other areas.

HAGEMANN, WALTER. **Zwischen la Plata und Hudson.** Berlin: Germania, 1927, 270 p.
Good on the political conditions of Argentina, Chile, Brazil and Mexico.

JONES, CLARENCE FIELDEN. **Commerce of South America.** Boston: Ginn, 1928, 600 p.
An exhaustive scholarly survey of the trade of the South American countries, one by one, with an interesting chapter on the United States and its competitors.

KOEBEL, WILLIAM HENRY. **South America: An Industrial and Commercial Field.**
London: Fisher Unwin, 1923, 360 p.
A new edition of a useful handbook, with an extended discussion of trade, English
interests and international competition.

LÜTGENS, RUDOLF. **Die A. B. C. Staaten.** Berlin: Zentral-Verlag, 1930, 102 p.
A brief economic study, with reference to the position of the A. B. C. states in the
economic scheme of the world.

NORMANO, JOÃO FREDERICO. **The Struggle for South America.** Boston: Houghton
Mifflin, 1931, 294 p.
A good book on South America and its place in the world, written by a lecturer at
Harvard.

SHANAHAN, EDWARD WILLIAM. **South America.** London: Methuen, 1927, 318 p.
An economic and regional geography, accurate and searching, and a good antidote to
over-sanguine accounts.

Territorial Problems; Tacna-Arica; Chaco; etc.

ACHÁ, JOSÉ AGUIRRE. **The Arbitration Zone in the Bolivian-Paraguayan Dispute.**
La Paz: 1929, 68 p.
A review of negotiations regarding the Chaco dispute with a view to determining just
what zone Bolivia would be prepared to submit to arbitration.

ALAMO YBARRA, CARLOS. **Nuestras Fronteras Occidentales.** Caracas: Editorial "Patria," 1927, 136 p.
A history of the Venezuelan-Colombian frontier dispute.

ANGULO Y PUENTE ARNAO, JUAN. **Historia de los Límites del Perú.** Lima: Imprenta de
la Intendencia General de Guerra, 1927, 312 p.
The Tacna-Arica problem from the Peruvian angle.

ARTEAGA, LUIS. **Las Negociaciones de Washington.** Santiago: Walker, 1922, 64 p.
The Chilean commissioner for the affairs of Tacna gives an account and defense of
the agreement of 1922, which he was active in effecting.

AYALA, ELÍAS. **Paraguay y Bolivia en el Chaco Boreal.** Asunción: Imprenta Nacional,
1929, 124 p.
A general review of the problem from the Paraguayan side, with much map material.

BARROS JARPA, ERNESTO. **Hacia la Solución.** Santiago: Imprenta Universitaria, 1922,
363 p.
An important account of the post-war negotiations between Chile and Peru, by the
Chilean Foreign Minister.

BELAUNDE, VÍCTOR ANDRÉS. **Nuestra Cuestión con Chile.** Lima: Sanmarti, 1919, 259 p.
The larger part of the volume is a review of the Tacna-Arica question from the War
of the Pacific on, written in refutation of the Chilean Red Book of 1909. The last chapters deal with later negotiations. A semi-official Peruvian statement.

BUSTAMENTE, DANIEL SÁNCHEZ. **Bolivia, Su Estructura y Sus Derechos en el Pacífico.**
La Paz: Arnó, 1919, 377 p.
A very able presentation of Bolivia's claim to an outlet on the Pacific, with consider-
able discussion of the new international order, the peaceful revision of treaties, etc.

CARRASCO, JOSÉ. **La Bolivie devant la Société des Nations.** Paris: Berger-Levrault,
1921, 207 p.
Really an historical review of Bolivian territorial claims and aspirations.

Chile y la Aspiración de Bolivia á Puerto en el Pacífico. Santiago: Imp. Universitaria, 1922, 160 p.
A collection of documents in support of the Chilean contention that Bolivia has no
right to go back on the treaty of 1904.

DEITRICK, JACKIE. **What Price Tacna-Arica?** Lima: West Coast Leader, 1926, 188 p.
A series of articles written by an American newspaperwoman for Peruvian papers
during the first months of the plebiscite in Arica.

DENNIS, WILLIAM JEFFERSON. **Tacna and Arica.** New Haven: Yale University Press,
1931, 350 p.
The best neutral treatment of the subject; a scholarly review of the whole evolution of
the problem down to the settlement of 1929. The volume is particularly well documented, and contains in appendices a complete set of the relevant treaties.

DIEZ DE MEDINA, EDUARDO. **Apuntes sobre Tópicos Internacionales.** La Paz: Arno,
1919, 163 p.
A collection of essays by a Bolivian diplomat, dealing with Bolivia's international
position and territorial aspirations.

DIEZ DE MEDINA, EDUARDO. **La Cuestión del Pacífico y la Política Internacional de
Bolivia.** La Paz: Unidas, 1923, 270 p.
A detailed reply to Barros Borgoño's "The Problem of the Pacific," of which the Span-
ish edition was published in 1922.

FRANCO, MODESTO CHÁVEZ. **Cartilla Patria.** Quito: Imprenta de "El Dia," 1922, 238 p.
An historical study of Peruvian territorial claims against Ecuador.

GÁLVEZ, JUAN IGNACIO. **International Conflicts.** Santiago de Chile: Sociedad Imprenta
Universo, 1920, 247 p.
A Chilean's indictment of Peruvian expansionist tendencies, as demonstrated in her
quarrels with Colombia, Ecuador and Chile.

MAURTUA, VICTOR MANUEL. **Sur le Pacifique du Sud.** Dijon: Darantière, 1922, 282 p.
Perhaps the best brief historical account from the Peruvian side of the Tacna-Arica
difficulty. Written by the former Peruvian delegate to the League of Nations.

MERCADO, MIGUEL. **El Chaco Boreal.** La Paz: 1920, 230 p.
A statement of Bolivian claims and a review of diplomatic negotiations to date.

El Problema de Tacna y Arica. Santiago de Chile: Imprenta Universitaria, 1919, 109 p.
A collection of a dozen expert opinions on the subject, assembled by *La Nación* of
Buenos Aires.

VARAS, CARLOS. **Tacna y Arica bajo la Soberanía Chilena.** Santiago: La Nación,
1922, 332 p.
Primarily an account of the development of the provinces and the achievement of the
Chilean administration. Illustrated.

Argentina

AYARRAGARAY, LUCAS. **Cuestiones y Problemas Argentinos Contemporáneos.**
Buenos Aires: Lajouane, 1930, 484 p.
The definitive edition of the writings of a prominent critic. The book contains essays
on constitutional problems, immigration, political life, etc.

BAS, ARTURO M. **El Derecho Federal Argentino.** Buenos Aires: Abeledo, 1927, 2 v.
The most exhaustive recent scholarly treatment on Argentine constitutional law.

BUNGE, ALEJANDRO E. **La Economía Argentina.** Buenos Aires: Agencia General de Librería, 1928, 2 v.
A collection of studies by an Argentine economist. They touch on many aspects of Argentine economic life, foreign capital, etc.

DENIS, PIERRE. **The Argentine Republic, Its Development and Progress.** New York: Scribner, 1922, 296 p.
A scholarly work, chiefly devoted to economic life and geographical resources.

DOMÍNGUEZ, EMILIO. **El 6 de Septiembre de 1930.** Buenos Aires: Agencia General de Librería, n. d., 304 p.
A study of the background of the revolution, together with much material in the way of speeches, proclamations, etc.

EMILIANI, RAFAEL P. **Reorganización Económica Política y Social.** Buenos Aires: Martino, 1920, 520 p.
A general review of Argentine financial, commercial and industrial problems in the light of the new conditions resulting from the World War.

GONZÁLEZ, JOAQUÍN VÍCTOR. **Patria y Democracia.** Buenos Aires: Menéndez, 1920, 174 p.
Chiefly a study of Argentine immigration and growing radicalism in social thought and politics.

GUTIÉRREZ DE MIGUEL, VALENTÍN. **La Revolución Argentina.** Madrid: Compañía General de Artes Gráficas, 1930, 259 p.
A narrative history of the revolution of September 1930, by the editor of *La Voz*.

JEFFERSON, MARK. **Peopling the Argentine Pampa.** New York: American Geographical Society, 1926, 211 p.
A study of the social and political background of the nation, and of the progress of colonization. Illustrated with many maps and photographs.

KIRKPATRICK, FREDERICK ALEXANDER. **A History of the Argentine Republic.** New York: Macmillan, 1931, 282 p.
Probably the best general history of Argentina available in English.

KOEBEL, WILLIAM HENRY. **The New Argentina.** New York: Dodd, Mead, 1923, 276 p.
Contains a mass of concrete information especially on resources, communications, trade, industry, labor problems, etc.

KURTZ, ROBERTO. **La Argentina ante Estados Unidos.** Buenos Aires: Librería del Colegio, 1928, 305 p.
A contrast between the United States and Argentina, followed by an analysis of North American superiority and Argentine weaknesses, and a discussion of Latin American hatred of the United States.

LAFOND, GEORGES. **La République Argentine.** Paris: Roger, 1927, 96 p.
A very brief, but helpful survey of Argentine conditions.

LESTARD, GASTÓN H. **Los Problemas de la Moneda y del Crédito.** Buenos Aires: Roldan, 1925, 61 p.
An authoritative discussion of Argentine monetary and banking problems.

MACIEL, CARLOS NÉSTOR. **La Italianización de la Argentina.** Buenos Aires: Menéndez, 1924, 235 p.
A cry of alarm lest the culture and nationality of Argentina become submerged by the Italians.

MATIENZO, JOSÉ NICOLÁS. **Nuevos Temas Políticos e Históricos.** Buenos Aires: La Facultad, 1928, 521 p.
A collection of essays by an Argentine professor, dealing chiefly with constitutional problems.

MORENO QUINTANA, LUCIO M. **La Diplomacia de Yrigoyen.** La Plata: Editorial Inca, 1928, 485 p.
A detailed, documented account of Argentine policy from 1916 to 1922.

MORENO QUINTANA, LUCIO M. **Inmigración.** Buenos Aires: Menéndez, 1920, 160 p.
A general review of the Argentine immigration problem in the light of the new situation created by the World War and the policy of the United States.

OTERO, JOSÉ PACÍFICO. **Nuestro Nacionalismo.** Buenos Aires: La Facultad, 1920, 186 p.
An interesting attempt to analyze the historical and social factors in Argentine nationalism.

PIÑERO, NORBERTO. **La Moneda, el Crédito y los Bancos en la Argentina.** Buenos Aires: Menéndez, 1921, 398 p.
A general scholarly history of money and banking in Argentina.

PIÑERO, NORBERTO. **La Política Internacional Argentina.** Buenos Aires: Menéndez, 1924, 300 p.
The best general account of Argentine foreign policy from the wars of independence to the present.

PUCCIO, LUIS FRISTACHI. **L'Évolution Constitutionnelle de la République Argentine et l'Évolution de l'Esprit Public.** Paris: Vie Universitaire, 1922, 166 p.
A superficial dissertation analyzing the Constitution and the Argentine political system.

ROWE, LEO STANTON. **The Federal System of the Argentine Republic.** Washington: Carnegie Institution, 1921.
A general analysis of the constitutional system of the Argentine, written by the president of the Pan-American Union and published under the auspices of the Carnegie Institution.

SOUWEINE, PAUL B. **L'Argentine au Seuil de l'Industrie.** Paris: Casterman, 1927, 644 p.
A detailed scholarly study of available labor, fuel, plant and credit resources, as well as of social and industrial legislation.

VERA Y GONZÁLEZ, ENRIQUE. **Historia de la República Argentina.** Buenos Aires: La Facultad, 1926, 3 v.
A general semi-popular history of Argentina from 1829 to the post-war period.

ZUKER, CARLOS. **Die Argentinische Nationalbank.** Weida: Thomas, 1928, 135 p.
A German dissertation reviewing the history of the bank from 1891 to 1926 and analyzing its credit policy.

Bolivia

See also (South America) Territorial Problems, p. 212.

ARGUEDAS, ALCIDES. **Historia General de Bolivia.** La Paz: Arno, 1922, 579 p.
An admirable general study of Bolivian development in the nineteenth century, but rather brief on the early twentieth. There is an abridged French edition, "Histoire Générale de la Bolivie" (Paris: Alcan, 1923, 157 p.).

HARMS ESPEJO, CARLOS. **Bolivia en Sus Diversas Fases.** Santiago de Chile: Castro, 1922, 284 p.
An elaborate report dealing chiefly with Bolivia's economic resources and life, by a former Chilean military attaché.

MARSH, MRS. MARGARET CHARLOTTE (ALEXANDER). **The Bankers in Bolivia.** New York: Vanguard, 1928, 233 p.

An excellent study of the country and the American investment. A volume of the "Studies in American Imperialism."

PAZ, JULIO. **Historia Económica de Bolivia.** La Paz: Ayacucho, 1927, 189 p.
The barest outline, very slight on the modern period.

Brazil

ATRI, ALESSANDRO D'. **L'État de São Paulo et le Renouvellement Économique de l'Europe.** Paris: Allard, 1926, 360 p.
Really a full account of the economic, political and social situation in Brazil.

BARROS, JOÃO DE. **Sentido do Atlantico.** Lisbon: Aillaud, 1921, 251 p.
Essays pleading for closer Portuguese-Brazilian relations and contacts.

DENIS, PIERRE. **Brazil.** London: Fisher Unwin, 5th ed., 1926, 388 p.
The latest edition of a well-known French descriptive study.

FUNKE, ALFRED. **Brasilien im 20-ten Jahrhundert.** Berlin: Hobbing, 1926, 435 p.
An excellent descriptive work, especially valuable for the account of German colonization.

JAMES, HERMAN GERLACH. **Brazil after a Century of Independence.** New York: Macmillan, 1925, 599 p.
An historical and descriptive manual, the best recent book in English.

JORGE, RICARDO. **Brasil! Brasil!** Lisbon: Fluminense, 1930, 162 p.
Lectures on the Brazilian movement in Portugal, and kindred subjects.

KOEHLER, FRITZ. **Brasilien Heute und Morgen.** Leipzig: Brockhaus, 1926, 272 p.
A general descriptive work with emphasis on economic aspects.

MALESANI, EMILIO. **Brasile.** Rome: Libreria Mantegazza, 1929, 894 p.
A large-scale descriptive work published by the Istituto Cristoforo Colombo.

NASH, ROY. **The Conquest of Brazil.** New York: Harcourt, 1926, 454 p.
One of the best general accounts of the development and present day conditions in Brazil.

NOGUEIRA, J. A. **Sonho de Gigante.** S. Paulo: Monteiro, 1922, 210 p.
Essays on various phases of Brazilian nationalism.

SCHÜLER, HEINRICH. **Brasilien.** Berlin: Verlags-Anstalt, 6th ed., 1924, 257 p.
One of the best surveys of Brazilian resources and economic life.

Chile

See also (South America) Territorial Problems, p. 212.

ALESSANDRI, ARTURO. **Parlementarisme et Régime Présidentiel.** Paris: Sirey, 1930, 163 p.
The constitutional, international, financial and social evolution of Chile, by the former President.

CABERO, ALBERTO. **Chile y los Chilenos.** Santiago: Nascimento, 1926, 440 p.
A course of lectures on the historical, cultural and economic evolution of Chile.

CONTRERAS, FRANCISCO. **Le Chili et la France.** Paris: Bossard, 1919, 164 p.
A brief survey of Chile's affairs and problems, with special treatment of her sympathies for France and the possibilities of further French propaganda.

Cousiño, Adolfo Calderón. **Short Diplomatic History of the Chilean-Peruvian Relations, 1819-1879.** Santiago de Chile: Imprenta Universitaria, 1920, 255 p.
A history, written from the Chilean point of view, of relations between Chile and Peru from the War of Liberation to the close of the World War.

Edwards, Alberto. **La Fronda Aristocrática en Chile.** Santiago: Imprenta Nacional, 1928, 308 p.
A series of articles on the rôle of the Chilean aristocracy in politics since 1810.

Elliott, Lilian Elwyn. **Chile Today and Tomorrow.** New York: Macmillan, 1922, 345 p.
A survey of Chilean history and civilization.

Fetter, Frank Whitson. **Monetary Inflation in Chile.** Princeton: Princeton University Press, 1931, 226 p.
Though this is essentially a financial study, the author does not leave out of account the political background. By a well-known American economist.

Guerra, José Guillermo. **La Constitución de 1925.** Santiago: Balcells, 1929, 569 p.
A standard commentary on the constitution, by a leading Chilean authority.

Martner, Daniel. **Estudio de Política Comercial Chilena.** Santiago: Imprenta Universitaria, 1923, 2 v.
A thorough economic history of Chile, with special attention to trade relations.

Ninni, Alessandro. **Cile.** Rome: Treves, n. d., 138 p.
One of the historical and descriptive studies published by the Istituto Cristoforo Colombo.

Pena, Leonardo. **Histoire du Chile.** Paris: Alcan, 1927, 278 p.
The best brief survey of Chilean history.

Subercaseaux, Guillermo. **El Sistema Monetario i la Organización Bancaria de Chile.** Santiago: Universo, 1920, 404 p.
A systematic historical study of the monetary and banking system, by a Chilean economist.

Van Deusen, W. M. **Banco Central de Chile.** Santiago: Imprenta Universitaria, 1927, 54 p.
A concise expert account of the working of the bank.

Colombia

See also (South America) Territorial Problems, p. 212.

Dollero, Adolfo. **Cultura Colombiana.** Bogotá: De Cromos, 1930, 868 p.
Chapters on Colombia's intellectual and scientific progress, followed by descriptive sections.

Humbert, Jules. **Histoire de la Colombie et du Venezuela.** Paris: Alcan, 1921, 220 p.
A general historical survey, very weak on the modern period.

Rippy, James Fred. **The Capitalists and Colombia.** New York: Vanguard Press, 1931, 288 p.
A competent study of foreign interests and activities in Colombia; a valuable contribution to the study of imperialism.

Uribe, Antonio José. **Colombia y los Estados Unidos. Colombia, Venezuela, Costa Rica, Ecuador, Brasil, Nicaragua y Panamá. Colombia y el Perú.** Bogotá: Minerva, 1931.
These three volumes, parts of a doctoral dissertation, cover the whole range of Colombia's international relations and form an important contribution to the literature of Latin American diplomacy.

Ecuador

See also (South America) Territorial Problems, p. 212.

NILES, MRS. BLAIR (RICE). **Casual Wanderings in Ecuador.** New York: Century, 1923, 249 p.
> Strictly a travel book, describing new experiences and new sights without any attempt to study social or political conditions.

UP DE GRAFF, FRITZ W. **Head Hunters of the Amazon.** New York: Duffield, 1923, 337 p.
> The record of seven years of exploration and adventure in the highlands of Ecuador and on the Upper Amazon.

Paraguay

See also (South America) Territorial Problems, p. 212.

BÁEZ, CECILIO. **Le Paraguay.** Paris: Alcan, 1927, 124 p.
> An historical and descriptive work of merit, by the rector of the National University, former minister to France and Great Britain.

BÜRGER, OTTO. **Paraguay, der "Garten Südamerikas," ein Wegweiser für Handel, Industrie und Einwanderung.** Leipzig: Dieterich'sche Verlagsbuchhandlung, 1927, 280 p.
> One of the series by the same author designed to inform prospective emigrants and investors regarding conditions and opportunities in various of the South American countries. The book reports mainly on the present status of agriculture and industry and their future possibilities.

MANGELS, H. **Paraguay.** Munich: Datterer, 1919, 255 p.
> A handbook dealing with economic and physical problems, by a former German consul.

ROMERO, GENARO. **Guía del Inmigrante.** Asunción: "Ariel," 1920, 70 p.
> Information on the opportunities offered agricultural immigrants by the Government of Paraguay, with the laws governing their admission and statistics on available public lands.

SCHUSTER, ADOLF N. **Paraguay.** Stuttgart: Strecker und Schröder, 1929, 667 p.
> An elaborate and exhaustive survey of the land and the people, their history and their economic life, written by the German consul and filled with valuable statistics and information.

Peru

See also (South America) Territorial Problems, p. 212.

BAUTISTA DE LAVALLE, JUAN. **El Perú y la Gran Guerra.** Lima: Imprenta Americana 1919, 439 p.
> Primarily a collection of documents and other materials dealing with Peru's international relations during the war.

DUNN, WILLIAM EDWARD. **Perú: Commercial and Industrial Handbook.** Washington: Department of Commerce, 1925, 530 p.
> A useful handbook prepared for the Bureau of Foreign and Domestic Commerce.

OLAECHEA, GUILLERMO U. **La Constitución del Perú.** Lima: Imprenta Americana, 1922, 647 p.
> An official text of constitution and organic laws, decrees, etc., with commentary.

Olivo, Juan Francisco, *comp.* **Constituciones Políticas del Perú.** Lima: Torres Aguirre, 1922, 383 p.
A useful collection of documents prepared for the Peruvian Chamber of Deputies in celebration of the centenary of the first constituent assembly.

Rowe, Leo Stanton. **Early Effects of the War upon the Finance, Commerce and Industry of Peru.** New York: Oxford, 1920, 60 p.
A study of economic conditions in 1915, published by the Carnegie Endowment.

Stuart, Graham Henry. **The Governmental System of Peru.** Washington: The Carnegie Institution, 1926, 160 p.
An admirable scholarly account of the Peruvian constitution and its workings. The best general treatment of Peruvian political life.

Ugarte, César Antonio. **Bosquejo de la Historia Económica del Perú.** Lima: Cabieses, 1926, 214 p.
A history of Peruvian economics and finance from the days of the Incas to the present, prepared as a textbook for a course given by the Faculty of Political and Economic Sciences of Lima. Contains a valuable bibliography, chiefly of works by Peruvian authors.

Uruguay

Buero, Juan Antonio. **El Uruguay en la Vida Internacional.** Montevideo: Renacimiento, 1919, 502 p.
Consists primarily of speeches and articles by the former Minister for Foreign Affairs, during the years 1914-1918.

Llobet, J. **La Constitution de l'Uruguay.** Toulouse: Douladoure, 1926, 138 p.
A French dissertation of the usual undocumented type, describing and restating the provisions of the 1917 constitution.

Morey Otero, Sebastián. **Constitución Anotada de la República Oriental del Uruguay.** Montevideo: Claudio García, 2nd ed., 1924, 440 p.
A standard text and commentary, for use in higher schools.

Vedia y Mitre, Mariano de. **El Gobierno del Uruguay.** Buenos Aires: Agencia General de Librería, 1919, 238 p.
An outline of Uruguayan constitutional history and an analysis of the reform of 1917, by an Argentine professor.

Venezuela

See also (South America) Territorial Problems, p. 212.

Bürger, Otto. **Venezuela.** Leipzig: Dieterich, 1922, 272 p.
One of the best studies of the country and its economic resources, by an authority.

García Naranjo, Nemesio. **Venezuela and Its Ruler.** New York: Carranza, 1927, 174 p.
A Mexican journalist's very flattering account of Gómez and his policy.

Landaeta, Leopoldo. **El Banco de Venezuela.** Caracas: Empresa el Cojo, 1924, 256 p.
A scholarly documented history of banking in Venezuela.

Márquez Bustillos, V. **Semblanza del General Juan Vicente Gómez.** Caracas: Litografía del Comercio, 1919, 228 p.
A general study of Gómez's career, by a warm admirer.

PACANIUS, G. M. **Jurisprudencia y Crítica de la Doctrina de la Casación Venezolana.** Caracas: Litografía del Comercio, 1925, 596 p.
An exhaustive treatment of Venezuelan financial policy from 1876 to 1923.

POCATERRA, JOSÉ RAFAEL. **Gómez, the Shame of America.** Paris: Delpeuch, 1929, 255 p.
The title indicates the viewpoint of this account of Venezuelan domestic politics.

ROLDÁN OLIARTE, ESTEBAN. **Venezuela Adentro.** San José: A. Reyes, 1928, 229 p.
Reminiscences of thirty years of Venezuelan politics.

FIFTH PART:

EUROPE

I. EUROPE IN GENERAL

POST-WAR HISTORY AND CONDITIONS

See also (The Peace Negotiations) Criticism and Proposals for Revision, p. 160.

AUBERT, LOUIS. **The Reconstruction of Europe.** New Haven: Yale University Press, 1925, 180 p.
Williamstown Lectures, 1924, ably presenting the French point of view of problems then current. The author has since become a leading French official in disarmament negotiations.

BAINVILLE, JACQUES. **Les Conséquences Politiques de la Paix.** Paris: Nouvelle Librairie Nationale, 1920, 198 p.
A French conservative's view of post-war problems—Franco-German relations, the Polish question, the Adriatic, and above all the position of France.

BAKELESS, JOHN EDWIN. **The Origin of the Next War.** New York: Viking Press, 1926, 318 p.
The author sees in post-war conditions an alarming similarity to conditions which resulted in the war of 1914.

BEARD, CHARLES AUSTIN. **Cross Currents in Europe To-day.** Boston: Marshall Jones, 1922, 278 p.
An analysis by an open-minded American historian.

BEYENS, NAPOLÉON EUGÈNE LOUIS, BARON. **L'Avenir des Petits États.** Paris: Van Oest, 1919, 261 p.
The author, a leading Belgian diplomat, discusses the situation of the Balkan States and in particular the international status of Belgium and the future value of neutrality.

BOLDYREV, N. V. and GESSEN, S. I. **Sovremennaia Evropa.** Leningrad: Seiatel', 1925, 255 p.
An economic and political survey of Western Europe in the post-war period.

BRAILSFORD, HENRY NOEL. **Across the Blockade.** New York: Harcourt, 1919, 174 p.
The observations of an experienced English newspaperman, with radical tendencies, during travels in Hungary, Poland, and Germany in the spring of 1919.

BRIEY, RENAUD, COMTE DE. **L'Épreuve du Feu.** Paris: Berger-Levrault, 1925, 240 p.
Original and interesting reflections on the political effects of the war on European politics, by a Belgian jurist.

BUELL, RAYMOND LESLIE. **Europe. A History of Ten Years.** New York: Macmillan, 1928, 428 p.
A brief introduction to the history of Europe since the peace settlement. The author reviews the treaties and general problems arising from them and then surveys the developments in each of the various European countries.

CHÉRADAME, ANDRÉ. **Les Vraies Raisons du Chaos Européen.** Évreux: Hérissey, 1924, 418 p.

A confirmed baiter of Germany tells of the entente of British and German interests which has supposedly ruined all that was gained by victory and which now threatens the world with a new "supercapitalism."

CHILD, RICHARD WASHBURN. **A Diplomat Looks at Europe.** New York: Duffield, 1925, 301 p.
The post-war experiences and impressions of an American ambassador to Italy. The book, while far from profound, throws sidelights on the Genoa Conference, the Lausanne Conference and the advent of Fascism in Italy.

CHISHOLM, ARCHIBALD. **The Healing of the Nations.** London: Student Christian Movement, 1926, 155 p.
A dispassionate criticism of some current social policies and problems.

CHURCHILL, WINSTON SPENCER. **The World Crisis. The Aftermath.** New York: Scribner, 1929, 516 p.
The concluding volume of Churchill's brilliant memoirs, covering the years 1918-1922, and discussing the Peace Conference, the Russian situation, the Near East crisis, the Irish problem, and other controversial matters. The impression left on the reader is an uninspiring one of indecision and bungling on the part of the Allies, who do not appear as great in victory as in the hour of trial. Churchill pictures himself as championing reconciliation with Germany from the very time of the armistice, but in a masterly way he recreates the general atmosphere then prevailing and shows why a more sensible policy was almost impossible.

D'ABERNON, EDGAR VINCENT, VISCOUNT. **The Diary of an Ambassador.** New York: Doubleday, 1929-1931, 3 v.
The important memoirs and impressions of the British ambassador to Berlin, covering the years 1920-1926. The author gives a full and critical account of the development of post-war Europe and sprinkles his work with keen reflections and character sketches. One of the really outstanding books on post-war Europe.

DALTON, HUGH. **Towards the Peace of Nations.** London: Routledge, 1928, 328 p.
A Laborite M. P.'s view of the post-war chaos, followed by a vigorous indictment of Conservative foreign policy. The author was Under-Secretary for Foreign Affairs, 1929-31.

DE CHAIRE, SOMERSET STRUBEN. **Divided Europe.** London: Cape, 1931, 224 p.
A stimulating essay, containing some radical and probably impracticable suggestions for revision of the treaties and the union of Europe.

DEMANGEON, ALBERT. **Le Déclin de l'Europe.** Paris: Payot, 1920, 314 p.
A pessimistic view of Europe's future in relation to the United States and Japan. A thoughtful book.

DICKINSON, THOMAS HERBERT. **The New Old-World.** New York: Dutton, 1923, 167 p.
An interesting, if occasionally superficial, summary of some of the novel trends and problems in post-war Europe, such as movements of people, economic, social and intellectual currents.

Europa. Edited by MICHAEL FARBMAN. London: Europa Publications, Ltd.
This useful survey and directory is now published in loose-leaf form, in two sections. The first is entitled "The Encyclopædia of Europe," the second "The European Who's Who."

FERRERO, GUGLIELMO. **La Tragedia della Pace.** Milan: Athena, 1923, 302 p.
A series of writings in which the prolific Italian historian discusses the Peace Conference, the treaties, and their aftermath.

GIBBS, SIR PHILIP. **Since Then.** New York: Harper, 1930, 476 p.
A readable account of the stormy post-war period, written by a well-known journalist.

GRAUX, LUCIEN. **Histoire des Violations du Traité de Paix.** Paris: Crès, 1921-1923, 3 v.
A full-length treatment of evasions of peace treaty provisions, covering the period June 1919-December 1922.

GURKO-KRIAZHIN, V. A. **Poslevoennye Mirovye Konflikty.** Moscow: Moskovskiĭ Rabochiĭ, 1924, 125 p.
A popular account of the aftermath of the World War.

HARDEN, MAXIMILIAN. **Germany, France and England.** New York: Brentano, 1924, 326 p.
A leading German journalist's pessimistic survey of the situation in Europe, with a plea for international coöperation.

HERRON, GEORGE DAVIS. **The Defeat in the Victory.** Boston: Christopher Publishing House, 1924, 202 p.
The disillusionment of one of Wilson's faithful followers.

HIGH, STANLEY. **Europe Turns the Corner.** New York: Abingdon Press, 1925, 308 p.
A rather racy account of what the author was certain was Europe's incipient convalescence.

HUDDLESTON, SISLEY. **Europe in Zigzags.** Philadelphia: Lippincott, 1929, 362 p.
Amiable chats on continental social, artistic and political affairs and tendencies, by the former Paris correspondent of the London *Times.*

KAREEV, NIKOLAĬ IVANOVICH. **Evropa do i Posle Voiny.** Petrograd: Sabashnikov, 1922, 84 p.
A popular account of the territorial changes wrought in Europe by the World War.

LE BON, GUSTAVE. **The World in Revolt.** New York: Macmillan, 1921.
General psychological studies of war and post-war Europe, with stress on popular illusions and the threatening revolutionary tempest.

LÉMONON, ERNEST. **La Nouvelle Europe et Son Bilan Économique.** Paris: Alcan, 1926, 178 p.
An excellent general survey by a well-known French writer on international affairs.

LEWINSOHN, RICHARD. **Histoire de l'Inflation; le Déplacement de la Richesse en Europe.** Paris: Payot, 1926, 448 p.
The translation, from the German, of an important study of the social effects of the war.

LLOYD GEORGE, DAVID. **Where Are We Going?** New York: Doran, 1923, 371 p.
A collection of the ex-Premier's speeches on European politics in 1922-1923. Contemporary French policy is roundly abused. There are also chapters on the inter-Allied debts, prohibition and social subjects.

LYON, LAURANCE. **When There Is No Peace.** New York: Doran, 1923, 416 p.
A gossipy and somewhat tedious sequel to "The Pomp of Power."

MACARTNEY, MAXWELL HENRY HAYES. **Five Years of European Chaos.** New York: Dutton, 1924, 242 p.
Interesting chapters of post-war history by an English journalist. There is a good treatment of Bolshevism in Hungary, the efforts of the Hapsburg to return, the Greek-Turkish muddle, the Upper Silesian problem and the Irish difficulty.

MAURRAS, CHARLES. **Le Mauvais Traité: De la Victoire à Locarno.** Paris: Éditions du Capitole, 1928, 2 v.
A brilliant French controversialist follows the fashion by writing a violent denunciation of European diplomacy from Versailles to Locarno.

MENDELSSOHN-BARTHOLDY, ALBRECHT. **The European Situation.** New Haven: Yale University Press, 1927, 123 p.
Williamstown lectures, by a prominent German writer and pacifist. Among other things he discusses the backward races and the prospects of a European commonwealth.

MONTGOMERY, BO GABRIEL DE. **Issues of European Statesmanship.** London: Routledge, 1926, 276 p.
A penetrating analysis of some of the outstanding problems.

MOORE, FREDERICK. **The Chaos in Europe.** New York: Putnam, 1919, 192 p.
A picture of conditions in Russia, the Balkans and Asia, by an American journalist who advocated international action to save the situation.

MOWAT, ROBERT BALMAIN. **A History of European Diplomacy, 1914-1925.** New York: Longmans, 1927, 351 p.
A useful survey which suffers somewhat from its brevity and consequent over-simplification.

MOWRER, PAUL SCOTT. **Balkanized Europe.** New York: Dutton, 1921, 349 p.
Written by the correspondent of the *Chicago Daily News*, this is one of the most readable of the early post-war surveys of political, economic and social conditions.

MUIR, RAMSAY. **The Political Consequences of the Great War.** London: Butterworth, 1930, 252 p.
Nationalism, internationalism, parliamentary government and other major post-war problems, discussed from a thorough-going English liberal viewpoint, by an observer who knows how to write.

NEVINSON, HENRY WOODD. **Last Changes, Last Chances.** New York: Harcourt, 1928, 361 p.
Observations and experiences of a well-known journalist, covering the war and post-war period, especially interesting on the Irish situation and the Ruhr occupation.

NITTI, FRANCESCO SAVERIO. **Bolshevism, Fascism and Democracy.** New York: Macmillan, 1927, 223 p.
The former Italian Premier demonstrates once again that Bolshevism and Fascism are alike products of the war and are bound to give way sooner or later to the normal system of civilized society—liberal democracy.

NITTI, FRANCESCO SAVERIO. **The Decadence of Europe.** New York: Holt, 1923, 302 p.
An angry indictment of present-day European politicians and all their works. The Italian statesman regards the peace treaties merely as instruments for continuing the war and adduces much evidence to support his interpretation.

NITTI, FRANCESCO SAVERIO. **They Make a Desert.** London: Dent, 1924, 270 p.
The third volume of the former Italian Premier's post-war "Jeremiad." He here continues his attack on French policy, with special reference to the Ruhr invasion.

NOYES, PIERREPONT B. **While Europe Waits for Peace.** New York: Macmillan, 1921, 99 p.
The American Rhineland Commissioner's picture of Europe in ruin, with a plea for American action.

ORMESSON, WLADIMIR, COMTE D'. **Dans la Nuit Européenne.** Paris: Champion, 1923, 291 p.
Collected articles by a very keen French observer. They range over many subjects, but deal chiefly with German, Polish and general Central European problems.

PEEL, GEORGE. **The Economic Impact of America.** New York: Macmillan, 1928, 340 p.
A well-reasoned discussion of European economic problems arising from the American conquest. A volume that attracted a good deal of attention in England.

PINON, RENÉ. **La Reconstruction de l'Europe Politique.** Paris: Perrin, 1920, 344 p.
The outlines of the new Europe as they appear to an intensely patriotic French political
writer.

PLUM, HARRY GRANT and BENJAMIN, GILBERT GIDDINGS. **Modern and Contemporary
European Civilization.** Philadelphia: Lippincott, 1923, 413 p.
An unusually sane and succinct manual, stressing social and economic factors and the
rise of modern nationalism.

POWELL, EDWARD ALEXANDER. **Thunder over Europe.** New York: Ives Washburn,
1931, 288 p.
A well-known correspondent reviews in a rather elementary way the racial, economic
and political questions which threaten the peace of Europe.

POWERS, JAMES H. **Years of Tumult.** New York: Norton, 1932, 345 p.
A survey of the course of events since the conclusion of the peace treaties.

PRICE, MORGAN PHILIPS. **The Economic Problems of Europe.** New York: Macmillan,
1928, 218 p.
An original book dealing largely with problems of foreign investments before and
after the war, the new industrial revolution, etc. The author has had wide experience
in continental countries as correspondent for the *Daily Herald* and other papers.

PRINGLE, W. HENDERSON, *ed.* **Economic Problems in Europe Today.** London: Black,
1928, 146 p.
A series of lectures at Birmingham Commercial College, including ones by Peel on
France, Salvemini on Italy, Seton-Watson on Czechoslovakia, Farbman on Russia,
Edwards on Germany, and Cammaerts on Belgium.

RAVAGE, MARCUS ELI. **The Malady of Europe.** New York: Macmillan, 1923, 250 p.
A critique of the present European situation from the liberal point of view, with
variations on the theme: "Too much victory and not enough peace."

RENARD, ALBERT. **Paix ou Guerre?** Paris: Alcan, 1931, 208 p.
A former French Senator and nationalist reviews some of the fundamental problems
of the Continent, such as Eupen-Malmedy, Alsace-Lorraine, the *Anschluss* and
Belgium.

REPINGTON, CHARLES À COURT. **After the War.** Boston: Houghton Mifflin, 1922, 477 p.
A diary of travel through Central and Southeastern Europe after the war, containing
gossip from most of the capitals.

RÉVÉSZ, ANDRÉS. **La Reconstitución de Europa y la Rusia de los Soviets.** Madrid:
Biblioteca Internacional, 1922.
Interesting comments of a Spanish publicist on the Genoa and The Hague Conferences.

RUFFIN, HENRY. **Reverrons-Nous la Guerre?** Paris: Budry, 1925.
A thoughtful consideration of the situation after Locarno.

SFORZA, CONTE CARLO. **Diplomatic Europe since the Treaty of Versailles.** New
Haven: Yale University Press, 1928, 137 p.
A series of brilliant lectures delivered before the Institute of Politics by the liberal
Italian statesman. The subjects treated are Franco-German and Polish-German re-
lations, the Succession States, the Turkish problem, and the position of the Catholic
Church.

SHADWELL, ARTHUR. **The Breakdown of Socialism.** Boston: Little, Brown, 1927, 272 p.
Perhaps the best general survey of the working of socialist governments in Europe,
written by a competent sociologist after extended visits to Russia, Germany, Austria,
Sweden, Czechoslovakia and Denmark.

SHADWELL, ARTHUR. **The Socialist Movement, 1824-1924.** London: Philip Allan, 1925,
2 v.
An excellent account of the socialist movement in various countries, especially in the
recent period.

SIMONDS, FRANK HERBERT. **Can Europe Keep the Peace?** New York: Harper, 1931,
373 p.
A balance-sheet of conditions and trends, by a veteran American journalist. Dismal
but realistic and well worth reading.

SIMONDS, FRANK HERBERT. **How Europe Made Peace without America.** New York:
Doubleday, 1927, 407 p.
A good general survey of post-war developments in Europe, by a well-known writer
of syndicated news and editorial articles.

SLOSSON, PRESTON WILLIAM. **Twentieth Century Europe.** Boston: Houghton Mifflin,
1927, 756 p.
A good conventional text, commendable for its open-mindedness.

SNOWDEN, ETHEL (ANNAKIN) SNOWDEN, VISCOUNTESS. **A Political Pilgrim in Europe.**
New York: Doran, 1921, 284 p.
The travels of an English feminist leader, wife of the British Chancellor of the Ex-
chequer, in the years following the peace. Interesting views of conditions in Austria,
Russia, Transcaucasia and the Balkans.

STANNARD, HAROLD MARTIN. **The Fabric of Europe.** New York: Knopf, 1923, 260 p.
An optimistic essay on the nature and causes of the present European confusion.

STODDARD, LOTHROP. **Social Classes in Post-War Europe.** New York: Scribner, 1925,
178 p.
Essays by a frequent writer on many and various sociological subjects, giving a good
picture of the social overturn and the twilight of the middle classes.

STRÖBEL, HEINRICH. **Socialization in Theory and Practice.** London: King, 1922, 341 p.
An objective study of the principal socialistic experiments in Europe since 1917.
Especially valuable for the German socialization program.

STRÖHLE, ALBERT. **Von Versailles bis zur Gegenwart.** Berlin: Zentralverlag, 1931,
118 p.
A concise account of the Treaty and its effects, supplied with numerous diagrams.

These Eventful Years: The Twentieth Century in the Making. New York: Encyclopædia Britannica, 1924, 2 v.
Eighty-four chapters on the origins, conduct and results of the war, the progress of
science, education and the arts, and including a look into the future by H. G. Wells.
Among the papers, which inevitably are of unequal value, are many of importance
and interest.

THOMSON, VALENTINE. **Young Europe.** New York: Doubleday, 1932, 342 p.
Stimulating observations by the daughter of a French politician.

VANDERLIP, FRANK ARTHUR. **What Next in Europe?** New York: Harcourt, 1922, 308 p.
A somewhat optimistic inventory. The author's proposal is to devote the Allied indebtedness to America to the aid of near-bankrupt European states.

VISSCHER, CHARLES DE. **The Stabilization of Europe.** Chicago: Chicago University
Press, 1924, 190 p.
Lectures dealing with problems of nationality, security and communication.

VODOVOZOV, V. V. **Zapadnaia Evropa i Amerika posle Voiny.** St. Petersburg: Gosizdat, 1922, 208 p.
A general statistical handbook of post-war Europe.

WALLACE, WILLIAM KAY. **Thirty Years of Modern History.** New York: Macmillan, 1926, 293 p.
An interpretative essay, aiming to show the growing preponderance of the economic over the purely political factors.

WEBSTER, MRS. NESTA H. **The Socialist Network.** London: Boswell, 1926, 165 p.
A comprehensive and useful survey of the socialist organization in the various countries of Europe and in the United States, if one leaves out of account certain hysterical passages.

WILLIAMSON, JAMES ALEXANDER. **Europe Overseas.** New York: Oxford University Press, 1925, 144 p.
A serviceable introduction to the subject of European expansion.

CONSTITUTIONAL PROBLEMS; DICTATORSHIPS

See also under Italy, Russia, Spain, Jugoslavia, Turkey, etc.

BONN, MORITZ JULIUS. **The Crisis of European Democracy.** New Haven: Yale University Press, 1925, 103 p.
Williamstown lectures. Penetrating generalizations on recent developments in Europe by a leading German economist.

CAMBÓ Y BATLLE, FRANCISCO DE ASÍS. **Les Dictatures.** Paris: Alcan, 1930, 210 p.
The French translation of one of the most searching studies of European dictatorship, by an eminent Spanish statesman.

COUNTS, GEORGE SYLVESTER, VILLARI, LUIGI and others. **Bolshevism, Fascism and Capitalism.** New Haven: Yale University Press, 1932, 274 p.
Williamstown lectures. By no means the least interesting part of the book is the long record of discussion.

DARESTE DE LA CHAVANNE, FRANÇOIS RODOLPHE and PIERRE. **Constitutions Modernes.** Fourth edition, completely revised by Joseph Delpech and Julien Laferrière. Paris: Sirey, 1928-1931, 3 v.
The new edition of a well-known handbook, brought up to date with critical notes.

Dictatorship on Trial. New York: Harcourt, 1930, 390 p.
A collection of essays, some adulatory and foolish (like that on Pilsudski), some analytical and interesting (like that on King Alexander). The majority, unfortunately, belong in the former category.

HEADLAM-MORLEY, AGNES. **The New Democratic Constitutions of Europe.** New York: Oxford University Press, 1928, 306 p.
A good study of the origins, influence and working of the new constitutions.

HERVÉ, GUSTAVE. **Nouvelle Histoire de l'Europe.** Paris: Éditions de la Victoire, 1931.
An essay stressing the growth of the revolutionary tradition and the danger of a cataclysm unless energetic action is taken by the world's leaders.

LANDAUER, KARL and HONEGGER, HANS, *ed.* **Internationaler Faschismus.** Karlsruhe: Braun, 1928, 163 p.
Essays for and against the Fascist movement in various countries, the object being to establish a common denominator and determine the essence of the thing.

LANGHANS-RATZEBURG, MANFRED. **Die Verfassungen des Erdballs.** Gotha: Perthes, 1927, 194 p.
Brief summaries of the world's constitutions, in convenient form for reference.

McBain, Howard Lee and Rogers, Lindsay. **The New Constitutions of Europe.** New York: Doubleday, 1922, 612 p.
A work which includes the texts of the new constitutions and a brief analysis of the political principles and innovations involved. A useful text.

Mirkin-Getsevich, Boris Sergieevich. **Les Constitutions de l'Europe Nouvelle.** Paris: Delagrave, 1928, 415 p.
An admirable handbook written by an authority. There is a good chapter dealing with general tendencies of constitutional development.

Munro, William Bennett. **The Governments of Europe.** New York: Macmillan, 1925, 792 p.
A well-known and widely used American text.

Nin, Andrés. **Les Dictadures dels Nostres Dies.** Barcelona: Librería Catalonia, 1930, 236 p.
The European dictatorships as a background for the study of the Primo de Rivera régime. The Spanish edition is entitled "Las Dictaduras de Nuestro Tiempo" (Madrid: Hoy, 1930, 211 p.).

Ruffini, Francesco. **Diritti di Libertà.** Turin: Gobetti, 1926.
An excellent review of the constitutional development of Europe by a former Italian Minister of Education.

Sforza, Conte Carlo. **European Dictatorships.** New York: Brentano, 1931, 273 p.
The former Italian Foreign Minister surveys the post-war dictatorships in a series of essays characterized by his usual understanding. He distinguishes carefully between the various manifestations of autocratic government seen in different parts of Europe today.

Tiltman, Hubert Hessell. **The Terror in Europe.** New York: Stokes, 1932, 413 p.
A study of the European dictatorships, especially in Russia, Poland and Italy.

Weber, Alfred. **Die Krise des Modernen Staatsgedankens in Europa.** Stuttgart: Deutsche Verlagsanstalt, 1925, 173 p.
A stimulating sociological study strongly tinged with Teutonism.

BIOGRAPHIES

See also under individual countries; also (World War) Biographies of Wartime Statesmen and Diplomats, p. 101.

Bagger, Eugene Szekeres. **Eminent Europeans.** New York: Putnam, 1922, 283 p.
Character studies of ten contemporary European personalities, some of them important, some unimportant but none the less interesting.

Box, Pelham Horton. **Three Master Builders and Another.** Philadelphia: Lippincott, 1925, 396 p.
Studies of Lenin, Mussolini, Venizelos and Wilson as representing anti-liberal and liberal forces and currents.

D'Abernon, Edgar Vincent, Viscount. **Portraits and Appreciations.** London: Hodder, 1931, 259 p.
This volume includes the introductions to the various volumes of D'Abernon's memoirs, together with some new character sketches of European leaders.

Fülöp-Miller, René. **Lenin and Gandhi.** New York: Putnam, 1927, 306 p.
A well-known writer holds up the Russian and the Indian leaders as our two typical contemporaries.

GLASGOW, GEORGE. **Continental Statesmen.** London: Bles, 1930, 238 p.
Interesting character sketches and appreciations by an English liberal.

GUERIN, THOMAS. **Caps and Crowns of Europe.** New York: Carrier, 1929, 290 p.
Intimate pictures of European rulers and statesmen by a Canadian writer.

HARDEN, MAXIMILIAN. **I Meet My Contemporaries.** New York: Holt, 1925, 287 p.
Unusually interesting biographical studies by a famous German journalist. Included are Wilson, Lloyd George, Clemenceau, Stinnes, Lenin.

HUDDLESTON, SISLEY. **Those Europeans.** New York: Putnam, 1924, 297 p.
Amiable and understanding sketches of many of Europe's leading post-war statesmen, by the former Paris correspondent of the London *Times*.

KLEIN, FRITZ. **Dreizehn Männer Regieren Europa.** Hamburg: Hanseatische Verlagsanstalt, 1930, 194 p.
The leaders of European politics described in a series of unusually discerning essays by the editor of the *Deutsche Allgemeine Zeitung*.

LANDAU, MARK ALEKSANDROVICH. **Portrety.** Berlin: Slovo, 1931, 236 p.
Character studies of Pilsudski and Briand, as well as some earlier figures.

MARCU, VALERIU. **Men and Forces of Our Time.** New York: Viking, 1931, 244 p.
Biographical sketches of Clemenceau, Lenin, Foch, Kemal Pasha and others, written with brilliance and penetration.

NOMAD, MAX, *pseud.* **Rebels and Renegades.** New York: Macmillan, 1932, 430 p.
Using a pseudonym, an experienced revolutionary writes of the careers of typical radical leaders like Briand, Scheidemann, MacDonald, Trotsky and Mussolini.

SFORZA, CONTE CARLO. **Makers of Modern Europe.** Indianapolis: Bobbs-Merrill, 1930, 420 p.
The former Italian Foreign Minister gives interesting impressions of Europe's leading figures as he came to know them through experience in various capitals.

VERGIN, FEDOR. **Das Unbewusste Europa.** Leipzig: Hess, 1931, 342 p.
European politicians psychoanalyzed.

PAN-EUROPEAN SCHEMES

See also (Central Europe) Middle European Schemes, p. 299.

COHEN-PORTHEIM, PAUL. **Der Geist Frankreichs und Europa.** Potsdam: Kiepenheuer, 1926, 209 p.
A German plea for a European spirit based upon French culture.

COUDENHOVE-KALERGI, RICHARD NIKOLAUS. **Pan-Europe.** New York: Knopf, 1926, 234 p.
The English translation of what is perhaps the best-known book on the subject, by the leading protagonist of the Pan-European idea.

DAHRIMAN, GEORGES. **Pour les États Confédérés d'Europe.** Paris: Argo, 1929, 121 p.
A discerning analysis of the forces making for federation and the methods by which a new organization might be evolved.

DRIEU LA ROCHELLE, PIERRE. **L'Europe contre les Patries.** Paris: Nouvelle Revue Française, 1931, 153 p.
The countries of western and central Europe are urged to rise above national strife and present a united front against Russia and America.

EBNER VON EBENTHALL, OSCAR. **S. O. S. Europa.** Vienna: Amalthea, 1930, 204 p.
A general discussion of the European problem. The writer favors some sort of British-European union.

FIMMEN, EDO. **Labour's Alternative: The United States of Europe, or Europe Limited.** London: Labour Publishing Company, 1924, 128 p.
The author advocates the conversion of Europe into a free union of proletarian republics as the only means of protecting the working classes.

FLEISSIG, ANDREAS. **Paneuropa.** Munich: Duncker und Humblot, 1930, 171 p.
Like most writers on the subject, the author approaches the problem from the economic and social standpoints. A substantial book.

HEERFORDT, CHRISTIAN FREDÉRIK. **The New Europe.** London: Allen and Unwin, 1926, 221 p.
A Danish plea for reorganization of the League to allow for a European federation.

HEIMANN, HANS, *ed.* **Europäische Zollunion.** Berlin: Hobbing, 1926, 278 p.
Twenty-two essays by industrialists and professors setting forth the problems of European tariffs as seen from the German side.

HERRIOT, ÉDOUARD. **The United States of Europe.** New York: Viking, 1930, 330 p.
After outlining the past history of the idea of European solidarity, the French radical statesman analyzes the contemporary problem. The approach is from the economic angle, with reference especially to the question of tariffs, cartels, international finance and labor. These factors, M. Herriot believes, impose a union upon the states of Europe. The union, to be successful, must be within the framework of the League, must respect national institutions, must be open to all states which wish to join, including England, in spite of her extra-European interests, and must give all members a position of equality. The primary purpose should be industrial concentration and the protection of the European market.

HOHLFELD, HANS HERBERT. **Zur Frage einer Europäischen Zollunion.** Leipzig: Ricker, 1929, 67 p.
An analysis of obstacles in the way of a customs union, by an able German historian.

HUTCHINSON, PAUL. **The United States of Europe.** Chicago: Willett, Clark and Colby, 1929, 225 p.
An account of the origin of the idea, with a description of tendencies and obstacles.

JOUVENEL, BERTRAND DE. **Vers les États-Unis d'Europe.** Paris: Valois, 1930.
An analysis of the ways of diplomacy, relegating the idea of a united Europe to the realm of dreams.

KAYSER, JACQUES, FRANCK, PAUL and LE MERCIER, CAMILLE. **Les États-Unis d'Europe.** Paris: Editeurs Associés, 1926.
A valuable contribution to the history of the security problem from Versailles to Locarno.

MARCHAL, JEAN. **Union Douanière et Organisation Européenne.** Paris: Sirey, 1929, 231 p.
A useful doctoral thesis reviewing the history of customs unions and analyzing various projects, pre-war and post-war, for partial or complete European union.

MIRKIN-GETSEVICH, BORIS SERGIEEVICH and SCELLE, GEORGES. **L'Union Européenne.** Paris: Delagrave, 1931, 334 p.
A semi-popular presentation of the problem, by two prominent international lawyers.

NOVELLIS, L. DE. **L'Unificazione Economica dell' Europa.** Milan: Treves, 1931, 304 p.
A scholarly study of the projects put forward for the economic union of Europe.

NUESCH, ARNOLD. **Souveräner Europäischer Bund.** Basel: Nuesch, 1930, 208 p.
An account of the legal aspects of the problem of a confederation.

POULIMENOS, ARISTOTELES. **Vereinigte Staaten Europas.** Leipzig: Schmidt, 2nd ed., 1929, 128 p.
A reconsideration of the European problem, with special emphasis on relations to England and America, by one of the earliest advocates of union.

QUARTARA, GIORGIO. **Gli Stati Uniti d'Europa e del Mondo.** Turin: Bocca, 1930.
A dialogue setting forth the advantages of union, based on the American example.

SCHWARZ, HANS. **Europa im Aufbruch.** Berlin: Ringverlag, 1926, 311 p.
An interesting essay on the development of the idea of European solidarity.

VOĬTINSKIĬ, VLADIMIR SAVEL'EVICH. **Tatsachen und Zahlen Europas.** Vienna: Paneuropa Verlag, 1930, 211 p.
An eminent economist examines the Pan-Europe scheme through a statistical examination of factors like cartels, population movements, food supply, raw materials, markets and colonies.

VOĬTINSKIĬ, VLADIMIR SAVEL'EVICH. **Die Vereinigten Staaten von Europa.** Berlin: Dietz, 1926, 186 p.
Another plea for economic union.

II. GREAT BRITAIN; IRELAND
IMPERIAL RELATIONS

See also under individual British dominions and colonies; also (Africa) British Possessions, p. 508.

ACWORTH, BERNARD. **The Navies of To-day and To-morrow.** London: Eyre and Spottiswoode, 1931, 277 p.
This book, written by a retired naval officer, is primarily a sharp criticism of recent British naval policy, with special reference to deficiencies in men and material.

AMERY, LEOPOLD CHARLES MAURICE STENNETT. **The Empire in the New Era.** London: Arnold, 1928, 306 p.
Speeches delivered during a tour of the Empire by the Secretary for Dominion Affairs and Colonies.

ASTON, SIR GEORGE GREY. **The Navy of To-day.** London: Methuen, 1927, 110 p.
A good general survey of contemporary facts and figures.

ASTON, SIR GEORGE GREY. **The Problem of Defence.** London: Allen, 1925, 180 p.
An interesting discussion by a competent critic, particularly valuable on the problem of Singapore.

BAKER, PHILIP JOHN NOEL. **The Present Judicial Status of the British Dominions in International Law.** New York: Longmans, 1929, 422 p.
One of the best and most lucid treatments of the problem. The author views the problem historically and examines in detail the position of the dominions as League members and in international law generally.

BERTRAM, SIR ANTON. **The Colonial Service.** New York: Macmillan, 1930, 291 p.
Based on a course of lectures at the London School of Economics. A survey of colonial government by an experienced official.

BOYCOTT, A. G. **The Elements of Imperial Defence.** London: Gale, 1931, 402 p.
The author examines the available material resources of the Empire, the problem of communications and the ways of coördinating action

BUCHET, EDMOND ÉDOUARD. **Les "Status" des Dominions Britanniques en Droit Constitutionnel et en Droit International.** Paris: Sirey, 1928, 137 p.
A documented review of the development and present international status of the dominions. The book has a good bibliography.

CHENG, SEYMOUR CHING YUAN. **Schemes for the Federation of the British Empire.** New York: Columbia University Press, 1931, 313 p.
A substantial scholarly analysis of the numerous schemes that have been advanced, and a discussion of the pros and cons of the matter.

CHEVALLIER, JEAN JACQUES. **L'Évolution de l'Empire Britannique.** Paris: Éditions Internationales, 1930, 2 v.
An exhaustive historical treatment of the Empire, with an analysis of its present status and problems.

COLE, DAVID HENRY. **Changing Conditions of Imperial Defence.** London: Sifton, Praed, 1930, 184 p.
Really an introductory discussion of the great problems of world politics, with special reference to the position of the Empire.

COLE, DAVID HENRY. **Imperial Military Geography.** London: Sifton, Praed, 1925, 406 p.
The geography of the Empire and a discussion of the military and economic factors of importance for its defense.

CORNISH, VAUGHAN. **A Geography of Imperial Defence.** London: Sifton, Praed, 1922, 154 p.
The author lays much stress on questions of distribution of population, communications, naval stations and the defense of India. A text for army examinations.

COUVE DE MURVILLE, HENRI. **Le Gouverneur dans les Dominions Britanniques.** Paris: Rousseau, 1929, 205 p.
A thorough piece of constitutional writing giving a documented account not only of the governor's powers and functions as head of the dominion government, but of his position as an imperial official.

DEMANGEON, ALBERT. **The British Empire.** New York: Harcourt, 1925, 298 p.
A translation of a good and reliable French survey of the history of British colonization and of present-day imperial problems.

DEWEY, ALEXANDER GORDON. **The Dominions and Diplomacy.** New York: Longmans, 1929, 2 v.
A scholarly study, by a Canadian jurist. Approaching the problem of imperial organization from the dominion side, he devotes the first volume to a review of the evolution of the Empire and traces the gradual disintegration since the time of the first Imperial Conference in 1887. In the second volume he gives a detailed study of the conduct of imperial international relations during the post-war period. He considers the conference of 1926 the final stage in the reorganization of the Empire as a confederacy of sovereign states.

DRAGE, GEOFFREY. **Sea Power.** London: Murray, 1931, 318 p.
A miscellaneous collection of letters and essays, some of considerable interest.

EASTWOOD, REGINALD ALLEN. **The Organization of a Britannic Partnership.** New York: Longmans, 1922, 148 p.
A stimulating discussion of forces making for a reorganization of the imperial machinery. The author suggests a conference of premiers, the appointment of resident dominion ministers and an imperial court of appeal.

EGERTON, HUGH EDWARD. **British Colonial Policy in the Twentieth Century.** London: Methuen, 1922, 259 p.

Really a treatment of the dominion problem and of the government of backward races, by a leading writer of the "sane imperialist" school.

ELLIOTT, WILLIAM YANDELL. **The New British Empire.** New York: McGraw-Hill, 1932, 519 p.
A book by an American scholar which will be welcome to many who have found it impossible to keep track of the rapidly changing relationships between different parts of the British Empire. Economic, religious and cultural factors are given full consideration, and the author succeeds in rising above the mere data to some very interesting judgments of the British system and its place in the general international scene.

FIDDES, SIR GEORGE VANDELEUR. **The Dominions and Colonial Offices.** New York: Putnam, 1926, 288 p.
Written by a former Under-Secretary for the Colonies, this is a useful survey of the organization and work of the Colonial Office and the technique of government.

FIEDLER, ELSA. **Die Englischen Rüstungsausgaben seit dem Weltkriege.** Leipzig: Akademische Verlagsgesellschaft, 1929, 97 p.
A succinct study of the British defense system, its pre-war and post-war costs, and its relations to the military expenditure of the United States and France.

FULLER, JOHN FREDERICK CHARLES. **Imperial Defence, 1588-1914.** London: Sifton, Praed, 1926, 110 p.
A useful brief survey of the facts, presented by an advocate of the balance of power.

GRIGG, SIR EDWARD. **The Greatest Experiment in History.** New Haven: Yale University Press, 1924, 216 p.
An able apology for British imperialism and imperial administration. Williamstown lectures.

GUEST, LESLIE HADEN. **The Labour Party and the Empire.** London: Labour Publishing Company, 1926, 95 p.
A leading Laborite discusses various imperial problems and defends his party's attitude towards them.

GUEST, LESLIE HADEN. **The New British Empire.** London: Murray, 1929, 334 p.
Observations and reflections of an English Laborite during an Empire tour. The book deals chiefly with Canada and Australia.

GUNN, HUGH, ed. **The British Empire.** London: Collins, 1924, 12 v.
A series surveying the history, resources and activities of the Empire, prepared for the British Empire Exhibition of 1924. Individual volumes are written by authorities like Lucas, Keith, Lewin, etc.

HALL, HESSEL DUNCAN. **The British Commonwealth of Nations.** London: Methuen, 1920, 393 p.
The historical evolution of the imperial problem, the effects of the war upon imperial relationships, and post-war aspects of dominion status. One of the best informed and best balanced brief treatments.

HALL, WALTER PHELPS. **Empire to Commonwealth.** New York: Holt, 1928, 536 p.
A sound study of the last thirty years of British history, in which the author attempts an interpretation of the forces at work and an appraisal of the present institutions of the Commonwealth.

HARRIS, SEYMOUR EDWIN. **Monetary Problems of the British Empire.** New York: Macmillan, 1931, 569 p.
The author deals in a scholarly way with the evolution of the English situation since the beginning of the war, and relates it to conditions in the dominions. There are detailed chapters on India, Australia, South Africa and Egypt, also a bibliography.

HEWINS, WILLIAM ALBERT SAMUEL. **The Apologia of an Imperialist.** London: Constable, 1929, 2 v.
Contains much information of value on the history of imperial policy, with special reference to the question of tariffs. The author was for many years secretary and chairman of the tariff commission and for a time Under-Secretary for the Colonies.

HUGHES, HECTOR. **National Sovereignty and Judicial Autonomy in the British Commonwealth of Nations.** London: King, 1931, 184 p.
A technical investigation of the position of the dominions in the judicial sphere.

HUGHES, WILLIAM MORRIS. **The Splendid Adventure.** London: Benn, 1929, 456 p.
The Australian statesman writes in his usual vigorous style about Empire relations and foreign policy, and finds much to criticize in the policy of the home government.

HURD, PERCY. **The Empire; a Family Affair.** London: P. Allan, 1924, 184 p.
A popular survey of dominions, colonies and mandates, betraying the feeling of solidarity wrought by the war.

HURST, SIR CECIL JAMES BARRINGTON, SMIDDY, TIMOTHY and others. **Great Britain and the Dominions.** Chicago: Chicago University Press, 1928, 520 p.
Lectures, on the Harris Foundation, surveying the Empire as an international unit and reviewing the problems of Ireland, Canada and Australia.

JEBB, RICHARD. **The Empire in Eclipse.** London: Chapman and Hall, 1926, 352 p.
An eloquent plea for further coöperation within the Empire in matters of foreign policy, defense and trade.

KEITH, ARTHUR BERRIEDALE. **Dominion Autonomy in Practice.** New York: Oxford University Press, 1930, 98 p.
This new edition of a splendid little work takes into account the epoch-making changes of the last few years.

KEITH, ARTHUR BERRIEDALE. **The Sovereignty of the British Dominions.** New York: Macmillan, 1929, 550 p.
This book sets forth the English rather than the colonial view. Professor Keith opposes the extreme interpretations placed upon the report of 1926, and denies the dominions full sovereignty in international relations. A standard treatment of the problem.

KING-HALL, STEPHEN. **Imperial Defence.** London: Allen and Unwin, 1926, 204 p.
A knotty problem attacked from the standpoint of the taxpayer. The author pleads for better coördination of forces and dilates on difficulties in the way of reductions of armaments at the present time.

KLEINSCHMIT VON LENGEFELD, WILHELM. **Der Geistige Gehalt im Britischen Imperialismus.** Marburg: Elwert, 1928, 176 p.
British imperialism as it appears from the writings in the *Round Table*.

KNOWLES, MRS. LILIAN CHARLOTTE ANNE (TOMN). **The Economic Development of the British Overseas Empire.** London: Routledge, 1924-1930, 2 v.
The treatment is uneven, but the book contains some good chapters on the economic development of India.

LEACOCK, STEPHEN. **Back to Prosperity.** New York: Macmillan, 1932, 108 p.
Further suggestions (not of a very concrete nature) of a Canadian economist for the development of Empire preference, written on the eve of the Ottawa Conference.

LEACOCK, STEPHEN. **Economic Prosperity in the British Empire.** London: Constable, 1930, 246 p.
A brilliant but not very closely reasoned attack upon the problem, from the imperialist point of view.

LUFFT, HERMANN A. L. **Das Britische Weltreich.** Leipzig: Bibliographisches Institut, 1930, 626 p.
One of the excellent and profusely illustrated descriptive works published by the famous German institute.

McDOUGALL, FRANK LIDGETT. **Sheltered Markets.** London: Murray, 1925, 148 p.
An able discussion of the value of Empire trade and preference.

MacINNES, CHARLES MALCOLM. **The British Commonwealth and Its Unsolved Problems.** New York: Longmans, 1925, 186 p.
A general review of the problems of dominion status, government of backward races, and the position of India, designed for the lay reader.

MAZZOLINI, GIAMBATTISTA. **L'Odierno Impera Britannica.** Pavia: University of Pavia, 1928, 142 p.
The author analyzes the organization of the Empire in 1914 and traces the changes brought about during the war and the post-war period.

MELCHETT, ALFRED MORITZ MOND, BARON. **Imperial Economic Unity.** London: Harrap, 1930, 196 p.
A prominent industrialist reviews the history of imperial preference and the evolution of trade within the Empire, with a plea for closer coöperation.

MONTGOMERY, BO GABRIEL DE. **Pax Britannica.** London: Methuen, 1928, 249 p.
A Swedish view of the British imperial problem and general international relations.

MORRIS, GUY WILFRID and WOOD, LEONARD SOUTHERDEN. **The English-Speaking Nations.** New York: Oxford University Press, 1924, 416 p.
An able review of the growth of the Empire and of the federative idea, with a brief chapter on the United States. The book is well illustrated.

MUIR, RAMSAY. **A Short History of the British Commonwealth.** Yonkers: World Book Co., 1922-23, 2 v.
Regarded by some critics as the best general history of the British Empire which has yet been produced by a single writer. The second volume is especially valuable as a history of Great Britain's foreign relations and imperial expansion.

NATHAN, MANFRED. **Empire Government.** Cambridge: Harvard University Press, 1929, 256 p.
A scholarly outline of the British imperial system.

PARGITER, ROBERT BEVERLEY and EADY, HAROLD GRIFFIN. **The Army and Sea Power.** London: Benn, 1927, 220 p.
A substantial study in strategy, showing the interdependence of the army and the navy throughout English history down to 1918.

PORRITT, EDWARD. **The Fiscal and Diplomatic Freedom of the British Overseas Dominions.** New York: Oxford University Press, 1922, 492 p.
A survey of the development of fiscal and administrative independence in the self-governing dominions, published for the Carnegie Endowment.

REPINGTON, CHARLES À COURT. **Policy and Arms.** London: Hutchinson, 1924, 322 p.
A series of essays on the most diverse questions, but dealing chiefly with problems of defense—American, French and especially British.

RICHMOND, SIR HERBERT WILLIAM. **National Policy and Naval Strength.** New York: Longmans, 1928, 373 p.
The commandant of the Imperial Defence College takes up the old problem of the relation of naval to military tactics, and the difficulties of Britain's position. Many of the chapters are historical.

ROBINSON, HOWARD. **The Development of the British Empire.** Boston: Houghton Mifflin, 1922, 475 p.
A reliable manual, progressive in tone, devoted mainly to the nineteenth century.

ROWELL, NEWTON WESLEY. **The British Empire and World Peace.** New York: Oxford University Press, 1922, 307 p.
A series of lectures dealing with international coöperation and the League, the organization of the British Empire, Canadian problems and policies, and the Church's place in the world. The work of a leading Canadian barrister.

SALT, ALEXANDER EDWARD WROTTESLEY. **Military Geography of the British Commonwealth.** London: Gale, 1925, 426 p.
An exhaustive scholarly work.

SCHILLER, FERDINAND CANNING SCOTT. **Cassandra; or, The Future of the British Empire.** New York: Dutton, 1926, 92 p.
A pessimistic forecast by a well-known English philosopher.

SCHLOSBERG, HERZL JOSHUA. **The King's Republics.** London: Stevens, 1929, 147 p.
The title is suggestive, for this nationalist South African writer goes, if anything, beyond Dewey in his view of the sovereignty of the dominions.

SCHUYLER, ROBERT LIVINGSTON. **Parliament and the British Empire.** New York: Columbia University Press, 1929, 285 p.
A scholarly review of some famous disputes in regard to the legislative authority of Parliament in colonial affairs, followed by an analysis of the present situation.

SETON, SIR MALCOLM COTTER CARISTON. **The India Office.** New York: Putnam, 1926, 299 p.
An excellent and well-written account of the organization and working of the office, by one of its high permanent officials.

SOMERVELL, DAVID CHURCHILL. **The British Empire.** London: Christophers, 1930, 345 p.
An introductory survey of a descriptive and factual nature. Includes the mandated territories.

STOKES, ROBERT. **New Imperial Ideas.** London: Murray, 1930, 314 p.
The author thinks the dominions must share in the control of the non-self-governing parts of the Empire if the Empire is to be kept together.

STRATHSPEY, TREVOR OGILVIE-GRANT, BARON. **The Case for Colonial Representation in Parliament.** London: Fleetway Press, 1923, 140 p.
A concrete proposal for colonial representation in Parliament, based upon historical and legal arguments.

TSIANG, TINGFU FULLER. **Labor and Empire.** New York: Longmans, 1923, 220 p.
A needed historical account of the attitude of the British Labor Party towards British overseas policy in the last forty years.

WEBSTER, MRS. NESTA H. **The Surrender of an Empire.** London: Boswell, 1931, 392 p.
The author is haunted by the idea of secret subversive organizations and influences, and attributes England's misfortunes in the past decade to the operation of these sinister forces.

WILLIAMS, BASIL. **The British Empire.** New York: Holt, 1928, 252 p.
One of the best brief accounts of the evolution and present status of the Empire.

WILLIAMSON, JAMES ALEXANDER. **A Short History of British Expansion.** London: Macmillan, 1922, 647 p.
A serious historical work.

ZIMMERN, ALFRED ECKHARD. **The Third British Empire.** New York: Oxford University Press, 1926, 148 p.
Three lectures by a well-known English writer, who examines the bases of the Empire and looks at the future optimistically.

ENGLAND
General Treatises and Histories

ANGELL, SIR NORMAN. **If Britain Is to Live.** New York: Putnam, 1923, 175 p.
A summary argument for the development of internationalism and the elimination of armaments, customs barriers and political boundaries for Britain's own good.

BASTIDE, CHARLES. **L'Angleterre Nouvelle.** Paris: Alcan, 1929, 236 p.
A general survey of English politics and society, of the type now fashionable.

BENN, SIR ERNEST JOHN PICKSTONE. **If I Were a Labour Leader.** New York: Scribner, 1926, 154 p.
An English capitalist's appeal for reason and a sense of responsibility.

CENTURION, *pseud.* (JOHN HARTMAN MORGAN). **The Man Who Didn't Win the War: An Exposure of Lloyd-Georgism.** London: National Review Office, 1923, 174 p.
A violent denunciation of Lloyd George's policies from 1904 to 1922, with an appeal for a return to ultra-conservatism and vigorous English imperialism.

CLAYTON, JOSEPH. **The Rise and Decline of Socialism in Great Britain.** London: Faber and Gwyer, 1926, 263 p.
An account of the English socialist movement from 1884 to 1924, as distinguished from the labor movement. Scholarly and well-informed.

COHEN-PORTHEIM, PAUL. **England, the Unknown Isle.** New York: Dutton, 1931, 237 p.
A readable and understanding descriptive interpretation, written by a young Austrian who was interned in England during the war.

DIBELIUS, WILHELM. **England.** New York: Harper, 1930, 569 p.
An interesting study of contemporary English life, institutions and problems. One of the best and most understanding post-war books on Britain.

FARBMAN, MICHAEL S., *ed.* **Political Britain.** London: Europa Publications, 1929, 194 p.
A useful compendium of parties, policies and politicians.

FLOURNOY, FRANCIS ROSEBRO. **Parliament and War.** London: King, 1927, 294 p.
A scholarly piece of research examining the part played by Parliament in determining questions of war in the last hundred years.

FYFE, HAMILTON. **The British Liberal Party.** London: Allen and Unwin, 1928, 272 p.
A general outline history of the party, setting forth the constant dissensions and the growing drift from original ideals.

GREENWOOD, ARTHUR. **The Labour Outlook.** London: Chapman, 1929, 246 p.
A concise statement of social, economic and international policy, by a Labor M. P.

GREENWOOD, GEORGE A. **England Today.** London: Allen and Unwin, 1922, 185 p.
An indictment of social waste, idleness and ostentation. A critique of the theory and practice of "the leisure class."

HEARNSHAW, FOSSEY JOHN COBB. **Democracy and Labour.** New York: Macmillan, 1924, 274 p.
Based on a series of lectures—a discussion of democracy and labor, and a critique of such false doctrine as socialism, syndicalism and anarchism.

INGE, WILLIAM RALPH. **England.** New York: Scribner, 1926, 302 p.
A characteristically pessimistic study, but stimulating if only because of its exaggerations.

KIRCHER, RUDOLF. **How They Do It in England.** London: E. Mathews and Marrot, 1930, 246 p.
The political, social and intellectual life of England in the era of democracy, by a German who knows his subject.

LYMINGTON, GERARD VERNON WALLOP, VISCOUNT. **Ich Dien. The Tory Path.** New York: R. R. Smith, 1931, 127 p.
A modern formulation of thorough-going Toryism, with special reference to economic problems.

MACDONAGH, MICHAEL. **The English King.** New York: J. Cape and H. Smith, 1929, 318 p.
A rather popular study of the monarchy and the royal family in its historical, constitutional and social aspects.

MASTERMAN, CHARLES FREDERICK GURNEY. **England after War.** New York: Harcourt, 1923, 311 p.
A trenchant attempt to estimate the effect of the war on English society.

NATHAN, HARRY LOUIS and HEATHCOTE-WILLIAMS, HAROLD, *eds.* **Liberal Points of View.** London: Benn, 1927, 328 p.
A series of addresses by a number of prominent Liberals, including Gilbert Murray, J. A. Spender, J. M. Keynes, R. Mins and others. The subjects are by no means all political, but cover problems such as Production, Free Trade, Unemployment and Foreign Policy. On the whole, an excellent survey of contemporary Liberal outlook.

PHILLIPS, HUBERT. **The Liberal Outlook.** London: Chapman, 1929, 189 p.
A vigorous restatement of post-war Liberal doctrine and policy, with an introduction by Lloyd George.

RUGGIERO, GUIDO DE. **L'Impero Britannico dopo la Guerra.** Florence: Vallecchi, 1921, 270 p.
One of the ablest foreign analyses on English and Imperial politics and British foreign policy.

SANDERSON, WILLIAM. **Statecraft.** London: Methuen, 1927, 146 p.
A provocative discussion of English politics, which the author looks upon as an expression of the race.

SPENDER, JOHN ALFRED. **The Public Life.** New York: Cassell, 1925, 2 v.
The mature reflections of one of the leading English publicists on politics and politicians, democracy, public opinion and the press.

TRACY, HERBERT, *ed.* **The Book of the Labour Party.** London: Caxton Publishing Company, 1925, 3 v.
Authoritative essays on the origins, history, policies and leaders of the Labor Party.

TROTSKIĬ, LEV. **Whither England?** New York: International Publishers, 1925, 192 p.
Chiefly an indictment of Fabianism and pink socialism of the non-revolutionary kind.

WERTHEIMER, EGON. **Portrait of the Labour Party.** New York: Putnam, 1929, 327 p.
The translation of a strikingly discerning German appraisal of the party, its doctrines, practices and prospects.

WINGFIELD-STRATFORD, ESMÉ CECIL. **The History of British Civilization.** New York: Harcourt, 1928, 2 v.
On the whole an excellent performance, marked throughout by understanding, impartiality and balance.

Economic Problems

See also (General International Relations) International Trade, Tariffs, Cartels, p. 13, and International Finance, p. 20; also (World War) Economic and Financial Aspects, War Costs, p. 153.

ANGELL, SIR NORMAN. **Must Britain Travel the Moscow Road?** London: Douglas, 1926, 190 p.
A discussion of the English economic crisis, with arguments against communism and revolution.

BARRON, CLARENCE WALKER. **A World Remaking.** New York: Harper, 1920, 243 p.
An American financial expert's impressions and opinions on Britain's economic difficulties as "the great war loser."

BATTEN, EDWARD. **National Economics.** London: Pitman, 1926, 217 p.
A study of the unemployment problem chiefly in its relation to foreign trade and government finance.

BERKELEY, REGINALD. **England's Opportunity.** London: Gollancz, 1931, 260 p.
The author, replying to Siegfried, advocates a new liberalism and something akin to a five-year plan. This is a book worth reading.

BONNET, GEORGE EDGAR. **La Politique Anglaise d'Assainissement Monétaire.** Paris: Sirey, 1923, 172 p.
A doctoral dissertation which reviews the developments of the currency problem between 1918 and 1922.

BROWN, WILLIAM ADAMS, JR. **England and the New Gold Standard.** New Haven: Yale University Press, 1929, 338 p.
A technical study of the evolution of the new gold standard, covering the years 1919 to 1926.

CRONER, FRITZ. **Sturm über England.** Berlin: Industrie-Beamten Verlag, 1926, 102 p.
An investigation of the English unemployment problem and the circumstances of the general strike.

CROSSLEY, ARTHUR. **An Opportunity for the Cotton Trade.** London: Christophers, 1932, 78 p.
A member of Parliament gives figures to support the view that imperial preference would enable Lancashire to regain most of her lost cotton piece goods trade.

DELATTRE, FLORIS. **L'Angleterre d'Après-Guerre et le Conflit Houiller.** Paris: Colin, 1930, 440 p.
The author takes the coal problem as a reflection of the social crisis in post-war England. After studying the coal industry and setting forth its place in the economic life of the country, he examines the causes of the post-war crisis, stressing the larger national and international factors as well as the narrower dispute between the owners and the workers.

FYFE, HAMILTON. **Behind the Scenes of the Great Strike.** London: Labour Publishing Company, 1926, 89 p.
Observations of the editor of the London *Daily Herald*.

GAUSSEL, GEORGES. **La Réforme Monétaire Anglaise.** Paris: Presses Universitaires, 1928, 163 p.
A scholarly review of the work of the Bradbury committee, the Gold Standard Act, and the more recent developments.

HENDERSON, W. **L'Exportation des Capitaux Anglais avant et après la Guerre.** Paris: La Vie Universitaire, 1924, 135 p.
A useful dissertation reviewing British loans before the war, the mobilization of foreign securities and capital exports during the war, and the effects of these policies on British trade.

HIRST, FRANCIS WRIGLEY. **From Adam Smith to Philip Snowden.** New York: Adelphi Co., 1925, 88 p.
A sympathetic outline of the history of free trade in Great Britain.

LACHAPELLE, GEORGES. **Les Finances Britanniques.** Paris: Sirey, 1920, 316 p.
A scholarly general treatment of the British financial system before the war and the ways in which the exigencies of the war period were met. There is a good criticism of these financial war moves.

LACOUT, GEORGES. **Le Retour à l'Étalon-Or.** Paris: Payot, 1926, 256 p.
An excellent critical account of English monetary history from 1914 to 1926, by a member of the economic staff of the Bank of France.

LAWRENCE, FREDERICK WILLIAM PETHICK. **The Gold Crisis.** London: Gollancz, 1931, 244 p.
The former financial adviser of the British Treasury reviews the development of the problem after the war and stresses its connections with debts, reparations, etc.

LAZARD, JEAN PIERRE. **Politique et Théories Monétaires Anglaises d'Après-Guerre.** Paris: Sirey, 1927, 125 p.
A stimulating essay, designed to introduce the theories and practice of the English to the French public.

LEUBUSCHER, CHARLOTTE. **Liberalismus und Protektionismus in der Englischen Wirtschaftspolitik seit dem Kriege.** Jena: Fischer, 1927, 224 p.
A scholarly review of the conflict between free trade and protectionism in England down to 1926.

LOVEDAY, ALEXANDER. **Britain and World Trade.** New York: Longmans, 1931, 229 p.
A collection of essays by the head of the economic intelligence service of the League.

MELCHETT, ALFRED MORITZ MOND, BARON. **Industry and Politics.** London: Macmillan, 1927, 337 p.
Speeches and essays by a leading British industrialist.

MILNER, ALFRED MILNER, VISCOUNT. **Questions of the Hour.** New York: Doran, 1923, 173 p.
Important essays on contemporary English economic problems by one of the most distinguished of English conservatives.

PEEL, GEORGE. **The Economic War.** London: Macmillan, 1930, 284 p.
A keen study of the world situation with special reference to Britain. The author urges the need of adjusting the economic armament at home before embarking on international economic action.

PERSÉGOL, LUCIEN. **Les Conséquences Économiques de la Guerre en Angleterre.** Blois: Breton, 1922, 213 p.
A dissertation reviewing the history of government control of industry during the war, the forms of protection after the war and the effects of this on England's leading export industries.

PLACHY, FRANK, JR. **Britain's Economic Plight.** Boston: Little, Brown, 1926, 249 p.
An American journalist's impressions of industrial England lead him to the conclusion that what England lacks is not resources or plant, but economic intelligence to turn them to account.

RECOULY, RAYMOND. **L'Angleterre Est-Elle en Décadence?** Paris: Éditions de France, 1931, 224 p.
Another volume called forth by Siegfried's critique. Lively writing by a facile French publicist.

SHAW, WILLIAM ARTHUR. **Currency, Credit and the Exchanges.** London: Harrap, 1927, 203 p.
A competent British writer reviews the years of confusion 1914-1926. A good general treatment.

SIEGFRIED, ANDRÉ. **England's Crisis.** New York: Harcourt, 1931, 317 p.
A valuable if not entirely novel estimate of England's post-war tribulation, by an able French writer who possesses psychological as well as factual grasp.

SIEGFRIED, ANDRÉ. **Post-War Britain.** New York: Dutton, 1925, 314 p.
An analysis primarily of England's economic position, though there is some consideration of political life and parties. A discerning book and one of the best critiques of the situation as it was at the time the author made his study.

WILLIAMS, HERBERT GERAINT. **Politics and Economics.** London: Murray, 1926, 179 p.
Really an exposition of the conservative view on present economic problems.

WITHERS, HARTLEY. **Bankers and Credit.** London: Nash, 1924, 294 p.
A review of the tribulations of the British monetary system, a survey of new monetary theories, and an argument for return to the gold standard, by a former Treasury official who writes frequently on investment and other problems.

Biographies and Addresses

See also (World War) Biographies of Wartime Statesmen and Diplomats, p. 101; also (Europe) Biographies, p. 228.

ANDREADĒS, ANDREAS MICHAĒL. **Philip Snowden.** London: King, 1930, 110 p.
A brief study, marked throughout by sympathy and understanding remarkable in a foreigner. The emphasis is on Snowden's financial policies.

ARTHUR, SIR GEORGE COMPTON ARCHIBALD. **George V.** New York: J. Cape and H. Smith, 1930, 326 p.
The king as a great ruler, in a rather uneven and very subjective biographical essay.

BALDWIN, STANLEY. **On England.** London: Allan, 1926, 275 p.
A collection of addresses on diverse subjects, including several on the Empire and several biographical studies of contemporaries.

BALDWIN, STANLEY. **Our Inheritance.** London: Hodder, 1928, 309 p.
A second collection of speeches, including fifteen on imperial matters.

BEGBIE, HAROLD. **Mirrors of Downing Street.** New York: Putnam, 1921, 171 p.
Biographical sketches, by a Liberal journalist. A book much talked of in its day.

BIRKENHEAD, FREDERICK EDWIN SMITH, EARL OF. **Contemporary Personalities.** London: Cassell, 1924, 326 p.
The leading political figures of the post-war era analyzed by an unusually keen diagnostician.

CECIL, ALGERNON. **British Foreign Secretaries, 1807-1916.** London: Bell, 1927, 390 p.
A fascinating review of the personalities and policies of British foreign ministers, provocative and written from a cosmopolitan standpoint.

CHAMBERLAIN, SIR AUSTEN. **Peace in Our Time.** London: Allan, 1928, 322 p.
Speeches of the former Foreign Minister.

EDWARDS, JOHN HUGH. **David Lloyd George.** New York: Sears, 1929, 2 v.
An authorized biography, not very critical, but useful.

EPHESIAN, *pseud.* (CARL ERIC BECHHOFER ROBERTS). **Philip Snowden.** London: Cassell, 1929, 246 p.
An impartial and sympathetic biography, of special interest for the account of the earlier phases of the Labor movement.

FISHER, HERBERT ALBERT LAURENS. **James Bryce.** New York: Macmillan, 1927, 2 v.
The authoritative biography, based on Bryce's correspondence and stressing especially his American connection. The author is a well-known English educator and statesman.

FYFE, HAMILTON. **Northcliffe. An Intimate Biography.** New York: Macmillan, 1930, 357 p.
A lively study of Northcliffe's character and work, by one of his admirers.

GERMAINS, VICTOR WALLACE. **The Tragedy of Winston Churchill.** London: Hurst, 1931, 288 p.
A bitter and telling attack upon Churchill, biographical in form but devoted to special episodes in his political career.

GUEDALLA, PHILIP. **A Gallery.** New York: Putnam, 1924, 285 p.
The well-known biographer includes here a dozen thumb nail studies of Conservative and Liberal political leaders.

HAGBERG, KNUT HJALMAR. **Kings, Churchills and Statesmen.** New York: Dodd, 1929, 235 p.
Excellent biographical studies covering the field from the Duke of Marlborough to Prime Minister Baldwin.

ICONOCLAST, *pseud.* (MRS. MARY AGNES HAMILTON). **England's Labour Rulers.** New York: Seltzer, 1924, 136 p.
Brief biographical sketches of the members of the Labor Party cabinet which took office in 1924.

ICONOCLAST, *pseud.* (MRS. MARY AGNES HAMILTON). **James Ramsay MacDonald.** London: Cape, 1931, 305 p.
An amplified edition of an able and warmly appreciative character study first published in 1924.

KIRCHER, RUDOLF. **Engländer.** New York: W. Collins, 1928, 307 p.
Interesting and penetrating sketches of leaders in contemporary English life.

MALCOLM, SIR IAN. **Vacant Thrones.** London: Macmillan, 1931, 220 p.
Attractive pen pictures of British statesmen of the past forty years, based chiefly on personal reminiscences and impressions.

MALLET, SIR CHARLES EDWARD. **Mr. Lloyd George: A Study.** London: Benn, 1930, 314 p.
A Liberal criticism of Lloyd George as a Liberal leader.

OXFORD AND ASQUITH, HERBERT HENRY ASQUITH, EARL OF. **Fifty Years of British Parliament.** Boston: Little, Brown, 1926, 2 v.
The parliamentary reminiscences of the former Prime Minister and Liberal leader, indispensable for a study of recent English political life.

SIDEBOTHAM, HERBERT. **Political Profiles.** Boston: Houghton Mifflin, 1921, 256 p.
Successful character sketches of most political leaders of the post-war period, by an experienced parliamentary and military correspondent.

SIMON, SIR JOHN. **Comments and Criticisms.** London: Hodder, 1930, 319 p.
Speeches on a variety of subjects, including the general strike, the International Court, the Empire and certain phases of the Indian problem.

SPENDER, JOHN ALFRED. **Life, Journalism and Politics.** London: Cassell, 1927, 2 v.
The reminiscences of the well-known Liberal and former editor of the *Westminster Gazette.* The presentation is charming and the viewpoint interesting, while there are a number of important contributions to the recent domestic and foreign history of the Empire.

STEED, HENRY WICKHAM. **The Real Stanley Baldwin.** London: Nisbet, 1930, 191 p.
A psychological study: an appreciation rather than a biography.

THOMPSON, EDWARD RAYMOND. **Mr. Lloyd George.** New York: Doran, 1922, 367 p.
  A friendly popular biography, by a prolific writer.

THOMPSON, EDWARD RAYMOND. **Portraits of the New Century.** New York: Doubleday,
  1928, 369 p.
  A well-written but rather superficial collection of biographical essays, usually in pairs.
  Those on Harmsworth and Pearson, Roberts and Kitchener, Fisher and Beresford,
  and Curzon and Cromer, are the most interesting.

TILTMAN, HUBERT HESSELL. **Ramsay MacDonald: Labor's Man of Destiny.** New
  York: Stokes, 1929, 466 p.
  Hardly a profound contribution, but a fair account of MacDonald's career.

VRIESLANDER, WISMANN. **Lloyd George.** Munich: Wieland-Verlag, 1923, 119 p.
  A German estimate of Lloyd George and his foreign policies.

WHYTE, ADAM GOWANS. **Stanley Baldwin.** London: Chapman, 1926, 176 p.
  An attempt to fathom an enigmatic personality. Based on Baldwin's speeches and
  pronouncements.

WILSON, ROBERT MCNAIR. **Lord Northcliffe: A Study.** Philadelphia: Lippincott, 1927,
  304 p.
  Written by a friend and admirer, this biography of the great journalist can hardly be
  regarded as a just appraisal of his real influence or importance, though it adds many
  interesting facts to our knowledge.

WRIGHT, PETER E. **Portraits and Criticisms.** London: Nash, 1925, 214 p.
  These essays, by a well-informed writer, deal very largely with the international
  activities of men like Asquith, Lloyd George, Balfour, Churchill and Curzon.

ZETLAND, LAWRENCE JOHN LUMLEY DUNDAS, MARQUESS OF. **The Life of Lord Curzon.**
  New York: Boni and Liveright, 1928, 3 v.
  The authoritative biography, based on the Curzon papers. This work was published
  while the author was still Earl of Ronaldshay, before he succeeded to his present title.

Foreign Policy

**Anglo-Sovetskie Otnosheniia so Dnia Podpisaniia Torgovogo Soglashenia do
  Razryva.** Moscow: Commissariat for Foreign Affairs, 1927, 172 p.
  A valuable collection of documents bearing on Anglo-Russian relations from 1921
  to 1927.

GLASGOW, GEORGE. **MacDonald as a Diplomatist.** London: Jonathan Cape, 1925,
  232 p.
  A eulogy of the Premier and his "gallant attempt to guide the steps of Europe into
  the paths of peace."

MAZZOLINI, GIAMBATTISTA. **L'Antagonismo Anglo-Russo in Asia.** Pavia: Facoltà di
  Scienze Politiche, 1927, 72 p.
  A much needed historical review of Anglo-Russian relations in Asia from 1907 to
  1927, unfortunately sketchy.

OBST, ERICH. **England, Europa und die Welt.** Berlin: Vowinckel, 1927, 356 p.
  An impressive study of England's political and economic relations and her dependence on the Continental countries, by a leading geographer.

PAYNE, GEORGE HENRY. **England: Her Treatment of America.** New York: Sears,
  1931, 343 p.
  The author reviews the English attitude towards America since the Revolution.

RICHTHOFEN, WILHELM, FREIHERR VON. **Brito-Germania die Erlösung Europas.** Berlin: Esche-Verlag, 1926, 184 p.
An appeal for close British-German friendship as an indispensable preliminary to recovery.

WILLERT, SIR ARTHUR. **Aspects of British Foreign Policy.** New Haven: Yale University Press, 1928, 141 p.
Lectures at Williamstown by the press officer at the British Foreign Office.

IRELAND

See also (Great Britain) Imperial Relations, p. 231.

BEASLEY, PIERCE. **Michael Collins and the Making of New Ireland.** New York: Harper, 1926, 2 v.
The standard biography of the Irish leader, written by a close associate on the basis of much unpublished material.

BLÁCAM, AODH DE. **What Sinn Fein Stands For.** London: Chapman, 1921, 247 p.
An historical sketch of the republican movement, followed by a concise analysis of its program and doctrine.

BRETHERTON, C. H. **The Real Ireland.** London: Black, 1925, 197 p.
An outspoken interpretation of the Irish troubles as a class struggle between bourgeoisie and proletariat.

BUTLER, HUGH D. **Irish Free State: Economic Survey.** Washington: Department of Commerce, 1928, 86 p.
A handbook surveying resources, industries, and transportation and banking facilities; prepared for the Bureau of Foreign and Domestic Commerce.

CLARKSON, JESSE DUNSMORE. **Labour and Nationalism in Ireland.** New York: Longmans, 1925, 502 p.
A scholarly examination of the relation of labor to the nationalist movement in Ireland, and in a larger sense a history of Ireland's domestic development in the nineteenth and twentieth centuries.

COLLINS, MICHAEL. **The Path to Freedom.** London: Fisher Unwin, 1923, 153 p.
Notes by the late leader of the Irish Free State dealing with the history and nature of the treaty with England.

CREEL, GEORGE. **Ireland's Fight for Freedom.** New York: Harper, 1919, 199 p.
The "facts" presented to secure wider support for Ireland among the non-Irish elements in America.

CROZIER, FRANK PERCY. **Impressions and Recollections.** London: Laurie, 1930, 330 p.
Light on the events in Ireland in the period just before and just after the war.

DESMOND, SHAW. **The Drama of Sinn Fein.** New York: Scribner, 1923, 494 p.
One of the most vivid and dramatic accounts, at the same time well-informed and fair.

FAUCON, GUILLAUME. **Le Statut de l'État Libre d'Irlande.** Paris: Rousseau, 1929, 252 p.
A competent study, dealing primarily with the international position of the Irish Free State.

FIGGIS, DARRELL. **The Irish Constitution Explained.** Dublin: Mellifont, 1922, 100 p.
A clear exposition.

FIGGIS, DARRELL. **Recollections of the Irish War.** London: Benn, 1927, 309 p.
An Irish literary man's experiences and impressions of the period 1914-1921.

FITZ-GERALD, WILLIAM GEORGE, *ed.* **The Voice of Ireland.** London: Heywood, 1924, 611 p.
A valuable collection of composite authorship representing all shades of opinion on contemporary Irish problems.

FRÉDÉRIX, PIERRE. **Irlande, Extrême Occident.** Paris: Gallimard, 1931, 216 p.
The book deals chiefly with the figures and problems of Ireland's struggle for liberty and the course of the civil war.

GOBLET, YANN MORVRAN. **L'Irlande dans la Crise Universelle, 1914-1920.** Paris: Alcan, 2nd ed., 1921, 462 p.
Home Rule and the war, the Easter rebellion, the war for independence. A well-informed French study.

GOOD, JAMES WINDER. **Ulster and Ireland.** London: Maunsel, 1919, 294 p.
A résumé of the factors in the Ulster question, by an Irish nationalist.

GWYNN, DENIS ROLLESTON. **The Irish Free State.** New York: Macmillan, 1928, 436 p.
A good survey of the course of events from 1922 to 1927, written by a supporter of the government.

GWYNN, DENIS ROLLESTON. **The Life and Death of Roger Casement.** London: Cape, 1930, 444 p.
A sympathetic study of a most unusual and tragic career.

GWYNN, STEPHEN. **Ireland.** London: Benn, 1924, 252 p.
A volume in the "Modern World" Series. A competent analysis of various aspects of Irish development in modern times.

HACKETT, FRANCIS. **The Story of the Irish Nation.** New York: Century, 1922, 402 p.
A readable outline, by a well-known literary critic.

HANNA, HENRY. **The Statute Law of the Irish Free State.** Dublin: Thom, 1929, 101 p.
A convenient review of the legislative activity of the new state since 1922.

HEALY, TIMOTHY MICHAEL. **Letters and Leaders of My Day.** New York: Stokes, 1929, 2 v.
The former Governor-General of the Irish Free State takes his letters to his father and brother as a basis for an interesting review of sixty years of the Irish question.

HENRY, ROBERT MITCHELL. **The Evolution of Sinn Fein.** New York: Huebsch, 1920, 318 p.
The author relates the modern movement to earlier organizations and efforts. A good brief account.

HULL, ELEANOR. **A History of Ireland and Her People.** London: Harrap, 1931, 487 p.
The second volume of a general history, covering the period from 1688 to the present, with special stress on the revolution and the establishment of the Free State.

Irish Free State Official Handbook. London: Benn, 1932, 323 p.
An official publication, prepared under the direction of the Ministry for Industry and Commerce, conveying information on all aspects of life in the Free State. Beautifully illustrated by Irish artists.

KERZHENTSEV, R. **Revoliutsionnaia Irlandiia.** Moscow: Gosizdat, 1923, 224 p.
The stormy post-war history of Ireland, with the usual communist emphasis on the class struggle and the iniquities of British imperialism.

LAZENBY, ELIZABETH. **Ireland. A Catspaw.** New York: Charter Pub. Co., 1929, 246 p.
The situation as the writer found it in the critical year 1922. The book is vividly written and reports some interesting conversations with Irish leaders.

LYND, ROBERT. **Ireland a Nation.** New York: Dodd, 1920, 299 p.
History and action called in to support the claim for Ireland's full nationhood.

McCARTAN, PATRICK. **With De Valera in America.** New York: Brentano, 1932, 284 p.
The best account of the part played by Irish-Americans from 1917 to 1920, by the "Envoy of the Irish Republic" in those years.

MacDONAGH, MICHAEL. **The Life of William O'Brien.** London: Benn, 1928, 281 p.
Based on information from O'Brien and on his papers, this is a valuable study not only of the man but of the nationalist movement in which he played such a part.

MacNEILL, JOHN GORDON SWIFT. **Studies in the Constitution of the Irish Free State.** Dublin: Talbot Press, 1925, 268 p.
An analysis of the constitution, article by article, with commentary on its implications not only for domestic but for imperial relations.

McNEILL, RONALD JOHN. **Ulster's Stand for Union.** London: Murray, 1922, 310 p.
The best single account of the Unionist movement, by an active participant.

MACREADY, SIR NEVIL. **Annals of an Active Life.** New York: Doran, 1925, 2 v.
Contains valuable material on conditions in Ireland during the last years of the British rule, by the commander of the British forces there in 1920-22.

MURRAY, ROBERT HENRY and LAW, HUGH ALEXANDER. **Ireland.** Boston: Houghton Mifflin, 1924, 286 p.
A volume in "The Nations of Today" Series. A good outline of Irish history and survey of post-war conditions and problems.

O'BRIEN, WILLIAM. **The Irish Revolution.** London: Allen, 1923, 462 p.
Chiefly a study of the period from 1910 to 1918, by a well-informed Irish participant.

O'CONNOR, BATT. **With Michael Collins in the Fight for Irish Independence.** London: Davies, 1930, 196 p.
A readable but of course partisan account of the Irish troubles.

O'FLAHERTY, LIAM. **The Life of Tim Healy.** New York: Harcourt, 1927, 319 p.
A contemptuous biography of the former Governor-General.

O'HEGARTY, P. S. **The Victory of Sinn Fein.** London: Simpkin, 1925, 226 p.
The impressions and reflections of an Irish nationalist rather than a systematic account of events.

PAUL-DUBOIS, LOUIS FRANÇOIS ALPHONSE. **Le Drame Irlandais et l'Irlande Nouvelle.** Paris: Perrin, 1927.
A general account of events in Ireland since 1914.

PHILLIPS, ALISON. **The Revolution in Ireland, 1906-1923.** New York: Longmans, 1926, 348 p.
The revised edition of the best account from the English side. The work of an eminent historian.

QUEKETT, SIR ARTHUR SCOTT. **The Constitution of Northern Ireland.** Belfast: H. M. S. O., 1928, 90 p.
A government official discusses the origin and development of the constitution.

RYNNE, MICHAEL. **Die Voelkerrechtliche Stellung Irlands.** Munich: Duncker und Humblot, 1930, 435 p.
An exhaustive scholarly study of dominion status and especially of Ireland's status in international law and as a League member.

SHEEHAN, DANIEL DESMOND. **Ireland since Parnell.** London: O'Connor, 1921, 326 p.
A well written narrative, fullest on the pre-war period.

SPINDLER, KARL. **The Mystery of the Casement Ship.** New York: Westermann, 1931, 282 p.
A valuable contribution, written by a German officer who commanded the blockade-runner *Libau* and who took part in the Easter insurrection.

TALBOT, HAYDEN, *ed.* **Michael Collins' Own Story.** London: Hutchinson, 1923, 256 p.
An important book.

TÉRY, SIMONE. **En Irlande.** Paris: Flammarion, 1923, 284 p.
A history of events from the Easter Rising to 1923, by a Frenchman who was on the Irish side.

TURNER, EDWARD RAYMOND. **Ireland and England in the Past and at Present.** New York: Century, 1920, 504 p.
Scholarly, but no longer up to date on recent movements. The author makes out a fair case for the British.

WARREN, RAOUL DE. **L'Irlande et Ses Institutions Politiques.** Paris: Berger-Levrault, 1928, 496 p.
A scholarly review of Anglo-Irish relations followed by a detailed analysis of present arrangements and problems. One of the good books on the subject.

WELLS, WARRE BRADLEY. **Irish Indiscretions.** London: Allen and Unwin, 1923, 230 p.
Really a history of the Irish troubles from 1914 on, as demonstrated by the policies and actions of the leaders.

WHITE, ALBERT CLEMENT. **The Irish Free State: Its Evolution and Possibilities.** London: Hutchinson, 1923, 160 p.
A brief sympathetic history of the Irish movement for independence by an English Liberal.

III. WESTERN EUROPE

HOLLAND

See also (World War) Neutrals and the War, p. 152; also (Far East) East Indies, p. 489.

ASSELIN, H. **L'Âme et la Vie d'un Peuple. La Hollande dans le Monde.** Paris: Perrin, 1921.
A sympathetic essay on the politics and culture of the Netherlands.

BARNOUW, ADRIAAN JACOB. **Holland under Queen Wilhelmina.** New York: Scribner, 1923, 320 p.
The only good history of contemporary Holland available in English, by the Professor of Dutch Language and Literature at Columbia University.

COLENBRANDER, HERMANN THEODOOR. **Nederland en België.** Hague: Nijhoff, 1927, 140 p.
A collection of essays on the post-war relations of Holland and Belgium, by a leading Dutch historian.

COLIJN, H. **Koloniale Vraagstukken.** Amsterdam: Dagblad de Standaard, 1928, 145 p.
An up-to-date and well-written volume on the colonial problem of the Dutch, by one of the men who knows it best.

DEMER, J. **Les Relations Hollando-Belges.** Paris: Presses Universitaires, 1922.
A dissertation on the Wieringen difficulty, giving a useful systematic survey of the chief points.

Es, W. J. L. van. **Holland-België.** Haarlem: Tjeenk Willink, 1926, 144 p.
Another general treatment of Dutch-Belgian relations and the problems left by the war.

Jitta, Abraham Carel Josephus. **Holland's Modern Renascence.** Hague: Nijhoff, 1930, 96 p.
A survey of Dutch commerce, industry and agriculture in the last fifty years, with stress on Holland's place in the modern world. An excellent little book.

Nemry, Léon. **Les Pays-Bas après la Guerre.** Brussels: De Wit, 1924, 371 p.
The economic effects of the war on Holland and the Dutch colonies.

Nygh, Willem Johannis Cornelis Anthony. **La Politique Financière des Pays-Bas pendant la Guerre.** Hague: Nijhoff, 1923, 130 p.
A thorough, scholarly treatment of the subject.

BELGIUM

General

See also (International Finance) Reparations and War Debts, p. 25; also (World War) Belgium, p. 125; also (France) Relations with Other Countries, p. 269; also (Africa) Belgian Possessions, p. 526.

Baudhuin, Fernand. **Finances Belges. La Stabilisation et Ses Conséquences.** Paris: Giard, 1928, 296 p.
An up-to-date study of the evolution of Belgian finance after the war.

Baudhuin, Fernand. **La Structure Économique de la Belgique.** Paris: Giraudon, 1926, 238 p.
A scholarly survey by a Louvain professor.

Berghe, E. van den. **Émile Vandervelde, Sa Doctrine, Son Action.** Courtrai: Vermant, 1928.
A sympathetic sketch of the career of an eminent socialist leader.

Cammaerts, Émile. **Belgium.** New York: Putnam, 1921, 357 p.
A volume in the "Story of the Nations" Series. A well-informed history of the country and its culture.

Collet, Octave. **La Question Financière en Belgique.** Brussels: Van Campenhout, 1922, 180 p.
A study of the stabilization and conversion of the franc.

Damoiseaux, M. **Les Institutions Nationales de la Belgique.** Tournai: Casterman, 3rd ed., 1922, 184 p.
The latest edition of a good survey of the Belgian constitutional and administrative system.

Des Ombiaux, Maurice. **La Politique Belge depuis l'Armistice.** Paris: Bossard, 1921, 195 p.
Controversial writing on post-war politics and problems.

Fournier, Henri. **La Réforme Financière et Monétaire en Belgique.** Paris: Giard, 1927, 261 p.
The best of several doctoral dissertations on the subject.

Franck, Louis. **La Stabilisation Monétaire en Belgique.** Paris: Payot, 1927, 176 p.
An authoritative study by the Governor of the Banque Nationale de Belgique.

GRAHAM, EVELYN. **Albert: King of the Belgians.** New York: Dodd, Mead, 1929, 314 p.
As good a biography of the King as can be expected at the present time.

Histoire de la Belgique Contemporaine, 1830-1914. Brussels: De Wit, 1928-1930, 3 v.
A splendid coöperative work, with chapters on the formation of the Kingdom, the evolution of institutions, and economic history. Attention should be called especially to the chapter on Belgium's relations to the Great Powers, written by Terlinden, the director of the Foreign Office.

KALKEN, FRANS VAN. **La Belgique Contemporaine.** Paris: Colin, 1930, 218 p.
An admirable survey by a Professor at the University of Brussels.

LEVY-ULLMANN, HENRI and MIRKIN-GETSEVICH, BORIS SERGIEEVICH. **Belgique.** Paris: Delagrave, 1931, 350 p.
An authoritative treatment of the constitution, political régime and international status of Belgium.

LINDEN, HERMAN VAN DER. **Belgium, the Making of a Nation.** Oxford: Clarendon, 1920, 356 p.
A competent general survey from earliest times onward, by a well known Belgian historian.

MAHAIM, ERNEST, *ed.* **La Belgique Restaurée.** Brussels: Lamertin, 1926, 687 p.
An extensive collaborative survey of post-war Belgium's economic resources and problems.

MARQUARDT, SIEGFRIED. **Verfall und Wiederaufrichtung der Belgischen Währung nach dem Weltkriege.** Berlin: Ebering, 1929, 106 p.
A careful monographic study of Belgium's post-war currency problem. An up-to-date and concise treatment.

MEEÜS, ADRIEN DE. **Histoire de Belgique Illustrée.** Paris: Van Oest, 1930, 246 p.
A lively, beautifully illustrated survey designed for the layman.

PIERARD, LOUIS. **Belgian Problems since the War.** New Haven: Yale University Press, 1929, 106 p.
Williamstown Lectures, dealing with the Flemish-Walloon problem, but especially with questions of labor and socialism. The author is a member of Parliament.

PIRENNE, HENRI. **Histoire de Belgique.** Brussels: Lamertin, 1922-1932, 7 v.
The standard history of Belgium, by one of the world's foremost historians. Volume VII covers the period from 1830 to 1914.

PIRENNE, HENRI. **Le Pangermanisme et la Belgique.** Brussels: Lamertin, 1919.
A discussion of the German annexationist plans, by an eminent Belgian scholar.

REED, THOMAS HARRISON. **The Government and Politics of Belgium.** Yonkers: World Book Company, 1924, 197 p.
The best general survey in English of parties, politics and the governmental system in the immediate post-war period.

SPEYER, H. **La Réforme de l'État en Belgique.** Brussels: Bruylant, 1927, 146 p.
A professor at the University of Brussels examines the working of the Belgian Government and makes constructive suggestions for future development.

WIDMER, ROBERT. **La Question Monétaire en Belgique depuis la Fin de la Guerre.** Paris: Presses Universitaires, 1928, 404 p.
The most exhaustive recent dissertation dealing with post-war monetary policies and problems.

The Flemish Question

BASSE, M. **De Vlaamsche Beweging van 1905 tot 1930.** Ghent: 1931.
A useful general survey of the Flemish question.

CLOUGH, SHEPARD BANCROFT. **A History of the Flemish Movement in Belgium.**
New York: R. R. Smith, 1930, 316 p.
This careful study in English fills a real need. It can be warmly recommended to all interested in one of the major movements of western Europe. The book contains an exhaustive bibliography.

DESTRÉE, JULES. **Wallons et Flamands. La Querelle Linguistique en Belgique.**
Paris: Plon, 1923, 186 p.
A Walloon account of the language difficulty and its dangers for the future of Belgium.

EGGEN VAN TERLAN, J. L. **Contribution à l'Histoire du Mouvement Flamand pendant la Guerre.** Brussels: L'Églantine, 1931, 96 p.
The account of an active Flemish agitator. Well-documented.

PUYMBROECK, H. VAN. **Het Vlaamsche Front en de Strijd voor de Vlaamsche Zelfstandigheid.** Antwerp: Volksheil, 1925.
A general account of the post-war development of the Flemish question.

LUXEMBOURG

ANDERS, JÉRÔME. **Le Grand-Duché de Luxembourg.** Brussels: Lamertin, 1919, 121 p.
A general introductory survey, historical, constitutional and economic.

LOUTSCH, HUBERT. **Le Grand-Duché de Luxembourg.** Luxembourg: St. Paul, 1919, 190 p.
An historical review and study of economic problems, together with a plea for maintenance of independence according to the treaties.

MOUNIER, JEAN. **L'État Actuel de la Question du Luxembourg.** Paris: Jouve, 1920, 96 p.
A dissertation devoted largely to a history of the Luxembourg question, the position of the Duchy during the war, and its present political and economic orientation.

PRUM, XAVIER. **The Problem of Luxemburg.** New York: Knickerbocker, 1919, 76 p.
A Luxembourger's plea for a separate status for the Duchy within the Belgian state.

SWITZERLAND

See also (World War) Neutrals and the War, p. 152; also (France) Relations with Switzerland,
p. 269.

BROOKS, ROBERT CLARKSON. **Civic Training in Switzerland.** Chicago: Chicago University Press, 1930, 436 p.
An excellent volume. The author deals with the functioning of democracy under the peculiar conditions of a multi-national country.

FUETER, EDUARD. **Die Schweiz seit 1848.** Zurich: Orell Füssli, 1928, 305 p.
A Swiss historian surveys his country's recent history, politics and economics. The best historical work on modern Switzerland.

GAGLIARDI, ERNST. **Geschichte der Schweiz.** Zurich: Orell Füssli, 1920-1927, 3 v.
An excellent general history of Switzerland. Volume III covers the period from 1848 to 1926.

HORBER, KARL. **Die Schweizerische Politik.** Zurich: Bopp, 1928, 296 p.
A useful handbook of present Swiss problems and policies.

LEDERREY, E. G. M. **L'Armée Suisse.** Geneva: Société d'Éditions Artistiques, 1929, 254 p.
A coöperative work surveying the history, organization and equipment of the Swiss army.

LUTH, RUDOLF ZU DER. **Die Schweiz, Ihre Militärpolitische Lage vor und nach dem Weltkriege.** Charlottenburg: Offene Worte, 1925, 374 p.
An exhaustive treatment of the Swiss military system.

MARTIN, WILLIAM. **A History of Switzerland.** London: G. Richards, 1931, 333 p.
The best general history of Switzerland in English, written attractively and based on sound knowledge of the subject.

RUCHTI, JACOB. **Geschichte der Schweiz während des Weltkrieges.** Bern: Haupt, 1928, 554 p.
Volume I of an authoritative history, dealing with the political history of Swiss neutrality.

WALDKIRCH, EDUARD OTTO VON. **Die Dauernde Neutralität der Schweiz.** Basel: Helbing und Lichtenhahn, 1925, 73 p.
A brief but good history of Swiss neutrality, with chapters on the legal and political aspects of the problem.

WEILENMANN, HERMANN. **Die Vielsprachige Schweiz.** Basel: Rhein-Verlag, 1925, 301 p.
A careful study of the Swiss solution of the nationality question with particular stress on the methods of overcoming friction between nationalities.

WERNLÉ, GABRIEL. **La Suisse et Nous.** Paris: Société Anonyme d'Éditions, 1923, 218 p.
An admirable survey of Swiss agriculture, manufacturing, and commerce.

WORNER, BERNARD. **La Suisse, Centre Financier Européen.** Paris: Chauny, 1932, 176 p.
A study of Switzerland's economic and financial position.

FRANCE

General

Annuaire Général de la France et de l'Étranger. Paris: Larousse. Annual.
An important French handbook.

BENOIST, CHARLES. **Les Lois de la Politique Française.** Paris: Fayard, 1928, 320 p.
A well-known French historian attempts to determine the underlying principles which condition the conduct of French policies.

BOURGIN, GEORGES, CARRÈRE, JEAN and GUÉRIN, ANDRÉ. **Manuel des Partis Politiques en France.** Paris: Rieder, 1928, 304 p.
One of the best guides to French politics.

BRIAND, ARISTIDE. **Paroles de Paix.** Paris: Figuière, 1927, 181 p.
Selections from the speeches of Briand to show that the key to his policy was always peace.

BUCHAN, JOHN, ed. **France.** London: Hodder and Stoughton, 1923, 366 p.
A volume in the "Nations of Today" Series, dealing mainly with the period since 1870.

BUREAU, PAUL. **Quinze Années de Séparation.** Paris: Bloud, 1921, 248 p.
A review of the history of the Law of Separation, showing how it failed in practice and how the Church managed to maintain itself.

CAILLAUX, JOSEPH. **Whither France? Whither Europe?** New York: Knopf, 1923, 186 p.
The former French Premier tries to answer the question: "How are we to adjust the political institutions founded by our fathers to the economic forces which have become our chaotic, all-powerful rulers?"

CATALOGNE, ÉDOUARD. **La Politique de l'Immigration en France depuis la Guerre.** Paris: Tournon, 1925, 175 p.
A doctoral dissertation which reviews the difficult immigration problem and the efforts that have been made to find a satisfactory solution.

CESTRE, CHARLES. **The Ideals of France.** New York: Abingdon, 1922, 325 p.
A series of lectures, in a somewhat mystical and very idealistic vein, stressing French leadership in faith, chivalry, reason, progress, equality, solidarity and peace.

CHARDON, HENRI. **L'Organisation de la République pour la Paix.** New Haven: Yale University Press, 1927, 163 p.
A volume of the Carnegie Series, giving an excellent survey of French governmental organization.

CLAUSS, MAX. **Das Politische Frankreich vor dem Kriege.** Karlsruhe: Braun, 1928, 162 p.
One of the best studies of pre-war France and French political alignments, with due stress on the conflict of forces, the disintegration of the Left Bloc, the new nationalism, etc.

CURTIUS, ERNST ROBERT and BERGSTRÄSSER, ARNOLD. **Frankreich.** Stuttgart: Deutsche Verlags-Anstalt, 1930, 2 v.
A book comparable to Dibelius's "England," surveying the cultural and economic-political life of France. The review of French politics, finance, industry and international relations is splendidly done.

DAUDET, LÉON A. **L'Agonie du Régime.** Paris: Nouvelle Librairie Nationale, 1925, 376 p.
Parliamentary reminiscences by a prominent Royalist leader, covering the post-war period.

DAUDET, LÉON A. **The Stupid XIXth Century.** New York: Payson and Clarke, 1928, 333 p.
The Royalist and Catholic leader's fierce attack on the development of democracy and critical thought in France since 1789.

DUHAMEL, MAURICE. **La Question Bretonne dans Son Cadre Européen.** Paris: Delpeuch, 1929, 235 p.
The spectre of self-expression raises its head even in France. Duhamel also sees the need for some sort of federalism.

FONCK, RENÉ. **L'Aviation et la Sécurité Française.** Paris: Bossard, 1924, 317 p.
An argument for making France's air forces the core of her future military defenses, by the president of the Ligue Aéronautique.

FRANÇOIS-PONCET, ANDRÉ. **Réflexions d'un Républicain Moderne.** Paris: Grasset, 1925, 135 p.
An eloquent summons to the bourgeoisie to awake to its duties, and for the republicans to find a program, political, economic and social, which shall put them abreast of modern needs.

FRØISLAND, FRØIS. **Fortellinger fra Fronten.** Oslo: Gyldendal, 1929, 238 p.
Reminiscences of the war years in France, by the editor of *Aftenposten*.

GOYAU, GEORGES. **L'Effort Catholique dans la France d'Aujourd'hui.** Paris: Revue des Jeunes, 1922, 152 p.
Three lectures, by a leading French historian of the Church, to demonstrate the new organization and the new intellectual and social currents.

GRESSENT, ALFRED GEORGES. **Le Fascisme.** Paris: Nouvelle Librairie Nationale, 1927, 164 p.
A leader of the French Fascist movement extols the beauties of the creed.

GRESSENT, ALFRED GEORGES. **La Politique de la Victoire.** Paris: Nouvelle Librairie Nationale, 1925.
The program of French Fascism, set forth by a well-known partisan.

GUEYDAN, B. E. **Les Rois de la République.** Paris: Perrin, 1925, 2 v.
An important study of French politics since 1905, with special reference to *Caillautism*.

GUY-GRAND, GEORGES. **Le Conflit des Idées dans la France d'Aujourd'hui.** Paris: Rivière, 1921, 268 p.
The French pre-war, war, and post-war mentality, by one of the keenest political writers.

GUY-GRAND, GEORGES, *ed*. **La Renaissance Religieuse.** Paris: Alcan, 1928, 272 p.
An admirable collection of essays by various writers dealing with the movement of ideas in the Catholic Church, among Protestants and among Jews.

GWYNN, DENIS ROLLESTON. **The Catholic Reaction in France.** New York: Macmillan, 1924, 186 p.
A well-written sympathetic interpretation of the revival of Catholicism in France since the war.

HAFFNER, LÉON. **Cent Ans de Marine de Guerre.** Paris: Payot, 1931, 332 p.
A useful brief survey of the development of French sea power, by the secretary of the Ligue Maritime.

HALÉVY, DANIEL. **Courrier de Paris.** Paris: Édition du Cavalier, 1932, 324 p.
The post-war political and intellectual development of France.

HARMSEN, HANS. **Bevoelkerungsprobleme Frankreichs.** Berlin: Vowinckel, 1927, 221 p.
On the whole the best general treatment of the French population problem, examining the decline of the birth rate, the measures taken to correct it, foreign immigration and its effects, and the larger evolution of the French population.

HAYES, CARLTON JOSEPH HUNTLEY. **France: A Nation of Patriots.** New York: Columbia University Press, 1930, 487 p.
A revealing study of education for patriotism in France, by an American authority. The book takes up in succession the influence of the government, the schools, the army and navy, the churches, the press, the radio and cinema, etc., and passes to a consideration of the organization of patriotism in societies, its stimulation by ceremonies, and its cultivation in Alsace-Lorraine.

HÖGEL, MAX. **Die Auswärtige Handelspolitik Frankreichs nach dem Kriege.** Jena: Fischer, 1929, 124 p.
A handy summary account of the evolution of post-war industry in France and the involutions of the French tariff.

HUDDLESTON, SISLEY. **France.** New York: Scribner, 1927, 613 p.
A storehouse of facts dealing with all phases of modern French life, by the former Paris correspondent of the London *Times*.

HUDDLESTON, SISLEY. **France and the French.** New York: Scribner, 1925, 348 p.
French life, presented in a favorable light by an experienced English observer.

LA BATUT, GUY DE, VICOMTE and FRIEDMANN, GEORGES. **A History of the French People.** New York: Dutton, 1923, 315 p.
A suggestive general history of France from the radical point of view.

LABÉ, CAMILLE. **Le Budget de la Guerre en France.** Strasbourg: Dernières Nouvelles, 1930, 216 p.
An analysis of French military expenditure, together with a study of the budgetary classification of these items.

LAMBERT, CHARLES. **La France et les Étrangers.** Paris: Delahaye, 1927, 155 p.
A book of considerable interest and importance. The writer, a deputy, discusses the vital problems of depopulation, immigration, naturalization, etc.

LA TOUR, ERNEST, VICOMTE DE. **Le Sentiment Français.** Paris: Peyronnet, 1928, 130 p.
Historical and philosophical studies of the French post-war mentality.

LAVISSE, ERNEST, *ed.* **Histoire de France Contemporaine depuis la Révolution jusqu'à la Paix de 1919.** Paris: Hachette, 1920-22, 10 v.
An important coöperative work by distinguished French historians. By far the best history of France in the nineteenth and twentieth centuries. Unfortunately the treatment of the Third Republic is rather drab.

MACDONALD, WILLIAM. **Reconstruction in France.** New York: Macmillan, 1922, 349 p.
A volume dealing with most aspects of French economic and social problems in the post-war period, giving many useful facts in readable form.

MARCELLIN, L. **Politique et Politiciens.** Paris: Renaissance du Livre, 1924, 3 v.
The diaries of a French journalist during the war and immediate post-war periods. Full of revelations and side-lights.

MARCELLIN, L. **Le Règne des Harangueurs.** Paris: Renaissance du Livre, 1928, 320 p.
A merciless survey of the past thirty years of French parliamentary life.

MERAN. **Anodin ou la République?** Paris: Renaissance Moderne, 1928, 361 p.
Yet another scathing and truculent satire on French democracy.

MONTEILHET, J. **Les Institutions Militaires de la France, 1814-1924.** Paris: Alcan, 1925, 413 p.
A good history of French army organization during the last hundred years.

MONTIGNY, JEAN. **La République Réaliste.** Paris: Renaissance du Livre, 1927.
The author, a French deputy of the radical school, reviews and criticizes the chief developments of recent French politics.

MOUSSET, ALBERT. **La France Vue de l'Étranger.** Paris: Île de France, 1926, 222 p.
A criticism and satire of the French methods in international relations.

NOUSSANNE, HENRI DE. **Vive l'Empereur! ou, Comment en Finir avec une République Folle.** Paris: Peyronnet, 1925, 93 p.
A characteristic demand, not for an Emperor, but for an authoritarian republic.

OGBURN, WILLIAM FIELDING and JAFFÉ, WILLIAM. **The Economic Development of Post-War France.** New York: Columbia University Press, 1929, 613 p.
An excellent volume that goes beyond the spectacular financial phenomena and analyzes the changes in agriculture and industry brought about by the war. Well-documented, and with an admirable bibliography.

PAON, MARCEL. **L'Immigration en France.** Paris: Payot, 1926, 224 p.
A competent investigation of the French problem, advocating restrictive legislation based on the experience of other states.

PINON, RENÉ. **Le Redressement de la Politique Française.** Paris: Perrin, 1923.
A friendly review of the achievements of Poincaré.

POINCARÉ, RAYMOND. **Histoire Politique, Chroniques de Quinzaine.** Paris: Plon, 1920-22, 4 v.

Articles on current politics published periodically in the *Revue des Deux Mondes* and covering the years 1920-1922, including the Premier's views on the Conferences of Washington and Cannes.

La Politique Républicaine. By a Group of Radical Leaders. Paris: Alcan, 1924, 587 p.
A study of the Radical program, by a number of prominent leaders. Particularly interesting in view of the victory of the Left in 1924.

Pomaret, Charles. **Depuis le 11 Mai.** Paris: Renaissance du Livre, 1927, 240 p.
A general survey of political developments in France since the election of May 1924.

Recouly, Raymond. **The Third Republic.** New York: Putnam, 1928, 390 p.
Perhaps the best brief account available in English of the Third Republic down to the year 1914, but journalistic in the treatment of economic and social questions.

Renouvin, Pierre. **The Forms of War Government in France.** New Haven: Yale University Press, 1927, 166 p.
The translation of one of the best studies in the Carnegie Series. A most valuable analysis of the effects of the war on French government institutions.

Romier, Lucien. **Explication de Notre Temps.** Paris: Grasset, 1925, 289 p.
A rather penetrating criticism of French life and ideas, by a competent and interesting writer.

Roques, L. **La Sécurité Française.** Paris: Occitania, 1929, 164 p.
The title is a misnomer. According to the writer, France has no security and urgent measures of defense must be taken. A typical French military view.

Sieburg, Friedrich. **Who Are These French?** New York: Macmillan, 1932, 303 p.
A brilliant analysis of the French make-up, written by the Paris correspondent of the *Frankfurter Zeitung*. Both the German original, "Gott in Frankreich," and the French translation attracted wide attention.

Siegfried, André. **France: A Study in Nationality.** New Haven: Yale University Press, 1930, 122 p.
A thoroughly satisfactory interpretation of French politics and the French political system, by a well-known author.

Soltau, Roger Henry. **French Parties and Politics, 1871-1930.** New York: Oxford University Press, 1930, 90 p.
This is the latest edition of a well-known survey, now brought up to date.

Soltau, Roger Henry. **French Political Thought in the Nineteenth Century.** New Haven: Yale University Press, 1931, 500 p.
One of the best books on the historical background of modern France, well-informed, scholarly and moderate.

Suarez, Georges. **De Poincaré à Poincaré.** Paris: Éditions de France, 1927, 246 p.
A review of French politics, in the stormy post-war period, with stress on the accomplishments of Poincaré.

Tardieu, André. **L'Épreuve du Pouvoir.** Paris: Flammarion, 1931, 282 p.
Largely extracts from Tardieu's public utterances during his tenure of the Premiership.

Théry, Edmond. **Conséquences Économiques de la Guerre pour la France.** Paris: Belin, 1922, 350 p.
An admirable compilation of facts on the economic situation in France today.

Tilley, Arthur. **Modern France.** Cambridge: Cambridge University Press, 1922, 850 p.

A voluminous and authoritative coöperative work outlining the history of France, her economic and social development, her contribution to law, religion, science and art from about 1500 to the end of the war.

UNGERN-STERNBERG, RODERICH VON. **Grundzüge der Französischen Volkswirt-schaft.** Frankenstein: Philipp, 1927, 254 p.
A survey of French economic development from 1913 to 1927, stressing the greater industrial activity, the decline of the lesser bourgeoisie, and the influx of foreign labor.

La Vie Publique dans la France Contemporaine. Paris: Alcan, 1925, 216 p.
A series of interesting lectures on French public life by a number of prominent professors.

WĘDKIEWICZ, STANISLAUS. **Dyktator.** Cracow: Krakowska Spólka Wydawnicza, 1927, 143 p.
A penetrating survey by a prominent Polish editor of the present tendencies in French politics and literature and forecasting the advent of some type of dictatorship.

WELTER, G. **La France Économique d'Aujourd'hui.** Paris: Payot, 1927, 368 p.
A splendid study of the economic situation, by an official of the department of foreign commerce.

WINTER, GUSTAV. **Kniha o Francii.** Praha: Aventrium, 1930, 484 p.
An interesting interpretation of the French scene, by a Czech journalist long resident in France.

ZÉVAÈS, ALEXANDRE BOURSON. **Histoire de la Troisième République.** Paris: George-Anquetil, 1926, 650 p.
One of the best general accounts of the history of the Third Republic, bringing the story down to 1926. Written from the Radical standpoint.

Financial Problems

See also (General International Relations) International Trade, Tariffs, Cartels, p. 13, and Reparations and War Debts, p. 25; also (World War) Economic and Financial Aspects and War Costs, p. 153.

BONNET, GEORGES ÉTIENNE. **Comment Avoir un Franc Stable.** Paris: Payot, 1926, 128 p.
An expert's discussion of the financial chaos and the problem of stabilization.

DUBOIN, JACQUES. **La Stabilisation du Franc.** Paris: Rivière, 1927, 268 p.
A collection of essays and speeches by a French authority.

DULLES, ELEANOR LANSING. **The French Franc, 1914-1928.** New York: Macmillan, 1929, 606 p.
A competent treatment of the history of the franc, laying particular stress on the psychological factor in depreciation and the tenability of modern theories.

Les Finances Publiques de la France. Paris: Alcan, 1927, 287 p.
A series of lectures at the École des Hautes Études Sociales, by such authorities as Bonnet, Homberg and Nogaro.

FISK, HARVEY EDWARD. **French Public Finance.** New York: Bankers Trust Company, 1922, 363 p.
A study of French war finance, of post-war reconstruction problems, of the budgetary system and French banking practices.

FRAYSSINNET, PIERRE. **La Politique Monétaire de la France, 1924-1928.** Paris: Sirey, 1928, 306 p.
A serious study covering the most critical years of the post-war crisis.

GRESSENT, ALFRED GEORGES. **L'État, les Finances et la Monnaie.** Paris: Nouvelle
Librairie Nationale, 1925, 630 p.
A detailed controversial account of the crisis after the war.

HAIG, ROBERT MURRAY. **The Public Finances of Post-War France.** New York: Colum-
bia University Press, 1929, 463 p.
One of the admirable treatises in the "Social and Economic Studies of Post-War
France." A dispassionate and reliable volume.

LACHAPELLE, GEORGES. **Les Batailles du Franc.** Paris: Alcan, 1928, 259 p.
Though reviewing the development of the crisis since 1914, the author concentrates
on the years 1924-1926, examining the theories and policies advanced by different
groups.

MARTIN, GERMAIN. **Les Finances Publiques de la France et la Fortune Privée.** Paris:
Payot, 1925, 444 p.
A leading French authority examines events since 1914 with reference to the French
credit structure, fiscal system, monetary questions, etc.

MENDÈS-FRANCE, PIERRE. **L'Œuvre Financière du Gouvernement Poincaré.** Paris:
Librairie Générale du Droit, 1928, 320 p.
A dispassionate account of the financial achievements of the Poincaré régime.

MOULTON, HAROLD GLENN and LEWIS, CLEONA. **The French Debt Problem.** New
York: Macmillan, 1925, 459 p.
The best treatment in English of the French financial crisis, lending support to the
French contention of inability to make debt payments on the scale demanded by the
American Debt Commission.

OESTERGAARD, PETER. **Inflation und Stabilisierung des Französischen Franc.**
Jena: Fischer, 1930, 178 p.
A scholarly study of the French monetary problem.

PEEL, GEORGE. **The Financial Crisis of France.** New York: Macmillan, 1925, 332 p.
The author reviews the development of the French system since 1789, with special
emphasis on the war period and the evolution of the crisis of 1924.

PERQUEL, JULES. **Les Vicissitudes des Placements Français à l'Étranger.** Paris:
Éditions du Capital, 1929, 120 p.
The editor of *Capital* tells the sad story of French foreign investments and their fate.

POINCARÉ, RAYMOND. **La Restauration Financière de la France.** Paris: Payot, 1928,
114 p.
The authentic text of the Premier's great speech of February 3-4, 1928, with all the
statistics and charts upon which he relied.

La Politique Financière et Monétaire de la France. Paris: Maison du Livre Français, 1922, 573 p.
A valuable collection of speeches, reports and resolutions of a group of experts. A
second collection was printed in 1927 under the title "La Stabilité Monétaire" (Paris:
Valois, 1927, 393 p.).

RAMON, GABRIEL G. **Histoire de la Banque de France.** Paris: Grasset, 1929, 501 p.
A general history of the Bank from Napoleonic times to the present. Based on original
documents.

ROGERS, JAMES HARVEY. **The Process of Inflation in France, 1914-1927.** New York:
Columbia University Press, 1929, 398 p.
Another admirable account of the inflation, in the series of "Social and Economic
Studies of Post-War France."

SCHMITZ, JOSEPH. **Inflation und Stabilisierung in Frankreich, 1924-28.** Bonn: Schroeder, 1930, 228 p.
A careful study, covering the years 1914 to 1928.

Biographies

See also (World War) Biographies of Wartime Statesmen and Diplomats, p. 101; also (Europe) Biographies, p. 228.

AUBERT, ALFRED. **Briand.** Paris: Chiron, 1928, 286 p.
A general biographical sketch, based in large measure on Briand's own writings and utterances.

DOMINIQUE, PIERRE. **Monsieur le Parlement.** Paris: Baudinière, 1928, 320 p.
Interesting and searching portraits of some of the leading French parliamentarians.

GIVET, J. S. DE. **Aristide Briand.** Paris: Éditions Prométhée, 1930, 162 p.
A real nationalist view of Briand, whose internationalist leanings are of course responsible for all the woes of France.

HAMBURGER, MAURICE. **Léon Bourgeois.** Paris: Rivière, 1931, 272 p.
A good biography of one of France's most experienced diplomats and statesmen, a leading advocate of international coöperation.

KOLB, ANNETTE. **Versuch über Briand.** Berlin: Rowohlt, 1929, 217 p.
An honest attempt to evaluate the work of Briand.

LÖWEGREN, GUNNAR. **Silhuettklipp av Nutida Franska Politici.** Lund: Gleerups, 1929.
Interesting pen pictures of French statesmen by a Swedish diplomat and writer.

MARGUERITTE, VICTOR. **Aristide Briand.** Paris: Flammarion, 1932, 360 p.
A full-length biography of Briand, by one of his close friends.

MARTIN, GASTON. **Joseph Caillaux.** Paris: Alcan, 1931, 208 p.
Though written by a friend of Caillaux, this is the work of an historian and gives a careful estimate of a controversial figure in French politics.

MAURRAS, CHARLES. **Casier Judiciaire d'Aristide Briand.** Paris: Éditions du Capital, 1931, 174 p.
An analysis and very vigorous condemnation of Briand's policy, by the royalist, nationalist leader.

MISSOFFE, MICHEL. **La Vie Volontaire d'André Tardieu.** Paris: Flammarion, 1930, 252 p.
An enthusiastic chronology.

PERSPICAX, A. **Der Rattenfänger von Europa.** Berlin: Brunnen Verlag, 1931, 109 p.
Briand deflated.

PRIVAT, MAURICE. **Pierre Laval.** Paris: Hachette, 1931, 235 p.
A popular sketch of the statesman's career.

SISCO, JOSEPH. **Aristide Briand.** Paris: Rivière, 1929, 154 p.
The author lays particular stress on Briand's less familiar early career.

SONOLET, LOUIS. **La Vie et l'Œuvre de Paul Deschanel.** Paris: Hachette, 1926, 318 p.
On the whole the best biography of the French statesman.

THOMSON, VALENTINE. **Briand, Man of Peace.** New York: Covici-Friede, 1930, 356 p.
This intimate biographical essay is full of interesting sidelights, but is in no way a critical contribution.

Foreign Relations

General

COTTEZ, ANDRÉ. **De l'Intervention du Pouvoir Exécutif et du Parlement dans la Conclusion et la Ratification des Traités.** Paris: Buscoz, 1920, 152 p.
A doctoral thesis analyzing the constitutional position of the executive and of parliament in the conclusion of treaties.

Notre Diplomatie Économique. Paris: Alcan, 1925, 256 p.
Valuable lectures by French experts, delivered at the École des Sciences Politiques.

PINON, RENÉ. **Histoire de la Nation Française.** Volume IX: **Histoire Diplomatique, 1515-1928.** Paris: Plon, 1929.
This volume, in a well-known series, is written by a professor at the École des Sciences Politiques. Despite this, it is an uncritical nationalistic account which does little credit to French scholarship.

RECOULY, RAYMOND. **De Bismarck à Poincaré.** Paris: Éditions de France, 1932, 548 p.
A well-known French journalist's account of French action at the various critical moments of the past sixty years.

SCHUMAN, FREDERICK LEWIS. **War and Diplomacy in the French Republic.** New York: McGraw-Hill, 1931, 469 p.
The purpose of this volume, as defined in the preface, is to give a "behavioristic account of all those patterns of social action which underlie French foreign policy and which have their counterparts in the foreign policies of all other Great Powers." After investigating French action in various crises, the author goes beyond the usual diplomatic narrative and devotes many chapters to foreign relations and the mechanism of French diplomacy, as well as to the rôle of parliament, the press and patriotic associations.

STREET, CECIL JOHN CHARLES. **The Treachery of France.** London: Allan, 1924, 179 p.
A violent criticism of French post-war policy, urging England's withdrawal from the Entente and closer coöperation with America.

Relations with England

BARDOUX, JACQUES. **De Paris à Spa.** Paris: Alcan, 1921, 396 p.
An interesting and well-informed narrative of the Franco-English estrangement and the development of the situation from the meeting of the Peace Conference through the Polish-Russian War.

BARDOUX, JACQUES. **Lloyd George et la France.** Paris: Alcan, 1923, 453 p.
A voluminous documented history of the diplomatic clashes between France and England since 1918. The author is critical of the arbitrary methods of both states.

BARDOUX, JACQUES. **Le Socialisme au Pouvoir. L'Expérience de 1924.** Paris: Firmin-Didot, 1930, 307 p.
M. Bardoux here continues his excellent studies of Anglo-French relations and attempts an analysis of the MacDonald and Herriot mentalities.

FABRE-LUCE, ALFRED. **La Crise des Alliances.** Paris: Grasset, 1922, 427 p.
A brilliant and unsparing account of the Anglo-French mésalliance from 1919 to 1922, by a French radical writer who stands for international coöperation.

GAIN, PAUL HENRY. **La Question du Tunnel sous la Manche.** Paris: Rousseau, 1932, 289 p.
A study of the proposal to build a tunnel between England and France.

GAUTIER, CHARLES. **L'Angleterre et Nous.** Paris: Grasset, 1922, 323 p.
An analysis of the post-war estrangement.

IVANOV, L. **Anglo-Frantsuskoe Sopernichestvo, 1918-1927.** Moscow: Gosizdat, 1928, 164 p.
The Anglo-French economic rivalry viewed as a typically capitalistic phenomenon.

PINON, RENÉ. **L'Avenir de l'Entente Franco-Anglaise.** Paris: Plon, 1924, 150 p.
A plea for mutual understanding, based on the assumption that a close alliance is rendered impractical by the divergent interests and methods of the two countries.

Relations with Germany

See also (War, Peace, Security and Disarmament) Locarno Pacts, p. 79; also (Germany) Post-War Germany, p. 321, and Foreign Policy, p. 334.

General

DIETRICH, ERICH. **Die Deutsch-Französischen Wirtschaftsverhandlungen der Nachkriegszeit.** Berlin: De Gruyter, 1931, 241 p.
A study of the surprisingly extensive Franco-German economic rapprochement during the early post-war period.

GONDER, GUSTAV. **Armes Deutschland, Armes Frankreich.** Metz: Even, 1930, 175 p.
A critique of projects for Franco-German rapprochement.

HALLER, JOHANNES. **Tausend Jahre Deutsch-Französischer Beziehungen.** Stuttgart: Cotta, 1930, 242 p.
An historian with an unusual gift for synthesis reviews the evolution of the Franco-German rivalry. One of the best general surveys from the German side.

HERVÉ, GUSTAVE. **France-Allemagne; la Réconciliation ou la Guerre.** Paris: Hachette, 1931, 251 p.
A prominent French radical pleads for a Franco-German understanding.

KELLER, RUDOLF. **Deutschland und Frankreich.** Munich: Piper, 1931, 112 p.
The editor of a German newspaper at Prague spares neither side in his discussion of the Franco-German problem.

KUCZYNSKI, ROBERT RENÉ, *ed.* **Deutschland und Frankreich.** Berlin: R. L. Prager, 1924, 410 p.
A well-known German economist's essays, aiming to improve the relations between the two countries by setting forth their common interests.

LAVERGNE, BERNARD. **Esquisse des Problèmes Franco-Allemands.** Paris: Gamber, 1931, 124 p.
The author warmly advocates economic collaboration.

LICHTENBERGER, HENRI. **Relations between France and Germany.** Washington: Carnegie Endowment for International Peace, 1923, 133 p.
A general survey of the diplomatic, political, economic and psychological bases of Franco-German relations between 1914 and 1922, by one of the Frenchmen who knows Germany best.

ORMESSON, WLADIMIR, COMTE D'. **La Confiance en l'Allemagne?** Paris: Nouvelle Revue Française, 1928, 250 p.
A stimulating essay on Franco-German relations. The author conceives the problem of an understanding as primarily psychological. After an analysis of the dangers inherent in the modern press system, he investigates the chief reasons for French distrust—German armaments, the patriotic societies, nationalism, the question of

Germany's European position. He thinks the questions at issue could be settled satisfactorily by a large-scale liquidation, leaving the road clear for a huge conservative Anglo-French-German combination guaranteeing the security of Europe.

RESPONDEK, ERWIN. **Wirtschaftliche Zusammenarbeit zwischen Deutschland und Frankreich.** Berlin: Heymann, 1929, 222 p.
Develops the interesting theme of Franco-German economic interdependence, and the conditions of coöperation.

ROHDE, HANS. **Deutsch-Französische Machtfaktoren.** Berlin: Berliner Börsenzeitung, 1932.
The author tries to show, by diagrams and statistics, that in almost every way France has greater military potentiality than Germany.

SCHAETZEL, WALTER. **Das Deutsch-Französische Gemischte Schiedsgericht.** Berlin: Stilke, 1930, 140 p.
The organizing and working of the mixed tribunal which has done much to smoothe out current friction.

SORB, COMMANDANT, *pseud.* **La Revanche de l'Allemagne.** Paris: Tallandier, 1928, 224 p.
Germany is preparing her revenge under the cover of peace pacts. France must look for an attack by air and with gas, the Hun coming through Belgium and backed by the Bolsheviks.

VALMIGÈRE, PIERRE. **Et Demain?** Paris: Figuière, 1929, 187 p.
An indictment of the French policy in the questions of Danzig and Silesia, which the author considers fundamentally mistaken.

WECHSSLER, EDUARD. **Esprit und Geist.** Bielefeld: Velhagen und Klasing, 1927, 604 p.
An interesting attempt to show the fundamental cultural unity of Frenchman and German by a survey of their development and institutions.

Alsace-Lorraine

BARRÈS, MAURICE. **La Lorraine Dévastée.** Paris: Alcan, 1919, 176 p.
Emotional pictures of Lorraine during the war, by the famous nationalist writer.

BATIFFOL, LOUIS. **L'Alsace Est Française.** Paris: Flammarion, 1919, 246 p.
An historical account, setting forth the traditional French views and claims, by a French historian.

BRONNER, FRITZ. **Die Verfassungsbestrebungen des Landesausschusses für Elsass-Lothringen, 1875-1911.** Heidelberg: Winter, 1926, 262 p.
A scientific contribution to the history of the Alsace-Lorraine problem in its constitutional aspects.

DELAHACHE, GEORGES, *pseud.* (LUCIEN AARON). **Les Débuts de l'Administration Française en Alsace et en Lorraine.** Paris: Hachette, 1921, 331 p.
An exhaustive digest, with commentary, of the new administrative system, legislation, etc.

FÉRENZY, OSCAR DE. **La Vérité sur l'Alsace.** Paris: Bloud et Gay, 1930, 500 p.
A critique of French policy, by an Alsatian editor.

FERVACQUE, PIERRE. **L'Alsace et le Vatican.** Paris: Fasquelle, 1930, 223 p.
The author sees in the autonomist movement nothing but a blind for the dangerous policy being pursued by the Church.

FERVACQUE, PIERRE. **L'Alsace Minée.** Paris: Fasquelle, 1929, 196 p.
An interesting essay on the Alsatian autonomist movement, from the French nationalist standpoint.

GILLOUIN, RENÉ. **Les Trois Crises.** Paris: Grasset, 1929, 254 p.
An illuminating discussion of such questions as the Alsatian problem, the case of the *Action Française*, etc.

HELMER, PAUL ALBERT. **France-Alsace.** Paris: Édition Française Illustrée, 1920, 314 p.
An Alsatian jurist and autonomist leader discusses the relation between the recovered provinces and France.

HELSEY, ÉDOUARD. **Notre Alsace.** Paris: Michel, 1926, 302 p.
An investigation of the autonomist troubles and a full account of the Colmar trial, by a firm believer in German designs.

HERBER, EDMOND. **Elsässisches Lust- und Leidbuch.** Strasbourg: Vomhoff, 1926, 109 p.
A record of the disillusionment of an Alsatian leader since 1918.

JAFFÉ, FRITZ. **Zwischen Deutschland und Frankreich.** Stuttgart: Cotta, 1931, 413 p.
A general outline of Alsatian history, cultural as well as political, from early times to the present.

MADELIN, LOUIS. **Les Heures Merveilleuses d'Alsace et de Lorraine.** Paris: Hachette, 1919, 247 p.
A French historian's rhapsodical account of the recovery of the lost provinces.

MILLERAND, ALEXANDRE. **Le Retour de l'Alsace-Lorraine à la France.** Paris: Charpentier, 1924, 248 p.
A study of the administrative, economic and cultural problems of the redeemed provinces as they confronted the French commissioner in 1919.

POHL, HEINRICH. **Die Elsass-Lothringische Frage.** Stuttgart: Enke, 1927, 63 p.
A short German survey of the problem as dealt with in the Peace Treaty and the Locarno Pact, together with a review of the autonomist movement.

REDSLOB, ROBERT. **Le Régime Politique de l'Alsace-Lorraine sous la Domination Allemande.** Paris: Giard, 1921.
An exposition of the German administration in the pre-war period.

RENOUARD, PIERRE. **L'Alsace-Lorraine, Sa Situation Juridique dans l'Empire Allemand, 1870-1918.** Paris: Dumoulin, 1919, 162 p.
A dissertation which gives a documented account of the constitutional development.

ROOS, KARL. **Politik und Gewaltpolitik in Elsass-Lothringen.** Zurich: Fricke, 1928, 169 p.
A survey of the Alsatian problem in the post-war period, with special reference to regionalist aspirations.

ROUX, GEORGES. **Divorce de l'Alsace?** Paris: La Nouvelle Revue Française, 1929, 116 p.
A dispassionate exposition of the incongruity of trying to incorporate a particularistic province in a rigidly centralized state. The solution lies in the revision of current French ideas as to the state.

SCHLENKER, MAX, *ed.* **Die Wirtschaftliche Entwicklung Elsass-Lothringens, 1871-1918.** Frankfurt: Elsass-Lothringen Institut, 1931, 652 p.
This elaborate and well-illustrated history of the German economic achievement in Alsace-Lorraine is the first volume of a comprehensive study of the German rule.

SCHMIDT, CHARLES. **A Revelation. Germany's Secret Views for Alsace-Lorraine, 1915-1918.** Paris: Berger-Levrault, 1924, 220 p.
Plans of the German command to wipe out French influence and interest. The documents are from the Imperial Alsace-Lorraine archives.

SPINDLER, CHARLES. **L'Alsace pendant la Guerre.** Strasbourg: Treuttel and Würtz, 1925, 763 p.
A detailed diary of events, full of the theme of German persecution.

VIOLLIS, ANDRÉE, *pseud.* (MME. ANDRÉE F. C. D'ARDENNE DE TIZAC). **Alsace et Lorraine au-dessus des Passions.** Paris: Ottinger, 1928, 208 p.
All is quiet along the Rhine and the Moselle. An account of the new French rule and the pacification.

WENTZCKE, PAUL. **Der Deutschen Einheit Schicksalsland.** Munich: Drei Masken, 1921, 228 p.
An excellent survey of the Alsace-Lorraine problem in the nineteenth and twentieth centuries. The author ends with a large question mark.

WOLF, GEORGES. **Das Elsässische Problem.** Leipzig: Fernau, 1926, 136 p.
Another volume characteristic of the growing agitation for autonomy.

Rhineland and Ruhr

ALLEN, HENRY TUREMAN. **My Rhineland Journal.** Boston: Houghton Mifflin, 1923, 593 p.
General Allen's detailed account of his duties, routine and otherwise, with the American Army of Occupation. Contains no revelations, but gives an interesting picture of conditions.

ALLEN, HENRY TUREMAN. **The Rhineland Occupation.** Indianapolis: Bobbs-Merrill, 1927, 347 p.
By the American commander on the Rhine, who shows frankness and breadth of view.

APEX, *pseud.* **The Uneasy Triangle.** London: Murray, 1931, 276 p.
The experiences and impressions of a British officer in the Cologne and Wiesbaden areas from 1920 to 1925.

AULNEAU, JOSEPH. **Le Rhin et la France.** Paris: Plon, 1922, 385 p.
One of the ablest and most complete French versions of the history of the Rhine problem, France's civilizing mission, and needs for defense.

BALDENSPERGER, J. and others. **La Rhénanie.** Paris: Alcan, 1922, 175 p.
An historical survey setting forth the traditional French view.

BARRÈS, MAURICE. **Le Génie du Rhin.** Paris: Plon, 1921, 259 p.
Five lectures delivered at the University of Strasbourg in which Barrès called for unity of spirit and policy on the part of the French.

BARRÈS, MAURICE. **Les Grandes Problèmes du Rhin.** Paris: Plon, 1930, 472 p.
These collected writings of the late nationalist leader set forth the ideas that underlay his important campaign in the years following 1919.

BARRÈS, MAURICE. **La Politique Rhénane, Discours Parlementaires.** Paris: Bloud et Gay, 1922, 143 p.
Passionate parliamentary appeals for a French "national policy" in "La Rhénanie."

BARRUCH, G. **Le Bilan de la Ruhr et les Réparations.** Brussels: Éditions du Flambeau, 1924.
A criticism of the French policy in the Ruhr.

BERTRAM, ERNST. **Rheingenius und Génie du Rhin.** Bonn: Cohen, 1922, 115 p.
A reply to Barrès' "Le Génie du Rhin."

BLONDEL, GEORGES. **La Rhénanie.** Paris: Plon, 1921, 260 p.
Its past, present and future.

Böhmer, Leo. **Die Rheinische Separatistenbewegung und die Französische Presse.** Stuttgart: Deutsche Verlagsanstalt, 1928, 128 p.

By using a mass of newspaper clippings the author makes an interesting attempt to prove that the French *Drang zum Rhein* was at the bottom of the Separatist movement.

Briey, Renaud, Comte de. **Le Rhin et le Problème d'Occident.** Brussels: De Wit, 1922, 225 p.

Another disquisition on the importance of the Rhine for France's security.

Coubé, Stéphen. **Alsace, Lorraine et France Rhénane.** Paris: Lethielleux, 1920, 181 p.

A history of the Left Bank of the Rhine and an exposition of France's historic right to the whole of it.

Coupaye, Joseph Marie Léon. **La Ruhr et l'Allemagne.** Paris: Dunod, 1922, 319 p.

A good study of the importance of the Ruhr in contemporary German industrial life.

Cuno, Rudolf. **Der Kampf um die Ruhr.** Leipzig: Koehler, 1923, 232 p.

A history of French policy in the Ruhr and of the first six months of the French occupation. The author predicts a "Waterloo" for France.

Darsy, Eugène. **Les Droits Historiques de la France sur la Rive Gauche du Rhin.** Paris: Sirey, 1919, 209 p.

Another historical sketch in justification of the French claims.

Djermanovitch, Rayko. **Le Traité de Versailles et les Matières Premières.** Paris: Jouve, 1927, 175 p.

A valuable monograph on the potash, coal and iron problem as it presents itself in Franco-German relations. The author analyzes suggested solutions proposed before 1919 and examines the terms and effects of the treaties.

Erdmann, Lothar. **Die Gewerkschaften im Ruhrkampfe.** Berlin: Verlagsgesellschaft des Allgemeinen Deutschen Gewerkschaftsbundes, 1924, 224 p.

Practically an official version of the part played by the Trade Unions, and an important contribution to the story of the occupation of the Ruhr.

Fillet, B. and others. **The Ruhr.** London: Labour Publishing Co., 1923, 64 p.

Represents the point of view of British labor.

Funck-Brentano, Frantz. **La France sur le Rhin.** Paris: Sirey, 1919, 499 p.

A documented history from the earliest days, with emphasis on French influence and accomplishment.

Gedye, George Eric Rowe. **The Revolver Republic.** London: Arrowsmith, 1930, 255 p.

The experiences of an English correspondent during the stormiest years of the Rhineland occupation. A very severe indictment of the French policy of Separatism.

Germann, Georg. **Im Gefängnis der Separatisten.** Nürnberg: Schmalz, 1927, 144 p.

More inside information on the Separatist movement in the Palatinate.

Greer, Guy. **The Ruhr-Lorraine Industrial Problem.** New York: Macmillan, 1925, 348 p.

A sound analysis of the Franco-German iron and coal problem, its connection with the reparations question, and its effects on French policy.

Gruben, Hervé, Baron de. **Les Belges sur le Rhin.** Brussels: De Wit, 1924.

A review of the Belgian occupation and of Belgian policy in relation to French aims.

Heyland, Karl. **Die Rechtsstellung der Besetzten Rheinlande.** Stuttgart: Kohlhammer, 1923, 271 p.

A detailed study of the legal position of the Rhineland under the peace treaties. The book is a reprint from the *Handbuch des Voelkerrechts.*

JAER, B. DE. **L'Armée Belge d'Occupation et Son Droit de Juridiction.** Liège: Thone, 1928, 135 p.
Primarily an analysis of pertinent clauses of the peace treaties.

JOHANNET, RENÉ. **France et Rhin.** Paris: Nouvelle Librairie Nationale, 1919, 237 p.
The philosophy of the natural frontiers. The Rhine as the "frontière naturelle, passionelle, stratégique" of France. An uncompromising statement of the extreme French view.

LACHMANN, KURT. **Das Schicksal des Ruhrgebietes.** Frankfurt: Frankfurter Societätsdruckerei, 1924, 72 p.
Based on a German socialist's impressions. A critical account of the French occupation of the Ruhr and of the policies of the great industrialists.

LECLÈRE, LÉON. **La Question d'Occident.** Brussels: Lamertin, 1921, 218 p.
A well-documented and learned Belgian account of the swinging pendulum of Franco-German competition for control of the Left Bank of the Rhine from 843 to 1921 A.D.

LINTZ, KARL HEINZ. **Grosskampftage aus der Separatistenzeit in der Pfalz.** Edenkoben: Südwestdeutscher Verlag, 1930, 200 p.
An interesting contribution to the story of the Separatist movement.

MARX, WILHELM, PFEIFFER, MAXIMILIAN and ONCKEN, HERMANN. **Pfalzfrage und Weltpolitik.** Heidelberg: Thoma, 1925, 64 p.
A series of essays by competent writers on various aspects of the Franco-German rivalry in the Palatinate, with special reference to the Separatist movement.

NAPP-ZINN, ANTON FELIX. **Rheinschiffahrt, 1913-1925.** Berlin: Springer, 1925, 223 p.
A study of the influence of the war and the peace settlement on Rhine shipping.

PANGE, JEAN DE, COMTE. **Les Libertés Rhénanes.** Paris: Perrin, 1922, 369 p.
The Rhine states have always struggled for autonomy and France has supported this movement. The author, arguing thus, studies the new régime in Alsace-Lorraine and the Saar, and the work of the Rhineland Commission.

Die Pfalz unter Französischer Besetzung. Munich: Süddeutsche Monatshefte, 1930, 453 p.
An official chronology of events in the Palatinate during the French occupation, 1918-1930.

PINON, RENÉ. **La Bataille de la Ruhr.** Paris: Perrin, 1924, 361 p.
A reprint of the bi-weekly survey of French policy in the *Revue des Deux Mondes*, by the man who succeeded Poincaré in charge of that task.

POUPARD, E. **L'Occupation de la Ruhr et le Droit des Gens.** Paris: Presses Universitaires, 1925, 256 p.
More than a defense of the French policy, this dissertation studies the administration and jurisdiction of the occupying forces and the general legal relationship between the army and the population.

PYSZKA, HANNES. **Der Ruhrkrieg.** Munich: Verlag für Kulturpolitik, 1923, 250 p.
Very largely a study of the legality or lack of legality of the French occupation.

REBOUL, JEAN MARIE PAUL. **Pourquoi Nous Sommes dans la Ruhr.** Paris: Berger-Levrault, 1923.
A vigorous defense of the French occupation by a high French officer.

RECOULY, RAYMOND. **La Ruhr.** Paris: Flammarion, 1923, 250 p.
Its significance for Germany and for France, with special reference to the reparations and coal problems, by a somewhat critical and disillusioned French journalist.

RHENANUS, *pseud.* (HEINZ GORRENZ). **Die Drahtzieher.** Berlin: Verlag für Presse, Wirtschaft und Politik, 1924, 207 p.
An important account of the Separatist movement in the Rhineland, based on numerous documents.

ROQUES, PAUL. **Le Contrôle Militaire Interallié en Allemagne.** Paris: Berger-Levrault, 1927, 152 p.
A systematic account of the military control, with stress on its legal aspects.

ROUSSEAU, JEAN. **La Haute Commission Interalliée des Territoires Rhénans.** Mainz: Walther, 1923, 238 p.
The first volume of an exhaustive technical study of the commission and its working, by one of its members.

SCHULTZE, ERNST, *ed.* **Ruhrbesetzung und Weltwirtschaft.** Leipzig: Gloeckner, 1927, 256 p.
A collection of studies on the effects of the occupation of the Ruhr on world commerce, by experts from various countries. From their investigations it appears that in its effects the French policy was second in importance only to the continental blockade.

SOLEMACHER-ANTWEILER, VIKTOR, FREIHERR VON. **Die Abgetretenen und Besetzten Gebiete im Deutschen Westen.** Berlin: Hobbing, 1925, 133 p.
A statistical handbook of Eupen-Malmédy, Saar and Rhineland.

SPETHMANN, HANS. **Die Grosswirtschaft an der Ruhr.** Breslau: Hirt, 1925, 283 p.
One of the best general accounts of the economic organization of the Ruhr area.

SPETHMANN, HANS. **Zwölf Jahre Ruhrbergbau.** Berlin: Hobbing, 1928-31, 5 v.
Covers the period 1914-1925. A huge and exhaustive study of the coal and other industries, with very extensive illustrative material. The last volume deals with the occupation of the Ruhr.

SPRINGER, MAX. **Loslösungsbestrebungen am Rhein.** Berlin: Vahlen, 1924, 168 p.
A general account of the Separatist movement in the Rhineland from 1918 to 1924.

STEGEMANN, HERMANN. **The Struggle for the Rhine.** New York: Knopf, 1927, 432 p.
An excellent general historical account in English of the Rhine problem. Written by a Swiss historian, but sympathetic to the German view.

STREET, CECIL JOHN CHARLES. **Rhineland and Ruhr.** London: Couldrey, 1923, 84 p.
An English journalist's snapshot of the French occupation, taken from a very hostile standpoint.

TIRARD, PAUL. **La France sur le Rhin.** Paris: Plon, 1930, 520 p.
The French commissioner reviews the French occupation of the Rhine country in what is practically an official statement. He deals with the administration, with policies and with economic questions. This is the most important account from the French side.

TUOHY, FERDINAND. **Occupied, 1918-1930.** London: Thornton, Butterworth, 1931, 318 p.
An Englishman's experiences of the occupation and his reflections on French policy and general Allied objectives.

VERGNET, PAUL. **La France au Rhin.** Paris: Renaissance du Livre, 1919, 128 p.
A collection of opinions of prominent Frenchmen, prepared to impress the Peace Conference with the urgent necessity of a decision in accord with French views.

VEYSSIÉ, ROBERT. **La Paix par la Ruhr.** Paris: Plon, 1923, 147 p.
The Ruhr occupation as an inescapable countermove to the anti-French policies and evasions of the coal barons and the German Government.

VOGELS, WERNER. **Die Verträge über Besetzung und Räumung des Rheinlandes.**
Berlin: Heymann, 1925, 398 p.
A valuable collection of documents and ordinances of the Rhineland Commission.

WACHENDORF, KARL. **Zehn Jahre Fremdherrschaft am Deutschen Rhein.** Berlin:
Hobbing, 1928, 290 p.
A well-documented review of the Ruhr occupation and the Separatist movement.

WENTZCKE, PAUL. **Rheinkampf.** Berlin: Vowinckel, 1925, 2 v.
Volume two is a substantial account of the problem of the Rhine since 1919.

WENTZCKE, PAUL. **Ruhrkampf.** Berlin: Hobbing, 1930-32, 2 v.
An authoritative account of the occupation of the Ruhr as seen from the German side.
The author, a trained historian, has consulted all the governmental records as well as
the archives of many of the leading industrial concerns which played a part in the
crisis. The work is not intended as propaganda, and is well-documented and dispassionate.

Saar

ALLOT, ALEXANDRE. **Le Bassin de la Sarre.** Paris: Berger-Levrault, 1924, 372 p.
A careful and well-documented doctoral thesis reviewing the making of the Saar
clauses of the Peace Treaty and analyzing the entire governmental system of the area.

BIESEL, EDWARD W. **Die Völkerrechtliche Stellung des Saargebiets.** Leipzig: Noske,
1929, 135 p.
A dissertation on the position of the Saar in international law.

COURSIER, HENRI. **Le Statut International du Territoire de la Sarre.** Nemours:
Lesot, 1925, 150 p.
Another thorough, scholarly study, with an examination of the criticisms that have
been directed against the post-war régime.

DONALD, SIR ROBERT. **A Danger Spot in Europe.** London: Parsons, 1925, 166 p.
An anti-French account of present conditions in the Saar and of the alleged policy
of Gallicization, by an English publicist who has many irons in the fire.

DONNADIEU, JACQUES. **La Liquidation de la Victoire.** Paris: Tallandier, 1930, 256 p.
The author reveals the machinations of the Germans in the Saar and exposes the disastrous policy of the French Government.

FITTBOGEN, GOTTFRIED. **Die Französischen Schulen im Saargebiet.** Berlin: Verlag
Rheinischer Beobachter, 1925, 122 p.
A detailed study of this crucial and much debated problem.

HERLY, ROBERT. **L'Introduction du Franc dans la Sarre.** Paris: Berger-Levrault,
1925, 240 p.
A carefully documented history of the checkered monetary experiences of the Saar,
from the depreciation of the mark to the introduction of the franc.

KATSCH, HELLMUT. **Regierung und Volksvertretung im Saargebiet.** Leipzig: Weicher,
1930, 173 p.
The author analyzes the governmental system as set up by the League in the Saar,
and criticizes the League as an administrative organ.

KLOEVEKORN, FRITZ, *ed.* **Das Saargebiet.** Saarbrücken: Hofer, 1929, 584 p.
The best descriptive and statistical work on the Saar area, with admirable maps.

MARVAUD, ANGEL. **Le Territoire de la Sarre.** Paris: Plon, 1924, 142 p.
An economic, political and cultural survey.

OSBORNE, SIDNEY. **The Saar Question; a Disease Spot in Europe.** London: Allen and Unwin, 1923, 384 p.
As the title shows, this work can make no claim to impartiality, but it does give much interesting information on the situation just after the beginning of the new régime.

PRIOU, JEAN. **Le Territoire de la Sarre.** Paris: Berger-Levrault, 1923, 223 p.
A study which deals less with political organization than with agriculture, food supply, industry, tariff problems and monetary difficulties.

REVIRE, JEAN. **Perdrons-Nous la Sarre?** Paris: Éditions Prométhée, 1930, 124 p.
A review of the question since 1919 and the policy of various French governments, which the author accuses of having failed to consider political factors and to prepare for the plebiscite.

ROOSEGAARDE-BISSCHOP, WILLEM. **The Saar Controversy.** London: Sweet and Maxwell, 1924, 186 p.
A competent historical and legal analysis of the régime instituted by the treaties.

ROY, CHARLES. **L'Organisation Financière des Mines de la Sarre.** Paris: Pichon, 1926, 330 p.
A technical treatise of real value.

Das Saargebiet unter der Herrschaft des Waffenstillstandsabkommens und des Vertrags von Versailles. Berlin: Stilke, 1921, 362 p.
An important collection of articles, speeches, despatches and newspaper notices, published by the German Government.

VIDAL DE LA BLACHE, PAUL and GALLOIS, LUCIEN LOUIS JOSEPH. **Le Bassin de la Sarre.** Paris: Colin, 2nd ed., 1923, 54 p.
Chiefly an economic and demographic study.

Relations with Italy

See also (Western Europe) Mediterranean Problems, p. 272; also (Italy: Foreign and Colonial Policies) General, p. 283, and Policy in the Mediterranean and Levant, p. 285; also (Africa) Algeria and Tunis, p. 515.

ANDREA, U. D'. **Posizioni ed Errori del Nazionalismo Francese.** Rome: Critica Fascista, 1931, 110 p.
An extremely nationalistic polemical essay on Franco-Italian relations.

BEDEL, MAURICE. **Fascisme An VII.** Paris: Nouvelle Revue Française, 1929, 122 p.
The author concerns himself chiefly with the reasons for the "mesentente cordiale" between France and Italy.

FOA, RODOLFO. **La Francia del Dopo-Guerra e il Problema delle Relazioni Franco-Italiane.** Milan: Société d'Éditions Unitas, 1922.
An analysis by an Italian journalist with keen perceptions.

GARIBALDI, EZIO. **Memoriale alla Francia.** Florence: Vallecchi, 1931, 168 p.
A famous revolutionary pleads the cause of Franco-Italian amity.

MARABINI, CAMILLO. **Le Problème France-Italie.** Paris: Hachette, 1931, 220 p.
The Franco-Italian tension and the way to a solution, as seen by a strong protagonist of good relations.

ROHDE, HANS. **Italien und Frankreich in Ihren Politischen, Militärischen und Wirtschaftlichen Gegensätzen.** Berlin: Mittler, 1931, 189 p.
An able analysis of the naval rivalry, colonial competition, and economic antagonism between France and Italy, with some consideration of questions of expansion, emigration and treaty revision.

SABINI, CANDIDO MARCELLO, CONTE. **Le Fond d'une Querelle: Documents Inédits sur les Relations Franco-Italiennes, 1914-21.** Paris: Grasset, 1921, 194 p.
A valuable body of material illustrating the growing rivalry between the two Latin nations.

SIMONATTI, MARIO. **On Prépare un Crime.** Paris: La Revue Mondiale, 1930, 222 p.
One of the ablest books outlining and analyzing the Franco-Italian problem, written by a leading Italian journalist resident in France since 1913.

SOLMI, ARRIGO. **Italia e Francia nei Problemi Attuali della Politica Europea.** Milan: Treves, 1931, 218 p.
A review of the Franco-Italian problem from the Italian side, written by a well-known historian.

Relations with Switzerland

See also Switzerland, p. 250.

BÉRARD, VICTOR. **Genève et les Traités.** Paris: Colin, 1930, 2 v.
The best and most complete study of the evolution of the free zone problem from 1589 to 1921, from the French standpoint. The book is meant as a reply to Pictet.

BÉRARD, VICTOR. **Genève, la France et la Suisse.** Paris: Colin, 1928, 4 v.
A well-known French political writer's report to the Senate on the free zone controversy. An immense mass of documentary material covering the period since 1815.

CRAMER, L. **La Question des Zones Franches de la Haute-Savoie et du Pays de Gex.** Berne: Rösch and Schatzmann, 1919, 113 p.
An outline of the Franco-Swiss controversy from the Swiss side.

GEISMAR, R. **Die Freizonen.** Leipzig: Noske, 1931, 85 p.
This monograph on the free zones deals primarily with the Franco-Swiss dispute, though there is considerable discussion of the free zone principle.

GRASSIN, H. **Les Zones Franches du Pays de Gex et de Savoie.** Paris: Jouve, 1924, 132 p.
Chiefly an analysis of the post-war situation.

PICTET, PAUL. **Zones Franches de la Haute-Savoie et du Pays de Gex.** Lausanne: Payot, 1928, 235 p.
An able commentary on the French view as advanced by Bérard.

TRÉMAUD, HENRY. **La Question des Zones Franches devant la Cour Permanente de Justice Internationale.** Paris: Sirey, 1931, 296 p.
An exhaustive scholarly study of the latest phase of the Franco-Swiss dispute.

Relations with Other Countries

See also (Vatican City) Relations with France, p. 291; also (Spain) Colonial Policy, the War in Morocco, p. 297.

DU MOURIEZ, F. **France et Pologne. La Paix Française dans l'Europe Orientale.** Paris: Payot, 1919.
A plea for close Franco-Polish relations in the interests of European peace.

EVAIN, E. **Le Problème de l'Indépendance de l'Ukraine et la France.** Paris: Alcan, 1931, 136 p.
A history of the question by a French deputy, strongly sympathetic to Ukrainian aspirations.

RIPAULT, LOUIS. **Pendant la Tourmente, 1914-1918. France et Pologne.** Paris: Quillet, 1927, 233 p.
Collected writings on various phases of Polish problems and French policy towards Poland in the years 1916 to 1921.

ROUQUETTE, LOUIS FRÉDÉRIC. **La Pologne et Nous.** Paris: Chapelot, 1919, 230 p.
Relations, historical and intellectual, between Poland and France.

SCHWENDEMANN, KARL. **Frankreich in Belgien.** Berlin: Deutsche Verlagsgesellschaft
für Politik und Geschichte, 1924, 58 p.
A study of French cultural influence in Belgium.

SEMENOV, MARC, *ed*. **Les Relations de la France avec les Soviets Russes.** Paris:
Delpeuch, 1923.
A valuable anthology of French and Russian opinions supporting and opposing the
resumption of diplomatic relations.

SMOGORZEWSKI, CASIMIR. **La Politique Polonaise de la France.** Paris: Gebethner and
Wolff, 1926, 120 p.
A collection of utterances by public men, publicists and scholars.

WOLF, M. **Un Siècle d'Amitié.** Paris: Renaissance du Livre, 1923.
An examination of Franco-Belgian relations since 1792.

Colonial Questions

*See also (Western Europe) Mediterranean Problems, p. 272; also (Far East) Indo-China,
p. 486; also (Africa) French Possessions, p. 514; etc.*

BEAUREGARD, VICTOR. **L'Empire Colonial de la France.** Paris: Challamel, 1924, 47 p.
A succinct history based on the doctrine that France possesses a special colonizing
genius, and that her future lies in her colonies.

BESSON, MAURICE. **Histoire des Colonies Françaises.** Paris: Boivin, 1931, 402 p.
For the general reader. A history of French colonial activity by periods, with stress on
the continuity of the colonial tradition.

BRUNEAU, ANDRÉ. **Traditions et Politique de la France au Levant.** Paris: Alcan,
1932, 440 p.
One of the best surveys of France's aims and accomplishments in the Near East.

DEWAVRIN, MAURICE L., DELIBERT, PAUL and HOUDARD, MARCEL. **Comment Mettre
en Valeur Notre Domaine Colonial?** Paris: Rivière, 1920, 188 p.
The authors examine, in a general way, the colonial resources, questions of concessions,
transport, banking and tariffs.

Le Domaine Colonial Français. Paris: Éditions du Cygne, 1929, 4 v.
A splendid illustrated coöperative survey of the French colonial empire.

DUCHÊNE, ALBERT. **La Politique Coloniale de la France.** Paris: Payot, 1928, 347 p.
The Director of Political Affairs of the Ministry for Colonies reviews the evolution of
the Ministry, and of French colonial policy in general since the time of Richelieu. An
important contribution.

FERDINAND-LOP, S. **Les Ressources du Domaine Colonial de la France.** Paris:
Dunod, 1924, 150 p.
A survey of the French colonial possessions, with a plea for a more constructive
colonial policy.

FRANÇOIS, GEORGES and MARIOL, HENRI. **Législation Coloniale.** Paris: Larose, 1929,
392 p.
A general handbook, written by an official of the French Ministry for Colonies, dealing
with political and financial administration and economic organization.

HANOTAUX, GABRIEL and MARTINEAU, ALFRED, *eds*. **Histoire des Colonies Françaises.**
Paris: Plon, 1929 ff.

A splendid coöperative undertaking, of which four volumes have appeared to date: I. French Colonies in America. II. Algeria. III. Morocco, Tunis, Syria. IV. French Equatorial Africa.

HARDY, GEORGES. **Histoire de la Colonisation Française.** Paris: Larose, 1928, 348 p. One of the best brief, semi-popular histories, with good bibliographies.

HARDY, GEORGES. **Géographie de la France Extérieure.** Paris: Larose, 1928, 378 p. A companion volume to the preceding.

HARDY, GEORGES. **Nos Grands Problèmes Coloniaux.** Paris: Colin, 1929, 216 p. The director of the École Coloniale attempts to arouse more popular interest in the French colonial empire.

HOMBERG, OCTAVE. **La France des Cinq Parties du Monde.** Paris: Plon, 1927, 320 p. A history and general survey of the French colonies, with a consideration of the spirit of French overseas expansion.

Législation et Finances Coloniales. Paris: Sirey, 1930, 784 p. An elaborate coöperative survey of the political and economic system of the colonies.

LYAUTEY, PIERRE. **L'Organisation de l'Empire Colonial Français.** Paris: Éditions de France, 1931, 540 p. An excellent volume in the series of special studies on the history of the Third Republic.

MEGGLÉ, ARMAND. **Le Domaine Colonial de la France. Ses Ressources et Ses Besoins.** Paris: Alcan, 1922, 344 p. Economic factors are emphasized in this handbook published under the auspices of the French Ministry of Commerce and Industry.

MÉRIGNHAC, ALEXANDRE. **Traité de Législation et d'Économie Coloniales.** Paris: Sirey, 2nd ed., 1925, 887 p. A standard treatment of political, judicial, economic organization and system of the colonies.

PAVLOVICH, M. *pseud.* (MIKHAIL VEL'TMAN). **Frantsuskiĭ Imperializm.** Moscow: 1926, 260 p. The leading Russian writer on imperialism reviews the building up and exploitation of the modern French colonial empire.

PIQUET, VICTOR. **Histoire des Colonies Françaises.** Paris: Payot, 1931, 350 p. This is perhaps the best single-volume survey of French colonial history among several that appeared in connection with the great exposition of 1931. The book is well-divided and stresses the modern period.

La Politique Coloniale de la France. Paris: Alcan, 1924, 280 p. A series of lectures, by different authorities, delivered at the École des Sciences Politiques and dealing with resources, communications, native policy, administration, etc.

RÉGISMANSET, CHARLES. **Questions Coloniales.** Paris: Larose, 1923, 2 v. A collection of articles on various phases of French colonial history and administration, written between 1912 and 1919.

ROBERTS, STEPHEN HENRY. **History of French Colonial Policy, 1870-1925.** London: King, 1929, 2 v. An exhaustive exposition, dealing with the economic and social as well as the purely political aspects. The best account in English.

RUNNER, JEAN. **Les Droits Politiques des Indigènes des Colonies.** Paris: Larose, 1927, 158 p. A study of the existing rights, followed by an argument against the extension of democratic, representative principles to the natives.

SARRAUT, ALBERT. **La Mise en Valeur des Colonies Françaises.** Paris: Payot, 1923, 656 p.
The French Minister for Colonies reviews the support given by the colonies in the war, analyzes their resources and possibilities, and maps out for each a program of development.

SOLUS, HENRY. **Traité de la Condition des Indigènes.** Paris: Sirey, 1927, 590 p.
An exhaustive legal treatise, dealing with all the colonies, protectorates and mandated areas under French control, but not with Algeria, Morocco and Tunis.

SOUTHWORTH, CONSTANT. **The French Colonial Adventure.** London: King, 1931, 216 p.
An attempt at a scientific evaluation of the French colonies, which comes to the conclusion that they have not been a paying proposition. One of the most original and valuable of recent books on colonization.

Monaco

AUREGLIA, LOUIS. **La Politique Monégasque.** Paris: Giard, 1927.
A general review of Monacan politics from 1911 to 1926.

PRAT, MICHEL. **La Principauté de Monaco et le Traité du 17 Juillet, 1918.** Aix: L'Association du Patronage St. Pierre, 1920, 160 p.
An historical sketch, followed by an analysis of the treaty of 1918 regulating the status of Monaco.

MEDITERRANEAN PROBLEMS

See also (France) Relations with Italy, p. 268, and Colonial Questions, p. 270; also (Italy) Policy in the Mediterranean and Levant, p. 285; also (Africa) Algeria and Tunis, p. 515, and Tangier Problem, p. 521.

ALBI, FERNANDO. **La Politica del Mediterraneo en la Postguerra.** Valencia: Quiles, 1931, 224 p.
An historical study of the evolution of Mediterranean questions from 1918 to 1928.

BENOIST, CHARLES. **La Question Méditerranéenne.** Paris: Attinger, 1928, 190 p.
The history of European policy in Morocco, Tunis, Tripoli and Asia Minor, by a prominent French historian.

HERRE, PAUL. **Weltgeschichte am Mittelmeer.** Potsdam: Athenaion, 1930, 455 p.
A beautifully illustrated scholarly history of the Mediterranean area. The best single treatment.

LUIGI, GIUSEPPE DE'. **Il Mediterraneo nella Politica Europea.** Naples: Jovene, 1925, 506 p.
An exhaustive scholarly treatment of Mediterranean and Near Eastern politics in their international aspects during the modern period.

MIGOT, ROBERT and GUSTHAL, COMTE. **La Guerre Est Là.** Paris: Soubiron, 1932.
The authors discuss the Mediterranean and North African roots of war.

NEWBIGIN, MARION ISABEL. **The Mediterranean Lands.** New York: Knopf, 1924, 222 p.
A suggestive treatment of the Mediterranean problem from the anthropo-geographical standpoint.

NEWMAN, EDWARD WILLIAM POLSON. **The Mediterranean and Its Problems.** London: Philpot, 1927, 346 p.

A survey of the Mediterranean problems in their larger connections. This is largely a collection of articles already published elsewhere, but all exhibiting a first-hand acquaintance which gives them permanent interest. The arrangement and construction are not all they might be.

SILVA, PIETRO. **Il Mediterraneo dall'Unità di Roma all'Unità d'Italia.** Milan: Mondadori, 1927, 447 p.
A serious work on the history of the Mediterranean problem.

ITALY

General

See also (World War) Austro-Italian Front, p. 132.

ALAZARD, JEAN. **L'Italie et le Conflit Européen 1914-16.** Paris: Alcan, 1924, 271 p.
A sketch of Italy's entry into the World War.

BERGMANN, H. **L'Italie.** Paris: Rieder, 1923, 184 p.
An interpretation of modern Italian society.

CARONCINI, A. **Problemi di Politica Nazionale.** Bari: Laterza, 1921, 304 p.
A collection of articles published in reviews before 1915 on various phases of Italian policy.

COOPER, CLAYTON SEDGWICK. **Understanding Italy.** New York: Century, 1923, 306 p.
A penetrating journalistic survey of contemporary Italian institutions and culture, with discussions of emigration, industrialism, hydroelectric power, foreign trade, agriculture, colonization, etc.

CORRADINI, ENRICO. **La Rinascita Nazionale.** Florence: Le Monnier, 1929, 350 p.
Collected writings of the nationalist leader, of interest for students of recent Italian history.

CROCE, BENEDETTO. **A History of Italy, 1871-1915.** New York: Oxford University Press, 1929, 333 p.
The best general history of modern Italy available in English. Written by a distinguished thinker, it shows breadth of view and is not disfigured by polemics.

CROCE, BENEDETTO. **Pagine sulla Guerra.** Bari: Laterza, 2nd ed., 1928, 358 p.
Collected writings of the eminent Italian philosopher and historian.

DORSO, GUIDO. **La Rivoluzione Meridionale.** Turin: Gobetti, 1925, 242 p.
A general review of the vexed question of Southern Italy in its political and economic aspects, together with an excellent analysis of the attitude of pre-war and post-war parties towards this special set of problems.

FERRERO, GUGLIELMO. **La Democrazia in Italia.** Milan: Rassegna Internazionale, 1925, 136 p.
Essays by a well-known historian.

GENTILE, GIOVANNI. **Guerra e Fede.** Naples: Ricciardi, 1919, 381 p.
Collected writings of the leading Italian philosopher who has accepted Fascist principles. They deal with such subjects as nationalism, socialism, the Church, the League of Nations, etc.

GENTILE, GIOVANNI. **Dopo la Vittoria.** Rome: La Voce, 1920, 216 p.
Further writings, touching on most of the burning questions faced by Italy on the dawn of peace.

HAUTECŒUR, LOUIS. **L'Italie sous le Ministère Orlando.** Paris: Bossard, 1919, **276 p.**
A chronicle of affairs from 1917 to 1919, based largely on the Italian newspaper and periodical press.

HAZARD, PAUL. **L'Italie Vivante.** Paris: Perrin, 1923, 285 p.
An illuminating diary of Italian travels and observations in 1921, with good sketches of socialists, populists, Fascists, etc.

LÉMONON, ERNEST. **L'Italie d'après Guerre, 1914-1921.** Paris: Alcan, 1922, 259 p.
The writer reviews Italian domestic and foreign policy, economic problems, social questions, the Roman Question, etc.

MALAPARTE, CURZIO. **Italia Barbara.** Turin: Gobetti, 1926, 128 p.
A searching criticism of European liberalism and Cavour's policy of importing it into Italy.

MALAPARTE, CURZIO. **L'Italie contre l'Europe.** Paris: Alcan, 1928, 158 p.
The writer, a protagonist of Fascism, demands a return to the essentially Italian, with emphasis on national costume and attention to the Italian peasant.

MALATESTA, ALBERTO. **I Socialisti Italiani durante la Guerra.** Milan: Mondadori, 1926, 303 p.
A much-needed study of a confused phase of Italian political life.

MARRIOTT, SIR JOHN ARTHUR RANSOME. **The Makers of Modern Italy.** New York: Oxford University Press, 1931, 228 p.
An entirely rewritten edition of a famous book; a brief history of Italy from Napoleon to Mussolini.

MEDA, FILIPPO. **Il Socialismo Politico in Italia.** Milan: Unitas, 1924, 203 p.
The rise and fall of the socialist wave in Italy. A brief outline of the party's history, by a Catholic leader.

MICHELS, ROBERT. **Italien von Heute.** Zurich: Füssli, 1930, 410 p.
The well-known German-Italian sociologist reviews the evolution of modern Italy. An informative and stimulating volume.

MICHELS, ROBERT. **Sozialismus und Faszismus als Politische Strömungen in Italien.** Munich: Meyer und Jessen, 1925, 323 p.
Really a study of various intellectual currents in the Italian socialist movement.

MICHELS, ROBERT. **Storia Critica del Movimento Socialista Italiano.** Florence: La Voce, 1926, 464 p.
The standard history of the development of Italian socialism, bringing the story to 1911.

MOWRER, EDGAR ANSEL. **Immortal Italy.** New York: Appleton, 1922, 418 p.
An interesting journalistic sketch of modern Italy with most of the space devoted to the period since 1914.

MURRI, ROMOLO. **Dalla Democrazia Cristiana al Partito Popolare Italiano.** Venice: La Nuova Italia, 1928, 210 p.
The author, a former Christian Democratic leader, throws light on the origins of the Italian peasant movement.

ROSSELLI, CARLO. **Socialisme Libéral.** Paris: Valois, 1930, 224 p.
A study of Marxian socialism, as reflected in the Italian situation after the war.

SPENCER, HENRY RUSSELL. **Government and Politics of Italy.** New York: World Book Co., 1932, 319 p.
The author mainly draws his information from Fascist sources but criticizes the régime from a liberal standpoint.

TITTONI, TOMMASO. **Modern Italy.** New York: Macmillan, 1922, 236 p.
Williamstown Lectures, by a leading Italian statesman of the old school. The subjects discussed are Italy's contribution to literature, art, science, jurisprudence, philosophy, international law, and various economic, social and populational problems.

VARANINI, V. **La Ricostruzione Fascista delle Forze Armate Italiane.** Milan: Libreria d'Italia, 1929, 301 p.
A good account of the Italian military machine as it has emerged from the Fascist forges.

VERCESI, ERNESTO. **Il Movimento Cattolico in Italia.** Florence: La Voce, 1923, 306 p.
A survey of the period after 1870, and especially of the pontificates of Pius X and Benedict, with emphasis on the emergence and history of the Popular Party.

VILLARI, LUIGI. **Italy.** New York: Scribner, 1929, 392 p.
A volume in the "Modern World" Series, expounding the history of Italy in recent times and the fundamentals of the present system. The viewpoint is Fascist.

VITI DE MARCO, ANTONIO DE. **Un Trentennio di Lotte Politiche: 1894-1922.** Rome: Meridionale, 1930, 480 p.
The collected essays and speeches of an Italian parliamentarian, a valuable contribution to the study of how problems were handled under the parliamentary system.

VOLPE, GIOACCHINO. **L'Italia in Cammino.** Milan: Treves, 1927, 278 p.
A sound critical history of the previous fifty years of Italian history. Next to Croce's book, the best thing on the period.

Biographies

See also (World War) Biographies of Wartime Statesmen and Diplomats, p. 101; also (Europe) Biographies, p. 228.

AMBRIS, ALCESTE DE. **Amendola: Fatti e Documenti.** Toulouse: Exoria, 1927.
An account of the Fascist treatment of the liberal leader.

BORGHI, ARMANDO. **Mussolini in Camicia.** New York: Edizioni Libertarie, 1927, 183 p.
Light on Il Duce's early career. Interesting though intensely hostile.

CILIBRIZZI, SAVERIO. **Francesco Saverio Nitti e l'Avvenire d'Italia.** Naples: Pierro, 1919, 334 p.
An understanding study of Nitti as an economist and a statesman, with special attention to his economic and social policies.

COZZANI, ETTORE. **Gabriele d'Annunzio.** Milan: L'Eroica, 1930, 167 p.
An enthusiastic account of D'Annunzio's war career and his part in the victory.

FIORI, VITTORIO ERMETE DE. **Mussolini: the Man of Destiny.** New York: Dutton, 1928, 242 p.
The writer served on the staff of Mussolini's paper. The book deals with Il Duce's earlier career. Its eulogistic nature is adequately indicated by the title.

Gabriele d'Annunzio Combattente al Servizio della Regia Marina. Rome: Poliografica Italiana, 1931, 309 p.
A detailed review of D'Annunzio's activities with the navy, published by the Italian Ministry of Marine.

KEMECHEY, L. **"Il Duce": The Life and Work of Benito Mussolini.** New York: R. R. Smith, 1930, 280 p.
The author, a former official in the Hungarian Legation at Rome, has had close relations with the dictator.

MATTEOTTI, GIACOMO. **Reliquie.** Milan: Corbaccio, 1924, 324 p.
A collection of Matteotti's writings covering the period from the March on Rome to his assassination.

MUSSOLINI, BENITO. **Diuturna.** Milan: Imperia, 1924, 475 p.
A valuable collection of Mussolini's newspaper writings from the beginning of the war to the March on Rome.

MUSSOLINI, BENITO. **Messaggi e Proclami.** Milan: Libreria d'Italia, 1929, 220 p.
A collection of proclamations and messages.

MUSSOLINI, BENITO. **My Autobiography.** New York: Scribner, 1928, 318 p.
A very general, superficial piece of work, adding little factual material and giving the impression of being produced second-hand.

MUSSOLINI, BENITO. **Tempi della Rivoluzione Fascista.** Milan: Alpes, 1930, 246 p.
Articles published in *Gerarchia* between 1920 and 1928.

NARDELLI, FEDERICO and LIVINGSTON, ARTHUR. **Gabriel, the Archangel; Gabriele d'Annunzio.** New York: Harcourt, 1931, 336 p.
A somewhat critical account of D'Annunzio, with special reference to his personal life and military activities. Signor Nardelli was a member of the Fiume government.

NITTI, VINCENZO. **L'Opera di Nitti.** Turin: Gobetti, 1924, 274 p.
There are chapters on the war, the 1919 elections, domestic policies, Fiume, reconstruction, and foreign policy.

OCCHINI, PIER LUDOVICO. **Enrico Corradini.** Florence: Vallecchi, 1925, 263 p.
A biography of the nationalist leader and an appraisal of his literary output. Written by a warm friend and partisan, this is a valuable contribution.

ORANO, PAOLO. **Mussolini da Vicino.** Rome: Casa Editrice Pinciana, 1928, 164 p.
Studies of Il Duce's character—his will to power, his religion—and select scenes from his dramatic career.

PETRIE, SIR CHARLES ALEXANDER. **Mussolini.** London: Holme, 1931, 186 p.
A popular sketch, written with enthusiasm.

ROBERTSON, ALEXANDER. **Mussolini and the New Italy.** New York: Revell, 1928, 156 p.
Brimming over with enthusiasm and admiration.

ROYA, LOUIS, *pseud.* (LOUIS TOESCA). **Histoire de Mussolini.** Paris: Sagittaire, 1926, 210 p.
Chiefly sensational revelations.

SAAGER, ADOLF. **Mussolini ohne Mythus.** Vienna: Hess, 1931, 276 p.
An honest attempt to explain the character and policy of Il Duce.

SARFATTI, MARGHERITA GRASSINI. **The Life of Benito Mussolini.** New York: Stokes, 1925, 352 p.
This volume contains much material on Mussolini's early career. The presentation is quite uncritical.

SODINI, ANGELO. **Ariel Armato.** Milan: Mondadori, 1931, 725 p.
A beautifully illustrated monumental life of D'Annunzio.

Vita di Giolitti. BY AN EX-DEPUTY. Ferrara: Ghelfi, 1929, 262 p.
A critical historical study.

Fascism

See also (Europe) Constitutional Problems, Dictatorships, p. 227.

ANDREA, U. D'. **Corradini e il Nazionalismo.** Rome: Augustea, 1928, 111 p.
A much-needed study of the origins of Italian nationalism in the pre-war years; useful for an understanding of Fascist backgrounds.

AVARNA DI GUALTIERI, CARLO. **Il Fascismo.** Turin: Gobetti, 1925, 236 p.
An able attack on Fascist ideas and practices.

BALABANOVA, ANGELICA. **Wesen und Werdegang der Italienischen Fascismus.**
Vienna: Hess, 1931, 286 p.
The author was associated with Mussolini when the latter was editor of the socialist
daily *Avanti*, and gives interesting, though very hostile, information about that
period.

Le Barbarie Rosse. Rome: Tip. Sociale, 1921, 110 p.
Fascist records of acts of violence committed by socialists, published by the Fascio
Italiano di Combattimento.

BARNES, JAMES STRACHEY. **Fascism.** New York: Holt, 1931, 252 p.
A sympathetic treatment of the Fascist movement, in the "Home University Library"
series.

BARNES, JAMES STRACHEY. **The Universal Aspects of Fascism.** London: Williams and
Norgate, 1927, 247 p.
One of the best generally favorable books on Fascism in English. The writer sees the
Fascist experiment as an attempt to reintegrate the national forces and realize a type
of industrial Christianity.

BEALS, CARLETON. **Rome or Death.** New York: Century, 1923, 347 p.
An impressionistic but enlightening sketch of the Fascist movement and the March
on Rome.

BECKERATH, ERWIN VON. **Wesen und Werden des Fascistischen Staates.** Berlin:
Springer, 1927, 155 p.
A philosophical disquisition. The author sees the Fascist state as the realization of the
authoritarian state aimed at in the eighteenth century and foresees attempts to
establish similar systems elsewhere in Europe as the economic and political tension
grows.

BERTELÈ, ALDO. **Aspetti Ideologici del Fascismo.** Turin: Druetto, 1930, 237 p.
The author discusses the connection between Fascism and the writings of men like
Sorel, Pareto, Gentile, etc.

BOLITHO, WILLIAM. **Italy under Mussolini.** New York: Macmillan, 1926, 129 p.
A very unfavorable and unfair report on Fascism and the Fascist system, by a special
correspondent of the New York *World*.

BONOMI, IVANOE. **From Socialism to Fascism.** London: Martin Hopkinson, 1924,
164 p.
A sane if uninspired examination of the origins and development of Fascism and the
failure of socialism in Italy, by a former Italian Prime Minister.

BRANDO, NICOLA. **Il Fascismo nella Storia.** Mantua: Mussolinia, 1931, 117 p.
Purporting to set forth the traditions of Italian politics and Fascism's place in Italian
and world history.

CAMBÓ Y BATLLE, FRANCISCO DE ASÍS. **Autour du Fascisme Italien.** Paris: Plon, 1925,
252 p.
A discussion of Fascism by a former Spanish minister.

CAPUANO, EDUARDO. **L'Italia Nuova.** Naples: Giannini, 1925, 177 p.
A glorification of Fascism and all that is Fascist.

CARLI, MARIO. **Fascismo Intransigente.** Florence: Bemporad, 1926, 267 p.
A rhapsodical account of the rise and victory of Fascism, by one of the leaders.

CHIURCO, G. A. **Storia della Rivoluzione Fascista.** Florence: Vallecchi, 1929, 5 v.
A rather confused day-by-day chronicle of events from March 1919 to October 1922.

CICCOTTI, ETTORE. **Il Fascismo e le Sue Fasi.** Milan: Unitas, 1925, 442 p.
A collection of writings covering the years 1916 to 1924, reflecting the rise of Fascism, its first period and its alleged degeneration.

CRESSWELL, C. M. **The Keystone of Fascism.** London: Besant, 1929, 336 p.
An exuberant review of Italian affairs since the war and the rise of Mussolini, prophet of the new discipline.

EBERLEIN, GUSTAV WILHELM. **Der Faschismus als Bewegung.** Berlin: Scherl, 1929, 141 p.
A scholarly monograph on the background of Fascism, its organization and leadership.

ELLIOTT, WILLIAM YANDELL. **The Pragmatic Revolt in Politics.** New York: Macmillan, 1928, 557 p.
A study of the philosophic aspects of the revolt against the omnipotence of the modern state and of the background of Fascist ideology and practice. A scholarly contribution to modern political theory.

FARINACCI, ROBERTO. **Andante Mosso.** Milan: Mondadori, 1929.
A reprint of articles from the *Cremona Nuova* covering the stormy and crucial period from June 1924 to March 1925.

Il Fascismo e i Partiti Politici. Bologna: Cappelli, 1924, v.p.
A collection of studies on the origins of the Fascist movement written in 1921 and 1922 by men of the most widely divergent views, under the leadership of an able socialist scholar, Prof. Rodolfo Mondolfo.

FERRARI, FRANCESCO LUIGI. **Le Régime Fasciste Italien.** Paris: Spès, 1928, 374 p.
A documented study of the Fascist system, by an objective though unfriendly critic.

FERRERO, GUGLIELMO. **Four Years of Fascism.** London: King, 1924, 138 p.
A collection of articles by a well-known Italian historian, giving a critical survey of events from 1919 to 1923.

FILARETI, GENERALE. **In Margine del Fascismo.** Milan: Unitas, 1925, 421 p.
A series of searching essays on the development and significance of the Fascist movement by a convinced monarchist who despairs of democratic systems.

GARIBALDI, EZIO. **Fascismo Garibaldino.** Rome: Camicia Rossa, 1928, 242 p.
From the red shirt to the black shirt; a discussion of the Garibaldian movement as a precursor of Fascism. Not very serious.

GAY, HARRY NELSON. **Strenuous Italy.** Boston: Houghton Mifflin, 1927, 226 p.
A record of the material and social progress made under the new régime, by a wholehearted American lover of Italy and sincere admirer of Il Duce.

GENTILE, GIOVANNI. **Che Cosa è il Fascismo?** Florence: Vallecchi, 1926, 262 p.
A collection of essays and speeches by an Italian philosopher and intellectual defender of Fascism.

GENTILE, GIOVANNI. **Fascismo e Cultura.** Milan: Treves, 1928, 208 p.
The official theorist of the movement enlarges on its non-political implications.

GENTILE, GIOVANNI. **Origini e Dottrina del Fascismo.** Rome: Littorio, 1929, 65 p.
A brief recapitulation of the history and party struggles of pre-war Italy, the emergence of Fascism and its philosophical bases.

GIAMPAOLI, M. **1919.** Rome: Littorio, 1928, 336 p.
Recollections of a Fascist leader, highly interesting and instructive.

GOAD, HAROLD ELSDALE. **The Making of the Corporate State.** London: Christophers, 1932, 167 p.
A concise and sympathetic study of Fascist development and organization.

GOBETTI, PIERO. **La Rivoluzione Liberale.** Bologna: Cappelli, 1924, 158 p.
An interesting study of Italian traditions, parties and party conflicts from which Fascism emerged.

GORGOLINI, PIETRO. **The Fascist Movement in Italian Life.** Boston: Little, Brown, 1923, 217 p.
A journalistic account of the rise and character of the movement, by an active Fascist. Declared by Mussolini to be "the best publication on Fascism" up to 1923.

GUTKIND, KURT SIGMAR, *ed.* **Mussolini und Sein Faschismus.** Heidelberg: Merlin Verlag, 1928, 410 p.
A coöperative study of the evolution of Fascism, of the revolution, and of the new system, by Fascist writers.

HELLER, HERMANN. **Europa und der Fascismus.** Berlin: De Gruyter, 1929, 137 p.
An analysis of the Fascist state and the mentality that produced it, with an attempt to determine its value for Europe at large.

KAMINSKI, HANNS ERICH. **Der Faschismus in Italien.** Berlin: Verlag für Sozialwissenschaft, 1925, 141 p.
A condensed survey of the origins and development of Fascism, written from the socialist standpoint.

KING, BOLTON. **Fascism in Italy.** London: Williams and Norgate, 1931, 100 p.
Written by a leading authority on Italian affairs, this little volume is one of the best critical accounts of the Fascist state and Fascist policy.

LABRIOLA, ARTURO. **Polemica Antifascista.** Naples: Ceccoli, 1925, 218 p.
The reactions of the famous socialist leader.

LION, ALINE. **The Pedigree of Fascism.** London: Sheed and Ward, 1927, 242 p.
The authoress, a French lady, traces the development of Italian political thought from the Renaissance and Machiavelli, seeks to interpret the influence of Croce and Gentile and finally discusses the evolution of Fascism.

MANNHARDT, JOHANN WILHELM. **Der Faschismus.** Munich: Beck, 1925, 411 p.
One of the most complete studies of pre-war Italy, the origins and rise of Fascism, and the Fascist system.

MARINETTI, FILIPPO TOMMASO. **Futurismo e Fascismo.** Foligno: Campitelli, 1924, 249 p.
A collection of extraordinary writings and proclamations by the leader of the Futurists, forerunners and supporters of the Fascists.

MATTEOTTI, GIACOMO. **Il Fascismo della Prima Ora.** Rome: Tipografia Italiana, 1924.
Documents on Mussolini's ultra-revolutionary activities in 1919 and 1920.

MATTEOTTI, GIACOMO. **The Fascisti Exposed.** London: Independent Labour Party Publication Department, 1924, 128 p.
A documented attack on Fascism by an opponent murdered in 1924.

MEHLIS, GEORG. **Die Idee Mussolinis und der Sinn des Faschismus.** Leipzig: Haberland, 1928, 156 p.
An able account of the origins of Fascism, its doctrine and its evolution, its struggles and success.

MEHLIS, GEORG. **Der Staat Mussolinis.** Leipzig: Haberland, 1929, 205 p.
A brief survey of the theory and practice of the Fascist state.

NENNI, PIETRO. **Ten Years of Tyranny in Italy.** London: Allen and Unwin, 1932, 218 p.
A violent attack on Fascism, by one of Mussolini's former associates who went into opposition and was imprisoned.

NICOLETTI, EDGARDO. **Da Nitti a Mussolini, 1919-1922.** Naples: Chiurazzi, 1927, 158 p.
A general review of the stormy post-war period and the events that led to the March on Rome.

OTTEN, JOHAN FRANCISCUS. **Het Fascisme.** Amsterdam: Paris, 1928, 340 p.
A well-documented dissertation analyzing the rise of Fascism and discussing in detail the constitutional system and policies.

PELLIZZI, CAMILLO. **Problemi e Realtà del Fascismo.** Florence: Vallecchi, 1924, 216 p.
An analysis of the nature and program of the Fascist movement by a philosophic adherent. The author stresses the relationship of bourgeois liberalism, socialism, syndicalism and nationalism, and the ideological background of the Fascist state

PINI, GIORGIO and BRESADOLA, FEDERICO. **Storia del Fascismo.** Rome: Littorio, 1928, 510 p.
A review of the history of the movement and the work of the régime.

POMBA, GIUSEPPE LUIGI, *ed.* **La Civiltà Fascista Illustrata nella Dottrina e nelle Opere.** Turin: Torinese, 1928, 685 p.
This important book consists of a large number of authoritative articles surveying all aspects of Fascist thought and activity. Among the contributions may be mentioned those by Volpi on the historical development of the movement, by Morello on the dissolution of the old régime, by Gorgolini on the March on Rome, by Gentile on the essence of Fascism, by Cian on the precursors of Fascism, by Torre on the new spirit of Italian foreign policy, by Rollini on the colonial policy, by Alberti on finances. There are other essays on religion, art, legislation, agriculture, industry, the coöperatives, syndicalism, the labor code, etc. With a bibliography.

POMPEIS, ETTORE DE. **Il Sistema Elettorale Maggioritario Proporzionale del Governo Fascista.** Castello: Unione Arti Grafiche, 1925, 415 p.
An account of the Fascist electoral law of 1923.

POR, ODON. **Fascism.** New York: Knopf, 1923, 270 p.
One of the best and most objective of the earlier accounts of the rise and character of Fascism.

PREZZOLINI, GIUSEPPE. **Fascism.** New York: Dutton, 1927, 201 p.
A clear and moderate statement of the problems of Italian politics, with emphasis on fundamental geographical, historical and psychological factors. The book is intended chiefly for the enlightenment of foreigners.

Le Procès de Rosa. Paris: Valois, 1930, 164 p.
The record of the famous Brussels trial, involving a serious indictment of the Fascists.

ROCCA, MASSIMO. **Le Fascisme et l'Anti-Fascisme en Italie.** Paris: Alcan, 1930, 230 p.
The rise, apogee and decline of Fascism as seen by a former Italian deputy and Fascist now in exile.

ROSSI, LEOPOLDO. **Da Cavour a Mussolini.** Milan: Corbaccio, 1929, 341 p.
A thoroughly Fascist book. The writer reviews the pre-war régime only to demonstrate the inadequacy of liberalism and to furnish a background for Fascism.

RUINI, MEUCCIO. **La Democrazia e l'Unione Nazionale.** Milan: Corbaccio, 1925, 299 p.
The position of the democratic parties under the Fascist régime. An interesting contribution to the story of the crisis following the Matteotti murder.

SALVEMINI, GAETANO. **The Fascist Dictatorship in Italy.** Volume I. New York: Holt, 1927, 328 p.

Written by one of the most uncompromising opponents of the Fascist régime, this book is likely to remain for a long time the classic formulation of the case against it. Professor Salvemini is a well-known historian, all of whose work has been characterized by painstaking and conscientious scholarship. The present book, though written with passion and with an outspoken hostility, is nevertheless done with the greatest care, the facts quoted being invariably supported by acceptable references.

SCHNEIDER, HERBERT WALLACE. **Making the Fascist State.** New York: Oxford University Press, 1928, 403 p.
One of the good books on the Fascist movement. The author approaches the subject without preconceived notions and without undue credulity. The reactions of nationalism, imperialism, futurism and syndicalism upon each other are clearly brought out. In describing the Fascist state the author is careful to stress the lack of a concise program and to bring out the various viewpoints within the movement. Extensive appendices and bibliography.

SCHNEIDER, HERBERT WALLACE and CLOUGH, SHEPARD BANCROFT. **Making Fascists.** Chicago: Chicago University Press, 1929, 226 p.
A valuable study, based largely on personal interviews and observation and throwing much light on Italian group attitudes, educational work, the Fascist party, the press, patriotic organizations, etc.

SILLANI, TOMASO. **La Vittoria dello Spirito.** Florence: Bemporad, 1925, 244 p.
Articles published in the *Rassegna Italiana* by its editor, between 1919 and 1924, furnishing a useful guide to the development of Italian opinion.

SILLANI, TOMASO, *ed.* **What Is Fascism and Why?** London: Benn, 1931, 359 p.
The English translation of a collection of statements by Fascist leaders, dealing with economic, social and cultural problems and achievements.

STURZO, LUIGI. **Italy and Fascismo.** New York: Harcourt, 1927, 317 p.
One of the outstanding books on Fascism, by the leader of the Catholic People's Party. The author reviews the whole development of the movement and its manifestations in a critical but objective way.

STURZO, LUIGI. **Popolarismo e Fascismo.** Turin: Gobetti, 1924, 398 p.
A collection of articles and speeches between 1919 and 1923.

TITTONI, TOMMASO. **International Economic and Political Problems of the Day and Some Aspects of Fascism.** London: Simpkin, 1926, 302 p.
A collection of the essays and addresses of the Italian statesman.

TRENTIN, SILVIO. **L'Aventure Italienne.** Paris: Presses Universitaires, 1928, 332 p.
A former Italian professor of law and ex-deputy reviews the post-war history of his country and deflates the claims of Fascism.

TRENTIN, SILVIO. **Les Transformations Récentes du Droit Public Italien.** Paris: Giard, 1929, 692 p.
The present volume is one of the few constitutional histories of Fascism written by a competent authority. Remembering that the constitution of 1848 is technically still in force, the author examines first the pre-war system and its functioning, but the larger part of the volume is taken up with a careful study of the Fascist régime in its relations to the preceding constitutional system.

TRENTIN, SILVIO. **Aux Sources du Fascisme.** Paris: Rivière, 1931, 212 p.
A penetrating analysis of Fascist evolution.

TURATI, AUGUSTO. **A Revolution and Its Leader.** London: Alexander-Ouseley, 1930, 206 p.
Speeches on various Fascist topics by one of the party's highest officials.

Villari, Luigi. **The Awakening of Italy.** London: Methuen, 1924, 292 p.
The story of Italy's regeneration through the victory of the Fascists over the Socialists.

Villari, Luigi. **The Fascist Experiment.** London: Faber and Gwyer, 1926, 269 p.
A review of the policies and programs of Fascism, designed to enlighten the English-speaking world regarding its merit.

Volpe, Gioacchino. **Guerra, Dopoguerra, Fascismo.** Venice: La Nuova Italia, 1928, 470 p.
A collection of writings covering the post-war years and ranging over a large variety of subjects, by one of the keenest Italian political writers.

Economic and Social Problems

Alessio, Giulio. **La Rivalutazione della Lira.** Milan: Libreria, 1926, 184 p.
A competent discussion of the entire monetary situation, the arguments for and against revalorization and stabilization, etc.

Arias, Gino. **La Questione Meridionale.** Bologna: Zanichelli, 1921, 2 v.
A study of the many problems, social and economic, confronting southern Italy.

Belluzzo, Giuseppe. **Ecconomia Fascista.** Rome: Libreria del Littorio, 1928, 262 p.
Speeches delivered by the author when he was Minister of Industry.

Bottai, Giuseppe. **Esperienza Corporativa.** Rome: Diritto del Lavoro, 1929.
A collection of speeches delivered by Bottai in his capacity as Minister of Labor.

Buozzi, Bruno and Nitti, Vincenzo. **Fascisme et Syndicalisme.** Paris: Valois, 1930, 292 p.
A condemnation of Fascist trade-unionism.

Cabiati, Attilio. **Il Ritorno all'Oro.** Milan: Corbaccio, 1926, 327 p.
Essays on Italy's financial problem, the cost of the war, etc.

Ferri, Carlo Emilio. **Aspetti Economici della Vita Italiana.** Milan: Acquati, 1927, 322 p.
A survey of developments from 1920 to 1925.

Foerster, Robert Franz. **The Italian Emigration of Our Times.** Cambridge: Harvard University Press, 1919, 556 p.
The best scholarly study of the Italian emigration problem. The author examines the causes, the history and especially the conditions of Italians abroad.

Fox, Sir Frank. **Italy To-day.** London: Jenkins, 1927, 285 p.
An appreciative account of the Fascist accomplishment, especially in the economic field. Journalistic.

Gangemi, Lello. **La Politica Economica e Finanziaria del Governo Fascista.** Bologna: Zanichelli, 1924, 507 p.
A treatment of the first phase of Fascist economic policy.

Gressent, Alfred Georges. **Finances Italiennes.** Paris: Valois, 1930, 172 p.
A condemnation of the financial and economic régime.

Haider, Carmen. **Capital and Labor under Fascism.** New York: Columbia University Press, 1930, 296 p.
Based upon documentary material, personal observation and consultation with adherents and opponents of the régime.

Joly, Henri. **Les Crises Sociales de l'Italie.** Paris: Perrin, 1925, 291 p.
An examination of the underlying causes for unrest in Italy.

McGuire, Constantine Edward. **Italy's International Economic Position.** New York: Macmillan, 1926, 606 p.

Published by the Institute of Economics. The author examines all aspects of Italian finance, national income, emigration, etc.

MAZZEI, JACOPO. **Il Cambio Italiano.** Florence: Vallecchi, 1926, 122 p.
A study of the causes of the recent fluctuations in the value of Italian currency.

MITZAKIS, MICHEL. **Les Grands Problèmes Italiens.** Paris: Alcan, 1931, 420 p.
Another detailed, documented study of the post-war economic and financial problems of Italy.

PANTALEONI, MAFFEO. **Bolcevismo Italiano.** Bari: Laterza, 1922, 276 p.
Essays on the financial, economic and social crisis in Italy from which Fascism emerged.

PARATORE, GIUSEPPE. **Alcune Note di Politica Monetaria.** Rome: Modernissima, 1925, 169 p.
Mildly criticizes the Fascist financial policy of the first three years.

PENNACHIO, ALBERTO. **The Corporative State.** New York: Italian Historical Society, 1927, 192 p.
A brief statement of the corporative organization of the Fascist state, with chief reference to labor legislation.

PERROUX, FRANÇOIS. **Contribution à l'Étude de l'Économie et des Finances Publiques de l'Italie depuis la Guerre.** Paris: Giard, 1929, 357 p.
A survey of the financial and economic difficulties of post-war Italy, with conclusions unfavorable to the Fascist régime.

La Ricostruzione Fascista. Novembre 1924-Gennaio 1925. Milan: Corbaccio, 1925, 220 p.
A pro-Fascist collection of documents on the working of the Fascist régime in its first phase.

SERPIERI, ARRIGO. **La Guerra e le Classi Rurali Italiane.** New Haven: Yale University Press, 1930, 503 p.
This monograph in the Carnegie Series strikes at one of the key problems of modern Italy. The account is carried through the years immediately following the war.

STEFANI, ALBERTO DE'. **La Restaurazione Finanziaria, 1922-1925.** Bologna: Zanichelli, 1926, 274 p.
A collection of the speeches of the former Italian Finance Minister.

STEFANI, ALBERTO DE'. **Vie Maestre.** Milan: Treves, 1927, 340 p.
Speeches and essays of the Italian statesman during 1926.

STEFANI, ALBERTO DE'. **Il Paese e lo Stato.** Milan: Treves, 1930, 334 p.
Collected articles, mainly from the *Corriere della Sera*, dealing chiefly with current economic problems.

WOOG, CLAUDE. **La Politique d'Émigration de l'Italie.** Paris: Presses Universitaires, 1931, 392 p.
A scientific study of the Italian Government's emigration policy, of legislation on the subject, and of international agreements touching it.

Foreign and Colonial Policies

General

See also (France) Relations with Italy, p. 268; also (Vatican City) Relations with Italy, p. 291; also (Africa) Italian Possessions, p. 525.

ADAMI, VITTORIO. **Storia Documentata dei Confini del Regno d'Italia.** Rome: Istituto Poligrafico dello Stato, 1919-1931, 4 v. in 5.
A huge work published by the historical section of the Italian General Staff. Richly equipped with documents and maps, the various volumes give in great detail the history and description of every part of the frontier.

ARENA, CELESTINO. **Italiani per il Mondo.** Milan: Alpes, 1927, 185 p.
The author discusses the emigration problem from the nationalist standpoint.

BISSOLATI, LEONIDA. **La Politica Estera dell'Italia dal 1897 al 1920.** Milan: Treves, 1923, 447 p.
A collection of papers and speeches by a leading Italian anti-imperialist.

CICCOTTI, ETTORE. **Cronache Quadriennali di Politica Italiana ed Estera, 1919-1923.** Milan: Unitas, 1924, 2 v.
A useful chronicle of events in Italy in the last years.

Fatti Europei e Politica Italiana, 1922-1924. Milan: Imperia, 1924, 196 p.
A survey of Italian foreign policy in the two years following the establishment of the Fascist régime.

GAIBI, AGOSTINO. **Manuale di Storia Politico-Militare delle Colonie Italiane.** Rome: Libreria dello Stato, 1928, 579 p.
A colonial history, with emphasis on the military phases, written and published under the supervision of the Italian General Staff. With many maps and plans.

GUYOT, GEORGES. **L'Italie devant le Problème Colonial.** Paris: Société d'Éditions Géographiques, 1927, 240 p.
A serious study of Italy's social and economic needs.

MARZIO, CORNELIO DI. **Popoli e Paesi.** Rome: Tiber, 1929, 334 p.
A discussion of the chief problems of Italian foreign policy from the Fascist viewpoint.

MONDAINI, GENNARO. **Manuale di Storia e Legislazione Coloniale del Regno d'Italia.** Rome: Sampaolese, 1927, 2 v.
The best systematic, scholarly history of Italian colonial history, devoting particular attention to the last ten years. Written by an outstanding authority, editor of *La Revista Coloniale*.

NAUDEAU, LUDOVIC. **L'Italie Fasciste ou l'Autre Danger.** Paris: Flammarion, 1927, 283 p.
A French *enquête* in Italy. Well-informed discussion of Fascist policies, especially foreign policy and the question of Italian-French relations.

REALE, EGIDIO. **La Politique Fasciste et la Société des Nations.** Paris: Pedone, 1932, 84 p.
A serious study of the doctrines of Fascism about war and peace, and of its changing attitudes towards the League of Nations. Count Sforza contributes a preface.

SALVEMINI, GAETANO. **Mussolini Diplomate.** Paris: Grasset, 1932, 338 p.
This book, written by the foremost authority on the history of Italian foreign policy, is based upon wide reading and draws heavily upon newspaper material as well as upon official documents. It supplies a critical survey of Italian policy under Fascist rule in all its aspects, and its conclusions deserve the careful attention of all who interest themselves in the development of the European situation.

SCHANZER, CARLO. **Sulla Conferenze di Genova e sulla Politica Estera dell'Italia.** Rome: Bardi, 1922, 177 p.
A collection of speeches by a former Italian Minister of Foreign Affairs.

TITTONI, TOMMASO. **Questioni del Giorno.** Milan: Treves, 1928, 215 p.
Miscellaneous essays by the late Italian statesman on Tunis, Abyssinia, Bessarabia, Libya, Jugoslavia and Albania.

TRENTIN, SILVIO. **Le Fascisme à Genève.** Paris: Rivière, 1932, 264 p.
A criticism of Italy's League and disarmament policy, by one of the ablest opponents of the régime.

VILLARI, LUIGI. **The Expansion of Italy.** London: Faber, 1930, 290 p.
An eloquent and thoroughly Fascist defense of Italian colonial policy and aspirations under Mussolini, covering territorial expansion in Africa and other regions, as well as giving an account of the expansion of the Italian people in all parts of the world.

ZOPPOLA, GIUSEPPE. **Imperialismo Spirituale e Imperialismo Materiale.** Venice: Istituto Manin, 1928, 144 p.
The spiritual kind is Fascist and Catholic, the materialistic type is Jewish and Masonic.

Policy in the Mediterranean and the Levant; the Dodecanese; the Malta Question

See also (Western Europe) Mediterranean Problems, p. 272; also (France) Relations with Italy, p. 268; also (Greece) General, p. 418; also (Africa) Algeria and Tunis, p. 515, and Tangier Problem, p. 521, and Italian Possessions, p. 525.

ALHADEFF, VITTORIO. **L'Ordinamento Giuridico di Rodi.** Milan: Istituto Editoriale Scientifico, 1927, 214 p.
The constitutional and legal status of Rhodes and the other Aegean Islands under Italian rule.

AMBROSINI, GASPARE. **L'Italia nel Mediterraneo.** Foligno: Campitelli, 1927, 303 p.
A professor at the University of Palermo gives an excellent account of Italian claims and policy from 1878 on, and discusses ways and means for realizing the national program in the Mediterranean.

BERTONELLI, FRANCESCO. **Il Nostro Mare.** Florence: Bemporad, 1930, 150 p.
Really an introductory study of Mediterranean problems as they affect Italy, written from a thoroughly Fascist standpoint.

BOOTH, CHARLES DOUGLAS GREAVES and ISABELLE BRIDGE. **Italy's Aegean Possessions.** London: Arrowsmith, 1928, 324 p.
An historical and descriptive outline of the Dodecanese, with a good discussion of Italian rule since the annexation.

CAPASSO, CARLO. **Italia e Oriente.** Florence: Nuova Italia, 1932, 290 p.
A strongly Fascist presentation of Italian interests in the east.

CIPPICO, ANTONIO, CONTE. **Italy, the Central Problem of the Mediterranean.** New Haven: Yale University Press, 1926, 121 p.
Williamstown Lectures, in which a prominent Fascist discusses the present Italian régime, and Italy's position and claims in the Mediterranean.

COLLINI, B. **Malta e la Politica Stricklandiana.** Livorno: Giusti, 1931, 164 p.
This latest contribution to the Maltese dispute contains a number of documents.

DANDRIA, ENRICO. **The Malta Crisis.** London: Surridge, 1930, 38 p.
An able presentation of the language problem and the shortcomings of British rule.

DESIO, A. **Le Isole Italiane dell'Egeo.** Rome: Libreria dello Stato, 1931, 534 p.
An elaborate and richly illustrated descriptive work.

GIANNI, GIUSEPPE. **Le Isole Italiane dell'Egeo.** Florence: Istituto Geografico Militare, 1928, 80 p.
A good survey of the islands and their inhabitants, with a description of the Italian government and military institutions. Excellent maps.

In Difesa della Civiltà Italiana a Malta. Livorno: Giusti, 1931, 147 p.
A collection of articles published in the organ of the National Maltese Party.

NAVA, S. **Il Problema dell'Espansione Italiana ed il Levante Islamico.** Padua: C. E. D. A. M., 1931, 254 p.
A scholarly account of Italian interests and aspirations in the Near East.

NOBILI, MASSUERO F. **Ombre e Luci di Due Continenti: Due Anni di Politica Coloniale e Mediterranea.** Milan: Alpes, 1926, 514 p.
A detailed study of colonial enterprise during the years 1923 and 1924.

PEDRAZZI, ORAZIO. **Il Levante Mediterraneo e l'Italia.** Milan: Alpes, 1925, 169 p.
Italy's interests and aspirations in the eastern Mediterranean described and defended.

ROGGERO, S. **Siamo Mediterranei.** Genoa: Istituto Editoriale Genovese, 1928, 200 p.
The why and the wherefor of a leading Fascist slogan.

ROSSI, ETTORE. **Lingua Italiana, Dialetto Maltese e Politica Britannica a Malta.** Livorno: Giusti, 1929, 118 p.
Perhaps the best Italian account of the political and language difficulties in Malta since 1881.

SCIUTI, G. **Visioni Mediterranee.** Catania: Etna, 1932, 115 p.
A brief recapitulation of Mediterranean problems and Italian aspirations.

SEYFULLAH, IBRAHIM. **Italien im Östlichen Mittelmeer.** Berlin: Vowinckel, 1930, 92 p.
The problem of the Dodecanese, with special reference to its economic aspects.

TSAKALAKIS, ANTHONY. **Le Dodécanèse.** Alexandria: Cassimatis, 1928, 97 p.
An outline of the history of the islands, followed by a study of their present position. The author prints all the relevant documents.

VOLONAKIS, MICHAEL D. **The Island of Roses and Her Eleven Sisters.** London: Macmillan, 1922, 438 p.
A general historical, geographical and cultural sketch of the Dodecanese, by the man who represented the inhabitants at the Peace Conference.

ZERVOS, SKEVOS GEORGES. **La Question du Dodécanèse et Ses Documents Diplomatiques.** Athens: Elefteroudakis, 2nd ed., 1928, 151 p.
A handy collection of documents designed to substantiate the Greek position, by a Dodecanesian leader now in exile in Athens.

Policy in the Adriatic

See also (The Balkan Area) General, p. 399; also (Jugoslavia) General, p. 407; also Albania, p. 416.

General

ADRIACUS, *pseud.* **From Trieste to Valona.** Rome: Alfieri and Lacroix, 1919, 124 p.
Italy's aspirations in the Adriatic.

ADRIATICUS, *pseud.* **La Question Adriatique.** Paris: Imprimerie Typographique, 1920, 158 p.
A collection of documents bearing on the problem.

ALIA, A. D'. **La Dalmazia.** Rome: Optima, 1928, 300 p.
The author proves to his own satisfaction that Dalmatia's connection with Italy has always been extremely close.

BENEDETTI, GIULIO. **Rivendicazioni Adriatiche.** Milan: Libreria d'Italia, 1929, 238 p.
The author revives the argument that the power controlling the west coast of the Adriatic must, for defensive, if for no other reasons, control also the eastern coast. He bemoans France's support of Jugoslav claims, and stresses the need for close Italian-Hungarian relations.

BERNARDY, AMY A. and FALORSI, VITTORIO. **La Questione Adriatica Vista d'Oltre Atlantico.** Bologna: Zanichelli, 1923, 335 p.
  Written by members of the Italian Embassy in Washington, this book adds some important documentary material to the story of the Adriatic problem and Wilson's policy.

BERTOTTI, EMILIO. **La Nostra Spedizione in Albania.** Milan: Unitas, 1926, 184 p.
  This is the first adequate account of the Italian expedition to Albania in 1915-1916, and throws light on the present Balkan policy of the Fascist government.

BISCOTTINI, UMBERTO. **Sull'Italianità della Dalmazia.** Livorno: Giusti, 1930, 130 p.
  A collation of evidence as to the Italian character of Dalmatia.

CANIGLIA, BENEDETTO. **Italia e Albania.** Rome: Brocato, 1925, 118 p.
  An able presentation of Italian relations with Albania from 1914 to 1920, by an Italian officer stationed there.

COLONNA DI CESARO, G. A. **L'Italia nell'Albania Meridionale.** Foligno: Campitelli, 1922, 374 p.
  A valuable documented study of Italian-Albanian relations in 1917 and 1918.

FABBRI, A. **Effetti delle Annessioni Territoriali.** Padua: C. E. D. A. M., 1931, 156 p.
  The author stresses especially the effects of the Fiume and Dalmatian questions on Italy's relations with Jugoslavia.

Italy and the Jugoslav Minority within Her Borders. Ljubljana: Minorities Institute, 1931, 62 p.
  A strong presentation of Jugoslav grievances regarding the treatment of the Slovene and Croat minorities in Italy.

JAQUIN, PIERRE. **La Question des Minorités entre l'Italie et la Yougoslavie.** Paris: Sirey, 1929, 220 p.
  A serious study of the problem of Jugoslav and Italian minorities, the provisions for their protection, and the actual working of these arrangements. Texts of the Treaty of Rapallo, the Nettuno Convention, etc., are included.

MARANELLI, CARLO and SALVEMINI, GAETANO. **La Questione dell'Adriatico.** Rome: La Voce, 1919, 374 p.
  A discussion of Italian aims and policies in the Adriatic as seen by two liberal Italians at the close of the war.

MENINI, GIULIO. **Passione Adriatica.** Bologna: Zanichelli, 1925, 237 p.
  An Italian nationalist's version of events in Dalmatia from 1918 to 1920.

NANI, UMBERTO. **Italia e Jugoslavia.** Milan: Libreria d'Italia, 1928, 144 p.
  A review of the relations between the two countries in the past decade.

SALVEMINI, GAETANO. **Dal Patto di Londra alla Pace di Roma.** Turin: Gobetti, 1925, 360 p.
  Salvemini (like Bissolati) during and after the war opposed the plan to annex Dalmatia to Italy. This volume gives the basis of his anti-imperialist campaign.

STOJANOVIĆ, STOJAN. **La Question de l'Adriatique et le Principe des Nationalités.** Grenoble: Aubert, 1923, 158 p.
  Discusses the Adriatic problem as it was dealt with in the London Pact, at the Peace Conference, and in the later Jugoslav-Italian agreements.

WOODHOUSE, EDWARD JAMES and CHASE GOING. **Italy and the Jugoslavs.** Boston: Badger, 1920, 394 p.
  An account of the development of the Jugoslav movement and of the Adriatic question, valuable for the information which it contains on negotiations at the Peace Conference and Italy's simultaneous manœuvres in Trieste, Fiume, Dalmatia and Montenegro.

The Fiume Question

AMBRIS, ALCESTE DE. **Dalla Frode al Fratricido.** Rome: La Fionda, 1921, 115 p.
A violent attack upon the Italian Government for its action against the D'Annunzio régime in Fiume.

ANNUNZIO, GABRIELE D'. **Il Sudore di Sangue.** Rome: La Fionda, 1930, 385 p.
Addresses, messages and appeals of D'Annunzio in the spring and summer of 1919, up to the time of his departure for Fiume.

BENEDETTI, GIULIO. **Fiume, Porto Baross e il Retroterra.** Rome: Maglione e Strini, 1921, 231 p.
A well-informed analysis of the post-war problem of Fiume.

BENEDETTI, GIULIO. **La Pace di Fiume.** Bologna: Zanichelli, 1924, 323 p.
This volume traces the Fiume question, especially its economic aspects, in the period from 1920 to 1924 and examines in great detail the settlement embodied in the final treaty.

BERRI, GINO. **La Gesta di Fiume.** Florence: Bemporad, 1920, 221 p.
An ecstatic chronicle of D'Annunzio's coming and his brief rule.

CARLI, MARIO. **Con D'Annunzio a Fiume.** Milan: Facchi, 1920, 158 p.
One of the best contemporary Italian accounts of the Fiume expedition.

ĆIRIĆ, SLAVKO M. **La Question de Fiume.** Paris: Jouve, 1924, 200 p.
A review of the development of the question from earliest times, based mainly on Jugoslav and French material.

DANIELE, NINO. **D'Annunzio Politico.** São Paulo: Tisi, 1929, 176 p.
A lively and interesting account of the preparation of the Fiume expedition, by one closely associated with the leader.

GIGANTE, SILVINO. **Storia del Comune di Fiume.** Florence: Bemporad, 1928, 284 p.
The author of this convenient general history lays special stress on the stirring events between 1918 and the annexation to Italy.

MACDONALD, J. N. **A Political Escapade.** London: Murray, 1921, 176 p.
The best general account in English of the famous filibustering expedition to Fiume.

MARGONARI, VITTORIO. **Il Comandante.** Milan: Pirola, 1926, 309 p.
Reminiscences of D'Annunzio's Fiume adventure, by one of his enthusiastic followers.

MARTINI, MARIO MARIA. **La Passione di Fiume.** Milan: Sonzogno, 1920, 243 p.
A diary of events during September and November 1919, together with proclamations, decrees, etc.

SUSMEL, EDOARDO. **La Città di Passione.** Milan: Treves, 1921, 358 p.
A stirring account of events in Fiume from 1914 to 1920, by an Italian resident of the city.

TORSIELLO, I. E. **Gli Ultimi Giorni di Fiume Dannunziana.** Bologna: Oberosler, 1921, 183 p.
A chronicle of events during the last days of D'Annunzio's rule, together with interesting documentary material of various sorts.

ZOLI, CORRADO. **Le Giornate di Fiume.** Bologna: Zanichelli, 1921, 138 p.
The notes and impressions of D'Annunzio's under-secretary for foreign affairs.

The South Tyrol Question

ALTROCK, CONSTANTIN VON. **Wetterleuchten im Süden und Osten.** Berlin: Mittler, 1926, 64 p.
An account of the sufferings of the Germans in Carinthia, the Southern Tyrol and Ticino.

BATTISTI, CARLO. **Popoli e Lingue nell'Alto Adige.** Florence: Bemporad, 1931, 400 p.
An elaborate restatement of the "Latinity" of the disputed region.

BORGESE, GIUSEPPE ANTONIO. **L'Alto Adige contro l'Italia.** Milan: Treves, 1921, 111 p.
Letters on conditions, and especially on the autonomist movement in the Tyrol. The author counsels a moderate Italian policy.

FINGELLER, HANS. **Die Wahrheit über Südtirol, 1918-1926.** Munich: Huber, 1926, 24 p.
An exposé of the Italian policy in the southern Tyrol.

FINGELLER, HANS. **Die Wahrheit über Südtirol, 1926-1927.** Innsbruck: Jenny, 1928, 68 p.
Supplementing the previous title.

GIURIATI, GIOVANNI. **La Vigilia.** Milan: Mondadori, 1930, 318 p.
The Fascist leader and former president of the Trento and Trieste Society tells the thrilling story of the society's irredentist activity and agitation in the period from January 1913 to Italy's entrance into the war. An important book.

HERFORD, CHARLES HAROLD, *ed.* **The Case of German South Tyrol against Italy.** London: Allen and Unwin, 1927, 96 p.
A collection of material aiming to set forth the evils of the Italian administration.

HERRE, PAUL. **Die Südtiroler Frage.** Munich: Beck, 1927, 430 p.
A well-known German historian examines the history and development of the problem. The best systematic treatment from the German side.

REUT-NICOLUSSI, EDUARD. **Tyrol under the Axe of Italian Fascism.** London: Allen and Unwin, 1930, 278 p.
The English translation of an effective indictment of the Italian policy, written by an exiled Tyrolese leader. A good formulation of the German grievances.

SONNTAG, JOSEF. **Mussolini's Sendung und die Wahrheit über Tirol.** Leipzig: Foerster, 1928, 111 p.
Another exposure of the Italian nationalist policy as it touches the Germans.

ZIEGER, ANTONIO. **Storia del Trentino e dell'Alto Adige.** Trent: Monauni, 1926, 239 p.
A general illustrated history, from a pronouncedly Italian standpoint.

VATICAN CITY

General

BAGNANI, GILBERT. **Rome and the Papacy.** London: Methuen, 1929, 260 p.
Reviewing the whole history of the Papacy down to the present time, the writer shows how things had to come out as they did. Not very illuminating, and slight on the modern period.

CAIROLI, LUIGI PASQUALE. **La Città del Vaticano.** Monza: Dossi, 1929, 66 p.
The international status of the new Vatican City.

FONTANELLE, R. and STRINATI, R. **S. S. Pio XI.** Rome: Dante Alighieri, 1929, 108 p.
A sober and interesting biography.

FREDIANI, G. **Pio XI.** Rome: Studium, 1929, 235 p.
A biography of the Pope, with much attention given to the recent settlement.

GIANNINI, AMEDEO. **I Concordati Postbellici.** Milan: Vita e Pensiero, 1929, 302 p.
A timely volume on the post-war agreements made by the Papacy.

HAYWARD, FERNAND. **A History of the Popes.** New York: Dutton, 1931, 405 p.
The translation of a general history in French. One of the few books of its kind that has something to say of the recent period.

JARRIGE, RENÉ. **La Condition Internationale du Saint-Siège avant et après les Accords du Latran.** Paris: Rousseau, 1931, 350 p.
Primarily a monographic study of the idea of sovereignty as it appears in the case of the Vatican.

JUDET, ERNEST. **Le Vatican et la Paix.** Paris: Delpeuch, 1927, 314 p.
An important work. The author, who has long been in touch with Vatican circles, attempts to show by elaborate documentation that the Popes, from Leo XIII to Pius XI, have followed undeviatingly a policy of peace.

LA BRIÈRE, YVES DE. **L'Organisation Internationale du Monde Contemporain et la Papauté Souveraine.** Paris: Spès, 1927-1930, 3 v.
A series of essays by a French Catholic scholar, dealing with the Papacy and its attitude to the work of the League, various special problems confronting the Papacy in the post-war period, and the genesis of the Lateran Treaties. A valuable collection.

LAMA, FRIEDRICH, RITTER VON. **Papst und Kurie in Ihrer Politik nach dem Weltkrieg.** Illertissen: Martinus, 1926.
An extensive examination of the position of the Papacy since the war, its activities in the various countries, and especially its relation to Germany. One of the important works on the modern history of the Church.

LE FUR, LOUIS. **Le Saint-Siège et le Droit des Gens.** Paris: Sirey, 1930, 291 p.
A contribution to the knotty problem of the international position of the Papacy, by a leading French jurist.

MÜLLER, JOSEF. **Das Friedenswerk der Kirche in den Letzten Drei Jahrhunderten.** Berlin: Deutsche Verlagsgesellschaft für Politik und Geschichte, 1927, 483 p.
Volume I of a monumental work based upon the Vatican papers. The author here gives about two hundred documents to illustrate the mediations and arbitrations carried through by the Church from 1598 to 1917.

PACELLI, EUGENIO. **Gesammelte Reden.** Berlin: Germania, 1930, 190 p.
Speeches of the former Nuncio to Munich and Berlin, now Papal Secretary of State, largely concerned with international peace and the position of the Papacy.

PERNOT, MAURICE. **Le Saint-Siège, l'Église Catholique et la Politique Mondiale.** Paris: Colin, 1924, 214 p.
A study of the part played by the Church in international affairs in the last twenty-five years, from the Gallican view. One of the best general treatments.

PRATI, CARLO. **Popes and Cardinals in Modern Rome.** New York: Dial, 1927, 233 p.
Largely sketches of life at the Curia and character studies of eminent churchmen.

SERGIUS, *pseud.* **Le Pape d'Hier, le Pape d'Aujourd'hui.** Paris: Delamain, 1922, 144 p.
A judicious analysis of the policies of Benedict XV and Pius XI.

Relations with France

See also (France) General, p. 251.

DELAHAYE, JULES AUGUSTIN. **La Reprise des Relations Diplomatiques avec le Vatican.** Paris: Plon, 1921, 322 p.
This volume consists chiefly of speeches and writings of a French clerical deputy on the vexed problem of French representation at Rome.

FONTAINE, NICOLAS. **Saint Siège, Action Française et Catholiques Intégraux.** Paris: Gamber, 1928, 210 p.
The writer throws light on the *dessous* of the famous conflict, tracing it back to 1903 in a most interesting and penetrating study.

GAY, J. **Les Deux Rome et l'Opinion Française.** Paris: Alcan, 1931, 248 p.
A review of Franco-Italian relations since 1915, with special reference to the French attitude in the Papal question.

LORULOT, ANDRÉ. **L'Église et la Guerre.** Paris: Lorulot, 1932, 180 p.
A French radical view of the policy of the Vatican, with special reference to relations with France and Austria.

Relations with Italy

CIMBALI, EDUARDO. **Roma Italiana e Roma Papale.** Catánia: Giannotta, 1928, 69 p.
An Italian jurist's proposals for a compromise to meet the needs of both Italian and international law.

CIVIS ROMANUS, *pseud.* **The Pope Is King.** New York: Putnam, 1929, 323 p.
A straightforward and detached account of how the Lateran agreements came about, with a description of some of the scenes attending the settlement.

COCHAUX, HENRI. **Le Pape et l'Italie.** Paris: Beauchesne, 1929, 186 p.
A Catholic summary of the Roman question, followed by an enthusiastic analysis of the agreements.

CURATULO, GIACOMO EMILIO. **La Questione Romana da Cavour a Mussolini.** Rome: Littorio, 1928, 235 p.
An historical outline.

Date a Dio. Vatican City: Osservatore Romano, 1930, 160 p.
An effective reply to Missiroli's "Date a Cesare—."

HEARLEY, JOHN. **Pope or Mussolini.** New York: Macaulay, 1929, 256 p.
An American's review of the Roman Question and the settlements of 1929. The author, critical of the policy and tactics on both sides, writes from a strictly liberal viewpoint.

JOHNSON, HUMPHREY JOHN THEWLIS. **The Papacy and the Kingdom of Italy.** London: Sheed and Ward, 1926, 124 p.
A well-informed Catholic account of the development of the Roman Question since 1870.

LOISEAU, CHARLES. **Saint-Siège et Fascisme.** Paris: Gamber, 1930, 240 p.
This is one of the most competent books on the Roman Question. The author begins with the development of the problem after 1870 and follows up this rather conventional account with a detailed review of the position of the Papacy during and after the World War. Stress is laid on relations with the Fascist Government and on the policy of Pius XI. The most important part of the volume is the analysis of the Lateran Treaties and the discussion of their probable political and religious results.

MANSUETI, CESARE. **Il Cardinale Ferrari e la Guerra Europea.** Clusone: Giudici, 1927, 110 p.
Based upon unpublished documents, this study of the activity of the Cardinal Archbishop of Milan is an important contribution to the story of Papal-Italian rapprochement.

MISSIROLI, MARIO. **Date a Cesare—.** Rome: Littorio, 1929, 462 p.
A fervent defense of the Fascist standpoint in the dispute with the Papacy after the signing of the treaty. The author publishes the original demands of the Holy See of 1926 to prove how good were the terms finally secured by the Government.

MOORE, THOMAS EWING. **Peter's City.** New York: Macmillan, 1930, 284 p.
Another well-informed account of the negotiations and the agreements of 1929, by an American diplomat.

NASALLI, ROCCA A. M. **Realismo Nazionale.** Rome: Marino, 1926, 346 p.
Outlines a feasible policy for the Italian Catholics.

ORESTANO, FRANCESCO. **Lo Stato e la Chiesa in Italia.** Rome: Optima, 1927.
An analysis of the Laws of Guarantees, with an examination of the possibilities for a settlement.

ORLANDO, VITTORIO EMANUELE. **Su Alcuni Miei Rapporti di Governo con la Santa Sede.** Naples: Sabina, 1930, 104 p.
The notes of the former Prime Minister throw light on the relations between the Italian Government and the Holy See before and during the war and immediately after.

PARSONS, WILFRID. **The Pope and Italy.** New York: America Press, 1929, 144 p.
A review of the Roman Question, the negotiations and the settlement, written from the Catholic standpoint.

PERTINAX, *pseud.* (ANDRÉ GERAUD). **Le Partage de Rome.** Paris: Grasset, 1929, 310 p.
This is one of the best post-war studies of the Roman Question. The author, the well-known political writer of the *Echo de Paris,* places the Lateran Treaties in their proper historical setting, showing them as a logical development in Vatican foreign policy during the last hundred years. Chapters are set aside for a discussion of the personalities of the Pope, Cardinal Gasparri and Premier Mussolini, while a final chapter reviews the relations of France with the Vatican. The work is documented throughout and shows both care and imagination.

PIOLA, ANDREA. **La Questione Romana nella Storia e nel Diritto.** Padua: C. E. D. A. M., 1931, 398 p.
A documented history of the Roman Question from Cavour to the Lateran Pact.

PUCCI, ENRICO. **La Pace del Vaticano.** Florence: Libreria Fiorentina, 1929, 215 p.
A Catholic study of the evolution of the Roman Question.

RIVET, LOUIS. **La Question Romaine et le Traité du Latran.** Paris: Sirey, 1931, 237 p.
A doctoral dissertation recapitulating the history and terms of the treaties. Contains a good bibliography.

TORRE, GIUSEPPE DALLA. **Postille.** Florence: Libreria Fiorentina, 1929, 162 p.
A collection of authoritative articles on the agreements of 1929, originally published in the *Osservatore Romano.*

TREZZI, G. **La Posizione Giuridica della Santa Sede nel Diritto Internazionale.** Rome: Desclée, 1929, 113 p.
The international aspect of the Lateran settlement, with the texts of the treaty and the concordat.

VOLTAS, PEDRO. **Ciudad del Vaticano e la Cuestión Romana.** Madrid: Corazón de María, 1931, 163 p.
A Spanish view of the settlement of the Roman Question.

WILLIAMSON, BENEDICT. **The Treaty of the Lateran.** London: Burns, Oates, 1929, 102 p.
A brief Catholic statement of the antecedents and negotiation of the agreement, with the pertinent documents.

SPAIN

The Directorate and the Revolution

General

See also (Europe) Constitutional Problems, Dictatorships, p. 227.

ALBA, SANTIAGO. **Espagne.** Paris: Valois, 1930, 174 p.
An important book by a former Spanish Minister of Foreign Affairs, later resident in Paris. He reviews the dictatorship and offers a program.

ALBORNOZ, ALVARO DE. **Intelectuales y Hombres de Acción.** Madrid: Hernández y Galo Sáez, 1927, 318 p.
The conflict between ideals and the hard facts of reality as reflected in the Spanish situation in the time of the dictatorship.

ALBORNOZ, ALVARO DE. **La Tragedia del Estado Español.** Madrid: Raggio, 1925, 256 p.
An analysis of the origins of the dictatorship, and its system.

ALTAMIRA Y CREVEA, RAFAEL. **A History of Spanish Civilization.** London: Constable, 1930, 277 p.
A brilliant synthesis, by an eminent Spanish historian.

ALTAMIRA Y CREVEA, RAFAEL. **Ideario Político.** Valencia: Prometeo, 1921, 227 p.
Notes and impressions, many of them dealing with international affairs of the pre-war and war periods.

ARAQUISTAIN, LUIS. **El Ocaso de un Régimen.** Madrid: Editorial España, 1930, 274 p.
The revised edition of a book written just after the war. A warmly partisan republican view of recent Spanish history, by a well-known journalist, later appointed Ambassador in Berlin.

ARMIÑÁN, JOSÉ MANUEL DE. **Epistolario del Dictador.** Madrid: Morata, 1930, 414 p.
A study of Primo de Rivera as he revealed himself in his letters.

BAELEN, JEAN. **Principaux Traits du Développement Économique de l'Espagne.** Paris: Sagot, 1924, 250 p.
An essay on the economic development of Spain, covering the period from the war to the beginning of the directorate.

BALLESTEROS Y BERETTA, ANTONIO. **Síntesis de Historia de España.** Madrid: Torres, 2nd ed., 1924, 497 p.
An interesting survey by one of the leading Spanish historians.

BISKAYA, LUIS DE. **Los Sembradores del Bien: España con el Directorio.** Madrid: Marzo, 1926, 203 p.
A defense of the directorate, with a survey of its legislative work.

BLASCO IBÁÑEZ, VICENTE. **Alfonso XIII Unmasked. The Military Terror in Spain.** New York: Dutton, 1924, 121 p.
A reprint of violently republican articles by the famous Spanish novelist.

BURGOS Y MAZO, MANUEL DE. **Al Servicio de la Doctrina Constitucional.** Madrid: Morata, 1930, 224 p.
Letters and memoranda of a Liberal senator bearing largely on the establishment of the directorate. The last chapter explains the author's stand in the spring of 1930.

CARRETERO, JOSÉ MARÍA. **España entre dos Libelos.** New York: Publicidad Hispánica, 1925, 100 p.
A reply to the attacks of Ibáñez.

COLA, JULIO. **El Rey y la Política.** Madrid: Gráfica Universal, 1930, 142 p.
The author tackles the vexed question of the King's position and policy.

COOPER, CLAYTON SEDGWICK. **Understanding Spain.** New York: Stokes, 1928, 318 p.
Spanish characteristics investigated by an American traveler and lecturer.

CORTÉS CAVANILLAS, JULIÁN. **La Dictadura y el Dictador.** Madrid: Velasco, 1929, 349 p.
A sympathetic account of the rise of the directorate and its accomplishments.

DEAKIN, FRANK B. **Spain Today.** New York: Knopf, 1924, 221 p.
A frank and critical survey of Spanish conditions today, by an attaché of the British Embassy. One of the best general treatments of Spanish post-war conditions.

DOMINIQUE, PIERRE. **Marche, Espagne.** Paris: Valois, 1931, 288 p.
This is what the French call an *enquête*, that is, a survey of the present state of affairs in Spain. It gives a good general picture of conditions at the birth of the republic.

UN ESPAÑOL NEUTRAL, *pseud.* **Réplica al Conde de Romanones sobre las Responsabilidades del Antiguo Régimen.** Madrid: Voluntad, 1925, 503 p.
A detailed, able reply to the attacks of the Liberal leader.

FALCÓN, CÉSAR. **Crítica de la Revolución Española.** Madrid: Aguilar, 1931, 264 p.
A Spanish communist's attempt to place the revolution in the general setting of Spanish history and the class struggle.

GARCÍA GALLEGO, JERÓNIMO. **Necesidad de Cortes Constituyentes.** Madrid: Asilo de Huérfanos, 1930, 352 p.
A reply to monarchist arguments and a strong presentation of the case against the constitution of 1876.

GARCÍA GALLEGO, JERÓNIMO. **La Quiebra de Nuestro Sistema Político y la Gestación de un Régimen Nuevo.** Vich: Editorial Seráfica, 1928, 810 p.
A critical review of Spanish affairs by a political leader.

GARCÍA GALLEGO, JERÓNIMO. **¿Por Dónde Se Sale?** Madrid: Tipografía de Archivos, 1931, 784 p.
The program of a Spanish leader.

GONZÁLEZ-RUANO, CÉSAR. **Vida, Pensamiento y Aventura de Miguel de Unamuno.** Madrid: Aguilar, 1930, 238 p.
The account of a remarkable career. A biographical sketch of one of Spain's intellectual leaders.

GREENFIELD, ERIC VILLE. **Spain Progresses.** Boston: Badger, 1932, 213 p.
Travel experiences and observations in the new Spain.

HERNÁNDEZ MIR, FRANCISCO. **Un Crimen de Lesa Patria.** Madrid: Compañía General de Artes Gráficas, 1931, 360 p.
The verdict of history on the dictatorship, as predicted by a Spanish liberal.

HUME, MARTIN. **Modern Spain.** London: Unwin, 1923, 598 p.
A new edition of a standard work, with supplementary chapters covering the period to 1918.

IGLESIAS, DALMACIO. **Política de la Dictadura.** Barcelona: Espasa Calpe, 1930, 224 p.
A criticism of the economic policy of the dictatorship, with suggestions for the future.

JOLICLERC, EUGÈNE. **L'Espagne Vivante.** Paris: Roger, 1921, 232 p.
One of the best general books on Spain at the beginning of the post-war period.

LEONHARDT, ERNST JOACHIM. **Währung und Banken in Spanien.** Jena: Fischer, 1925, 190 p.
A general scholarly study of the banks and currency of Spain. The larger part is devoted to the war and post-war period.

McCABE, JOSEPH. **Spain in Revolt.** London: Lane, 1931, 246 p.
A popular survey of the evolution of the Spanish attitude towards the monarchy and the Church during the last century.

MADARIAGA, SALVADOR DE. **Spain.** New York: Scribner, 1930, 507 p.
A volume in the "Modern World" Series, by an internationally-known Spanish writer and statesman. Madariaga reviews the history and culture of the Spaniards by way of preface to an analysis of the great problems of the post-war period. The writer is frankly on the constitutional side.

MAURA Y GAMAZO, GABRIEL, CONDE DE LA MORTERA. **Bosquejo Histórico de la Dictadura.** Madrid: Tipografía de Archivos, 1930, 2 v.
Written by a prominent Spanish statesman and historian, this is one of the best detailed accounts of the dictatorship, from its inception to its fall.

MAURIN, JOAQUÍN. **Los Hombres de la Dictadura.** Madrid: Cenit, 1930, 241 p.
This volume contains biographical sketches of Sánchez Guerra, Cambó, Iglesias, Largo Caballero, Lerroux and Melquiades Alvarez, men much in the public eye.

NICOLAU D'OLWER, LLUIS. **La Lliçó de la Dictadura.** Barcelona: Edición Catalonia, 1931, 244 p.
A prominent republican's collected writings, dealing with problems of liberty and liberalism, the state, the Catalan question, the religious issue, etc.

ORTEGA Y GASSET, EDUARDO. **La Verdad sobre la Dictadura.** Paris: Librairie Cervantes, 1925, 340 p.
A contribution to the recent history of Spain, highly hostile to the dictatorship, by a leading political philosopher.

ORTEGA Y GASSET, JOSÉ. **Rectificación de la República.** Madrid: Revista de Occidente, 1931, 170 p.
A collection of speeches and articles.

ORTEGA Y GASSET, JOSÉ. **La Redención de las Provincias y la Decencia Nacional.** Madrid: Revista de Occidente, 1931, 218 p.
A collection of articles on the constitutional question, written between 1927 and 1930 by one of the intellectual leaders of the Spanish revolution.

PEMARTIN, JOSÉ. **Los Valores Históricos en la Dictadura Española.** Santander: Arte y Ciencia, 1928, 656 p.
A suggestive study of the dictatorship in its larger historical setting.

PÉREZ, DIONISIO. **La Dictadura a Través de Sus Notas Oficiosas.** Madrid: Compañía General de Artes Gráficas, 1930, 339 p.
A useful compendium of the leading decrees of the Rivera period.

PILAR, PRINCESS OF BAVARIA and CHAPMAN-HUSTON, DESMOND. **Every Inch a King.** New York: Dutton, 1931, 485 p.
Though written by a relative of the King and designed to exonerate him, this biography of Alfonso XIII is a serious book that repays reading.

RECASÉNS SICHES, LUIS. **El Poder Constituyente.** Madrid: Morata, 1931, 191 p.
A philosophical disquisition on the theory of constituent power, and on the justification for revolution, with reference to Spanish problems.

REPARAZ, GONZALO. **Los Borbones de España.** Madrid: Morata, 1931, 298 p.
The subtitle of this book is: "The Pathological History of a Degenerate Dynasty."

RIGGS, ARTHUR STANLEY. **The Spanish Pageant.** Indianapolis: Bobbs-Merrill, 1928, 416 p.
Impressions formed during twenty-five years of study and residence.

ROMANONES, ALVARO FIGUEROA Y TORRES, CONDE DE. **Las Responsabilidades Políticas del Antiguo Régimen de 1875 a 1923.** Madrid: Renacimiento, 1924, 363 p.
Written by a Liberal monarchist statesman, this is one of the most important critical reviews of the last fifty years of Spanish history. It contains, among other things, an admirable survey of Spanish foreign policy.

ROMANONES, ALVARO FIGUEROA Y TORRES, CONDE DE. **Las Últimas Horas de una Monarquía.** Madrid: Morata, 1931, 136 p.
A collection of writings by the well-known Spanish statesman, a member of the last ministry of the monarchy.

SÁNCHEZ GUERRA, RAFAEL. **Dictadura, Indiferencia, República.** Madrid: Compañía General de Artes Gráficas, 1931, 285 p.
A collection of writings, several dealing with international relations, by an able and active republican publicist.

SANTA CARA, JOAQUÍN ARGAMASILLA DE LA CERDA Y BAYONA, MARQUÉS DE. **En Honor de la Verdad.** Madrid: Pueyo, 1930, 214 p.
In defense of the dictatorship.

SEDGWICK, HENRY DWIGHT. **Spain, a Short History of Its Politics, Literature and Art.** Boston: Little, Brown, 1925, 419 p.
An excellent brief survey, by a competent American essayist and historian.

SENCOURT, ROBERT. **The Spanish Crown.** New York: Scribner, 1932, 399 p.
A sympathetic account of the Spanish monarchy in the nineteenth and twentieth centuries.

TARDUCHY, EMILIO R. **Psicología del Dictador y Caracteres Más Salientes de la Dictadura en España.** Madrid: Junta de Propaganda Patriótica, 1929, 320 p.
More evidence of the rising tide of resentment that swept Primo de Rivera away.

THARAUD, JÉRÔME and JEAN. **Rendez-vous Espagnols.** Paris: Plon, 1925, 84 p.
The well-known politico-novelists reach Spain. Stimulating and original reflections on currents and events.

TORRUBIANO RIPOLL, JAIME. **Política Religiosa de la Democracia Española.** Madrid: Morata, 1931, 326 p.
A good exposition and critique of one of the most important aspects of republican policy.

VILLANUEVA, FRANCISCO. **El Momento Constitucional.** Madrid: Morata, 1929, 390 p.
An analysis of the attitude of Spanish groups towards the program of the future, with a discussion of various past constitutions and of new projects.

VILLANUEVA, FRANCISCO. **Obstáculos Tradicionales.** Madrid: Atlántida, 1930, 270 p.
The first volume of an extensive polemical chronicle of the dictatorship and the revolution. The later volumes are "La Dictadura Militar" (Madrid: Morata, 1930, 232 p.); "¿Qué Ha Pasado Aquí?" (ibid. 1930, 188 p.); "¡No Pasa Nada!" (ibid. 1931, 222 p.); "¿Ha Pasado Algo?" (ibid. 1931, 227 p.).

The Catalan Question

BROUSSE, GEORGES. **La Question Catalane.** Perpignan: Indépendant, 1928, 96 p.
An excellent survey of one of the most urgent constitutional questions of Spain.

La Catalogne Rebelle. Paris: Agence Mondiale, 1927.
An important volume containing documents on the Catalan nationalist movement.

DOMINGO, MARCELINO. ¿ **On Va Catalunya?** Barcelona: Llansás, 1927, 228 p.
An important contribution to the history of the movement.

DWELSHAUVERS, GEORGES. **La Catalogne et le Problème Catalan.** Paris: Alcan, 1926, 236 p.
A full treatment of the Catalan side.

ESTELRICH, JUAN LUIS. **De la Dictadura a la República.** Barcelona: Librería Catalónia, 1931, 221 p.
Essays and speeches dealing with the Catalonian problem.

LARCEGUÍ, FRANCISCO DE S. **Cataluña y la Nacionalidad Española.** Madrid: Agencia General de Librería, 1927, 228 p.
A general review of Catalan and Spanish history and culture, to show that Catalonia is only a region within the larger Spain.

NANCY, AD. **La Catalogne et Sa Lutte pour la Liberté Nationale.** Paris: Les Documents Européens, 1924, 44 p.
The geography, economics and culture of Catalonia, together with a strongly partisan account of the nationalist movement.

PICÓN, JOSÉ GAYA. **La Jornada Histórica de Barcelona.** Madrid: Castro, 1931, 123 p.
The author discusses the problem of autonomy as against centralization, and reviews the Catalan negotiations with Madrid.

PUJOLS, FRANCISCO. **La Solució Cambó.** Barcelona: Librería Catalónia, 1931, 197 p.
An interview with one of the most prominent Catalan leaders.

ROVIRA I VIRGILI, ANTONI. **Catalunya i la República.** Barcelona: Librería Catalónia, 1931, 271 p.
Contains a large number of interesting documents touching on the question of Catalan autonomy in the last fifty years.

Foreign Policy

See also (Latin America) Pan-Hispanism, p. 199; also (Africa) Tangier Problem, p. 521.

UN ESPAÑOL NEUTRAL, *pseud.* **España en la Política Internacional.** Madrid: Talleres, 1926, 248 p.
The best general review of the international position of Spain, with an introduction by Don Gabriel Maura.

MOUSSET, ALBERT. **L'Espagne dans la Politique Mondiale.** Paris: Bossard, 1923, 348 p.
A review of the foreign policy of Spain in the last half-century by a former attaché of the French Embassy at Madrid. The most serviceable general study.

Colonial Policy; the War in Morocco

See also (Africa: French Possessions) Morocco, p. 517.

ALFARO Y ZARABOZO, SABAS. **Geografía de Marruecos.** Toledo: Colegio de María Cristina, 1920, 159 p.
Really a demographic study not only of Morocco, but of the western Sahara and Spanish Guinea as well.

Arija, Julio. **La Guinea Española y Sus Riquezas.** Madrid: Espasa Calpe, 1930, 229 p.
An excellent book on the Spanish possessions in West Africa.

Armiñán, José Manuel de and Luis de. **Francia, el Dictador y el Moro.** Madrid: Morata, 1930, 233 p.
An historical reconsideration of French and Spanish policy in Morocco during the dictatorship. The "truth" about Primo de Rivera's action and a severe indictment of the Spanish directorate.

Berenguer, General. **Campañas en el Rif y Yebala, 1921-1922.** Madrid: Velasco, 1923, 267 p.
Diaries and notes of a Spanish commander, of great value for the study of the Spanish campaign.

Bueno y Nuñez de Prado, Emilio. **Historia de la Acción de España en Marruecos.** Madrid: Ibérica, 1929, 255 p.
Discusses the evolution of Spanish policy in Morocco from 1904 to 1927.

Cansino Roldán, Luis. **Recuerdos de Marruecos.** Málaga: Zambrana, 1923, 330 p.
Travels in Northern Morocco, with some discerning remarks on historical and political aspects.

Carpio, Julio del. **Por Ceuta, Tetuán y Tánger.** Madrid: Nieto, 1925, 101 p.
Experiences with the Spanish troops in North Africa.

España, Juan de. **La Actuación de España en Marruecos.** Madrid: Velasco, 1926, 369 p.
An extended account of Spanish interests and policies in Morocco to 1925.

Gómez Hidalgo, F. **Marruecos, la Tragedia Prevista.** Madrid: Pueyo, 1921, 296 p.
An important criticism of the Spanish command and the campaign under General Berenguer.

Hernández Mir, Francisco. **Del Desastre a la Victoria.** Madrid: Fe, 1927, 259 p.
The Spanish campaign in the Rif from 1921 to 1926.

Hernández Mir, Francisco. **La Dictadura en Marruecos.** Madrid: Morata, 1930, 244 p.
A detailed and well-informed indictment of the Moroccan policy of the dictatorship in 1923-1924.

López Rienda, Rafael. **Raisuni.** Madrid: Sociedad General Española de Librería, 1923, 297 p.
A study more especially of Raisuni's relations with the Spaniards.

Martinez de Campos, Arsenio. **Melilla 1921.** Ciudad Real: El Pueblo Manchego, 1922, 365 p.
A Spanish politician's speeches on the Moroccan problem, together with miscellaneous notes on the campaign, discussion of financial aspects, etc.

Queipo de Llano, G. **El General Queipo de Llano Perseguido por la Dictadura.** Madrid: Morata, 1930, 247 p.
The apology and defense of one of the Spanish commanders in the Riffian War.

Reparaz, Gonzalo. **Alfonso XIII y Sus Cómplices.** Madrid: Morata, 1931, 471 p.
An important book, written by the former Spanish special commissioner in Morocco. A bitter and violent attack on Alfonso and his military advisers.

Sánchez, José G. **Nuestro Protectorado.** Madrid: Fuentenebro, 1930, 346 p.
Chiefly a geographical and descriptive study of the Rif.

PORTUGAL

See also (South America) Brazil, p. 216; also (Africa) Portuguese Possessions, p. 528.

GARCITORAL, ALICIO. **Notas sobre Portugal.** Barcelona: Sociedad General Española, 1928, 105 p.
Political observations on the Portuguese dictatorship.

GUYOMARD, GEORGES. **La Dictature Militaire au Portugal.** Paris: Presses Universitaires, 1927, 112 p.
A Frenchman's dispassionate account of his observations in Portugal. One of the best general studies.

LEGRAND, THÉODORIC. **Histoire du Portugal.** Paris: Payot, 1928, 175 p.
A general outline, brief on the nineteenth and twentieth centuries.

NUNES, LEOPOLDO. **A Ditadura Militar.** Lisbon: Anuário Comercial, 1928, 298 p.
A Portuguese journalist's record of the events of 1926 to 1928.

SARDINHA, ANTONIO. **La Alianza Peninsular.** Madrid: Junta de Propaganda Patriótica, 1930, 378 p.
Essays by a Portuguese leader, setting forth the idea of Peninsula unity and solidarity.

VASCONCELLOS, ERNESTO DE. **As Colónias Portuguesas.** Lisbon: Teixeira, 1921, 658 p.
A detailed survey of the Portuguese colonial empire in its geographic, economic, political and administrative aspects. The third edition of a standard work.

IV. CENTRAL EUROPE

GENERAL; MIDDLE EUROPEAN SCHEMES, ETC.

See also (Europe) Pan-European Schemes, p. 229; also (Central Europe) The Little Entente, p. 304; also (Austria) The Anschluss Problem, p. 307.

AULNEAU, JOSEPH. **Histoire de l'Europe Centrale.** Paris: Payot, 1926, 656 p.
An attempt to present the history of Central Europe as a whole. A useful textbook, though slight on the modern period.

BAROLIN, JOHANNES CARL and SCHECHNER, KURT. **Für und wider die Donauföderation.** Vienna: Braumüller, 1926, 150 p.
Two suggestive essays. The first author pleads for a confederation for economic reasons; the second deprecates it for national reasons.

BUDAY, KÁLMAN. **The International Position of Hungary and the Succession States.** Budapest: Légrády, 1931, 118 p.
A study of the situation created by the Treaty of Trianon's violation of "economic imperatives," with emphasis on the League's activities in the resulting situation.

CSIKAY, PÁL. **L'Europe Centrale Économique et Sociale.** Paris: Alcan, 1931, 160 p.
This book is in reality only another presentation of the Hungarian problem and an argument for revision of the treaties.

EISENMANN, LOUIS and others. **Les Problèmes de l'Europe Centrale.** Paris: Alcan, 1923, 202 p.
A collection of lectures on various phases of Central European problems by leading French authorities.

GEDYE, GEORGE ERIC ROWE. **Heirs to the Habsburgs.** London: Arrowsmith, 1932, 291 p.
The Succession States described rather subjectively by an English correspondent.

GRAHAM, MALBONE WATSON. **The New Governments of Central Europe.** New York: Holt, 1927, 826 p.
A description of the new constitutions of Germany, Austria, Hungary, Czechoslovakia and Jugoslavia.

GRÁTZ, GUSZTÁV and SCHÜLLER, RICHARD. **Äussere Wirtschaftspolitik Österreich-Ungarns: Mitteleuropäische Pläne.** New Haven: Yale University Press, 1925, 334 p.
One of the outstanding books in the Carnegie Series. The authors, high Austrian officials, enter upon a detailed discussion of Austro-German economic negotiations and schemes for pooling the resources of Central Europe.

GÜRGE, WILHELM and GOTKOPP, W., *eds.* **Grossraumwirtschaft.** Berlin: Organisation, 1931, 160 p.
A collection of essays on the economic union of Central and Southeastern Europe, which the writers believe to be the only solution of the continent's ills.

GUEST, LESLIE HADEN. **The Struggle for Power in Europe, 1917-1921.** London: Hodder and Stoughton, 1922, 318 p.
An interesting but only fairly judicious survey of post-war developments in Central and Eastern Europe, by a British Laborite.

HANTOS, ELEMÉR. **Die Handelspolitik in Mitteleuropa.** Jena: Fischer, 1925, 111 p.
An indictment of the existing methods of exclusion and a plea for lower tariffs or tariff union.

HANTOS, ELEMÉR. **Mitteleuropäische Eisenbahnpolitik. Mitteleuropäische Wasserstrassenpolitik. Mitteleuropäischer Postverein.** Vienna: Braumüller, 1929, 112, 194, 85 p.
Three monographic studies by a leading advocate of the economic union of Central Europe.

HANTOS, ELEMÉR. **Mitteleuropäische Kartelle im Dienste des Industriellen Zusammenschlusses.** Berlin: Organisation, 1931, 86 p.
A discussion of the significance of large industrial combines in binding together the European nations.

HANTOS, ELEMÉR. **L'Europe Centrale.** Paris: Alcan, 1932, 258 p.
A persistent Hungarian protagonist of *Mitteleuropa* draws together his suggestions for a new economic organization of the region.

KÁSZONYI, FRANZ. **Rassenverwandtschaft der Donauvoelker.** Vienna: Amalthea, 1931, 271 p.
This is not a scientific treatise, but rather a plea for the cultivation of common ideals and a new brotherliness among the Danube peoples, to replace rampant and disastrous nationalism.

LÉMONON, ERNEST. **La Nouvelle Europe Centrale et Son Bilan Économique, 1919-1930.** Paris: Alcan, 1931, 260 p.
An authoritative review of the developments in Austria, Hungary, Czechoslovakia, Jugoslavia, Rumania, Poland and Italy to the time of the Young Plan and the Hague Conference.

LYON, LAURANCE. **The Fruits of Folly.** London: Hutchinson, 1929, 320 p.
Impressions of the situation in Central Europe, by the author of "The Pomp of Power."

ORMESSON, WLADIMIR, COMTE D'. **Nos Illusions sur l'Europe Centrale.** Paris: Plon, 1923, 142 p.
A survey of contemporary conditions in Central Europe, with a convincing plea for a more constructive international policy towards that area.

PASVOLSKY, LEO. **Economic Nationalism of the Danubian States.** New York: Macmillan, 1929, 636 p.
A volume surveying the pre-war situation, the consequences of the dissolution of the Hapsburg Monarchy, and the work of reconstruction. One of the most valuable treatments in English.

SCHACHER, GERHARD. **Die Nachfolgestaaten und Ihre Wirtschaftlichen Kräfte.** Stuttgart: Enke, 1932, 286 p.
The author, who has already written an excellent book on the economic resources of the Balkan states, here surveys Austria, Hungary and Czechoslovakia.

SEBESS, DÉNES. **Die Neuen Agrardemokratien.** Lugos: Husvéth und Hoffer, 1926, 110 p.
The economic situation in the Succession States, set forth in the style of Count Teleki.

SOULANGE-BODIN, ANDRÉ. **À Travers la Nouvelle Europe.** Paris: Perrin, 1925, 294 p.
The experiences of a French diplomat, important in the study of the history of the Danubian countries since the war.

THOMSON, CHRISTOPHER BIRDWOOD THOMSON, BARON. **Victors and Vanquished.** London: Cape, 1924, 124 p.
A survey of political conditions and international relations in Central Europe and the Balkans, by an observer affiliated with the Labor Party.

TÖRÖK, ARPÁD. **Die Wirtschaftskrise in Mitteleuropa.** Novivrbas: Pleesz, 1925, 99 p.
The economic situation in the Danubian countries described from the Magyar viewpoint.

WIRSING, GISELHER. **Zwischeneuropa und die Deutsche Zukunft.** Jena: Diederich, 1932, 329 p.
An exposition of the facts that call for the introduction of federalism in Central Europe.

X 7, *pseud.* **The Return of the Kings. Facts about the Conspiracy for the Restoration of Monarchy in Central Europe.** New York: Dodd, 1925, 271 p.
Sensational and unconvincing revelations.

ZIEGLER, WILHELM. **Mitteleuropäischer Zollvergleich.** Vienna: Braumüller, 1932, 104 p.
An Austrian diplomat brings forward original and stimulating suggestions for the reorganization of Central Europe on the basis of tariff adjustments.

ZINGARELLI, ITALO. **Das Erbe von Versailles.** Vienna: Amalthea, 1930, 405 p.
An Italian correspondent surveys the wreckage in Central Europe and the Balkans.

THE COLLAPSE OF THE HAPSBURG EMPIRE

See also (World War) Biographies of Wartime Statesmen and Diplomats, p. 101, and Military Memoirs and Biographies, p. 117, and Russian Front, p. 130, and Austro-Italian Front, p. 132; also (Peace Negotiations) Preliminary Discussions and Armistice Negotiations, p. 156; also Hungary, p. 308; also (Czechoslovakia) Establishment of the State, p. 313; also (Poland) Resurrection of the State, p. 347; also (Jugoslavia) General, p. 407; etc.

AUERBACH, BERTRAND. **L'Autriche et la Hongrie pendant la Guerre.** Paris: Alcan, 1925, 627 p.
An objective and understanding analysis of the main movements and opinions of the war period, based on newspaper files and other published materials.

BAGGER, EUGENE SZEKERES. **Francis Joseph.** New York: Putnam, 1927, 572 p.
A general biography, written by a Hungarian-American and reflecting the Hungarian view. Now superseded by the biographies of Redlich and Tschuppik.

BAUER, OTTO. **Die Oesterreichische Revolution.** Vienna: Verlag der Wiener Volksbuchhandlung, 1923, 293 p.
A general study of the war years, the conflict of nationalities and the class struggle, by an Austrian socialist leader.

CHLUMECKÝ, LEOPOLD, FREIHERR VON. **Erzherzog Franz Ferdinands Wirken und Wollen.** Berlin: Verlag für Kulturpolitik, 1929, 378 p.
This study of the Archduke, written by one who was closely associated with him, is the best that has been published. The emphasis is laid particularly on the Archduke's plan for a reorganization of the Empire on trialistic basis.

CLOPOŢEL, I. **Revoluţia din 1918 şi Unirea Ardealului cu România.** Cluj, 1926, 174 p.
A Rumanian's account of the collapse of Central Europe in 1918 and the circumstances of Transylvania's union with Rumania.

DEUTSCH, JULIUS. **Aus Oesterreichs Revolution.** Vienna: Volksbuchhandlung, 1921, 147 p.
An important contribution to the story of the stormy winter of 1918-1919, by a former Austrian minister.

EISENMENGER, VICTOR. **Archduke Francis Ferdinand.** London: Selwyn, 1931, 285 p.
An unvarnished character study, by the Archduke's personal physician. Not very important.

FREI, BRUNO. **Die Roten Matrosen von Cattaro.** Vienna: Verlag der Wiener Volksbuchhandlung, 1927, 84 p.
A little-known episode in the history of the war, the Austrian naval mutiny of February 1, 1918, during which 6,000 sailors raised the red flag, formed sailors' councils and accepted the "fourteen points."

GARGAS, SIGISMUND. **Le Problème du Fédéralisme en Autriche-Hongrie.** Paris: Giard, 1927, 44 p.
An interesting essay on the much-discussed question of the constitutional organization of the old monarchy.

GLAISE VON HORSTENAU, EDMUND. **The Collapse of the Austro-Hungarian Empire.** London: Dent, 1930, 348 p.
Probably the best single account of the Empire's collapse from the Austrian side. Written by the director of the Vienna war archives. In this English edition some changes and omissions have been made.

GOPČEVIĆ, SPIRIDION. **Oesterreichs Untergang.** Berlin: Siegismund, 1920, 343 p.
An unscientific and rather sensational account of the transgressions of Francis Joseph and his government.

GRÁTZ, GUSZTÁV and SCHÜLLER, RICHARD. **Der Wirtschaftliche Zusammenbruch Oesterreich-Ungarns.** New Haven: Yale University Press, 1930, 308 p.
A volume in the Carnegie Series, and an important addition to the literature on Austria's collapse. The authors outline the early economic history of the monarchy and study in detail the food shortage and other phenomena. Important documents in the appendix.

HEVESY, ANDRÉ DE. **L'Agonie d'un Empire: L'Autriche-Hongrie.** Paris: Perrin, 1923, 281 p.
A general survey of the decline and fall of the Hapsburg Empire, written from the liberal Hungarian standpoint. Contains some interesting material from the Tisza papers.

JÁSZI, OSZKÁR. **The Dissolution of the Habsburg Monarchy.** Chicago: Chicago University Press, 1929, 512 p.
The author had distinguished himself before the war by his enlightened writings on the Hapsburg problem, and served as Minister of National Minorities in the ill-fated Károlyi cabinet of 1919. He here discusses the historical development of the question, laying stress not only on the racial aspect, but on economic and psychological factors. The book shows grasp and breadth of view. With an extensive bibliography.

KLEINWÄCHTER, FRIEDRICH VON. **Der Untergang der Oesterreich-Ungarischen Monarchie.** Leipzig: Koehler, 1920, 331 p.
One of the earliest and still one of the best general treatments of the collapse.

MARGUTTI, ALBERT, FREIHERR VON. **The Emperor Francis Joseph and His Times.** London: Hutchinson, 1921, 379 p.
An understanding study of the Emperor in the years 1900-1917, by one who was in close touch with him.

MOLISCH, PAUL. **Geschichte der Deutschnationalen Bewegung in Oesterreich von Ihren Anfängen bis zum Verfall der Monarchie.** Jena: Fischer, 1926, 278 p.
A standard history of the German nationalist movement in Austria to 1918.

NIKITSCH, PAUL. **Vor dem Sturm.** Berlin: Verlag für Kulturpolitik, 1925, 203 p.
Reminiscences of Francis Ferdinand, by his secretary.

NOWAK, KARL FRIEDRICH. **The Collapse of Central Europe.** New York: Dutton, 1924, 365 p.
One of the most vivid pictures of events in Germany and especially in Austria-Hungary from Brest-Litovsk to the breakdown of the Central Powers. Written by a journalist attached to headquarters.

OPOČENSKÝ, JAN. **Umsturz in Mitteleuropa.** Hellerau: Avalun, 1932, 464 p.
The German translation of an important Czech work on the downfall of the Hapsburg Monarchy and the rise of the Succession States.

POLZER-HODITZ und WOLFRAMITZ, ARTHUR, GRAF VON. **Life of Emperor Karl.** New York: Putnam, 1930, 470 p.
The English translation of the best biography of the last Austrian Emperor, written by his Chief of Cabinet and containing much new information.

POPOVICS, ALEXANDER. **Das Geldwesen im Kriege.** New Haven: Yale University Press, 1925, 185 p.
An authoritative financial history of the Dual Monarchy during the war, in the Carnegie Series.

REDLICH, JOSEF. **Austrian War Government.** New Haven: Yale University Press, 1929, 187 p.
The translation of one of the best and most valuable volumes in the Carnegie Series, by the last Austro-Hungarian Minister of Finance, an internationally known authority on constitutional law.

REDLICH, JOSEF. **Emperor Francis Joseph of Austria.** New York: Macmillan, 1929, 547 p.
The life of Francis Joseph is inseparable from the history of his time and his country, and this book is at the same time a fine character study and a searching analysis of the whole Austro-Hungarian problem. All in all, this is the best biography of the Emperor and one of the most enlightening books on the decline of the Hapsburg Empire.

SETON-WATSON, ROBERT WILLIAM. **Europe in the Melting Pot.** London: Macmillan, 1919, 400 p.

Miscellaneous papers on political questions, men and events, mainly in Central Europe in the war period. Many of them appeared originally in *The New Europe*, of which Dr. Seton-Watson was the editor.

SOSNOSKY, THEODOR VON. **Franz Ferdinand.** Munich: Oldenbourg, 1929, 255 p.
A first-rate study of the Archduke, by an able historian. The stress is on the ideas of the Archduke in matters of foreign policy. The author explodes the idea that Francis Ferdinand was the leader of a war party or that he desired war at any time.

STEINITZ, EDUARD, RITTER VON, *ed.* **Erinnerungen an Kaiser Franz Joseph I.** Berlin: Verlag für Kulturpolitik, 1930, 438 p.
A valuable collection of essays on various aspects of Franz Joseph's activities, written by those who were closely associated with him.

SZILASSY, GYULA, BÁRÓ. **Der Untergang der Donau-Monarchie.** Berlin: Berger, 1921, 422 p.
The recollections of an Austro-Hungarian diplomatist, covering the years 1908 to 1919. The relation of Berchtold to Serbian policy is illuminated.

TOSTI, AMEDEO. **Come Ci Vide l'Austria Imperiale.** Milan: Mondadori, 1930, 310 p.
A well-documented general history, military and political, of the war period and the collapse.

TROUD, JÉRÔME. **Charles I, Empereur d'Autriche, Roi de Hongrie.** Paris: Plon, 1931, 244 p.
Really a plea for the restoration of the unity of the Hapsburg dominions. The viewpoint is that of the Hungarian loyalists.

TSCHUPPIK, KARL. **Francis Joseph I.** New York: Harcourt, 1930, 509 p.
A creditable and interestingly written biography, not as profound as Redlich's, but fuller in many ways, especially on the later period.

WIESER, FRIEDRICH, FREIHERR VON. **Oesterreichs Ende.** Berlin: Ullstein, 1919, 317 p.
A former Austrian official reviews the nationalities problem and the social antagonisms, and gives a general account of the catastrophic end of the monarchy.

WINDISCH-GRAETZ, LAJOS, HERCZEG. **My Memoirs.** London: Allen and Unwin, 1921, 350 p.
The memoirs of a member of the Austrian Foreign Office at the time of the collapse, throwing considerable light on the confused events of 1918-1919 in Hungary.

THE LITTLE ENTENTE

See also (Central Europe) Middle European Schemes, p. 299; also (Czechoslovakia) Post-War History, Foreign and Domestic Problems, p. 315; also (Rumania) General, p. 402; also (Jugoslavia) General, p. 407.

CODRESCO, FLORIN. **La Petite Entente.** Paris: Les Presses Modernes, 1930, 710 p.
An excellent doctoral dissertation, by far the most detailed and complete treatment of the subject. The author has consulted not only the bound literature, but many newspapers. The work contains an exhaustive bibliography.

CRANE, JOHN OLIVER. **The Little Entente.** New York: Macmillan, 1931, 239 p.
A good general survey, reviewing the steps by which the treaties were made and setting forth the present situation in Central and Eastern Europe. The viewpoint is quite pronouncedly Czech.

MACHRAY, ROBERT. **The Little Entente.** New York: R. R. Smith, 1929, 394 p.
An account of the making of the treaties and the action of the Little Entente to 1928. The chief merit of the book is in the setting. The author gives enough of Central and Southeastern European history to make the combination and its action understandable.

MALYNSKI, EMMANUEL, COUNT. **Les Problèmes de l'Est et la Petite Entente.** Paris: Éditions Hispano-Françaises, 1931, 560 p.
A description of the post-war situation in Eastern Europe, especially as it affects Poland, and of the present status of the Little Entente.

MOUSSET, ALBERT. **La Petite Entente.** Paris: Bossard, 1923, 192 p.
A competent early account of the making of the treaties and the first positive actions of the combination. By a Frenchman resident for some time in Belgrade.

AUSTRIA

General

See also (Italy) The South Tyrol Question, p. 289.

ADAMOVICH, LUDWIG. **Grundriss des Oesterreichischen Staatsrechtes.** Vienna: Staatsdruckerei, 1927, 647 p.
An exposition of the constitution and administrative law of the new republic.

BASCH, ANTONIN and DVOŘÁČEK, JAN. **Austria and Its Economic Existence.** Prague: Orbis, 1925, 106 p.
A brief review of Austria's sources of income and economic structure. The authors recommend a system of preferential duties among the Succession States.

BOUSQUET, GEORGES HENRI. **La Restauration Monétaire et Financière de l'Autriche.** Paris: Rivière, 1926, 158 p.
A substantial and reliable account by the former secretary of control.

DECOUDU, JEAN. **Le Partage des Dettes Publiques Autrichiennes et Hongroises, 1918-1926.** Paris: Sagot, 1926, 157 p.
A dissertation which reviews the settlement of the Austrian debt through the peace treaties, the action of the reparations commission, and the association of bondholders.

DUNAN, MARCEL. **L'Autriche.** Paris: Rieder, 1921, 125 p.
A general descriptive study of the new Austria, by the special correspondent of the Paris *Temps.*

EISENMANN, CHARLES. **Dix Ans d'Histoire Constitutionelle Autrichienne.** Paris: Giard, 1928, 73 p.
A brief survey, by a leading French authority.

FEILER, ARTHUR. **Das Neue Österreich.** Frankfurt: Frankfurter Societätsdruckerei, 1924, 120 p.
By the editor of the *Frankfurter Zeitung;* a discerning critical survey of the Austrian scene after the restorative action of the League.

FRANCK, PAUL. **La Reconstitution Financière de l'Autriche.** Paris: Rhea, 1925, 263 p.
An investigation of the work done by the League, with all the important documents.

HUDECZEK, KARL. **The Economic Resources of Austria.** London: Dawson, 1922, 74 p.
A brief picture of Austria's economic situation and the obstacles in the way of its development.

KELSEN, HANS. **Die Verfassungsgesetze der Republik Deutschoesterreich.** Vienna: Deuticke, 1919, 248 p.
The best edition of the Austrian constitution, with expert commentary.

KERVÉGAN, JEAN. **L'Autriche en 1920.** Paris: Messein, 1921, 122 p.
Dancing while Rome burns—a not very convincing study of the situation and the people.

KLEINSCHMIED, OSKAR. **Schober.** Vienna: Manz, 1930, 323 p.
An excellent general biography, stressing Schober's reforms as minister of police and his contribution to the economic salvation of Austria.

LOVCHEVIĆ, JOVAN. **La Restauration des Finances Autrichiennes.** Paris: Vie Universitaire, 1924, 299 p.
A well-documented dissertation analyzing the bases of Austria's economic crisis and the action of the League.

MACARTNEY, CARLILE AYLMER. **The Social Revolution in Austria.** New York: Macmillan, 1927, 288 p.
A detailed and judicious account of the internal developments in Austria since 1914. The best work on the subject in English.

MERKL, ADOLF. **Die Verfassung der Republik Deutschoesterreich.** Vienna: Deuticke, 1919, 184 p.
A commentary on the constitution by an official who took part in the drafting.

MIRKIN-GETSEVICH, BORIS SERGIEEVICH and TIBAL, ANDRÉ. **L'Autriche.** Paris: Delagrave, 1932, 142 p.
An excellent French survey, with a useful collection of documents.

MORGAIN, GEORGES. **La Couronne Autrichienne depuis le Traité de Saint-Germain.** Paris: Sirey, 1927, 331 p.
A detailed dissertation on the collapse and stabilization of the Austrian currency between 1919 and 1924.

NEUMANN, LUDWIG. **Oesterreichs Wirtschaftliche Gegenwart und Zukunft.** Vienna: Halm und Goldmann, 1927, 83 p.
An industrialist surveys the situation and suggests remedies.

SCHEICHELBAUER, BERNHARDT. **Aufrichtigkeit, Klarheit, Verständigung.** Klagenfurt: Leon Sen, 1932, 104 p.
An Austrian reply to complaints made by the Slovene minorities in Austria.

SCHWARZ, ROBERT PH. **L'Autriche de 1919-1924.** Paris: Pedone, 1926, 152 p.
A survey of the economic and financial problems in the critical post-war lustrum.

SEIPEL, IGNAZ. **Der Kampf um die Oesterreichische Verfassung.** Vienna: Braumüller, 1930, 379 p.
Speeches and essays by the Austrian statesman.

SOZIUS, *pseud.* (ELI RUBIN). **Ignaz Seipel.** Vienna: Wiener Volksschriften, 1929, 144 p.
An appreciative but rather sensational and scrappy study of Seipel's achievement.

TRAZIT, RENÉ. **La Constitution d'Autriche.** Toulouse: Société Méridionale, 1925, 322 p.
A well-documented analysis, with historical background.

WALRÉ DE BORDES, J. VAN. **The Austrian Crown.** London: King, 1924, 252 p.
A good detailed study of the depreciation of the crown and the work of stabilization, by a member of the League secretariat.

The *Anschluss* Problem

See also (Central Europe) Middle European Schemes, p. 299, and The Little Entente, p. 304; also (Post-War Germany) General, p. 321.

ARGUS, *pseud*. **The Economic Aspect of the Austro-German Customs Union.**
Prague: Orbis, 1931, 85 p.
Practically an official presentation of the Czech objections on the economic side. Contains useful statistics.

AUERBACH, BERTRAND. **Le Rattachement de l'Autriche à l'Allemagne.** Paris: Berger-Levrault, 1927, 190 p.
A detailed study of the problem as it arose at the Peace Conference and as it developed up to 1926. A special chapter discusses the French attitude and policy.

BITTERMAN, M. **Austria and the Customs Union.** Prague: Orbis, 1931, 121 p.
A Czech author proves to the Austrians that the customs union would do them no good.

DARCY, PAUL. **La République Pan-Germaniste et l'Autriche.** Paris: Éditions et Librairie, 1919, 157 p.
Of the type of war-time over-statement. The French objections in extreme form.

DONNADIEU, JACQUES. **Où Va l'Autriche?** Paris: Tallandier, 1932, 287 p.
The author reviews the problem and sounds a note of warning.

ESCALLIER, E. **L'Anschluss de l'Autriche à l'Allemagne.** Paris: Sirey, 1930.
A dissertation recapitulating the main phases in the development of the problem.

HÖPER, GERHARD. **Oesterreichs Weg zum Anschluss.** Berlin: Reimar Hobbing, 1928, 168 p.
The desirability of economic union as the necessary first step to political union.

IMMANUEL, FRIEDRICH. **Schicksalsgemeinschaft.** Munich: Bayerischer Volksverlag, 1928, 400 p.
The author elaborates the theme of Austro-German community before and during the war, in connection with the questions of war guilt and *Anschluss*.

KLEINWÄCHTER, FRIEDRICH F. G. **Der Deutsch-Osterreichische Mensch und der Anschluss.** Vienna: Eckart Verlag, 1926, 240 p.
Setting forth the cultural, economic and political advantages of the *Anschluss*.

KLEINWÄCHTER, FRIEDRICH F. G. **Self-Determination for Austria.** London: Allen and Unwin, 1929, 74 p.
A forceful presentation of the case for the *Anschluss*, which the author considers the only feasible solution of the Austrian dilemma.

KLEINWÄCHTER, FRIEDRICH F. G. and PALLER, HEINZ VON, *eds*. **Die Anschlussfrage in Ihrer Kulturellen, Politischen und Wirtschaftlichen Bedeutung.** Vienna: Braumüller, 1930, 656 p.
This weighty volume is all that the title implies. It is, in fact, the best single thing yet produced on the *Anschlussfrage*. The editors have collected a large number of statements from competent people throughout the world, so that the reader finds here a most exhaustive presentation of every conceivable angle of the question, historical, political, economic, social, cultural, etc. The volume makes an effective plea for the consummation of the *Anschluss*.

PALLER, HEINZ VON. **Der Grossdeutsche Gedanke.** Leipzig: Hofstetter, 1928, 163 p.
A history of the Greater German idea, with special reference to the question of *Anschluss*.

PAPOUŠEK, JAROSLAV. **Politischer Hintergrund der Deutsche-Österreichischen Zollunion.** Prague: Orbis, 1931, 60 p.
The political side of the question which is discussed from the economic point of view in the volumes by "Argus" and Bitterman.

SCALA, OTTO ERWIN VON. **Die Wirtschaftlichen Vorteile des Anschlusses.** Vienna: Braumüller, 1929, 112 p.
A prominent authority sets forth the evidence to show that the *Anschluss* would be to the economic advantage not only of Germany and Austria, but of all Central Europe.

SCHEFFER, EGON. **Oesterreichs Wirtschaftliche Sendung.** Vienna: Hölder-Pichler-Tempsky, 1927, 298 p.
A monograph setting forth the possibilities of a Pan-German economic union.

TERSANNES, JEAN. **Le Problème Autrichien et la Menace du Rattachement à l'Allemagne.** Paris: Bossard, 1921, 189 p.
The author pictures the *Anschluss* movement as a product of Pan-German propaganda, and shows why the union is both undesirable and unnecessary.

HUNGARY

See also (Central Europe) Middle European Schemes, p. 299, and The Little Entente, p. 304.

APPONYI, ALBERT, GRÓF and others. **Justice for Hungary.** London: Longmans, 1928, 376 p.
The Hungarian view of the Treaty of Trianon, of course with an eloquent plea for revision. Contains an ethnographic map by Count Teleki.

BALASSA, IMRE. **A Magyar Királytragédia.** Budapest: Madách, 1930, 252 p.
A stirring popular account of the trials and tribulations of the last Hapsburg Emperor. More than ten thousand copies have been sold in Hungary.

BATTHYÁNY, THEODOR, GRÓF. **Für Ungarn gegen Hohenzollern.** Vienna: Amalthea, 1930, 261 p.
Really an autobiography in which the Hungarian statesman expounds his policy of Hungary for the Hungarians as against the influence of both Hapsburgs and Hohenzollerns. The writer, a leader of the Hungarian opposition, covers the pre-war, war and revolutionary periods.

BIRINYI, LOUIS KOSSUTH. **The Tragedy of Hungary.** Cleveland: Author, 1924, 346 p.
A nationalist outline of Hungarian history and of the mutilation of Hungary in 1919, which the author ascribes largely to the hostility of the international financiers.

BIRÓ, KARL. **Die Ungarische Arbeiterbewegung seit dem Sturz der Räterrepublik.** Hamburg: Hoym, 1925, 157 p.
A systematic account of the labor movement since the disappearance of Bela Kun.

BIZONY, LADISLAO. **133 Giorni di Bolschevismo Ungherese.** Bologna: Capelli, 1920.
A concise account of events from March to August 1919, by a Hungarian journalist.

BLEYER, JAKOB, ed. **Das Deutschtum in Rumpf-Ungarn.** Budapest: Sonntagsblatt, 1928, 196 p.
A statistical analysis of the German element in present-day Hungary, with admirable maps.

BOROVICZÉNY, ALADÁR VON. **Der König und Sein Reichsverweser.** Munich: Verlag für Kulturpolitik, 1924, 361 p.
An inside history of the last attempt of Emperor Charles to regain his throne in Hungary. The author aims to prove that the plan was backed by the French Government and was frustrated solely by Horthy's reluctance to surrender his power.

BRANDIS, KLEMENS, GRAF ZU. **Die Ungarische Seele.** Vienna: Amalthea, 1926, 155 p.
A thoroughly conservative interpretation of Hungarian development.

BUDAY, LÁSZLÓ. **Dismembered Hungary.** London: Grant Richards, 1923, 288 p.
A survey of Hungary—her position during and after the war, her land, people, social
conditions and nationality questions—buttressed by much statistical material.

CHÉLARD, RAOUL. **Responsabilité de la Hongrie.** Paris: Bossard, 1930, 192 p.
The recollections of an agent of the French Foreign Office, on mission to Hungary.

CSEKONICS, ERSÉBET, GRÓFNÖ. **Hungary New and Old.** Budapest: Csáthy, 1926, 194 p.
A general descriptive work.

CUCCHETTI, GINO. **Nel Cuore dei Magiari. L'Ungheria d'Oggi.** Milan: Hoepli, 1929,
312 p.
This volume of travel impressions is enriched with the record of conversations with
Hungarian statesmen like Bethlen and Andrássy, and with an interesting discussion
of Hungarian-Italian relations, past and present.

DAMI, ALDO. **La Hongrie de Demain.** Paris: Delpeuch, 1929, 227 p.
The author, in disagreement with some of the proposals of Lord Rothermere and the
revisionists, makes suggestions of his own for the autonomous organization of the
minorities of Upper Hungary and Transylvania. A fair and dispassionate book.

DINER, JÓZSEF. **La Hongrie.** Paris: Librairie des Sciences Politiques, 1927, 171 p.
A survey of Hungarian history, written by the former Secretary of State of the Károlyi
government, who sees the past and present as a conflict of the bourgeoisie and peas-
ants with the strongly entrenched and selfish landowning oligarchy.

DOMANOVSZKY, SÁNDOR. **Die Geschichte Ungarns.** Munich: Paetel, 1923, 379 p.
A general introductory history of Hungary, by a professor at the University of Budapest.

DOMÁNY, GYULA. **A Magyar Szanálás.** Budapest: Grill-Benkö, 1927, 157 p.
A competent discussion of the financial evolution of post-war Hungary, with consideration of the budget and tax systems and a strong plea for economic union of the Danube
states.

DONALD, SIR ROBERT. **The Tragedy of Trianon.** London: Butterworth, 1928, 348 p.
An exposition of Hungary's case, showing signs of very incomplete documentation.

DUPUIS, RENÉ. **Le Problème Hongrois.** Paris: Éditions Internationales, 1931, 214 p.
The writer pleads for Polish and French initiative in bringing about a solution of the
problem of Hungarian minorities and a revision of Central European tariffs. Failing
action, Hungary is certain to be driven into the arms of Germany.

ECKHART, FERENC. **A Short History of the Hungarian People.** London: Grant
Richards, 1931, 244 p.
By the director of the Hungarian Institute of Vienna; a general survey, with stress on
social, institutional and economic factors. Perhaps the best introduction to Hungarian
history in a western language.

EISENMANN, LOUIS. **La Hongrie Contemporaine, 1867-1918.** Paris: Delagrave, 1921.
The best account of Hungary's political history after the compromise of 1867, well-
documented and well-balanced, by a French authority on Central Europe.

ESZTERHÁZY, NIKOLAUS, GRÓF. **Meine Erlebnisse und Eindrücke aus der Zeit vom
1 November 1918 bis 2 August 1919.** Budapest: St. Stephan, 1921, 126 p.
A Hungarian nobleman's story of his experiences during the stormy period of the
Károlyi ministry and the Bolshevik régime.

FALUHELYI, FERENC. **Magyarország Közjoga.** Pécs: Karl, 1926, 2 v.
A standard treatment of the Hungarian constitution, with a chronological collection of important documents from the Golden Bull to the present.

FRACCAROLI, ARNOLDO. **Ungheria Bolscevica.** Milan: Sonzogno, 1920, 196 p.
The notes of an Italian eye-witness of the confused period of Bolshevik ascendancy.

GRÁTZ, GUSZTÁV, *ed.* **A Bolsevizmus Magyarországon.** Budapest: Franklin, 1921, 861 p.
A huge collaborative work on the Bolshevik interlude, with essays by Julius Andrássy, Albert von Berzeviczy and others.

GRÁTZ, GUSZTÁV, *ed.* **Ungarisches Wirtschafts-Jahrbuch.** Berlin: Hobbing, 1925 ff.
An annual containing valuable articles on all aspects of Hungary's economic condition.

GUILLEMAIN, JEAN. **L'Assainissement et le Redressement des Finances Hongroises après la Guerre de 1914-18.** Paris: Presses Universitaires, 1925, 174 p.
A systematic review of the economic crisis and the work accomplished by the League of Nations.

HALMAY, E., *ed.* **La Hongrie d'Aujourd'hui.** Budapest: Kelet-Népe, 1925, 224 p.
More than forty articles by Apponyi, Bárány, Berzeviczy, etc., surveying the political, religious, artistic, educational and economic life of the new Hungary.

HASAS, ÉMILE. **La Revision du Traité de Trianon et les Difficultés Suscitées par la Hongrie en Ce Qui Concerne Son Application.** Paris: Picart, 1928, 179 p.
Hostile to the Hungarian claims; the writer reviews the attempts at restoration of the Hapsburgs, the St. Gotthard affair and especially the Rothermere campaign, all to prove Hungary a disturber of the peace.

HEGEDÜS, LORÁNT. **Harc a Magyar Igazságért.** Budapest: Légrády, 1928, 174 p.
Collected essays of a former Hungarian finance minister, dealing intimately with most of the fundamental foreign problems of Hungary in the post-war period.

HERCZEG, FERENCZ. **Két Arczkép. Tisza István, Károlyi Mihály.** Budapest: Singer and Wolfner, 1920.
The biographical sketches of Tisza and Károlyi, by an Hungarian poet.

HERCZEG, GÉZA. **Béla Kun. Eine Historische Grimasse.** Berlin: Verlag für Kulturpolitik, 1928, 188 p.
A journalistic and very hostile account of the communist leader's career, without much reference to the setting or to larger implications.

HEVESY, ANDRÉ DE. **Nationalities in Hungary.** London: Unwin, 1919, 246 p.
A general review of the nationalities problem, with criticism of the government's pre-war policy and a plea for a return to the spirit of Deák.

HORVÁTH, JENÖ. **Magyar diplomácia.** Budapest: Pfeifer, 1928, 202 p.
An excellent review of Hungary's international position from 1815 to 1918.

HORVÁTH, JENÖ. **Modern Hungary, 1660-1920.** Budapest: Külügyi Társaság, 1922, 232 p.
An authoritative account, with useful bibliography, but written from a pronouncedly national standpoint.

JÁSZI, OSZKÁR. **Revolution and Counter-Revolution in Hungary.** London: King, 1924, 236 p.
An interesting and important account of the three Hungarian revolutions of 1918-19, by one of Károlyi's ministers.

KAAS, ALBERT, BÁRÓ and LAZAROVICS, FEDOR VON. **Der Bolschewismus in Ungarn.** Munich: Dresler, 1930, 315 p.
Though this book contains no new material it is of value as a convenient summary of an important episode. Many proclamations and decrees are textually reprinted.

KÁROLYI, MICHAEL, GRÓF. **Fighting the World.** New York: Boni, 1925, 464 p.
A surprisingly moderate account by the former President of the Hungarian Republic of his activities during the war. An important and interesting contribution.

KRISZTICS, SÁNDOR. **A Békeszerzodések Reviziója.** Budapest: Grill-féle Könyvkereskedés, 1927, 508 p.
The author, a member of the Hungarian delegation to the Peace Conference, here prints a collection of lectures on war guilt, the methods and prospects of treaty revision, and the new balance of power in Europe.

LEBOURG, PAUL and JEAN. **Les Consciences Se Reveillent.** Paris: Delpeuch, 1930, 178 p.
A strong presentation of the orthodox Hungarian argument for revision. The authors claim that minorities were better treated in the old Hungary than in the new states and call for at least partial rectification of the frontiers.

LUDWIG, ERNEST. **Le Sort des Minorités Nationales en Hongrie et en Tchécoslovaquie.** Budapest: Presse des Associations Scientifiques Hongroises, 1922, 125 p.
A defense of Hungarian policy towards minorities, and an attack upon the attitude of the Czechs and the Great Powers towards the fate of Hungarians in Czechoslovakia.

LUKÁCS, GYÖRGY, *ed.* **La Hongrie et la Civilisation.** Paris: Renaissance du Livre, 1929, 3 v.
A collaborative work, by Hungarian and French scholars, dealing with the history, geography, ethnography, government and foreign policy, as well as artistic and social life. While the articles are frequently too specialized or short, the collection is a mine of information.

MAILÁTH, JÓZSEF, GRÓF. **Erlebnisse und Erfahrungen nach dem Kriege.** Budapest: Benko, 1919-1925, 3 v.
Vivid and penetrating observations of a great Hungarian magnate during the Károlyi and Bela Kun régimes, with special reference to events in the provinces.

MÁLYUSZ, ELEMÉR. **Sturm auf Ungarn.** Munich: Dresler, 1931, 295 p.
A study of the activities of Hungarian communist, socialist and radical emigrés against the existing régime. The book, though one-sided, contains much material throwing light on the struggle.

MITZAKIS, MICHEL. **Le Relèvement Financier de la Hongrie et la Société des Nations.** Paris: Presses Universitaires, 1926, 418 p.
A study based on sound knowledge and extensive use of first hand statistical material. The author reviews the financial history of Austria-Hungary during the war, the provisions of the treaties, and the inflation, before discussing the work of recovery.

MOLNÁR, KÁLMÁN. **Magyar Közjog.** Pécs: Danubia, 1926-28, 2 v.
An authoritative treatise on Hungarian constitutional law.

MOSCA, RODOLFO. **Problemi Politici. L'Ungheria Contemporanea.** Bologna: Zanichelli, 1928, 293 p.
The author reviews the war period and the revolutions of 1918-1919, discusses the problems arising from the peace treaty, and analyzes the position of Hungary in Italian policy as a make-weight against the Slavs.

NYIRI, J. **Die Regierung Károlyi in Ungarn, 1918-1919.** Budapest: Száthy, 1926, 136 p.
A polemic against the Károlyi régime, advancing the argument that the system, not even democratic in itself, only paved the way for Bolshevik rule.

PÉTHÖ, SÁNDOR. **Le Comte Albert Apponyi.** Paris: Œuvres Representatives, 1931, 256 p.
A laudatory biography, with a supplement containing Apponyi's Geneva speeches.

PÉTHÖ, SÁNDOR. **Viharos Emberöltö.** Budapest: Stadium, 1928, 243 p.
Biographical sketches of eminent Hungarian political figures of recent times, including Andrássy, Apponyi and Tisza.

PÉTHÖ, SÁNDOR. **Világostól Trianonig.** Budapest: Enciklopedia, 1926, 324 p.
A survey of Hungarian history from 1849 to 1920, brilliantly written but concerned chiefly with Hungarian parliamentary struggles.

PILCH, JENÖ. **Horthy Miklós.** Budapest: Athenaeum, 1928, 408 p.
The best biography of Admiral Horthy, and at the same time a contribution to the story of the counter-revolution of 1919-1920 of which he was a leader.

POGÁNY, JOSEF. **Der Weisse Terror in Ungarn.** Vienna: Neue Erde, 1920, 192 p.
An account of the aftermath of Bolshevism and the repressive policy and persecution initiated by the returned feudalists.

RÁKOSI, JENÖ. **Trianontól Rothermereig.** Budapest: Horizont, 1928, 203 p.
A Hungarian journalist's account of the campaign for revision of the Trianon Treaty conducted by Lord Rothermere and the *Daily Mail*. An interesting contribution to the technique of modern propaganda.

RIETH, ADOLF. **Die Geographische Verbreitung des Deutschtums in Rumpf-Ungarn.** Stuttgart: Ausland und Heimat, 1927, 102 p.
A dissertation which gives a good historical and statistical study of the Germans in Hungary, their distribution, occupation, condition, etc.

SANGIORGI, GIORGIO M. **L'Ungheria.** Bologna: Zanichelli, 1927, 227 p.
A good brief survey of the course of events in Hungary from the time of the Károlyi régime to the establishment of the Horthy regency.

SCHMIDT-PAULI, EDGAR VON. **Graf Stefan Bethlen.** Berlin: Hobbing, 1931, 299 p.
This book is more than a biography of Bethlen, being really a succinct account of the history of post-war Hungary, written by a well-informed author.

SIMEONI, A. and BUCCHI, G. **Trianon.** Rome: Sapientia, 1931, 304 p.
A sympathetic account of the disastrous effects of the Trianon Treaty for Hungary.

STREET, CECIL JOHN CHARLES. **Hungary and Democracy.** London: Fisher Unwin, 1923, 207 p.
An indictment of the Hungarian régime from 1867 to 1914, with reference to the oppressed nationalities, social reaction and Magyar "imperialism."

SZÁNTÓ, BÉLA. **Klassenkämpfe und Diktatur des Proletariats in Ungarn.** Berlin: Arbeiterbuchhandlung, 1920, 115 p.
A communist account of the Bela Kun régime.

SZENDE, ZOLTÁN. **Die Ungarn im Zusammenbruch 1918.** Oldenburg: Schwartz, 1931, 227 p.
A collection of material to illustrate the demoralization of the Hungarian army, its dissolution and the policy of the Károlyi Government.

TELEKI, PÁL, GRÓF. **The Evolution of Hungary and Its Place in European Politics.** New York: Macmillan, 1923, 312 p.
A moderate pro-Magyar exposition of Hungarian history and economic problems, with the emphasis on the period since 1867. It has many maps and a bibliography.

THARAUD, JÉRÔME and JEAN. **When Israel Is King.** New York: McBride, 1924, 248 p.
A brilliant but biassed book, consisting primarily of a bitter anti-Semitic attack upon the Bolshevik episode.

TORMAY, CÉCILE. **An Outlaw's Diary.** London: P. Allan, 1924, 2 v.
A vivid and sensational picture of Hungary during the Károlyi and Bela Kun régimes, by a prominent woman of the aristocracy who was deeply involved. The book went through many Hungarian editions.

Ungheria. Rome: Istituto per l'Europa Orientale, 1929, 454 p.
A splendidly illustrated coöperative work surveying Hungarian history and culture, written by eminent Hungarian scholars.

VARGA, SIGISMOND. **La Tragédie d'un Pays Millénaire.** Paris: Source, 1932, 129 p.
The author recalls the past relations of France and Hungary and pleads eloquently for French aid in the revision of the treaties.

WELTNER, JAKAB. **Forradalom, Bolsevizmus, Emigráció.** Budapest: Author, 1929, 317 p.
The recollections of the editor of the official socialist paper during the Károlyi and Bolshevik régimes; a valuable addition to the literature of this stormy period.

CZECHOSLOVAKIA
Establishment of the State

See also (World War) Siberia, p. 139; also (Central Europe) Collapse of the Hapsburg Empire, p. 301; also (Russia) Counter-Revolution and Intervention, p. 367.

ADAMOVICH, LUDWIG. **Grundriss des Tschechoslowakischen Staatsrechtes.** Vienna: Oesterreichische Staatsdruckerei, 1929, 517 p.
A systematic analysis of the constitution, based in part on Masaryk's political views during the war with regard to the future Czechoslovak state.

BENEŠ, EDVARD. **Světová Válka a Naše Revolucie.** Prague: Orbis, 1927-1928, 3 v.
A detailed study of the Czech movement for independence during the war. The memoirs of Masaryk's chief lieutenant and one of the fundamental sources. There is a French translation of volumes I and II ("Souvenirs de Guerre et la Révolution," Paris: Leroux, 1928-1929). The German translation ("Der Aufstand der Nationen," Berlin: Cassirer, 1928, 755 p.) is somewhat abridged, and the English edition ("My War Memoirs," London: Allen and Unwin, 1928, 512 p.) considerably so.

BENEŠ, VOJTA. **Československá Amerika v Odboji.** Prague: Pokrok, 1931, 425 p.
Memoirs of one of the chief organizers of the Czechoslovak movement in the United States. An important supplement to the story as told by Masaryk and Edvard Beneš.

ČAPEK, KAREL. **Hovory s T. G. Masarykem.** Prague: Čin, 1931, 171 p.
A useful anthology of Masaryk's utterances.

CHALOUPECKÝ, VÁCLAV. **Zápas o Slovensko 1918.** Prague: Čin, 1930, 251 p.
The most recent and best history of the struggle between the Czechs and the Hungarians for the possession of Slovakia. The book is based on Czech, Slovak and Hungarian memoirs and material, and is written from the Czech standpoint.

DOLEŽAL, JAROMÍR. **Masarykova Cesta Žlvotem.** Brno: Polygrafia, 1920-21, 2 v.
Masaryk's life, a standard biography.

FISCHEL, ALFRED. **Das Tschechische Volk.** Breslau: Priebatsch, 1928, 234 p.
An outline of Czech history, written by a leading German authority.

FOURNIER-FABRE, ÉMILE. **La Vie et l'Œuvre Politique et Sociale de M. Thomas Garrigue Masaryk.** Paris: Ficker, 1927, 345 p.
A good biographical sketch supplemented with a discussion of Masaryk's scholarly work.

HERBEN, JAN. **T. G. Masaryk.** Prague: 1926-27, 3 v.
The most extensive biographical study yet made of the eminent Czech statesman.

JEŘÁBEK, ČESTMÍR. **Le Monde en Flammes.** Paris: Valois, 1930, 300 p.
A portrayal of the Czechs during the war. A psychological study which has been awarded an important prize.

LAZAREVSKIĬ, VLADIMIR. **Rossiia i Chekhoslovatskoe Vozrozhdenie.** Berlin: Grad Kitezh, 1927, 176 p.
A study of Russia's policy and part in the Czechoslovak revival, 1914-18.

LOWRIE, DONALD ALEXANDER. **Masaryk of Czechoslovakia.** New York: Oxford University Press, 1930, 216 p.
A character study that comes very near to hero worship.

Masaryk, Staatsmann und Denker. Prague: Orbis, 1930, 251 p.
A series of appreciations of Masaryk, among the most interesting being those which discuss his relations to other European countries.

MASARYK, TOMÁŠ GARRIGUE. **The Making of a State.** New York: Stokes, 1927, 538 p.
The English translation of the memoirs of the great Czech leader. While reviewing his own remarkable career and outlining the stages in the evolution of the Czechoslovak state, Masaryk indulges in many digressions of a political-philosophical nature. For insight and perspective it is hardly equalled by any book dealing with the larger causes of the world conflict.

MAURICE, CHARLES EDMUND. **Bohemia.** London: Fisher Unwin, 1922, 565 p.
A revised edition of a standard work. The section on the period since 1848 is still brief and inadequate.

MOLISCH, PAUL. **Vom Kampf der Tschechen um Ihren Staat.** Vienna: Braumüller, 1929, 164 p.
With the use of unpublished material, the author, who is state librarian in Vienna, reviews the Czech struggle for independence. A book to be read as an antidote to Masaryk, Beneš, Opočenský, and Papoušek.

NANI, UMBERTO. **T. G. Masaryk e l'Unità Cecoslovacca.** Milan: Treves, 1931, 260 p.
The resurrection of the Czech state described by one of the most competent Italian students of eastern affairs. A book characterized throughout by knowledge and breadth of view.

NEJEDLÝ, ZDENĚK. **T. G. Masaryk.** Prague: Melantrich, 1930-1931, V. I, pts. 1 and 2.
This is the best critical treatment of Masaryk's career. Contains the most complete bibliography on the subject and is partly based on unpublished documents.

NOŠEK, VLADIMIR. **The Spirit of Bohemia.** London: Allen, 1926, 379 p.
A general review of Czech history, literature and art, for the orientation of the English reader.

OPOČENSKÝ, JAN. **The Collapse of the Austro-Hungarian Monarchy and the Rise of the Czechoslovak State.** Prague: Orbis, 1928, 216 p.
A good review of the Czech epic as it emerges from the memoirs of Masaryk and Beneš, and from other material.

PAPOUŠEK, JAROSLAV. **The Czechoslovak Nation's Struggle for Independence.** Prague: Orbis, 1928, 95 p.
A general survey of the Czech movement before and during the war and an account of the activity of Masaryk and Beneš abroad.

PAPOUŠEK, JAROSLAV. **Masaryk a Revoluční Armáda.** Prague: Čin, 1922, 239 p.
A collection of Masaryk's speeches.

PERGLER, CHARLES. **America in the Struggle for Czechoslovak Independence.**
Philadelphia: Dorrance, 1926, 113 p.
A summary of American policy toward the Czech question during the war.

PROKEŠ, JAROSLAV. **Histoire Tchécoslovaque.** Prague: Orbis, 1927, 374 p.
A general survey of Czechoslovak history, stressing the fundamental unity of the component parts. The chapter on the World War and the establishment of the new state is by Papoušek.

RAUBAL, STANISLAS. **Formation de la Frontière entre la Pologne et la Tchécoslovaquie.** Paris: Presses Modernes, 1928, 189 p.
A detailed monographic treatment of geographic and historic claims, the question of self-determination and the final delimiting of the frontier.

RYCHNOVSKY, ERNST. **Masaryk.** Prague: Staatliche Verlagsanstalt, 1931, 338 p.
One of the best of the books about the Czech statesman published on the occasion of his eightieth birthday; a popular biography, based largely on Masaryk's writings and utterances. Text in German.

SOUKUP, FRANTIŠEK. **28 Řijen 1918.** Prague: Orbis, 1928.
An eloquent account of the revolution of October, 1918, by a socialist leader.

STREET, CECIL JOHN CHARLES. **President Masaryk.** London: Bles, 1930, 256 p.
Masaryk in the setting of the Czech resurrection, by a sympathetic English journalist.

TSCHUPPIK, WALTER. **Die Tschechische Revolution.** Leipzig: Tal, 1920, 162 p.
Really a collection of newspaper articles dealing with various stages in the evolution of Czech independence. Well-informed but rather smart.

WEIL, FRITZ. **Das Werden eines Volkes und der Weg eines Mannes.** Dresden: Reissner, 1930, 265 p.
A good critical review of Czech history and the problem of Czech independence, followed by an appreciative study of the career of Beneš.

WEISS, LOUISE. **La République Tchéco-Slovaque.** Paris: Payot, 1919, 233 p.
An able analysis of the Czech problem and the Czech agitation during the war, by a discerning French political writer, editor of *L'Europe Nouvelle*.

Post-War History; Foreign and Domestic Problems

See also (Central Europe) Middle European Schemes, p. 299, and The Little Entente, p. 304;
also (Austria) The Anschluss Problem, p. 307; also Hungary, p. 308.

BALTHASAR, ELSE. **Die Staatsfinanzen der Tschechoslowakei.** Leipzig: 1929, 149 p.
A German dissertation, based on Czech materials, heavily documented and covering the period 1918 to 1928. The book has an exhaustive bibliography.

BOROVIČKA, JOSEF. **Ten Years of Czechoslovak Politics.** Prague: Orbis, 1929, 131 p.
An excellent brief handbook recounting how the state was established and giving the principal facts of its post-war history. The volume is in a sense a continuation of Papoušek's book.

ČAPEK, E. **Politická Příručka Csr.** Prague: Melantrich, 1931, 206 p.
An excellent sociological introduction to Czechoslovak conditions, stressing density of population, nationalistic and religious factors, emigration and historical evolution.

CHANAL, A. **Monnaie et Économie Nationale en Tchécoslovaquie.** Paris: Giard, 1929, 318 p.
Traces the economic evolution of the new state since its foundation. A substantial documented dissertation, reviewing the establishment and ultimate stabilization of the crown. Based in large part on Czech materials.

CHMELAŘ, JOSEF. **Political Parties in Czechoslovakia.** Prague: Orbis, 1926, 102 p.
An admirable review of the parties, leaders, press and general politics of the state.

CÍSAŘ, JAROSLAV and POKORNÝ, FRANTIŠEK. **The Czechoslovak Republic.** London: Fisher Unwin, 1922, 276 p.
A handbook about the land and the people, the economic resources and life, the political system, education, literature, etc.

EISENMANN, LOUIS. **La Tchécoslovaquie.** Paris: Rieder, 1921, 126 p.
Probably the best work available on Czechoslovakia. An admirable survey of the new republic, written by a French authority on Hapsburg history.

GEORGES-PICOT, GEORGES MARIE ERNEST. **La Politique de Déflation en Tchécoslovaquie.** Paris: Presses Universitaires, 1925, 90 p.
A scholarly presentation of the effects of the financial policy pursued by Rašín, the author stressing constantly the importance of foreign policy for Czechoslovakia's well-being.

GRUBER, JOSEF, *ed.* **Czechoslovakia.** New York: Macmillan, 1924, 256 p.
A competent analysis of social and economic conditions.

HARTMANN, PAUL. **Die Politische Partei in der Tschechoslowakischen Republik.** Brno: Rohrer, 1931, 260 p.
A juristic analysis of the party system in Czechoslovakia.

HASSINGER, HUGO. **Die Tschechoslowakei.** Vienna: Rikola, 1925, 619 p.
An exhaustive standard monograph, written by a Swiss professor. The author examines, from a German viewpoint, the geographic, economic, social and political structure of the state, and has much to say of the nationalities problem.

IOACHIMESCU, I. and KUDRNÁČ, A. **Republica Cehoslovacă.** Bucharest: Cultura Naţionala, 1924, 123 p.
A survey of Czechoslovak history, political life, social and educational policy, artistic accomplishment, economic activity, etc.

JEHLIČKA, FRANTIŠEK. **Une Étape du Calvaire Slovaque. Le Procès Tuka.** Paris: Argo, 1930, 120 p.
A piece of violent polemical writing which throws light on the difficulties between the Czechs and the Slovaks.

KUTZSCHER, GERHARD. **Die Natürlichen und Nationalen Grundlagen des Tschechoslowakischen Staates.** Leipzig: Noske, 1927, 134 p.
A systematic treatment of the geographic and national lines and influences.

MIRKIN-GETSEVICH, BORIS SERGIEEVICH and TIBAL, ANDRÉ. **La Tchécoslovaquie.** Paris: Delagrave, 1929, 119 p.
A general political survey, with an admirable collection of documents dealing with international agreements, constitutional matters, agrarian legislation, minorities, etc.

MOTHERSOLE, JESSIE. **Czechoslovakia. The Land of an Unconquerable Ideal.** New York: Dodd, 1926, 320 p.
One of the better general travel books on Czechoslovakia, beautifully illustrated.

NÁRODNI, SHROMÁŽDENI. **Republiky Československé v Prvém Desítiletí.** Prague: Sněmovna, 1928, 1251 p.
A valuable summary and collection of documents relating to the activity of the Czechoslovak Parliament since the war.

PAPÁNEK, JÁN. **La Tchécoslovaquie.** Prague: Orbis, 1923, 96 p.
Primarily a constitutional study of how the state was established and how the new system works.

PEROUTKA, FERDINAND. **Boje o Dnešek.** Prague: Borový, 1925, 282 p.
Essays on political and social problems of Czechoslovakia, by an able Czech journalist.

PIOT, ANDRÉ. **La Couronne Tchécoslovaque.** Paris: La Vie Universitaire, 1923, 260 p.
A complete study of Czechoslovak monetary history from 1918 to 1923, with stress on Rašín's policy.

PROCHÁZKA, ADOLF. **Právní Případ dra K. Perglera.** Prague: Orbis, 1931, 52 p.
An analysis of the *cause célèbre* of the Czechoslovak judicial system, involving a prominent Czechoslovak-American revolutionary worker.

RÁDL, EMANUEL. **La Question Religieuse en Tchécoslovaquie.** Prague: Gazette de Prague, 1922, 63 p.
A semi-official summary, with emphasis on the efforts to form an independent Czechoslovak church at the expense of the Roman Catholic Church.

RAŠÍN, ALOÏS. **The Financial Policy of Czechoslovakia.** Oxford: Clarendon Press, 1923, 160 p.
A technical analysis in the Carnegie Series, written by the Czech Minister of Finance.

RIVET, CHARLES. **Chez les Slaves Libérés. Les Tchécoslovaques.** Paris: Perrin, 1921, 322 p.
An *enquête* by a special correspondent of the Paris *Temps*, interesting and instructive.

SCHMIDT-FRIEDLÄNDER, REINHARD. **Die Währungspolitik der Tschechoslowakei.** Reichenberg: Stiepel, 1929, 211 p.
A technical study of the Czech currency problem, thoroughly documented, with emphasis on post-war currency problems.

SETON-WATSON, ROBERT WILLIAM. **The New Slovakia.** Prague: Borový, 1924, 131 p.
A competent description by one of the leading authorities on Eastern Europe.

SETON-WATSON, ROBERT WILLIAM, *ed.* **Slovakia, Then and Now.** London: Allen and Unwin, 1931, 356 p.
The most complete survey of Slovak affairs yet published in a western language. The general discussion by Seton-Watson is followed by statements from twenty-five Slovak experts, and the whole goes to show that conditions are vastly improved and generally satisfactory.

STREET, CECIL JOHN CHARLES. **East of Prague.** London: Bles, 1924, 288 p.
An Englishman's observations in the new Slovakia.

SZANA, ALEXANDER. **Die Geschichte der Slowakei.** Bratislava: Grenzbote, 1930, 327 p.
This book consists largely of anthologies of opinions and documents intended to demonstrate the nationalist view of Slovak history.

SZANA, ALEXANDER. **Zum Ewigen Frieden.** Bratislava: Grenzbote, 1931, 167 p.
An historical survey of Slovakia's struggle for freedom.

La Tchécoslovaquie. Paris: Crès, 1921, 206 p.
Lectures delivered at the Union Française by authorities like Brunhes, Eisenmann and Jelínek.

URBAN, K. **Kurze Zusammenstellung über die Tschechoslowakische Armee.** Berlin: Eisenschmidt, 1929, 111 p.
A reliable survey of Czechoslovak military forces and organization.

WEIL, FRIEDRICH. **Tschechoslowakei.** Gotha: Perthes, 1924, 186 p.
One of the best brief handbooks, with emphasis on politics and economics.

WEINGART, MILOŠ, *ed.* **Současná Filosofie u Slovanů.** Prague: Slovanský Ustav, 1932, 173 p.
A series of lectures on the problems of the Slavic nations, delivered under the auspices of the Slavonic Institute at Prague.

WEYR, FRANZ. **Soustava Československého Práva Státního.** Prague: Borový, 1924, 476 p.
A critical analytical study of the Czechoslovak constitutional system, with emphasis on the theoretical aspects. Written by a leading authority.

Minorities

See also (The League of Nations) Minorities, p. 60; also (Germany) Minorities Abroad, p. 337.

KAINDL, RAIMUND FRIEDRICH. **Der Voelkerkampf und Sprachenstreit in Böhmen.** Vienna: Braumüller, 1928, 72 p.
An admirable historical sketch of the development of the national question in Bohemia prior to 1918, followed by a collection of the most important documents.

KLEPETAŘ, HARRY. **Der Sprachenkampf in den Sudetenländern.** Warnsdorf: Strache, 1930, 152 p.
An enlightening study of the language difficulties in Czechoslovakia.

NADOLNY, RUDOLF. **Germanisierung oder Slavisierung?** Berlin: Stollberg, 1928, 208 p.
A reply to Masaryk's "The Making of a State."

PETERS, GUSTAV. **Der Neue Herr von Böhmen.** Berlin: Deutsche Rundschau, 1927, 134 p.
A book comparable to that of Rádl, both stressing, from different standpoints, the urgent need for a new spirit of coöperation and union of forces for the general good of the new state.

RÁDL, EMANUEL. **Der Kampf zwischen Tschechen und Deutschen.** Reichenberg: Stiepel, 1928, 208 p.
An eminently sane book, in which a Czech professor fulminates against the exaggeration of the national idea and calls for intelligent coöperation between the Czechs and the German minority.

SOBOTA, EMIL. **Das Tschechoslowakische Nationalitätenrecht.** Prague: Orbis, 1931, 461 p.
The German translation of a very full collection of documentary material bearing on the nationalities laws of Czechoslovakia.

STEIER, LAJOS. **Ungarns Vergewaltigung. Oberungarn unter Tschechischer Herrschaft.** Vienna: Amalthea, 1928, 1007 p.
A tremendous mass of material—laws, memoranda, newspaper articles, etc.—to illustrate Czech rule. The second part of the book contains a good account of the autonomist movement since 1918.

WINTER, EDUARD, ed. **Die Deutschen in der Slowakei und in Karpatho-Russland.** Münster: Aschendorff, 1926, 96 p.
A coöperative handbook of considerable value.

GERMANY

Old Régime and Revolution

See also World War, p. 87; also (Central Europe) Collapse of the Hapsburg Empire, p. 301.

ANDLER, CHARLES. **La Décomposition Politique du Socialisme Allemand.** Paris: Bossard, 1919, 282 p.
A documented account of the German Socialists during the war and the Revolution.

BAUMONT, MAURICE. **The Fall of the Kaiser.** New York: Knopf, 1931, 270 p.
An impartial account of the Emperor's abdication. The best single book on the subject.

BERNSTEIN, EDUARD. **Die Deutsche Revolution.** Berlin: Verlag für Gesellschaft und Erziehung, 1921, 198 p.
Written by the moderate German Socialist leader, this volume, covering the story through the events of March 1919, was intended as the first installment of a larger work.

BOUTON, STEPHEN MILES. **And the Kaiser Abdicates.** New Haven: Yale University Press, rev. ed., 1921, 332 p.
An American correspondent's view of the German Revolution.

DAWSON, WILLIAM HARBUTT. **The German Empire, 1867-1914.** New York: Macmillan, 1919, 2 v.
Still one of the best histories available in English. The presentation is not very good, but the book contains much information.

DITTMANN, WILHELM. **Die Marine-Justizmorde von 1917 und die Admirals-Rebellion von 1918.** Berlin: Dietz, 1926, 104 p.
A distinctly partisan account, but based upon secret documents laid before the German parliamentary commission.

GENTIZON, PAUL. **La Révolution Allemande, 1918-1919.** Paris: Payot, 1919, 240 p.
A valuable contemporary record covering the period from November 1918 to January 1919, by the special correspondent of the Paris *Temps*.

GIEREN, GERHARD. **Vorkriegs- und Kriegssünden.** Leipzig: Thalacker und Schwarz, 1926, 310 p.
A popular but suggestive description of the old military system, the politico-military conflicts and the chief operations of the war.

GOT, AMBROISE. **La Terreur en Bavière.** Paris: Perrin, 1922, 306 p.
An able account of the radical phase of the Bavarian overturn and the victory of reaction. The author regards events in Munich as the best illustration of the forces working in Germany in 1918-1919.

GRISHIN, M. I. **Krasnaia Bavariia.** Moscow: Molodaia Gvardiia, 1925, 154 p.
The Soviet Republic of 1919 in Bavaria; a communist account.

HARMS, PAUL. **Vier Jahrzehnte Reichspolitik, 1878-1919.** Leipzig: Quelle und Meyer, 1924, 209 p.
A study of the causes of Germany's collapse and the conditions of recovery; an able and interesting discussion.

HARTUNG, FRITZ. **Deutsche Geschichte.** Bonn: Schroeder, 3rd ed., 1930, 416 p.
The best one-volume survey of German history from 1871 to 1919.

HERZFELD, HANS. **Die Deutsche Sozialdemokratie und die Auflösung der Nationalen Einheitsfront im Weltkriege.** Leipzig: Quelle und Meyer, 1928, 425 p.
One of the best studies of the domestic history of Germany during the war. The writer traces, in a scholarly way, the influence of conditions and the influence of Socialist leaders in preparing the breakdown of the old régime. Like Rosenberg, Herzfeld concludes that the failure of Social Democracy in the war had much to do with the disastrous outcome so far as Germany was concerned.

KARL, JOSEF, *comp.* **Die Schreckensherrschaft in München.** Munich: Hochschulverlag, 1919, 296 p.
A valuable diary and collection of edicts, proclamations, etc., covering the period of communist rule in Bavaria.

KNESEBECK, LUDOLF GOTTSCHALK VON DEM. **Die Wahrheit über den Propaganda-feldzug und Deutschlands Zusammenbruch.** Munich: Fortschrittliche Buchhandlung, 1927, 168 p.
Deals especially with the part played by the press, and publishes some new letters of Ludendorff to the editor of the *Königsberger Allgemeine Zeitung*, throwing considerable light on such important matters as the dismissal of Falkenhayn.

LÉMONON, ERNEST. **L'Allemagne Vaincue.** Paris: Bossard, 1919, 220 p.
A general survey of Germany in defeat, with emphasis on material factors.

LUTZ, RALPH HASWELL. **The German Revolution, 1918-1919.** Stanford: Stanford University Press, 1922, 186 p.
The first authoritative account in English, based on an intimate acquaintance with the material then available.

MAERCKER, LUDWIG RUDOLF GEORG. **Vom Kaiserheer zur Reichswehr.** Leipzig: Koehler, 1922, 382 p.
The story of the volunteer corps organized and commanded by Maercker. An important contribution to the history of the German Revolution, especially in central Germany.

MEINECKE, FRIEDRICH. **Nach der Revolution.** Munich: Oldenbourg, 1919, 144 p.
A series of essays on the German Revolution, by one of the greatest German historians and political theorists.

MÜLLER, RICHARD. **Der Bürgerkrieg in Deutschland.** Berlin: Phöbus, 1925, 244 p.
A good brief outline of the German Revolution with emphasis on the struggle with the extreme radicals.

NEU, HEINRICH. **Die Revolutionäre Bewegung auf der Deutschen Flotte, 1917-1918.** Stuttgart: Kohlhammer, 1930, 82 p.
A scholarly investigation of a rather obscure subject. The author attributes responsibility for the naval mutinies to the representatives of the Independent Socialists.

NIEMANN, ALFRED. **Kaiser und Revolution.** Berlin: Scherl, 1922, 159 p.
A detailed account of events in the months preceding the Revolution and especially of the critical days at Spa headquarters. Practically the authorized version of the Emperor.

NIEMANN, ALFRED. **Revolution von Oben—Umsturz von Unten.** Berlin: Verlag für Kulturpolitik, 1927, 448 p.
An attempt to explain the origins and course of the German Revolution exclusively by the actions of individuals. A very incomplete picture, though interesting in spots.

ROSENBERG, ARTHUR. **The Birth of the German Republic.** New York: Oxford University Press, 1931, 294 p.
The secretary of the parliamentary investigating committee gives an admirable analysis of the domestic developments since 1871. This is one of the outstanding studies of the German Revolution.

SCHULTZE-PFAELZER, GERHARD. **Von Spa nach Weimar.** Leipzig: Grethlein, 1929, 386 p.
A detailed account of the critical period from the armistice to the making of the German Constitution, well-written and moderate, but not documented.

STEINHAUSEN, GEORG. **Der Politische Niedergang Deutschlands in Seinen Tieferen Ursachen.** Osterwieck: Zickfeldt, 1927, 206 p.
A detached examination of the fundamental structure of the old régime.

STRÖBEL, HEINRICH. **The German Revolution and After.** London: Jarrold, 1923, 320 p.
A general exposition, somewhat critical in tone, now outdated by books like Rosenberg's and Schultze-Pfaelzer's.

Die Ursachen des Deutschen Zusammenbruches im Jahre 1918. Berlin: Deutsche
Verlagsgesellschaft für Politik und Geschichte, 1926-1929, 12 v.
The proceedings of the German parliamentary committee to investigate the causes
of Germany's collapse. Series IV deals with the domestic situation and comprises an
invaluable collection of documents and testimony.

VOLKMANN, ERICH OTTO. **Revolution über Deutschland.** Oldenburg: Stalling, 1930,
393 p.
Not so much an account of the German Revolution as a discussion of the deeper
forces and aims. A very stimulating book.

YOUNG, GEORGE. **The New Germany.** London: Constable, 1920, 333 p.
A very keen and discerning analysis of the situation in Germany after the armistice,
by an Englishman who even then realized the grievous errors of the Allies.

ZIEKURSCH, JOHANNES. **Politische Geschichte des Neuen Deutschen Kaiserreiches.**
Frankfurt: Frankfurter Societäts-Druckerei, 1925-1930, 3 v.
A general history of the German Empire from 1860 to 1918. Well-informed and docu-
mentary. On the whole the best extended account.

Post-War Germany

General

ASSMANN. **Unser Reichsheer.** Leipzig: Paul, 1930, 160 p.
A brief survey of contemporary German military forces.

AULNEAU, JOSEPH. **Le Drame de l'Allemagne.** Paris: Alcan, 1924, 258 p.
A thorough but uninspiring account of developments in Germany from 1918 to 1924.

BAUMONT, MAURICE and BERTHELOT, MARCEL. **L'Allemagne; Lendemains de Guerre
et de Révolution.** Paris: Colin, 1922, 292 p.
A relatively impartial analysis of German developments since 1918 by two keen
French observers. One of the best works in French on contemporary Germany.

BENARY, A. **Unsere Reichswehr.** Berlin: Neufeld und Henius, 1932, 256 p.
A popular survey of the armed forces of the German Republic.

BENOIST, CHARLES. **Les Nouvelles Frontières d'Allemagne.** Paris: Plon, 1920, 189 p.
An analysis of the provisions of the peace treaties, with good maps and bibliography.

BERGSTRÄSSER, LUDWIG, comp. **Der Politische Katholizismus.** Munich: Drei Masken
Verlag, 1921-1923, 2 v.
A valuable collection of documents, preceded by an admirable introduction on the
economic, social, and political policy of the Catholic leaders in Germany since 1914.

BLUN, GEORGES. **L'Allemagne Mise à Nu.** Paris: Société d'Éditions, 1928, 183 p.
Germany as seen by the Berlin correspondent of the Paris *Journal*.

BRAUER, ERWIN. **Der Ruhraufstand von 1920.** Berlin: Internationaler Arbeiterverlag,
1930, 112 p.
The rising in the Ruhr in 1920, told from the communist viewpoint.

CABALZAR, F. G. **Sigfrido, 1932.** Genoa: Tipografía Nazionale, 1931, 116 p.
Hitlerism, its theory and the forces behind it, together with a keen comparison between
it and Fascism.

CLARKE, CHARLES H. **Germany Yesterday and To-morrow.** London: Selwyn, 1923,
143 p.
A rather pessimistic account of affairs in the new Germany and a lugubrious prognosis
of a German-Russian economic alliance.

COAR, JOHN FIRMAN. **The Old and the New Germany.** New York: Knopf, 1924, 288 p.
A survey of changes in German society and institutions since 1917.

COLIN, PAUL. **Allemagne.** New York: Brentano, 1923, 286 p.
A journalistic but astute description of post-war conditions in Germany, with special reference to intellectual movements and artistic life.

DANIELS, HAROLD GRIFFITH. **The Rise of the German Republic.** London: Nisbet, 1927, 304 p.
The author, correspondent of the London *Times* in Berlin since the war, gives an objective account of the Revolution, setting forth the policies of the Majority and Minority Socialists, and then traces the various stages in the establishment of the Republic. The chapters dealing with German domestic history during the occupation of the Ruhr are especially enlightening.

DANTON, GEORGE HENRY. **Germany Ten Years After.** Boston: Houghton Mifflin, 1928, 305 p.
A sympathetic popular evaluation of contemporary German thought by an exchange professor at the University of Leipzig.

DENVIGNES, JOSEPH CYRILLE MAGDELAINE. **Ce Que J'Ai Vu et Entendu en Allemagne; la Guerre ou la Paix?** Paris: Tallandier, 1927, 320 p.
The results of six years' observation in Germany by a French general, member of the Allied Military Control. The writer sounds a note of caution to his countrymen and advises keeping the powder dry until the moral disarmament of Germany is complete.

DIESEL, EUGEN. **Germany and the Germans.** New York: Macmillan, 1931, 315 p.
A keen and discerning book. The author surveys the geographical, biological and climatic characteristics of Germany, discusses the people, their mode of life, their activities and their mentality. The last section the author devotes to the complex problems of Germany's collapse and resurrection, the industrial changes, the new psychology, the new political organizations.

DUMAINE, ALFRED. **Choses d'Allemagne.** Paris: Fayard, 1925, 288 p.
The recollections and impressions of a French diplomat who served in Berlin, Munich and Vienna.

EBERS, GODEHARD JOSEF. **Staat und Kirche im Neuen Deutschland.** Munich: Hueber, 1930, 432 p.
A standard treatment, well-documented, on the relations of Church and State since the Revolution.

FRANCKE, KUNO. **German After-War Problems.** Cambridge: Harvard University Press, 1927, 134 p.
Four essays by a Harvard professor, dealing chiefly with intellectual and cultural trends in the new Germany.

GALÉRA, KARL SIEGMAR, BARON VON. **Geschichte Unserer Zeit.** Leipzig: Schlüter, 1930, 4 v.
A detailed, illustrated history of Germany from 1916 on, for popular consumption.

GARCÍA CALDERÓN, FRANCISCO. **El Espíritu de la Nueva Alemania.** Barcelona: Maucci, n. d., 238 p.
Interesting essays on Germany's intellectual life—studies of Eucken, Rathenau, Spengler, Keyserling, etc.—by a distinguished Peruvian diplomat.

GENTIZON, PAUL. **L'Allemagne en République.** Paris: Payot, 1920, 254 p.
Observations and reflections by the special correspondent of the *Temps*, covering the years 1919 and 1920, in continuation of his "La Révolution Allemande."

GOOCH, GEORGE PEABODY. **Germany.** New York: Scribner, 1925, 360 p.
A volume in the Modern World Series, one of the best introductions to the study of post-war Germany. Written by a sympathetic English scholar.

GOT, AMBROISE. **L'Allemagne après la Débâcle.** Strasbourg: Imprimerie Strasbourgeoise, 1920, 262 p.
The experiences and impressions of a French military attaché. They throw considerable light on the communist movement and the danger of radical revolution.

GOT, AMBROISE. **La Contre-Révolution Allemande.** Strasbourg: Imprimerie Strasbourgeoise, 1920, 210 p.
In this second installment of observations, the author deals with the aftermath of the Treaty, the Kapp Putsch, etc.

GOT, AMBROISE. **L'Allemagne à Nu.** Paris: La Pensée Française, 1923, 248 p.
The author continues his recollections.

Die Grossen Bewegungen des Neuen Deutschland. Würzen: Unikum, 1926, 64 p.
The programs of the leading parties, by the party leaders.

GUMBEL, EMIL JULIUS. **Verschwörer.** Berlin: Malik Verlag, 1924, 224 p.
A study of German nationalist secret societies.

HARMS, BERNHARD, *ed.* **Volk und Reich der Deutschen.** Berlin: Hobbing, 1929, 3 v.
The finest sort of coöperative descriptive work. The three volumes contain fifty-eight essays written by leading German authorities and dealing with all phases of the political, economic, social and intellectual activities of the new republic.

HELLPACH, WILLY. **Politische Prognose für Deutschland.** Berlin: Fischer, 1928, 520 p.
A sociological survey, followed by a criticism of current shibboleths. The writer discounts ideas of European solidarity and preaches faith in Germany's own abilities.

HESNARD, O. **Les Partis Politiques en Allemagne.** Paris: Crès, 1923, 250 p.
An account of the effect of the war and the Revolution on German political parties; clear and impartial.

HEUSS, THEODOR. **Hitler's Weg.** Stuttgart: Union, 1932, 167 p.
A dispassionate inquiry into the historical and political significance of the National Socialist movement.

HONNORAT, ANDRÉ. **Un des Problèmes de la Paix; le Désarmement de l'Allemagne.** Paris: Costes, 1924, 148 p.
Largely a collection of texts and documents, with elucidations by a member of the French military mission.

HORKENVACH, CUNO. **Das Deutsche Reich von 1918 bis Heute.** Berlin: Verlag für Presse, Wirtschaft und Politik, 1931, 852 p.
A huge handbook of modern Germany, drawn up with the aid of official bureaus, party organizations and all sorts of associations.

HUGENBERG, ALFRED. **Streiflichter aus Vergangenheit und Gegenwart.** Berlin: Scherl, 1927, 311 p.
An important volume of reminiscences by a prominent industrialist and nationalist leader.

JÄCKH, ERNST. **The New Germany.** New York: Oxford University Press, 1927, 103 p.
Three lectures emphasizing particularly Germany's new place in the world, by the president of the Hochschule für Politik.

KANDLER, JOHANNES. **Der Deutsche Heeresetat vor und nach dem Kriege.** Leipzig: Akademische Verlagsgesellschaft, 1930, 98 p.
A monographic study of pre-war and post-war German military budgets.

KERN, FRITZ. **Auf die Barrikaden?** Hamburg: Hanseatische Verlagsanstalt, 1931, 116 p.
The editor of a leading German paper reviews the personalities and currents of modern Germany and urges a European policy to render a revolution unnecessary.

KESSLER, HARRY, GRAF VON. **Germany and Europe.** New Haven: Yale University Press, 1924, 150 p.
A review of post-war German developments, the security problem, the Ruhr episode, etc. Williamstown Lectures.

KNITTEL, JEAN. **L'Allemagne au Carrefour.** Strasbourg: Dernières Nouvelles, 1930.
An illuminating study of the German situation, by the editor of an important Alsatian newspaper.

KRAUS, HERBERT. **Germany in Transition.** Chicago: Chicago University Press, 1924, 236 p.
Lectures by a German professor, surveying political tendencies, reparations, Germany's attitude to the League, separatism, etc.

KÜHLMANN, RICHARD VON. **Thoughts on Germany.** New York: Macmillan, 1932, 315 p.
This is one of the important books on modern Germany. The former Foreign Minister of the Empire writes without rancor and as a man of the world. The book contains interesting reflections on German policy before the war, also on the party conflicts of contemporary Germany and such questions as treaty revision and reparations.

LAPORTE, MAURICE. **Sous le Casque d'Acier.** Paris: Redier, 1931, 324 p.
Startling revelations regarding German military societies and preparations for war.

LAURET, RENÉ. **Les Conditions de la Vie en Allemagne.** Paris: Crès, 1923, 174 p.
One of the best French surveys of the situation in Germany during the year 1922.

LOTE, RENÉ. **L'Allemagne d'Après-Guerre.** Paris: Alcan, 1928, 318 p.
A professor at Grenoble gives a straightforward account of the national revival, and a somewhat over-sanguine view of Germany's possibilities.

LUEHR, ELMER. **The New German Republic.** New York: Minton, Balch, 1929, 442 p.
A review of the development of the German Republic from the Revolution to the present time. One of the best general histories written by a non-German.

MORDACQ, JEAN JULES HENRI. **La Mentalité Allemande.** Paris: Plon, 1926, 284 p.
The observations of a French general on the Rhine during the five years from 1921 to 1926. He believes the Germans unrepentant.

MORGAN, JOHN HARTMAN. **The Present State of Germany.** Boston: Small, Maynard, 1924, 107 p.
An interesting brief survey with stress on economic conditions.

MÜLLER, ERNST. **Bolschevismus, Faschismus oder Freistaat?** Munich: Wittkop, 1931, 301 p.
A telling critique of the German post-war régime.

MÜLLER-FREIENFELS, RICHARD. **Die Psychologie des Deutschen Menschen und Seiner Kultur.** Munich: Beck, 2nd, rev. ed., 1929, 245 p.
A valuable attempt to analyze the psychology of the German race and German culture, emphasizing especially its bearing on political life and institutions.

NEY, E. L. **L'Autre Allemagne.** Paris: Berger-Levrault, 1930, 268 p.
An exposure of the German revenge movement, by a French officer on mission. Covering the period from 1921 on, he gives a detailed account of secret arms caches, organizations and intrigues.

NORDICUS, *pseud.* **Hitlerism, the Iron Fist in Germany.** New York: Mohawk Press, 1932, 243 p.
A well-informed, rather sober analysis of the Nazi movement.

OTTWALDT, ERNST. **Deutschland Erwache!** Leipzig: Hess, 1932, 392 p.
A strongly partisan account of the National Socialist movement and its leader.

PERNOT, MAURICE. **L'Allemagne Aujourd'hui.** Paris: Hachette, 1927, 202 p.
In this panoramic view of present-day Germany an able French commentator discusses the new moral outlook and touches on social changes, financial evolution, educational development, political conditions, the problems of federalism and decentrali-
zation, foreign policy and commercial expansion. He suggests that the Franco-German
rapprochement begin in the economic field.

PIAZZA, GIUSEPPE. **La Germania fra l'Europa e l'Antieuropa.** Rome: Campitelli,
1931, 320 p.
An Italian journalist's reports from Berlin.

POSSE, ERNST H. **Die Politischen Kampfbünde Deutschlands.** Berlin: Junker und
Dünnhaupt, 1930, 89 p.
A very compact survey of the militant political organizations of Germany.

PRICE, MORGAN PHILIPS. **Germany in Transition.** London: Labour Publishing Co.,
1924, 262 p.
A study of the social and economic ch anges since 1919 by a moderate British Laborite.
This is one of the best of the earlier b ooks on the revolutionary period.

QUAATZ, REINHOLD GEORG and SPAHN, MARTIN. **Deutschland unter Militär-, Finanz-
und Wirtschaftskontrolle.** Berlin: Stilke, 1925, 146 p.
A concise presentation of the system of control as established by the peace treaties
and the London Agreement.

QUIGLEY, HUGH and CLARK, R. T. **Republican Germany.** New York: Dodd, 1928,
332 p.
A well-informed and sympathetic review of the first decade of post-war Germany.
The authors emphasize especially the conflict with nationalist movements, and the
great economic issues.

REBOUL, JEAN MARIE PAUL. **L'Allemagne et Ses Camouflages.** Paris: Berger-Levrault,
1921, 182 p.
A special military commentator for the *Temps* reports that Germany in 1921 was
what she was in 1914, unable to recognize her own faults or to respect the rights of
others.

REVENTLOW, ERNST, GRAF ZU. **Monarchie?** Leipzig: Hammer, 1926, 124 p.
A criticism of the old régime coming to the conclusion that the monarchy will be
possible only if based on the national idea.

ROHRBACH, PAUL. **Deutschland. Tod oder Leben?** Munich: Bruckmann, 1930, 256 p.
A well-known nationalist writer looks for a national regeneration through electoral
reform, federalism, etc.

SCHEUMANN, WALTHER. **Der Nationalsozialismus.** Berlin: Der Neue Geist, 1931, 143 p.
One of the best brief accounts of the Hitler movement.

SCHNEE, HEINRICH, DRAEGER, HANS and others, *eds.* **Zehn Jahre Versailles.** Berlin:
Brückenverlag, 1929-1930, 3 v.
A collection of essays by prominent Germans, dealing with the economic and political
results of the treaty, as well as with the arguments in favor of revision.

SHUSTER, GEORGE N. **The Germans. An Inquiry and an Estimate.** New York: Dial,
1932, 334 p.
A sound appraisal of the mental and moral state of present-day Germany.

SPETHMANN, HANS. **Die Rothe Armee an Ruhr und Rhein.** Berlin: Hobbing, 1930, 251 p.
An important contribution to the history of the Kapp Putsch of 1920, by an authority on the history of the Ruhr and the Ruhr industries.

TACITUS REDIVIVUS, *pseud.* **Die Grosse Trommel.** Berlin: Deutsch-Schweizerische Verlagsanstalt, 1930, 155 p.
The Hitlerite movement approached in a humorously sarcastic spirit.

VERMEIL, EDMOND. **L'Allemagne Contemporaine.** Paris: Alcan, 1925, 255 p.
A general political, economic and social history of the new Germany, with emphasis on the conflict of economic classes.

VERMEIL, EDMOND, BROUILHET, CHARLES and others. **L'Allemagne depuis la Guerre.** Paris: Librairie Générale de Droit, 1926, 121 p.
A series of substantial essays on juridical, political and economic aspects.

VIBRAYE, RÉGIS DE, COMTE. **Allemagne 1930.** Bordeaux: Feret, 1930, 158 p.
A general survey, followed by a plea for Franco-German coöperation.

VIÉNOT, PIERRE. **Is Germany Finished?** New York: Macmillan, 1932, 141 p.
A translation of an admirable little book, in which a sympathetic French observer tries to make clear to his countrymen the extent and nature of the German *Kulturkrise.*

WERTHEIMER, FRIEDRICH. **Von Deutschen Parteien und Parteiführern im Ausland.** Berlin: Zentralverlag, 1927, 251 p.
Really a survey of the political position of the Germans in adjacent countries.

WINNIG, AUGUST. **Das Reich als Republik, 1918-1928.** Stuttgart: Cotta, 1928, 361 p.
The former governor of East Prussia paints a rather lugubrious picture of the past ten years and bemoans the mistakes that have been made.

WOLF, HANS and SEIDLER, FRITZ. **Die Deutsche Politik seit 1918.** Karlsruhe: Müller und Gräf, 1928, 95 p.
A documentary survey of events, bringing the story to December 1927. The authors' plan included annual supplements.

Zehn Jahre Deutsche Geschichte, 1918-1928. Berlin: Stollberg, 1928, 556 p.
A coöperative survey of German history and problems since 1918. Oncken writes on the historical development, Noske on the defense against Bolshevism, Gessler on the organization of the new army, Rheinbaben on foreign policy, Müller on social legislation and Dooifel on the German press.

Constitutional Problems

ANSCHÜTZ, GERHARD. **Die Verfassung des Deutschen Reichs.** Berlin: Stilke, 8th ed., 1928, 453 p.
An adequate commentary on the constitution.

AUBRY, MAURICE. **La Constitution Prussienne du 30 Novembre 1920.** Paris: La Vie Universitaire, 1922, 216 p.
A systematic analysis, reprinting the text.

BECKER, OTTO. **Weimarer Reichsverfassung und Nationale Entwicklung.** Berlin: Heymann, 1931, 122 p.
The German historian points out the historical position of the constitution and argues for evolution as against revolutionary change in meeting new requirements.

BLACHLY, FREDERICK FRANK and OATMAN, MIRIAM EULALIE. **The Government and Administration of Germany.** Baltimore: Johns Hopkins University Press, 1928, 770 p.
A useful guide, published by the Institute for Government Research.

BREDT, JOHANNES VICTOR. **Der Geist der Deutschen Reichsverfassung.** Berlin: Stilke, 1924, 465 p.
A study of the fundamental principles embodied in the constitution.

BRUNET, RENÉ. **The New German Constitution.** New York: Knopf, 1922, 339 p.
Still one of the best commentaries and expositions.

EMERSON, RUPERT. **State and Sovereignty in Modern Germany.** New Haven: Yale University Press, 1928, 293 p.
An admirable work reviewing the political theories of the German jurists in the period since 1871.

FREYTAGH-LORINGHOVEN, AXEL, FREIHERR VON. **Die Weimarer Verfassung.** Munich: Lehmann, 1924, 424 D.
A scholarly review of the provisions of the constitution and the machinery of government.

GOLDSCHMIDT, HANS. **Das Reich und Preussen im Kampf um die Führung.** Berlin: Heymann, 1931.
A volume of documents and commentary covering the constitutional problem in Germany from Bismarck's time to 1918.

HARMS, BERNHARD, *ed.* **Recht und Staat im Neuen Deutschland.** Berlin: Hobbing, 1929, 2 v.
A valuable series of lectures on the German constitution, economic and social legislation, and international relations, by such authorities as Driesch, Oncken, Jellinek, Stier-Somlo and Mendelssohn Bartholdy.

MATTERN, JOHANNES. **Principles of the Constitutional Jurisprudence of the German National Republic.** Baltimore: Johns Hopkins University Press, 1928, 682 p.
A scholarly study of the fundamental principles of the German constitution, preceded by a survey of German constitutional development prior to 1918.

MEISSNER, OTTO. **Das Neue Staatsrecht des Reichs und Seiner Länder.** Berlin: Hobbing, 1921, 359 p.
The best brief treatment of German constitutional law.

OPPENHEIMER, HEINRICH. **The Constitution of the German Republic.** London: Stevens, 1923, 260 p.
A critical exposition and analysis of considerable value.

PREUSS, HUGO. **Staat, Recht und Freiheit.** Tübingen: Mohr, 1926, 588 p.
Essays and writings of the German jurist who was the father of the new constitution.

SCHULZE, ALFRED. **Das Neue Deutsche Reich.** Dresden: Jess, 1927, 259 p.
A high Saxon official gives an instructive survey of the constitutional situation.

VERMEIL, EDMOND. **La Constitution de Weimar et le Principe de la Démocratie Allemande.** Strasbourg: Librairie Istra, 1923, 473 p.
An interpretation of the present German political system in the light of the constitutional history of the last century. A well-documented analysis of the new constitution.

Financial and Economic Problems

See also (International Finance) Reparations and War Debts, p. 25.

ABRAMOVICI, ARTHUR. **Étude sur les Transformations du Système Monétaire Allemand de 1919 à 1925 et Ses Conséquences Économiques.** Paris: Jouve, 1926, 243 p.

A substantial dissertation, treating especially the effects of the government's monetary policy on taxes, banks, and stock exchange.

AGAHD, ERNST. **Planeta. Wir und die Weltwirtschaft.** Berlin: Weitsicht-Verlag, 1931, 356 p.
A critique of German investments and banking activities in pre-war Russia.

ANGELL, JAMES WATERHOUSE. **The Recovery of Germany.** New Haven: Yale University Press, 1932, 442 p.
The revised edition of the best study in English of German economic development in the post-war period. The author bases his account not only on the great mass of statistical material, but also on the results of extensive personal investigation. Published for the Council on Foreign Relations.

BAUMGARTNER, WILFRID. **Le Rentenmark, 15 Octobre 1923-11 Octobre 1924.** Paris: Presses Universitaires, 1925, 175 p.
A good French treatment of the establishment of the Rentenmark, its effects on public and private finance, and finally the return to the gold standard.

BECKERATH, HERBERT VON. **Reparationsagent und Deutsche Wirtschaft.** Bonn: Schroeder, 1928, 107 p.
A telling critique of the present German economic system, by a leading economist.

Die Bedeutung der Rationalisierung für das Deutsche Wirtschaftsleben. Berlin: Stilke, 1928, 460 p.
An important symposium on nationalization in all its aspects, by a group of experts.

BEUSCH, PAUL. **Währungszerfall und Währungsstabilisierung.** Berlin: Springer, 1928, 181 p.
A posthumous account of the stabilization, by a high official of the finance ministry. The book contains a number of valuable documents.

BÜCHER, HERMANN. **Finanz- und Wirtschaftsentwicklung Deutschlands in den Jahren 1921 bis 1925.** Berlin: Heymann, 1925, 203 p.
Speeches on reparations, the Dawes plan, the Rentenbank, etc., by the influential ex-president of the "Reichsverband der Deutschen Industrie."

BÜSCHER, GUSTAV. **Die Inflation und Ihre Lehren.** Zurich: Rudolf, 1926, 187 p.
A very critical discussion of the inflation and its effects, especially in respect to the destruction of property.

CAMBON, VICTOR. **L'Allemagne Nouvelle.** Paris: Roger, 1923, 287 p.
Observations of a well-known French writer on German economic life. The author attempts to show the completeness and rapidity of Germany's economic recovery.

DALBERG, RUDOLF. **Deutsche Währungs- und Kreditpolitik, 1923-1926.** Berlin: Hobbing, 1926, 161 p.
A collection of speeches and essays on German monetary history, by a high official of the Ministry for Economics.

DAWSON, SIR PHILIP. **Germany's Industrial Revival.** London: Williams and Norgate, 1926, 276 p.
A series of articles by an English expert. They deal chiefly with the fiscal and economic policies of post-war Germany and their effects on industry.

DERNIS, GEORGES. **La Renaissance du Crédit en Allemagne.** Paris: Presses Universitaires, 1927, 140 p.
A well-documented examination of the reëstablishment of credit in Germany, the general purpose being to discredit the idea of revaluation.

ELSTER, KARL. **Von der Mark zur Reichsmark.** Jena: Fischer, 1928, 480 p.
A scientific and documented history of the Germany currency from 1914 to 1924, the more valuable as the author discusses the inflation in conjunction with the effects of the peace treaties, the economic dislocation, the reparations tangle, etc.

FLINK, SALOMON. **The German Reichsbank and Economic Germany.** New York: Harper, 1930, 277 p.
The history of the Reichsbank, treated with special reference to its part in the handling of reparations and reconstruction problems.

FOURGEAUD, ANDRÉ. **La Dépréciation et la Revalorisation du Mark Allemand.** Paris: Payot, 1926, 304 p.
A good dissertation, treating the collapse of the mark and its economic and social consequences, followed by an analysis of the stabilization.

GEYER, CURT. **Drei Verderber Deutschlands.** Berlin: Dietz, 1924, 230 p.
A severe attack upon the financial policies of Havenstein, Helfferich and Stinnes, which the author regards as responsible for the wretched state of German finances.

GIUSTINIANI, GASTON. **Le Commerce et l'Industrie devant la Dépréciation et la Stabilisation Monétaire.** Paris: Alcan, 1927, 211 p.
A scholarly investigation of German economic life as affected by the financial crisis.

HAAS, HERMANN, OTT, ROLF and HOLZMANN, WILHELM. **Auslandsanleihen und Reparationen.** Jena: Fischer, 1929, 256 p.
Three essays, by German experts, dealing with foreign loans and their effects on economic life, and with the effects upon exchange of measures taken by the Agent-General for Reparation Payments.

HENNIG, CURT. **Die Struktur der Deutschen Reichsbank und Ihre Geld- und Kreditpolitik unter der Herrschaft des Dawes-Planes.** Berlin: Ebering, 1930, 202 p.
A technical study, covering the operations of the Reichsbank from 1924 to 1928.

HERMANT, MAX. **Les Paradoxes Économiques de l'Allemagne Moderne, 1918-1931.** Paris: Colin, 1931, 202 p.
Interesting especially for its light on the German financial crisis. The author reviews the economic history of Germany since the war and explains the present difficulties as the result of rationalization.

KNICKERBOCKER, HUBERT RENFRO. **The German Crisis.** New York: Farrar and Rinehart, 1932, 262 p.
A well-known American correspondent's investigation of the situation of the moment.

KOLLBACH, PAUL. **Deutsche Handelsflotte und Versailler Vertrag.** Berlin: Dümmler, 1929, 176 p.
A survey of the destruction and reconstruction of the German merchant marine with special reference to the provisions of the peace treaties.

LÖFFLER, WERNER. **Die Moderne Konzernierung.** Frankenstein: Philipp, 1926, 143 p.
An account of the German combinations in big business in the post-war period.

LOTZ, WALTHER. **Die Deutsche Staatsfinanzwirtschaft im Kriege.** New Haven: Yale University Press, 1927, 151 p.
The writer, a well-known German economist, shows to how large an extent the war was financed by the German government by means of loans, and explains why the system of greater taxation was difficult. A volume in the Carnegie Series.

LÜTHGEN, HELMUT. **Das Rheinisch-Westfälische Kohlensyndikat.** Leipzig: Deichert, 1926, 238 p.
A brief history of the great coal syndicate, covering the pre-war as well as the post-war period.

LUTHER, HANS. **Feste Mark—Solide Wirtschaft.** Berlin: Otto Stollberg, 1924.
A popular exposition of the former Chancellor's financial policy.

MEAKIN, WALTER. **The New Industrial Revolution.** London: Gollancz, 1928, 284 p.
A sound study of the post-war tendencies of capital and labor, with special reference to the reorganization and revival of German industry.

MENZEL, CURT. **Das Deutsche Vorkriegsvermögen in Russland und der Deutsche Entschädigungsvorbehalt.** Berlin: De Gruyter, 1931, 236 p.
A technical discussion of the evolution of the problem of German investments in Russia.

MEYER, WALTHER. **Die Deutschen Auslandsanleihen in der Nachkriegszeit.** Berlin: Särchen, 1928, 106 p.
The author of this heavily documented dissertation discusses the period 1924-1926, studying the reasons for German loans, the technique followed, and the consequences. Special attention is given to the loans from the United States.

MICHELS, RUDOLF KARL. **Cartels, Combines and Trusts in Post-War Germany.** New York: Columbia University Press, 1928, 183 p.
A survey of the movement and an analysis of its working in the leading industries. The book is brief and to the point and should be welcomed by students of international economics.

PFITZNER, JOHANNES. **Deutschlands Auslandsanleihen.** Berlin: Heymann, 1928, 174 p.
A manual of German indebtedness. The author deals with local and city loans, industrials, etc.

PRIESKER, HANS E. **Der Wiederaufbau der Deutschen Handelsschiffahrt.** Berlin: Springer, 1926, 152 p.
An account of the recovery of Germany's merchant marine.

RAAB, FRIEDRICH. **Die Entwicklung der Reichsfinanzen seit 1924.** Berlin: Zentralverlag, 1929, 127 p.
Perhaps the best general treatment of the German budgetary situation since the introduction of the Dawes Plan.

RAFFEGEAU, P. C. and LACOUT, A. **Établissement des Bilans-Or.** Paris: Payot, 1926, 149 p.
The authors are concerned mainly with a study of business and banking under the inflation and the depreciated currency. The third part discusses the modalities of the return to the gold standard.

Rationalization of German Industry. New York: National Industrial Conference Board, 1931, 182 p.
A valuable survey of the great changes in the leading German industries since the war.

Die Reichsbank, 1901-1925. Berlin: Reichsbank, 1925, 184 p.
A valuable official history of the Bank, its organization and activity, with much statistical material.

REINHOLD, PETER P. **The Economic, Financial and Political State of Germany since the War.** New Haven: Yale University Press, 1928, 143 p.
Williamstown lectures of the former German Finance Minister. The book discusses the reparations question, the financial problem, the aftermath of stabilization, the transfer question, etc.

RIVAUD, ALBERT. **Les Crises Allemandes, 1919-1931.** Paris: Colin, 1932, 218 p.
This little popular survey, concerned primarily with economic matters, comes to the usual French conclusions, namely that Germany is a military menace and that she must be made to pay.

SCHACHT, HJALMAR. **The Stabilization of the Mark.** New York: Adelphi Co., 1927, 247 p.

The President of the Reichsbank tells his story, based in large part on unpublished material. Probably the most important single book on the history of the post-war German currency.

SOMBART, WERNER, *ed*. **Volk und Raum.** Hamburg: Hanseatische Verlagsanstalt, 1928, 218 p.
Authoritative opinions on the question whether German territory will support a growing population.

TARLÉ, ANTOINE DE. **La Préparation de la Lutte Économique par l'Allemagne.** Paris: Payot, 1919, 284 p.
An early French cry of alarm. A report on the situation of German industry and its organization for regaining lost markets.

THALHEIM, KARL E. **Das Deutsche Auswanderungsproblem der Nachkriegszeit.** Crimmitschau: Rohland und Berthold, 1926, 173 p.
The first adequate treatment of the German emigration problem after the war.

WELTER, ERICH. **Die Ursachen des Kapitalmangels in Deutschland.** Tübingen: Mohr, 1931, 221 p.
A pioneer study of the dearth of capital in Germany and its causes.

Zahlen zur Geldentwertung in Deutschland, 1914-1923. Berlin: Hobbing, 1925, 54 p.
Figures published by the Statistical Office to illustrate the course of the mark, the wholesale and retail prices, salaries, etc.

Biographies

See also (World War) Biographies of Wartime Statesmen and Diplomats, p. 101; also (Europe) Biographies, p. 228.

ALTER, JUNIUS. **Nationalisten.** Leipzig: Koehler, 1930, 214 p.
Character sketches of German nationalist leaders like Kapp, Reventlow, Hitler, Hugenberg and Ludendorff.

BAUER, HEINRICH. **Stresemann.** Berlin: Stilke, 1930, 268 p.
A good, if not very critical study of Stresemann's political career and achievements, based in part on conversations with Stresemann.

BEER, RÜDIGER ROBERT. **Heinrich Brüning.** Berlin: Politisch-Wissenschaftlicher Verlag, 1931, 70 p.
A biographical sketch by one of Brüning's admirers.

BRINCKMEYER, HERMANN. **Die Rathenaus.** Munich: Wieland-Verlag, 1923, 97 p.
A study of the careers of Emil and Walther Rathenau in relation to the economic development of modern Germany.

BROCKDORFF-RANTZAU, ULRICH KARL CHRISTIAN, GRAF. **Dokumente.** Berlin: Deutsche Verlagsgesellschaft für Politik und Geschichte, 2nd ed., 1922, 278 p.
Declarations and statements of policy by the German peace envoy (1918-1921) revealing a new German policy—"ein Zukunftsprogramm"—based on the consolidation of German democracy and coöperation with the small nations.

EBERT, FRIEDRICH. **Schriften, Aufzeichnungen, Reden.** Dresden: Reissner, 1926, 2 v.
An excellent edition of the speeches and writings of the first President of the Republic, with some interesting recollections.

EISNER, KURT. **Gesammelte Schriften.** Berlin: Cassirer, 1919, 2 v.
The standard edition of the writings of the famous leader of the Bavarian Revolution.

EULENBERG, HERBERT. **The Hohenzollerns.** New York: Century, 1929, 364 p.
Feuilletonistic essays in the style of Ludwig, with emphasis on all that is scandalous.

FÜRSTENBERG, CARL. **Die Lebensgeschichte eines Deutschen Bankiers.** Berlin: Ullstein, 1931, 577 p.
The biography of a prominent German banker; an important contribution to the history of German finance and industry.

GOLDSMITH, MARGARET LELAND and VOIGT, FREDERICK. **Hindenburg, the Man and the Legend.** New York: Morrow, 1930, 304 p.
A biographical study which leaves little of Hindenburg but the legend.

HAASE, ERNST, *ed.* **Hugo Haase.** Berlin: Ottens, 1929, 254 p.
This brief biography of the socialist leader, followed by letters, articles and speeches, throws light on the attitude of the Socialist Party at the outbreak of the war, during the war period, and in the Revolution.

HITLER, ADOLF. **Mein Kampf.** Munich: Eher, 1925, 2 v.
Hitler's story of his rise. An unimpressive but widely read work.

KESSLER, HARRY, GRAF VON. **Walther Rathenau.** New York: Harcourt, 1930, 379 p.
The best biography of the German statesman. The author, while saying little of Rathenau as an industrial leader, analyzes his writings in detail and discusses fully his career as a statesman. The book throws considerable light on the Genoa negotiations, the Rapallo Treaty, etc.

KOHLHAAS, FRAU ETTA (FEDERN). **Walther Rathenau.** Dresden: Reissner, 1927, 256 p.
A sympathetic picture of Rathenau as a man, but hardly critical enough to be an authoritative study of his teaching.

LACOUR-GAYET, GEORGES. **Guillaume II, le Vaincu.** Paris: Hachette, 1920, 341 p.
Not so much a biography as a study of the Emperor's attitude and policy in various matters.

LENGYEL, EMIL. **Hitler.** New York: Dial, 1932, 256 p.
A study of Hitler's career and the development of the Hitler movement. One of the best accounts available in English.

LEWIS, WYNDHAM. **Hitler.** London: Chatto and Windus, 1931, 202 p.
A brilliant estimate of a religion and its prophet.

LIEBKNECHT, KARL PAUL AUGUST FRIEDRICH. **Reden und Aufsätze.** Hamburg: Hoym, 1921, 374 p.
Utterances and writings of the German communist leader, arranged topically. A valuable collection.

LUDWIG, EMIL. **Wilhelm Hohenzollern.** New York: Putnam, 1927, 528 p.
The most widely-read biography. Lively in style and showing occasional flashes of insight, but journalistic and sensational.

LUMM, KARL VON. **Karl Helfferich als Währungspolitiker und Gelehrter.** Leipzig: Hirschfeld, 1926, 164 p.
A sympathetic study by one of Helfferich's collaborators. Especially important for the history of the stabilization of the German currency.

LUXEMBURG, ROSA. **Letters to Karl and Luise Kautsky, 1896-1918.** New York: McBride, 1925, 238 p.
Correspondence of the famous Spartacist leader, important for the history of the communist movement in Germany.

MICHAELIS, GEORG. **Für Staat und Volk.** Berlin: Furche Verlag, 1922, 440 p.
The unimpressive memoirs of the unimpressive successor of Bethmann-Hollweg.

MURET, MAURICE. **Guillaume II.** Paris: Éditions des Portiques, 1930, 379 p.
A general biography, based upon the innumerable biographies and diaries of associates that have appeared since the war. An honest book, undocumented but containing a very full bibliography.

NIEMANN, ALFRED. **Wanderungen mit Kaiser Wilhelm II.** Leipzig: Koehler, 1924, 128 p.
Conversations with William II after the war. They deal with a variety of subjects and may be taken as a kind of supplement to the ex-Emperor's own memoirs.

NOBEL, ALPHONS. **Brüning.** Leipzig: Kitler, 1932, 88 p.
A brief sketch, emphasizing the international aspects of Brüning's policies.

NOSKE, GUSTAV. **Von Kiel bis Kapp.** Berlin: Verlag für Politik und Wirtschaft, 1920, 210 p.
A detailed account and apology for the writer's activity as Minister of Defense. One of the important sources for the history of the years 1918 to 1920.

OLDEN, RUDOLF. **Stresemann.** New York: Dutton, 1930, 235 p.
The English translation of one of the best biographies of the late statesman; written with understanding and psychological grasp.

RAPHAËL, GASTON. **Le Roi de la Ruhr; Hugo Stinnes, l'Homme.** Paris: Payot, 1923, 205 p.
A typical French product of the days of the Ruhr invasion. Stinnes pictured as the evil spirit who must be punished.

RATHENAU, WALTHER. **Politische Briefe.** Dresden: Reissner, 1929, 348 p.
These letters cover the period from 1913 to 1922, and constitute a valuable source for the study of Rathenau's views and policies.

RHEINBABEN, ROCHUS, FREIHERR VON. **Stresemann.** New York: Appleton, 1929, 322 p.
A general biographical sketch, but with the emphasis on Stresemann's political career, and especially on his foreign policies. On the whole a well informed and fair estimate.

SCHEIDEMANN, PHILIPP. **The Making of New Germany.** New York: Appleton, 1929, 2 v.
The autobiography of the Socialist leader, dealing very largely with the pre-war period. The book throws light on the history of German Social-Democracy.

SCHEIDEMANN, PHILIPP. **Der Zusammenbruch.** Berlin: Verlag für Sozialwissenschaft, 1921, 251 p.
Reminiscences and experiences of the war period and the Revolution, by a Socialist leader. An important account.

SCHULTZE-PFAELZER, GERHARD. **Hindenburg.** Glasgow: P. Allan, 1931, 368 p.
A somewhat journalistic biography, with much emphasis on Hindenburg's post-war political career.

SEECKT, HANS VON. **Thoughts of a Soldier.** London: Benn, 1930, 161 p.
Reflections upon military and other affairs by the famous German general, who at times seems to exaggerate the novelty of his views.

SEECKT, HANS VON. **The Future of the German Empire.** New York: Dutton, 1930, 187 p.
In continuation of "Thoughts of a Soldier," these essays are interesting chiefly for the discussion of the question of the police and the army.

SEVERING, CARL. **1919-1920, im Wetter- und Watterwinkel.** Bielefeld: Volkswacht, 1927, 253 p.
Valuable notes and reminiscences of the years 1919-1920, the Kapp Putsch and the Ruhr strike, by the commissar in the Rhenish-Westphalian industrial area.

STERN-RUBARTH, EDGAR. **Graf Brockdorff-Rantzau.** Berlin: Hobbing, 1929, 174 p.
An important biography of the German diplomat who was first Foreign Minister of the German Republic and served from 1922 to 1928 as Ambassador to Russia. Written by an intimate friend.

STERN-RUBARTH, EDGAR. **Stresemann, der Europäer.** Berlin: Hobbing, 1930, 100 p.
Not a biography, but a revealing study of Stresemann's policy and aspirations in the larger setting, written by one of his collaborators.

STRESEMANN, GUSTAV. **Essays and Speeches on Various Subjects.** London: Butterworth, 1930, 306 p.
A happy selection of papers and addresses illustrating the revolution of the ideas of the late German Foreign Minister. Contains a biographical introduction by von Rheinbaben.

STRESEMANN, GUSTAV. **Reden und Schriften.** Dresden: Reissner, 1926, 2 v.
Addresses and writings of the German Foreign Minister from 1897 to 1926.

STRESEMANN, GUSTAV. **Vermächtnis.** Berlin: Ullstein, 1932, 643 p.
The first of three volumes of Stresemann's writings, published and unpublished, on which he himself intended to base his autobiography. An important source for the history of post-war Europe.

THOMPSON, DOROTHY. **I Saw Hitler.** New York: Farrar and Rinehart, 1932, 43 p.
A clever snapshot, with a telescope lens.

UFERMANN, PAUL. **Könige der Inflation.** Berlin: Verlag für Sozialwissenschaft, 1924.
Critical biographical portraits of some of the leading German industrial magnates.

VALLENTIN, ANTONINA. **Stresemann.** New York: R. R. Smith, 1931, 359 p.
This book, based upon intimate knowledge, is a real contribution to the story of Stresemann's leadership.

WETERSTETTEN, RUDOLPH and WATSON, A. M. K. **The Biography of President von Hindenburg.** New York: Macmillan, 1930, 276 p.
A sympathetic biography in which the civil as well as the military career of the German President is given due consideration.

WILHELM II, EX-EMPEROR OF GERMANY. **Memoirs, 1888-1918.** New York: Harper, 1922, 348 p.
A disappointing book, superficial and undocumented, but not to be passed over since it gives the Emperor's account of critical episodes in his reign.

YBARRA, THOMAS RUSSELL. **Hindenburg, the Man with Three Lives.** New York: Duffield and Green, 1932, 329 p.
A sympathetic biography stressing the extraordinary fluctuations in Hindenburg's career and outlook.

Foreign Policy

See also (War, Peace, Security and Disarmament) Locarno Pacts, p. 79; also (France) Relations with Germany, p.260; also (Austria) The Anschluss Problem, p. 307; also (Northern Europe) Baltic States, p. 340; also (Poland) The Corridor and Danzig, p. 354.

BOSCHMANS, RAYMOND. **Les Ailes Repoussent. Comment l'Allemagne Prépare Sa Revanche.** Paris: Charles-Lavauzelle, 1921, 107 p.
The title adequately describes the book. A French *cri d'alarme* at Germany's sinister plans.

CHÉRADAME, ANDRÉ. **The Mystification of the Allied Peoples. Why? How? By Whom?** Évreux: Author, 1923, 404 p.

Another exposé by a well-known nationalist writer. He this time reveals how the Germans have managed to evade the treaties and how German and British financial interests have combined to dupe the trusting French.

DEWALL, WOLF VON. **Der Kampf um den Frieden.** Frankfurt: Frankfurter Societäts-druckerei, 1929, 244 p.
Fundamental problems of German foreign policy described, with stress on the necessity of Franco-German understanding.

ERUSALIMSKIĬ, A. **Germaniia, Antanta i S. S. S. R.** Moscow: Communist Academy, 1928, 187 p.
The position of Germany in the policy of the Entente to encircle Russia.

GÖHRE, PAUL. **Deutschlands Weltpolitische Zukunft.** Berlin: Vowinckel, 1925, 176 p.
A plea by a former Prussian minister for Germany's entrance into the League, as the most effective way for Germany to regain her position.

GOTTSCHALK, HERMANN. **Deutschland Neutral.** Leipzig: Fleischer, 1929, 150 p.
The way to real freedom lies in Germany's voluntary abstention from international disputes.

HAUSHOFER, K. and TRAMPLER, K. **Deutschlands Weg an der Zeitwende.** Munich: Hugendubel, 1931, 238 p.
Essays by experts, including men like Treviranus and Schnee, reviewing the German position in eastern and western Europe, the colonial problem, reparations and armaments, domestic, economic and political questions and Germany's position in the world.

HOETZSCH, OTTO. **Germany's Domestic and Foreign Policies.** New Haven: Yale University Press, 1929, 116 p.
Williamstown lectures, by a German scholar, editor of *Osteuropa*. The most important are those dealing with Germany's position in Europe, her relations with Russia, and her policy towards the League.

Der Kampf um die Deutsche Aussenpolitik. Leipzig: Liszt, 1931, 425 p.
A review and study of the course of German foreign policy since the war.

KOCH-WESER, ERICH. **Germany in the Post-War World.** Philadelphia: Dorrance, 1930, 222 p.
A translation of one of the sanest discussions of German policy in the past decade.

KRAUS, HERBERT. **Der Auswärtige Dienst des Deutschen Reiches.** Berlin: Stilke, 1932, 1216 p.
An elaborate account of the German foreign service, published by the Foreign Office.

LOISEAU, HIPPOLYTE. **Le Pangermanisme, Ce Qu'Il Fut—Ce Qu'Il Est.** Paris: Payot, 1921, 170 p.
Intended as a warning to the French people that Madame de Staël was wrong, that the Germans are double-faced, and that the Pan-German menace still exists.

MERSMANN-SOEST, O. and WOHL, PAUL. **Die Deutsch-Russischen Verträge vom 12 Oktober 1925.** Berlin: Vahlen, 1926, 372 p.
Perhaps the best of a number of studies on the commercial treaties of 1925, containing the texts of all pertinent laws.

METZ, FRIEDRICH, *ed.* **Probleme des Deutschen Westens.** Berlin: Hobbing, 1928, 160 p.
A series of essays by eminent German historians discussing Rhine policies and the problems of the Saar, Eupen-Malmedy and Luxembourg.

NIEKISCH, ERNST. **Entscheidung.** Berlin: Widerstands-Verlag, 1930, 186 p.
Germany must regain her complete independence by scaring Europe with the bogey of a Russian-Asiatic deluge.

REVENTLOW, ERNST, GRAF ZU. **Minister Stresemann als Staatsmann und Anwalt des Weltgewissens.** Munich: Lehmann, 1925, 98 p.
A very able attack on Stresemann's foreign policy by a well-known nationalist.

RHEINBABEN, WERNER KARL FERDINAND, FREIHERR VON. **Von Versailles zur Freiheit.** Hamburg: Hanseatische Verlagsanstalt, 1927, 254 p.
A brief survey of the course of German foreign policy since Versailles.

SCHMIDT, AUGUST. **Das Neue Deutschland in der Weltpolitik und Weltwirtschaft.** Berlin: Hobbing, 1925, 429 p.
An able study of German foreign policy and economic policy in the larger setting of "global" problems.

SCHÜCKING, WALTHER. **Die Nationalen Aufgaben Unserer Auswärtigen Politik.** Berlin: Hensel, 1926, 74 p.
A collection of essays by the famous German writer and protagonist of the League.

SONTER, RICHARD. **Der Neue Deutsche Imperialismus.** Hamburg: Hoym, 1928, 192 p.
A Socialist tirade against the new imperialism.

STEGEMANN, HERMANN. **Deutschland und Europa.** Berlin: Deutsche Verlagsanstalt, 1932, 448 p.
A study of the German problem in its European setting, by a leading political writer.

WAHL, KURT HARTWIG. **Die Deutschen Länder in der Aussenpolitik.** Stuttgart: Enke, 1930, 162 p.
The author studies the treaty-making power of the German lands under the Weimar Constitution and its effect on German foreign policy.

The Question of Colonies

See also (League of Nations) Mandates, p. 58.

ABS, JOSEPH MARIA. **Der Kampf um Unsere Schutzgebiete.** Düsseldorf: Floeder, 1926, 382 p.
A series of essays on various aspects of German colonial enterprise and administration, followed by an account of Allied rule and conditions in the mandated territories.

DIX, ARTHUR. **Weltkrise und Kolonialpolitik.** Berlin: Neff, 1931, 347 p.
Germany's urgent need for colonies if she is again to become a good customer in world trade.

POESCHEL, HANS, *comp.* **Die Kolonialfrage im Frieden von Versailles.** Berlin: Mittler, 1920, 246 p.
A valuable collection of documents dealing with the treaty settlements of the German colonies, together with texts of debates in the Reichstag, and many excerpts from the world's press.

SALESSE, CAPITAINE. **Le Problème Colonial Allemand.** Paris: Charles-Lavauzelle, 1931, 130 p.
The familiar French argument against the return of colonies to Germany.

SCHNEE, HEINRICH. **German Colonization Past and Present.** New York: Knopf, 1926, 176 p.
The best general account of the German colonial problem. The author, formerly governor of East Africa, defends the German administration, exposes what he considers were the real objects of the Allies in taking the colonies, and severely criticizes their post-war government of the former German possessions.

SEILLIÈRE, ERNEST, BARON. **Les Pangermanistes d'Après-Guerre.** Paris: Alcan, 1924.
The well-known French philosopher of imperialism examines some post-war German doctrines of expansion.

TOWNSEND, MARY EVELYN. **The Rise and Fall of Germany's Colonial Empire.**
New York: Macmillan, 1930, 442 p.
An excellent scholarly study of Germany's short-lived empire. On the whole the best single-volume account.

ZASTROW, R. VON and DANNERT, EDUARD, *eds.* **Deutschland Braucht Kolonien!**
Berlin: Deutsche Volksgemeinschaft, 1925, 48 p.
A coöperative appeal for colonies, by men like Schnee, Seitz and Solf.

Minorities Abroad; the Upper Silesia and Schleswig Questions

See also (The League of Nations) Minorities, p. 60; also (Czechoslovakia) Minorities, p. 318;
also (Northern Europe) Baltic States, p. 340; also (Poland) Minorities, p. 356.

ADRIATICUS, *pseud.* **Deutschlands Gerechte Grenzen.** Berlin: Dietrich-Reimer, 1925,
116 p.
A general survey of the German claims to frontier rectifications on the principle of nationality.

ALNOR, KARL. **Handbuch der Schleswigschen Frage.** Neumünster: Wachholtz, 1926-
1930, 3 v.
An important historical handbook. Volume II covers the Schleswig question during the war, and volume III the problem as it was dealt with at the Peace Conference.

BOEHM, MAX HILDEBERT. **Die Deutschen Grenzlande.** Berlin: Hobbing, 1930, 346 p.
A new revised edition of the best descriptive work on the German border lands and their problems.

BOELITZ, OTTO. **Das Grenz- und Auslanddeutschtum.** Munich: Oldenbourg, 1926,
196 p.
A good general handbook of the Germans outside the Reich.

COUSSANGE, JACQUES DE, *pseud.* (MME. BARBE DE QUIRIELLE). **Det Slesvigske Sporgs-
maal og Selvbestemmelsesretten.** Copenhagen: Slesvigsk Forlag, 1929, 211 p.
The Schleswig question approached from the standpoint of self-determination.

DÉCORET, JACQUES. **La Question de Haute-Silésie et Son Règlement.** Lyon: 1924,
196 p.
A dissertation dealing chiefly with the interpretation of the League plebiscite in 1921.

FIRICH, CHARLES T. **Polish Character of Upper Silesia.** Warsaw: Central Polish
Plebiscite Committee, 1921, 37 p.
The Polish interpretation of the plebiscite results; a collection of statistical and diagrammatic material.

HEISS, FRIEDRICH and ZIEGFELD, A. H. **Kampf um Preussenland.** Berlin: Volk und
Reich, 1931, 230 p.
The German view of the Danzig and East Prussian questions.

HUTCHISON, GRAHAM SETON. **Silesia Revisited.** London: Simpkin, 1929, 112 p.
An illuminating study of the problems arising from the region's partition, and the relation of the Silesian situation to the British coal industry. The author was secretary to the British member of the Upper Silesian Commission in 1920-1921.

KUSTER, R. **Die Polnische Irredenta in West-Oberschlesien.** Berlin: Hallig, 1931, 178 p.
An account of Polish propaganda by a man long resident in the disputed area. The book quotes extensively from the Polish press.

LAUBERT, MANFRED. **Deutsch oder Slavisch.** Berlin: Deutscher Ostbund, 1928, 182 p.
The trials and tribulations of the German minorities in the east.

LAUBERT, MANFRED. **Nationalität und Volkswille im Preussischen Osten.** Breslau: Hirt, 1925, 72 p.
An investigation of ethnographic, political and other conditions on the eastern frontier.

LOESCH, KARL CHRISTIAN VON and BOEHM, MAX HILDEBERT, *eds.* **Grenzdeutschland seit Versailles.** Berlin: Brückenverlag, 1930, 450 p.
An extensive German study of the lot of the German minorities under the peace treaties. The authors review the claims of Germany's enemies, the modes of settlement and the condition of the German populations ceded to other states.

NICOLAI, HELMUT. **Oberschlesien im Ringen der Voelker.** Breslau: Grass, Barth, 1930, 126 p.
The Silesian question as seen from the German side.

OLBRICH, HEINRICH O. **Der Leidensweg des Oberschlesischen Volkes.** Breslau: Priebatsch, 1929, 308 p.
An account of the crucial years 1919-1922 in Upper Silesia, based upon all available sources.

OSBORNE, SIDNEY, *ed.* **The Problem of Upper Silesia.** London: Allen, 1921, 180 p.
A collection of essays, in which, in addition to Osborne's contributions, are included J. H. Harley's "The Case for Poland," Walther Schotte's "The Future of the Upper Silesian Industry," and Vladimir Sacharczewski's "Autonomy for Upper Silesia." The book is equipped with excellent detailed maps.

OSBORNE, SIDNEY. **The Upper Silesian Question and Germany's Coal Problem.** London: Allen, 2nd rev. ed., 1921, 285 p.
The best account and analysis of the complex Upper Silesian problem available in English.

ROHRBACH, PAUL. **Deutschtum in Not.** Berlin: Andermann, 1926, 416 p.
The well-known writer paints a lurid picture of the condition of the oppressed Germans outside the Reich.

La Silésie Polonaise. Paris: Gebethner et Wolff, 1932, 328 p.
A collection of addresses on the history, geography, demography and economic life of Upper Silesia, by eminent French and Polish scholars. The study of the plebiscite is by Smorgorzewski. This is the best presentation of the subject from the Polish standpoint.

SZPOTAŃSKI, STANISLAW. **Sprawa Górnego Ślaska na Konferencji Pokojowej.** Warsaw: Perzyński, Niklewicz, 1922, 111 p.
The question of Upper Silesia at the Peace Conference, with some good sidelights on the personalities and activities of the Polish delegation.

TARDIEU, ANDRÉ and JESSEN, F. DE. **Le Slesvig et la Paix.** Paris: Meynial, 1928, 393 p.
A detailed account of the problem in 1919 as seen from the Allied standpoint.

VOGEL, RUDOLF. **Deutsche Presse und Propaganda des Abstimmungskampfes in Oberschlesien.** Beuthen: Oberschlesische Zeitung, 1931, 182 p.
A detailed analysis of the German press campaign at the time of the Upper Silesian plebiscite. A valuable contribution to the study of modern propaganda technique.

VOLZ, WILHELM. **The Economic-Geographical Foundations of the Upper Silesian Question.** Berlin: Stilke, 1921, 91 p.
An able German study, by the director of the Geographical Institute at Breslau.

WARDERHOLT, J. P. **Das Minderheitenrecht in Oberschlesien.** Berlin: Brückenverlag, 1930, 451 p.
A general discussion of the question of protection of minorities followed by an analysis of the decisions of the President of the Mixed Commission from 1922 to 1929.

Zum Oberschlesischen Problem. Gleiwitz: Oberschlesische Volksstimme, 1930, 147 p.
A collection of scientific papers dealing with various aspects of the question, presented to Wilhelm Volz.

V. NORTHERN EUROPE

SCANDINAVIAN STATES

See also (World War) Neutrals and the War, p. 152; also (Germany) Minorities Abroad, the Upper Silesia and Schleswig Questions, p. 337; also (Finland) General, p. 345, and Aaland Islands, p. 346; also Polar Regions, p. 498.

BELLQUIST, ERIC CYRIL. **Some Aspects of the Recent Foreign Policy of Sweden.** Berkeley: University of California Press, 1929, 127 p.
Apart from a discussion of the Åland Islands question, the book is concerned chiefly with a scholarly presentation of Sweden's activities in the League of Nations.

BLOMSTEDT, MAGNUS and BÖÖK, FREDRIK, *eds.* **Sweden of Today.** Stockholm: Tullberg, 1930, 402 p.
A splendid, beautifully illustrated survey of the country, its constitution, defense system, religious and educational life, and scientific, economic and intellectual activity, by many authors.

COHN, EINAR DAVID. **Danmark under den Store Krig.** Copenhagen: Gad, 1928, 333 p.
A general economic study of the effects of the World War upon Denmark.

COSTE-FLORET, GEORGES. **La Situation Internationale de la Norvège.** Lyon: Bosc, 1929, 178 p.
A dissertation which reviews the separation of Norway and Sweden and outlines developments since 1905, with special reference to Spitzbergen and the question of neutralization.

Denmark. Copenhagen: Ministry for Foreign Affairs. Annual.
An official handbook.

EGAN, MAURICE FRANCIS. **Ten Years near the German Frontier.** New York: Doran, 1919, 364 p.
Reminiscences and impressions of an American minister to Denmark. Contains much about German influence and intrigues, and about American negotiations over the Virgin Islands.

FRIIS, AAGE, LINVALD, AXEL and MACKEPRANG, MOURITZ, *eds.* **Det Danske Folks Historie.** Copenhagen: Erichsen, 1927-1929, 8 v.
A history of the Danish people, by a large number of historians. A good work, well illustrated.

GATHORNE-HARDY, GEOFFREY MALCOLM. **Norway.** New York: Scribner, 1925, 324 p.
A volume in the "Modern World" Series. The best account in English of recent Norwegian history and cultural development.

GJERSET, KNUT. **History of Iceland.** New York: Macmillan, 1924, 482 p.
The standard history of Iceland; the author gives due consideration to economic and cultural aspects.

HALLENDORFF, CARL and SCHÜCK, ADOLF. **History of Sweden.** London: Cassell, 1929, 466 p.
The best general one-volume history of Sweden.

HILDEBRAND, EMIL and STAVENOW, LUDVIG, *eds.* **Sveriges Historia.** Stockholm: Norstedt, 1919-1926, 14 v.
The standard history of Sweden; a collaborative undertaking covering the history of the Swedes from earliest times to the present.

JOHANNSEN, UDO. **Die Skandinavische Münzunion in der Entwicklung des Dänischen Geldwesens.** Nürnberg: Hochschulbuchhandlung, 1926, 91 p.
A general historical sketch of the Scandinavian monetary union, followed by a study of Danish inflation between 1914 and 1924.

LECARPENTIER, GEORGES. **Pays Scandinaves et Finlande.** Paris: Roger, 1921, 246 p.
General descriptive studies, with some consideration of Baltic problems.

MORRIS, IRA NELSON. **From an American Legation.** New York: Knopf, 1923, 287 p.
On the fringe of the World War. Interesting reminiscences of an American Minister to Stockholm.

NEUSTÄTTER, HANNA. **Schwedische Währung während des Weltkrieges.** Munich: Drei Masken, 1920, 111 p.
A scientific study of Swedish currency during the war, with much statistical material.

Norway Year Book. Oslo: Sverre Mortensen. Annual.
A general statistical and political handbook.

Sveriges Läge ur Internationellträttslig och Politisk Synspunkt. Stockholm: Beckmans Bokförlag, 1930, 130 p.
A summary of the memorandum on the post-war political and military position of Sweden, prepared by an advisory commission which was appointed in March 1929 by the Conservative Ministry of Admiral Lindman.

Sweden Yearbook. Stockholm: Almquist and Wiksells. Annual.
Detailed statistical information concerning the political, economic and social life of Sweden.

BALTIC STATES
General

See also (Eastern Europe) General, p. 347; also (Russia) The War and the Revolution, p. 360, and Foreign Policy, p. 393.

Baltisches Handbuch. Danzig: Danziger Zeitungsverlagsgesellschaft, 1930, 250 p.
A valuable collection of essays on the policies of Estonia, Latvia, Danzig, Denmark, Sweden and Lithuania, written chiefly by prominent Baltic statesmen.

BRAATZ, KURT VON. **Fürst Anatol Pawlowitsch Lieven.** Stuttgart: Belser, 1926, 165 p.
An important contribution to the history of the revolution in the Baltic provinces.

ESSÉN, RÜTGER. **Europas Tillfrisknande.** Stockholm: 1929, 330 p.
An optimistic survey of some important political problems of Europe, with special reference to the Baltic States.

FRIEDRICHSEN, MAX. **Finnland, Estland und Lettland, Litauen.** Breslau: Hirt, 1924, 144 p.
A popular but withal compact and excellent descriptive survey of the new Baltic States, their people, resources, and economic life.

GAILLARD, GASTON. **L'Allemagne et le Baltikum.** Paris: Chapelot, 1919, 278 p.
Deals chiefly with German activities and policies in all the Baltic areas during the war. A useful and well-informed narrative of the confused events of that period.

GOLTZ, RÜDIGER, GRAF VON DER. **Meine Sendung in Finnland und im Baltikum.** Leipzig: Koehler, 1920, 312 p.
The story of the German commander in Finland and the Baltic in 1918-1919. A most important source for the history of the formative period of the new Baltic States.

KÜRBS, FRIEDRICH. **Die Osteuropäischen Staaten.** Stuttgart: Enke, 1931, 266 p.
Reports drawn up for the Reichsverband der Deutschen Industrie, chiefly economic in character and covering the Baltic states and Poland.

LEHNICH, OSWALD. **Währung und Wirtschaft in Polen, Litauen, Lettland und Estland.** Berlin: R. L. Prager Verlag, 1924, 356 p.
A serious study of economic problems confronting some of the new states of Eastern Europe.

NEWMAN, EDWARD WILLIAM POLSON. **Britain and the Baltic.** London: Methuen, 1930, 276 p.
A complete survey of the Baltic problem. The author takes up in turn the outstanding questions in the history and politics of the various new states, concentrating quite naturally on the two crucial points, Vilna and Danzig. He stresses especially the danger of an eventual Russian-German combination directed against these new states, particularly Poland, for he does not believe that the Russian bear has changed his skin, or that the Soviet Government will be able to avoid permanently the great question of securing access to the Baltic.

La Pologne et la Baltique. Paris: Gebethner et Wolff, 1931, 360 p.
This collection of lectures, delivered at the Bibliothèque Polonaise by a number of French scholars, touches upon several urgent problems of the Baltic area.

POPOV, GEORGII KONSTANTINOVICH. **L'Invasion Moscovite.** Paris: Plon, 1929, 248 p.
A thrilling account of five months under Bolshevik rule in an unnamed Baltic city.

ROLNIK, HIRSCH. **Die Baltischen Staaten Litauen, Lettland und Estland und Ihr Verfassungsrecht.** Leipzig: Noske, 1927, 148 p.
A good general survey of the constitutions of the Baltic states, by a Lithuanian.

RUHL, ARTHUR. **The New Masters of the Baltic.** New York: Dutton, 1921, 239 p.
A readable popular account of the Baltic area in the post-war period.

RUTENBERG, GREGOR. **Die Baltischen Staaten und das Voelkerrecht.** Riga: Löffler, 1929, 156 p.
Chiefly a study of the international complications attending the establishment of the Baltic states.

RUTTER, OWEN. **The New Baltic States and Their Future.** Boston: Houghton Mifflin, 1926, 274 p.
A survey written primarily from the geographical standpoint. One of the best descriptive works.

SCOTT, ALEXANDER MACCALLUM. **Beyond the Baltic.** New York: Doran, 1926, 316 p.
Interesting travel impressions of the Baltic area and Russia.

SOBOLEVITCH, E. **Les États Baltes et la Russie Soviétique.** Paris: Presses Universitaires, 1930, 267 p.
A study of the political and economic relations of Russia and the Baltic states from 1918 to 1928.

VILLECOURT, LOUIS. **La Protection des Minorités dans les Pays Baltiques et la Société des Nations.** Bordeaux: Bière, 1925, 135 p.
A dissertation which reëxamines the provisions for protection and criticizes them on the ground that they were unjustified and unnecessary.

WINNIG, AUGUST. **Am Ausgang der Deutschen Ostpolitik.** Berlin: Staatspolitischer Verlag, 1921, 125 p.
Letters and notes of a German trade-union leader who was on mission in Estonia and Latvia in 1918 and 1919.

Estonia

HALTENBERGER, MICHAEL. **Landeskunde von Eesti.** Tartu: Krüger, 1926, 204 p.
The first scientific treatment of Estonia from the physical, ethnical and economic standpoints.

MARTNA, M. **Estland, die Esten und die Estnische Frage.** Olten: Trösch, 1919, 200 p.
A description of the country and its problems, and a narrative of the stormy period of its resurrection, by a high Estonian official.

PULLERITS, ALBERT, *ed.* **Estland.** Tallinn: Kluge und Ströhm, 1931, 356 p.
An admirable reference book.

VILLECOURT, LOUIS. **L'Estonie.** Paris: Rieder, 1932, 128 p.
An historical and descriptive survey by a French professor.

Latvia

BERG, ARVED. **Latvia and Russia.** London: Dent, 1920, 93 p.
An argument for settlement of the Lettish problem irrespective of Russian wishes, and a vehement rejection of the idea of inclusion in a Russian Federation.

BIHLMANS, ALFRED. **Latvia in the Making, 1918-1928.** Riga: Riga Times, 1928, 160 p.
The best general survey of Latvia's development during the first decade of independence.

DREWS, HANS. **Die Lettische Revolution und das Baltentum.** Riga: Jonck und Poliewsky, 1927, 104 p.
The part of the Germans in the development of the Latvian question.

DUPARQUET, LIEUTENANT-COLONEL. **Der Drang nach Osten. L'Aventure Allemande en Lettonie.** Paris: Lavauzelle, 1926, 346 p.
A useful history of German policy in Latvia.

HELSTEIN, MAX CH. **La Constitution de la République de Lettonie.** Paris: Sirey, 1930, 275 p.
The best study of the Latvian constitution.

MEYER, PERCY. **Latvia's Economic Life.** Riga: East-Service, 1925, 220 p.
A competent survey of all aspects of Latvian economic life.

PLANTIÉ-CAZÉJUS, ARMAND. **La Constitution de la Lettonie.** Toulouse: Imp. Régionale, 1925, 228 p.
A geographic and historical survey followed by the text of the constitution and some commentary. An unimpressive dissertation.

Rosenberg, Eduard, Baron von. **Für Deutschtum und Fortschritt in Lettland.** Riga: Salamandra, 1928, 199 p.
One of the Baltic barons writes of the situation in Latvia, and urges the necessity of abandoning the oligarchic type of leadership if anything is to be accomplished in the German cause.

Siew, Benjamin. **Lettlands Volks- und Staatswirtschaft.** Riga: Müllersche Buchhandlung, 1925, 298 p.
A survey of Latvia's economic condition, with particular emphasis on finance and trade, but with some consideration of industry and agriculture.

Toupine, Arthur. **La Guerre et la Vérité.** Paris: Éditions de l'Affranchi, 1919, 221 p.
Chapters on Latvia's struggles in the war.

Walters, Michel. **Lettland.** Riga: Walters und Rapa, 1924, 500 p.
A study of the cultural and economic development of the Letts, their literature, art and intellectual achievement. There is a French translation: "Le Peuple Letton" (same place and publisher, 1926).

Walters, Michel. **Lettland: Seine Entwicklung zum Staat und die Baltischen Fragen.** Rome: Privately printed, 1923, 510 p.
The most extensive general history of the Letts and the Latvian problem in the past century, with emphasis on the clash with the German element and due attention to the great agrarian problem.

Zalts, Albert. **Latvian Political Economy.** Riga: Riga Times, 1928, 180 p.
An able review of Latvia's economic development in the first ten years.

Lithuania and Memel

See also (Poland) *The Vilna Problem, p. 354.*

Borch, Nicolas, Comte de. **Le Principe des Nationalités et la Question Lithuanienne.** Louvain: Ceuterick, 1925, 139 p.
An historical sketch of Lithuanian history and the connection with Poland, which the author believes to be the only solution of present difficulties.

Chambon, Henry de. **La Lithuanie pendant la Conférence de la Paix.** Paris: Mercure Universel, 1931, 185 p.
This account of Lithuania's resurrection is written by the editor of the *Revue Parlementaire* and is based upon his own papers.

Deu, Fred H. **Das Schicksal des Deutschen Memelgebietes.** Berlin: Verlag der Neuen Gesellschaft, 1927, 105 p.
A survey of developments, both political and economic, since the revolution.

Ehret, Joseph. **La Lituanie, Passé, Présent, Avenir.** Geneva: Atar, 1919, 480 p.
A series of essays, historical and descriptive, by a Swiss writer with warm Lithuanian sympathies.

Friesecke, Ernst. **Das Memelgebiet.** Stuttgart: Enke, 1928, 76 p.
An interesting study of the international and political position of the disputed territory.

Gabrys, Juozas. **Vers l'Indépendance Lituanienne.** Lausanne: Librairie des Nationalités, 1920, 304 p.
Impressions and reminiscences of Lithuania's struggle for freedom, from 1905 to 1920.

Ganss, Johannes. **Die Völkischen Verhältnisse des Memellandes.** Berlin: Memelland-Verlag, 1925, 144 p.
A general survey of the history of the Memel problem and the post-war status of the territory with special reference to the position of the Germans. Contains much statistical matter.

HARRISON, E. J., *ed*. **Lithuania, 1928.** London: Hazell, 1928, 383 p.
An excellent general reference book.

HARRISON, E. J. **Lithuania Past and Present.** New York: McBride, 1922, 230 p.
By a British consul in Lithuania. A well-informed and sympathetic survey of history, economic life, literature, etc. The best single book in English.

HEBERLE, RUDOLF. **Die Deutschen in Litauen.** Stuttgart: Ausland und Heimat, 1927, 159 p.
A socio-political survey, with abundant statistics.

JAHN, LOUIS. **Memel als Hafen- und Handelsstadt, 1913-1922.** Jena: Fischer, 1926, 141 p.
A scholarly investigation of the economic life of Memel and the changes wrought by the war in its trade relations.

JANZ, FRIEDRICH. **Die Entstehung des Memelgebietes.** Berlin: 1928, 134 p.
A good review of the circumstances which led to the establishment of the present Memel territory.

KLIMAS, PETRAS. **Le Développement de l'État Lithuanien.** Paris: Langlois, 1919, 277 p.
A history of the Lithuanian problem from 1915 to the formation of the provisional government in November 1918. A valuable account based on official documents.

MAUCLÈRE, JEAN. **Le Pays du Chevalier Blanc.** Paris: Spès, 1930, 272 p.
A lively and readable essay on the history of Lithuania and the national renaissance.

MAUCLÈRE, JEAN. **Sous le Ciel Pâle de Lithuanie.** Paris: Plon, 1926, 212 p.
An interesting travel book.

MORTENSEN, HANS. **Litauen.** Hamburg: Friedrichsen, 1926, 321 p.
A pioneer geographic study of the new Lithuanian state.

ROBINSON, NEHEMIA. **Die Finanzwirtschaft Litauens als eines Neuen Staates.** Prague: Mercy, 1928, 121 p.
A general study of the budgetary and tax systems, based upon extensive use of Lithuanian material.

ROGGE, ALBRECHT. **Die Verfassung des Memelgebiets.** Berlin: Deutsche Rundschau, 1928, 493 p.
An invaluable collection of documents on the international position of Memel, together with commentary. The book contains an exhaustive bibliography.

ROUZIER, A. **La Constitution de la Lithuanie et le Statut de Memel.** Toulouse: Les Frères Douladoure, 1926, 303 p.
An historical and geographical survey, followed by an extended commentary on the constitution. The best work on the subject.

ŠALKAUSKIS, STASYS. **Sur les Confins de Deux Mondes.** Geneva: Atar, 1919, 271 p.
One of the best books on Lithuania. The author studies the Eastern and Western influences in the formation of the national character and sets forth his ideas of Lithuania's mission between East and West.

SCHIERENBERG, ROLF. **Die Memelfrage als Randstaatenproblem.** Berlin: Vowinckel, 1925, 197 p.
A discussion of the history and geographical factors in the problem, with the pertinent documents.

SKORUPSKIS, COLONEL. **Le Résurrection d'un Peuple, 1918-1927.** Paris: Charles-Lavauzelle, 1931, 150 p.

A review of Lithuanian history in the 19th century, with a more detailed account of the World War, of Lithuanian relations with Russia and Germany. The last chapters are devoted to an extended discussion of the Vilna problem.

VANLANDE, RENÉ. **Avec le Général Niessel en Prusse et en Lithuanie.** Paris: Charles-Lavauzelle, 1922, 184 p.
A lively account of the work of the inter-Allied military mission in the Baltic area and the final disposition of von der Goltz' troops.

Finland

General

See also (Russia) The War and the Revolution, p. 360.

ATCHLEY, T. W. **Finland.** London: Sidgwick and Jackson, 1931, 244 p.
A geographical and demographic survey of Finland, followed by an admirable account of the cultural and political history. Written by a professor of English in the University of Helsingfors; one of the best general books.

BJÖRKSTEN, S. R. **Das Wassergebiet Finnlands in Voelkerrechtlicher Hinsicht.** Helsingfors: Tilgmann, 1925, 253 p.
An exhaustive treatise on the international status of the Gulfs of Finland and Bothnia.

Conditions Sociales en Finlande. Helsingfors: Imprimerie du Gouvernement, 1926, 150 p.
A coöperative work by competent scholars, setting forth various aspects of social problems in Finland.

ESTLANDER, BERNHARD. **Elva Årtionden ur Finlands Historia.** Stockholm: Geber, 1930, 419 p.
Volume V of a great history of Finland since 1808. It deals with the period 1917-1918. This is the standard history, written from the Swedish viewpoint, but very understanding of Finnish aspirations.

Finland: The Country, Its People and Institutions. Helsingfors: Otava, 1926, 600 p.
The abbreviated edition of the best Finnish descriptive work. The volume contains over eighty articles by experts on all phases of structure and life in the new Finland.

Finliandskaia Revoliutsiia. Moscow: Gosizdat, 1920, 115 p.
A series of essays dealing with various phases of the Finnish class struggle, written mostly by Finnish "Red" leaders in exile.

FOX, SIR FRANK. **Finland To-day.** London: Black, 1926, 198 p.
Written by one of the most observant English travellers, this book gives a vivid and reliable picture of present-day Finland.

HAMBURGER, REBECCA CATHARINA SOPHIA. **Twee Rechtsvragen Aangaande Finland.** Utrecht: Boer, 1925, 145 p.
A Dutch dissertation reviewing the problems of demilitarizing the Aaland Islands and the autonomy of East Carelia.

IGEL'STROM, V. A. **Finliandiia.** Moscow: Gosizdat, 1925, 69 p.
A brief but well-packed Russian survey of the history, geography, economic life, etc.

JÄRVINEN, KYÖSTI NESTOR. **The Trade and Industry of Finland.** Helsingfors: Simelius, 1922, 746 p.
A description of the economic life and opportunities of Finland.

La Chesnais, Pierre Georget. **La Guerre Civile en Finlande.** Paris: Bossard, 1920, 198 p.
A systematic account of the period January to April 1918, based on Russian documents left behind by the Bolsheviks. Over one hundred of them are here printed.

Laporte, Henry. **La Guerre des Rouges et des Blancs; le Premier Échec des Rouges; Russie, Finlande (Janvier-Mai 1918).** Paris: Payot, 1929, 192 p.
A fascinating though not sympathetic story of the first months of the Bolshevik régime, with special reference to the conflict in Finland.

Öhquist, Johannes. **Finnland.** Berlin: Vowinckel, 2nd ed., 1928, 257 p.
The best German handbook.

Pavolini, Alessandro. **L'Independenza Finlandese.** Rome: Anonima Romana Editoriale, 1928, 95 p.
A brief but scholarly and reliable history of the Finnish struggle for independence.

Schybergson, Magnus Gottfrid. **Politische Geschichte Finnlands, 1809-1919.** Stuttgart: Perthes, 1925, 500 p.
Easily the best one-volume history of modern Finland, especially detailed for the period following 1905.

Söderhjelm, Henning. **The Red Insurrection in Finland in 1918.** London: Harrison, 1919, 159 p.
A general study of the civil war of 1918, based upon "Red" documents that fell into the hands of the victorious "Whites."

Svechnikov, S. **Revoliutsiia i Grazhdanskaia Voǐna v Finliandii.** Moscow: Gosizdat, 1923, 122 p.
The best Russian account of the civil war, based on documents and personal experiences, with stress on military operations.

Van Cleef, Eugene. **Finland—the Republic Farthest North.** Columbus: Ohio State University Press, 1929, 235 p.
A well-written anthropo-geographical study of the history and life of the Finns.

Werner, Fritz. **Die Finnische Wirtschaft.** Berlin: Ost-Europa Verlag, 1931, 104 p.
A thorough, scholarly monograph, based on Finnish material and containing much statistical matter.

Wuorinen, John Henry. **Nationalism in Modern Finland.** New York: Columbia University Press, 1931, 312 p.
Nothing just like this contribution to the history of modern nationalism has appeared in any western language. The author has made available a mass of material, unpublished and published, in Finnish and Swedish, bearing on the evolution of the national movement in the 19th and 20th centuries.

Aaland Islands

Boursot, Raymond. **La Question des Îles d'Aland.** Dijon: Bernigaud et Privat, 1923, 354 p.
A rather wordy dissertation which attempts to place the question in the larger setting of the principle of self-determination.

Jégou du Laz, René. **La Question des Îles d'Aland.** Rennes: Carhaix: P. le Troadec, 1923, 126 p.
A fair, documented dissertation giving the essentials of the problem down to the Convention of 1921.

Maury, Pierre. **La Question des Îles d'Aland.** Paris: Presses Universitaires, 1930, 209 p.
The most recent of many French dissertations on the question.

VI. EASTERN EUROPE

GENERAL

See also (Central Europe) Middle European Schemes, p. 299; also (Baltic States) General, p. 340; also (The Balkan Area) General, p. 399.

BOURGEOIS, ÉMILE and others. **Aperçus Européens.** Paris: Alcan, 1932, 148 p.
A series of lectures under the auspices of the École des Sciences Politiques, dealing with Poland, Jugoslavia and Czechoslovakia.

CHOPIN, JULES, *pseud.* (JULES E. PICHON). **De l'Elbe aux Balkans.** Paris: Baudinière, 1929, 253 p.
The situation in Eastern Europe does not promise well for peace, according to this well-known French journalist.

GIANNINI, AMEDEO. **Le Costituzioni degli Stati dell'Europa Orientale.** Rome: Istituto per l'Europa Orientale, 1930, 2 v.
An up-to-date handbook for the constitutions of the new Eastern Europe. The text of each document is preceded by an introductory commentary, ably done.

GRAHAM, MALBONE WATSON. **New Governments of Eastern Europe.** New York: Holt, 1927, 835 p.
Supplementing the author's book on the governments of Central Europe and presenting in convenient form the essential information regarding Russia, Poland, and the Baltic States.

MALYNSKI, EMMANUEL, COUNT. **Les Problèmes de l'Est et la Petite Entente.** Paris: Cervantes, 1931, 560 p.
Primarily a discussion of the Polish-Russian conflict and its aftermath. There are several chapters on the Succession States, but very little on the Little Entente.

NANI, UMBERTO. **Oriente Europeo.** Foligno: Campitelli, 1930, 246 p.
A general survey of the situation in Eastern Europe, written from a Fascist view.

STEINMETZ, SEBALD RUDOLF. **De Nationaliteiten in Europa.** Amsterdam: Van Looy, 1920, 514 p.
Part I of a standard work, containing an elaborate political and sociological description of the nationalities of Eastern and Southeastern Europe.

POLAND

Resurrection of the State

See also (Central Europe) Collapse of the Hapsburg Empire, p. 301.

ASKENAZY, SZYMON. **Uwagi.** Warsaw: Wende, 1924, 496 p.
A collection of essays published in Polish, French and English during the war by an eminent Polish historian.

BAGIŃSKI, HENRYK. **Wojsko Polskie na Wschodzie, 1914-1920.** Warsaw: Główna Ksiegarnia Wojskowa, 1921, 598 p.
The best general account of the vicissitudes of the various Polish military forces in Russia during the war.

BENSON, EDWARD FREDERIC. **The White Eagle of Poland.** New York: Doran, 1919, 255 p.
The first half of the book is devoted to arguments for the reconstitution of Poland, needed as a barrier to German expansion in the East.

BLOCISZEWSKI, JOSEPH. **La Restauration de la Pologne et la Diplomatie Européenne.**
Paris: Pedone, 1927, 234 p.
An authoritative account of the Polish question from 1914 to 1923, written by the
late professor at the École des Sciences Politiques.

BOBRZYŃSKI, MICHAŁ. **Wskrzeszenie Państwa Polskiego.** Cracow: Krakowska Spólka
Wydawnicza, 1920, 1925, 2 v.
The first complete history of the restoration of Poland, written by an eminent Galician
historian and politician. He is distinctly pro-Austrian in view and stresses the contribution of Austrian Poles. The story is carried through the war with Russia, down to
the recognition of the frontiers in 1923.

CAPASSO, CARLO. **La Polonia e la Guerra Mondiale.** Rome: Garroni, 1927, 269 p.
A heavily documented monograph on the Polish question during the war. Based on
extensive use of Polish and other materials, this is one of the best scholarly treatments
of a very difficult subject.

DMOWSKI, ROMAN. **Polityka Polska i Odbudowanie Państwa.** Warsaw: Perzyński,
Niklewicz, 1925, 632 p.
A vivid account of the Polish question, written by the eminent National Democrat
leader.

DYBOSKI, ROMAN. **Outlines of Polish History.** London: Allen and Unwin, 2nd ed., 1931,
283 p.
Perhaps the best brief survey available in English. Commendably open-minded.

FILASIEWICZ, STANISLAS, *ed.* **La Question Polonaise pendant la Guerre Mondiale.**
Paris: Comité National Polonais, 1920, 592 p.
A valuable and rare collection of documents dealing with the Polish question during
the war, not complete, but well edited with explanatory notes.

FLAES, R. **Das Problem der Territorialkonflikte.** Amsterdam: Paris, 1929, 352 p.
This is really a survey of the territorial history of Poland, which is taken as the basis
for a discussion of ways and means of settling territorial conflicts in general.

GRAPPIN, HENRI. **Histoire de la Pologne des Origines à 1922.** Paris: Larousse, 1924,
425 p.
One of the best brief histories of Poland, reaching, however, only to the outbreak of
the World War.

KONOPCZYŃSKI, WŁADYSŁAW. **A Brief Outline of Polish History.** Geneva: Atar, 1919,
140 p.
A brief, outspokenly nationalist survey, by a professor at the University of Cracow.

KOROSTOVETS, VLADIMIR KONSTANTINOVICH. **The Rebirth of Poland.** London: Bles,
1928, 318 p.
The Poles in a rather unfavorable light, as seen in the post-war years by a Russian
official and newspaper correspondent.

KUMANIECKI, KAZIMIERZ WŁADYSŁAW. **Odbudowa Państwowości Polskiej.** Warsaw:
Czernecki, 1924, 782 p.
A collection of over three hundred documents dealing with foreign and domestic
aspects of the Polish question from 1912 to 1924.

KUTRZEBA, STANISŁAW. **Polska Odrodzona.** Cracow: Gebethner i Wolff, 1922, 264 p.
A concise account of Poland during the war, and of the restoration, written by a professor at the University of Cracow who acted as an expert at the Peace Conference.

LEBRETON, JULES. **La Résurrection de la Pologne.** Paris: Bloud et Gay, 1919, 259 p.
A collection of articles written on the Polish question during the war by a French
Polonophil.

MECH, WANDA. **La Reconstitution de l'État Polonais, 1880-1919.** Toulouse: Perry, 1929, 191 p.
A pedestrian dissertation, valuable only for its use of Polish materials.

RECKE, WALTHER. **Die Polnische Frage als Problem der Europäischen Politik.** Berlin: Stilke, 1927, 399 p.
The best non-Polish treatment of the Polish problem as a key question of international relations in the 19th and 20th centuries. Heavily documented and based on extensive materials, Polish, Russian, German and others.

ROTH, PAUL. **Die Entstehung des Polnischen Staates.** Berlin: Liebmann, 1926, 168 p.
A documented study, based on material in all languages, analyzing the international negotiations that led to the reconstitution of Poland.

Russko-Pol'skie Otnosheniia. Moscow: Moskovskiĭ Rabochiĭ, 1926, 158 p.
An important collection of documents, published by the Tsentrarkhiv, bearing on Russia's Polish policy during the war.

RZEPECKI, KAROL. **Oswobodzenie Poznania.** Posen: Ksiegarnia Rzepeckiego, 1923, 104 p.
A concise account of the insurrection in Posnania in December 1918 and the conquest of the area by the Poles.

SEYDA, MARYAN. **Polska na Przelomie Dziejów.** Posen: Ksiegarnia św. Wojciecha, 1927, 664 p.
Volume I of a great history of the restoration of Poland. The author, a prominent National Democrat, writes impartially and with heavy documentation, of the ups and downs of the problem to the time of the entrance of the United States into the war.

SMOGORZEWSKI, CASIMIR. **La Pologne Restaurée.** Paris: Gebethner et Wolff, 1927, 360 p.
A mine of information on conditions in Poland during the war, the reëstablishment of independence, and present day domestic and foreign problems.

SMOGORZEWSKI, CASIMIR. **La Pologne et la Guerre à travers les Livres Polonais.** Paris: Gebethner et Wolff, 1929, 96 p.
A very useful résumé of some thirty-five Polish books dealing with the war period.

SMOGORZEWSKI, CASIMIR. **L'Union Sacrée Polonaise.** Paris: Gebethner et Wolff, 1929, 71 p.
The story of the Polish organization during the war, based on unpublished material.

SROKOWSKI, KONSTANTY. **N. K. N. Zarys Historji Naczelnego Komitetu Narodowego.** Cracow: Krakowska Spólka Wydawnicza, 1923, 380 p.
A brilliantly written history of the National Supreme Committee, by its secretary-general. The author covers the period to the autumn of 1915 and throws much light on the activity of the Polish-Austrian group.

TARNOWSKI, JAN. **Nasze Przedstawicielstwo Polityczne w Paryżu i w Petersburgu.** Warsaw: Czcrnecki, 1923, 125 p.
Largely a polemic against the policy and activity of Dmowski and the Polish National Committee at Paris.

TOMMASINI, FRANCESCO. **La Risurrezione della Polonia.** Milan: Treves, 1925, 365 p.
Very shrewd and agreeably frank reminiscences by the Italian Minister to Poland during the period of the war with Soviet Russia, with light on the Jewish and ethnic minorities problem as well as political matters.

WALISZEWSKI, KAZIMIERZ. **Poland the Unknown.** London: Heinemann, 1919, 263 p.
A noted historian reviews Polish history, stressing the native viewpoint, in a brilliant and stimulating volume.

Biographies

CARENCY, JACQUES DE. **Joseph Pilsudski.** Paris: Renaissance du Livre, 1929, 279 p.
Pilsudski as the incarnation of the Polish spirit. A moderate biographical study, based in large part upon Polish material.

DASZYŃSKI, IGNACY. **Pamiętniki.** Cracow: Drukarnia Ludowa, 1925-26, 2 v.
The memoirs of the Polish National Socialist leader. An important contribution to the history of the Polish question during the war, and of Pilsudski's activities and policy.

HOŁÓWKO, TADEUSZ. **Prezydent Gabrjel Narutowicz.** Warsaw: Ignis, 1924, 221 p.
A general biography of the Polish statesman.

KLINGSLAND, SIGISMOND S. **Pilsudski.** Paris: Kra, 1929, 186 p.
Rhapsodical.

LANDAU, ROM. **Pilsudski and Poland.** New York: Dial, 1929, 311 p.
Heroic and poetic; a dramatized epic.

LEDNICKI, ALEKSANDER. **Z Lat Wojny.** Warsaw: Hoesick, 1921, 288 p.
Collected papers and addresses of a prominent Polish democrat who exercised a considerable influence in Russia during the war, especially in 1917.

LIGOCKI, EDWARD. **O Jósefie Hallerze.** Warsaw: Gebethner i Wolff, 1923, 360 p.
A dramatized account of Gen. Haller's career, first as commander of the Polish legions in Galicia, then as commander of the Polish army in France. Based on information from Haller.

PIŁSUDSKI, JÓZEF. **The Memories of a Polish Revolutionary and Soldier.** London: Faber, 1931, 377 p.
This volume includes a translation of the next title, but in addition a good many other autobiographical writings, notes and articles by the Marshal.

PIŁSUDSKI, JÓZEF. **Moje Pierwsze Boje.** Warsaw: Bibljoteka Polska, 1925, 186 p.
A highly impressionistic account of the early phases of the war, written at Magdeburg in 1917. More revealing with respect to Pilsudski's character than to the evolution of the Polish question.

SOSNOWSKI, JERZY JAN. **Prawda Dziejowa, 1914-1917.** Warsaw: Gebethner i Wolff, 1925, 736 p.
Rambling recollections of a member of the Russian mission to the United States for the purchase of war supplies.

New Poland

BOSWELL, ALEXANDER BRUCE. **Poland and the Poles.** New York: Dodd, 1919, 313 p.
A general descriptive study and estimate, by an English scholar long resident in Poland.

BUGIEL, V. **La Pologne et les Polonais.** Paris: Bossard, 1921, 390 p.
An outline of Polish history and a survey of the literature and arts, with a short section on social and economic conditions.

BUJAK, FRANCISZEK. **Poland's Economic Development.** London: Allen and Unwin, 1926, 67 p.
A reliable sketch of Polish economic history by a Polish professor.

COSTA DE BEAUREGARD, LOUIS. **L'Évolution Économique de la Pologne et les Réformes Monétaires depuis 1920.** Paris: Vrin, 1928, 156 p.
A dissertation outlining and analyzing the financial reforms and their effects.

CROZAT, CHARLES. **Les Constitutions de la Pologne et de Dantzig.** Toulouse: Bonnet, 1923, 273 p.
A dissertation giving the historical background of the constitutions and analyzing their provisions.

CZARNOMSKI, FRANCIS BAUER, *ed.* **The Polish Handbook.** London: Eyre and Spottis-woode, 1925, 704 p.
A complete statistical work, unusually well done.

DEVEREUX, RAY, *pseud.* (MRS. ROY PEMBER-DEVEREUX). **Poland Reborn.** New York: Dutton, 1922, 256 p.
A fair presentation of the evolution of the new Poland, its territorial problems and its economic and intellectual aspects.

DULLES, JOHN FOSTER, *comp.* **Poland: Plan of Financial Stabilization, 1927.** New York: Sullivan and Cromwell, 1928, 241 p.
The English text of the Polish Plan of Financial Stabilization, together with many relevant documents.

DYBOSKI, ROMAN. **Poland Old and New.** New York: Oxford University Press, 1926, 68 p.
Three brilliant lectures on various aspects of Polish life.

ETCHEGOYEN, OLIVIER, COMTE D'. **Pologne, Pologne . . .** Paris: Delpeuch, 1925, 321 p.
Realistic, somewhat too smart, travel impressions and experiences.

GUTTMANN, FRITZ. **Polnische Wirtschaftsprobleme.** Posen: Kosmos, 1927, 63 p.
A plea for international coöperation in solving such problems as those of industriali-zation and the intensification of agriculture.

HOFFMANN, WILHELM. **Inflation und Stabilisierung der Polnischen Währung.** Leipzig: 1925, 125 p.
A dissertation which affords a documented systematic review of the monetary prob-lems of the new state.

Informacyjny Kalendarz Wojskowy "Polski Zbrojnej." Warsaw: Polska Zbrojna, 1928, 422 p.
This calendar contains, among other things, a detailed description of the modern Polish army.

KARSKI, STEFAN. **Poland, Past and Present.** Warsaw: Drukarnia Krajowa, 1927, 160 p.
A competent survey of the institutions and conditions in the new Poland, with special emphasis, in each case, on the historical background.

KEMPNER, STANISŁAW ALEKSANDER. **Rozwój Gospodarczy Polski.** Warsaw: Bibljoteka Polska, 1924, 345 p.
An outline of Polish history followed by a survey of the various sections of the new Poland.

KERN, ELGA. **Vom Alten und Neuen Polen.** Zurich: Rascher, 1931, 168 p.
Miscellaneous studies of a high order, touching Polish economics, education, city life, minorities, etc.

KUMANIECKI, KAZIMIERZ WŁADYSŁAW. **Ustrój Państwowych Władz Administra-cyjnych na Ziemiach Polski.** Cracow: Frommer, 1920, 197 p.
A commentary on the Polish constitution and administration.

LAFOND, GEORGES and DESFEUILLES, PAUL. **La Pologne au Travail.** Paris: Reger, 1925.
A survey of Polish conditions, written with a Polish bias.

MACHRAY, ROBERT. **Poland, 1914-1931.** London: Allen and Unwin, 1932, 447 p.
Though written in a sympathetic vein, especially as regards Pilsudski, this is one of the best general accounts in English of recent Polish history and problems.

MARTIN, PIERRE GEORGES. **La Stabilisation et le Retour à la Monnaie Or.** Paris: Guillon, 1925, 220 p.
A scholarly monetary history of Poland, Germany and Danzig since the war.

MINCER, TADEUSZ. **Le Zloty Polonais.** Paris: Pedone, 1927, 150 p.
A scholarly treatment of the financial reforms and their effects.

OERTZEN, FRIEDRICH WILHELM VON. **Das Ist Polen.** Munich: Müller, 1932, 241 p.
The evolution of the new Poland as seen by a not too friendly German.

PERNOT, MAURICE. **L'Épreuve de la Pologne.** Paris: Plon, 1921, 311 p.
A general survey, by one of the ablest French travellers and political writers.

PHILLIPS, CHARLES. **The New Poland.** New York: Macmillan, 1923, 383 p.
An impressionistic sketch of the new Polish state, based on personal experiences, by a member of the American Red Cross Commission.

SKRZYŃSKI, ALEKSANDER JÓZEF, COUNT. **Poland and Peace.** London: Allen and Unwin, 1923, 154 p.
Written by a Polish Minister of Foreign Affairs, this is a general survey of the New Poland and its problems, intended for the enlightenment of the English public.

SMOGORZEWSKI, CASIMIR. **Le Jeu Complexe des Partis en Pologne.** Paris: Gebethner et Wolff, 1928, 40 p.
A convenient handbook of political and party life.

STUDNICKI, WŁADYSŁAW. **Die Wirtschaftliche und Kulturelle Entwicklung des Wiederauferstandenen Polens.** Berlin: Voelkermagazin, 1930, 150 p.
The economic side of the new Poland, in a succinct survey.

STYRA, ROBERT. **Das Polnische Parteiwesen und Seine Presse.** Plauen: Verlag Junges Volk, 1926, 169 p.
A survey of Polish party alignments and the political affiliations of the press.

SVIATOPOLK-MIRSKIĬ, MIKHAIL, KNIAZ'. **Les Origines de la Crise Monétaire en Pologne.** Paris: Vrin, 1929, 136 p.
A dissertation devoted primarily to an examination of the effects of inflation on private debts.

SZAWLESKI, MIECZYSŁAW. **Polska na tle Gospodarki Swiatowej.** Warsaw: Gebethner i Wolff, 1928, 432 p.
Studies, by an expert, of some of the leading economic problems of Poland and Europe.

SZEPS, SAMUEL. **Die Währungs- und Notenbankpolitik der Republik Polen.** Basel: Helbing, 1926, 132 p.
Sections of an extensive Swiss dissertation on the monetary problems and policies of post-war Poland.

TENNANT, A. E. **Studies in Polish Life and History.** London: Allen and Unwin, 1924, 254 p.
A sympathetic contribution to Polish history, culture and economic life.

TRIEBE, IMMANUEL G. **Zehn Jahre Polnische Währung, 1918-1928.** Berlin: Sack, 1929, 111 p.
A scholarly history of Poland's monetary problem, published by the Osteuropa Institut. One of the best monographs on the subject.

WINTER, NEVIN OTTO. **The New Poland.** Boston: Page, 1923, 369 p.
An interesting, popular pro-Polish work.

ZDZIECHOWSKI, JERZY. **The Finances of Poland, 1924-1925.** London: Published by the Polish Government, 1925, 172 p.
Practically an official statement, written by the chairman of the budget committee of the Polish Sejm.

Foreign Relations

General

See also (France) Relations with Other Countries, p. 269; also (Baltic States) General, p. 340.

Durand, L. **La Pologne Actuelle—Les Rapports Franco-Polonais. La Politique de M. Lloyd George.** Paris: Desclée, 1922.
A series of essays, centering on the conflict of French and English policy in the matter of Polish claims in Upper Silesia.

Makowski, Juljan. **Zobowiązamia Międzynarodowe Polski, 1919-1929.** Warsaw: Lazarski, 1929, 313 p.
The international engagements of Poland since the war.

Sarolea, Charles. **Letters on Polish Affairs.** Edinburgh: Oliver, 1922, 140 p.
Letters of an English publicist dealing chiefly with Poland's international position, frontier difficulties and foreign policy. Pronouncedly Polonophil.

Sobanski, Ladislas, Comte. **Tour d'Horizon.** Paris: Gebethner et Wolff, 1931, 123 p.
The European scene viewed from Warsaw.

Relations with Russia; the War of 1919-1920

D'Abernon, Edgar Vincent, Viscount. **The Eighteenth Decisive Battle of the World.** London: Hodder, 1931, 178 p.
D'Abernon was with the Anglo-French mission in the Polish-Russian war of 1920. He bases his account on his own recollections and on the works of Pilsudski and others.

Drunin, V. P. **Pol'sha, Rossiia i S. S. S. R.** Moscow: Gosizdat, 1928, 219 p.
The relations between Russia and Poland, historically considered.

Ezovitov, K. **Belorussy i Poliaki.** Kaunas: Skaryny, 1919, 124 p.
Documents and materials for the history of the Polish occupation of White Russia in 1918-1919.

Krasnaia Kniga. Moscow: Gosizdat, 1920, 112 p.
The Russian collection of documents bearing on Russian-Polish relations in the years 1918-1920.

Murray, Kenneth Malcolm. **Wings over Poland.** New York: Appleton, 1932, 363 p.
A hurried, superficial yet glamorous story of the Kosciuszko Squadron and the Polish war against the Bolshevists.

Piłsudski, Józef. **L'Année 1920.** Paris: Renaissance du Livre, 1929, 332 p.
Fundamental for a study of the Russian-Polish conflict. Pilsudski's own account of the decisive struggle with Russia.

Pomarański, Stefan, ed. **Pierwsza Wojna Polska, 1918-1920.** Warsaw: Główna Księgarnia Wojskowa, 1920, 355 p.
Correspondence of the Polish Staff and other important material bearing on the military operations.

Przybylski, Adam. **La Pologne en Lutte pour Ses Frontières, 1918-1920.** Paris: Gebethner et Wolff, 1929, 172 p.
A translation of the best general account of the military operations, written by an officer in the historical section of the staff and based on unpublished materials in the war office.

SAINT-DIDIER, G. V. **L'Aigle Blanc contre l'Étoile Rouge.** Paris: Berger-Levrault, 1931, 144 p.
A short military history of the Polish-Russian conflict.

SIKORSKI, WŁADISŁAW. **La Campagne Polono-Russe de 1920.** Paris: Payot, 1928, 320 p.
On the whole the best monographic study of the Polish-Russian campaign, written by one of the Polish generals.

SUSLOV, P. V. **Politicheskoe Obespechenie Sovetsko-Pol'skoĭ Kampanii 1920 goda.** Moscow: Gosizdat, 1930, 174 p.
A study of the political side of the war and especially of the work of the political agents with the Red Army.

WALISZEWSKI, KAZIMIERZ. **Polonais et Russes.** Paris: Plon, 1919, 312 p.
A review of Russia's Polish policy since 1863 and of the situation at the end of the World War, by a Polish historian who warns his compatriots against overmuch trust in Russia.

The Vilna Problem

See also (Baltic States) General, p. 340, and Lithuania, p. 343.

GORZUCHOWSKI, XAVIER. **Les Rapports Politiques de la Pologne et de la Lithuanie.** Paris: Presses Modernes, 1927, 198 p.
A well-documented dissertation reviewing the whole history of the Polish-Lithuanian connection and arguing that the new Lithuania is merely a province of the Old Poland.

GRAUŽINIS, CASIMIR. **La Question de Vilna.** Paris: Jouve, 1927, 206 p.
A dissertation which goes over much the same ground, stressing the Lithuanian view and claim.

MERIGGI, LEA. **Il Conflitto Lituano-Polacco e la Questione di Vilna.** Milan: Istituto Editoriale Scientifico, 1930, 117 p.
A careful and impartial study. One of the best monographic treatments of the subject.

MORESTHE, GEORGES. **Vilna et le Problème de l'Est Européen.** Paris: Bossard, 1921, 130 p.
A pro-Polish survey of the Vilna question.

NATKEVIČIUS, LADAS. **Aspect Politique et Juridique du Différend Polono-Lithuanien.** Paris: Jouve, 1930, 351 p.
The best account from the Lithuanian side of the interminable Vilna problem. A well-documented dissertation based on extensive Polish and Lithuanian material.

The Corridor and Danzig

See also (Germany) Foreign Policy, p. 334; also (Baltic States) General, p. 340.

ASKENAZY, SZYMON. **Dantzig and Poland.** London: Allen and Unwin, 1921, 132 p.
A survey of Danzig's history, written by a leading Polish historian in 1919 in anticipation of the city's union with Poland.

AUGUR, *pseud.* (VLADIMIR POLIAKOFF). **Eagles Black and White.** New York: Appleton, 1929, 206 p.
A well-known publicist tells why Germany must accept the Polish corridor and learn to treat Poland as an equal.

AUGUR, *pseud.* (VLADIMIR POLIAKOFF). **A Bulwark of Democracy.** New York: Appleton, 1931, 207 p.
The subject of this latest book by "Augur" is the position of Poznań, historically considered, as a focus of the Polish national idea.

BAUER, HANNS and MILLACK, WALTER, *eds*. **Danzigs Handel.** Danzig: Kafemann, 1925, 185 p.
A collection of scientific studies, dealing mostly with Danzig's commerce in the past, but also discussing the post-war situation.

BOUCHEREAU, ABEL. **Le Statut de Dantzig.** Poitiers: Poitou, 1924, 143 p.
A dissertation analyzing the provisions of Danzig's charter.

DONALD, SIR ROBERT. **The Polish Corridor and the Consequences.** London: Butterworth, 1929, 302 p.
The author of "The Tragedy of Trianon," much criticized for its bias, takes up another European problem in a spirit equally hostile to the peace settlements.

FLAKOWSKI, GERHARD. **Der Ökonomische Aspekt des Danzig-Problems.** Heidelberg: Lamade, 1927, 175 p.
A German dissertation. The author reviews Danzig's trade connections before the war, the changes wrought by the treaties, the economic relations with Poland, etc.

FÜRST, JOHANN. **Der Widersinn des Polnischen Korridors.** Berlin: Deutsche Rundschau, 1926, 147 p.
An able reply to Slawski's "Poland's Access to the Sea."

HANSEN, ERNST R. B. **Poland's Westward Trend.** London: Allen and Unwin, 1928, 92 p.
Basing his remarks on Polish ambitions as expressed by Polish writers, the author writes a rather unconvincing essay on the menace of Polish aspirations.

HARDER, HANS ADOLF. **Danzig, Polen und der Voelkerbund.** Berlin: Stilke, 1928, 134 p.
A fair, well-documented account of the whole Danzig problem. The author examines the city's position in international law, the Polish military and naval base, Danzig's foreign policy and trade, etc.

KEYSER, ERICH, *ed*. **Der Kampf um die Weichsel.** Berlin: Deutsche Verlags-Anstalt, 1926, 178 p.
A series of essays, by German scholars, examining the ethnic situation in the Corridor from earliest times to the present.

LEVESQUE, GENEVIÈVE. **La Situation Internationale de Dantzig.** Paris: Pedone, 1924, 178 p.
A documented dissertation analyzing not only the city's legal status, but its economic and political position also.

LEWINSKY, HERMANN and WAGNER, RICHARD. **Danziger Staats- und Voelkerrecht.** Berlin: Stilke, 1927, 668 p.
Practically an official publication dealing with the constitutional and international law of Danzig. It is particularly interesting on the legal relations with Poland.

MAKOWSKI, JULJAN. **La Situation Juridique du Territoire de la Ville Libre de Dantzig.** Paris: Bossard, 1925, 56 p.
A Polish professor's enquiry into the legal standing of Danzig as an international entity. He finds the statute and present situation thoroughly unsatisfactory and calls for larger control by Poland in Danzig's own interest.

MARTEL, RENÉ. **The Eastern Frontiers of Germany.** London: Williams and Norgate, 1930, 199 p.
A serious effort to illuminate the problem. The author presents the two conflicting views and tries to get at the truth.

MÜHLENFELS, ALBERT VON. **Ostpreussen, Danzig und der Polnische Korridor als Verkehrsproblem.** Berlin: Osteuropa Verlag, 1930, 61 p.

This publication of the Osteuropa Institut is a treatment of the extremely difficult question of communications across the Corridor.

ROSINSKI, WIKTOR. **La Pologne et la Mer Baltique.** Paris: Gebethner et Wolff, 1928, 253 p.
The Polish need for an outlet to the sea once more set forth with the usual eloquence and warmth.

SCHROEDER, KARL LUDWIG. **Die Voelkerrechtliche Stellung Danzigs.** Breslau: Kern, 1927, 96 p.
Another study of the vexed problem of the status of Danzig in international law. One of the best scholarly treatments.

SIEBENEICHEN, ALFRED. **Gdańsk a Polska.** Warsaw: Hoesick, 1923, 124 p.
A scholarly study of Danzig's connection with Poland, as it is defined in the treaties and conventions.

SLAWSKI, STANISLAW. **Poland's Access to the Sea.** London: Eyre and Spottiswoode, 1925, 62 p.
Essentially an official restatement of the Polish position, by a member of the Danzig Harbor Board.

SMOGORZEWSKI, CASIMIR. **Poland, Germany and the Corridor.** London: Williams and Norgate, 1930, 164 p.
A careful and authoritative presentation of the Polish view regarding the Corridor.

Minorities

See also (League of Nations) Minorities, p. 60; also (Germany) Minorities Abroad, the Upper Silesia and Schleswig Questions, p. 337.

FELINSKI, M. **The Ukrainians in Poland.** London: Author, 1931, 173 p.
The Polish view of the Ukrainian problem.

GLIKSMAN, GEORGES. **L'Aspect Économique de la Question Juive en Pologne.** Paris: Rieder, 1929, 195 p.
A sad picture of the Jewish situation, with much valuable statistical material.

GOODHART, ARTHUR LEHMAN. **Poland and the Minority Races.** New York: Brentano, 1922, 194 p.
The diary of a member of the commission sent in 1919 to investigate pogroms and maltreatment of minorities. A valuable document.

KOŹMIŃSKI, TADEUSZ. **Sprawa Mniejszości.** Warsaw: Perzyński, Niklewicz, 1922, 162 p.
A good study of the negotiations at Paris regarding protection of minorities in Poland, with some consideration of the treatment of the problem by the Sejm and government.

KUHN, WALTER. **Die Jungen Deutschen Sprachinseln in Galizien.** Münster: Aschendorff, 1930, 244 p.
A scientific description and analysis of the German linguistic islands in Galicia.

KUTRZEBA, STANISŁAW. **Mniejszości w Najnowszem Prawie Międzynarodowem.** Warsaw: Ossolińskich, 1925, 132 p.
. A treatment of the minority question, especially in Poland, by a professor at the University of Cracow.

LAPRADELLE, ALBERT GEOUFFRE DE. **La Loi Polonaise de 1920 sur la Nationalité et les Traités de Versailles.** Paris: Comité des Délégations Juives, 1924, 27 p.
A criticism of contemporary Polish policy toward minority peoples in Poland, by a professor of international law at the University of Paris.

MORNIK, STANISLAUS. **Polens Kampf gegen Seine Nichtpolnischen Volksgruppen.**
Berlin: De Gruyter, 1931, 154 p.
The author gives an account of the Polish linguistic, religious and economic campaign
against the non-Polish population groups.

RAUSCHNING, HERMANN. **Die Entdeutschung Westpreussens und Posens.** Berlin:
Hobbing, 1930, 405 p.
A critical account of Polish policy during the past decade. The best scholarly treat-
ment from the German side.

SEYDA, MARYAN. **Territoires Polonais sous la Domination Prussienne.** Paris: Section
de Presse du Comité National Polonais, 1919, 137 p.
An analysis of the anti-Polish policy of the Prussian government before the war and
the organization of the Polish defense; written from an advanced Polish nationalist
viewpoint, by the former editor of the *Kuryer Poznański.*

SMOGORZEWSKI, CASIMIR. **La Poméranie Polonaise.** Paris: Gebethner et Wolff, 1932,
400 p.
A thorough-going study of Polish Pomerania, written by a leading Polish publicist.

STOLIŃSKI, ZYGMUNT. **Die Deutsche Minderheit in Polen.** Warsaw: Institut zur
Erforschung der Minderheitenfragen, 1928, 132 p.
A very favorable report on the post-war conditions of the Germans as regards political
activity, economic activity, religious freedom, education, etc.

RUSSIA

General Treatises; the Old Régime

BELETSKIĬ, S. P. **Grigoriĭ Rasputin.** Leningrad: Byloe, 1923, 101 p.
Rasputin as he appears in the notes of the director of the police department. An interesting contribution.

BIKOV, P. M. **Les Derniers Jours des Romanov.** Paris: Payot, 1931, 192 p.
The author was in 1918 president of the Ural Soviet which carried through the execution of Nicholas II and his family. This is one of the important records of the last
days of the imperial family.

BLOK, ALEKSANDR ALEKSANDROVĬCH. **Les Derniers Jours du Régime Impérial.**
Paris: La Nouvelle Revue Française, 1931, 223 p.
This book was written in 1917, and is primarily an abstract of the proceedings of the
revolutionary committee which investigated the conduct of the old régime.

BOTKIN, GLEB. **The Real Romanovs.** New York: Revell, 1931, 336 p.
The imperial family as seen by the court physician. The volume deals chiefly with
the war and revolutionary periods.

BURTSEV, V. **Bor'ba za Svobodnuiu Rossiiu.** Berlin: Gamaiun, 1923, 382 p.
Recollections of an active Russian journalist and revolutionary.

FÜLÖP-MILLER, RENÉ. **Rasputin the Holy Devil.** New York: Viking, 1928, 386 p.
The English translation of a striking book by a well-known writer. While not trying
to whitewash Rasputin, the author attempts to put him in his proper setting and to
reach a sane estimate of his influence.

GILLIARD, PIERRE. **Thirteen Years at the Russian Court.** London: Hutchinson, 3rd
ed., n. d., 304 p.
One of the best-known and most faithful records of life at court, by the French tutor
of the Tsarevich. Deals primarily with the years 1911-1918.

GOLDER, FRANK ALFRED, *ed.* **Documents of Russian History, 1914-1917.** New York: Century, 1927, 679 p.
A series of important documents, extracts from diaries and letters to illustrate the history of Russia down to the time of the Bolshevik Revolution. The editing and the annotations are excellent.

HANBURY-WILLIAMS, SIR JOHN. **The Emperor Nicholas II as I Knew Him.** London: Humphreys, 1922, 271 p.
A valuable study of the Emperor and the Russian situation in the years 1914 to 1917, by the chief of the British military mission.

HEDENSTRÖM, ALFRED VON. **Geschichte Russlands von 1878 bis 1918.** Stuttgart: Deutsche Verlags-Anstalt, 1922, 348 p.
One of the best histories of pre-war Russia. Critical of the old régime, though by no means radical.

IUSUPOV, FELIKS FELIKSOVICH, KNIAZ'. **Rasputin.** London: Cape, 1927, 256 p.
The murder of Rasputin, told by one of his assassins.

KOMAROV-KURLOV, P. G. **Das Ende des Russischen Kaisertums.** Berlin: Scherl, 1920, 367 p.
The memoirs of the chief of the Russian secret police, dealing chiefly with the years 1905 to 1917.

KORFF, SERGIEĬ ALEKSANDROVICH, BARON. **Autocracy and Revolution in Russia.** New York: Macmillan, 1923, 161 p.
An interpretation of the leading trends in Russian internal history since 1870 with special reference to the Revolutions of 1905 and 1918.

KOVAŘIK, FEDOR. **Žážitky a Dojmy Ruského Čecha za Carství.** Prague: Slovanský Ústav, 1932, 346 p.
Clever and occasionally brilliant studies of Tsarist Russia.

Letters of the Tsaritsa to the Tsar, 1914-1916. London: Duckworth, 1923, 478 p.
These letters, like those of the Tsar to the Tsaritsa, are of great interest to the student of the Revolution. They show conclusively the Empress' influence over her husband and reflect the court view of the domestic and international situation.

Letters of the Tsar to the Tsaritsa, 1914-1917. New York: Dodd, 1929, 324 p.
The indispensable complement to the preceding item.

Lettres des Grands-Ducs à Nicolas II. Paris: Payot, 1926, 265 p.
These letters, dealing with the pre-war and war periods, are another important source for the history of the Russian court on the eve of the Revolution.

LIUBOSH, S. B. **Russkii Fashist Vladimir Purishkevich.** Leningrad: Byloe, 1925, 56 p.
A brief sketch of the career of the Black Leader and murderer of Rasputin.

MARKOW, ALEXIS. **Rasputin und Die um Ihn.** Königsberg: Hartung'sche Zeitung, 1928, 144 p.
The author views Rasputin as an unscrupulous and clever peasant rather than as a holy devil. An account based on the voluminous Russian material now available.

MARYE, GEORGE THOMAS. **Nearing the End in Imperial Russia.** Philadelphia: Dorrance, 1929, 479 p.
The contemporary notes and impressions of the American Ambassador to Russia from 1914 to 1916.

MASARYK, TOMÁŠ GARRIGUE. **The Spirit of Russia.** New York: Macmillan, 1919, 2 v.
Russian intellectual history and life, viewed in its religious, philosophical, social and political aspects. This standard work by a leading interpreter of things Slavic contains an excellent discussion of Russian socialism and the revolutionary movement.

MILLER, MARGARET STEVENSON. **The Economic Development of Russia, 1905-1914.**
London: King, 1926, 325 p.
An investigation of pre-war developments in trade, industry and finance.

O'HARA, VALENTINE and MAKEEF, N. **Russia.** New York: Scribner, 1925, 346 p.
One of the best popular outlines of Russian history in the 20th century. A volume
in the Modern World Series.

Padenie Tsarskogo Rezhima. Moscow: Gosizdat, 1925-27, 7 v.
The all-important stenographic reports of the hearings before the investigating commission of the Provisional Government in 1917. There is an abridged French edition,
giving most of the important material: "La Chute du Régime Tsariste; Interrogatoires"
(Paris: Payot, 1927, 577 p.).

PARES, SIR BERNARD. **History of Russia.** New York: Knopf, 1930, 564 p.
This general history of Russia enters more fully than most into the pre-war and revolutionary periods, and is for that reason especially useful for students of modern Russia.

PARES, SIR BERNARD. **My Russian Memoirs.** London: Cape, 1931, 623 p.
Sir Bernard Pares knew Russia as few Englishmen knew it in the pre-war and war
periods. His memoirs are a mine of information on personalities and events.

PAVLOVSKIĬ, GEORGIĬ. **Agricultural Russia on the Eve of the Revolution.** London:
Routledge, 1930, 340 p.
Chiefly a study of agricultural methods, conditions and policies. An able and useful
monograph.

PIONTKOVSKIĬ, S. **Ocherki Istorii Rossii v XIX-XX Vekakh.** Kharkov: no pub., 1930,
488 p.
A general history of Russia, from the Marxist viewpoint.

PROTOPOPOV, A. D. **Predsmertnaia Zapiska A. D. Protopopova.** Paris: Karbasnikov,
1926, 30 p.
Highly interesting notes written by the former Russian Minister of the Interior just
before his death.

PURISHKEVICH, V. M. **Ubiĭstvo Rasputina.** Moscow: no pub., 1923, 88 p.
The story of Rasputin's assassination, as drawn from the diary of Purishkevich, one
of the murderers.

ROBINSON, GEROID TANQUARY. **Rural Russia under the Old Régime.** New York:
Longmans, 1932, 342 p.
An admirable study of the old régime in its economic and social aspects. A fundamental
work, based on long and careful research in the voluminous Russian sources.

RODZIANKO, MIKHAIL VLADIMIROVICH. **The Reign of Rasputin.** London: Philpot, 1927,
292 p.
Memoirs of the Octobrist leader and president of the Duma. An important contribution to the story of Russian political life in the immediate pre-revolutionary period,
and a severe indictment of the old régime.

SHIDLOVSKIĬ, S. I. **Vospominaniia.** Berlin: Kirchner, 1923, 2 v.
The autobiography and political memoirs of an important member of the Duma.
They throw considerable light on the war and revolutionary periods.

SIMANOVICH, ARON. **Rasputin, der Allmächtige Bauer.** Berlin: Hensel, 1928, 360 p.
A sympathetic and valuable account written by Rasputin's adviser and collaborator.

SMIRNOV, SERGIEĬ NIKOLAEVICH. **Autour de l'Assassinat des Grands-Ducs.** Paris:
Payot, 1928, 281 p.
The account of the murders by a gentleman of the imperial court. A valuable addition
to the material in the Sokolov report.

SOKOLOV, NIKOLAĬ ALEKSIEEVICH. **Enquête Judiciaire sur l'Assassinat de la Famille Impériale Russe.** Paris: Payot, 1924, 339 p.
An important record of the murder of the imperial family, by an investigating official of the Kolchak government.

SPIRIDOVICH, ALEKSANDR IVANOVICH. **Histoire du Terrorisme Russe, 1886-1917.** Paris: Payot, 1930, 672 p.
The most complete account of the activities of the Social Revolutionary group, from 1886 to the Revolution of 1917.

SVIATOPOLK-MIRSKIĬ, DMITRIĬ PETROVICH, KNIAZ'. **Russia, a Social History.** London: Cresset, 1931, 312 p.
An admirable introduction to the study of present-day Russia.

TELBERG, GEORGE GUSTAV and WILTON, ROBERT, *eds.* **The Last Days of the Romanovs.** New York: Doran, 1920, 428 p.
A collection of depositions on the Ekaterinburg crime, together with Wilton's narrative, based on the investigation by Sokolov.

VASIL'EV, ALEKSIEĬ TIKHONOVICH. **The Ochrana.** Philadelphia: Lippincott, 1930, 320 p.
The sensational activities of the secret police of the old régime, from the papers of the last director.

VERNADSKIĬ, GEORGIĬ VLADIMIROVICH. **A History of Russia.** New Haven: Yale University Press, 1929, 416 p.
A good general history of Russia, stressing the modern period and the domestic problems.

VRANGEL, NIKOLAĬ EGOROVICH, BARON. **From Serfdom to Bolshevism.** Philadelphia: Lippincott, 1927, 324 p.
The autobiography of a Russian nobleman and landlord. An intimate picture of old Russian life.

The War and the Revolution

See also World War, p. 87; also (Baltic States) General, p. 340; also (Finland) General, p. 345; also (Poland) Resurrection of the State, p. 347; also (Far East) Siberia, p. 485.

AKHUN, M. I. and PETROV, V. A. **Bolcheviki i Armiia v 1905-1917.** Leningrad: Krasnaia Gazeta, 1929, 348 p.
An instructive account of the Bolshevik propaganda among the troops before and during the war.

ALEKSEEV, S. A., *ed.* **Revoliutsiia i Grazdanskaia Voĭna.** Moscow: Gosizdat, 1926-1930, 6 v.
An invaluable collection of memoirs, diaries, etc., bearing on the period 1917-1920 and written by revolutionary and counter-revolutionary leaders.

ALEKSINSKIĬ, GRIGORIĬ. **Du Tsarisme au Communisme.** Paris: Colin, 1923, 288 p.
A commentary on the war, the Revolution and the Soviet régime. Intended as a sequel to the author's "Russia and the War."

ANET, CLAUDE, *pseud.* (JEAN SCHOPFER). **La Révolution Russe.** Paris: Payot, 1918-1919, 4 v.
One of the best-known and most vivid journalistic accounts of the great crisis.

BACH, LYDIA. **Histoire de la Révolution Russe.** Paris: Valois, 1930, 370 p.
The first volume of what promises to be one of the best histories of the Revolution. This volume goes to the November Revolution of 1917.

BONCH-BRUEVICH, VLADIMIR DMITRIEVICH. **Na Boevykh Postakh Fevral'skoĭ i Oktiabr'skoĭ Revoliutsii.** Moscow: Federatsiia, 1930, 412 p.
Interesting recollections of Lenin and his activity in the October Revolution, by a close associate.

BRESHKO-BRESHKOVSKAIA, EKATERINA KONSTANTINOVNA (VERIGO). **Hidden Springs of the Russian Revolution.** Stanford: Stanford University Press, 1931, 369 p.
An important contribution to the history of the Russian revolutionary movement, written by the famous woman leader.

BUKHARIN, NIKOLAĬ IVANOVICH. **Ot Krusheniia Tsarizma do Padeniia Burzhuazii.** Kharkov: Proletarii, 1923, 144 p.
The Revolution from February to November 1917, by a leading Bolshevik intellectual.

BULLARD, ARTHUR. **The Russian Pendulum.** New York: Macmillan, 1919, 256 p.
Events in Russia and Siberia in 1917-1918 as seen by a member of the American Committee on Public Information.

CHERNOV, VIKTOR. **Mes Tribulations en Russie Soviétique.** Paris: Povoluzki, 1922, 339 p.
The memoirs of the leader of the Social Revolutionaries. A valuable contribution to the study of Soviet treatment of dissenting parties.

CIANCI DI SANSEVERINO, MANFREDI. **In Russia durante la Rivoluzione.** Naples: Mondana, 1926, 198 p.
The recollections of the Italian military attaché, covering the critical period from April 1917 to April 1918.

CLAUS, RUDOLF. **Die Kriegswirtschaft Russlands.** Bonn: Schroeder, 1922, 161 p.
This scholarly study of industry and commerce in war-time Russia serves as a good background to the Bolshevik system.

DANILOV, IURIĬ NIKIFOROVICH. **Dem Zusammenbruch Entgegen.** Hannover: Hahn, 1928, 189 p.
The Russian general's version of the downfall of the Empire. Covering the period 1905 to 1917, he stresses the weakness of the ruler, the failure to consult the "people," and other shortcomings of the régime.

DENIKIN, ANTON IVANOVICH. **The Russian Turmoil.** London: Hutchinson, 1922, 344 p.
Memoirs of the anti-Bolshevik leader dealing with the Russian army and the first Revolution of 1917, through the Kornilov episode.

DESTRÉE, JULES. **Les Fondeurs de Neige.** Paris: Van Oest, 1920, 306 p.
Vivid pen-pictures of events and conditions in Petrograd in the first months of the Bolshevik rule.

DOSCH-FLEUROT, ARNO WALTER. **Through War to Revolution.** London: Lane, 1931, 242 p.
The experiences of a newspaperman in Russia from 1914 to 1920.

DUBROVSKIĬ, S. M. **Die Bauernbewegung in der Russischen Revolution 1917.** Berlin: Parey, 1929, 206 p.
One of the better brief histories of the Revolution. The author goes back to the reforms of 1861 and carries his story to 1923. Based on unpublished as well as published material.

EPHESIAN, *pseud.* (CARL ERIC BECHHOFER ROBERTS). **In Denikin's Russia.** London: Collins, 1921, 324 p.
An interesting picture, by an English journalist, of the situation in the Caucasus and South Russia in 1919-1920.

FLORINSKIĬ, MIKHAIL TIMOFEEVICH. **The End of the Russian Empire.** New Haven: Yale University Press, 1931, 272 p.
A volume in the Carnegie Series, one of the best studies of Russian history during the great conflict.

FRANTZ, GUNTHER. **Russland auf dem Wege zur Katastrophe.** Berlin: Verlagsgesellschaft für Politik und Geschichte, 1926, 343 p.
In the introductory section Frantz discusses Russia's preparation for war and the personalities of Russian commanders. The body of the book consists of a translation of General Polivanov's diary and the letters of the Grand Dukes to the Tsar.

GAYDA, VIRGINIO. **Il Crollo Russo.** Turin: Bocca, 1920, 434 p.
The situation in Russia before and during the war, the Revolution and the Bolshevik triumph, as seen by an Italian journalist.

GRONSKIĬ, PAVEL P. and ASTROV, NIKOLAI I. **The War and the Russian Government.** New Haven: Yale University Press, 1929, 331 p.
Another volume in the Carnegie Series, reviewing Russian political life to the time of the Bolshevik overturn in November 1917.

GURKO, VASILIĬ IOSIFOVICH. **War and Revolution in Russia, 1914-1917.** New York: Macmillan, 1919, 420 p.
The experiences and observations of a high Russian officer.

HINDUS, MAURICE GERSCHON. **The Russian Peasant and the Revolution.** New York: Holt, 1920, 327 p.
A vivid picture of peasant life, followed by a description of the evolution of the agrarian problem during the Revolution.

HOARE, SIR SAMUEL JOHN GURNEY. **The Fourth Seal.** London: Heinemann, 1930, 377 p.
Russia in 1916, as seen by a member of the English secret service. An excellent picture of the country on the eve of revolution.

HURWICZ, ELIAS. **Geschichte der Jüngsten Russischen Revolution.** Berlin: Firn, 1922, 208 p.
One of the best of the earlier histories of the Revolution, based on all material then available.

IAKOVLEV, I. A., *ed.* **Razlozhenie Armii v 1917 Godu.** Moscow: Gosizdat, 1925, 190 p.
A collection of documentary material dealing with the disintegration of the Russian army in 1917.

IAROSLAVSKIĬ, E. **Partiia Bol'shevikov v 1917 Godu.** Moscow: Gosizdat, 1927, 107 p.
A general study of the activity of the Bolshevik group during the Revolution until its seizure of power.

ILIN-ZHENEVSKIĬ, A. F. **From the February Revolution to the October Revolution, 1917.** New York: International Publishers, 1931, 121 p.
Recollections of 1918 by the former secretary at the Commissariat of War.

JENNŸ, E. **Wie Russland Bolschewistisch Wurde.** Berlin: De Gruyter, 1921, 128 p.
The old régime and its gradual collapse, and the revolutions of 1917, described by an observer long resident in Russia who attributes the catastrophic developments to the clash of western and eastern influences.

KAKURIN, N. **Kak Srazhalas Revoliutsiia.** Moscow: Gosizdat, 1925-1926, 2 v.
An exhaustive documented military history of the Revolution and Civil War, published by the Military Academy.

KARABCHEVSKIĬ, NIKOLAĬ PLATONOVICH. **La Révolution et la Russie.** Paris: Berger-Levrault, 1921, 316 p.
Reminiscences of 1918, by a Russian judge. Very hostile to the Soviet régime.

KEHLER, HENNING. **Chroniques Russes. Les Premiers Temps du Bolchevisme, 1917-1919.** Paris: Perrin, 1928, 269 p.
A translation of a Danish diary covering the first phase of the Soviet régime.

KERENSKIĬ, ALEKSANDR FEDOROVICH. **The Catastrophe.** New York: Appleton, 1927, 377 p.
This account by the Russian revolutionary leader is on the whole rather thin and disappointing, but nevertheless takes its place as an important document.

KERENSKIĬ, ALEKSANDR FEDOROVICH. **The Prelude to Bolshevism.** New York: Dodd, 1919, 312 p.
A source of first rate importance. Kerensky's own story of the Kornilov rising of the summer of 1917.

KRAMÁŘ, KAREL. **Die Russische Krisis.** Munich: Duncker, 1925, 689 p.
Written by a Czech leader in 1921, this is an elaborate philosophical investigation into the conditions under the old régime, the issues and events of the Revolution, and the character of Bolshevism.

Krest'ianskoe Dvizhenie v 1917 Godu. Moscow: Gosizdat, 1927, 442 p.
A detailed chronicle of the peasant question in 1917, together with some important documentary material. Published by the Tsentrarkiv.

KRICHEVSKIĬ, BORIS. **Vers la Catastrophe Russe, 1917-1918.** Paris: Alcan, 1919, 271 p.
Vivid and interesting letters covering the period from October 1917 to February 1918, written by the special correspondent of the communist Paris paper *L'Humanité*.

KRITSMAN, L. **Geroicheskiĭ Period Velikoĭ Russkoĭ Revoliutsii.** Moscow: Gosizdat, 1926, 272 p.
Not a systematic history of the Revolution, but a documented analysis of various phases and phenomena.

LAWTON, LANCELOT. **The Russian Revolution.** New York: Macmillan, 1927, 534 p.
A British journalist's account of the Revolution and the Soviet system to 1926. Well-informed, topical, rather impressionistic.

LONG, ROBERT EDWARD CROZIER. **Russian Revolution Aspects.** New York: Dutton, 1919, 294 p.
Observations of the representative of the Associated Press, covering the Kerensky period.

LUKOMSKIĬ, ALEKSANDR SERGIEEVICH. **Memoirs of the Russian Revolution.** London: T. Fisher Unwin, 1922, 256 p.
The memoirs of the general who was assistant war minister in 1915 and chief of staff to Brussilov and Kornilov during the Revolution cover the whole period from 1914 to 1920 and deal with the Counter-Revolution as well as with the events of 1917.

MALAPARTE, CURZIO. **Intelligenza di Lenin.** Milan: Treves, 1930, 174 p.
An able Italian study of the Russian situation, with emphasis on the psychology of the Revolution as represented by Lenin and his followers.

MALATESTA, M. **Dall'Impero degli Zar al Governo dei Sovieti.** Rome: Tiber, 1929.
The first volume of a pretentious study of the Russian Revolution.

MARTOV, IULIĬ, *pseud.* (IU. TSEDERBAUM). **Zapiski Sotsialdemokrata.** Berlin: Grschebin, 1922, 2 v.
An excellent set of memoirs dealing with the development of Russian Social Democracy by a leader in the movement.

MARTYNOV, EVGENIĬ IVANOVICH. **Tsarskaia Armiia v Fevral'skom Perevorote.** Moscow: Izdanie Voennoĭ Tipografii, 1927, 212 p.

An important account of the part played by the army in the February Revolution, published by the Russian General Staff.

MAVOR, JAMES. **The Russian Revolution.** New York: Macmillan, 1928, 472 p.
One of the best general histories available in English; scholarly, well-informed and sufficiently stressing the economic aspects.

MEL'GUNOV, SERGIEĬ PETROVICH. **Na Putiakh k Dvortzovomu Perevorotu.** Paris: La Source, 1931, 231 p.
A series of scholarly essays on the projected palace revolution in 1916-1917. A unique treatment.

MEYENDORFF, ALEKSANDR FELIKSOVICH, BARON. **The Background of the Russian Revolution.** New York: Holt, 1929, 212 p.
A series of lectures by the former vice-president of the Duma.

MILIUKOV, PAVEL NIKOLAEVICH. **Istoriia Vtoroĭ Russkoĭ Revoliutsii.** Sofia: Rossiĭsko-Bolgarskoe Knigoizdatel'stvo, 1921-1924, 3 pts.
Written by the eminent Russian historian and Cadet leader. A detailed history of the February Revolution and the course of events to the Bolshevik overturn. One of the most important accounts.

MIRKIN-GETSEVICH, BORIS SERGIEEVICH. **Les Juifs et la Révolution Russe.** Paris: Povolozky, 1921, 70 p.
A strong refutation of the theory that the Jews were largely responsible for the disaster.

Mirnye Peregovory v Brest-Litovske. Moscow: Komissariat Inostrannykh Del, 1920, 268 p.
The official Russian report on the peace negotiations at Brest-Litovsk.

NABOKOV, KONSTANTIN. **The Ordeal of a Diplomat.** London: Duckworth, 1921, 320 p.
The memoirs of the Russian representative in London. Interesting for the light thrown on the repercussions of the Revolution abroad.

NOL'DE, BORIS EMMANUILOVICH, BARON. **L'Ancien Régime et la Révolution Russes.** Paris: Colin, 1928, 214 p.
An admirable, well-balanced and dispassionate outline of the background and course of the Revolution, which the author conceives as a purely Russian movement.

OL'DENBURG, SERGIEĬ SERGIEEVICH, *ed.* **Le Coup d'État Bolcheviste.** Paris: Payot, 1929, 527 p.
An extremely useful collection of Russian documents in translation. The editor has taken them from very diverse sources, Bolshevik and non-Bolshevik, in order to give a documentary picture of the period October 20 to December 3, 1917.

PERSKY, SERGE M. **De Nicolas II à Lénine.** Paris: Payot, 1919, 368 p.
A general narrative of events in the crowded years 1917-1918.

PLEKHANOV, GEORGIĬ VALENTINOVICH. **God na Rodinie.** Paris: Povolozky, 1921, 2 v.
A collection of the essays and addresses of the noted Social Democratic leader, dating from the year 1917.

PLESKOV, V. A. and CHUZHAK, N. F. **Tsarskiĭ Flot pod Krasnym Stiagom.** Moscow: no pub., 1931, 253 p.
A valuable study of the revolution in the navy.

POKROVSKIĬ, MIKHAIL NIKOLAEVICH. **Imperialistskaia Voĭna.** Moscow: Communist Academy, 1931, 340 p.
A collection of essays, by a leading communist historian, dealing chiefly with the war period of Russian history.

POKROVSKIĬ, MIKHAIL NIKOLAEVICH, *ed.* **Ocherki po Istorii Oktiabr'skoĭ Revoliutsii.**
Moscow: Gosizdat, 1927, 2 v.
The first parts of a standard coöperative history, scholarly and well-documented, from
the communist viewpoint. These two volumes discuss the situation during the war,
the February Revolution and the Kerensky régime to July 1917.

POKROVSKIĬ, MIKHAIL NIKOLAEVICH. **Ocherki po Istorii Revoliutsionnogo Dvizhenia
v Rossii v XIX i XX v. v.** Moscow: Gosizdat, 2nd ed., 1927, 200 p.
One of the best brief histories of the Russian revolutionary movement from the
Bolshevik viewpoint.

POKROVSKIĬ, MIKHAIL NIKOLAEVICH. **Oktiabr'skaia Revoliutsiia.** Moscow: Communist
Academy, 1929, 419 p.
A collection of articles by the eminent Bolshevik historian.

Rabochee Dvizhenie v 1917 Godu. Moscow: Gosizdat, 1926, 371 p.
An important collection of documents and other source material bearing on the workers
and their organizations in the overturns of 1917.

Razlozhenie Armii v 1917 Godu. Moscow: Gosizdat, 1925, 190 p.
A collection of valuable documents published by the Tsentrarkiv to illustrate the
breakdown of the old Tsarist army and the part of the soldiers in the revolutions of 1917.

REED, JOHN. **Ten Days that Shook the World.** New York: International Publishers,
1926, 371 p.
A new edition of a sympathetic observer's chronicle of events in November 1917.

ROLLIN, HENRY. **La Révolution Russe.** Paris: Delagrave, 1931, 3 v.
Really a series of studies on the history and philosophy of Bolshevism. Well-informed
and moderate. Well worth reading.

ROSS, EDWARD ALSWORTH. **The Russian Bolshevik Revolution.** New York: Century,
1921, 302 p.
A history of the Kerensky period and October Revolutions, written in a detached
way by an American sociologist. One of the best early accounts.

SADOUL, JACQUES. **Notes sur la Révolution Bolchévique.** Paris: Sirène, 1920, 465 p.
Discerning observations of a member of the French military mission, as contained
in his letters to his fellow socialist, Albert Thomas.

SISSON, EDGAR GRANT. **100 Red Days.** New Haven: Yale University Press, 1931, 502 p.
Written by President Wilson's representative in Russia. A valuable day-by-day record
of events in the first three months of Bolshevik rule.

SMILG-BENARIO, MICHAEL. **Der Zusammenbruch der Zarenmonarchie.** Vienna:
Amalthea, 1927, 302 p.
A beautifully illustrated book, in which the author contests the thesis of Miliukov
that the Russian Revolution was a national rising to save Russia from defeat, and
stresses the social factors, both agrarian and proletarian.

SMILG-BENARIO, MICHAEL. **Von Kerenski zu Lenin.** Vienna: Amalthea, 1929, 324 p.
A continuation of the preceding title; purely political, but stressing the importance
of foreign policy in the collapse of the first revolution.

SPARGO, JOHN. **Bolshevism.** New York: Harper, 1919, 389 p.
A straightforward account of the history of Bolshevism and the Bolshevik revolution,
by a critical American labor leader.

STALIN, IOSIF VISSARIONOVICH. **Na Putiakh k Oktiabriu.** Moscow: Gosizdat, 1925,
280 p.
A collection of speeches and essays from the period March to October 1917.

STROKOWSKI, KONSTANTY. **Elita Bolszewicka.** Cracow: Krakowska Spolka Wydawnicza, 1927, 124 p.
A leading Polish journalist attempts to explain why a small group of intellectuals succeeded in securing and keeping control of Russia.

SUKHANOV, NIKOLAĬ. **Zapiski o Revoliutsii.** Berlin: Grschebin, 1922-1923, 7 v.
This is probably the most extensive diary of the Russian Revolution yet published. The seven volumes cover the period from February to November 1917.

SVERCHKOV, D. F. **Kerenskiĭ.** Leningrad: Priboĭ, 1927, 133 p.
A more than critical account of Kerensky and his policy in 1917.

TARASOV-RODIONOV, ALEKSANDR IGNAT'EVICH. **February 1917.** New York: Covici, Friede, 1931, 378 p.
The overthrow of Tsarism and the return as recounted by a Red writer.

TROTSKIĬ, LEV. **The History of the Russian Revolution.** New York: Simon and Schuster, 1932, 544 p.
The first volume, reaching July 1917, of a most interesting story of the overturn, written in exile by the famous Bolshevik leader.

VAUCHER, ROBERT. **L'Enfer Bolchevik. À Petrograd sous la Commune et la Terreur Rouge.** Paris: Perrin, 1919, 434 p.
An eye-witness account of the first months of Bolshevik rule in Petrograd.

VULLIAMY, COLWYN EDWARD, *ed.* **The Red Archives.** London: Bles, 1929, 320 p.
A useful selection of documents on the history of Russia from 1915 to 1918, taken from the *Krasnyĭ Arkhiv* and throwing much light on the background of the revolution in its earlier phase.

VYRUBOVA, ANNA ALEKSANDROVNA (TANIEEVA). **Journal Secret.** Paris: Payot, 1928, 384 p.
The extraordinary diary of one of the closest associates of the imperial family. An important record of court life during the "reign of Rasputin."

WALSH, EDMUND ALOYSIUS. **The Fall of the Russian Empire.** Boston: Little, Brown, 1928, 357 p.
A well-written and well-informed study of the Russian collapse and the triumph of the Bolsheviks, by an American Roman Catholic priest who was long in Russia.

WILCOX, E. H. **Russia's Ruin.** New York: Scribner, 1919, 316 p.
The account of an English resident, covering the war and revolutionary period, and drawing upon newspapers and other Russian material.

WILLIAMS, ALBERT RHYS. **Through the Russian Revolution.** New York: Boni, 1921, 311 p.
A most sympathetic history of the great class struggle in 1917, by a well-known American newspaper correspondent.

WILLIAMS, MRS. ARIADNA (TYRKÓVA). **From Liberty to Brest-Litovsk.** New York: Macmillan, 1919, 526 p.
A vividly written and informative early account, by the Russian wife of an English correspondent.

ZVORYKIN, NIKOLAĬ NIKOLAEVICH. **La Révolution et le Bolchévisme en Russie.** Paris: Perrin, 1920, 310 p.
A general account of the Revolution and the rise of Bolshevism, with some discussion of the system, by a prominent Russian agriculturist.

Counter-Revolution and Intervention

See also (World War) Russian Front, p. 130, and Siberia, p. 139; also (Poland) Relations with Russia, the War of 1919-1920, p. 353.

ALBERTSON, RALPH. **Fighting without a War.** New York: Harcourt, 1920, 138 p.
A general layman's account of the Allied intervention in Northern Russia.

Les Alliés contre la Russie. Paris: Delpeuch, 1926, 391 p.
Essays by various Russian emigrés on the Allied policy towards Russia during and after the war.

Antanta i Vrangel. Moscow: no pub., 1923, 260 p.
A collection of essays on Wrangel and his relations with the Allies.

BOLDYREV, V. G. **Direktoriia, Kolchak, Interventy.** Novo-sibirsk: Gosizdat, 1925, 565 p.
Recollections of the Kolchak episode and of Allied intervention.

Bor'ba za Kazan. Kazan: no pub., 1924, 256 p.
A collection of material bearing on the intervention of the Czech legions in 1918.

Bor'ba za Petrograd. Petrograd: Gosizdat, 1920, 320 p.
Largely a collection of documentary material on the struggle for the capital in October and November 1919.

Bor'ba za Ural i Sibir'. Moscow: Gosizdat, 1926, 390 p.
The recollections and reports of participants in the struggle against Kolchak.

CANTACUZÈNE, JULIA (GRANT), PRINCESS. **Russian People.** New York: Scribner, 1920, 321 p.
Recollections and observations of the Revolution in the villages, the Counter-Revolution in the South, and the Siberian adventure of Kolchak. A reprint of magazine articles.

COLQUHOUN, JAMES. **Adventures in Red Russia.** London: Murray, 1926, 193 p.
Interesting experiences in the Caucasus and South Russia during the war and the Counter-Revolution.

CUDAHY, JOHN. **Archangel; the American War with Russia.** Chicago: McClurg, 1924, 216 p.
A very readable and well-informed narrative of the American expedition to Northern Russia.

DAWATZ, WLADIMIR. **Fünf Sturmjahre mit General Wrangel.** Berlin: Verlag für Kulturpolitik, 1927, 249 p.
A substantial contribution to our knowledge of the organization of the counter-revolutionary forces.

DENIKIN, ANTON IVANOVICH. **The White Army.** London: Cape, 1930, 368 p.
An abstract of the author's five-volume work in Russian, and a very important contribution to the history of the Russian Counter-Revolution.

DENISOV, GENERAL. **Zapiski.** Constantinople: no pub., 1921, 120 p.
Recollections and notes on the civil war in South Russia, by one of Wrangel's commanders.

DOBRYNIN, GENERAL. **Bor'ba s Bolshevikami na Iuge Rossii.** Prague: Slav-Isdat, 1921, 123 p.
Memoirs of a prominent White Russian commander.

DREIER, V. VON. **Krestnyi Put' vo Imia Rodiny.** No place, no pub., 1921, 145 p.
Reminiscences of the Counter-Revolution in Kuban and Caucasus regions and of the Denikin-Wrangel operations.

FINK, PAVEL. **Bílý Admirál.** Prague: Grégra, 1921, 303 p.
A Czech journalist's experiences and impressions while with the Kolchak forces.

GINS, G. K. **Sibir', Soiuzniki i Kolchak.** Peking: Litografiia Russkhoĭ Dukhovnoĭ Missii, 1922, 2 v.
A well-documented work on the anti-Bolshevik campaigns in Siberia, favorable to the White leaders.

GORN, V. **Grazhdanskaia Voĭna na Severo-Zapade Rossii.** Berlin: Gamaiun, 1923, 416 p.
A detailed account of the civil war in Northwest Russia, by a participant.

Grazhdanskaia Voĭna v Sibiri i Severnoĭ Oblasti. Moscow: Gosizdat, 1927, 480 p.
Primarily a collection of memoirs on the civil war in Siberia and North Russia.

GUKOVSKIĬ, A. I. **Antanta i Oktiabr'skaia Revoliutsia.** Moscow: no pub., 1931, 158 p.
A popular account of the Allied intervention and its relation to the Revolution.

GUKOVSKIĬ, A. I. **Frantsuskaia Interventsiia na Iuge Rossii, 1918-1919.** Moscow: Gosizdat, 1928, 267 p.
A concise history of French intervention in behalf of the Counter-Revolution in South Russia.

HARD, WILLIAM. **Raymond Robins' Own Story.** New York: Harper, 1920, 247 p.
An interesting contribution to the early history of the Bolshevik régime. The critical narrative of an American Red Cross officer who acted as intermediary in negotiation with Lenin, especially in matters of intervention.

IAKUSHKIN, E. and POLUNIN, S. **Angliĭskaia Interventsiia v 1918-1920 gg.** Moscow: Gosizdat, 1928, 106 p.
A careful monographic study of British policy and activity in the interest of the Counter-Revolution

KAKURIN, N. **Kak Srazhalas Revoliutsiia?** Moscow: Gosizdat, 1925-26, 2 v.
The most extensive history of the civil war, covering the years 1917-1920.

KRYLENKO, NIKOLAĬ VASIL'EVICH. **Za Piat' Let.** Moscow: Gosizdat, 1923, 527 p.
The speeches and arguments of the Bolshevik prosecutor in cases of counter-revolutionaries between 1918 and 1922.

LASIES, JOSEPH. **La Tragédie Sibérienne.** Paris: Crès, 1920, 255 p.
The Siberian experiences of a member of the French military mission.

LEVIDOV, MIKHAIL. **K Istorii Soiuznoĭ Interventsii v Rossii.** Leningrad: Priboĭ, 1925, 181 p.
A systematic account of the diplomacy of intervention in Russia from August 1917 to August 1918, based on documents and on extensive use of newspapers and memoirs.

MARGULIES, MANUIL SERGIEEVICH. **God Interventsii.** Berlin: Grschebin, 1923, 3 v.
A detailed account of Allied intervention in Russia in 1918 and 1919.

MARTY, ANDRÉ. **La Révolte de la Mer Noire.** Paris: Bureau d'Éditions, n. d., 2 v.
The French intervention in South Russia, the White Terror, the mutinies in the fleet; a dramatic story based on the accounts of participants and written by a leading radical among the sailors.

MAYNARD, SIR CHARLES CLARKSON MARTIN. **The Murmansk Venture.** London: Hodder, 1928, 334 p.
The British Commander-in-Chief gives a vivid account of the campaign and adds materially to our knowledge of this phase of the war.

MEL'GUNOV, SERGIEĬ PETROVICH. **The Red Terror in Russia.** London: Dent, 1925, 271 p.

A detailed, heavily documented account of the terror in 1919, especially in southern and southwestern Russia.

MEL'GUNOV, SERGIEĬ PETROVICH. **Tragediia Admirala Kolchaka.** Belgrade: Russkaia Biblioteka, 1930, 3 v.
The first parts of an exhaustive work on the Kolchak movement. The author here covers the years 1917-18, and gives a documented account of the situation in Siberia.

MILIUKOV, PAVEL NIKOLAEVICH. **Rossiia na Perelomie.** Paris: La Source, 1927, 2 v.
The history of the Revolution from the fall of the Kerensky government to the end of the civil war, by the well-known historian and Cadet leader.

MINK, I. **Angliĭskaia Interventsiia i Severnaia Kontrrevoliutsiia.** Moscow: no pub., 1931, 256 p.
A detailed study of the English action in North Russia in 1918.

MONTAUDON, G. **Deux Ans chez Koltchak et chez les Bolchéviques.** Paris: Alcan, 1922.
The experiences and impressions of a Red Cross official in the years 1919-1921.

POKROVSKIĬ, GEORGIĬ. **Denikinshchina.** Berlin: Grschebin, 1923, 279 p.
A careful study of the political and economic situation in the Kuban region in 1918-1919.

Poslednie Dni Kolchakovshchiny. Moscow: Gosizdat, 1926, 231 p.
Material published by the Soviet archive administration and bearing on the last phases of the Kolchak episode.

RAKOVSKIĬ, G. N. **V Stanie Bielykh.** Constantinople: Pressa, 1920, 340 p.
A general account of the counter-revolutionary movement in South Russia and the Kuban.

ROSS, EDWARD ALSWORTH. **The Russian Soviet Republic, 1918-1922.** New York: Century, 1923, 405 p.
An American sociologist's well-informed account of developments from Brest-Litovsk to 1922, with a survey of Bolshevik policies. In its day an excellent book.

ROUQUEROL, JEAN JOSEPH. **La Guerre des Rouges et des Blancs; l'Aventure de l'Amiral Koltchak.** Paris: Payot, 1929, 187 p.
A valuable military study of an important chapter of the Russian civil war.

SAKHAROV, KONSTANTIN VON. **Das Weisse Sibirien.** Munich: Laubereau, 1925, 386 p.
The civil war in Siberia, in the recollections of a White general.

SAVCHENKO, IL'IA. **Les Insurgés du Kouban.** Paris: Payot, 1929, 259 p.
An important narrative of stormy events in the northern Caucasus, by one of the leaders.

SOKOLOV, KONSTANTIN NIKOLAEVICH. **Pravlenie Generala Denikina.** Sofia: Ross-Bolg. Izdat, 1921, 292 p.
Reminiscences of the Denikin episode, by one of Denikin's associates.

TROTSKIĬ, LEV. **Materialy i Dokumenty po Istorii Krasnoĭ Armii. Kak Vooruzhalas' Revoliutsiia.** Moscow: Vysshiĭ Voennyĭ Redaktsionnyĭ Sovet, 1923-1925, 3 v.
An immense, heavily documented account of the organization and campaigns of the Russian Red Army.

VINAVER, M. **Nashe Pravitel'stvo.** Paris: Voltaire, 1928, 240 p.
The memoirs of a leader in the Crimea and a valuable contribution to the history of the stormy years 1918-1919 in South Russia.

VRANGEL, PETR NIKOLAEVICH, BARON. **Memoirs.** London: Williams and Norgate, 1929, 356 p.

The famous White leader's account of the counter-revolutionary movement. A valuable source, in diary form and rather scrappy.

WARD, JOHN. **With the "Die-Hards" in Siberia.** London: Cassell, 1920, 278 p.
The experiences and impressions of an English officer in Siberia, very critical of Allied policy towards Kolchak.

WRANGELL, WILHELM, BARON. **Geschichte des Baltenregiments.** Tallinn: Wassermann, 1928, 160 p.
An authoritative account of the struggle of the Baltic Germans against the Bolshevists, by the commander of the famous Baltic regiment.

ZENZINOV, VLADIMIR MIKHAĬLOVICH. **Gosudarstvennyĭ Perevorot Admirala Kolchaka v Omske.** Paris: Povolotzky, 1919, 193 p.
Documents bearing on Kolchak's coup d'état of November 1918.

The Emigrés

BUMGARDNER, EUGENIA S. **Undaunted Exiles.** Staunton: McClure, 1925, 230 p.
The sad story of the remnants of Wrangel's army and the tribulations of the refugees, especially in Constantinople.

DELAGE, JEAN. **La Russie en Exil.** Paris: Delagrave, 1930, 175 p.
Pictures and sketches of the emigration in Paris, which, according to the writer, represents the "true" Russia.

Dieti Emigratsii. Prague: Pedagogicheskoe Biuro, 1925, 251 p.
A series of essays on the educational problem of the Russian emigration.

RIMSCHA, HANS VON. **Russland jenseits der Grenzen.** Jena: Frommann, 1927, 238 p.
The best general study of the Russian emigration, its groups, organizations and activities.

TERSKOĬ, ALEKSANDR. **V Strane Proizvola i Bespraviia.** Moscow: Gosizdat, 1924, 181 p.
A study of Russian emigré activities in Bulgaria in the time of Stambuliski and his overturn.

VETLUGIN, A. **Tret'ia Rossiia.** Paris: Presse Franco-Russe, 1922, 395 p.
Pictures of the Russian emigration in Paris.

Bolshevism

General Theory and System of Government

See also (Europe) Constitutional Problems, Dictatorships, p. 227; also (Russia: Post-War Conditions) General, p. 380.

ANANOV, I. N. **Ocherki Federal'nogo Upravleniia.** Leningrad: Gosizdat, 1925, 211 p.
One of the best documented studies of the federal structure and operation of the Russian machine, and the working of the central organs.

ANTONELLI, ETIENNE. **Bolshevik Russia.** New York: Knopf, 1920. 307 p.
One of the best informed and most detached studies of the principles and practices of Bolshevism.

AUGUR, *pseud.* (VLADIMIR POLIAKOFF). **Soviet versus Civilization.** New York: Appleton, 1927, 106 p.
A virulent attack upon Bolshevism, and a plea for united action against the Soviet menace, by a voluminous if not always profound publicist.

BACH, LYDIA. **Le Droit et les Institutions de la Russie Soviétique.** Paris: Librairie Générale de Droit et de Jurisprudence, 1923, 338 p.
An impartial study of the political institutions of Soviet Russia.

BATSELL, WALTER RUSSELL. **Soviet Rule in Russia.** New York: Macmillan, 1929, 866 p.
An elaborate study of the theory and practice of Soviet Government, making available in English a large mass of hitherto untranslated documentary material.

BERDIAEV, NIKOLAĬ ALEKSANDROVICH. **Un Nouveau Moyen Âge.** Paris: Plon, 1927, 292 p.
An attempt to put Russian developments into a larger cultural synthesis. The author is a Russian philosopher expelled by the Bolsheviks for his religious views.

BOGOLEPOFF, A., BRUTZKUS, BORIS, and BUBNOFF, S. VON. **Der Staat, das Recht und die Wirtschaft des Bolschewismus.** Berlin: Rothschild, 1925, 350 p.
An interesting discussion of the theories of Bolshevism and the organization of the Soviet state.

BOURDEAU, JEAN. **La Dernière Évolution du Socialisme au Communisme.** Paris: Alcan, 1927, 184 p.
A useful account of the more recent teachings of the socialist school.

BRAILSFORD, HENRY NOEL. **How the Soviets Work.** New York: Vanguard, 1927, 169 p.
One of the best popular outlines, by an English radical.

BUKHARIN, NIKOLAĬ IVANOVICH. **K Voprosu o Trotskizme.** Moscow: Gosizdat, 1925, 192 p.
The case against Trotsky and his heresies, drawn by a leading communist intellectual.

BUKHARIN, NIKOLAĬ IVANOVICH and PREOBRAZHENSKIĬ, EVGENIĬ ALEKSIEEVICH. **The A. B. C. of Communism. A Popular Explanation of the Programme of the Communist Party of Russia.** London: Communist Party of England, 1922, 422 p.
The classic formulation of Russian communist doctrine.

CAMPODONICO, ALDEMIRO. **La Russia dei Soviets.** Florence: Vallecchi, 1920, 370 p.
A careful analysis of the fundamental legislative measures of the Bolsheviks, especially in economic, social and military matters.

CHUGUNOV, SERGIEĬ IVANOVICH. **Voprosy Organizatsii i Deiatel'nosti Sel'skikh Sovetov.** Leningrad: Gosizdat, 1925, 159 p.
An important monograph on the evolution, organization and working of the village Soviet.

CHUGUNOV, SERGIEĬ IVANOVICH. **Voprosy Organizatsii i Deiatel'nosti Nizovogo Sovetskogo Apparata. Gorodskie Sovety.** Moscow: Gosizdat, 1927, 225 p.
A complementary study to the preceding. A detailed study of the structure and working of the town soviets.

COLTON, ETHAN THEODORE. **The X Y Z of Communism.** New York: Macmillan, 1931, 423 p.
The principles of communism when translated into action, as seen by a man who has had long and wide experience with the Y. M. C. A. in Russia.

DALIN, D. **Posle Voĭn i Revoliutsiĭ.** Berlin: Grani, 1922, 287 p.
An essay on Bolshevism and what it implies, with special attention to the place of the phenomenon in the larger European setting.

DNEPROV, SERGEĬ. **Die Krise des Bolschewismus.** Berlin: Verlag der Kulturliga, 1922, 64 p.
A study of the transformation of Bolshevik policies under the pressure of economic necessity.

DRANITSYN, S. N. **Konstitutsiia S. S. S. R. i R. S. F. S. R.** Leningrad: Priboĭ, 1924, 232 p.
A catechism of the constitution, with excellent diagrams.

EASTMAN, MAX. **Marx, Lenin and the Science of Revolution.** New York: Boni, 1927, 263 p.
A suggestive criticism of Marxian teaching and Lenin's tactics, by a leading American sympathizer.

ECKARDT, HANS VON. **Die Sozialpolitik in der Union der Sozialistischen Sovĕtrepubliken.** Berlin: Sack, 1925, 35 p.
A brief outline of Bolshevik social legislation and policy, by a very competent German writer.

ENGEL', E. A. **Osnovy Sovetskoĭ Konstitutsii.** Moscow: Gosizdat, 1923, 248 p.
A syllabus of lectures on Soviet constitutional law.

AN ENGLISH EUROPASIAN, *pseud.* **Russia in Resurrection.** London: Routledge, 1928, 282 p.
Russian development in broad sweeps, stressing the failure of both Tsarism and Bolshevism and setting forth the Europasian program — political, economic, religious — which the author states to be steadily growing in influence.

FARBMAN, MICHAEL S. **After Lenin, the New Phase in Russia.** London: Parsons, 1925, 280 p.
Predicts a gradual return to something resembling the old order, with improvements made by the Bolsheviks.

GURIAN, WALDEMAR. **Bolshevism: Theory and Practice.** New York: Macmillan, 1932, 402 p.
A critical comparison of Bolshevik theory and practice, political, economic and social. One of the best books for the serious student.

GURVICH, G. S. **Istoriia Sovetskoĭ Konstitutsii.** Moscow: Socialist Academy, 1923, 216 p.
An account of the work of the constitutional commission and the birth of the Soviet constitution. Contains some of the earlier drafts and is indispensable for the student of the subject.

GURVICH, G. S. **Osnovy Sovetskoĭ Konstitutsii.** Moscow: Gosizdat, 5th ed., 1926, 206 p.
One of the best general introductions to the study of the constitution.

HAHN, WALTER and LILIENFELD-TOAL, ANATOL VON. **Der Neue Kurs in Russland: Wirtschaftsgesetze der Sowjetregierung.** Jena: Fischer, 1923, 108 p.
A brief documentary study of modifications of thoroughgoing Communism under the NEP policy.

HANS, NICHOLAS A. and HESSEN, SERGIEĬ IOSIFOVICH. **Educational Policy in Soviet Russia.** London: King, 1930, 236 p.
A monograph on an important plank in the Bolskevik platform.

HARPER, SAMUEL NORTHRUP. **Civic Training in Soviet Russia.** Chicago: Chicago University Press, 1929, 401 p.
One of the most scholarly books on Soviet Russia, and a veritable mine of information on the technique of Soviet propaganda in Russia itself.

HAUMANT, ÉMILE. **Le Problème de l'Unité Russe.** Paris: Bossard, 1922, 128 p.
An able argument for the reconstitution of Russia as a confederation, democratic and republican, based on the constitution of the United States.

HOPPER, BRUCE CAMPBELL. **Pan-Sovietism.** Boston: Houghton Mifflin, 1931, 288 p. Lowell Lectures. The author, an American scholar with first-hand information on Soviet Russia, analyzes the historic background of the Soviet system and deals in detail with later policies, like the Five Year Plan. In the last chapter he contrasts the Russian and American systems and points out the importance of the Far East as an eventual battleground.

IGNAT'EV, V. I. **Sovetskii Stroĭ.** Moscow: Gosizdat, 1928, 148 p. The first part of a larger work on the Soviet system, covering the origin and development of the Constitution.

ISSAKOVITCH, DRAGOMIR. **Le Pouvoir Central et le Système Électoral d'après la Constitution Soviétique Russe.** Paris: Jouve, 1927, 308 p. A dissertation, based largely on Russian secondary works, giving a convenient outline of the central government system and the mechanism of elections.

KOTLIAREVSKIĬ, SERGIEĬ ANDREEVICH. **S. S. S. R. i Soiuznye Respubliki.** Moscow: Gosizdat, 1926, 141 p. A learned discussion of the federalist organization, with special reference to foreign policy, war, international economic problems, etc.

LANDAU, MARK ALEKSANDROVICH. **Deux Révolutions.** Paris: Union, 1921, 119 p. An interesting comparison of the French and Russian Revolutions, with emphasis on social aspects, tactics and foreign policy.

LANGHANS-RATZEBURG, MANFRED. **Vom Absolutismus zum Rätefreistaat.** Leipzig: Hirschfeld, 1925, 160 p. A very satisfactory outline of Russian constitutional development since 1918.

LASKI, HAROLD JOSEPH. **Communism.** New York: Holt, 1927, 256 p. A convenient and thoroughly competent treatment, in the Home University Library series, by a well-known English essayist and liberal.

LENIN, NIKOLAĬ, BUKHARIN, NIKOLAĬ IVANOVICH and RUTGERS, S. J. **The New Policies of Soviet Russia.** Chicago: Kerr, 1922, 127 p. Authoritative apologia.

LESCURE, JEAN. **La Révolution Russe, le Bolchevisme.** Paris: Gamber, 1929, 356 p. Primarily a study of Soviet organization and an analysis of the NEP.

LODER, JOHN DE VERE. **Bolshevism in Perspective.** London: Allen and Unwin, 1931, 256 p. A study of the historical evolution of Bolshevism, with some consideration of its probable future development.

MAGEROVSKIĬ, D. A. **Soiuz Sovetskikh Sotsialisticheskikh Respublik.** Moscow: Iuridicheskoe Izdatel'stvo, 1931, 185 p. A study of the Russian constitution, with reference especially to the evolution of the federal principle. Many key documents are printed.

MALEVSKIĬ-MALEVICH, P. N. **A New Party in Russia.** London: Routledge, 1928, 126 p. The first extended account of the "Europasian movement," which accepts the Russian Revolution as a necessary break with imperial ("Westernized") Russia, views the rule of communism ("a Western doctrine") as a phase to be somehow endured, and looks forward to a new order to be based on the moral and religious forces of the Russian masses, strengthened by new bonds with the civilizations of the East.

MALINSKIĬ, ALEKSANDR. **Sovetskaia Konstitutsiia.** Kharkov: Iuridicheskoe Izdatel'stvo, 1925, 440 p. A standard general treatment of the principles and constitutional structure of the Soviet system, with relevant texts.

MARTOV, IULIĬ, *pseud.* (IU. TSEDERBAUM). **Geschichte der Russischen Sozialdemo-kratie.** Berlin: Dietz, 1926, 340 p.
The German translation of the standard Russian work on the subject, written from the Menshevik standpoint.

Materialy po Istorii Sovetskogo Stroitel'stva. Moscow: Communist Academy, 1928, 2 v.
A collection of documentary material to illustrate the evolution of the Soviet system of government in the critical period of 1917.

MAUTNER, WILHELM. **Der Bolschewismus.** Berlin: Kohlhammer, 1920, 368 p.
One of the ablest early studies of the origin and theory of Bolshevism.

MILIUKOV, PAVEL NIKOLAEVICH. **Bolshevism: an International Danger.** London: Allen, 1920, 303 p.
An able exposition of the danger threatening from the Internationale and from Bolshevik propaganda throughout the world, by an eminent liberal statesman.

MIRKIN-GETSEVICH, BORIS SERGIEEVICH. **La Théorie Générale de l'État Soviétique.** Paris: Giard, 1928, 200 p.
An admirable account of Soviet political theory by a former professor of law at the University of Petrograd.

NEARING, SCOTT. **Education in Soviet Russia.** New York: International Publishers, 1926, 159 p.
A sympathetic account by a well-known radical writer.

Ob Ekonomicheskoĭ Platforme Oppozitsii. Moscow: Gosizdat, 1926, 446 p.
A collection of articles by authoritative writers, published in reply to the heretical economic doctrines of Trotsky.

PALMIERI, AURELIO. **La Geografía Política della Russia Sovietista.** Rome: Garroni, 1926, 163 p.
A good handbook, by an outstanding Italian authority.

PARANDOWSKI, JAN. **Bolszewizm i Bolszewicy.** Warsaw: Wende, 1919, 159 p.
Articles by a Polish journalist, dealing chiefly with the Bolshevik ideology and the Soviet system in actual practice.

PINKEVICH, AL'BERT PETROVICH. **The New Education in the Soviet Republic.** New York: Day, 1929, 416 p.
The English translation of an important book by the president of the Second State University of Moscow.

POSTGATE, RAYMOND WILLIAM. **The Bolshevik Theory.** New York: Dodd, 1920, 240 p.
Why the Bolsheviks are revolutionaries and what their aims and principles are. A competent and interesting, though rather disjointed study.

Pravo Sovetskoĭ Rossii. Prague: Plamia, 1925, 2 v.
A collection of essays, by Russian scholars, on many phases of Soviet constitutional and administrative law.

PREOBRAZHENSKIĬ, EVGENIĬ ALEKSIEEVICH. **Novaia Ekonomika.** Moscow: Communist Academy, 1926, 336 p.
A purely theoretical treatise on Bolshevik economics.

REICHEL, M. **Soiuz Sovetskikh Sotsialisticheskikh Respublik.** Kharkov: no pub., 1925, 186 p.
An introduction to the federal constitution of the Soviet Republics.

RUNDT, ARTHUR. **Der Mensch Wird Umgebaut.** Berlin: Rowohlt, 1932, 198 p.
An analysis of the effects of the Bolshevik system upon the individual.

RUSSELL, BERTRAND RUSSELL, EARL. **Bolshevism; Practice and Theory.** New York: Harcourt, 1920, 192 p.
An interesting critique, written by an eminent English student and radical.

SERTOLI, MARIO. **La Costituzione Russa.** Florence: Le Monnier, 1928, 435 p.
The first of three volumes of a scholarly treatise analyzing in great detail the constitutional structure and practice of Russia.

Der Staat, das Recht und die Wirtschaft des Bolschewismus. Berlin: Rothschild, 1925, 350 p.
An important and valuable collection of studies, by Russian and German scholars, dealing with the principles, the legal theories and the economic policies of Bolshevism.

STALIN, IOSIF VISSARIONOVICH. **Leninism.** New York: International Publishers, 1928, 472 p.
The translation of an important collection of speeches and articles expressing the views of the Russian leader.

STEINBERG, I. **Als Ich Volkskommissar War.** Munich: Piper, 1929, 255 p.
The former Commissar of Justice extols Lenin and Trotsky and bemoans the shortcomings of their successors.

VISHNIAK, MARK VEN'IAMINOVICH. **Le Régime Soviétiste.** Paris: Union, 1920, 102 p.
A Social-Revolutionary view of the Soviet Constitution, with stress on the practice and on the ineluctable conflict between Bolshevism and democracy.

WIEDENFELD, KURT. **The Remaking of Russia.** London: Labour Publishing Company, 1924, 116 p.
An excellent brief account of communist theory and the organization of the Soviet State, by a former German Ambassador to Russia.

WOODY, THOMAS. **New Minds: New Men?** New York: Macmillan, 1932, 528 p.
A well-documented study of the Bolshevik educational system, based upon many months of careful investigation. A useful book.

Za Leninizm. Moscow: Gosizdat, 1925, 488 p.
More than twenty essays, by various authoritative writers. A tremendous broadside aimed at Trotsky.

ZAGORSKIĬ, SEMEN OSIPOVICH. **L'Évolution Actuelle du Bolchévisme Russe.** Paris: Povolozky, 1921, 149 p.
One of the ablest among the early critiques of the Bolshevik régime.

ZASZTOWT-SUKIENNICKA, HALINA. **Fédéralisme en Europe Orientale.** Paris: Presses Universitaires, 1926, 280 p.
A scholarly study of the federalist system in Soviet Russia.

The Communist Party and the Third Internationale

Die Bauerninternationale. Berlin: Neues Dorf, 1926, 186 p.
Twenty essays published by the International Peasant Council in Moscow, setting forth the agrarian problems of Europe from the Bolshevik standpoint.

GARGAS, SIGISMUND. **Die Grüne Internationale.** Halberstadt: Meyer, 1927, 55 p.
A good brief outline of the organization of the Peasant Internationale, its aims and its activities.

GUREVICH, A. **Vozniknovenie i Razvitie Kommunicheskogo Internatsionala.** Kharkov: Gosizdat, 1925, 224 p.
The origin and development of the Third Internationale. A good general treatment from the communist side.

IAROSLAVSKIĬ, E. **Aus der Geschichte der Kommunistischen Partei der Sowjet-union.** Berlin: Hoym, 1929-1931, 2 v.
The German translation of a standard and authoritative history of the Party. These volumes cover the period from the Populists to about 1921. A third volume, going to 1930, is to follow.

IVANOVICH, ST. **V K P. Desiat' Let Kommunisticheskoĭ Monopolii.** Paris: Société d'Éditions Franco-Slaves, 1928, 256 p.
A critical history of the Communist Party in the ten years after its victory.

Der Kampf um die Kommunistische Internationale. Berlin: Fahne des Kommunismus, 1928, 176 p.
Purporting to be a collection of documents from those in opposition to Stalin.

KAUTSKY, KARL. **Die Internationale und Sowjetrussland.** Berlin: Dietz, 1925, 62 p.
The German socialist calls for a new crusade against absolutism in the shape of Bolshevism, but deprecates the use of force.

KERZHENTSEV, P. M. **Stranitsy Istorii R K P.** Leningrad: Priboĭ, 4th ed., 1928, 187 p.
The congresses and conferences of the Communist Party from 1898 to 1915.

KOLESNIKOV, N. N. **R. K. P. i Komintern.** Moscow: Gosizdat, 1925, 230 p.
The Communist Party and the Internationale. The traditional communist statement of the organization and its purpose.

KURELLA, ALFRED. **Gründung und Aufbau der Kommunistischen Jugendinternationale.** Berlin: Verlag der Jugendinternationale, 1930, 253 p.
An interesting account of the efforts being made to educate the youth of the proletariat in the ways of Bolshevism.

POPOV, N. N. **Ocherk Istorii Vsesoiuznoĭ Kommunisticheskoĭ Partii.** Moscow: Gosizdat, 3rd ed., 1927.
A general popular survey of the party history, one of the best of its kind.

RÉZANOV, A. **La Troisième Internationale Communiste.** Paris: Bossard, 1922, 127 p.
Written by a Tsarist officer and published on the eve of the Genoa Conference to warn the world against a system directed by the "General Staff of the World Revolution."

TROTSKIĬ, LEV. **L'Internationale Communiste après Lénine.** Paris: Rieder, 1930, 438 p.
The latest product of the Trotsky-Stalin duel. Trotsky views with disgust the running down of the machinery of world revolution.

TROTSKIĬ, LEV. **Piat' Let Kominterna.** Moscow: Gosizdat, 2nd ed., 1925, 660 p.
Five years of the Internationale; a detailed account of its organization and work by one of its most enthusiastic supporters.

TROTSKIĬ, LEV. **Voĭna i Revoliutsiia.** Moscow: Gosizdat, 2nd ed., 1923, 2 v.
The breakdown of the Second Internationale and the beginnings of the Third; a most important source.

ZINOV'EV, GRIGORIĬ. **L'Internationale Communiste au Travail.** Paris: Librairie de l'Humanité, 1923, 187 p.
A classic statement of the aims and activities of the Internationale, by one of its leading figures.

ZINOV'EV, GRIGORIĬ. **Istoriia Rossiĭskoĭ Kommunisticheskoĭ Partii.** Moscow: Gosizdat, 1924.
A general history of the Party, by one of its most prominent leaders.

The Red Army

IVANOVICH, ST. **Krasnaia Armiia.** Paris: Sovremennyia Zapiski, 1931, 244 p.
A study of the military system and its place in the general Soviet structure.

IWANOW, A. N. **Kurze Zusammenstellung über die Russische Armee.** Berlin: Eisenschmidt, 1929, 135 p.
A good brief survey of Russia's armed forces and their organization.

MOVCHIN, N. **Komplektovanie Krasnoĭ Armii.** Moscow: Voennaia Tipografiia, 1926, 292 p.
Published by the Russian staff. A technical historical study of the Red Army.

SCHULHÖFER, FRANZ LUDWIG. **Der Russische Bolschewismus und das Rüstungsproblem.** Heidelberg: Brunner, 1928, 100 p.
A dissertation; a good scientific study of the communist attitude towards armaments and war and of the organization of the Red forces.

TAL, B. **Istoriia Krasnoĭ Armii.** Moscow: Gosizdat, 4th ed., 1928, 196 p.
The best general account of the origin and organization of the Red forces.

TECHOW, FRITZ. **Die Rote Armee.** Berlin: Sack, 1925, 55 p.
An excellent short outline of the Bolshevik army.

VISHNIAKOV, N. **Ustroĭstvo Vooruzhennykh sil S. S. S. R.** Moscow: Gosizdat, 1930, 392 p.
The most recent general study of the military, naval and aeronautic forces of the Soviet Union.

Vooruzhennyĭ Narod. Moscow: Gosizdat, 1925, 179 p.
A collection of authoritative essays by various writers dealing with many aspects of Russian military organization. With a good bibliography.

Cheka and Ogpu

AGABEKOV, GEORGIĬ. **Ogpu.** New York: Brentano, 1931, 277 p.
The Russian secret service in the light of the experiences of one of its agents in Afghanistan, Persia, Turkey and Arabia. An illuminating book.

BAJANOV, BORIS. **L'Enlèvement du Général Koutepov.** Paris: Spès, 1930, 86 p.
A detailed account of the famous kidnapping case.

BESEDOVSKIĬ, GRIGORIĬ ZINOVIEEVICH. **Oui, J'Accuse.** Paris: Redier, 1930, 265 p.
An illuminating indictment of Bolshevik activities, by a former Soviet diplomatic representative.

BRUNOVSKIĬ, VLADIMIR KHRISTIANOVICH. **The Methods of the Ogpu.** London: Harper, 1931, 255 p.
The horrible experiences of an agricultural expert who spent years in the Solovetski prison camp.

CEDERHOLM, BORIS. **In the Clutches of the Tcheka.** Boston: Houghton Mifflin, 1929, 350 p.
The appalling adventures of a foreign trade agent who fell into the hands of the Cheka in 1923 and spent many months in the Solovetski camp.

Che-Ka. Berlin: Novaia Rossiia, 1922, 225 p.
A collection of personal accounts and essays on the work of the Cheka, by exiled Social Revolutionaries.

DUMBADZE, E. **Na Sluzhbe Cheka i Kominterna.** Paris: Michen, 1930, 164 p.
Another revelation of Russian machinations in Georgia and Turkey.

Les Faussaires contre les Soviets. Paris: Librairie du Travail, 1926, 140 p.
An exposé of anti-Bolshevik propaganda, especially in the matter of the Zinoviev letter.

LUCIETO, CHARLES. **La Vierge Rouge du Kremlin.** Paris: Berger-Levrault, 1927, 444 p.
A rather sensational account of the work of the Cheka, by a member of the French intelligence service.

MITAREVSKIĬ, N. **World-Wide Soviet Plots.** Tientsin: Tientsin Press, 1928, 211 p.
The activities of Soviet agents in Asia, as they appear from the documents seized in the Russian Embassy at Peiping.

ORLOV, VLADIMIR GRIGOR'EVICH. **Underworld and Soviet.** New York: Dial, 1931, 274 p.
Thrilling experiences of a Russian secret service agent under the Tsars and under the Bolsheviks.

POPOV, GEORGIĬ KONSTANTINOVICH. **The Tcheka: the Red Inquisition.** London: Philpot, 1925, 308 p.
The experiences of a correspondent who fell into the hands of the secret police in 1922. A vigorous indictment of the methods of this "state within the state."

RÉZANOV, A. **Le Travail Secret des Agents Bolchévistes.** Paris: Bossard, 1926, 200 p.
A hostile exploitation of Bolshevik documents.

Biographies

See also (World War) Biographies of Wartime Statesmen and Diplomats, p. 101; also (Europe) Constitutional Problems, Dictatorships, p. 227, and Biographies, p. 228.

BESEDOVSKIĬ, GRIGORIĬ ZINOVIEEVICH and LAPORTE, MAURICE. **Staline, l'Homme d'Acier.** Paris: Revue Française, 1932.
A racy and distinctly partial biography.

BRYANT, LOUISE. **Mirrors of Moscow.** New York: Seltzer, 1923, 209 p.
Portraits of the leading figures in Bolshevik Russia.

CHASLES, PIERRE. **La Vie de Lénine.** Paris: Plon, 1929, 248 p.
One of the best accounts of Lenin as a revolutionary leader, by an author who knows Russia and Russian well.

EASTMAN, MAX. **Since Lenin Died.** New York: Boni and Liveright, 1925, 158 p.
A vindication of Trotsky in his struggle with the triumvirate since Lenin's death.

ESSAD BEY. **Stalin: The Career of a Fanatic.** New York: Viking, 1932, 399 p.
A translation from the German of a sensational account of the dictator's rise to power. Unreliable.

FERVACQUE, PIERRE. **La Vie Orgueilleuse de Trotsky.** Paris: Fasquelle, 1929, 190 p.
Trotsky as the incarnation of the spirit of destruction. An inadequate sketch based upon non-Russian sources.

GRAHAM, STEPHEN. **Stalin.** London: Benn, 1931, 148 p.
A straightforward narrative of the conventional kind adding little that is new, by a writer familiar with both pre-war and post-war Russia.

IAROSLAVSKIĬ, E. **Zhizn' i Rabota V. I. Lenina.** Leningrad: Gosizdat, 5th ed., 1926, 357 p.
One of the best general biographies of the great leader, by a leading communist journalist, editor of *Bezbozhnik.*

KRASIN, MME. LUBOV. **Leonid Krassin.** London: Skeffington, 1929, 284 p.
The late Russian trade envoy is pictured by his widow as a true Russian patriot and Bolshevik *malgré lui.* A book of considerable interest and value.

KRUPSKAIA, NADEZHDA KONSTANTINOVNA. **Memories of Lenin.** New York: International Publishers, 1930, 220 p.
These recollections of Lenin by his widow throw much light on his earlier career and the evolution of his ideas.

LARSONS, M. J., *pseud.* (MAURICE LASERSON). **Im Sowjet-Labyrinth.** Berlin: Transmare, 1931, 255 p.
This volume, written by a former Bolshevik official, contains interesting sketches of Krestinski, Joffe, Chicherin and other leaders.

LENIN, NIKOLAĬ. **Sobranie Sochineniĭ.** Moscow: Gosizdat, 1921-1926, 20 v.
The standard, authorized edition of Lenin's collected works. An English translation is in course of publication under the title "Collected Works of V. I. Lenin" (New York: International Publishers, 1929 ff.).

Leonid Borisovich Krasin. Moscow: Gosizdat, 1928, 397 p.
Essays and reminiscences by various writers, together with much other material for the biography of Krasin.

LEVINE, ISAAC DON. **The Man Lenin.** New York: Seltzer, 1924, 209 p.
The first discriminating biography in English.

LEVINE, ISAAC DON. **Stalin.** New York: Cosmopolitan, 1931, 421 p.
Though it does not answer all questions that arise in connection with Stalin's position, this book gives a clear account of the externals of his career and of his relations with the other Bolshevik leaders.

LUNACHARSKIĬ, ANATOLIĬ VASIL'EVICH. **Revoliutsionnye Siluety.** Moscow: Tranposektsiia, 1923, 79 p.
Short character sketches of Lenin, Trotsky, Zinoviev, Plekhanov, Sverdlov and others, by one of their collaborators, later Commissar for Education.

MARCU, VALERIU. **Lenin.** New York: Macmillan, 1928, 412 p.
A noteworthy book, giving a most interesting appreciation of the man and the statesman. Well illustrated.

POPOV, N. N. and IAKOVLEV, I. A. **Das Leben Lenins und der Leninismus.** Moscow: Zentral-Voelkerverlag, 1926, 136 p.
The life of the saint for popular consumption.

STALIN, IOSIF VISSARIONOVICH. **Ob Oppozitsii.** Moscow: Gosizdat, 1928, 750 p.
A collection of speeches and essays of the years 1921-27.

SVIATOPOLK-MIRSKIĬ, DMITRIĬ PETROVICH, KNIAZ'. **Lenin.** Boston: Little, Brown, 1931, 247 p.
In this biography more stress is laid on the evolution of Lenin's personality. An interesting volume.

TROTSKIĬ, LEV. **Lenin.** New York: Minton Balch, 1925, 236 p.
Deals chiefly with the years 1900-1903 and 1917-1918 and consists of interesting if somewhat disjointed reminiscences and appreciations.

TROTSKIĬ, LEV. **My Life.** New York: Scribner, 1930, 613 p.
A full-length autobiography by one of the most astonishing men of our time. A bitter polemic against the present rulers of Russia and against the emasculators (according to Trotsky) of the work accomplished by Lenin and himself.

TROTSKIĬ, LEV. **Sochineniia.** Moscow: Gosizdat, 1923 ff.
The collected writings of Trotsky. Parts of twenty-one volumes were published up to 1927.

VEALE, F. J. P. **The Man from the Volga.** London: Constable, 1932, 304 p.
The author is concerned chiefly with clearing up the main facts of Lenin's career.

Vernadskiǐ, Georgiǐ Vladimirovich. **Lenin, Red Dictator.** New Haven: Yale University Press, 1931, 351 p.
　　Certainly one of the best biographies of Lenin, written with understanding if not with sympathy.

Williams, Albert Rhys. **Lenin. The Man and His Work.** New York: Scott and Seltzer, 1919, 197 p.
　　A valiant attempt at a just estimate. The book is based in large measure on personal contacts and includes impressions of Lenin by Raymond Robins and Arthur Ransome.

Windecke, Christian. **Der Rote Zar.** Leipzig: Quelle und Meyer, 1932, 231 p.
　　One of the better biographies of Stalin, objective and detailed.

Zinov'ev, Grigoriǐ. **Lenin.** Leningrad: Gosizdat, 2nd ed., 1925, 312 p.
　　A sympathetic study of the communist dictator, by one of his close associates.

Zinov'ev, Grigoriǐ. **Sochineniia.** Moscow: Gosizdat, 1923 ff.
　　Collected writings of Zinoviev. Parts of sixteen volumes have been published to date.

Post-War Conditions

General

See also (Bolshevism) General Theory and System of Government, p. 370.

Abramowitsch, R. **Der Terror gegen die Sozialistischen Parteien in Russland und Georgien.** Berlin: Dietz, 1925, 134 p.
　　Contains interesting contributions by some of the socialist leaders.

Alvarez del Vayo, Julio. **Rusia á los Doce Años.** Madrid: Espasa-Calpe, 1929, 162 p.
　　A sympathetic portrayal of the Russian scene after twelve years of Bolshevik rule, by a Spanish radical, subsequently Ambassador to Mexico.

Aquara, Lucio d'. **L'Isola Rossa.** Bologna: La Voce, 1928, 188 p.
　　A brief but vivid survey of affairs, by an Italian Fascist.

Ashmead-Bartlett, Ellis. **The Riddle of Russia.** London: Cassell, 1929, 276 p.
　　Vivid impressions of Leningrad and Moscow, the result of a short visit by an English correspondent.

Baǐkalov, Anatoliǐ. **In the Land of Communist Dictatorship.** London: Cape, 1929, 286 p.
　　A Russian socialist condemns the Bolshevik régime on the strength of Bolshevik sources, with special reference to labor and social reform.

Baldwin, Roger Nash. **Liberty under the Soviets.** New York: Vanguard, 1928, 272 p.
　　The problem described in a friendly way by an American radical.

Béraud, Henri. **The Truth about Moscow.** London: Faber, 1926, 261 p.
　　A French worker's unfavorable observations of the régime.

Berkman, Alexander. **The Bolshevik Myth.** New York: Boni and Liveright, 1925, 319 p.
　　The diary of a revolutionary deportee who became disillusioned.

Bol'shakov, A. M. **Derevnia, 1917-1927.** Moscow: Rabotnik Prosveshcheniia, 1927, 470 p.
　　A detailed study of the Russian village in the first ten years of Bolshevik rule. An interesting contribution.

Borders, Karl. **Village Life under the Soviets.** New York: Vanguard, 1927, 191 p.
　　An excellent introduction to the agrarian problem, by a man who has spent years in rural Russia.

BRASOL, BORIS LEO. **The Balance Sheet of Sovietism.** New York: Duffield, 1922, 272 p.
A strong indictment of Bolshevik policies—political, economic and foreign—which, according to the author, have proved the ruin of Russia.

BROWN, WILLIAM ADAMS, JR. **The Groping Giant.** New Haven: Yale University Press, 1920, 204 p.
A largely psychological study of social groups—the masses, the Bolsheviki, the intelligentsia—by a member of the American Committee on Public Information.

CHAMBERLIN, WILLIAM HENRY. **Soviet Russia.** Boston: Little, Brown, 1930, 461 p.
One of the best accounts of Soviet Russia, written in a spirit of detachment by the correspondent of the *Christian Science Monitor.*

DARLING, JAY NORWOOD. **Ding Goes to Russia.** New York: McGraw-Hill, 1932, 204 p.
Observations of a well-known American cartoonist, with some clever sketches.

DESPREAUX, ÉLISE. **Trois Ans chez les Tzars Rouges.** Paris: Spès, 1931, 248 p.
The disillusioning experiences of an enthusiast for the cause.

DEWEY, JOHN. **Impressions of Soviet Russia and the Revolutionary World.** New York: New Republic, 1929, 270 p.
An educator's impressions (some of them first-hand) of conditions in Russia, Mexico, China and Turkey. Rather superficial.

DILLON, EMILE JOSEPH. **Russia Today and Yesterday.** New York: Doubleday, 1930, 325 p.
Dillon has known Russia for fifty years, and writes very sympathetically of the cultural work of the new régime and its effects.

DOUILLET, JOSEPH. **Moscow Unmasked.** London: Pilot Press, 1930, 222 p.
The late Belgian consul gives his observations and impressions of Russia after nine years there. His conclusions are not very complimentary.

DUKES, SIR PAUL. **Red Dusk and the Morrow.** New York: Doubleday, 1922, 322 p.
Experiences and impressions of Bolshevik Russia in 1918, by the chief of the British Intelligence Service in Russia.

DUMAS, CHARLES. **La Vérité sur les Bolcheviki.** Paris: Édition Franco-Slave, 1919, 141 p.
A French socialist deputy, after fifteen months in Russia, warns the workingman against Bolshevism.

DURANTY, WALTER. **The Curious Lottery.** New York: Coward-McCann, 1929, 237 p.
The able correspondent of the *New York Times* reviews a number of cases which throw light on the working of justice under the Soviets.

ECKARDT, HANS VON. **Russia.** New York: Knopf, 1932, 711 p.
One of the best general books on modern Russia. The author outlines the country's history and discusses in great detail the Revolution, the Bolshevik system, economic policies and conditions, etc.

EDDY, SHERWOOD. **The Challenge of Russia.** New York: Farrar and Rinehart, 1931, 278 p.
A well-known Y. M. C. A. worker and publicist gives his views about Russia.

EDELHERTZ, BERNARD. **The Russian Paradox.** New York: Walton, 1930, 165 p.
A first-hand study of life under the Soviets.

EPHESIAN, *pseud.* (CARL ERIC BECHHOFER ROBERTS). **Through Starving Russia.** London: Methuen, 1921, 165 p.
An English journalist's observations in the famine-stricken Volga regions.

FABRE-LUCE, ALFRED. **Russie, 1927.** Paris: Grasset, 1927, 264 p.
A brilliant picture by a well-known French writer frankly bourgeois in his views.

FAIRBURN, WILLIAM ARMSTRONG. **Russia, the Utopia in Chains.** New York: Nation, 1931, 476 p.
A series of articles and essays on forced labor, the peasant problem, the world revolution and the question of American recognition.

FARBMAN, MICHAEL S. **Bolshevism in Retreat.** London: Collins, 1923, 312 p.
This able book is really a history of the Bolshevik régime and its effects during the first five years. The author sees the NEP as the beginning of the end.

FEDOROV, MIKHAIL, *ed.* **La Russie sous le Régime Communiste.** Paris: Nouvelle Librairie Nationale, 1926, 592 p.
A reply to the report of the British Trade Union delegation, in the form of articles based on Bolshevik documents and written by twenty-three Russian scholars.

FEILER, ARTHUR. **The Experiment of Bolshevism.** London: Allen and Unwin, 1930, 256 p.
By the editor of the *Frankfurter Zeitung.* One of the most open-minded and discerning critiques of Bolshevism.

FISHER, HAROLD HENRY. **The Famine in Soviet Russia, 1919-1923.** New York: Macmillan, 1927, 619 p.
The authoritative record of the operations of the American Relief Administration.

FÜLÖP-MILLER, RENÉ. **The Mind and Face of Bolshevism.** New York: Knopf, 1929, 308 p.
The English translation of one of the best accounts of cultural developments under the Bolshevik régime. Beautifully illustrated.

GAVRONSKIĬ, DMITRIĬ. **Die Bilanz des Russischen Bolchewismus.** Berlin: Cassirer, 1919, 88 p.
With the use of Bolshevik material and newspaper evidence, the writer, a Social Revolutionary leader, makes out a strong case against the new régime.

GODDEN, GERTRUDE M. **Russia under the Red Flag.** London: Oates, 1929, 194 p.
Bolshevik horrors luridly presented.

GOLDER, FRANK ALFRED and HUTCHINSON, LINCOLN. **On the Trail of the Russian Famine.** Stanford: Stanford University Press, 1927, 331 p.
An interesting story, told by two competent observers, members of the Relief Administration.

GOLDMAN, EMMA. **My Disillusionment in Russia.** New York: Doubleday, 1923, 242 p.
The disappointments of a well-known radical after many months of Bolshevik rule.

GOMPERS, SAMUEL and WALLING, WILLIAM ENGLISH. **Out of Their Own Mouths.** New York: Dutton, 1921, 265 p.
Uncompromising condemnation of Bolshevism, its theories and methods, by the head of the American Federation of Labor and a well-known American socialist.

GOODE, WILLIAM THOMAS. **Bolshevism at Work.** New York: Harcourt, 1920, 142 p.
An understanding investigation of the Soviet system and policies, by the correspondent of the *Manchester Guardian.*

GORDIN, MORRIS. **Utopia in Chains.** Boston: Houghton Mifflin, 1927, 287 p.
The Russian experiences of another disillusioned communist.

GRADY, MRS. EVE GARRETTE. **Seeing Red.** New York: Brewer, 1931, 307 p.
Pointers for the prospective visitor to Russia. Racy observations on contemporary life.

GRAHAM, STEPHEN. **The Dividing Line of Europe.** New York: Appleton, 1925, 309 p.
Sketches of affairs in the Baltic States and Poland, of the Russian emigration in Paris, and of certain aspects of the Bolshevik régime.

GREDESKUL, N. A. **Rossiia Prezhde i Tepez'.** Moscow: Gosizdat, 1926, 255 p.
Proceeding on the theory that Old Russia was not Russia at all, the author traces the cultural changes of recent years.

GUEST, LESLIE HADEN. **The New Russia.** London: Butterworth, 1926, 488 p.
A general survey, based in part on personal observation, by an English Laborite. The book makes use of much Bolshevik material.

HARPER, SAMUEL NORTHRUP. **Making Bolsheviks.** Chicago: Chicago University Press, 1931, 186 p.
The author studies representative groups on which Bolshevik power depends.

HARRISON, MRS. MARGUERITE ELTON (BAKER). **Marooned in Moscow.** New York: Doran, 1921, 322 p.
Unembittered views of Russian life and conditions by an American journalist who spent ten of her eighteen months in prison.

HERRIOT, ÉDOUARD. **La Russie Nouvelle.** Paris: Ferenczi, 1923, 302 p.
The report of a visit to Russia. The French statesman discusses at length the economic theories, practices and problems, records his conversations with leaders, and lightly surveys social and artistic conditions.

Das Heutige Russland. Berlin: Frenkel, 1923, 2 pts.
A general review of all aspects of Russian cultural and economic life, written by a group of Russian experts and scholars.

HINDUS, MAURICE GERSCHON. **Broken Earth.** New York: International Publishers, 1926, 288 p.
An excellent picture of life in the village in the first years of Bolshevik rule.

HINDUS, MAURICE GERSCHON. **Humanity Uprooted.** New York: Cape and Smith, 1929, 369 p.
The author writes of the Russian scene with sympathy and sweet reasonableness.

IL'IN, IVAN ALEKSANDROVICH, *ed.* **Welt vor dem Abgrund.** Berlin: Eckart, 1931, 576 p.
An exhaustive review of the communist régime, written by more than a dozen Russian emigré scholars.

ISTRATI, PANAÏT. **Vers l'Autre Flamme.** Paris: Rieder, 1929, 3 v.
Strongly written and very revealing experiences and impressions of a disillusioned revolutionist, after sixteen months with the Soviets.

IVANOV, SERGIEÏ. **La Famine en Russie Bolcheviste.** Paris: Nouvelle Librairie Nationale, 1924, 228 p.
A diary of the great famine of 1921-1922.

JUST, ARTUR W. **Die Presse der Sowjetunion.** Berlin: Duncker, 1931, 304 p.
A careful study of Russian journalism, prepared under the auspices of the German Institute for Journalism.

JUVIN, LUCIEN. **La République Juive des Soviets.** Nantes: Chaillous, 1922, 172 p.
An unsympathetic account of two years (1919-1921) under the "Jewish" Dictatorship.

KARLGREN, ANTON. **Bolshevist Russia.** New York: Macmillan, 1927, 311 p.
The author, a Danish professor, has long been intimately connected with Russia. This book is one of the best studies of cultural changes and conditions.

KEELING, H. V. **Bolshevism.** London: Hodder, 1919, 212 p.
A disillusioning account of conditions in Russia, by an English workingman who was employed there for five years.

KOCH-WESER, ERICH. **Russland von Heute.** Dresden: Reissner, 1928, 200 p.
A general survey of conditions, classes and policies, by an able German statesman.

KOKOVTSOV, VLADIMIR NIKOLAEVICH, GRAF. **Le Bolchevisme à l'Œuvre.** Paris: Giard, 1931, 378 p.
The former Russian Minister of Finance and President of the Council of Ministers surveys the moral and economic ruin of Russia under the Bolshevik régime.

LANSBURY, GEORGE. **What I Saw in Russia.** London: Parsons, 1920, 172 p.
A hopeful report on conditions, by an English Laborite.

LEE, IVY LEDBETTER. **Present-Day Russia.** New York: Macmillan, 1928, 214 p.
Though only a short time in Russia, the author has written an open-minded account.

LONDON, GEO. **Red Russia after Ten Years.** London: Methuen, 1928, 182 p.
Brilliant pen-pictures of ordinary scenes and ordinary life, by the correspondent of the Paris *Journal*.

McCORMICK, MRS. ANNE (O'HARE). **The Hammer and the Scythe.** New York: Knopf, 1928, 312 p.
Chiefly a reprint of articles written for the *New York Times*. Clear and well-balanced.

McCULLAGH, FRANCIS. **A Prisoner of the Reds.** London: Murray, 1921, 346 p.
The experiences of an English correspondent after the collapse of the White Army in Siberia.

MALONE, CECIL L'ESTRANGE. **The Russian Republic.** New York: Harcourt, 1920, 149 p.
An English M. P.'s account of the first achievements of the Bolsheviks, and an extremely critical review of Allied policy.

MAL'SAGOV, S. A. **An Island Hell.** London: Philpot, 1926, 223 p.
A detailed and circumstantial account of the Solovetski prison, by an escaped prisoner.

MARX, MAGDELEINE, *pseud.* (MME. MAGDELEINE PAZ). **The Romance of New Russia.** New York: Seltzer, 1924, 225 p.
A rhapsodical account of life and experiences in millennial Russia.

MASLOV, S. S. **Russia after Four Years of Revolution.** London: King, 1923, 237 p.
A general survey of the country and the people in 1921, by a well-informed member of the coöperative movement.

MILIUKOV, PAVEL NIKOLAEVICH. **Russia, Today and Tomorrow.** New York: Macmillan, 1922, 392 p.
This volume, written by a Cadet leader, consists chiefly of Lowell Lectures in which the author reviews the rise of Bolshevism and discusses at some length the chief national and international problems of post-war Russia.

MONZIE, ANATOLE PIERRE ARMAND DE. **Petit Manuel de la Russie Nouvelle.** Paris: Firmin-Didot, 1931, 338 p.
A general handbook by a French statesman closely connected with Russian affairs.

MULDAVIN, ALBERT. **The Red Fog Lifts.** New York: Appleton, 1931, 311 p.
Racy, intimate pictures of life in contemporary Russia.

NANSEN, FRIDTJOF. **Russia and Peace.** New York: Macmillan, 1924, 162 p.
A not especially profound study, with emphasis on the economic and social sides.

POLLOCK, JOHN. **The Bolshevik Adventure.** London: Constable, 1919, 279 p.
The experiences of an English relief worker, with very hostile criticism of the Bolshevik régime.

Popov, Georgiǐ Konstantinovich. **Sous l'Étoile des Soviets.** Paris: Plon, 1925, 249 p.
After a year's travelling in Russia the author, himself a native, sees little to commend.

Puccio, Guido. **Al Centro della Macchina Sovietica.** Foligno: Campitelli, 1930, 336 p.
Keen observations by an unconvinced visitor.

Ransome, Arthur. **Russia in 1919.** New York: Huebsch, 1919, 232 p.
The record of a brief visit to Russia and of talks with Bolshevik leaders. A most favorable picture of the aims of the communists.

Ransome, Arthur. **The Crisis in Russia.** New York: Huebsch, 1921, 201 p.
This volume continues the story begun in the preceding item.

Rukeyser, Walter Arnold. **Working for the Soviets.** New York: Covici Friede, 1932, 301 p.
The experiences of an American engineer in Bolshevik service in Siberian mines.

La Russie d'Aujourd'hui et de Demain. Paris: Attinger, 1920, 202 p.
A series of essays, by able writers like Denis, Kramař, Miliukov, Rostovtsev and Struve, dealing with various international and domestic problems of post-war Russia.

Sarolea, Charles. **Impressions of Soviet Russia.** London: Nash and Grayson, 1924, 276 p.
An English publicist, long acquainted with Russia, paints an unedifying picture of the new régime.

Scheffer, Paul. **Seven Years in Soviet Russia.** New York: Putnam, 1931, 358 p.
The author, Russian correspondent of the *Berliner Tageblatt* during most of the period from 1921 to 1929, reënforced his penetrating observations in the capital by extensive travel in all parts of the union. He probably knows post-revolutionary Russia as well as any foreigner. This book, based on his despatches to his newspaper, is not a diatribe, but the calm and considered report of happenings by a competent person. Interesting chapters deal with the evolution of Russian foreign policy.

Seibert, Theodor. **Red Russia.** New York: Century, 1932, 422 p.
Typical views of politics and life, by a German correspondent in Moscow. A very hostile book, ably done.

Shul'gin, Vasiliǐ. **La Resurrection de la Russie.** Paris: Payot, 1927, 304 p.
The impressions of a former Russian deputy while on a secret visit to Russia. One of the better surveys of conditions.

Snowden, Ethel (Annakin) Snowden, Viscountess. **Through Bolshevik Russia.** London: Cassell, 1920, 188 p.
Moderate and understanding reports, by a member of the British Delegation of the Trades Union Congress.

Soviet Union Year-Book. London: Allen and Unwin. Annual since 1925.
Information on the economic and political life of Soviet Russia.

Spargo, John. **"The Greatest Failure in All History."** New York: Harper, 1920, 486 p.
A critical review of Bolshevism in practice, by an American Socialist.

Šrom, J. **Sovetske Rusko.** Prague: Orbis, 1924.
A sound review of political, economic and intellectual conditions, by the correspondent of the *Prager Presse*.

Strong, Anna Louise. **The First Time in History.** New York: Boni and Liveright, 1924, 249 p.
A partisan statement of Bolshevik aims and attainments. The book contains a discussion of the NEP and of cultural developments.

THOMPSON, DOROTHY. **The New Russia.** New York: Holt, 1928, 330 p.
Snapshots of the Russian scene by an American correspondent emphasizing psychological factors and currents.

TROTSKIĬ, LEV. **Problems of Life.** New York: Doran, 1924, 114 p.
A discussion of Bolshevik efforts to reconstruct the daily life of the Russians.

TROTSKIĬ, LEV. **The Real Situation in Russia.** New York: Harcourt, 1928, 364 p.
The case against Stalin and his policy, vigorously set forth in speeches and memoranda by the exiled leader of the opposition.

VISHNIAK, MARK VEN'IAMINOVICH. **Chernyi God.** Paris: Franko-Russkaia Pechat', 1922, 294 p.
Well-written essays, by an anti-Bolshevik journalist, covering various aspects of the first years of Bolshevik rule.

VOL'SKIĬ, STANISLAV. **Dans le Royaume de la Famine et de la Haine.** Paris: Union, 1920, 155 p.
Observations on the Bolshevik economic and social system by a former Bolshevik journalist.

VORST, HANS. **Das Bolschewistische Russland.** Leipzig: Der Neue Geist, 1919, 264 p.
The Soviet system in practice, as seen in the autumn of 1918 by the special correspondent of the *Berliner Tageblatt.*

WELLS, HERBERT GEORGE. **Russia in the Shadows.** New York: Doran, 1921, 179 p.
The record of a leading novelist's impressions of a very short visit to Russia and a long talk with Lenin.

WHITE, WILLIAM CHAPMAN. **These Russians.** New York: Scribner, 1931, 376 p.
The author presents a picture of conditions through the accounts of a number of representative inhabitants.

WICKSTEED, ALEXANDER. **Life under the Soviets.** London: Lane, 1928, 214 p.
The author, after five years' residence in Moscow, writes simply but shrewdly about everyday life under the new régime.

WILLIAMS, ALBERT RHYS. **The Russian Land.** New York: New Republic, 1928, 294 p.
Interesting, sometimes amusing, intimate pictures of life in the village.

YOUKIEVITCH, SIMEON. **Dans la Peur.** Paris: Plon-Nourrit, 1925, 248 p.
Experiences of a Russian bourgeois under the Bolshevik régime.

Economic Problems

General

AKSEL'ROD, ALEKSANDR. **L'Œuvre Économique des Soviets.** Paris: Povolozky, 1920, 146 p.
One of the soundest early analyses of the economic régime, based upon experience as well as study, by a critically minded socialist.

AMERICAN TRADE UNION DELEGATION. **Russia after Ten Years.** New York: International Publishers, 1927, 96 p.
This report naturally deals chiefly with unions, wages, labor, housing conditions, etc.

ASMIS, RUDOLF ALBERT AUGUST WILHELM. **Als Wirtschaftspionier in Russisch-Asien.** Berlin: Stilke, 1924, 234 p.
Reliable observations on the industrial situation in Siberia and Turkestan.

ATHOLL, KATHARINE MARJORY, DUCHESS OF. **The Conscription of a People.** New York: Columbia University Press, 1931, 216 p.

This study, based on Russian and British government documents and on the testimony of refugees, makes out a strong case against the Bolshevik policy of drafting labor for the timber camps and industry, mines and railroads, the whole amounting to a system of slavery.

BAROU, NOAH. **Russian Co-operation Abroad.** London: King, 1930, 96 p.
A treatise on the development of Russian foreign trade since 1912.

BEAUCHAMP, JOAN. **Agriculture in Soviet Russia.** London: Gollancz, 1931, 126 p.
A glowing account of the progress of the state farms.

BICHENKO, A. **Khrestomatiia Spravochnik po Istorii Kollektivnogo Zemledeliia v S. S. S. R.** Moscow: Novaia Derevnia, 1925, 603 p.
A collection of material for the history of collective agriculture between 1918 and 1924.

BLANC, ELSIE TERRY. **The Coöperative Movement in Russia.** New York: Macmillan, 1924, 324 p.
The first thorough study of this important subject in English.

BOL'SHAKOV, A. M. and ROZHKOV, NIKOLAĬ ALEKSANDROVICH. **Istoriia Khoziaĭstva Rossii.** Moscow: Gosizdat, 1925.
A large collection of archive and other documentary material on Russian economic history to 1925.

BRITISH TRADES UNION DELEGATION TO RUSSIA AND CAUCASIA, 1924. **Russia Today: The Official Report.** New York: International Publishers, 1925, 284 p.
The report of the British delegation of November 1924, containing valuable information on contemporary conditions.

BRON, SAUL G. **Soviet Economic Development and American Business.** New York: Liveright, 1930, 160 p.
An authoritative Bolshevik statement, by an official of the Amtorg in New York.

BRONSKIĬ, M. **Problemy Ekonomicheskoĭ Politiki S. S. S. R.** Moscow: Gosizdat, 1928, 164 p.
Really an outline of Bolshevik economic policy from the Revolution through the NEP and the Trotzkian opposition to planning.

BRUTSKUS, BORIS. **Agrarentwicklung und Agrarrevolution in Russland.** Berlin: Sack, 1925, 249 p.
An important scholarly contribution to the history of the agrarian question, by a former professor at the Petrograd Agricultural College.

BUDISH, JACOB M. and SHIPMAN, SAMUEL SAUL. **Soviet Foreign Trade.** New York: Liveright, 1931, 288 p.
Practically an official presentation of the Bolshevik thesis regarding dumping and convict labor, together with a survey of the possibilities of Russian-American trade after the completion of the Five Year Plan.

BURNS, EMILE. **Russia's Productive System.** New York: Dutton, 1930, 288 p.
Another useful and dispassionate presentation of Bolshevik economic policy.

BUROV, IA. **Derevnia na Perelome.** Moscow: Gosizdat, 1926, 278 p.
The situation in Russian agriculture, by a Bolshevik who worked on the farm for a year.

Ce Qu'Il Faut Savoir de la Russie Économique. Paris: Dunod, 1923.
A semi-official French compilation which constitutes a remarkably complete and accurate book of reference on natural resources and industries.

CHASE, STUART and others, *eds*. **Soviet Russia in the Second Decade.** New York: Day, 1928, 387 p.
A joint survey by the technical staff of the first American Trade Union Delegation.

CHERNYSHEV, I. V. **Sel'skoe Khoziaĭstvo Dovoennoĭ Rossii i S. S. S. R.** Moscow: Gosizdat, 1926, 200 p.
A general survey of Russian agriculture under the old and new régimes.

DOBB, MAURICE HERBERT and STEVENS, HENRY CHARLES. **Russian Economic Development since the Revolution.** New York: Dutton, 1928, 427 p.
One of the best general treatments, thoroughly objective and scientific.

DUNN, ROBERT WILLIAMS. **Soviet Trade Unions.** New York: Vanguard, 1928, 257 p.
One of the useful little handbooks published in the Vanguard series.

ELIASHEV, BORIS. **Le Dumping Soviétique.** Paris: Giard, 1931, 230 p.
A scholarly monograph on a burning question. The author reviews the Bolshevik system of production, the effect of dumping on the countries concerned, and possible methods of defense.

ELSTER, KARL. **Vom Rubel zum Tscherwonjez.** Jena: Fischer, 1930, 316 p.
Probably the best scholarly treatment, from a neutral source, of the evolution of the Russian currency under the Bolshevik régime.

GERSCHUNI, GERSON. **Die Konzessionspolitik Sowjetrusslands.** Berlin: Prager, 1927, 133 p.
A sober treatise on the Soviet theory and practice of concessions.

GOLDSCHMIDT, ALFONS. **Die Wirtschaftsorganisation Sowjet-Russlands.** Berlin: Rowohlt, 1920, 306 p.
A sympathetic study of Bolshevik organization and control of industry, which the author regards as the beginning of a new era.

GORDON, EZEKIEL. **La Réforme Monétaire dans la Russie des Soviets.** Paris: Povolozky, 1924, 61 p.
Sharp criticism, by an emigré, of the Bolshevik monetary policy, the introduction of the chervonets, etc.

HAENSEL, PAVEL PETROVICH. **The Economic Policy of Soviet Russia.** London: King, 1930, 190 p.
An authoritative statement written by a former professor and financial expert under the Bolshevik régime, later a member of the faculty at Northwestern University. An important book.

HAENSEL, PAVEL PETROVICH. **Das Steuersystem Sowjetrusslands.** Berlin: Preiss, 1926, 176 p.
The best single book on the Russian tax system.

HELLER, ABRAHAM AARON. **The Industrial Revival in Soviet Russia.** New York: Seltzer, 1922, 241 p.
Observations during a tour of the country. The author gives an account of the origins of the NEP and an enthusiastic report on its effects.

HESSEN, WLADIMIR. **Das Staatsbudget Sovetrusslands.** Berlin: Sack, 1925, 114 p.
A substantial monograph published by the Osteuropa Institut.

HOOVER, CALVIN BRYCE. **The Economic Life of Soviet Russia.** New York: Macmillan, 1931, 361 p.
A useful book that touches on almost all phases of the subject and attempts to treat them objectively.

IUGOV, ARON. **Economic Trends in Soviet Russia.** New York: R. R. Smith, 1930, 350 p.
The translation of an admirable and well-documented Russian work which sets forth
the futility of the Bolshevik efforts at socialization.

IUROVSKIĬ, LEONID NAUMOVICH. **Denezhnaia Politika Sovetskoĭ Vlasti.** Moscow:
Finansovoe Izdatelstvo, 1928, 400 p.
The standard Bolshevik account of the currency and monetary policy after 1917.
This work is more detailed than an earlier one translated into English under the
title: "Currency Problems and Policy of the Soviet Union" (London: Parsons, 1925,
152 p.).

IZHBOLDIN, BORIS. **Die Russische Handelspolitik der Gegenwart.** Jena: Fischer, 1930,
240 p.
A scholarly critique of the state monopoly of foreign trade, which, the writer concludes, was introduced and is maintained for political rather than economic reasons.

KATSENELENBAUM, ZAKHARIĬ SOLOMONOVICH. **Russian Currency and Banking.** London: King, 1925, 198 p.
Like the preceding item, this is an authoritative treatment covering the years from
the beginning of the war to the introduction of the chervonets.

KAVRAĬSKIĬ, V. and NUSINOV, I. **Klassy i Klassovye Otnosheniia v Sovremennoĭ
Sovetskoĭ Derevne.** Novosibirsk: Sibkraĭizdat, 1929, 215 p.
A study of social classes in the Russian village, with much statistical material.

KONDURUSHKIN, I. S. **Chastnyĭ Kapital pered Sovetskim Sudom.** Moscow: Gosizdat,
1927, 240 p.
An important study of the evolution of private capital under the NEP.

KRETSCHMANN, JENNY GRIZIOTTI. **La Questione Agraria in Russia.** Piacenza: Federa-
zione Italiana dei Consorzi Agrari, 1926, 330 p.
A documented monograph based largely on Russian materials. The author examines
the conditions of agriculture, the causes for crises, the agrarian legislation, etc.

KRYLENKO, NIKOLAĬ VASIL'EVICH, *ed.* **Ekonomicheskaia Kontr-revoliutsiia v Don-
basse.** Moscow: Iuridicheskoe Izdatel'stvo, 1928, 306 p.
A collection of essays by various authors, followed by documents bearing on the so-
called "economic counter-revolution" and the trials of suspects.

LABRY, RAOUL. **L'Industrie Russe et la Révolution.** Paris: Payot, 1919, 285 p.
Largely a study of the ruin of Russian industry as a result of the Revolution and
especially because of Bolshevik policies.

LARIN, I. **Chastnyĭ Kapital v S. S. S. R.** Moscow: Gosizdat, 1927, 310 p.
A careful study of the part played by private capital in the various phases of Soviet
economic life.

LARIN, I. **Sovetskaia Derevnia.** Moscow: Ekonomicheskaia Zhizn', 1925, 385 p.
One of the best studies of the development of the agrarian problem and the conflict
between private enterprise and government control.

LEHRFREUND, LUDWIG. **Die Entwicklung der Deutsch-Russischen Handelsbezie-
hungen.** Leipzig: Bitterling, 1921, 105 p.
A documented sketch of the important economic link between Germany and Russia,
from earliest times to the post-war period.

LEITES, KUSSIEL. **Recent Economic Developments in Russia.** New York: Oxford University Press, 1922, 240 p.
A technical monograph published by the Carnegie Endowment. The author, a Russian
financial expert, reviews the effects of the war, discusses Bolshevik policy, and examines the situation in 1920.

MASLOV, PETR PAVLOVICH. **Agrarnyĭ Vopros v Rossii.** Moscow: Gosizdat, 1926, 431 p.
A documented and statistical study of the agrarian problem in all its aspects.

MAVOR, JAMES. **An Economic History of Russia.** New York: Dutton, 1925, 2 v.
A second edition of a standard work.

MILIUTIN, VLADIMIR PAVLOVICH. **Istoriia Ekonomicheskogo Razvitiia S. S. S. R.**
Moscow: Gosizdat, 1928, 491 p.
One of the best accounts of the economic development of Russia from 1917 to 1927,
by a Bolshevik expert.

PASVOLSKY, LEO. **The Economics of Communism.** New York: Macmillan, 1921, 312 p.
A dispassionate treatment, based largely on Soviet publications, dealing with economic
ideas and practices in Soviet Russia, as well as their results.

PASVOLSKY, LEO and MOULTON, HAROLD GLENN. **Russian Debts and Russian Reconstruction.** New York: McGraw-Hill, 1924, 247 p.
A first-rate study of Russia's foreign debts in relation to her economic recovery. This
is a fundamental work, often quoted by Bolshevik writers.

PETROV, PETR and PETROVA, IRMA. **Die Wirtschaftliche Entwicklung der Sowjet-
Union.** Berlin: Handelsvertretung der U. S. S. R. in Deutschland, 1926, 313 p.
An official account of the economic organization and situation in Russia.

PRICE, GEORGE MOSES. **Labor Protection in Soviet Russia.** New York: International
Publishers, 1928, 128 p.
A well-balanced study, by a former investigator for the United States Department ot
Labor.

PROKOPOVICH, SERGIEĬ NIKOLAEVICH. **The Economic Condition of Soviet Russia.**
London: King, 1924, 230 p.
A scholarly documented treatment of the background and implications of the NEP.

RAFFALOVICH, ARTHUR, APOSTOL, PAUL and others. **Le Problème Financier Russe.
La Dette Publique de la Russie.** Paris: Payot, 1922, 240 p.
Data on the fiscal history of contemporary Russia. One of the most competent studies
of the subject.

ROZHKOV, NIKOLAĬ ALEKSANDROVICH. **Ocherk Istorii Truda v Rossii.** Moscow: Kniga,
1924, 123 p.
A good brief survey of Russian labor, from the beginnings of the Russian state to
the revolutions of 1917.

SARAB'IANOV, VLADIMIR. **Ekonomika i Economicheskaia Politika S. S. S. R.** Moscow:
Gosizdat, 1926, 455 p.
A general historical text of Soviet economics, with good bibliographical aids.

SCHILLER, OTTO. **Die Kollektivbewegung in der Sowjetunion.** Berlin: Ost-Europa
Verlag, 1931, 120 p.
A valuable study of the movement toward collectivism. With an excellent bibliog-
raphy.

SCHKAFF, EUGÈNE. **La Question Agraire en Russie.** Paris: Rousseau, 1923, 336 p.
A good dissertation, surveying the peasant and agrarian problem from the beginning
to 1922.

SOKOL'NIKOV, GRIGORIĬ IAKOVLEVICH and others. **Soviet Policy in Public Finance,
1917-1928.** Stanford: Stanford University Press, 1931, 470 p.
An authoritative study covering the years 1917 to 1928, written under the direction
of the former Commissar for Finance. A book for financial experts.

Soviet Russia. London: King, n.d., 174 p.
A series of essays on the conditions of industrial and commercial activity in Soviet Russia, by experts like Apostol, Kokovtsev, Gronsky and others.

STRONG, ANNA LOUISE. **The Soviets Conquer Wheat.** New York: Holt, 1931, 288 p.
An enthusiastic account of the revolutionary experiment in Russian agriculture, by a disciple of Sovietism.

TROTSKIĬ, LEV. **Whither Russia?** New York: International Publishers, 1926, 150 p.
A defense of communist economics in their larger world setting.

ZAGORSKIĬ, SEMEN OSIPOVICH. **L'Évolution Actuelle du Bolchevisme Russe.** Paris: Povolozky, 1921, 152 p.
A well-documented, critical analysis of Bolshevik policies, with special stress on agrarian problems, exchange, industry, labor and finance. Written by a Russian economist, this is one of the best treatments of the NEP.

ZAGORSKIĬ, SEMEN OSIPOVICH. **La République des Soviets.** Paris: Payot, 1921, 352 p.
An expert's painstaking and detailed study of the economic aspects of the régime.

ZAGORSKIĬ, SEMEN OSIPOVICH. **La Renaissance du Capitalisme dans la Russie des Soviets.** Paris: Giard, 1924, 443 p.
In this well-documented work the Russian scholar continues his investigations of economic life under the Soviets and deals exhaustively with the effects of the NEP.

ZAGORSKIĬ, SEMEN OSIPOVICH. **Où Va la Russie?** Paris: Petit Journal, 1928, 338 p.
After surveying the economic and social problems of the régime, the Russian economist still predicts a turn to something resembling capitalism.

ZIMAND, SAVEL. **State Capitalism in Russia.** New York: Foreign Policy Association, 1926, 77 p.
A reliable brief survey of economic developments.

The Five Year Plan

BOGOLEPOV, MIKHAIL IVANOVICH. **Finansovyĭ Plan Piatiletiia.** Moscow: Planovoe Khoziaĭstvo, 1929, 172 p.
A competent analysis of the financial aspects of the Five Year Plan and the proposed technique of operation.

BRUTSKUS, BORIS. **Der Fünfjahresplan und Seine Erfüllung.** Leipzig: Wissenschaftliche Buchhandlung, 1932, 106 p.
The German translation of an important Russian book.

CHAMBERLIN, WILLIAM HENRY. **The Soviet Planned Economic Order.** Boston: World Peace Foundation, 1931, 258 p.
A dispassionate statement of the Five Year Plan and its working, with a useful appendix of documents, by the correspondent of the *Christian Science Monitor*.

COUNTS, GEORGE SYLVESTER. **The Soviet Challenge to America.** New York: Day, 1931, 387 p.
The Five Year Plan and its implications, as seen by a friendly American professor.

GLAESER, ERNST and WEISKOPF, FRANZ. **Der Staat ohne Arbeitslose.** Berlin: Kiepenheuer, 1931, 198 p.
A richly illustrated survey of the working of the Five Year Plan.

GRIN'KO, GRIGORIĬ FEDOROVICH. **The Five Year Plan of the Soviet Union.** New York: International Publishers, 1930, 340 p.
One of the best statements in English, written by the vice-chairman of the Soviet planning commission.

IAKOVLEV, IAKOV ARKAD'EVICH. **Red Villages.** New York: International Publishers, 1931, 128 p.
An authoritative discussion of the Five Year Plan as it affects farming, by the Commissar of Agriculture.

KAUTSKY, KARL. **Bolshevism at a Deadlock.** New York: Rand School Press, 1931, 193 p.
One of the most eminent socialist critics of the Soviet régime demonstrates the inevitable failure of the Five Year Plan.

KNICKERBOCKER, HUBERT RENFRO. **The Red Trade Menace.** New York: Dodd, 1931, 295 p.
The story of how the five year program is working, by the correspondent of the *New York Evening Post.*

LEONT'EV, ALEKSANDR GRIGOR'EVICH. **Osnovnye Ustanovki Piatiletki.** Moscow: Gosizdat, 1930, 112 p.
One of the best of innumerable semi-popular books in Russian dealing with the Five Year Plan.

MOLOTOV, VIACHESLAV MIKHAÏLOVICH. **The Success of the Five Year Plan.** New York: International Publishers, 1931, 77 p.
The chairman of the Council of People's Commissars discusses not only the Plan, but replies to accusations of dumping, employment of forced labor, etc.

POLLOCK, FRIEDRICH. **Die Planwirtschaftlichen Versuche in der Sowjetunion.** Leipzig: Hirschfeld, 1929, 411 p.
One of the best general accounts of the economic experiments of the Bolsheviks along the lines of national planning.

ROZENTAL', K. **Promyshlennost' v Piatiletnem Plane.** Moscow: Gosizdat, 1930, 207 p.
A review of past mistakes and a good general outline of the Plan.

The Soviet Union Looks Ahead. New York: Liveright, 1929, 275 p.
A very welcome English translation of the Five Year Plan.

WALSH, EDMUND ALOYSIUS. **The Last Stand.** Boston: Little, Brown, 1931, 359 p.
One of the severest critics of the present régime examines the Plan, which he regards as the last phase of Bolshevik strategy in revolutionizing the world.

The Religious Question

BURY, HERBERT. **Russia from Within.** London: Churchman, 1927, 247 p.
The impressions of an English ecclesiastic long acquainted with Russia. The book, while general, deals very largely with the religious problem. The author, formerly Anglican bishop for Northern Europe, is now Assistant Bishop of London.

COOKE, RICHARD JOSEPH. **Religion in Russia under the Soviets.** New York: Abingdon Press, 1924, 311 p.
An honest account of the evolution of the religious problem since 1917, by a Methodist bishop.

EMHARDT, WILLIAM CHAUNCEY. **Religion in Soviet Russia.** Milwaukee: Morehouse, 1929, 405 p.
A survey of developments from 1917 to 1928, including organizations abroad. The author, a clergyman in the Episcopal Church, has been active in negotiations between that body and the Orthodox Church. The second part is a translation of Sergius Troitsky's "The Living Church."

FEDOTOV, GRIGORIĬ PETROVICH. **The Russian Church since the Revolution.** New York: Macmillan, 1928, 102 p.
On the whole the best brief survey of Russian church history since 1917.

FIOLETOV, N. N. **Tserkov' i Gosudarstvo.** Saratov: no pub., 1923, 87 p.
A brief study of the documents regulating the relations of church and state.

HECKER, JULIUS FRIEDRICH. **Religion under the Soviets.** New York: Vanguard, 1927, 207 p.
This study by the professor of social ethics at the Moscow Theological Academy is the best apologia for the government policy.

McCULLAGH, FRANCIS. **The Bolshevik Persecution of Christianity.** New York: Dutton, 1924, 401 p.
An American journalist's account of the campaign against the Church and the situation resulting therefrom.

MACKENZIE, FREDERICK ARTHUR. **The Russian Crucifixion.** London: Jarrolds, 1930, 140 p.
One of the better accounts of the relations of the Russian Government with the Church since the revolution, based in large measure upon personal observation.

SPINKA, MATTHEW. **The Church and the Russian Revolution.** New York: Macmillan, 1927, 342 p.
A scholarly critical study of the Orthodox Church since about 1905, with detailed treatment of the revolutionary period and the schism.

VALENTINOV, A. A., *comp.* **The Assault of Heaven.** London: Boswell, 1925, 266 p.
Source material from the communist press on the religious persecution in Russia.

Foreign Policy

General

See also Polar Regions, p. 498.

ALEKSEEV, N. N. and ZAĬTSEV, LEO. **Sowjetstaat und Voelkerrecht.** Breslau: Kern, 1931, 77 p.
A scholarly treatment of the position of Russia in international law.

ARNOT, ROBERT PAGE. **Soviet Russia and Her Neighbors.** New York: Vanguard, 1927, 175 p.
An excellent little survey of Russia in world affairs, written by a British Laborite who draws a sharp distinction between the Soviet Government and the Internationale.

BESEDOVSKIĬ, GRIGORIĬ. **Revelations of a Soviet Diplomat.** London: Williams and Norgate, 1932, 276 p.
An instructive account of Soviet diplomacy, by one formerly in its service.

DASZYNSKI, S. **Imperialistischer Kreuzzug gegen den Kommunismus.** Hamburg: Hoym, 1929, 240 p.
This translation expresses very well the prevalent fear of a capitalist crusade against the Soviets.

DENNIS, ALFRED LEWIS PINNEO. **The Foreign Policies of Soviet Russia.** New York: Dutton, 1924, 501 p.
A scholarly and reasonably objective book. Still useful for quotations from periodical and other obscure material.

FISCHER, LOUIS. **The Soviets in World Affairs.** New York: Cape and Smith, 1930, 2 v.
This is the most extensive treatment of Bolshevik foreign policy, and its intrinsic

value is enhanced by the fact that it is based in large measure on Russian sources. The author has had the advantage of using Russian documents and of friendship with leading Russian diplomats.

GOODE, WILLIAM THOMAS. **Is Intervention in Russia a Myth?** London: Williams and Norgate, 1931, 126 p.
The former correspondent of the *Manchester Guardian* in the Baltic States and Russia believes the Moscow trial of 1930 demonstrates the real danger of intervention.

KLIUCHNIKOV, Y. V. and SABANIN, ANDREĬ. **Mezhdunarodnaia Politika.** Moscow: Litizdat, 1925-1929, 3 v.
An important collection of treaties, agreements and diplomatic documents. Volumes II and III cover the period of the World War and Soviet rule to 1927.

KŎLLONTAĬ, MME. ALEKSANDRA. **Po Burzhuaznoĭ Evrope.** Kazan: Gosizdat, 1921, 183 p.
Notes of a Bolshevik woman diplomat in western Europe.

KOROVIN, EVSEVIĬ ALEKSANDROVICH. **Das Voelkerrecht der Übergangszeit.** Berlin: Rothschild, 1929, 142 p.
A German translation of one of the best Russian studies of Soviet foreign policy.

METZLER, WILHELM VON. **Die Auswärtige Gewalt der Sowjetunion.** Berlin: Rothschild, 1930, 88 p.
A technical study of the position of Russia in international affairs, of the organization of the foreign service, the status of Russian agents abroad, etc.

PAVLOVICH, M., *pseud.* (MIKHAIL VEL'TMAN). **RSFSR v Imperialisticheskom Okruzhenii.** Moscow: Gosizdat, 1922.
Contains: Part I. Soviet Russia and Capitalist France. Part II. Russia and Capitalist England. Part III. Russia and Capitalist America from 1780 on. Written by one of the ablest communist historians of imperialism.

RADEK, KARL. **Vneshniaia Politika Sovetskoĭ Rossii.** Moscow: Gosizdat, 1923, 111 p.
A classic account of the history of Soviet diplomacy from Brest-Litovsk to the Genoa Conference of 1922. The author subsequently became an editor of *Izvestiia*.

SOLOMON, GEORGIĬ ALEKSANDROVICH. **Sredi Krasnykh Vozhdeĭ.** Paris: Michen, 1930, 615 p.
The recollections of a Soviet diplomat at Berlin, Riga and London.

The Soviet Union and Peace. New York: International Publishers, 1929, 291 p.
A collection of lively and argumentative decrees, appeals, declarations and conventions designed to show the consistent and vigorous activity of the Soviet Government in the interests of peace and disarmament.

TANIN, M. **Mezhdunarodnaia Politika S. S. S. R.** Moscow: Rabotnik Prosveshcheniia, 1925, 107 p.
A brief survey of Russian foreign policy from 1917 to 1924, arranged by countries.

VAKS, B. **Ot Oktiabria do Genui.** Moscow: Commissariat for Foreign Affairs, 1922, 130 p.
A reference book on Russian policy, 1917-1922.

Relations with Specific Countries

See also (United States) Relations with Europe, p. 184; also (Baltic States) General, p. 340; also (Poland) Relations with Russia, p. 353; also (Rumania) Bessarabia, p. 405; also (Turkey) Foreign Policy, the Straits Question, p. 431; also (Near East) Persia, p. 442; also (Central Asia and India) Central Asia and Turkestan, p. 443; also (China) The Revolution and the Republic, p. 467; etc.

ARSEN'EV, VLADIMIR K. **Russen und Chinesen in Ostsibirien.** Berlin: Scherl, 1926, 229 p.
Mainly a sociological study of native conditions.

BACH, M. G. **Politiko-ekonomicheskie Vzaimootnosheniia mezhdu S. S. S. R. i Pribaltikoĭ za Desiat' Let.** Moscow: Communist Academy, 1928, 166 p.
The political and economic relations between the Soviets and the Baltic States from 1917 to 1927, viewed as one aspect of the capitalist encirclement of Russia.

BENN, SIR ERNEST JOHN PICKSTONE. **About Russia.** New York: Appleton, 1930, 168 p.
This might well have been called "Around Russia," for it surveys chiefly the situation in the Baltic States and their attitude towards their colossal and dangerous neighbor.

COATES, CHARLES H. **The Red Theology in the Far East.** London: Thynne and Jarvis, 1927, 202 p.
The title adequately characterizes the work, which is a study of Red propaganda in China and its effects.

CUMMING, CAROLINE KING and PETTIT, WALTER WILLIAM. **Russian-American Relations, March 1917-March 1920.** New York: Harcourt, 1920, 375 p.
A selection of Russian documents bearing on American relations with Russia during the revolutionary and counter-revolutionary periods.

GOL'DFARB, AN. **Frantsiia i S. S. S. R.** Moscow: Molodaia Gvardiia, 1925, 157 p.
A brief survey of French relations with Russia before the war, the intervention, and the post-war negotiations.

HARRISON, MRS. MARGUERITE ELTON (BAKER). **Red Bear or Yellow Dragon.** New York: Doran, 1924, 296 p.
A racy journalistic story of the struggle between Russia and Japan for raw materials and investments in China and Central Asia.

IAKHONTOV, VICTOR A. **Russia and the Soviet Union in the Far East.** New York: Coward-McCann, 1931, 454 p.
General Iakhontov, who has had long experience of Far Eastern affairs under various régimes, has based this study upon the writings of Russian, European and American scholars. He writes in a good-natured way and with fairness, though he is sometimes rather hard on the Japanese. It is of the utmost value to have this Russian slant on the Pacific problem. There is an admirable bibliography.

MISSION SCIENTIFIQUE DU MAROC, TANGIER. **Le Bolchevisme et l'Islam.** Paris: Leroux, 1922, 2 v.
A valuable, though somewhat prejudiced, analysis of the relations between Bolshevik Russia and the Turks.

PALMIERI, AURELIO. **La Politica Asiatica dei Bolscevichi.** Bologna: Zanichelli, 1924.
An interesting and well-informed account of Bolshevik policy in Asia, by an experienced Italian writer.

PASVOLSKY, LEO. **Russia in the Far East.** New York: Macmillan, 1922, 181 p.
A general account of Russian policy in the period before the Revolution, and of the short-lived Far Eastern Republic.

QUISLING, VIDKUN. **Russia and Ourselves.** London: Hodder, 1931, 284 p.
The Norwegian Minister of Defense, who has spent much of his time since 1917 in Russia, calls for a Scandinavian-British union for resistance to Bolshevism.

SAVVIN, V. P. **Vzaimootnosheniia Tsarskoĭ Rossii i SSSR s Kitaem.** Moscow: Gosizdat, 1930, 152 p.
A concise but important review of Russian relations with China.

SCHROEDER, HERBERT. **Russland und die Ostsee.** Riga: Löffler, 1927, 277 p.
A study of the situation created by Russia's exclusion from the Baltic.

SHLIAPNIKOV, A. P., *ed.* **Kto Dolzhnik?** Moscow: Avioizdatel'stvo, 1926, 587 p.
A collection of documented essays on Russia's relations with France and the Entente in 1914, during the war, and after the war.

VÉRIDICUS, *pseud.* **Suisse et Soviets.** Paris: Delpeuch, 1926, 128 p.
The story of the Russo-Swiss conflict which arose from the assassination of Vorovsky, told from the Russian side.

Minorities

Dva Gody Natsianalnai Raboty v B.S.S.R. Minsk: Natsianalnai Kommissii, 1929, 168 p.
Two years of the nationalities policy of the Soviet Republic of Ruthenia.

LANGHANS-RATZEBURG, MANFRED. **Die Wolgadeutschen.** Berlin: Ost-Europa Verlag, 1929, 190 p.
The status of the Volga Germans under the Soviet system, with special reference to Bolshevik treatment of minorities. An admirable documented account.

MARGOLIN, ARNOL'D DAVIDOVICH. **The Jews of Eastern Europe.** New York: Seltzer, 1926, 292 p.
Comparing the lot of the Jews before and since the Revolution.

MILIUKOV, PAVEL NIKOLAEVICH. **Natsional'nyĭ Vopros.** Prague: Svobodnaia Rossiia, 1925, 192 p.
An eminent Russian liberal historian reviews the question of nationalities, with special reference to Russia. The treatment is largely historical.

POPOV, N. N. **Natsional'naia Politika Sovetskoĭ Vlasti.** Moscow: Krasnaia Nov', 1924, 127 p.
A series of lectures reviewing the policy of the Tsarist Government toward subject nationalities, the evolution of this question during the Revolution, and the gradual formulation of the Bolshevik solution.

Rossiia i Evrei. Berlin: Osnova, 1924, 228 p.
The Jews in the Russian Revolution and under the Bolshevik régime. A collection of articles by various writers.

SCHLEUNING, JOHANNES. **In Kampf und Todesnot.** Berlin: Bernard und Graefe, 1930, 255 p.
The sufferings of the German colonies in Russia under the Bolshevik régime.

SHUL'GIN, VASILIĬ. **"Chto nam v nikh ne nravitsia . . ."** Paris: Pascal, 1929, 330 p.
A study of anti-semitism in Russia, with considerable documentary material.

STARZYŃSKI, STEFAN. **Zagadnienie Narodowościowe w Rosji Sowietskei.** Warsaw: Ignis, 1924, 98 p.
A thorough critical study of the Soviet policy toward national minorities.

YARMOLINSKY, AVRAHM. **The Jews and Other Minor Nationalities under the Soviets.** New York: Vanguard, 1929, 206 p.
The best brief treatment in English of a much discussed question.

Ukraine, Georgia, and Other Divisions of the Union

See also (World War) Near and Middle Eastern Front, p. 137; also (Central Asia and India) Central Asia and Turkestan, p. 443; also (Far East) Siberia, p. 485.

ADIL KHAN ZIATKHAN. **Aperçu sur l'Histoire, la Littérature et la Politique de l'Azerbaidjan.** Baku: no pub., 1919, 101 p.
A brief outline prepared as background for the Azerbaidjan claims after the war.

AFRIC, LEO, *pseud.* (LOUIS COQUET). **Les Héritiers de la "Toison d'Or."** Paris: Maisonneuve, 1931, 256 p.
A general history of Georgia, with special reference to the stormy war and post-war years.

ALIEV, UMAR. **Natsional'nyĭ Vopros i Natsional'naia Kul'tura.** Rostov: Kraĭnatsizdat, 1926, 128 p.
A review of the national question in the northern Caucausus, under Bolshevik rule.

ATAGULOV, S. **Bashkiriia.** Moscow: Gosizdat, 1925, 123 p.
A general survey in the series Respubliki i Oblasti S. S. S. R.

AVALOV, Z. **Nezavisimost' Gruzii v Meshdunarodnoĭ Politike, 1918-1921.** Paris: Navarre, 1924, 319 p.
Recollections of an active life in the struggle for Georgia's independence. One of the most detailed accounts.

BAMMATE, HAÏDAR. **Le Caucase et la Révolution Russe.** Paris: Union Nationale des Emigrés de la République du Caucase du Nord, 1929, 72 p.
Throws considerable light on the political side of the revolution in this area.

BARBUSSE, HENRI. **Voici Ce Qu'On A Fait de la Géorgie.** Paris: Flammarion, 1929, 324 p.
The famous French writer, now a convert to Bolshevism, finds everything thoroughly satisfactory on a trip through Georgia.

BIELARUS, V. **Narysy Historii, Ekonomiki, Kulturnaha i Revoliucyĭnaha Ruchu.** Minsk: no pub., 1924, 323 p.
A general history and survey of White Russia.

BONKÁLÓ, ALEXANDER. **Az Ukrán Mozgalom Története.** Budapest: Pfeifer, 1923, 223 p.
A thorough study of the Ukrainian movement, from 1917 to 1922, published by the Hungarian Society for Foreign Affairs.

BORISOV, T. **Kalmykia.** Moscow: Gosizdat, 1926, 100 p.
A political and social history of the Kalmucks.

BUXTON, HAROLD JOCELYN. **Transcaucasia.** London: Faith Press, 1926, 98 p.
An excellent outline of the history of the region, with emphasis on the war and post-war periods, by a British relief worker.

CHARACHIDZÉ, D. H. **Barbusse, les Soviets et la Géorgie.** Paris: Pascal, 1930, 212 p.
A Georgian writes an able reply to Barbusse's defense of Bolshevik policy in Transcaucasia.

DRABKINA, EL. **Gruzinskaia Kontr-revoliutsiia.** Leningrad: Priboĭ, 1928, 177 p.
A Bolshevik account of the social-democratic régime in Georgia. Well-documented.

DUBREUIL, CHARLES. **Deux Années en Ukraine, 1917-1919.** Paris: Paulin, 1919, 143 p.
The author's experiences, followed by a description of the country and people.

DUGUET, RAYMOND. **Moscou et la Géorgie Martyre.** Paris: Tallandier, 1927, 224 p.
Personal recollections of stormy days of Bolshevik rule in Georgia.

GABIDULLIN, C. **Tatarstan za Sem' Let.** Kazan: Gosizdat, 1927, 92 p.
Seven years of the autonomous Tartar Republic, 1920-1927.

GENTIZON, PAUL. **La Résurrection Géorgienne.** Paris: Leroux, 1921, 320 p.
A general review of conditions and developments, by the special correspondent of the Paris *Temps*. Documents in the appendix.

GRAHAM, STEPHEN. **Russia in Division.** New York: Macmillan, 1925, 293 p.
Random but useful observations on conditions in the border states of Russia.

GRUSHEVSKIĬ, MIKHAIL SERGEEVICH. **Abrégé de l'Histoire de l'Ukraine.** Paris: Giard, 1920, 253 p.
Written by the greatest authority on Ukrainian history, and about the only brief general treatment of the subject.

IAVORSKI, M. **Istoriia Ukrainy v Styslomu Narysi.** Kharkov: Gosizdat, 1928, 339 p.
A concise history of the Ukraine.

IGNATOVSKI, V. **Historiia Bielarusi v XIX v Pachatku XX Stalietsia.** Minsk: Gosizdat, 2nd ed., 1926, 252 p.
A general history of White Russia in the last century, written by a Russian professor.

KAUTSKY, KARL. **Georgia.** London: International Bookshops, 1922, 112 p.
The record of a journey to the social-democrat republic in 1920, by a well-known German socialist.

KUHNE, EMMANUEL. **La Géorgie Libre.** Geneva: La Tribune de Genève, 1920, 96 p.
A review of Georgian history followed by a brief discussion of the situation after the war.

LA CHESNAIS, PIERRE GEORGET. **Les Peuples de la Transcaucasie pendant la Guerre et devant la Paix.** Paris: Bossard, 1921, 218 p.
The author foresees Armenia, Azerbaidjan and Georgia as autonomous republics in a democratic Russian fedération.

LORIS-MELIKOV, IVAN. **La Révolution Russe et les Nouvelles Républiques Transcaucasiennes.** Paris: Alcan, 1920, 211 p.
One of the best outline histories of the area and its vicissitudes during the Revolution and Counter-Revolution.

MARGOLIN, ARNOL'D DAVIDOVICH. **Ukraïna i Politika Antanty.** Berlin: Efron, 1922, 397 p.
An account of the Ukrainian movement and of the efforts made by Ukrainian groups to secure action from the Powers.

MARTEL, RENÉ. **Les Blancs-Russes.** Paris: Delpeuch, 1929, 174 p.
An historical, political and economic study of the White Russians.

NANSEN, FRIDTJOF. **Through the Caucasus to the Volga.** New York: Norton, 1931, 255 p.
The record of a journey made in 1925 by the famous Arctic explorer. Well illustrated.

NIPPOLD, OTFRIED. **La Géorgie du Point de Vue du Droit International.** Berne: Iseli, 1920, 78 p.
A neutral study of the Georgian claims to independence.

RYSKULOV, T. R. **Kazakstan.** Moscow: Gosizdat, 1927, 96 p.
The autonomous Kirghiz Republik; a general descriptive study.

SAMURSKIĬ, N. **Dagestan.** Moscow: Gosizdat, 1925, 150 p.
A general survey in the series Respubliki i Oblasti S. S. S. R.

SAVCHENKO, IL'IA. **La Révolte des Cosaques du Kouban.** Paris: Payot, 1929, 272 p.
A participant writes of the little-known revolt of the Cossacks against the Bolsheviks.

SILBERFARB, M. **Dos Idische Ministerium un di Idische Autonomie in Ukraine.** Kiev: Folksverlag, 1919, 166 p.
The author, who was minister for Jewish affairs in the Ukraine in 1918, tells of the establishment and abrogation of the system of autonomy. The appendix contains a number of documents.

STAVROVSKIĬ, A. **Zakavkaz'e posle Oktiabria.** Moscow: Gosizdat, 1925, 120 p.
The Transcaucasian states after the October Revolution, with special references to
their relations with Turkey.

TROTSKIĬ, LEV. **Between Red and White.** London: Communist Party, n. d., 104 p.
Post-war Georgia as the center of Menshevism and counter-revolution. A classic
Bolshevik indictment of the "democratic" régime and of Allied intrigue.

TSARINNYĬ, A. **Ukrainskoe Dvizhenie.** Berlin: Zinaburg, 1925, 232 p.
A general history of the Ukrainian movement, with emphasis on the checkered history
from 1917 to 1920.

TURUK, F. **Belorusskoe Dvizhenie.** Moscow: Gosizdat, 1921, 145 p.
An outline of the history of the White Russian movement in its national and revolutionary aspects.

VOĬTINSKIĬ, VLADIMIR SAVEL'EVICH. **La Démocratie Géorgienne.** Paris: Lévy, 1921,
304 p.
One of the best surveys of the Georgian democratic republic and its stormy history
in the first few years following the war.

VOLKONSKIĬ, ALEKSANDR, KNIAZ'. **The Ukraine Question.** Rome: Armani, 1920, 239 p.
A counterblast to Ukrainian separatist propaganda.

ZETKIN, CLARA. **Im Befreiten Kaukasus.** Berlin: Verlag für Literatur und Politik,
1926, 312 p.
A glowing account of the development of the Caucasus under Bolshevik rule, by a
leading German communist.

VII. THE BALKAN AREA

GENERAL

*See also (World War) Balkan Front, p. 133; also (Italy) Policy in the Adriatic, p. 286; also
(Central Europe) Middle European Schemes, p. 299, and The Little Entente, p. 304; also
(Eastern Europe) General, p. 347.*

ANCEL, JACQUES. **Les Balkans Face à l'Italie.** Paris: Delagrave, 1928, 124 p.
An excellent brief account of Balkan history in the post-war decade, with special
attention to the Italian policy of expansion in the Mediterranean.

ANCEL, JACQUES. **Peuples et Nations des Balkans.** Paris: Colin, 1926, 221 p.
A short semi-popular approach from the geographic standpoint.

ARMSTRONG, HAMILTON FISH. **The New Balkans.** New York: Harper, 1926, 180 p.
A study of post-war Balkan problems and of their international significance, with
chapters on Jugoslav unity, Albania, Fiume, Saloniki, Bessarabia, etc.

ARMSTRONG, HAMILTON FISH. **Where the East Begins.** New York: Harper, 1929, 139 p.
The author discusses the key problems of the various states, with particular emphasis
on the royal dictatorship in Jugoslavia, the return of Venizelos to power in Greece,
the peasant régime in Rumania, and the Albanian problem in its international aspects.

BOBTSHEV, S. S. **Slavianski Sviat.** Sofia: Bibliothèque Slave, 1923.
A useful statistical collection of material bearing on most phases of Balkan culture and
economic life.

DEAMBROSIS, DELFINO. **I Confini Militari della Balcania Propriamente Detta.** Rome:
Istituto per l'Europa Orientale, 1929.
A scientific study of military boundaries, including those of Jugoslavia, Albania and
Bulgaria.

Durham, Mary Edith. **Twenty Years of Balkan Tangle.** London: Allen and Unwin, 1920, 295 p.
Recollections and impressions of an indefatigable Balkan traveler, throwing interesting if uneven light on Balkan pre-war intrigues and resulting animosities, in which the author makes no pretense not to share. She comes to the conclusion that Russia was primarily responsible for the disastrous course of events which led to the war.

Evelpidi, C. **Les États Balkaniques.** Paris: Rousseau, 1930, 395 p.
A comparative survey, with emphasis on the non-political problems.

Freri, Orlando. **Questioni Balcaniche e Dodecaneso.** Modena: Tipografica Modanese, 1922, 173 p.
A general review of post-war problems in the Balkans, with special reference to Italian interests and policies. Space is also given to the Dodecanese question.

Gallois, L. **Les Populations Slaves de la Péninsule des Balkans.** Paris: Colin, 1920, 434 p.
An elaborate ethnographic study, which, however, does not replace Cvijić's standard work, "La Péninsule Balkanique" (Paris, 1918).

Genève, Paul. **Un Français à Constantinople.** Paris: Lesot, 1923, 414 p.
Valuable memoirs of a distinguished French journalist, dealing with Balkan conditions during the decade from 1912 to 1923.

Gross, Hermann, *ed.* **Mittel- und Südost-Europäische Wirtschaftsfragen.** Leipzig: Böttger, 1931, 183 p.
A series of essays on the economic life of the Balkans and Turkey.

Heathcote, Dudley. **My Wanderings in the Balkans.** London: Hutchinson, 1925, 328 p.
Readable diverse observations by an English traveler.

Hoffmann, Walter. **Südost-Europa.** Leipzig: Londner, 1932, 248 p.
A survey of Jugoslavia, Bulgaria and Rumania, valuable for its detailed information on economic and trade matters.

Hurwicz, Elias. **Der Neue Osten.** Berlin: Mittler, 1927, 201 p.
An examination of the origins of the new states of eastern Europe along broad lines.

Iorga, Nicoláe. **Histoire des États Balcaniques jusqu'à 1924.** Paris: Gamber, 1925, 575 p.
A standard work, by a Rumanian historian, statesman and publicist. Probably the best general manual available, though the treatment is not always even.

Ivanchev, Konstantin. **L'Idée des États-Unis d'Europe et les Projets d'une Confédération Balkanique.** Paris: Gamber, 1930, 184 p.
An interesting essay on the long-mooted idea of Balkan Confederation and its place in a larger union of European states.

Kerner, Robert Joseph. **Social Sciences in the Balkans and in Turkey.** Berkeley: University of California Press, 1930, 137 p.
A handbook of existing resources for study and research in Jugoslavia, Rumania, Bulgaria, Greece and Turkey.

Kutschbach, Albin. **Der Brandherd Europas.** Leipzig: Haberland, 1929, 455 p.
Fifty years of Balkan reminiscences by a German journalist. While containing some interesting bits, they are not as illuminating as they should be.

Lamouche, Léon. **Quinze Ans d'Histoire Balkanique, 1904-1918.** Paris: Payot, 1928, 234 p.
A good account, written by a French officer long active in Macedonia and Bulgaria. Slightly weighted in favor of the Bulgarians.

LYALL, ARCHIBALD. **The Balkan Road.** London: Methuen, 1930, 244 p.
A pleasant travel book, with occasional penetrating observations on political and racial matters.

MACH, RICHARD VON. **Aus Bewegter Balkanzeit, 1879-1918.** Berlin: Mittler, 1928, 274 p.
Highly interesting and instructive memoirs of the representative of the *Kölnische Zeitung* in Sofia.

NAPIER, HENRY DUNDAS. **The Experiences of a Military Attaché in the Balkans.** London: Drane, 1923, 293 p.
A British officer's note-book in 1914-1915, throwing light on Allied efforts to win over Bulgaria, together with a brief account of Balkan developments with which the author was connected from 1915 to 1923.

NOEL-BUXTON, EDWARD, BARON and LEESE, C. LEONARD. **Balkan Problems and European Peace.** New York: Scribner, 1919, 135 p.
A brief account of Allied diplomacy in the Balkans in the war, mainly centering about Bulgaria, for which country the authors are disposed to make many allowances.

PANARETOFF, STEPHEN. **Near Eastern Affairs and Conditions.** New York: Macmillan, 1922, 216 p.
An exposition of Balkan history, politics and diplomacy from the standpoint of a scholarly Bulgarian, Minister in Washington during the World War.

PERNOT, MAURICE. **Balkans Nouveaux.** Paris: Hachette, 1929, 250 p.
Greece, Bulgaria, Rumania and Jugoslavia, as seen by a competent French journalist and traveler.

POWELL, EDWARD ALEXANDER. **The New Frontiers of Freedom.** New York: Scribner, 1920, 263 p.
Superficial observations on a journey through the Balkans in 1919.

RANDI, OSCAR. **I Popoli Balcanici.** Rome: Cremonese, 1929, 177 p.
One of the best Italian surveys of the Balkan states—political, economic, cultural.

RINDOFF, CONSTANTIN H. **Les États-Unis des Balkans.** Paris: Jouve, 1930, 218 p.
A critical study of the possibility of a political-economic understanding and federative union. The author was formerly secretary of the Macedonian Federal Organization.

SCHACHER, GERHARD. **Der Balkan und Seine Wirtschaftlichen Kräfte.** Stuttgart: Enke, 1930, 266 p.
The author stresses the neglected economic possibilities of the Balkan states. The book is an excellent general manual of the region.

SCHEVILL, FERDINAND. **A History of the Balkan Peninsula from the Earliest Times to the Present Day.** New York: Harcourt, 1922, 558 p.
Written by an authority, and probably the best on the list of none-too-satisfactory histories of the Balkans in the English language. The pre-war period occupies all but two chapters.

SPELLANZON, CESARE. **Vinti e Vincitori nei Balcani.** Milan: Corbaccio, 1926, 374 p.
A general survey of the Eastern Question and its development during the Great War, followed by a narrative of post-war happenings down to the Treaty of Lausanne.

SPENDER, HAROLD. **The Cauldron of Europe.** London: Witherby, 1925, 272 p.
A well-known English publicist's travel experiences in the Balkans. Not very deep.

STANOJEVIĆ, MILIVOJ STOJAN, *comp.* **Slavonic Nations of Yesterday and Today.** New York: Wilson, 1925, 461 p.
A reprint of miscellaneous articles on the Slavic nations, with a bibliography.

Vopicka, Charles J. **Secrets of the Balkans.** Chicago: Rand McNally, 1921, 330 p.
Rather disjointed memoirs and memoranda by the war-time American Minister to
Rumania, Serbia and Bulgaria.

Zingarelli, Italo. **Der Gross-Balkan.** Vienna: Amalthea, 1927, 395 p.
Journalistic travelogues on Rumania, Greece, Jugoslavia, Hungary and Austria, by
an able Italian correspondent.

RUMANIA

General

See also (World War) Russian Front, p. 130, and Balkan Front, p. 133; also (Central Europe)
Middle European Schemes, p. 299, and The Little Entente, p. 304.

Angelesco, Nicolas. **L'Expérience Monétaire Roumaine, 1914-1927.** Paris: Jouve,
1928, 259 p.
One of the best of many French dissertations on the subject.

Antipa, Gregor. **L'Occupation Ennemie de la Roumanie et Ses Conséquences
Économiques et Sociales.** New Haven: Yale University Press, 1930, 185 p.
A volume in the Carnegie Series, which throws much light not only on the methods of
the German command, but also on the difficult problem of Rumanian reconstruction.

Basilescu, Nicolas. **La Roumanie dans la Guerre et dans la Paix.** Paris: Alcan,
1919, 2 v.
The best general account of Rumanian history during the war. The second volume
is devoted to a discussion of the great problems confronting the new Rumania in 1919.

Berkowitz, Joseph. **La Question des Israélites en Roumanie.** Paris: Jouve, 1923,
799 p.
A scholarly treatment of this important problem in its historical development down
to 1919.

Clark, Charles Upson. **Greater Roumania.** New York: Dodd, 1922, 477 p.
An account of the geography, peoples, resources and recent history of Rumania,
written in an over-friendly vein.

Clark, Charles Upson. **United Roumania.** New York: Dodd, 1932, 432 p.
A convenient and well-informed survey of modern Rumania and its recent history,
from a sympathetic standpoint.

Evans, Ifor Leslie. **The Agrarian Revolution in Roumania.** New York: Macmillan,
1924, 197 p.
The new agrarian laws, and the changes resulting from their application.

Forter, Norman L. and Rostovsky, Demeter B. **The Roumanian Handbook.**
London: Simpkin, 1931, 320 p.
An up-to-date general manual and guide.

Gheorghiu, Démètre J. **Les Finances de la Roumanie après la Guerre.** Bucharest:
Cartea Romaneasca, 1930, 105 p.
The most convenient brief summary of Rumanian financial history, by an official of the
Rumanian National Bank.

Gillard, Marcel. **La Roumanie Nouvelle.** Paris: Alcan, 1922, 216 p.
A useful survey of the post-war situation, with special reference to social classes,
minorities, economic problems and political life.

HALLUNGA, ALEXANDRE. **L'Évolution et la Révision Récente du Tarif Douanier en Roumanie.** Paris: Dalloz, 1927, 348 p.
A doctoral thesis outlining the history of the Rumanian tariff and analyzing the law of April 1927.

IANCOULESCO, AUREL P. **La Roumanie Nouvelle et Ses Richesses Minières.** Paris: Gamber, 1928, 384 p.
A thorough account of the country's resources in petrol, coal, natural gases, etc.

IANCOVICI, D. **Take Jonesco.** Paris: Payot, 1919, 160 p.
A brief general biography of the Rumanian statesman who from the first favored intervention on the side of the Allies, and who later as Foreign Minister was one of the founders of the Little Entente.

IONESCU, TAKE and others. **Les Questions Roumaines du Temps Présent.** Paris: Alcan, 1921, 186 p.
A valuable collection of essays, by Rumanian scholars and statesmen, dealing with Rumanian territorial claims, policy toward minorities, and international policy.

IORGA, NICOLAE. **A History of Roumania.** London: T. Fisher Unwin, 1926, 284 p.
The standard account, in English, of Rumanian characteristics and national history. Not particularly well organized, and rather slight on the recent period.

IVANOF, ALEXANDRE IONESCO. **La Réforme Monétaire Roumaine.** Paris: Sirey, 1929, 142 p.
A doctoral thesis analyzing the important reforms of 1929.

LUPU, NICHOLAS. **La Roumanie Nouvelle et Ses Problèmes Vitaux.** Paris: P. Dupont, 1919, 36 p.
A leader of the peasant forces describes their characteristics and aims, and discusses briefly the history of some of Rumania's recently acquired territories.

MADGEARU, VIRGIL. **Rumania's New Economic Policy.** London: King, 1930, 63 p.
A Rumanian Minister of Finance explains the attitude of the régime toward agriculture, tariff, capital, etc.

MANOLIOU, F. **La Reconstruction Économique et Financière de la Roumanie.** Paris: Gamber, 1931, 304 p.
A volume dealing chiefly with the attitude of the Rumanian parties toward reconstruction problems.

MARIE, DOWAGER QUEEN OF RUMANIA. **The Country That I Love.** New York: Brentano, 1925, 175 p.
Chatty sketches of people and places, including shrewd appraisals of the former Rumanian rulers, King Charles and "Carmen Sylva."

MARTINEAU, MRS. ALICE (VAUGHAN-WILLIAMS). **Roumania and Her Rulers.** London: Paul, 1927, 226 p.
Sketches of court life, in which the indefatigable Queen Marie figures chiefly.

MEHEDINTI, SIMEON. **Le Pays et le Peuple Roumain.** Bucharest: Cartea Romaneasca, 1930, 133 p.
By a professor of geography, member of the Rumanian parliament, and former Minister of Instruction.

MITRANY, DAVID. **The Land and the Peasant in Rumania.** New Haven: Yale University Press, 1930, 627 p.
The agrarian problem is given its historical and social setting, after which the provisions of the new land law are described, as well as the effects. A scholarly study in the Carnegie Series.

MUZET, ALPHONSE. **La Roumanie Nouvelle.** Paris: Roger, 1920, 272 p.
A convenient summary of Rumanian government and the resources of the new Rumania, by a French engineer.

NETTA, XENOFON. **Die Rumänische Nationalbank.** Leipzig: Deichert, 1929, 241 p.
A dissertation which studies the organization and activity of the bank in the general setting of Rumanian economic life. The best treatment of the subject.

PARKINSON, MAUDE REA. **Twenty Years in Roumania.** London: Allen and Unwin, 1921, 255 p.
A general picture of Rumanian life and culture, rather interesting but not important.

PÉTAIN, HENRI PHILIPPE. **Le Drame Roumain, 1916-1918.** Paris: Payot, 1931, 3 v.
A detailed and largely technical account of military events in Rumania after that country entered the war, by the chief of the French military mission.

PIZANTY, MIHAIL. **Petroleum in Roumania.** Bucharest: Cultura Naţională, 1930, 100 p.
A general statistical and illustrated survey, published by the Rumanian Economic Institute.

Politica Externa a Romaniei. Bucharest: Cultura Naţională, 1927, 706 p.
Interesting lectures published by the Rumanian Institute of Social Science.

RADULESCO, SAVEL. **La Politique Financière de la Roumanie depuis 1914.** Paris: Presses Universitaires, 1923, 2 v.
The most extensive scholarly study of Rumanian war finance and of the financial policy of the post-war period (to 1922).

ROMIER, LUCIEN. **Le Carrefour des Empires Morts.** Paris: Hachette, 1931, 253 p.
Travel impressions and observations in the new Rumania, by an able and often brilliant publicist.

ROMMENHÖLLER, CAROL GUSTAVE. **La Grande Roumanie.** Hague: Nijhoff, 1926, 634 p.
An exhaustive general treatment of Rumanian conditions and problems, dealing largely with economic questions. Written by a Rumanian consular official.

ROUČEK, JOSEPH SLABEY. **Contemporary Roumania and Her Problems.** Stanford: Stanford University Press, 1932, 447 p.
Probably the best general work on Rumanian conditions now available in English, opening with a brief historical outline, followed by detailed studies of political organizations, foreign policy, the minorities question, and constitutional matters. There is also extended examination of Rumanian economic resources, and a good bibliography.

Roumania Ten Years After. Boston: Beacon Press, 1928, 152 p.
Social and political conditions as seen through the eyes of the American Committee on the Rights of Religious Minorities. The report stresses the need for a change of Rumanian policy toward minorities.

STAHEL DE CAPITANI, HERMANN J. **Rumänien.** Zurich: Tschopp, 1925, 143 p.
A general traveler's handbook, by a Swiss consular official.

STERIAN, PAUL. **La Roumanie et la Réparation des Dommages de Guerre.** Paris: Librairie Générale de Droit, 1929, 142 p.
A dissertation which stresses the Rumanian claims to reparations on the basis of damages done, and urges the extreme need of such reparations for the work of reconstruction.

TIBAL, ANDRÉ. **La Roumanie.** Paris: Rieder, 1930, 154 p.
A brief survey of the conventional kind, dealing with the people, the government, economics and intellectual life.

TROTSKIĬ, LEV and RAKOVSKIĬ, KH. **Ocherki Politicheskoĭ Rumynii.** Moscow: Gosizdat, 1922, 151 p.
Political sketches on Rumania, setting forth the Bolshevik view on the Bessarabian question and envisaging the ultimate victory of communism.

ZIMMERMANN, OTTO. **Die Rumänischen Währungsverhältnisse in der Kriegs- und Nachkriegszeit.** Leipzig: Helm, 1928, 238 p.
A German dissertation. On the whole the best brief treatment of the Rumanian currency since the beginning of the war. Contains many documents.

Territorial Problems

Bessarabia

See also (Russia) Foreign Policy, p. 393.

ALEKSANDRI, L. N. **Bessarabiia i Bessarabskiĭ Vopros.** Moscow: Gozisdat, n. d., 104 p.
A presentation of the Russian view, with a collection of documents.

BABEL, ANTONY. **La Bessarabie.** Paris: Alcan, 1926, 360 p.
One of the best general historical, ethnographic and economic surveys of the territory, though inclined to emphasize the Rumanian viewpoint and enlarge on Rumanian benefits.

BOLDUR, ALEXANDRE. **La Bessarabie et les Relations Russo-Roumaines.** Paris: Gamber, 1927, 412 p.
An exhaustive documented study by a native of Bessarabia and former professor at Petrograd. The author believes the union with Rumania not only necessary but just.

CLARK, CHARLES UPSON. **Bessarabia: Russia and Roumania on the Black Sea.** New York: Dodd, 1927, 333 p.
An historical and descriptive study of the problem, by an American writer on the Rumanian side.

DEMBO, V. **Bessarabskiĭ Vopros.** Moscow: Gosizdat, 1924, 185 p.
A general survey of the basic factors in the problem, with an outline of historical developments.

OKHOTNIKOV, J. and BACHINSKIĬ, N. **La Bessarabie et la Paix Européenne.** Paris: Librairie du Travail, 1927, 160 p.
A strong restatement of the Russian claim.

PELIVAN, ION G. **La Bessarabie sous le Régime Russe.** Paris: Lahure, 1919, 2 pts.
A survey of Bessarabian history from 1812 to 1918 and a severe indictment of Russian rule. The second part deals with Bessarabia's reunion with the "mother country."

POPOVICI, ANDREI. **The Political Status of Bessarabia.** Washington: Ransdell, 1931, 288 p.
A well-informed and careful presentation of the Rumanian claims to Bessarabia, historical, political and economic.

RAKOVSKIĬ, KHRISTIAN GEORGIEVICH. **Roumania and Bessarabia.** London: Coates, 1925, 64 p.
A classic statement of the Russian claims, by the Soviet Ambassador in London.

UHLIG, CARL LUDWIG GUSTAV. **Die Bessarabische Frage.** Breslau: Hirt, 1926, 107 p.
The problem approached from the geopolitical angle. One of the most impartial analyses.

Transylvania

See also (Central Europe) Collapse of the Hapsburg Empire, p. 301; also Hungary, p. 308.

ANTONESCU, MIHAI. **Reginul Agrar Român și Chestiunea Optanților Unguri.** Bucharest: România Nouă, 1928, 288 p.
A straightforward presentation of Rumania's legal standpoint and a history of the optants' dispute to 1928.

BAERLEIN, HENRY. **And Then to Transylvania.** London: Shaylor, 1931, 253 p.
Another travel book by a familiar writer on eastern European countries.

CABOT, JOHN MOORS. **The Racial Conflict in Transylvania.** Boston: Beacon Press, 1926, 213 p.
A painstaking and sincere work. The author considers the desires of the population, its ability to govern itself, and economic, geographical, historical and strategic considerations. In his opinion conflict can be avoided only by making Hungary satisfied, which means rectifying the frontier.

CORNISH, LOUIS CRAIG, *comp.* **Transylvania in 1922.** Boston: Beacon Press, 1923, 169 p.
Material on ecclesiastical and educational institutions and policies, gathered by the Commission of the American and British Unitarian Churches. Hardly impartial.

DEÁK, FRANCIS. **The Hungarian-Rumanian Land Dispute.** New York: Columbia University Press, 1928, 286 p.
A scholarly Hungarian's exposition of the well-known controversy, with particular reference to questions of treaty interpretation, the relation between international law and national legislation, the authority of the League, etc. The best single book on the optants' dispute from the Hungarian viewpoint.

DRAGOMIR, SYLVIUS. **The Ethnical Minorities in Transylvania.** Geneva: Sonor Printing Company, 1927, 131 p.
A Rumanian professor demolishes the book by Szász and confounds him with quotations from Hungarian authorities. This little book is restrained in tone and packed with information.

JANCSÓ, BENEDEK. **A Román Irredentista Mozgalmak Története.** Budapest: Pfeifer, 1920, 502 p.
A history of the Rumanian irredentist movement, as seen from Hungary.

MARBURG, ERNST. **Der Rumänisch-Ungarische Optantenstreit.** Leipzig: Noske, 1928, 113 p.
A German scholar views the Rumanian-Hungarian embroglio primarily from the League standpoint.

MATHEOVITS, FERENC. **A Magyar-román Virtokper.** Budapest: Grill, 1929, 272 p.
A recent Hungarian study of the optants' dispute; less complete than Deák's work, but containing an interesting collection of utterances on the subject by authorities on international law.

SZÁSZ, ZSOMBOR. **The Minorities in Roumanian Transylvania.** London: Richards, 1927, 414 p.
The author, a Hungarian publicist, reviews the provisions for protection of minorities, examines the actual policy of the government and adduces Rumanian material to support his severe indictment of the new régime.

TEUTSCH, FRIEDRICH. **Die Siebenbürger Sachsen in den Letzten 50 Jahren.** Hermannstadt: Krafft, 1926, 430 p.
The fourth and concluding volume of the classic history of the Saxons in Transylvania. The period here covered is 1868 to 1919.

Transilvania, Banatul, Crişana, Maramureşul, 1918-1929. Bucharest: Cultura Naţională, 1929, 3 v.
A huge collaborative work touching on almost all phases of conditions in the newly acquired territories. Published in celebration of the tenth anniversary of Greater Rumania.

URBAN, R. **Československi v Rumunsku.** Prague: Československý Ústav Zahranični, 1930, 191 p.
A description of the Czechoslovak minority in Rumania.

VELLANI-DIONISI, F. **Il Problema Territoriale Transilvano.** Bologna: Zanichelli, 1932, 232 p.
A study of the land question between Rumania and Hungary as it developed and as it stands.

WITTSTOCK, OSKAR, *ed.* **Die Offene Wunde Europas.** Hermannstadt: Krafft, 1930, 192 p.
A collection of twenty contributions touching various aspects of the minorities problems, with special attention to the Transylvanian difficulty.

Dobruja

See also Bulgaria, p. 413.

COMNÈNE, N. P. **La Dobrogea.** Paris: Payot, 1920, 207 p.
An essay on the region's history, ethnography, economic resources and political importance.

GABÉ, PETKO. **La Question de la Dobroudja dans Son Essence.** Sofia: Glushkov, 1925, 96 p.
Discusses primarily the expropriation measures of the Rumanian government.

ISHIRKOV, ANASTAS. **Les Bulgares en Dobroudja.** Berne: Pochon-Jent, 1919, 189 p.
Historical and ethnographical material to support Bulgarian claims.

KOLAROV, IVAN. **La Loi Roumaine pour la Nouvelle Dobroudja.** Sofia: Bojinoff, 1928, 152 p.
A Bulgarian protest against the land laws of the Rumanian régime.

Le Régime de la Propriété Rurale dans la Dobrudja du Sud. Sofia: L'Union Bulgare pour la Paix et pour la Société des Nations, 1929, 206 p.
A Bulgarian examination of Rumanian opinions on the land question.

JUGOSLAVIA
General

See also (World War) Balkan Front, p. 133; also (Europe) Constitutional Problems, Dictatorships, p. 227; also (Italy) Policy in the Adriatic, p. 286; also (Central Europe) Middle European Schemes, p. 299, Collapse of the Hapsburg Empire, p. 301, and The Little Entente, p. 304; also (Greece) General, p. 418.

AUERHAN, JAN. **Československá Větev v Jugoslavii.** Prague: Československý Ústav Zahranični, 1930, 403 p.
A description of the Czechoslovak minority in Jugoslavia, by the leading Czechoslovak authority.

BAERLEIN, HENRY. **The Birth of Yugoslavia.** London: Parsons, 1922, 2 v.
Pro-Jugoslav and voluminous description of Serbia before the war, the struggle for unification and the post-war difficulties.

BASSI, MARIO. **La Crisi Politica in Jugoslavia.** Rome: Istituto per l'Europa Orientale, 1930, 300 p.
A review of developments since 1919, with an analysis of the work of the dictatorship to date. Competent and scholarly.

BEARD, CHARLES AUSTIN and RADIN, GEORGE. **The Balkan Pivot: Jugoslavia.** New York: Macmillan, 1929, 333 p.
A complete and excellent survey of the Jugoslav government and administration as it existed until King Alexander's coup d'état.

BESOZZI, A. and MARTINI, V. A. **La Jugoslavia e la Pace Europea.** Milan: Unitas, 1930, 260 p.
The conventional Italian view of the Southern Slav question during the war, at the Peace Conference, and since, with emphasis on Serb imperialism.

BOGIĆEVIĆ, MILOŠ. **Le Procès de Salonique.** Paris: Delpeuch, 1927, 168 p.
A reëxamination of the evidence in connection with the famous war-time trial, by a Germanophile Serbian ex-diplomat. An important book for students of Balkan affairs, though not entirely trustworthy.

BUCHAN, JOHN, ed. **Yugoslavia.** London: Hodder, 1923, 283 p.
A volume in the Nations of Today series, giving an historical survey and outline of resources and conditions.

CHABOSEAU, AUGUSTIN. **Les Serbes, Croates et Slovènes.** Paris: Bossard, 1919, 110 p.
A brief popular introduction to modern Serbia and her problems at the Peace Conference.

CHAMBRY, RENÉ. **La Barrière Serbe.** Amsterdam: Van Holkema, 1920, 104 p.
The author revives the old argument for the need of a bulwark against German expansion toward the East.

CHANTIĆ-CHANDAN, K. S. **L'Unité Yougoslave et le Roi Alexandre I.** Paris: Publications Contemporaines, 1932, 210 p.
A study of Jugoslav politics and of current domestic problems.

CVIJIĆ, JOVAN and others. **La Question du Banat, de la Batchka et la Baranya.** Paris: Imprimerie Yougoslavia, 1919, 36 p.
Expert statistical description and propaganda, covering three questions discussed at the Peace Conference.

DENIS, ERNEST. **Du Vardar à la Sotcha.** Paris: Bossard, 1923, 351 p.
A series of historical, political and ethnographical articles published during the war by a well-known French friend of all things Slavic, and especially Serbian.

HAUMANT, ÉMILE. **La Formation de la Yougoslavie.** Paris: Bossard, 1930, 754 p.
A general history of the Southern Slav peoples from the 15th century to the end of the war, with emphasis on the later period. Well informed and detailed, but unfortunately not adequately documented. It none the less is the soundest and most complete general treatment in a western tongue.

HINKOVIĆ, HINKO. **Iz Velikog Doba.** Zagreb: Komisionalna Naklada, 1927, 432 p.
A Croatian leader's account of his work against Austria-Hungary during the war, incidentally throwing some light on the activities of the Serbian government at Corfu and on the "Saloniki trial." Hinković was a Croatian deputy in the Budapest parliament, and after the war became identified with the republican movement in Jugoslavia.

HOLZER, ERWIN. **Die Entstehung des Jugoslawischen Staates.** Berlin: Gunther Thon, 1929, 107 p.
The author is concerned only with the war and immediate post-war periods, and approaches the subject from a purely constitutional standpoint.

HORVATSKI, MILAN. **La Constitution de "Vidovdan."** Grenoble: Aubert, 1923, 277 p.
A dissertation which hardly goes beyond an analysis of the pertinent documents.

JAQUIN, PIERRE. **L'Effort Yougoslave.** Paris: Alcan, 1932, 180 p.
A useful compendium of information, with not particularly discriminating comment.

JOVANOVIĆ, MILUTIN. **Le Régime Absolu Yougoslave.** Paris: Bossuet, 1930, 200 p.
A survey of the developments of the past two years, with an interesting chapter on political conditions before King Alexander took full control.

JOVANOVIĆ, N. **La Constitution du Royaume des Serbes, Croates, et Slovènes.** Paris: Sagot, 1925, 428 p.
An authoritative examination of the whole constitutional development from 1914 onward.

Ko Je Ko u Jugoslaviji. Zagreb: Nove Evrope, 1928, 168 p.
The first edition of a Jugoslav "Who's Who." Carefully edited and quite complete.

KOSIER, LJUBOMIR. **La Bosnie et l'Herzégovine.** Zagreb: Bankarstvo, 1927-1928, 3 v.
A general historical and descriptive study, largely economic, by the director of an economic review in Zagreb.

KOSIER, LJUBOMIR. **Les Juifs en Yougoslavie et en Bulgarie.** Zagreb: Bankarstvo, 1929, 406 p.
Stresses the economic life and social status of the Jewish element.

KSIUNIN, A., *ed.* **Krv Slovenstva.** Belgrade: Radenkovitch, 1924, 132 p.
A patriotic Slavic collection, including the much-discussed article by Ljuba Jovanović suggesting that he had foreknowledge of the Sarajevo plot.

LAFFAN, ROBERT GEORGE DALRYMPLE. **Yugoslavia since 1918.** London: Yugoslav Society, 1929.
A good survey, by a professor at the University of Cambridge.

LAGGER, HANS, *ed.* **Abwehrkampf und Volksabstimmung in Kärnten, 1918-1920.** Berlin: Dietz, 1930, 160 p.
A detailed account of the plebiscite in Carinthia.

LONCHAREVIĆ, DUSHAN A. **Jugoslawiens Entstehung.** Vienna: Amalthea, 1928, 672 p.
The author, a Serb official, has written an admirable account of the economic and political struggle with Austria and the emergence of the new state. On the whole the best and most scholarly study from the Jugoslav point of view.

MARKOVIĆ, LAZAR, *ed.* **Serbia and Europe, 1914-1920.** London: Allen and Unwin, 1921, 355 p.
A collection of articles of unequal value, covering Serbian policy during the war, the achievement of Jugoslav union, subsequent problems, and relations with Bulgaria, Italy, etc., prepared by a Serbian politician and journalist.

MOROCUTTI, CAMILLO. **Gross-Deutschland, Gross-Südslawien.** Vienna: Braumüller, 1928, 103 p.
A strange book, in which a leader of the German minority in Slovenia describes the wrongs of his people and then proposes the formation of a new Mitteleuropa based upon the rapprochement of Germany and Austria on the one hand and Jugoslavia and Bulgaria on the other, the two sections to be bound together by economic and other agreements.

MOUSSET, ALBERT. **Le Royaume Serbe-Croate-Slovène.** Paris: Bossard, 1926, 270 p.
The first volume of a new and completely rewritten edition of the author's "Le Royaume des Serbes, Croates et Slovènes" (Paris: Bossard, 1921). In this useful volume the author surveys the political organization and life, the press, the theatre, etc.

PAVELIĆ, ANTE. **Aus den Kämpfen um den Selbständigen Staat Kroatien.** Vienna: Hölzl, 1931, 127 p.
Pictures and documents of the Croatian struggle, by an opponent of the present Jugoslav régime.

PAVLOVIĆ, BOJA L. **La Législation sur la Liberté de la Presse en Yougoslavie.** Paris: Sagot, 1928, 260 p.
A legal and political study of considerable merit.

RANDI, OSCAR. **La Jugoslavia.** Naples: Ricciardi, 1922, 582 p.
An elaborate and well-informed general survey, political and economic.

RIVET, CHARLES. **Chez les Slaves Libérés en Yougoslavie.** Paris: Perrin, 1921, 322 p.
An account of a journey in 1918, by a well-known French correspondent.

RUBIĆ, IVO. **Les Italiens sur le Littoral du Royaume Yougoslavie.** Split: Bureau Yougoslave d'Informations pour l'Étranger, 1931, 63 p.
The documented results of an investigation into the ethnic composition of the Dalmatian population, designed to refute Italian claims.

SELESKOVIĆ, MOMČILO T. **La Serbie dans l'Opinion Allemande Contemporaine.** Paris: Jouve, 1919, 292 p.
An interesting if not profound dissertation, digesting German and Austrian opinion on Serbian aspirations, responsibility for the war, etc.

SHISHIĆ, FERDO, *ed.* **Dokumenti o postanku kraljevine Srba, Hrvata i Slovenaca, 1914-1919.** Zagreb: Matice Hrvatske, 1920, 329 p.
A useful collection of documents, manifestoes, declarations, etc., dealing with the Southern Slav question during the war.

STAMENKOVIĆ, CHRISTA. **L'Émigration Yougoslave.** Paris: Derre, 1929, 395 p.
An excellent dissertation on Jugoslav emigration in Europe and overseas, its causes, and the government's policy. The book has an exhaustive bibliography and is easily the best thing on the subject.

STANOJEVIĆ, STANOJE. **Histoire Nationale Succincte des Serbes, des Croates et des Slovènes.** Paris: Bloud et Gay, 1919, 146 p.
A popular sketch, by a competent Serbian historian.

TAYSEN, FRIEDRICH VON. **Das Jugoslawische Problem.** Berlin: Mittler, 1927, 120 p.
Travel impressions and general considerations, of which the best are those dealing with economic problems and foreign policy.

TOMIĆ, ZORAN S. **La Formation de l'État Yougoslave.** Paris: Presses Modernes, 1927, 244 p.
A rather inadequate treatment of developments during the war and the organization of the new state.

VESNIĆ, MILENKO RADOMIR. **La Serbie à travers la Grande Guerre.** Paris: Bossard, 1920, 161 p.
A collection of writings and addresses, by the war-time Serbian Minister in Paris, setting forth Serbian hopes and claims.

VOJNOVIĆ, LUJO, COUNT. **Dalmatia and the Jugoslav Movement.** New York: Scribner, 1919, 320 p.
The story of Dalmatia's struggle against Venice and the Hapsburgs, and its part in the Serbo-Croat movement, by a Ragusan patriot and scholar.

VOSHNJAK, BOGUMIL. **A Bulwark against Germany.** New York: Revell, 1919, 283 p.
The fight of the Slovenes for national existence, by one of their war-time spokesmen.

WENDEL, HERMANN. **Aus der Welt der Südslawen.** Berlin: Dietz, 1926, 282 p.
Political, historical and sociological studies, by a careful German journalist.

WENDEL, HERMANN. **Der Kampf der Südslawen um Freiheit und Einheit.** Frankfurt: Frankfurter Societätsdruckerei, 1925, 798 p.
The most pretentious and detailed account of the Southern Slav movement yet published. Anti-Austrian in tone, but thoroughly well informed.

WENDEL, HERMANN, *ed.* **Südslawien.** Frankfurt: Hauser, 1922, 83 p.
An excellent survey and handbook, by various Serbian scholars, published for the Frankfurt fair.

WUTTE, MARTIN and LOBMEYR, OSKAR. **Die Lage der Minderheiten in Kärnten und in Slowenien.** Klagenfurt: Kollitsch, 1926, 79 p.
Another cry of anguish from the German minorities.

Economic and Financial

ALEKSANDER, BRANKO. **Das Jugoslavische Bankwesen.** Zagreb: no pub., 1926, 173 p.
A Swiss dissertation covering the banking and currency problem since 1914.

ARANITOVIĆ, RELJA. **Les Ressources et l'Activité Économique de la Yougoslavie.** Paris: Bossuet, 1930, 503 p.
A dissertation which gives an admirable detailed account of Jugoslav economic life—agriculture, trade, industry, finance and communication. The volume contains much statistical material.

DJULIZIBARIĆ, DRAGOLJUB. **Le Dinar Serbe et l'Évolution Financière de la Serbie depuis 1914.** Nancy: Imprimerie Nanceienne, 1925, 192 p.
A slight and rather pedestrian dissertation

FILIPIĆ, ANTONIJE. **La Jugoslavia Economica.** Milan: Treves, 1922, 297 p.
A study of Jugoslavia's geography, resources and commercial relations.

JOVANOVIĆ, DRAGOLJUB K. **Les Effets Économiques et Sociaux de la Guerre en Serbie.** New Haven: Yale University Press, 1930, 334 p.
A scholarly appraisal, by a professor of economics at Belgrade. The statistical material covers population changes, changes in rural and city economy, changes in cultural and intellectual life, etc.

MATL, JOSEF. **Die Agrarreform in Jugoslawien.** Berlin: Sack, 1927, 137 p.
A useful work by a professor at Graz. The book has a full account of the agrarian legislation and a summary of native criticism.

MIHAJLOVIĆ, DRAGOSLAV P. **Le Problème Monétaire en Yougoslavie.** Strasbourg: Union, 1928, 135 p.
A dissertation based chiefly on Serbian material. The best general account in a western language.

PATTON, KENNETH STUART. **Kingdom of Serbs, Croats, and Slovenes: Commercial and Industrial Handbook.** Washington: Department of Commerce, 1928, 261 p.
A useful handbook discussing the economic development of the country and providing valuable statistical material on industry and trade, prepared for the Bureau of Foreign and Domestic Commerce.

PROTIĆ, MILAN. **Banque Nationale du Royaume des Serbes, Croates et Slovènes.** Paris: Cadet, 1921, 255 p.
A thesis reviewing the Serbian currency problem before, during and after the war.

The Macedonian Problem

See also Bulgaria, p. 413.

ANCEL, JACQUES. **La Macédoine.** Paris: Delagrave, 1931, 352 p.
An illustrated handbook, probably the best general work on the subject.

BELIĆ, ALEKSANDAR. **La Macédoine.** Paris: Bloud et Gay, 1919, 278 p.
A study of Macedonian national feeling, ethnography and language, all designed to support the Serb claims.

COLOCOTRONIS, V. **La Macédoine et l'Hellénisme.** Paris: Berger-Levrault, 1919, 658 p.
A most extensive, heavily documented, historical and ethnographical study of Macedonia, from the Greek viewpoint.

DJORDJEVIĆ, TIHOMIR R. **La Macédoine.** Paris: Grasset, 1919, 275 p.
A résumé of ethnic and historical material to prove the region's Serbian character.

GOFF, A. and FAWCETT, HUGH ALDERSON. **Macedonia, a Plea for the Primitive.** London: Lane, 1921, 274 p.
A rather random non-political description, based on three years of travel and observation.

IARANOV, D. **La Macédoine Économique.** Sofia: Institut Scientifique Macédonien, 1931.
A Bulgarian review of the region's natural resources, communications, commerce and population.

IVANOV, IORDAN. **La Question Macédonienne.** Paris: Gamber, 1920, 292 p.
An historical and ethnographical study, by a Bulgarian professor.

JACOB, WALTER. **Die Makedonische Frage.** Berlin: Beltz, 1931, 57 p.
A geographical approach.

KARADJIĆ, C. **Le Banditisme et Ses Agissements contre la Paix Balkanique.** Belgrade: no pub., 1930.
Revelations of a former member of the I. M. R. O.

La Macédoine et les Macédoniens. Corfu: Imprimerie Nationale du Royaume de Serbie, 1920, 125 p.
The Macedonian problem from the official Serbian viewpoint.

PERRIGAULT, JEAN. **Bandits d'Orient.** Paris: Valois, 1931.
Highly-colored revelations of the activities of the Macedonian committees.

Pro Macedonia. Vienna: Makedon, 1925, 51 p.
A series of articles on the Macedonian question, by Bulgarian leaders.

RAPPOPORT, ALFRED. **Au Pays des Martyrs.** Paris: Gamber, 1927, 137 p.
The reminiscences of a former Austrian consul-general, covering the years 1904-1909. Important for the study of the Macedonian reform problem.

REISS, RODOLPHE ARCHIBALD. **The Comitadji Question in Southern Serbia.** London: Hazell, 1924, 156 p.
An account, by a Swiss professor friendly to the Serbian cause, of the Macedonian Revolutionary Organization and its post-war activities.

SCHULTZE, LEONHARD SIGISMUND. **Makedonien.** Jena: Fischer, 1927, 250 p.
An outstanding book on Macedonia, richly illustrated and comprehensive, written by a German geographer and based upon data taken during the war and in 1922.

STRUPP, KARL. **La Situation Juridique des Macédoniens en Yougoslavie.** Paris: Presses Universitaires, 1930, 140 p.
A German jurist reviews the vexed Macedonian problem and comes to the conclusion that the Macedonians are really a Bulgarian minority and that the Jugoslav policy is subject to provisions of the minorities treaties. Much statistical and map material.

WEIGAND, GUSTAV. **Ethnographie von Makedonien.** Leipzig: Brandstetter, 1925, 104 p.
An authoritative account of racial and philological conditions.

WENDEL, HERMANN. **Makedonien und der Friede.** Munich: Musarion, 1919, 113 p.
A competent review of the problem as it presented itself during the war, with emphasis on its economic aspects.

Montenegro

BAJZA, JÓZSEF DE. **La Questione Montenegrina.** Budapest: Pallas, 1928.
A reconsideration of obscure elements in the Montenegrin question.

BRESSE, LOUIS. **Le Monténégro Inconnu.** Paris: Berger-Levrault, 1920, 111 p.
Recollections and impressions of the Balkan Wars and the World War, by a well-known French correspondent.

CHOTCH, PIERRE G. **Le Monténégro.** Paris: Figuière, 1920, 89 p.
A statement by one of Nicholas' ministers.

KOSIER, LJUBOMIR. **Le Monténégro.** Zagreb: Bankarstvo, 1931, 300 p.
The author, director of the economic review *Bankarstvo*, deals primarily with the war period and the union with Serbia.

La Question Monténégrine. Paris: L'Émancipatrice, 1919, 47 p.
A brief statement of the events leading up to the absorption of Montenegro in the Jugoslav state, prepared by the Radović group hostile to King Nicholas.

WARREN, WHITNEY. **Montenegro; the Crime of the Peace Conference.** New York: Brentano, 1922, 64 p.
An angry indictment of the Peace Conference's treatment of King Nicholas and his people, by d'Annunzio's former New York representative.

BULGARIA

See also (World War) Balkan Front, p. 133; also (Rumania) Dobruja, p. 407; also (Jugoslavia)
The Macedonian Problem, p. 411.

ANCEL, JACQUES. **L'Unité de la Politique Bulgare, 1870-1919.** Paris: Bossard, 1919, 75 p.
A strongly hostile account of Bulgarian policy from 1870 to 1919. To be classed as war-time propaganda.

BUCHAN, JOHN, *ed.* **Bulgaria and Roumania.** London: Hodder, 1924, 318 p.
A volume in the Nations of Today series. The treatment in this case is largely historical, with a rather brief review of economic life and conditions.

BULACEL, A. **Ocherki Socialno-Politicheskoi Shizni Sovremennoi Bolgarii.** Moscow: Gosizdat, 1925, 136 p.
The political and social scene in post-war Bulgaria, from the Bolshevik viewpoint.

La Bulgarie. Paris: La Vie Technique, 1921, 92 p.
A compact survey of the economic resources and conditions of post-war Bulgaria.

La Bulgarie sous le Régime de l'Assassinat. Paris: Société Nouvelle Édition, 1925, 479 p.
The Bulgarian terror as pictured by the exiled leaders of the Stambuliski group.

BUXTON, LELAND. **The Black Sheep of the Balkans.** London: Nisbet, 1920, 191 p.
A review of the situation in the Balkans, with much criticism of Allied policy toward Bulgaria and Turkey, by an authority long friendly to the Bulgarian people.

CHRISTOFF, THEODOR. **Das Heutige Bulgarien.** Berlin: Runge, 1931, 93 p.
A brief popular survey of modern Bulgaria.

La Conspiration Bolcheviste contre la Bulgarie. Sofia: Imprimerie de la Cour, 1925, 108 p.
A government publication, with documents and opinions to prove the seriousness of the communist menace.

DESBONS, GEORGES. **La Bulgarie après le Traité de Neuilly.** Paris: Rivière, 1930, 463 p.
A review of recent history, with a pronounced Bulgarian bias. The author gives a good account of the Bulgarian side of the Macedonian question, the problem of access to the sea, reparations, exchange of populations, the communist danger, etc.

Les Droits des Minorités Bulgares et la Société des Nations. Lausanne: no pub., 1929, 94 p.
A survey of the peace treaties and provisions for minority protection, followed by a review of conditions in the Balkans in 1928 and proposals for more effective action by the League.

ELIEV, ATANASA T. **Spomeni.** Sofia: Glushkov, 1926, 468 p.
Important reminiscences, covering the entire period of modern Bulgarian history, from 1850 to 1922.

FOCARILE, ANGELO. **Bulgaria d'Oggi.** Milan: Hoepli, 1929, 371 p.
The usual type of general survey, social, political and economic.

GENTIZON, PAUL. **Le Drame Bulgare.** Paris: Payot, 1924, 256 p.
A journalistic account of the unsettled situation from 1918 to 1923, by the special correspondent of the Paris *Temps*.

GESHOV, IVAN EVSTRATIEV. **Spomeni i Studii.** Sofia: Glushkov, 1928, 393 p.
Essays and reminiscences of the well-known Bulgarian statesman. Many of them deal with economic conditions and problems.

GORRINI, G. **Boris III, Tzar dei Bulgari.** Voghera: Gabetta, 1930, 173 p.
Personal impressions and reminiscences of the present ruler.

GROTHE, HUGO. **Bulgarien.** Vienna: Seidel, 1921, 155 p.
A digest of material on geographic, ethnographic, governmental and economic aspects of modern Bulgaria.

IOTZOFF, DMITRI. **Zar Ferdinand von Bulgarien.** Berlin: Oestergaard, 1927, 295 p.
A biographical study of the ruler and of the historical setting of his activities, from 1886 to the end of the war.

IVANOV, IORDAN. **Les Bulgares devant le Congrès de la Paix.** Berne: Haupt, 1919, 304 p.
A collection of historic, ethnographic and political data to fortify the Bulgarian case at the Peace Conference. Written by a Bulgarian professor.

KAPTCHEFF, G. I. **La Débâcle Nationale Bulgare devant la Haute-Cour.** Paris: Voltaire, 1925, 280 p.
An important study of Bulgarian policy in the war period. The book is largely a digest of testimony on the causes for Bulgaria's disaster presented to the parliamentary investigating commission.

KEREKOFF, GEORGES. **Les Minorités Étrangères Ethniques et Religieuses en Bulgarie.** Sofia: Imprimerie de la Cour, 1925, 57 p.
A succinct survey of the status of Armenians, Moslems, Greeks, Rumanians, Jews, Catholics and Protestants.

KUHNE, VICTOR, *comp.* **Bulgaria Self-Revealed.** London: Constable, 1919, 292 p.
A picture of Bulgarian war-aims and mentality, based mainly on quotations from Bulgarian sources, which are interpreted in a most hostile sense.

KUNZER, GEORG EUGEN. **Bulgarien.** Gotha: Perthes, 1919, 168 p.
An excellent brief historical and descriptive study, with much emphasis on economic resources and organization.

LAMOUCHE, LÉON. **La Bulgarie.** Paris: Rieder, 1922, 126 p.
A well-documented book, sympathetic with the Bulgarian point of view. The author, long resident in Bulgaria, gives a brief survey of the history and post-war situation.

LOGIO, GEORGE CLENTON. **Bulgaria, Problems and Politics.** London: Heinemann, 1919, 285 p.
A general review of Bulgarian politics before and during the war, by an author violently opposed to Ferdinand and the militarists and warmly sympathetic to Stambuliski and his group.

LONDRES, ALBERT. **Les Comitadjis.** Paris: Michel, 1932, 256 p.
A French journalist's anecdotal but revealing sketch of the formidable I. M. R. O. and its influence in Bulgarian politics.

MADOL, HANS ROGER. **Ferdinand von Bulgarien.** Berlin: Universitäts-Verlag, 1931, 310 p.
An admiring biography of the ex-Tsar, based upon material from the Berlin and Vienna archives and upon information given by Ferdinand himself.

Les Minorités en Bulgarie. Sofia: Association Bulgare pour la Paix, 1927.
A statistical study of nationalities, their location, religion, school arrangements, etc.

NURIGIANI, GIORGIO. **Dieci Anni di Vita Bulgara.** Sofia: no pub., 1931, 224 p.
A survey of the ten years since the peace treaties. The author was press attaché of the Italian Legation at Sofia.

PASVOLSKY, LEO. **Bulgaria's Economic Position.** Washington: Brookings Institution, 1930, 409 p.
This volume gives a complete survey of the subject, with special reference to the reparations problem and the action of the League. One of the excellent studies made by the Brookings Institution.

PETKOF, JOSEPH. **Prix, Circulation et Change en Bulgarie.** Paris: Jouve, 1926, 164 p.
A thesis which gives a convenient survey of Bulgarian price and currency problems from 1890 to 1924.

PETROV, MME. SULTANE. **Trente Ans à la Cour de Bulgarie, 1887-1918.** Paris: Berger-Levrault, 1927, 284 p.
An account of the inside history of the Bulgarian court, covering the years from 1887 to 1918. While interesting in itself it does not add materially to our knowledge of political developments.

POPOFF, KIRIL G. **La Bulgarie Économique, 1879-1911.** Sofia: Imprimerie de la Cour, 1920, 527 p.
An elaborate and scholarly descriptive and analytical study, covering the period from 1879 to the war.

PROST, HENRI. **La Liquidation Financière de la Guerre en Bulgarie.** Paris: Giard, 1925, 232 p.
A useful thesis, making available a good deal of Bulgarian material on the financial and reparations problems.

SAKAZOV, IVAN. **Bulgarische Wirtschaftsgeschichte.** Berlin: De Gruyter, 1929, 294 p.
A valuable pioneer work in a field of which comparatively little is known.

SCIPCOVENSKY, MINKO. **La Bulgaria.** Milan: Alpes, 1931, 400 p.
A general survey of Bulgarian history, with emphasis upon the present reign.

La Situation Financière de la Bulgarie et la Dette Bulgare des Réparations.
Sofia: Commissariat des Réparations, 1923, 126 p.
An official exposé.

SLIVENSKY, IVAN. **La Bulgarie depuis le Traité de Berlin et de la Paix dans les Balkans.** Paris: Jouve, 1927, 222 p.
A good brief survey, rather weak on the war period, but enlightening on the question of Macedonia and relations with Italy, Jugoslavia and Albania.

SOGRAFOFF, A. **Bulgarien unter der Reparation.** Sofia: Glushkov, 1930, 168 p.
The author analyzes the effects of the reparations problem upon the development of Bulgaria since the war.

SPISSAREVSKI, K. D. **La Bulgarie au Travail.** Marseilles: Sémaphore, 1930, 450 p.
An extensive descriptive study of political, economic and social life. Contains an extensive bibliography. Written by a Bulgarian politician and publicist.

STANEV, NIKOLA. **Najnova Istorija na B'lgarija, 1878-1918.** Sofia: no pub., 1924-1925, 2 v.
The best general history of Bulgaria since the Congress of Berlin. Volume II is devoted to the period of the Balkan and World Wars.

STANEV, NIKOLA. **Istoriia na Nova B'lgarija, 1878-1928.** Sofia: Chipev, 1929, 520 p.
A general treatment, briefer than the author's other work, and carried down to 1928.

STEPHANOVE, CONSTANTINE. **The Bulgarians and Anglo-Saxondom.** Berne: Haupt, 1919, 384 p.
Largely a collection of statements from British and American writers supporting Bulgarian claims in 1878 and in later years.

TROTSKIĬ, LEV and KABAKCHIEV, C. **Ocherki Politicheskoĭ Bolgarii.** Moscow: Gosizdat, 1923, 203 p.
Political essays on Bulgarian affairs, as viewed from Moscow.

ZLATANOFF, EMMANOÏL. **La Constitution Bulgare et Ses Principes.** Paris: Labor, 1926, 155 p.
A doctoral dissertation, primarily descriptive and analytical.

ALBANIA

See also (Italy) Policy in the Adriatic, p. 286; also (Jugoslavia) General, p. 407.

ALMAGIÀ, ROBERTO. **L'Albania.** Rome: Cremonese, 1930, 296 p.
A general handbook, containing a good bibliography.

BAERLEIN, HENRY. **A Difficult Frontier.** London: Leonard Parsons, 1922, 155 p.
The general relations between the Serbs and Albanians as a setting for a discussion of the Serbo-Albanian frontier established by the Ambassadors' Conference in November 1921. The author is critical of these boundaries.

BALDACCI, ANTONIO. **L'Albania.** Rome: Istituto per l'Europa Orientale, 1929, 463 p.
A brief and rather inadequate historical introduction, followed by a survey of the minutiæ of present conditions and problems.

BAREILLES, BERTRAND, DURHAM, MARY EDITH and others. **Albania and the Albanians.** Paris: Chapelot, 1920, 73 p.
A general survey of land and people, by sympathetic writers.

BASRÎ BEG, OF DUKAGJIN. **L'Albanie Indépendante et l'Empire Khalifal Ottoman.** Paris: Perrin, 1920, 84 p.
The author was an Ottoman deputy, and afterwards became President of the second Albanian national government, 1915-1916. His book is a rather disjointed study of the development of affairs, together with reminiscences and reflections.

BOURCART, JACQUES. **L'Albanie et les Albanais.** Paris: Bossard, 1921, 264 p.
A former member of the Albanian boundary commission gives a review of conditions at the close of the war.

CASSAVETES, N. J. **Epirus and Albania, 1919.** New York: Oxford University Press, 1919, 172 p.
The Northern Epirus question as it was stated at Paris by Greece, published for the Pan-Epirotic Union of America.

CHEKREZI, CONSTANTIN ANASTASI. **Albania Past and Present.** New York: Macmillan, 1919, 255 p.
Probably the most satisfactory general treatment in English; the expansion of a thesis prepared by an Albanian student at Harvard, with emphasis on events during and just after the World War. The author is now a well-known Albanian journalist.

GIULIANI, SANDRO. **Assestamento e Rinascita dell'Albania.** Milan: Popolo d'Italia, 1929, 102 p.
Italy's share in the reconstruction of Albania.

GODART, JUSTIN. **L'Albanie en 1921.** Paris: Presses Universitaires, 1922, 374 p.
A general study of Albanian history and the struggle for independence, by the sympathetic French minister.

ISMAÏL KÉMAL BEY. **Memoirs.** London: Constable, 1920, 410 p.
A picture of old-school diplomacy by an Albanian statesman, cousin of the Grand Vizier, Ferid Pasha Vlora, and himself at one time in Turkish service. He played an important part in preparing Albanian independence and was Premier in the first cabinet in 1912.

LOUIS, HERBERT. **Albanien.** Stuttgart: Engelhorn, 1927, 164 p.
One of the few up-to-date scientific surveys, largely geographical.

MACCAS, LÉON. **La Question Gréco-Albanaise.** Paris: Berger-Levrault, 1921, 242 p.
The author was the delegate of the Epirotes of America to the Paris Peace Conference. He examines the history of Northern Epirus and adduces documents and opinions to buttress the Greek claim.

MOUSSET, ALBERT. **L'Albanie devant l'Europe.** Paris: Delagrave, 1930, 128 p.
A leading French writer on Balkan affairs reviews the political and social evolution of Albania since 1912, stressing what he regards as the mistaken connection which has been developed with Italy.

NIKITOVIĆ, TCHASLAV M. **L'Affaire du Monastère de Saint-Naoum.** Paris: Jouve, 1927, 144 p.
A study of an important post-war frontier dispute between Jugoslavia and Albania, with an account of the settlement.

NIKOLIĆ, DRAGUTIN. **Les Différends de Frontières de l'Albanie et le Traité Italo-Albanais du 27 Novembre, 1926.** Paris: Pedone, 1927, 231 p.
A study primarily of the legal and territorial status of Albania since 1878, with a discussion of disputes with Jugoslavia, Greece and Italy.

SELENICA, T. **Shqipria më 1927.** Tirana: Shtypshkronja "Tirina," 1928, 573 p.
Albania in 1927, an exhaustive descriptive work.

STICKNEY, EDITH PIERPONT. **Southern Albania or Northern Epirus in European International Affairs, 1912-1923.** Stanford: Stanford University Press, 1926, 195 p.
A painstaking scholarly treatment of the vexed problem of Albanian and Greek claims in Epirus.

STRAVROU, S. **Étude sur l'Albanie.** Paris: no pub., 1922, 226 p.
A dissertation on conditions and problems in Albania, 1878-1922. A work of no great merit, undocumented, but providing occasional interesting details.

SWIRE, JOSEPH. **Albania. The Rise of a Kingdom.** London: Williams and Norgate, 1929, 560 p.
The most extensive history of modern Albania, but in form hardly more than a chronological handbook. The author has used all available authorities and newspapers, but his conclusions are sometimes naïve.

TRAGLIA, GUSTAVO. **L'Albania di Re Zog.** Rome: Tiber, 1930, 160 p.
A general descriptive book.

VUJEVIĆ, ILIJA. **La Question de Scutari.** Paris: Jouve, 1924, 104 p.
A dissertation reviewing the geographical and economic factors and the general history of the question from 1912 to 1918. Rather slight.

GREECE
General

See also (World War) Greek Problem, p. 136; also (Italy) Policy in the Mediterranean and Levant, the Dodecanese, the Malta Question, p. 285; also Albania, p. 416; also (Near East) General, p. 422; also (Turkey) The War with Greece, p. 430.

ALTIAR, EL. **La Tragi-Comédie Grecque.** Paris: Perrin, 1922, 335 p.
Letters on affairs in Greece in 1920-1921, throwing an unfavorable light on the liberal régime.

ALTINOFF, IVAN. **La Thrace Interalliée.** Sofia: Union des Savants, 1922, 295 p.
Written by an attaché of the inter-Allied mission in Thrace in 1919-1920.

ANDREADĒS, ANDREAS MICHAĒL and others. **Les Effets Économiques et Sociaux de la Guerre en Grèce.** New Haven: Yale University Press, 1929, 324 p.
A volume in the Carnegie Series which throws much light on the non-political aspects of the Greek problem.

ANDREW, PRINCE OF GREECE. **Towards Disaster.** London: Murray, 1930, 320 p.
The writer discusses the part played by the army in Greek politics after 1909 and at the same time illuminates the causes of the great disaster in Asia Minor in 1922.

BRISTOYANNIS, DÉMOSTHÈNE GEORGES. **La Politique de la Banque Nationale de Grèce.** Paris: Sagot, 1929, 338 p.
A dissertation which is more than its title implies. The author studies the whole monetary situation from 1914 on.

COUCLÉLIS, ALEXANDRE P. **Les Régimes Gouvernementaux de la Grèce, de 1821 à Nos Jours.** Paris: Sirey, 1921, 159 p.
A review of the constitutional systems of modern Greece, arranged by types, with suggestions regarding a council of state and an upper chamber.

CUNLIFFE-OWEN, BETTY. **Silhouettes of Republican Greece.** London: Hutchinson, 1928, 278 p.
Chats on post-war Greek life and conditions, with special reference to the refugee problem.

DAMIRIS, C. J. **Le Système Monétaire Grec et le Change.** Paris: Giard, 1920, 3 v.
An extraordinarily detailed study, covering chiefly the period from 1910 to 1919.

DERTILIS, PANAGIOTIS B. **La Reconstruction Financière de la Grèce et la Société des Nations.** Paris: Rousseau, 1928, 240 p.
A dissertation reviewing the post-war financial problem and analyzing the League's work. One of the best treatments.

DERTILIS, PANAGIOTIS B. **La Zone Franche de Salonique et les Accords Gréco-Yougoslaves.** Paris: Rousseau, 1928, 89 p.
A legal study, from the Greek point of view, of the recent agreements about the Saloniki free zone.

DEWING, HENRY BRONSON and CAPPS, EDWARD. **Greece and the Great Powers.** Washington: American Friends of Greece, 1924, 96 p.
A brief survey of developments in Greece during and after the war. Really propaganda.

DJIRAS, ALEXANDRE C. **L'Organisation Politique de la Grèce.** Paris: Presses Modernes, 1927, 176 p.
A dissertation analyzing the republican constitution of September 1925.

DRIAULT, ÉDOUARD. **Le Roi Constantin.** Versailles: Author, 1930, 309 p.
An eminent French historian enters the lists in behalf of a much-maligned king. This important book is based in part upon French archive material.

DRIAULT, ÉDOUARD and LHÉRITIER, MICHEL. **Histoire Diplomatique de la Grèce de 1821 à Nos Jours.** Paris: Presses Universitaires, 1925-1926, 5 v.
The standard history of Greek diplomacy, based on extensive use of unpublished French and Greek material. The last volume deals with the years 1908 to 1923.

GLOSE, FRIEDRICH. **Der Griechisch-Bulgarische Streit vor dem Voelkerbundsgerichtshof.** Münster: Helios, 1928, 89 p.
A dissertation analyzing the action of the League in the Greco-Bulgarian dispute of October 1925.

La Grèce. Paris: La Vie Technique, 1927, 150 p.
A general survey, published under the auspices of the Greek Foreign Office.

KAPSALIS, THANOS S. **La Balance des Comptes de la Grèce.** Paris: Payot, 1927, 252 p.
An excellent monograph on the Greek trade balance, giving consideration to trade, funds from emigrants, tourists, etc., as well as debts.

LASTUREL, PIERRE. **L'Affaire Gréco-Italienne de 1923.** Paris: Île de France, 1925, 190 p.
Probably the best monographic treatment of the Corfu affair, based on Greek and League documents, newspapers, etc.

LEWINSOHN, RICHARD. **The Mystery Man of Europe, Sir Basil Zaharoff.** Philadelphia: Lippincott, 1929, 241 p.
A rather over-dramatized life of the Anglo-Greek financier and armaments contractor, with emphasis on his rôle during the war.

LHÉRITIER, MICHEL. **La Grèce.** Paris: Rieder, 1921, 127 p.
A brief historical and descriptive survey, admirably done, by a leading French scholar.

MAVROGORDATO, JOHN. **Modern Greece.** New York: Macmillan, 1931, 251 p.
A good introduction, with emphasis on the war and post-war periods.

MEARS, ELIOT GRINNELL. **Greece Today.** Stanford: Stanford University Press, 1929, 358 p.
An excellent survey setting forth the post-war problems, with emphasis on economic questions.

MILLER, WILLIAM. **A History of the Greek People, 1821-1921.** London: Methuen, 1922, 184 p.
A readable brief summary by a distinguished authority. Over half of the work is devoted to the period since 1878. Moderately philhellenic in tone.

MILLER, WILLIAM. **Greece.** New York: Scribner, 1928, 352 p.
The best single historical treatment in English. This volume, by a well-known historian, is published in the "Modern World" Series.

MOSCHOPOULOS, NICEPHORE. **La Question de Thrace.** Athens: no pub., 1922, 510 p.
Written by a Greek authority on Turkish affairs.

NICHOLAS, PRINCE OF GREECE. **My Fifty Years.** London: Hutchinson, 1926, 328 p.
A moderate book, and a useful antidote to Venezelism.

NICOGLOU, STEPHAN. **L'Affaire de Corfou et la Société des Nations.** Dijon: Rey, 1925, 112 p.
A competent study of the Corfu incident.

PUAUX, RENÉ. **L'Égéide.** Paris: Payot, 1919, 123 p.
The Greek situation and conditions just after the war in the Aegean and among the Greeks of Asia Minor, as described by a *Temps* correspondent.

SARAILIEFF, GEORGES V. **Le Conflit Gréco-Bulgare d'Octobre 1925.** Paris: Berger-Levrault, 1927, 165 p.
A systematic treatment of the dispute and of the work of the League in settling it.

TSOUDEROS, E. J. **Le Relèvement Économique de la Grèce.** Paris: Berger-Levrault, 1919, 254 p.
The author, a member of the Greek delegation to the Peace Conference, describes the economic resources and problems of contemporary Greece.

VILIMANOVIĆ, M. **Zone Libre Serbe à Salonique.** Paris: Rousseau, 1926, 130 p.
An account of Jugoslav commerce through Saloniki, and the negotiations leading up to the 1923 convention between Jugoslavia and Greece.

ZOLOTAS, XENOPHON. **Griechenland auf dem Wege zur Industrialisierung.** Leipzig: Teubner, 1926, 144 p.
A complete though brief survey of the entire economic situation in Greece.

Exchange of Populations

DEIMEZIS, A. **Situation Sociale Créée en Grèce à la Suite de l'Échange des Populations.** Paris: Budry, 1927, 83 p.
A dissertation, with the usual defects, but bringing together valuable material on the method of colonization, resultant financial difficulties, the Greek political crisis, etc.

DEVEDJI, ALEXANDRE. **L'Échange Obligatoire des Minorités Grecques et Turques.** Paris: Éditions et Publications Contemporaines, 1930, 230 p.
A dissertation which gives a brief historical account of the Greeks in the Ottoman Empire and then analyzes the Lausanne Convention of January 30, 1923.

EDDY, CHARLES B. **Greece and the Greek Refugees.** London: Allen and Unwin, 1931, 280 p.
The last head of the Greek Refugee Settlement Commission gives a dispassionate account of the problems with which he became familiar during his service in Greece.

KIOSSÉOGLOU, TH. P. **L'Échange Forcé des Minorités d'après le Traité de Lausanne.** Nancy: Imprimerie Nanceienne, 1926, 218 p.
A doctoral thesis; primarily an analysis of the convention of January 30, 1923.

LADAS, STEPHEN PERICLES. **The Exchange of Minorities.** New York: Macmillan, 1932, 847 p.
The best and most complete account of the exchange of populations between Greece, Bulgaria and Turkey. Future writers are unlikely to be able to add much to the factual material or seriously question the author's scholarship. With maps and bibliography.

MACARTNEY, CARLILE AYLMER. **Refugees.** London: League of Nations Union, 1931, 127 p.
A compact survey of the exchange of populations between Greece and Bulgaria.

MORGENTHAU, HENRY. **I Was Sent to Athens.** New York: Doubleday, 1929, 327 p.
A eulogy of Greek post-war achievements, and of the work of the Greek Refugee Settlement Commission, by that body's first chairman.

WURFBAIN, ANDRÉ. **L'Échange Gréco-Bulgare des Minorités Ethniques.** Paris: Payot, 1930, 217 p.
A competent general study of the problem, now more or less superseded by Ladas' exhaustive treatment.

SIXTH PART:
ASIA

I. NEAR EAST
GENERAL

See also (World War) Near and Middle Eastern Front, p. 137; also (Russia) Foreign Policy, p. 393.

ALLEN, WILLIAM EDWARD DAVID. **The Turks in Europe.** New York: Scribner, 1920, 256 p.
The briefest sort of outline of the Ottoman Empire. Best on the period 1875 to 1914.

ANCEL, JACQUES. **Manuel Historique de la Question d'Orient, 1792-1930.** Paris: Delagrave, 1931, 386 p.
The fourth edition of a standard, conventional textbook.

BARTON, JAMES LEVI. **Story of Near East Relief.** New York: Macmillan, 1930, 501 p.
A complete record of a stupendous philanthropic enterprise.

BASRÎ BEG, OF DUKAGJIN. **Le Monde Oriental et l'Avenir de la Paix.** Paris: Perrin, 1920, 320 p.
Consideration of many Near Eastern problems by an Albanian Turk with Entente sympathies.

BURRIDGE, J. H. **Near East Politics and the Bible.** Birmingham: Old Gospel Press, 1930, 152 p.
The title indicates the nature of the book.

CHIROL, SIR VALENTINE. **The Occident and the Orient.** Chicago: Chicago University Press, 1924, 228 p.
Lectures by one of the most competent authorities on the Near East.

COSTOPOULO, STAVRO. **L'Empire de l'Orient.** Paris: Île de France, 1925, 263 p.
A very sketchy history of the Eastern question with particular emphasis on ethnic, economic and geographical factors.

DAVIS, WILLIAM STEARNS. **A Short History of the Near East.** New York: Macmillan, 1922, 408 p.
An interestingly written, if not authoritative, narrative. Unsatisfactory on the modern period.

DRIAULT, ÉDOUARD. **La Grande Idée, la Renaissance de l'Hellénisme.** Paris: Alcan, 1920, 242 p.
A misleading title. The book is really an outline of the Eastern question, with special reference to Greek aspirations and French and German policy.

DRIAULT, ÉDOUARD. **La Question d'Orient.** Paris: Alcan, 1921, 479 p.
The eighth and latest edition of the best-known French manual, carrying the story to 1920.

DURDENEVSKIĬ, VSEVOLOD NIKOLAEVICH and LUDSHUVEĬT, E. F. **Konstitutsii Vostoka.** Moscow: Gosizdat, 1926, 180 p.
The constitutions of Egypt, Turkey, Persia, Afghanistan, India, China, Mongolia and Japan.

FILIPPUCCI-GIUSTINIANI, G. **Dieci Anni di Viaggi Politici in Oriente: Turchia, Grecia, Egitto, Palestina, Siria, 1914-1924.** Rome: Egeria, 1924, 300 p.
Discerning observations on life in the old Ottoman Empire, mainly during the war period.

FORBES, MRS. ROSITA (TORR). **Conflict: Angora to Afghanistan.** New York: Stokes, 1931, 333 p.
Racial, religious, political and social conflicts in the new Near East, as seen by an indefatigable traveller in Turkey, Syria, Palestine, Iraq, Persia and the Transcaucasus region.

GURKO-KRIAZHIN, V. A. **Blizhnii Vostok i Derzhavy.** Moscow: Nauchnaia Assotsiatsiia Vostokovedeniia, 1925, 243 p.
The story of international rivalries and capitalist exploitation in the Near East before and during the war, and the development of modern Turkey and Arabia. A well-documented communist account.

HANS, JOSEF. **Geld und Gold in Asien.** Vienna: Author, 1930, 148 p.
An account of the currencies of the Near, Middle and Far Eastern countries. A unique volume.

HOCKING, WILLIAM ERNEST. **The Spirit of World Politics.** New York: Macmillan, 1932, 585 p.
Largely an examination of the situation in Egypt, Syria and Palestine, with a plea for the redefinition of the West's relationship to the so-called backward peoples.

IKBĀL 'ALĪ SHĀH, SIRDAR. **Westward to Mecca.** London: Witherby, 1928, 224 p.
Thrilling adventures in Afghanistan, Turkestan, Persia, Iraq and Hejaz. The author throws light on the Bolshevik régime on the Indian frontier.

KOHN, HANS. **A History of Nationalism in the East.** New York: Harcourt, 1929, 476 p.
One of the few really outstanding books on recent developments in the Near East and India. The work is based throughout on sound knowledge of the history and literature of this area and is buttressed with an extensive bibliography which is almost unique in this field. The discussion of the position of the Great Powers, like Great Britain and Russia, is especially illuminating, and is presented with great detachment.

KOHN, HANS. **Nationalism and Imperialism in the Hither East.** New York: Harcourt, 1932, 347 p.
In this second book the author touches on some of the great forces in the Near East, and then reviews the situation in Egypt, Palestine, Syria, Iraq and Arabia since 1914.

LAURENT-VIBERT, ROBERT. **Ce Que J'Ai Vu en Orient.** Paris: Crès, 1924, 303 p.
A survey of political conditions in the Near East by a French nationalist.

LODER, JOHN DE VERE. **The Truth about Mesopotamia, Palestine and Syria.** London: Allen and Unwin, 1923, 221 p.
A non-controversial study of the Arab movement during the war and the effects of the peace settlements in Syria, Mesopotamia and Palestine. A commendably sound introduction.

LUQUET, JEAN. **La Politique des Mandats dans le Levant.** Paris: Éditions de la Vie Universitaire, 1924, 284 p.
The Near East mandates and the clash of Anglo-French interests.

LYAUTEY, PIERRE. **Le Drame Oriental et le Rôle de la France.** Paris: Société d'Éditions Géographiques Maritimes et Coloniales, 1924, 259 p.
A history of the struggles of Germany and England for the hegemony of the Near East, with a plea for a more determined French policy.

MARRIOTT, SIR JOHN ARTHUR RANSOME. **The Eastern Question.** New York: Oxford University Press, 1930, 564 p.
The third and latest edition of a well-known text.

MATHEWS, BASIL. **The Riddle of Nearer Asia.** New York: Doran, 1919, 216 p.
A handbook for missionaries, containing much useful information, but colored by anti-Turkish bias.

MOTT, JOHN RALEIGH, *ed.* **The Moslem World of To-day.** New York: Doran, 1925, 435 p.
An excellent study from the non-political standpoint, edited by a Y. M. C. A. leader.

NEWMAN, EDWARD WILLIAM POLSON. **The Middle East.** London: Bles, 1926, 300 p.
This volume, written by a war correspondent during the Syrian rising of 1925, gives an interesting survey of the situation in Palestine, Syria, Transjordania, Iraq and Persia.

PASSIDIS, AUGUSTIN. **La Question d'Orient et la Grèce.** Paris: Presses Modernes, 1929, 339 p.
A perfectly conventional account of the Eastern question since the Greek War of Independence, with more detailed treatment of Greek-Turkish disputes.

POWELL, EDWARD ALEXANDER. **The Struggle for Power in Moslem Asia.** New York: Century, 1924, 320 p.
A review of the situation by an experienced correspondent, and at the same time a telling attack upon the anti-Turk imperialism of the Powers, especially England.

RAFAIL, M. **Blizhniĭ Vostok.** Moscow: Gosizdat, 1926, 266 p.
The third edition of a standard Russian survey of the Near Eastern situation after the war.

RIHBANY, ABRAHAM MITRIE. **Wise Men from the East and from the West.** Boston: Houghton Mifflin, 1922, 309 p.
A somewhat mystical defense of the civilization of the hither Orient, attacking western imperialism and discussing in detail the situation in Western Asia since the Peace Conference.

ROSS, FRANK ALEXANDER and others. **The Near East and American Philanthropy.** New York: Columbia University Press, 1929, 321 p.
A survey of conditions in all the countries of the Near East, drawn up under the auspices of Near East Relief as a basis for a program of further work.

Der Vordere Orient. Königsberg: Gräfe und Unzer, 1931, 140 p.
A collection of lectures by authorities, including Bergsträsser, Hartmann and Lohr.

WRATISLAW, ALBERT CHARLES. **A Consul in the East.** London: Blackwood, 1924, 361 p.
A well-written book, important for a knowledge of recent diplomacy and the prominent figures of the day in the Near East.

WYON, O. **An Eastern Palimpsest.** London: World Dominion Press, n. d., 115 p.
An admirable missionary survey of Turkey, Syria, Palestine, Transjordania and Egypt.

ISLAM; THE CALIPHATE

ABBAS, M. H. **All about the Khalifat.** Calcutta: Ray and Ray Choudhury, 1924, 368 p.
The problem of the Caliphate from the point of view of an Indian Moslem.

UN AFRICAIN, *pseud.* **Manuel de Politique Musulmane.** Paris: Bossard, 1924, 190 p.
An indispensable handbook for those interested in Moslem countries.

AMĪR'ALĪ, MAULAVĪ SǍIYID. **The Spirit of Islam.** New York: Doran, 1923, 515 p.
The rôle of Mohammedanism in religious and political history as described by a pro-Islamic writer.

ARNOLD, SIR THOMAS WALKER. **The Caliphate.** Oxford: Clarendon Press, 1924, 223 p.
The most competent and one of the most recent historical studies of the Caliphate as an institution.

CHAUVELOT, ROBERT. **Où Va l'Islam?** Paris: Tallandier, 1931, 194 p.
A review of the situation in Turkey, Syria, Palestine, Egypt and Morocco as it touches on the relations of Moslem and Christian.

INSABATO, ENRICO. **L'Islam et la Politique des Alliés.** Paris: Berger-Levrault, 1920, 265 p.
This book has little to do with the Allies. The author surveys important currents in Islam, such as mysticism, schismatic movements and orthodoxy.

JUNG, EUGÈNE. **L'Islam et l'Asie devant l'Impérialisme.** Paris: Marpon, 1927, 316 p.
The writer predicts a war of races and religions unless more consideration is introduced into the relations of the western nations with the so-called backward peoples.

LAMMENS, HENRI. **Islam: Beliefs and Institutions.** London: Methuen, 1929, 256 p.
An excellent survey of the history of Islam, its institutions, sects, movements, etc.

O'LEARY, DE LACY EVANS. **Islam at the Cross-Roads.** New York: Dutton, 1923, 218 p.
A suggestive analysis of the newer tendencies in the Mohammedan world and of European methods in dealing with Islam.

PERNOT, MAURICE. **En Asie Musulmane.** Paris: Hachette, 1927, 243 p.
A competent French writer records conditions in the Middle East. A valuable book, in spite of its pronounced anti-English bias.

REDAN, PIERRE, *pseud.* (PIERRE J. ANDRÉ). **L'Islam et les Races.** Paris: Geuthner, 1922, 2 v.
A curious medley of religious and political studies of the Islamic countries, by one who has travelled widely in the Near East.

SABA, JEAN S. **L'Islam et la Nationalité.** Paris: Chauny et Quinsac, 1931, 166 p.
A keen analysis of the difficulties in the way of nationalism in Islamic countries.

SANHOURY, A. **Le Califat.** Paris: Geuthner, 1926, 627 p.
One of the best books on the Caliphate, dealing with its doctrine and history and attempting a forecast of the future.

SÉKALY, ACHILLE. **Le Congrès du Khalifat.** Paris: Leroux, 1927, 220 p.
A report of the Caliphate congress at Cairo in May 1926 and the Congress of the Moslem World in June 1926.

STODDARD, LOTHROP. **The New World of Islam.** New York: Scribner, 1921, 362 p.
A broad essay on Moslem conditions and problems in the post-war period. Stimulating and often suggestive.

VÁLYI, FÉLIX. **Spiritual and Political Revolutions in Islam.** London: Kegan Paul, 1925, 240 p.
A sympathetic but not profound account of the regeneration of Turkey, stressing particularly its spiritual aspects.

ZINGARELLI, ITALO. **Il Risveglio dell'Islam.** Milan: Treves, 1928, 261 p.
Though not particularly novel, the theme of the Mohammedan revival is treated in this book with moderation and understanding.

ZWEMER, SAMUEL MARINUS. **Across the World of Islam.** New York: Revell, 1929, 382 p.
The editor of the *Moslem World* reviews the problems arising from the awakening of the Moslem masses.

TURKEY

General

See also (World War) Dardanelles, p. 135, and Near and Middle Eastern Front, p. 137.

ARMSTRONG, HAROLD. **Turkey in Travail.** London: Lane, 1925, 292 p.
A most valuable record of experiences and observations in Turkey between 1916 and 1923, by an English officer captured at Kut.

ARMSTRONG, HAROLD. **Turkey and Syria Reborn.** London: Lane, 1930, 270 p.
In this later volume the author sums up his impressions of two more years of travel. This is one of the soundest accounts of the present stage in Turkish and Syrian development.

BELLO, C. **Notes et Réflexions sur la Turquie.** Paris: Rivière, 1920, 123 p.
The book is largely a discussion of English and French policy, with special reference to the fate of Constantinople.

BRERETON, FREDERICK SADLEIR. **On the Road to Bagdad.** London: Blackie, 1929, 384 p.
Travel impressions of a former medical officer in the British army.

DJEMAL, AHMAD, PASHA. **Memories of a Turkish Statesman, 1913-1919.** New York: Doran, 1922, 302 p.
The most important volume of memoirs about Turkey in the war period, written by one of the controlling Triumvirate.

ELLISON, GRACE. **An Englishwoman in Angora.** New York: Dutton, 1923, 344 p.
A light-hearted account of a journey through Asia Minor, full of observations of an interesting if not very profound nature.

ELLISON, GRACE. **Turkey Today.** London: Hutchinson, 1928, 288 p.
An enthusiastic picture of Turkey under the new régime.

EMIN, AHMED. **Turkey in the World War.** New Haven: Yale University Press, 1930, 310 p.
This volume in the Carnegie Series fills an important gap in the history of the Near East. After tracing the breakdown of the old régime and the rise of the Young Turks, the author surveys economic aspects of the war, takes up the racial problems, the questions of reform, education and health, and ends with a succinct analysis of the new nationalist movement. An invaluable book for students of Near Eastern affairs.

EVERSLEY, GEORGE JOHN SHAW-LEFEVRE, BARON and CHIROL, SIR VALENTINE. **The Turkish Empire.** London: T. Fisher Unwin, 1923, 456 p.
A new edition of a general narrative. The second part, by Chirol, covers the period 1914-1922.

FIKRY, FÉRIDOUN. **Le Mouvement Constitutionnel en Turquie et la Loi sur l'Organisation Fondamentale d'Angora.** Paris: Presses Universitaires, 1923, 98 p.
A doctoral thesis reviewing the constitution of 1876 and its modifications in 1909 and 1912, and then analyzing the present Organic Law.

FRANCO, GAD. **Développements Constitutionnels en Turquie.** Paris: Rousseau, 1926, 160 p.
A fairly good historical sketch of Ottoman constitutional development in the 19th and 20th centuries, with most space devoted to the work of Midhat Pasha, the Organic Law, the abolition of the Caliphate, and the Angora Constitution of 1924.

GAILLARD, GASTON. **Les Turcs et l'Europe.** Paris: Chapelot, 1920, 384 p.
A general, well-informed history of Turkey in the war period, the collapse of the Empire, and its dismemberment.

GENTIZON, PAUL. **Mustapha Kemal ou l'Orient en Marche.** Paris: Bossard, 1929, 350 p.
A well-known French publicist, who has been a resident in the Near East for years, traces the whole Turkish revival, which, he believes, is profound and genuine.

GEORGES-GAULIS, BERTHE. **Angora, Constantinople, Londres; Moustafa Kémal et la Politique Anglaise en Orient.** Paris: Colin, 1922, 257 p.
A brilliant account of the rise and success of the Turkish nationalist movement.

GEORGES-GAULIS, BERTHE. **La Question Turque.** Paris: Berger-Levrault, 1931, 376 p.
Madame Gaulis is one of the most interesting writers on Near Eastern affairs. In this volume she reviews the events in Turkey since the end of the war.

GURKO-KRIAZHIN, V. A. **Istoriia Revoliutsii v Turtsii.** Moscow: Mir, 1923, 195 p.
A general survey of the Turkish nationalist movement and the revolution, by a well-informed Soviet writer.

HĀLIDAH ADĪB, KHĀNUM. **Turkey Faces West.** New Haven: Yale University Press, 1930, 273 p.
A Turkish feminist reviews briefly the rise and evolution of the Ottoman power and the problems raised by the infiltration of western influence since the later eighteenth century. Full of condemnation for the régime of Abdul Hamid, she discusses in a dispassionate way the Young Turk movement, the tribulations of the war period and the rise of the new nationalist movement. Stress is laid less on political developments than on the vicissitudes of the Turkish people and their cultural progress.

HĀLIDAH ADĪB, KHĀNUM. **The Turkish Ordeal.** New York: Century, 1928, 407 p.
The second volume of the memoirs of a prominent Turkish feminist, covering the period of the national revival.

HOWARD, HARRY. **The Partition of Turkey, 1913-1923.** Norman: University of Oklahoma Press, 1913, 486 p.
A careful study of the immense amount of diplomatic correspondence published during the period in question. The author takes up the situation on the eve of the war, Turkey's entrance into the conflict, the Constantinople Treaty, the claims of the Balkan states, the secret treaties and the attempts to realize upon them, the Greek-Turkish conflict, the Lausanne negotiations, and the mandates. The author is not very successful in synthesizing his material.

IASHUNSKIĬ, M. S. and LUDSHUVEĬT, E. F. **Ocherk Gosudarstvennogo Ustroĭstva Turetskoĭ Respubliki.** Moscow: Nauchnaia Assotsiatsiia Vostokovedeniia, 1925, 70 p.
A careful study of the constitution and administrative system of the new Turkey.

IZZET, AHMED, PASHA. **Denkwürdigkeiten.** Leipzig: Koehler, 1927, 309 p.
The memoirs of the former Turkish Chief of Staff and Grand Vizir. An important volume for the study of the last twenty years of Turkish history.

JÄSCHKE, GOTTHARD and PRITSCH, ERICH. **Die Türkei seit dem Weltkriege.** Berlin: Deutsche Gesellschaft für Islamkunde, 1929, 154 p.
A valuable chronology of events from 1918 to 1928, supplemented with a bibliography and political handbook. There have been supplements since 1928.

JOHNSON, CLARENCE RICHARD, *ed.* **Constantinople To-day.** New York: Macmillan, 1922, 418 p.
A sociological study of the pivotal area of the Near East, with chapters on special aspects by various authors.

KIAZIM, OMER. **L'Aventure Kémaliste.** Paris: Éditions Universelles, 1921, 106 p.
The author stresses the danger of Kemalism for Europe as well as for the Near East.

LEVONIAN, LUTFĪ. **The Moslem Mind.** Boston: Pilgrim Press, 1929, 245 p.
An unusual and highly interesting discussion of Turkish mentality and the background of recent changes, by the Dean of the School of Religion at Athens.

LOTI, PIERRE, *pseud.* (JULIEN VIAUD). **La Mort de Notre Chère France en Orient.** Paris: Calmann-Lévy, 1920, 295 p.
Described by the famous author as "an incoherent mass of documents and testimony," all of it designed to save the Turk and effect a change in French policy.

LUKE, HARRY CHARLES. **Anatolica.** London: Macmillan, 1924, 210 p.
A descriptive book of high merit on Cyprus, Asia Minor and the Caucasus area.

MARCHAND, RENÉ. **Le Réveil d'une Race.** Paris: Nouvelle Société d'Éditions, 1927, 229 p.
The well-known French radical returns, duly impressed, from a visit to the land of Mustapha Kemal Pasha.

MARY-ROUSSELIÈRE, ANDRÉ. **La Turquie Constitutionnelle.** Rennes: Imprimeries Réunies, 1925, 360 p.
A dissertation giving an historical account of Turkish constitutional development from 1876 to 1924 against the background of general domestic politics.

MARZIO, CORNELIO DI. **La Turchia di Kemal.** Milan: Alpes, 1926, 326 p.
A general account of conditions, with useful maps and statistics.

MEARS, ELIOT GRINNELL. **Modern Turkey.** New York: Macmillan, 1924, 779 p.
A coöperative work, perhaps the most useful book on modern Turkey in English.

MÉLIA, JEAN. **Mustapha Kémal; ou, La Rénovation de la Turquie.** Paris: Fasquelle, 1929, 240 p.
A sympathetic study of the dictator and of his reforming activities, by the former director of the French commissariat in Syria.

MIKUSCH, DAGOBERT VON. **Mustapha Kemal.** New York: Doubleday, 1931, 390 p.
Probably the best biography of Mustapha yet published, based upon Turkish as well as western sources, and viewing his career in the general setting of the last twenty-five years of Turkish history.

MILLER, WILLIAM. **The Ottoman Empire and Its Successors, 1801-1927.** Cambridge: Cambridge University Press, 1927, 616 p.
The revision of one of the standard English books on the subject, crammed with factual material. The author stresses Greek aspects somewhat heavily.

MUFTY-ZADE, K. ZIA, BEY. **Speaking of the Turks.** New York: Duffield, 1922, 271 p.
A young Turk, resident ten years in the United States, goes back to Constantinople and describes the changes since the war in Turkish habits and outlook.

MUSTAFĀ KĀMAL, PASHA. **Die Neue Türkei, 1919-1927.** Leipzig: Koehler, 1929, 397 p.
The famous speech of 1927, in which the national leader reviews the whole rise and establishment of the new régime.

NAHID, HACHIM. **Les Symptômes de la Crise Turque et Son Remède.** Paris: Librairie Philosophique, 1931, 88 p.
A telling critique and exposé of the weaknesses of the new Turkish régime.

OSTRORÓG, LEON, HRABIA. **The Angora Reform.** London: University of London Press, 1928, 99 p.
Three splendid lectures, in which the author reviews the rise of Turkish nationalism resulting from the treaty of Sèvres, discusses the reasons for the overthrow of the Sultanate, and surveys the great reforms.

PAILLARÈS, MICHEL. **Le Kémalisme devant les Alliés.** Constantinople: Édition du Bosphore, 1922, 494 p.
The Kemalist movement, the Treaty of Sèvres and the Angora Pact, described in a rather rambling way by an observer who saw in Turkish nationalism a grave menace.

PERNOT, MAURICE. **La Question Turque.** Paris: Grasset, 1923, 320 p.
An able analysis of the Turkish problem indicating the conditions believed essential to Turkish stability and prosperity. Written by a French correspondent.

PITTARD, EUGÈNE. **Le Visage Nouveau de la Turquie.** Paris: Société d'Éditions Géographiques, 1930, 314 p.
A well-known geographer surveys Asia Minor and estimates the accomplishments of the present Turkish government.

PRICE, CLAIR. **The Rebirth of Turkey.** New York: Seltzer, 1923, 234 p.
A survey of the development of the new régime in Turkey from 1908 to 1923. One of the best of the earlier books.

REDAN, PIERRE, *pseud.* (PIERRE J. ANDRÉ). **La Cilicie et le Problème Ottoman.** Paris: Gauthier-Villars, 1921, 144 p.
An argument for a more vigorous French policy in the Levant and against the abandonment of Cilicia.

SCHLICKLIN, JEAN. **Angora: l'Aube de la Turquie Nouvelle, 1919-1922.** Paris: Berger-Levrault, 1923, 349 p.
An excellent account of the Turkish revival and of the new statesmen and the new policies, by a fervent admirer of Mustapha Kemal.

SHERIDAN, MRS. CLARE (FREWEN). **The Turkish Kaleidoscope.** London: Duckworth, 1926, 223 p.
Disillusioning sidelights on conditions in present-day Turkey.

TOYNBEE, ARNOLD JOSEPH. **The Western Question in Greece and Turkey.** London: Constable, 1922, 420 p.
An indispensable book, stressing the growing Oriental impatience with Western interference, and indicating the disastrous results of Allied bungling in the Near East.

TOYNBEE, ARNOLD JOSEPH and KIRKWOOD, KENNETH. **Turkey.** New York: Scribner, 1927, 329 p.
A valuable though not entirely impartial account of happenings, chiefly since the nationalist revival. A volume in the "Modern World" series.

WAUGH, SIR TELFORD. **Turkey: Yesterday, To-day, and To-morrow.** London: Chapman and Hall, 1930, 306 p.
A former British consul-general at Constantinople reviews his experiences over a long period of service in Turkey. A valuable and interesting book.

WILLIAMS, TALCOTT. **Turkey, a World Problem of To-day.** New York: Doubleday, 1921, 336 p.
Based upon Lowell Lectures, this book discusses the history of Islam and Turkey, the governmental system, national problems, etc.

WORTHAM, HUGH EVELYN. **Mustapha Kemal of Turkey.** Boston: Little, Brown, 1931, 258 p.
A rather slight, but spirited biographical sketch of Mustapha's checkered career.

ZIEMKE, KURT. **Die Neue Türkei.** Berlin: Deutsche Verlagsanstalt, 1930, 550 p.
Probably the best systematic scholarly history of Turkey since 1914.

Economic and Financial Problems

ALPHAND, HERVÉ. **Le Partage de la Dette Ottomane et Son Règlement.** Paris: Éditions Internationales, 1928, 207 p.
An historical outline of the post-war problem of the Ottoman Debt and the efforts made to solve it.

BLAISDELL, DONALD CHRISTY. **European Financial Control in the Ottoman Empire.** New York: Columbia University Press, 1929, 243 p.
Based upon unpublished papers in the archives of the Ottoman Public Debt Commission. A most important study of European financial control in the Near East before the war.

MOUHIDDIN, TAHSIN. **La Réforme Financière en Turquie.** Paris: Rousseau, 1930, 224 p.
A scientific study of the Turkish monetary problem.

MOUTAL, MOSCHÉ. **L'Avenir Économique de la Turquie Nouvelle.** Paris: Jouve, 1924, 222 p.
This thesis merely digests the material on agriculture, mines and industry contained in standard works of earlier date.

RASCHID, SCHEWKET. **Die Türkische Landwirtschaft als Grundlage der Türkischen Volkswirtschaft.** Berlin: De Gruyter, 1932, 202 p.
A competent if rather ponderous treatise on Turkish economy and the outlook for agricultural development.

ROUMANI, ADIB. **Essai Historique et Technique sur la Dette Publique Ottomane.** Paris: Imprimerie Administrative, 1927, 332 p.
A dissertation reviewing the Ottoman debts since the Crimean War and especially the decree of Moharrem. The later period is only sketchily treated.

The War with Greece and the Lausanne Treaty

See also (World War) Greek Problem, p. 136; also (Greece) General, p. 418, and Exchange of Populations, p. 420.

BAREILLES, BERTRAND. **D'Athènes à Angora. Le Drame Oriental.** Paris: Bossard, 1923, 272 p.
A French journalist's account of the Greek campaign.

BUJAC, ÉMILE. **Les Campagnes de l'Armée Hellénique, 1918-1922.** Paris: Lavauzelle, 1930, 348 p.
The best general account of the Greek campaigns in Asia Minor from 1918 to 1922.

COLRAT, RAYMOND. **Lausanne et les Vieillards.** Paris: Librairie Littéraire et Scientifique, 1923.
A vigorous criticism of the diplomacy at the Lausanne Conference.

DOURMOUSSIS, EVDOKIMOS. **La Vérité sur un Drame Historique.** Paris: Coffin, 1928, 160 p.
An indictment of the Turks in the matter of the Smyrna catastrophe.

DUFAYARD, CHARLES. **L'Asie Mineure et l'Hellénisme.** Paris: Alcan, 1919, 103 p.
The ethnological, historical, economic and moral claims of the Greeks.

GEORGES-GAULIS, BERTHE. **La Nouvelle Turquie.** Paris: Colin, 1924, 282 p.
Further observations on the Turkish situation, with special reference to the Greek disaster and the two Lausanne Conferences.

GONTAUT-BIRON, ROGER DE, COMTE and LE RÉVÉREND, L. **D'Angora à Lausanne.**
Paris: Plon, 1925, 230 p.
An attack on Allied and especially British policy, with a discussion of problems left
unsettled at Lausanne.

HORTON, GEORGE. **The Blight of Asia.** Indianapolis: Bobbs, 1926, 292 p.
An unvarnished account of the massacres and the burning of Smyrna, by an American
consul in the Near East.

The Lausanne Treaty and Kemalist Turkey. New York: American Committee for
the Independence of Armenia, 1924, 79 p.
A collection of violently anti-Turkish papers.

The Lausanne Treaty, Turkey and Armenia. New York: American Committee Opposed to the Lausanne Treaty, 1926, 204 p.
A number of vigorous statements against the treaty, by American men of affairs.

MACCAS, LÉON. **L'Hellénisme de l'Asie Mineure.** Paris: Berger-Levrault, 1919, 233 p.
Chiefly a history of the Greeks of Asia Minor. High-grade propaganda to support the
Greek claims.

NICOL, E. **Angora et la France.** Paris: Société Générale d'Imprimerie, 1922, 200 p.
A reply to Franklin-Bouillon.

OECONOMOS, LYSIMACHOS, *comp.* **The Martyrdom of Smyrna and Eastern Christen-
dom.** London: Allen and Unwin, 1923, 237 p.
A Greek scholar's vigorous indictment of Turkish activities in Asia Minor, assigning
responsibility in part to Allied diplomacy.

PAVLOVICH, M., *pseud.* (MIKHAIL VEL'TMAN), GURKO-KRIAZHIN, V. A. and RASKOL'NIKOV, F.
Turtsiia v Bor'be za Nezavisimost'. Moscow: Nauchnaia Assotsiatsiia Vostokovedeniia, 1925, 152 p.
One of the series of studies of nationalist movements published by a group of competent Russian writers.

PECH, EDGAR. **Les Alliés et la Turquie.** Paris: Presses Universitaires, 1925, 267 p.
Letters from Turkey covering the period from 1918 to 1925 and dealing largely with
French policy before and after Lausanne.

Foreign Policy; the Straits Question; the Capitulations

ABELOUS, FRÉDÉRIC. **L'Évolution de la Turquie dans Ses Rapports avec les Étrangers.** Paris: Rivière, 1928, 297 p.
The author studies in detail the capitulatory system, its final abolition and the present
status of foreigners. A better thesis than most.

ABI-CHAHLA, HABIB. **L'Extinction des Capitulations en Turquie et dans les
Régions Arabes.** Paris: Picart, 1924, 333 p.
A discussion of the capitulations as an anachronism in international law.

GRAVES, PHILIP PERCEVAL. **The Question of the Straits.** London: Benn, 1931, 216 p.
A brief and rather sketchy survey of the development of the Straits Question from
earliest times to the present.

KABBARA, SAMY. **Le Régime des Détroits avant et depuis le Traité de Lausanne.**
Lyon: Bosc, 1929, 172 p.
A dissertation outlining and analyzing the modern agreements on the Straits.

KIAZIM, OMER. **Angora et Berlin: Le Complot Germano-Kémaliste contre le Traité de Versailles.** Paris: L'Édition Universelle, 1922, 174 p.
Recent Near Eastern diplomacy treated from the anti-German point of view.

KRÜGER, KARL. **Kemalist Turkey and the Middle East.** London: Allen and Unwin, 1932, 224 p.
The best parts of this volume are the chapters dealing with Turkey's relations with Russia and her neighbors to the south and east. The sections on economic problems rely too uncritically on Turkish statistics.

MAZARD, JEAN ALBERT. **Le Régime des Capitulations en Turquie pendant la Guerre de 1914.** Algiers: Gaudet, 1923, 259 p.
A doctoral dissertation, giving a useful review of the problem during the war, and down to the Lausanne settlement.

MILEV, MILU. **La Bulgarie et les Détroits.** Paris: Jouve, 1927, 196 p.
A recapitulation of the evolution of the problem since 1878. The author of this thesis regards Bulgarian policy as revolving around the Straits Question and the attitude of the Powers towards it.

ROTSTEÏN, F., *ed.* **Proliyi.** Moscow: Krasnaia Nov', 1923, 101 p.
Five essays by various Soviet authors. They deal with the Constantinople and Black Sea problems and with the economic aspects of the Straits Question.

SCHLESINGER, NATHAN. **Le Nouveau Régime des Détroits.** Paris: Jouve, 1926, 119 p.
A doctoral thesis dealing chiefly with the legal aspects of the Lausanne settlement.

Armenia

See also (World War) Near and Middle Eastern Front, p. 137; also (Russia) Ukraine, Georgia and Other Divisions of the Union, p. 396.

ASLAN, KEVORK. **Armenia and the Armenians.** New York: Macmillan, 1920, 138 p.
A brief but reliable sketch of Armenian history from the beginning to the World War.

BARRY, H. **Les Extravagances Bolcheviques et l'Épopée Arménienne. Paris:** Michel, 1919.
A general account of the Armenian Question in the stormy post-war period.

BASMADJIAN, K. J. **Histoire Moderne des Arméniens, 1375-1920.** Paris: Gamber, 1922.
Generally reliable, if somewhat nationalistic in tone. The best brief introduction.

BOR'IAN, B. A. **Armeniia, Mezhdunarodnaia Diplomatiia i S. S. S. R.** Moscow: Gosizdat, 1928-1929, 2 v.
An exhaustive treatment of the Armenian question from the beginning, the diplomacy of the Powers and the policy of the Bolsheviks.

BURTT, JOSEPH. **The People of Ararat.** London: Hogarth, 1926, 184 p.
A brief and very sympathetic account of the vicissitudes of the Armenians.

CHAMBERS, WILLIAM NESBITT. **Yoljuluk; Random Thoughts on a Life in Imperial Turkey.** London: Simpkin, Marshall, 1929, 125 p.
Memoirs of thirty years of missionary activity in Armenia and Kurdistan.

ELLIOTT, MABEL EVELYN. **Beginning Again at Ararat.** New York: Revell, 1924, 341 p.
The experiences of a medical adviser of the Near East Relief in Armenia and the Caucasus.

IORGA, NICOLAE. **L'Arménie Cilicienne.** Paris: Gamber, 1930, 160 p.
Historical lectures on Little Armenia, by the noted Rumanian historian.

KRISCHTSCHIAN, MELKON. **Deutschland und die Ausrottung der Armenier in der Türkei.** Potsdam: Missionshandlung, 1930, 94 p.
A volume exonerating the Germans of any responsibility in the Armenian massacres.

LEPSIUS, JOHANNES, *ed.* **Deutschland und Armenien, 1914-1918.** Berlin: Tempelverlag, 1919, 541 p.
The German reports on the great massacres during the war, published by a persistent pacifist and champion of the Armenians.

MACLER, FRÉDÉRIC. **La Nation Arménienne.** Paris: Fischbacher, 1923, 110 p.
A brilliant synthesis of Armenian history and culture, by an eminent scholar.

MANDEL'SHTAM, ANDREÏ NIKOLAEVICH. **Das Armenische Problem im Lichte des Voelker- und Menschenrechts.** Berlin: Stilke, 1931, 149 p.
Really a general, documented survey of the action of the Powers in the Armenian Question, with special stress on the war and post-war periods.

MANDEL'SHTAM, ANDREÏ NIKOLAEVICH. **La Société des Nations et les Puissances devant le Problème Arménien.** Paris: Pedone, 1925, 355 p.
The first adequate examination of the Armenian question in its later stages.

MORGAN, JACQUES DE. **Histoire du Peuple Arménien.** Paris: Berger-Levrault, 1919, 410 p.
An authoritative general history, but weak on the modern period.

NAAYEM, JOSEPH. **Shall This Nation Die?** New York: Chaldean Rescue, 1921, 318 p.
A circumstantial account of the massacres during the war.

NANSEN, FRIDTJOF. **Armenia and the Near East.** London: Allen and Unwin, 1928, 328 p.
The people and their history, together with the writer's observations as a representative of the League investigating the possibility of re-settling the Armenians.

TCHALKHOUCHIAN, G. **Le Livre Rouge.** Paris: Veradzenount, 1919, 112 p.
A review of the Armenian question and the massacres during the war.

VARANDIAN, MIKAEL. **Le Conflit Arméno-Géorgien et la Guerre du Caucase.** Paris: Flinikowski, 1919, 153 p.
A straightforward narrative of the chaotic developments in 1918 and 1919.

VIERBÜCHER, HEINRICH. **Was die Kaiserliche Regierung den Deutschen Untertanen Verschwiegen Hat.** Hamburg: Fackelreiter, 1930, 84 p.
The Armenian massacres of 1915 and the ignorance of the German people.

PALESTINE

See also (Civilizations and Race Conflicts) Jewish Problem, p. 5; also (League of Nations) Mandates, p. 58; also (World War) Near and Middle Eastern Front, p. 137.

ANDREWS, MRS. FANNIE FERN (PHILLIPS). **The Holy Land under Mandate.** Boston: Houghton Mifflin, 1931, 2 v.
These volumes give information on almost every phase of the situation in Palestine, from conditions of travel to the actual workings of the Jewish settlements. There is a discussion of the Zionist movement and Jewish aspirations, while in other chapters the Arab claims are quite as conscientiously presented. Attention is also given to the policies of the mandatory Powers.

ASHBEE, CHARLES ROBERT. **A Palestine Notebook, 1918-1923.** New York: Doubleday, 1923, 278 p.
A frank record of experiences and observations in Palestine, 1918-1923, by a British official.

BALFOUR, ARTHUR JAMES BALFOUR, EARL OF. **Speeches on Zionism.** London: Arrowsmith, 1928, 128 p.
A convenient collection of statements and addresses.

BAUMKOLLER, ABRAHAM. **Le Mandat sur la Palestine.** Paris: Rousseau, 1931, 354 p.
A scholarly study of the peculiarity of the Palestine mandate, and of the interaction of the mandatory system and the provision of a national home for the Jews.

BEN-AVI, ITTAMR. **L'Enclave.** Paris: Rieder, 1931, 240 p.
An account of the Palestine tragedy as it unfolded itself in recent years.

BENTWICH, NORMAN DE MATTOS. **England in Palestine.** London: Kegan Paul, 1932, 358 p.
An accounting of the British stewardship by a man long a high official in the administration. One of the most important books on post-war Palestine.

BENTWICH, NORMAN DE MATTOS. **Palestine and the Jews.** London: Kegan Paul, 1919, 288 p.
A brief and sympathetic treatment of Zionism and the Jewish revival, the Palestine colonies and the Holy Cities.

BERNFELD, MARCEL. **Le Sionisme.** Paris: Jouve, 1920, 458 p.
A well-documented dissertation which reviews the whole Jewish question in the 19th century, as well as discussing the Modern Zionist movement and the national home in Palestine.

BREUER, ISAAC. **The Jewish National Home.** London: Agudas Israel World Organization, 1926, 105 p.
A reconsideration of the attitude of Orthodoxy towards the Zionist movement.

COHN, JOSEF. **England und Palästina.** Berlin: Vowinckel, 1931, 327 p.
A useful book on the Palestine question, giving a scholarly survey of the development of British policy from the very beginning, as well as an account of the establishment of the mandate and the evolution of the Zionist question in recent years.

CONWAY, SIR WILLIAM MARTIN. **Palestine and Morocco.** London: Arnold, 1923, 296 p.
A comparative study of the effect of European intervention and enterprise, with a general survey of problems and politics in Palestine.

ELAZARI-VOLKANI, I. **The Communistic Settlements in the Jewish Colonization in Palestine.** Tel-Aviv: "Hapoel Hazair," 1927, 139 p.
One of the Palestine Economic Society's publications.

GINZBERG, ASHER. **Ten Essays on Zionism and Judaism.** London: Routledge, 1922, 256 p.
A selection of writings by a great intellectual leader and advocate of the spiritual renaissance.

GRANOVSKY, ABRAHAM. **Land Problems in Palestine.** London: Routledge, 1926, 120 p.
Ten essays by an authoritative writer, dealing with the land policy of the National Fund, the need for preventing speculation and the necessity for public ownership.

GRANOVSKY, ABRAHAM. **Land Settlement in Palestine.** London: Gollancz, 1930, 224 p.
A continuation of the author's studies of the all-important land question.

GRANOVSKY, ABRAHAM. **Die Bodenfrage und der Jüdische Aufbau in Palästina.** Vienna: Barth, 1931, 178 p.
Granovsky's latest contribution, not yet translated into English.

GRAVES, PHILIP PERCEVAL. **Palestine: The Land of Three Faiths.** London: Cape, 1923, 286 p.

Written by a correspondent of the London *Times*, this book attempts to present the Palestine problem in its larger geographical and political setting and to give a critical account of British, Zionist and Arab policies. One of the better early books.

HARRY, MIRIAM, *pseud*. **A Springtime in Palestine.** Boston: Houghton Mifflin, 1924, 206 p.
Somewhat rhapsodical impressions of the great work of reconstruction being carried on by the Jews.

HOLDHEIM, GERHARD. **Palästina: Idee, Probleme, Tatsachen.** Berlin: Schwetschke, 1928, 180 p.
The idea of a national home and the obstacles in the way of its realization.

HOLMES, JOHN HAYNES. **Palestine To-day and To-morrow.** New York: Macmillan, 1929, 289 p.
An American religious leader's impressions after a visit to the Holy Land and conversations with the resident spokesmen of the Jews, Arabs and English.

JANNAWAY, FRANK GEORGE. **Palestine and the World.** London: Sampson Low, 1922, 268 p.
The author studies the Jewish claims in Palestine, the achievements of Zionist colonies and the policies of the various Powers.

JARVIS, CLAUD S. **Yesterday and To-day in Sinai.** London: Blackwood, 1931, 312 p.
Entertaining and informative pages by the governor of the region.

JASTROW, MORRIS. **Zionism and the Future of Palestine.** New York: Macmillan, 1919, 159 p.
A critique of political Zionism and a plea for the establishment of Palestine as a state not distinctively Jewish.

JUNG, EUGÈNE. **Les Arabes et l'Islam en Face des Nouvelles Croisades.** Paris: Jung, 1931, 80 p.
A rather brilliant presentation of the Arab-Jewish antagonism in Palestine by a sympathizer with the Arabs.

KALLEN, HORACE MEYER. **Zionism and World Politics.** New York: Doubleday, 1921, 345 p.
An excellent review and interpretation of the nationalist movement and Zionism, together with a discussion of the position of the Jews in Europe at the end of the war. The author is connected with the New School for Social Research.

LOEB, MRS. SOPHIE IRENE (SIMON). **Palestine Awake.** New York: Century, 1926, 249 p.
Collected newspaper articles on the new Palestine, by an American social worker.

LUKE, HARRY CHARLES and KEITH-ROACH, EDWARD. **The Handbook of Palestine and Trans-Jordan.** London: Macmillan, 1930, 505 p.
An authoritative survey of conditions in contemporary Palestine. The second edition of the best manual in English.

McCRACKAN, WILLIAM DENISON. **The New Palestine.** Boston: Page, 1922, 392 p.
A vivid picture of personalities and conditions in Palestine at the end of the war.

PREISS, LUDWIG and ROHRBACH, PAUL. **Palestine and Transjordania.** New York: Macmillan, 1926, 230 p.
One of the most substantial and competent books on the subject.

RAPPOPORT, ANGELO S. **History of Palestine.** New York: Dutton, 1931, 368 p.
A general history, well-informed and attractively written.

ROMANO, MARIO. **Problèmes Politiques de l'Organisation Sioniste.** Paris: Rieder, 1927, 128 p.
A plea for the maintenance of the entente with England and for an understanding with the Arabs.

RUPPIN, ARTHUR. **Die Landwirtschaftliche Kolonisation der Zionistischen Organisation in Palästina.** Berlin: Aufbau, 1925, 205 p.
A competent study of the land policy and its first accomplishments, with considerable discussion of disputed points.

SAAD, LAMEC. **Palästina Erinnerungen.** Berlin: Mulzer und Cleemann, 1930, 143 p.
Interesting pre-war and post-war reminiscences of a Turkish doctor in Palestine.

SAMPTER, JESSIE ETHEL, *ed*. **A Guide to Zionism.** New York: Zionist Organization, 1920, 262 p.
A convenient handbook on the history and status of Zionism and the general situation in Palestine.

SAMUEL, HORACE BARNETT. **Unholy Memories of the Holy Land.** London: Hogarth, 1930, 314 p.
A provocative book on the British administration, written on the basis of a long official experience.

SAMUEL, MAURICE. **On the Rim of the Wilderness.** New York: Liveright, 1931, 247 p.
The whole Palestine situation reviewed by a competent representative of the Jewish standpoint, with special stress on the Jewish-Arab problem.

SAMUEL, MAURICE. **What Happened in Palestine?** Boston: Stratford, 1929, 222 p.
A discussion of the events of August 1929, and of their background.

SEIDEL, HANS JOACHIM. **Der Britische Mandatstaat Palästina im Rahmen der Weltwirtschaft.** Berlin: De Gruyter, 1926, 136 p.
An able analysis of Palestine's resources, productive system and general potentialities in industry and commerce.

SIMON, LEON and STEIN, LEONARD. **Awakening Palestine.** London: Murray, 1923, 318 p.
A composite work by experts dealing with the contemporary problems of the new Palestine, the significance of the Zionist program, and the obstacles to its realization.

SIMON, LEON. **Studies in Jewish Nationalism.** New York: Longmans, 1920, 174 p.
A series of essays on various aspects and implications of the Jewish renaissance and Zionism, by a brilliant English Zionist.

SOKOLOW, NAHUM. **History of Zionism, 1600-1918.** New York: Longmans, 1919, 2 v.
A detailed, authoritative history of the movement.

STEIN, LEONARD. **Zionism.** London: Benn, 1925, 218 p.
One of the best-informed popular historical accounts of the movement and of the establishment of the Jews in Palestine.

STOYANOVSKY, J. **The Mandate for Palestine.** New York: Longmans, 1928, 414 p.
A thorough technical study of the Palestine Mandate in the larger setting of the mandates system and in connection with the problem of a national home. On the whole the best book on the subject.

TRITONJ, ROMOLO. **Come Va Risolta la Questione dei Luoghi Santi.** Rome: Rassegna Italiana, 1925, 398 p.
A competent documented study of the historical evolution of the question of the Holy Places, with a discussion of methods of settlement within the mandate.

VANDERVELDE, ÉMILE. **Le Pays d'Israël.** Paris: Rieder, 1929, 256 p.
The Belgian socialist statesman views conditions in Palestine chiefly from the standpoint of the class struggle and the national conflict.

WALDSTEIN, ABRAHAM SOLOMON. **Modern Palestine.** New York: Bloch, 1927, 229 p.
A general review of present conditions and problems.

WEDGWOOD, JOSIAH CLEMENT. **The Seventh Dominion.** London: Labour Publishing Company, 1928, 131 p.
A Labor M. P. criticizes the working of the mandate system in Palestine and calls for its organization on a Dominion basis.

WIENER, ALFRED. **Kritische Reise durch Palästina.** Berlin: Philo, 1927, 156 p.
A survey of conditions and problems, by an author who guards against overstatement and extravagant hopes.

WISE, STEPHEN SAMUEL and DE HAAS, JACOB. **The Great Betrayal.** New York: Brentano, 1930, 315 p.
The authors picture the changing attitude of England, emphasizing in particular the emasculation of the Balfour Declaration and the "betrayal" of the Passfield Paper.

WORSFOLD, WILLIAM BASIL. **Palestine of the Mandate.** London: T. Fisher Unwin, 1925, 275 p.
A survey of developments since 1919, especially in their economic aspects. One of the most substantial studies of the achievements of the British and the Zionists in the first years.

SYRIA

See also (League of Nations) Mandates, p. 58; also (World War) Near and Middle Eastern Front, p. 137.

ABOUSSOUAN, BENOÎT. **Le Problème Politique Syrien.** Paris: Chauny et Quinsac, 1924, 324 p.
A doctoral thesis, very lightly documented. The author discusses chiefly the constitutional problem and the clauses of the Lausanne Treaty relating to Syria.

ARSLAN, AMIR EMIN. **La Revolución Siria contra el Mandato Francés.** Buenos Aires: Menendez, n. d., 159 p.
A bitter attack on the French policy, by an Arab educated in France and formerly a supporter of the mandate.

BEAUPLAN, ROBERT DE. **Où Va la Syrie?** Paris: Tallandier, 1929, 224 p.
"Shall France keep the mandate?" asks one of the best writers of *L'Illustration.*

BONARDI, PIERRE. **L'Imbroglio Syrien.** Paris: Rieder, 1927, 160 p.
Personal experiences during the troubles of 1925.

BOURON, NARCISSE. **Les Druzes.** Paris: Berger-Levrault, 1930, 424 p.
A serious, documented history of the Druses, with an analysis of their religion, social structure and customs.

BURCKHARD, CHARLES. **Le Mandat Français en Syrie et au Liban.** Paris: Fabre, 1925, 198 p.
A dissertation, in which the author gives a fairly good account of the establishment and organization of the mandate government.

CLERGET, PIERRE. **La Syrie sous le Mandat Français.** Paris: Revue Économique Internationale, 1923.
An excellent, if enthusiastic, brochure describing the establishment and early results of the French mandate.

DAVID, PHILIPPE. **Un Gouvernement Arabe à Damas, le Congrès Syrien.** Paris: Giard, 1923, 154 p.
How the Sherifian government was established in the pre-mandate days.

GEORGES-GAULIS, BERTHE. **La Question Arabe.** Paris: Berger-Levrault, 1930, 310 p.
The larger part of the book is devoted to a study of the historical development of Syria since 1920, with special attention to the rising of 1925 and the further growth of Syrian nationalism.

GONTAUT-BIRON, ROGER DE, COMTE. **Comment la France S'Est Installée en Syrie, 1918-1919.** Paris: Plon, 1922, 354 p.
Strongly anti-English in tone, but very valuable as a history and interpretation of the French post-war policy in the Near East. The author was closely associated with the French commissioner and his account is of prime importance.

GONTAUT-BIRON, ROGER DE, COMTE. **Sur les Routes de Syrie après Neuf Ans de Mandat.** Paris: Plon, 1928, 220 p.
A veritable handbook of the Syrian question in the later period, cataloguing the French accomplishments and the present problems.

LAMMENS, R. P. **Petite Histoire de Syrie et du Liban.** Beyrouth: Imprimerie Catholique, 1924, 150 p.
A well-organized summary of the history of Syria and the Lebanon by an eminent scholar.

MACCALLUM, ELIZABETH PAULINE. **The Nationalist Crusade in Syria.** New York: Foreign Policy Association, 1928, 299 p.
The best available treatment of the great rising of 1925-1927, based upon good command of the material and sound understanding of the issues involved.

MAESTRACCI, NOËL. **La Syrie Contemporaine.** Paris: Charles-Lavauzelle, 1930, 228 p.
A general descriptive work devoted chiefly to governmental organization.

MÉLIA, JEAN. **Chez les Chrétiens d'Orient.** Paris: Fasquelle, 1928, 215 p.
An interesting account by the former director of the French commissariat in Syria.

MUSIL, ALOIS. **Palmyrena: A Topographical Itinerary.** New York: American Geographical Society, 1928, 367 p.
Travels of a well-known student of Arabia in central Syria between 1908 and 1915.

NAVA, SANTI. **Il Mandato Francese in Siria dalle Sue Origine al 1929.** Genoa: Milani, 1930, 269 p.
A sharp criticism of the French policy.

NIELSEN, ALFRED. **Muhammedansk Tankegang i Vore Dage.** Copenhagen: Gads, 1930, 182 p.
A detailed study of the Moslem press of Damascus since the war, reflecting the evolution of public opinion in Syria.

O'ZOUX, RAYMOND. **Les États du Levant sous Mandat Français.** Paris: Larose, 1931, 332 p.
Primarily a descriptive study of Syria, well-documented and reliable, and equipped with a full bibliography.

PIC, PAUL. **Syrie et Palestine, Mandats Français et Anglais dans le Proche-Orient.** Paris: Champion, 1924, 235 p.
A study of the mandate system as applied in the Near East with emphasis on the development of nationalism in Syria and the reaction against Zionism in Palestine.

RABBATH, E. **L'Évolution Politique de la Syrie sous Mandat.** Paris: Rivière, 1928, 280 p.
One of the best of many theses on the mandatory organization. Well-documented.

REDAN, PIERRE, *pseud.* (PIERRE J. ANDRÉ) and PINON, RENÉ. **La Cilicie et le Problème Ottoman.** Paris: Gauthier, 1921, 144 p.

A review of the geography, ethnography, history and religious status of Cilicia, and a report on the eagerness of the population for French rule.

SAINT-POINT, V. DE. **La Vérité sur la Syrie.** Paris: Cahiers de France, 1929, 242 p.
A semi-popular review of the situation after the subsidence of the great rising.

SAMNÉ, GEORGES. **La Syrie.** Paris: Bossard, 1921, 733 p.
An extensive, documented historical and descriptive survey, by the secretary-general of the Syrian Central Committee.

SOREL, JEAN ALBERT. **Le Mandat Français et l'Expansion Économique de la Syrie et du Liban.** Paris: Giard, 1929, 259 p.
A dissertation concerned chiefly with an analysis of the resources of Syria and the economic development of the country since 1920.

STEIN, LEONARD. **Syria.** London: Benn, 1926, 94 p.
A clear account of events since 1918, with an exposition of racial and religious problems.

WETTERLÉ, ÉMILE. **En Syrie avec le Général Gouraud.** Paris: Flammarion, 1924, 248 p.
A sympathetic study of the French régime.

ARABIA

See also (World War) Near and Middle Eastern Front, p. 137.

Araviia i Evropeiĭskie Derzhavy. Moscow: Krasnaia Nov', 1924, 224 p.
A collection of articles on Arabia and its relations with the Powers.

BROUCKE, JEANNE. **L'Empire Arabe d'Ibn Séoud.** Brussels: Falk, 1929, 89 p.
A scholarly sketch of the history of the Wahabit movement before and during the war.

CHEESMAN, ROBERT ERNEST. **In Unknown Arabia.** New York: Macmillan, 1926, 467 p.
A fascinating narrative of travel in Eastern Arabia, chiefly scientific, but offering interesting sidelights on Ibn Sa'ud and his régime.

COKE, RICHARD. **The Arab's Place in the Sun.** London: Butterworth, 1929, 318 p.
A succinct history of the Arabs, emphasizing the more recent period and the contacts with European imperialisms.

HARRISON, PAUL W. **The Arab at Home.** New York: Crowell, 1924, 345 p.
Written by an American medical missionary of long experience; an interesting study of Mesopotamia and the east coast tribes.

HOGARTH, DAVID GEORGE. **Arabia.** New York: Oxford University Press, 1922, 139 p.
A good historical introduction, from earliest times to the Arab participation in the World War, by a recognized authority.

JACOB, HAROLD FENTON. **The Kings of Arabia: The Rise and Set of the Turkish Sovranty in the Arabian Peninsula.** London: Mills and Boon, 1923, 294 p.
An excellent sketch of the history and present situation of the Yemen, by a British representative.

JUNG, EUGÈNE. **La Révolte Arabe.** Paris: Colbert, 1924-1925, 2 v.
Continues the author's excellent earlier book on the Arab revival. These volumes carry the story from 1906 to 1924.

KHAIRALLAH, K. T. **Les Régions Arabes Libérées.** Paris: Leroux, 1919, 133 p.
A review of the Arab revival, the supposed aims of the Powers in the war, and the Arab claims to independence.

Musil, Alois. **Arabia Deserta: A Topographical Itinerary.** New York: American Geographical Society, 1927, 631 p.
A veteran traveller's record of life and politics among the Bedouins, throwing light also on the early reaction of the tribesmen to the World War. Other volumes on Arabia by the same author, published by the same publisher, include: "Northern Neğd" (1928, 368 p.), "The Northern Heğâz" (1926, 374 p.), and "The Manners and Customs of the Rwala Bedouins" (1928. 712 p.).

Philby, Harry St. John Bridger. **Arabia.** New York: Scribner, 1930, 387 p.
A general history of Arabia in the last few centuries, with special reference to the rise of the Wahabis and the post-war period. An excellent volume in the "Modern World" series. The author, a former member of the Indian Civil Service, served in Mesopotamia and Arabia during and after the war.

Philby, Harry St. John Bridger. **The Heart of Arabia.** New York: Putnam, 1923, 2 v.
A detailed account of travel at the end of the war in little-known parts of Nejd, which the author was the first European to visit.

Philby, Harry St. John Bridger. **Arabia of the Wahhabis.** London: Constable, 1928, 438 p.
A fascinating book, continuing the author's "Heart of Arabia" and recounting his mission to Ibn Sa'ud in 1918.

Rihani, Ameen Fares. **Arabian Peak and Desert.** Boston: Houghton Mifflin, 1930, 280 p.
Though a travel book, this volume gives a full description of the politics and general conditions in the Yemen.

Rihani, Ameen Fares. **Around the Coasts of Arabia.** Boston: Houghton Mifflin, 1930, 374 p.
A well-known Arab-American recounts his observations on an extensive trip around Arabia. The book is full of interesting information on the little-known states of the eastern and Persian Gulf coasts. There are also chapters on Hejaz and Asir.

Rihani, Ameen Fares. **Maker of Modern Arabia.** Boston: Houghton Mifflin, 1928, 370 p.
The author was entertained by Ibn Sa'ud, and gives us a sympathetic picture of this strong man of the desert. What he has to say about the Wahabis themselves is both novel and important.

Rutter, Eldon. **The Holy Cities of Arabia.** New York: Putnam, 1928, 2 v.
A detailed narrative of a pilgrimage to Mecca and Medina in 1925.

Seabrook, William Buehler. **Adventures in Arabia.** New York: Harcourt, 1927, 347 p.
These travels among Bedouins and Druses throw much light on religious sects and little known aspects of Arab life.

Thomas, Bertram. **Alarms and Excursions in Arabia.** Indianapolis: Bobbs, 1931, 296 p.
A narrative of the war and post-war periods by a man who played an active part in Arabian affairs, especially in southeastern Arabia.

Topf, Erich. **Die Staatenbildungen in den Arabischen Teilen der Türkei seit dem Weltkriege.** Hamburg: De Gruyter, 1929, 260 p.
Really an examination of the Arabian national movement since the beginning of the struggle against the Turks, followed by a review of the present mandated and non-mandated territories, and concluding with an elaborate bibliography and selection of documents. Easily the best scholarly, documented study of the new states.

IRAQ; THE MOSUL QUESTION

See also (League of Nations) Mandates, p. 58; also (World War) Near and Middle Eastern Front, p. 137.

BELL, GERTRUDE LOWTHIAN. **Letters.** New York: Boni and Liveright, 1927, 2 v.
The correspondence of a remarkable woman and one of the most arresting figures in the recent history of the Near East. It makes absorbing reading.

BOMLI, PIETER ELIAS JOHANNES. **L'Affaire de Mossoul.** Amsterdam: Paris, 1929, 252 p.
A competent study of the development of the Mosul question since the war.

COKE, RICHARD. **The Heart of the Middle East.** London: Butterworth, 1925, 320 p.
An excellent history of Mesopotamia, especially detailed on the recent period.

CRUTIANSKY, LÉON. **La Question de Mossoul.** Paris: Presses Modernes, 1927, 143 p.
A dissertation giving in brief form the story of the struggle for oil and the action of the League.

GONTAUT-BIRON, ROGER DE, COMTE. **La France et la Question de Mossoul.** Paris: Société d'Études et d'Informations Économiques, 1923.
A sketch of the struggle of France and England for the possession of this important oil district.

HALDANE, SIR AYLMER LOWTHROP. **The Insurrection in Mesopotamia, 1920.** London: Blackwood, 1922, 352 p.
The authoritative history of the crisis, written by an experienced British officer who was commander-in-chief in Mesopotamia at the time.

HESSE, FRITZ. **Die Mossulfrage.** Berlin: Vowinckel, 1925, 68 p.
A careful study of the question in its geophysical aspect.

HOOPER, CHARLES ARTHUR, *ed.* **The Constitutional Law of 'Iraq.** Baghdad: MacKenzie, 1928, 277 p.
A valuable historical introduction, followed by an authoritative analysis of the constitution of 1925, by the president of the Court of First Instance in Iraq.

HOOPER, CHARLES ARTHUR. **L'Iraq et la Société des Nations.** Paris: Pedone, 1928, 108 p.
A well-documented discussion of the evolution of modern Iraq, and its relationship with the League and with England. The author analyzes in some detail the Mosul and Kurd questions.

LUKE, HARRY CHARLES. **Mosul, and Its Minorities.** London: Hopkinson, 1925, 161 p.
An excellent first-hand account of the Christian minorities and their difficult position, by a high British official.

LYELL, THOMAS. **The Ins and Outs of Mesopotamia.** London: Philpot, 1923, 237 p.
Though unfriendly to Islamic teachings and ideals, this book gives one of the best expositions of conditions in Iraq and of England's situation there.

MANN, JAMES SAUMAREZ. **An Administration in the Making.** New York: Longmans, 1921, 330 p.
Contains a young British official's letters bearing on the beginnings of the new Iraq and the rising of 1920.

MUSIL, ALOIS. **The Middle Euphrates: A Topographical Itinerary.** New York: American Geographical Society, 1927, 426 p.
The narrative of journeys in 1912 and 1915 along the Euphrates and into the interior of Mesopotamia.

STEVENS, ETHEL STEFANA. **By Tigris and Euphrates.** London: Hurst and Blackett, 1923, 349 p.
An interesting work on modern Mesopotamia, with emphasis on religious aspects.

PERSIA

See also (World War) Near and Middle Eastern Front, p. 137.

AFSCHAR, MAHMOUD. **La Politique Européenne en Perse.** Berlin: Nay, 1921, 276 p.
A detached scholarly account of a most confused chapter in modern imperialism. A Swiss dissertation.

BALFOUR, JAMES MONCREIFF. **Recent Happenings in Persia.** London: Blackwood, 1922, 307 p.
Written by the assistant to the financial adviser of the Persian government. An excellent critical account of contemporary affairs.

FATEH, MOUSTAFA KHAN. **The Economic Position of Persia.** London: King, 1926, 98 p.
A good general survey of resources, economic activities and possibilities for development. The best book on the subject.

FORBES-LEITH, FRANCIS ARTHUR CORNELIUS. **Checkmate.** London: Harrap, 1927, 242 p.
Life and experiences in post-war Persia by an Englishman in the service of one of the great nobles.

HESSE, FRITZ. **Persien. Entwicklung und Gegenwart.** Berlin: Zentral-Verlag, 1932, 92 p.
The latest volume in an admirable German series of surveys.

IḰBĀL 'ALĪ SHĀH, SIRDAR. **Eastward to Persia.** London: Wright and Brown, 1931, 292 p.
Interesting and informative pictures of Persian life, by a competent Persian writer.

LESUEUR, ÉMILE. **Les Anglais en Perse.** Paris: Renaissance du Livre, 1922, 192 p.
A none-too-friendly survey of British policies and interests.

LITTEN, WILHELM. **Persien.** Berlin: De Gruyter, 1920, 396 p.
A most valuable collection of documentary and other material to illustrate the "pacific penetration" of Persia before the war, together with some discussion of the political and economic situation.

MARTCHENKO, M. **Un Voyage en Perse.** Paris: Berger-Levrault, 1920, 99 p.
A vivid picture of the anarchy in Persia during the Russian Revolution, by a Russian officer who denounces German machinations.

MATINE-DAFTARY, AHMAD KHAN. **La Suppression des Capitulations en Perse.** Paris: Presses Universitaires, 1930, 266 p.
A Persian judge and high official studies the régime of the capitulations and the methods of its abrogation. Easily the best book on the subject.

MILLSPAUGH, ARTHUR CHESTER. **The American Task in Persia.** New York: Century, 1925, 336 p.
The story of the American Financial Mission established in 1922, told by the chief of the mission. The book gives an excellent picture of the post-war problems of Persia and the obstacles in the way of reform.

MOHR, ANTON. **Den Persiske Bukt.** Oslo: Aschehoug, 1929, 173 p.
A political-geographic study showing the important rôle of the Persian Gulf in modern world politics.

PAVLOVICH, M., *pseud*. (MIKHAIL VEL'TMAN) and IRANSKIĬ, S. **Persiia v Bor'be za Neza-visimost'**. Moscow: Nauchnaia Assotsiatsiia Vostokovedeniia, 1925, 184 p.
Written by a leading communist student of imperialism, this is one of a series of studies of the struggle of exploited peoples for their independence.

POIDEBARD, A. **Au Carrefour des Routes de Perse**. Paris: Crès, 1923, 322 p.
An excellent account of the geography of Persia and valuable material on diplomatic and military events in the Near East in 1918-19.

ROSS, SIR EDWARD DENISON. **The Persians**. New York: Oxford University Press, 1931, 142 p.
A compact and serviceable little survey of the history, the country and the culture of the Persians.

SHEEAN, VINCENT. **The New Persia**. New York: Century, 1927, 344 p.
The author discusses the latest revolution and what it stands for, but takes a rather pessimistic view of the future of Persia, which, he thinks, will inevitably become again a bone of contention between England and Russia.

SIASSI, ALI AKBAR. **La Perse au Contact de l'Occident**. Paris: Leroux, 1931, 273 p.
A dissertation. The author gives a well-informed and dispassionate, though unfortunately brief survey of Persia in international relations in modern times, and studies the cultural as well as the political effects of contact with the West.

SYKES, SIR PERCY MOLESWORTH. **A History of Persia**. London: Macmillan, 3rd ed., 1930, 2 v.
The latest edition of the standard history, carrying the story of Persia through the World War.

VACALA, R. **Le Golfe Persique**. Paris: Rousseau, 1920, 151 p.
A survey of the history and economic life of the Gulf, with a full bibliography.

WILSON, SIR ARNOLD TALBOT. **The Persian Gulf**. New York: Oxford University Press, 1928, 344 p.
A well-written and highly interesting account of international rivalry for control of the Gulf. Unfortunately rather sketchy for the later period.

II. CENTRAL ASIA AND INDIA

CENTRAL ASIA AND TURKESTAN

See also (Russia) Foreign Policy, p. 393.

BACH, LYDIA. **Orient Soviétique**. Paris: Valois, 1931, 300 p.
A competent French writer pictures the renaissance of Central Asia under Soviet rule.

CABLE, MILDRED and others. **The Challenge of Central Asia**. New York: World Dominion Press, 1929, 136 p.
A survey of Tibet, Mongolia and Turkestan for missionary purposes, with stress on the menace of Bolshevik domination.

ETHERTON, PERCY THOMAS. **In the Heart of Asia**. London: Constable, 1925, 305 p.
An important narrative of events and experiences in Chinese Turkestan in the post-war period, by the British Consul-General and political resident. There is an interesting discussion of Soviet agitation in that region.

LATTIMORE, OWEN. **High Tartary**. Boston: Little, Brown, 1930, 360 p.
Travels and observations in Chinese Turkestan, continuing the author's well-known "The Desert Road to Turkestan" (Little, Brown, 1929, 373 p.).

Ocherki Revoliutsionnogo Dvizheniia v Srednei Azii. Moscow: Nauchnaia Assotsiatsiia Vostokovedeniia, 1926, 152 p.
A series of essays on the revolutionary movement in Central Asia.

SERVET, CLAUDE. **Le Turkestan Soviétique.** Paris: Bureau d'Éditions, 1932, 132 p.
An interesting description of present-day Turkestan.

SKRINE, CLARMONT PERCIVAL. **Chinese Central Asia.** Boston: Houghton Mifflin, 1926,
322 p.
An excellent descriptive work on Chinese Turkestan, by the former British Consul-
General in Kashgar.

STRONG, ANNA LOUISE. **Red Star in Samarkand.** New York: Coward-McCann, 1929,
329 p.
One of our most persistent travellers gives an unvarnished picture of Central Asia
under communist rule.

STRONG, ANNA LOUISE. **The Road to the Grey Pamir.** Boston: Little, Brown, 1931,
289 p.
These pages of adventure by a Soviet sympathizer are interesting in themselves, but
also throw light upon Soviet workings in the more remote areas of Asia.

AFGHANISTAN

L'Afghanistan Nouveau. Paris: Cosmos, 1924, 95 p.
History, international relations, political and economic status.

FOUCHET, MAURICE. **Notes sur l'Afghanistan.** Paris: Maisonneuve, 1932, 228 p.
An excellent introduction to the people and politics of Afghanistan, written by the
late French minister.

FURON, RAYMOND. **L'Afghanistan.** Paris: Blanchard, 1926, 132 p.
A geographical and historical sketch, followed by descriptive matter, by a French
representative resident in Afghanistan for two years.

IKBĀL 'ALĪ SHĀH, SIRDAR. **Afghanistan of the Afghans.** London: Diamond Press,
1928, 272 p.
A general description of the customs and traditions of the Afghans, by a Persian
writer.

KATRAK, SORAB K. H. **Through Amanullah's Afghanistan.** London: Luzac, 1930,
415 p.
A travel book, well illustrated, written by an enthusiastic supporter of Amanullah
and his reform policy.

MACMUNN, SIR GEORGE FLETCHER. **Afghanistan, from Darius to Amanullah.**
London: Bell, 1929, 360 p.
One of the best general surveys of the checkered history of Afghanistan.

MÉLIA, JEAN. **Visages Royaux d'Orient.** Paris: Fasquelle, 1929, 206 p.
Interesting pen sketches of Amanullah, Reza Shah Pehlevi, Feisal, Ibn Sa'ud, etc.

RYBITSCHKA, EMIL. **Im Gottgegebenen Afghanistan.** Leipzig: Brockhaus, 1927, 296 p.
One of the most vivid accounts of developments in modern Afghanistan, by a German
prisoner who escaped from Russia and spent years in the country.

SNESAREV, A. E. **Afganistan.** Moscow: Gosizdat, 1921, 244 p.
A general descriptive study in Russian.

THOMAS, LOWELL. **Beyond Khyber Pass.** New York: Century, 1925, 272 p.
An entertaining and profusely illustrated travel book.

TIBET

BELL, SIR CHARLES ALFRED. **Tibet, Past and Present.** Oxford: Clarendon Press, 1925, 340 p.
An extremely valuable account of the developments of the last twenty years, by a high British official often employed on missions to Tibet.

BELL, SIR CHARLES ALFRED. **The People of Tibet.** Oxford: Clarendon Press, 1928, 329 p.
The best descriptive work on Tibet, written by an eminent authority.

BOSSHARD, WALTER. **Durch Tibet und Turkistan.** Stuttgart: Strecker, 1930, 246 p.
A lavishly illustrated record of travel in Tibet, Pamir and Central Asia.

FILCHNER, WILHELM. **Quer durch Ost-Tibet.** Berlin: Mittler, 1925, 195 p.
This report of a scientific expedition throws much light on conditions and reasons for unrest in eastern Tibet.

FILCHNER, WILHELM, *ed.* **Sturm über Asien.** Berlin: Neufeld, 1924, 311 p.
The narrative of an important Russian agent in Tibet, covering the period from 1900 to 1918.

HEBER, A. REEVE and MRS. KATHLEEN MARY. **In Himalayan Tibet.** Philadelphia: Lippincott, 1926, 283 p.
Experiences and observations based on twelve years' residence.

KING, MRS. RIN-CHEN LHA-MO. **We Tibetans.** London: Seeley Service, 1926, 228 p.
A simple, straightforward account of life, beliefs and customs, by a Tibetan woman who married an English consul.

MACDONALD, DAVID. **The Land of the Lama.** London: Seeley Service, 1929, 283 p.
One of the most valuable intimate pictures of Tibet and Tibetan life, by a man who was for fifteen years British trade agent in the country.

MCGOVERN, WILLIAM MONTGOMERY. **To Lhasa in Disguise.** New York: Century, 1924, 462 p.
The author, an English scientist, travelled as a coolie in a caravan. His account gives a valuable picture of Tibet in transformation.

ROERICH, GEORGE NICHOLAS. **Trails to Inmost Asia.** New Haven: Yale University Press, 1931, 504 p.
The account of a five-year expedition through Central Asia and Mongolia.

SHERAP, PAUL. **A Tibetan on Tibet.** London: T. Fisher Unwin, 1926, 212 p.
The travels of a Tibetan free lance, giving excellent insight into conditions and customs of the country.

TEICHMAN, ERIC. **Travels of a Consular Officer in Eastern Tibet.** New York: Macmillan, 1922, 248 p.
A valuable survey of Tibet's relations with China and India, to 1918, followed by a record of travel in 1918 to establish peace on the Chinese-Tibetan frontier.

TRINKLER, EMIL. **The Storm-Swept Roof of Asia.** Philadelphia: Lippincott, 1931, 312 p.
The report of a journey through Tibet and Turkestan to India.

INDIA
British Rule and Reform
See also (Great Britain) Imperial Relations, p. 231.

AHMAD, TOFAIL. **Responsible Government and the Solution of Hindu-Muslim Problem.** London: Probsthain, 1928, 157 p.
The author surveys British rule and finds that it has degenerated. He calls upon the present-day English "to come out of their palaces and help India in her struggle" to become an equal member in the Commonwealth.

ANTONOWICZ, S. **Les États Indigènes dans l'Inde Anglaise.** Paris: Rousseau, 1931, 215 p.
A careful analysis of the vexed problem of the native states.

ARCHBOLD, WILLIAM ARTHUR JOBSON. **Outlines of Indian Constitutional History.** London: King, 1926, 367 p.
A substantial but not very readable work. The approach is historical, and little is said of local government, taxation or finance. The author was for some years a leading educator in India.

BANERJEE, DEBENDRA NATH. **The Indian Constitution and Its Actual Working.** New York: Longmans, 1926, 497 p.
An able, documented study of the new constitution in operation, intended as a text.

BANERJEE, DEBENDRA NATH. **India's Nation Builders.** London: Headley, 1919, 234 p.
A series of biographical studies of Indian leaders in intellectual and political life, including Tagore, Gokhale, Gandhi, Tilak, Pal, Ghose and others.

BASHIR AL-DĪN MAHMŪD AHMAD. **Some Suggestions for the Solution of the Indian Problem.** London: Probsthain, 1930, 459 p.
The head of the Ahmadiyya Community writes appreciatively of English rule and proposes that India be given dominion status.

BESANT, MRS. ANNIE (WOOD). **The Future of Indian Politics.** London: Theosophical Publishing House, 1922, 351 p.
The struggle over the reforms in the war and post-war periods, reviewed by an extreme protagonist of nationalism and Home Rule, President of the Theosophical Society.

BESANT, MRS. ANNIE (WOOD). **India: A Nation.** Madras: Theosophical Publishing House, 1930, 226 p.
An historical account of the national movement, with consideration of religious, economic, and educational factors and a plea for self-government.

BESANT, MRS. ANNIE (WOOD). **India, Bond or Free?** New York: Putnam, 1926, 216 p.
How the Indian race has been stunted, stultified and impoverished by British rule.

BEVAN, EDWYN ROBERT. **Thoughts on Indian Discontents.** London: Allen and Unwin, 1929, 178 p.
The psychological side of the Anglo-Indian problem, viewed in a detached spirit and with sweet reasonableness.

BHĀLACHANDRA GANGĀDHARA SAPRE. **The Growth of Indian Constitution and Administration.** Bombay: Tutorial Press, 3rd ed., 1929, 548 p.
A good text, with a detailed treatment of the reforms of 1919 in operation.

Bridging the Gulf. London: King, 1930, 182 p.
A review of the factors in the Anglo-Indian dilemma, by an Indian who believes in coöperation and stresses the need for economic improvement as the best way to remove discontent.

The British Crown and the Indian States. London: King, 1929, 244 p.
A well-balanced and reliable statement of the case of the native princes, prepared for the Butler Committee by the standing committee of the Chamber of Princes.

BRITISH-INDIA MERCHANT, *pseud.* **India on the Brink.** London: King, 1931, 122 p.
A spirited defense of England's work in India, and a plea for a strong stand against the demands of extremists.

BROCKWAY, ARCHIBALD FENNER. **The Indian Crisis.** London: Gollancz, 1930, 208 p.
An English radical M. P. analyzes the problems raised by the nationalist movement and calls for positive action to meet India's desires.

CARTHILL, AL, *pseud.* **The Lost Dominion.** New York: Putnam, 1925, 357 p.
An important and forceful book describing the decline of British power in India, the work of an English official writing under a pseudonym.

CHIROL, SIR VALENTINE. **India, Old and New.** New York: Macmillan, 1922, 319 p.
The author, formerly foreign editor of the London *Times*, summarizes the history of India and analyzes sympathetically the recent British reforms.

CHIROL, SIR VALENTINE. **India.** New York: Scribner, 1926, 359 p.
A general treatment by one of the world's foremost authorities. A volume in the "Modern World" series.

CHUDGAR, P. L. **Indian Princes under British Protection.** London: Williams and Norgate, 1929, 240 p.
A vigorous, but rather uncritical indictment of the native rulers, whom the writer, as a nationalist, dislikes as cordially as he does the British themselves.

CHURCHILL, WINSTON SPENCER. **India.** London: Butterworth, 1931, 141 p.
Churchill's speeches on the Indian situation, with an introduction.

COLVIN, IAN DUNCAN. **The Life of General Dyer.** London: Blackwood, 1929, 345 p.
All that can be said in favor of the man responsible for the Amritsar shooting. The author is a leader writer on the *Morning Post*.

COUSINS, MRS. MARGARET E. **The Awakening of Asian Womanhood.** Madras: Ganesh, 1923, 160 p.
A sympathetic study of the beginnings of the emancipation and enfranchisement of women in the Orient. The chief emphasis is laid on India.

CRADDOCK, SIR REGINALD HENRY. **The Dilemma in India.** London: Constable, 1929, 380 p.
An official long in the Indian service reviews the reforms of the past period and analyzes their effect upon the administrative system. An excellent and noteworthy analysis of present problems and their historical evolution.

CRINIVASA AIYANGAR, P. T. **A Short History of India.** New York: Oxford University Press, 1931, 214 p.
A compact, non-controversial manual.

CROSS, CECIL MERNE PUTNAM. **The Development of Self-Government in India, 1858-1914.** Chicago: University of Chicago Press, 1922, 248 p.
A thorough documented study of the various reform measures from 1858 to the World War.

CURTIS, LIONEL. **Papers Relating to the Application of the Principle of Dyarchy to the Government of India.** New York: Oxford University Press, 1920, 606 p.
A valuable and authoritative collection of documents, with an extensive introduction. The author is a member of the *Round Table* group.

CURZON, GEORGE NATHANIEL CURZON, MARQUIS. **British Government in India.** New York: Cassell, 1925, 2 v.
An historical study by the famous Viceroy dealing with his predecessors and with Government House.

DAS, TARAKNATH. **India in World Politics.** New York: Huebsch, 1923, 135 p.
A well-informed essay on India and its influence on British world policy, by a writer who wastes no sympathy on imperialism.

DODWELL, HENRY HERBERT. **A Sketch of the History of India, from 1858 to 1918.** New York: Longmans, 1925, 326 p.
A competent, readable outline and a good introduction to the post-war developments.

DUMBELL, PERCY HAROLD, *ed.* **Loyal India.** New York: Cape and Smith, 1930, 244 p.
A useful collection of important documents to illustrate the evolution and working of British policy since the great mutiny.

DUNCAN, ARTHUR. **India in Crisis.** New York: Putnam, 1931, 271 p.
A well-informed, popular introduction to the Indian problem and the development of affairs since about 1911.

DUTT, RAJANI PALME. **Modern India.** Bombay: Sunshine Publishing Company, 1926, 211 p.
British rule in India as seen by a Bolshevik.

ELLAM, J. E. **Swaraj, the Problem of India.** London: Hutchinson, 1930, 288 p.
This book is really a survey of Indian history, with three chapters on the present unrest, which the author attributes to the agitation of a few intellectuals and for which he believes the only remedy to be stronger direct rule by Britain.

FULLER, JOHN FREDERIC CHARLES. **India in Revolt.** London: Eyre and Spottiswoode, 1931, 272 p.
A rather diffuse, but nevertheless thoughtful and stimulating discussion of the fundamental causes of the post-war unrest.

GARRATT, GEOFFREY THEODORE. **An Indian Commentary.** London: Cape, rev. ed., 1930, 335 p.
A solid book of facts, well-presented and impartial. The author surveys the situation in India, the relations of India to England, the causes of estrangement, and finally reviews various possible solutions.

GWYNN, JOHN TUDOR. **Indian Politics: A Survey.** London: Nisbet, 1924, 344 p.
A realistic description of contemporary Indian conditions and of the growth of disaffection towards English rule, by the correspondent of the *Manchester Guardian.*

HAKSAR, KAILAS NARAYAN and KERALA PUTRA, *pseud.* (KAVALAM MADHAVA PANIKKAR). **Federal India.** London: Hopkinson, 1930, 212 p.
The claims of the native princes in the future organization of India, expounded by two of their leading spokesmen.

HILL, SIR CLAUDE HAMILTON ARCHER. **India—Stepmother.** London: Blackwood, 1929, 333 p.
The reminiscences and reflections of a high British official. Interesting and valuable especially for the war period and the 1919 reforms.

HORNE, ERIC ARTHUR. **The Political System of British India.** Oxford: Clarendon Press, 1922, 184 p.
Based upon lectures delivered at Harvard by a member of the Indian Educational Service. One of the best brief expositions of Indian constitutional development, the Montagu-Chelmsford reforms, and general post-war problems.

HOROVITZ, JOSEF. **Indien unter Britischer Herrschaft.** Leipzig: Teubner, 1928, 136 p.
A well-balanced historical and analytical study, by a German who lived for eight years in India. He believes dominion status to be all that India is prepared for or apt to get.

HULL, WILLIAM ISAAC. **India's Political Crisis.** Baltimore: Johns Hopkins Press, 1930, 250 p.
A study of the All Parties Conference and the National Congress of 1928-1929.

IDRIS AHMAD. **Britain in India: Have We Benefited?** Lucknow: Seth, 1923, 226 p.
An appreciation of what England has done for India.

ILBERT, SIR COURTENAY PEREGRINE. **The Government of India.** Oxford: Oxford University Press, 1922, 144 p.
A succinct historical summary of imperial legislation by an authority.

ILBERT, SIR COURTENAY PEREGRINE and MESTON, JAMES SCORGIE MESTON, BARON. **The New Constitution of India.** London: University of London Press, 1923, 212 p.
Six lectures by experts in the subject, dealing with the history and main provisions of the new system.

INDIAN MOHAMMEDAN, *pseud.* **British India from Queen Elizabeth to Lord Reading.** London: Pitman, 1926, 594 p.
A good conventional account.

Indian Year Book. Bombay: Bennett, Coleman. Annual, since 1914.
A standard book of reference. A "Who's Who in India" is included.

INDO-BRITISH ASSOCIATION, LONDON. **The Crumbling of an Empire.** London: Author, 1922, 100 p.
A severe and well-documented indictment of British policy in India since 1916.

KENWORTHY, JOSEPH MONTAGUE. **India: A Warning.** London: Mathews, 1931, 117 p.
The author, a Labor M. P., considers the Round Table Conference and its recommendations.

KERALA PUTRA, *pseud.* (KAVALAM MADHAVA PANIKKAR). **An Introduction to the Study of the Relations of Indian States with the Government of India.** London: Hopkinson, 1927, 201 p.
An able and forceful study, the author concentrating on an examination of the relations of the leading states.

KERALA PUTRA, *pseud.* (KAVALAM MADHAVA PANIKKAR). **The Working of Dyarchy in India.** Bombay: Taraporevala, 1928, 159 p.
A systematic survey of results, by an Indian professor. The author finds that the constitution proved a source of great political progress, but a complete failure as an introduction to self-government. He envisages a new system to pave the way to dominion status.

KHŪB DEKHTĀ ĀGE, *pseud.* **India To-morrow.** New York: Oxford University Press, 1927, 87 p.
A stimulating examination of the problems which have arisen from the introduction of dyarchy. Written in anticipation of the appointment of the Constitutional Commission.

KRAUS, WOLFGANG. **Die Staats- und Voelkerrechtliche Stellung Britisch-Indiens.** Leipzig: Noske, 1930, 226 p.
A documented study of the relation of India to Great Britain and the Empire, and of India's status in international law. One of the best scholarly treatments.

LājPAT Rāya. **The Political Future of India.** New York: Huebsch, 1919, 237 p.
An extreme nationalist argument, written by a prominent leader.

MacDonald, James Ramsay. **The Government of India.** New York: Huebsch, 1920, 291 p.
A survey of the government, the constitutional relationships, financial and educational policies. Writing before the Montagu-Chelmsford reforms, MacDonald urges the need of changes to meet the demands of the new India.

MacMunn, Sir George Fletcher. **The Romance of the Indian Frontiers.** London: Cape, 1931, 349 p.
A well-known military historian reviews the story of India's frontier struggles.

Marvin, Francis Sydney. **India and the West.** New York: Longmans, 1927, 190 p.
The author emphasizes the opportunities offered India by her membership in the League of Nations, and urges an attitude of coöperation.

Montagu, Edwin Samuel. **An Indian Diary.** London: Heinemann, 1930, 410 p.
The private diary of the man whose name is associated with the Montagu-Chelmsford reforms. A valuable part of the literature of the subject.

Nicholson, Arthur Pole. **Scraps of Paper.** London: Benn, 1930, 355 p.
Purports to be the truthful record of England's high-handed treatment of the Indian states. The book is not documented.

O'Dwyer, Sir Michael Francis. **India as I Knew It, 1885-1925.** London: Constable, 1925, 464 p.
A rather narrow-minded interpretation of the Indian problem by a former Governor-General of the Punjab.

O'Malley, Lewis Sydney Steward. **The Indian Civil Service.** London: Murray, 1931, 310 p.
A succinct, sympathetic history of the service and its accomplishments.

Osburn, Arthur Carr. **Must England Lose India?** New York: Knopf, 1930, 280 p.
A highly controversial book, in which the author alleges that British arrogance of manner and contempt for the native are determining factors in the present unrest.

Palmer, Julian. **Sovereignty and Paramountcy in India.** London: Stevens, 1931, 104 p.
A study of the legal relations of the Indian states to the rest of India.

Pankhurst, Estelle Sylvia. **India and the Earthly Paradise.** Bombay: Sunshine Publishing Company, 1926, 638 p.
A wild communistic attack upon the existing régime.

Paul, Kanakarayan T. **The British Connection with India.** London: S. C. M., 1927, 224 p.
A well-written and suggestive essay, discussing the problems arising from the advent of the English and the introduction of western methods in India. The author stresses the importance of the non-political ties and attempts to show that, though changes may be made, a close interdependence of England and India is inevitable.

Pradhan, R. G. **Principles of the Constitution of the United States of India.** Poona: Aryabhushan, 1931, 114 p.
A vigorous discussion of the problems of defense and the position of the native states.

The Problem of Indian Administration. Baltimore: Johns Hopkins Press, 1928, 894 p.
One of the exhaustive publications of the Institute for Government Research.

Ranga Iyer, C. S. **India in the Crucible.** London: Selwyn, 1928, 336 p.
A discussion of the Simon Commission and the results of dyarchy, by a member of the Legislative Assembly and able exponent of the moderate Indian view.

RANGA IYER, C. S. **India: Peace or War?** London: Harrap, 1930, 256 p.
One of the moderate members of the Indian Legislative Assembly makes out a strong case for eventual dominion status. He deals with the national movement, the problem of the native princes, and the London Conference.

RAO, B. SHIVA and POLE, DAVID GRAHAM. **The Problem of India.** London: Labour Publishing Company, 1926, 96 p.
A presentation of the nationalist point of view.

RATCLIFFE, SAMUEL KERKHAM. **Sir William Wedderburn and the Indian Reform Movement.** London: Allen and Unwin, 1923, 192 p.
A well written account of the services of the most eminent and active English advocate of a liberal policy in Anglo-Indian relations.

RICE, STANLEY PITCAIRN. **Life of Sayaji Rao III, Maharaja of Baroda.** New York: Oxford University Press, 1931, 2 v.
An excellent biography of one of the most able and progressive of the Indian rulers.

ROY, MANABENDRA NATH. **La Libération Nationale des Indes.** Paris: Éditions Sociales Internationales, 1927, 108 p.
A Hindu presents the case against independence.

RUTHERFORD, VICKERMAN HENZELL. **Modern India. Its Problems and Their Solution.** London: Labour Publishing Company, 1928, 268 p.
A radical critique of the English administration and an appeal for complete self-government.

SCHOMERUS, HILKO WIARDO. **Indien und das Abendland.** Wernigerode: Die Aue, 1925, 160 p.
A competent brief review of European influences upon India, both political and religious.

SETON, SIR MALCOLM COTTER CARISTON. **The India Office.** New York: Putnam, 1926, 299 p.
A reliable brief treatment of the history and organization of the Home Government of India, by the Under-Secretary of the India Office.

SIMON, SIR JOHN. **India and the Simon Report.** New York: Coward-McCann, 1930, 56 p.
A brief statement by the chairman of the Statutory Commission.

SINGH, GURMUKH NIHAL. **Indian States and British India.** Benares: Nand Kishore, 1930, 380 p.
A moderate and competent discussion of one of the most knotty problems in the Indian situation. Half the book is devoted to documents.

SIVASVĀMI AIYAR, SIR PARAMANHĪRI SUNDARAM. **Indian Constitutional Problems.** Bombay: Taraporevala, 1928, 384 p.
An able survey of the main problems that were to come before the Simon Commission. A course of lectures by a retired member of the Madras Executive Council.

SKRINE, FRANCIS HENRY. **India's Hope.** London: Thacker, 1929, 61 p.
Reminiscences of a retired British official, together with a sympathetic study of the intelligentsia and a reply to India's detractors.

SMITH, VINCENT ARTHUR. **The Oxford History of India.** Oxford: Clarendon Press, 2nd rev. ed., 1928, 814 p.
The best general history of India, from earliest times to the present.

SPENDER, JOHN ALFRED. **The Changing East.** New York: Stokes, 1926, 256 p.
A well-balanced and competent survey dealing chiefly with India and Egypt.

SUNDERLAND, JABEZ THOMAS. **India in Bondage.** New York: Lewis Copeland, 1929, 554 p.
A vigorous refutation of the English claim to rule India for India's good, by the editor of *Young India.*

THAKORE, BALVANTRAI KALLIANRAI. **Indian Administration to the Dawn of Responsible Government, 1765-1920.** Bombay: Taraporevala, 1922, 471 p.
A dispassionate and on the whole well-balanced study, covering the years 1765 to 1920. Written by a professor at Deccan College.

THOMPSON, EDWARD. **Reconstructing India.** New York: Dial, 1930, 416 p.
The author reviews the history of the British in India, makes a calm assessment of their accomplishments, expounds the views of the nationalists, and points out the great difficulties in the way of a satisfactory settlement. One of the best books on present-day Indian problems.

VAN TYNE, CLAUDE HALSTEAD. **India in Ferment.** New York: Appleton, 1923, 252 p.
An American historian, unsympathetic with the Gandhi movement, makes a clear analysis of the situation and pleads for a gradual solution of Anglo-Indian relations by coöperation.

WAGENVOORT, MAURITS. **In het Voetspoor der Vaderen.** Amsterdam: Mees-Santpoort, 1930, 152 p.
A Dutch historian's interesting observations on the problems raised by British rule.

WHYTE, SIR ALEXANDER FREDERICK. **India. A Federation?** Delhi: Home Department, 1926, 326 p.
A well-balanced study of existing federal constitutions, with reference to their possible introduction in India, by a former president of the Indian Legislative Assembly.

YOUNGHUSBAND, SIR FRANCIS EDWARD. **Dawn in India.** New York: Stokes, 1931, 331 p.
Written by a well-known authority on things Indian. An admirable survey of the characteristics of British rule and the origins of the new Indian movements, with stress on spiritual forces.

YŪSUF 'ALĪ, 'ABD ALLĀH. **India and Europe.** London: Dranes, 1927, 132 p.
An attempt to pave the way to better understanding by setting forth the obstacles. A series of stimulating lectures contrasting European and Indian history, society, art and education.

YŪSUF 'ALĪ, 'ABD ALLĀH. **The Making of India.** London: Black, 1925, 318 p.
An interesting historical study which aims to lay due emphasis upon social, economic and religious factors.

Nationalism and *Swaraj*

ANDREWS, CHARLES FREER. **India and the Simon Report.** New York: Macmillan, 1930, 192 p.
This really is less an examination of the Simon Report than an interesting exposition of the views of Gandhi.

ANDREWS, CHARLES FREER. **Mahatma Gandhi's Ideas.** New York: Macmillan, 1930, 382 p.
A close friend of the Indian leader supplies an excellent selection from his speeches and articles, with explanatory comment.

ANDREWS, CHARLES FREER, *ed.* **Mahatma Gandhi, His Own Story.** New York: Macmillan, 1930, 372 p.
A selection from the two volumes of Gandhi's autobiography and his account of his experiences in South Africa.

BANERJEE, SIR SURENDRANATH. **A Nation in the Making.** New York: Oxford University Press, 1925, 435 p.
A sane history of Indian national development in the last half century, by a man long active in public life.

BHAGAVĀN DĀS. **The Philosophy of Non-Co-operation.** Madras: Tagore, 1922, 118 p.
A series of critical newspaper articles on Swaraj, political and spiritual, its aims and program—or lack of program.

BOSE, PRAMATHA NATH. **Swaraj—Cultural and Political.** Calcutta: Newman, 1929, 290 p.
The extreme nationalist view.

DAS, CHITTA RANJAN. **The Way to Swaraj.** Madras: Tamil-Nadu Swarajya Party, 1923, 260 p.
A collection of speeches by an independent and critical leader of the national movement.

DAS, KRISHNA. **Seven Months with Mahatma Gandhi.** Madras: Ganesan, 1928, 2 v.
The inside view of the non-coöperation movement of 1921-1922, by a fervent admirer.

DUTT, SUKUMAR. **Problem of Indian Nationality.** Calcutta: University of Calcutta, 1926, 199 p.
A university prize essay. A careful documented study.

GANDHI, MOHANDAS KARAMCHAND. **The Story of My Experiments with Truth.** Ahmedabad: Navajivan Press, 1927-1929, 2 v.
The autobiography of the leader.

GANDHI, MOHANDAS KARAMCHAND. **Young India, 1919-1922.** New York: Huebsch, 1923, 1199 p.
The authoritative exposition by the leader of the non-coöperation movement and his associates. A collection of speeches and writings.

GANDHI, MOHANDAS KARAMCHAND. **Young India, 1924-1926.** New York: Viking, 1927, 999 p.
Selections from the leader's contributions to the journal *Young India* in the years from 1924 to 1926.

GILCHRIST, ROBERT NIVEN. **Indian Nationality.** New York: Longmans, 1920, 246 p.
A stimulating study of race, language, religion and caste as factors in the making of Indian nationalism.

KOCH, D. M. G. **Herleving.** Weltevreden: Kolff, 1922, 486 p.
A detailed and well-informed history of the national movement in India, by a Dutch East-Indian publicist.

LÉVI, SYLVAIN. **L'Inde et le Monde.** Paris: Champion, 1926, 175 p.
Interesting essays in which the author combats the idea of a distinctive Indian culture and stresses Indian dependence on other nations and cultures.

LOVETT, SIR HARRINGTON VERNEY. **A History of the Indian Nationalist Movement.** London: Murray, 1920, 285 p.
A most interesting study of the earlier development of the movement, written by an official of long experience.

MESTON, JAMES SCORGIE MESTON, BARON. **Nationhood for India.** New York: Oxford University Press, 1931, 120 p.
Lectures delivered at Williamstown by a former Indian official, dealing largely with Hinduism and Nationalism.

PAVLOVICH, M., *pseud.* (MIKHAIL VEL'TMAN), GURKO-KRIAZHIN, V. A. and VEL'TMAN, L. **Indiia v Bor'be za Nezavisimost'.** Moscow: Nauchnaia Assotsiatsia Vostokovedeniia, 1925, 117 p.
A brief survey of the nationalist movement by Bolshevik writers, one of them the editor of *Novyĭ Vostok*.

PIRACÉS, AGUSTÍN. **Gandhi.** Barcelona: Iberia, 1930, 222 p.
A Spanish account of the Indian leader's life, work and doctrine.

POLAK, MRS. MILLIE GRAHAM. **Mr. Gandhi: the Man.** London: Allen and Unwin, 1931, 186 p.
Non-political reminiscences and impressions, written by the wife of one of Gandhi's chief assistants during the South Africa period.

PURKAYASTHA, K. M. **The Burden of Swaraj.** Calcutta: The Book Company, 1931, 192 p.
A moderate nationalist statement.

RĀDHĀKAMALA MUKHOPĀDHYĀYA. **Nationalism in Hindu Culture.** London: Theosophical Publishing House, 1921, 104 p.
A series of lectures delivered at Mysore University, dealing with the bases of patriotism and nationalism in Hindu literature and religion.

RAJAGOPALACHAR, C. and KUMARAPPA, J. C., *eds*. **The Nation's Voice.** Ahmedabad: Navajivan Press, 1932, 340 p.
Gandhi's speeches in England, with an account of his visit.

RAY, PRITHWIS CHANDRA. **Life and Times of C. R. Das.** New York: Oxford University Press, 1928, 329 p.
A valuable contribution to the history of Bengal in the period after 1900, with special reference to the growth of nationalism.

ROLLAND, ROMAIN. **Mahatma Gandhi.** New York: Century, 1924, 250 p.
A most sympathetic biographical sketch by one of the European writers best fitted to understand the Indian leader.

SANKARAN NAIR, SIR CHETTUR. **Gandhi and Anarchy.** Madras: Tagore, 1922, 262 p.
An Indian publicist's critical analysis.

SARMA, S. K. **Towards Swaraj.** Madras: Iyengar, 1929, 428 p.
The extreme nationalist and anti-British view of the situation and the future solution.

A Searchlight on Gandhi. London: King, 1931, 139 p.
A telling attack on Gandhi and his teachings, by the author of "India on the Brink."

SEN, RAJEN and SEN, B. K. **Deshabandhu Chitta Ranjan.** Calcutta: Karim Bux, 1926, 337 p.
A sketch of the life of the Bengalese leader C. R. Das, followed by a useful collection of his speeches.

SEN, SOCHIN. **Political Philosophy of Rabindranath.** Calcutta: Asher, 1929, 226 p.
The poet's utterances on political and social problems, gleaned from his writings.

STANDENRATH, FRANZISKA. **Indiens Freiheitskampf 1930; Vier Monate Gast Mahatma Gandhis.** Vienna: Leuschner und Lubensky, 1931, 478 p.
One of the Mahatma's admirers recounts the course of the struggle during 1930, and prints a number of Gandhi's letters from prison.

VIOLLIS, ANDRÉE, *pseud.* (ANDRÉE FRANÇOISE CAROLINE D'ARDENNE DE TIZAC). **L'Inde contre les Anglais.** Paris: Éditions des Portiques, 1931, 270 p.
A history of the nationalist movement, dramatically written.

WINSLOW, JACK C. and ELWIN, VERRIER. **Gandhi: The Dawn of Indian Freedom.**
New York: Revell, 1931, 224 p.
Two missionaries give a sympathetic account of Gandhi and his teaching.

YOUNG, PHILIP NORTON FRUSHARD and FERRERS, AGNES. **India in Conflict.** New York:
Macmillan, 1920, 153 p.
The Indian scene and the work of the missions, by the vice-principal of St. Stephen's
College at Delhi.

General Conditions

See also (Indo-China, Malay Peninsula, East Indies) Burma, p. 486.

ALEXANDER, HORACE GUNDRY. **The Indian Ferment.** London: Williams and Norgate,
1929, 253 p.
Letters of a traveller in India, touching especially on racial problems and intellectual
currents.

BOSSHARD, WALTER. **Indien Kämpft!** Stuttgart: Strecker und Schröder, 1931, 290 p.
Penetrating travel observations made during 1930.

BRAILSFORD, HENRY NOEL. **Rebel India.** New York: The New Republic, 1931, 274 p.
A socialist's observations in Northern India, betraying a strong leaning to the nationalist cause. A good study of village conditions and general social factors.

BROWN, ALFRED CLAUDE. **The Ordinary Man's India.** London: Palmer, 1927, 295 p.
A book written from the unofficial European view and intended as an introductory
account of the main aspects of Indian life.

BURDWAN, SIR BIJAY CHAND MAHTAB, MAHARAJADHIRAJA BAHADUR OF. **The Indian
Horizon.** London: Benn, 1932, 106 p.
A series of lectures delivered in the United States. The author stresses especially
the Hindu-Moslem antagonism.

BURR, AGNES RUSH. **Neighbour India.** New York: Revell, 1929, 200 p.
Largely a non-missionary's appreciation of the aims and achievements of missionary
activity.

BUTLER, SIR HARCOURT. **India Insistent.** London: Heinemann, 1931, 125 p.
The author, who has had forty years of experience in Indian affairs, surveys the land,
the people and the religions of India, and describes recent developments. This is un-
doubtedly one of the best books on the Indian problem.

CARTHILL, AL, *pseud.* **The Garden of Adonis.** London: Blackwood, 1927, 360 p.
A capable and arresting survey. The author, well-known for his "The Lost Dominion,"
here continues his pessimistic prognostications.

CATON, ANNIE ROSE, *ed.* **The Key of Progress.** New York: Oxford University Press,
1930, 250 p.
A dispassionate presentation of the facts regarding the position of women in India,
written by a number of competent persons.

CHAKRABERTY, CHANDRA. **National Problems.** Calcutta: Chakraberty, 1923, 155 p.
The author looks to progress in education, industry and hygiene to solve the problem
of India. An interesting survey of conditions.

CHAUVELOT, ROBERT. **L'Inde Mystérieuse.** Paris: Chapelot, 1920, 222 p.
Travels and observations, with stress on the religious and exotic.

CHRISTLIEB, MARIE LUISE. **Uphill Steps in India.** Boston: Houghton Mifflin, 1931, 254 p.
Very human and frequently amusing letters of a missionary, covering a long period of close observation.

CUMMING, SIR JOHN GHEST, *ed.* **Modern India.** New York: Oxford University Press, 1931, 310 p.
Valuable essays on all aspects of the Indian situation, written by English experts.

DARLING, MALCOLM LYALL. **Rusticus Loquitur.** New York: Oxford University Press, 1930, 400 p.
A valuable contribution to the study of the outlook of the Indian peasant.

DURANT, WILL. **The Case for India.** New York: Simon and Schuster, 1930, 238 p.
Not overloaded with knowledge of the subject, but pronounced in viewpoint and eloquent in pleading the cause of the Indian.

EMERSON, GERTRUDE. **Voiceless India.** New York: Doubleday, 1930, 458 p.
One of the most interesting books on India. The writer spent a year living with the inhabitants of a small village, and gives an excellent picture of village life.

FISHER, FREDERICK BOHN. **India's Silent Revolution.** New York: Macmillan, 1919, 192 p.
An able study of economic, social, religious and political conditions as they emerged after the World War.

HARCOURT, HENRY. **Sidelights on the Crisis in India.** London: Longmans, 1924, 118 p.
A suggestive reconsideration of the principal points at issue.

HOYLAND, JOHN SOMERVELL. **The Case for India.** New York: Dutton, 1929, 180 p.
An eloquent plea in behalf of the Indian standpoint, written on the basis of fifteen years' experience in India.

India in 1917-1918, and Later Years. Calcutta: Government Printing Office, 1919 ff.
A valuable annual report on conditions and progress, published under government auspices.

KENDALL, PATRICIA. **Come with Me to India.** New York: Scribner, 1931, 467 p.
The author, who is well-informed, identifies the nationalist movement with Hindu and Moslem opposition to the western influences on which Indian welfare depends.

KLÖTZEL, CHESKEL ZIVI. **Indien im Schmelztiegel.** Leipzig: Brockhaus, 1930, 285 p.
Observations on the Indian ferment by the correspondent of the *Berliner Tageblatt.*

MAYHEW, ARTHUR. **Christianity and the Government of India.** London: Faber and Gwyer, 1929, 260 p.
A scholarly and detached discussion of the relations between the British Government and the Christian Missions from 1600 to 1920, by the former Director of Public Instruction of the Central Provinces.

MAYO, KATHERINE. **Mother India.** New York: Harcourt, 1927, 454 p.
Probably the most discussed book about India written since the war. A disillusioning picture of social conditions and an unsparing criticism of Indian views of life. Among the many replies published may be mentioned: Ranga Iyer, C. S.: "Father India" (London: Selwyn, 1927); Mukerji, Dhan Gopal: "A Son of Mother India Answers" (New York: Dutton, 1928); Wood, Ernest: "An Englishman Defends Mother India" (New York: Tantrik, 1930); Natarajan, K.: "Miss Mayo's Mother India" (Madras: Natesan, 1928); Lājpat Rāya: "Unhappy India" (Calcutta: Banna, 1928); Chakravarty, Syam S.: "My Mother's Picture" (London: Thacker, 1930); Saund, Dalip Singh: "My Mother India" (Los Angeles: Wetzel, 1930); Chapman, J. A.: "The

Character of India" (Oxford: Blackwell, 1928). These and other criticisms have been examined and the argument of Miss Mayo restated by Field, Harry H.: "After Mother India" (New York: Harcourt, 1929).

MAYO, KATHERINE. **Volume Two.** New York: Harcourt, 1931, 313 p.
More evidence to support the contentions of Miss Mayo's previous book.

MUKERJI, DHAN GOPAL. **Disillusioned India.** New York: Dutton, 1930, 224 p.
A well-known Indian writer sets forth the results of recent investigations on the spot.

PARANJPYE, RAGHUNATH PURUSHOTTAM. **The Crux of the Indian Problem.** London: Watts, 1931, 116 p.
The crux, as the author sees it, is in the religious antagonism, which can only be overcome by a spread of rationalism.

PINCH, TREVOR. **Stark India.** New York: Appleton, 1931, 288 p.
Sociological, in the vein of Miss Mayo, by an English editor.

PYM, MICHAEL. **The Power of India.** New York: Putnam, 1930, 317 p.
Suggestive if not profound observations of an American newspaper woman with considerable experience of India.

RANADIVE, BHALCHANDRA TRIMBAK. **The Population Problem of India.** New York: Longmans, 1930, 216 p.
Though not directly concerned with politics, this book will serve to give an understanding of some of the deeper factors in the present crisis.

REED, SIR STANLEY and CADELL, PATRICK ROBERT. **India: The New Phase.** London: Allan, 1928, 175 p.
Written by the former editor of *The Times of India* and intended as a popular introduction to the conditions and problems of India, for the English voter.

SARKAR, BENOY KUMAR. **The Political Institutions and Theories of the Hindus.** Leipzig: Verlag von Markert und Petters, 1922, 242 p.
A stimulating survey containing frequent comparisons with the institutions of Western Europe.

The Times Book of India. London: The Times, 1930, 288 p.
As a general survey of conditions this collection by some thirty-odd experts can hardly be improved upon.

UNDERWOOD, ALFRED CLAIR. **Contemporary Thought of India.** New York: Knopf, 1931, 235 p.
A competent survey of political, social and religious currents.

WHITEHEAD, HENRY. **Indian Problems in Religion, Education and Politics.** London: Constable, 1924, 335 p.
A valuable work by the Bishop of Madras, resident in India for forty years.

WILLIAMS, MRS. GERTRUDE (MARVIN). **Understanding India.** New York: Coward-McCann, 1928, 342 p.
These impressions of extensive travels, by a woman with insight and discrimination, may well be read with Miss Mayo's book, as the viewpoint is very different.

WINGFIELD-STRATFORD, BARBARA (ERRINGTON). **India and the English.** London: Cape, 1922, 223 p.
A fair and understanding picture of Indian and Anglo-Indian life and culture.

WOOLACOTT, JOHN EVANS. **India on Trial.** London: Macmillan, 1929, 258 p.
The former Delhi correspondent of the London *Times* gives a lucid discussion of the present discontent, the religious antagonisms and the economic problems.

ZETLAND, LAWRENCE JOHN LUMLEY DUNDAS, MARQUIS OF. **India: A Bird's-Eye View.**
Boston: Houghton Mifflin, 1924, 322 p.
Intended as a general introduction. An excellent historical and descriptive study of
Indian life and its problems. The author, the biographer of Lord Curzon, wrote as
the Earl of Ronaldshay until his accession to his present title in 1929.

ZETLAND, LAWRENCE JOHN LUMLEY DUNDAS, MARQUIS OF. **The Heart of Âryâvarta.
A Study of the Psychology of Indian Unrest.** Boston: Houghton Mifflin, 1925,
262 p.
An unusually penetrating study of the causes of unrest, by a former Governor-
General of Bengal. The author pays especial attention to the position of the Hindu
intelligentsia.

ZIMAND, SAVEL. **Living India.** New York: Longmans, 1928, 296 p.
A good popular book. The author is not profound, but gives a fair and unsensational
survey of the history of the country, the social structure and the political situation.
The volume has an excellent bibliography.

Economic Problems

AMBEDKAR, BHIVRAM RAMJI. **The Problem of the Rupee.** London: King, 1923, 309 p.
A history and technical discussion of the currency, the gold standard and the gold
exchange standard.

ANSTEY, MRS. VERA (POWELL). **The Economic Development of India.** New York:
Longmans, 2nd ed., 1931, 581 p.
This elaborately documented and very competent study is, on the whole, the most
complete and reliable treatment of the subject.

BANERJEA, PRAMATHANATH. **Fiscal Policy in India.** New York: Macmillan, 1922, 256 p.
Lectures by a leading Indian economist, giving a good documented account of fiscal
development.

BROUGHTON, GLADYS MARY. **Labour in Indian Industries.** New York: Oxford University Press, 1924, 214 p.
An English dissertation. The author gives a well-documented account of the industrial revolution, the labor demand and supply, conditions of employment, amelio-
rative measures, etc.

CHAND, GYAN. **The Financial System of India.** London: Kegan Paul, 1926, 464 p.
A scholarly investigation.

COYAJEE, SIR JEHANGIR COOVERJEE. **The Indian Currency System, 1835-1926.**
Madras: Minerva, 1930, 326 p.
A series of lectures on the historical evolution of the currency problem.

DADACHANJI, B. E. **History of Indian Currency and Exchange.** Bombay: Taraporevala, 1931, 247 p.
The second edition of a good introductory text.

JATHER, G. B. and BERI, S. G. **Indian Economics.** New York: Oxford University
Press, 2nd ed., rev., 1930, 440 p.
A systematic handbook of Indian economic life and problems, by two Indian scholars.

JEVONS, HERBERT STANLEY. **Money, Banking and Exchange in India.** Simla: Government Central Press, 1922, 330 p.
A general text, for the layman.

Joshi, Ramchandra Mahadev. **Indian Export Trade.** Bombay: Sydenham College of Commerce and Economics, 1923, 195 p.
A compilation containng illuminating charts and statistics.

Lupton, Arnold. **Happy India.** London: Allen, 1922, 188 p.
India "as it might be if guided by modern science." A very critical account of Indian economics, with special reference to agriculture and irrigation.

Mukherji, Panchanandas. **The Coöperative Movement in India.** Calcutta: Thacker and Spink, 1923, 468 p.
A largely rewritten edition of the standard work on Indian coöperation.

Narain, Brij. **Essays on Indian Economic Problems.** Lahore: Punjab Printing Works, 1922, 547 p.
These able essays deal very largely with prices, currency and banking, and the problem of protection.

Pal, Bipin Chandra. **The New Economic Menace to India.** Madras: Ganesh, 1920, 250 p.
A warning to Indian patriots that the menace of English economic exploitation is perhaps even greater than the menace of political oppression.

Pillai, Purushottama Padmanabha. **Economic Conditions in India.** London: Routledge, 1925, 330 p.
A well-documented scholarly monograph, devoted chiefly to the problems of industrial development.

Read, Margaret. **The Indian Peasant Uprooted.** New York: Longmans, 1931, 256 p.
A vivid and depressing picture of labor in the new factories and in the fields, based chiefly on the eighteen-volume Report of the Royal Commission on Labor in India.

Shah, Khushal Talaksi. **Federal Finance in India.** London: King, 1929, 334 p.
A semi-popular lecture, delivered at Patna University.

Shirras, George Findlay. **Indian Finance and Banking.** New York: Macmillan, 1920, 535 p.
A scholarly history of the currency and banking systems, by a leading economist and statistician, professor in the University of Bombay.

Vakil, Chandulal Nagindas. **Financial Developments in Modern India, 1860-1924.** London: King, 1925, 640 p.
A solid piece of work, equipped with charts and tables.

Vakil, Chandulal Nagindas and Muranjan, Sumant K. **Currency and Prices in India.** London: King, 1927, 549 p.
The second volume in the author's series of studies on Indian financial history.

Wadia, Pestonji Ardesir and Joshi, Gulabbhai Naranji. **Money and the Money Market in India.** New York: Macmillan, 1926, 440 p.
Written by two Indian professors; one of the best historical and analytical studies of monetary policy, currency and banking.

Wadia, Pestonji Ardesir and Joshi, Gulabbhai Naranji. **The Wealth of India.** New York: Macmillan, 1925, 437 p.
A general survey of India's economic life and its evolution, together with a program of development designed to utilize the lessons learned by the West.

III. FAR EAST

GENERAL

See also (General International Relations) Civilizations and Race Conflicts, p. 4; also (United States) Far Eastern Policy, p. 186, and Immigration and Race Problems, p. 191; also (Russia) Foreign Policy, p. 393.

BAIN, H. FOSTER. **Ores and Industry in the Far East.** New York: Council on Foreign Relations, 1927, 229 p.
An authoritative description of the influence of key mineral resources on the development of Oriental civilization, by the secretary of the American Institute of Mining and Metallurgical Engineers. An illuminating volume.

BLAND, JOHN OTWAY PERCY. **China, Japan and Korea.** New York: Scribner, 1921, 327 p.
A well-informed study of events after 1910, and impressions of the post-war situation.

CHIROL, SIR VALENTINE and others. **The Reawakening of the Orient, and Other Addresses.** New Haven: Yale University Press, 1925, 176 p.
Williamstown lectures, including two by Mr. Tsurumi and two by Sir Arthur Salter.

Christian Missions and Oriental Civilizations. New York: Stechert, 1924, 604 p.
An exhaustive treatment of fundamental problems of the missionary in Eastern countries.

CIPOLLA, ARNALDO. **Nella Grande Asia Rivoluzionaria.** Turin: Paravia, 1931, 254 p.
Observations of a leading Italian writer on foreign affairs during an extended journey through the Far East.

CLOSE, UPTON, *pseud.* (JOSEF WASHINGTON HALL). **The Revolt of Asia.** New York: Putnam, 1927, 338 p.
The writer discusses the end of the white domination and speculates on possible future developments. A lively and interesting analysis.

CLOSE, UPTON, *pseud.* (JOSEF WASHINGTON HALL). **Eminent Asians.** New York: Appleton, 1929, 510 p.
The author of "The Revolt of Asia" draws vivid portraits of Sun Yat Sen, Yamagata, Ito, Mustapha Kemal, Stalin, and Gandhi.

DENNERY, ÉTIENNE. **Asia's Teeming Millions.** London: Cape, 1931, 248 p.
A stimulating discussion of the population problem, which the author regards as the most urgent presented by the Far East.

DUTCHER, GEORGE MATTHEW. **The Political Awakening of the East.** New York: Abingdon, 1925, 372 p.
A study of the influence of western political ideals on the nations of the East. A series of lectures on Egypt, India, China, Japan and the Philippines.

ELDRIDGE, FRANK REED. **Trading with Asia.** New York: Appleton, 1921, 474 p.
An important work on the resources, commerce and commercial policies of the Philippines and Eastern Asia.

ESSÉN, RÜTGER. **Från Asiens Oroshärdar.** Stockholm: Bonniers, 1931, 215 p.
Impressions of a journey to the Far East in 1930, with some interesting discussion of the important rôle of the Europeans in India and China.

FOTH, WERNER. **Der Politische Kampf im Fernen Osten.** Gotha: Perthes, 1919, 116 p.
A concise review of the policies of the various Powers in the Far East, with special reference to Chinese finance.

FRANKE, OTTO. **Die Grossmächte in Ostasien, 1894-1914.** Hamburg: Westermann, 1924, 408 p.
A valuable survey of the relation of imperialism in the Far East to the causes of the World War. Though somewhat outdated, this perhaps is still the best scholarly account of European diplomacy in the Far East.

GIBBONS, HERBERT ADAMS. **The New Map of Asia, 1900-1919.** New York: Century, 1919, 571 p.
A vivid but not entirely well-balanced account of the development of the Far Eastern problem, just before and during the war.

GOWEN, HERBERT HENRY. **Asia, a Short History from the Earliest Times to the Present Day.** Boston: Little, Brown, 1926, 456 p.
A general text, furnishing a reliable introduction to the subject.

GROUSSET, RENÉ. **Histoire de l'Extrême Orient.** Paris: Geuthner, 1929, 2 v.
An outstanding scholarly treatment, written by the curator of the Guimet Museum.

GUÉNON, RENÉ. **Orient et Occident.** Paris: Payot, 1924, 249 p.
A study of methods of establishing better relations between eastern and western peoples. The author upholds the superiority of Oriental culture.

HARRIS, NORMAN DWIGHT. **Europe and the East.** Boston: Houghton Mifflin, 1926, 619 p.
A survey of the foreign relations of Asiatic states in recent times. The book covers the whole Asiatic field and is useful only as an introduction.

HARRISON, MRS. MARGUERITE ELTON (BAKER). **Asia Reborn.** New York: Harper, 1928, 398 p.
A popular survey of conditions in Asia since the recent national revivals. As the whole continent is discussed, from Asia Minor to Japan, the treatment sometimes is superficial. There is nothing new in the book, but the oft-told story is presented readably.

HUNT, FRAZIER. **The Rising Temper of the East.** Indianapolis: Bobbs, 1922, 247 p.
A vivid, but impressionistic, sketch of the rise of democratic and nationalistic sentiment in India and the Far East. Written in sympathetic mood.

HUNTINGTON, ELLSWORTH. **West of the Pacific.** New York: Scribner, 1925, 453 p.
Valuable observations on the Far East by a well-known geographer and anthropologist.

KING-HALL, STEPHEN. **Western Civilization and the Far East.** New York: Scribner, 1924, 385 p.
One of the best-informed and best-written general surveys of domestic and international developments in the Far East during the last generation.

KOMOROWSKI, WŁADYSŁAW. **Daleki Wschód w Miedzynarodowej Polityce Gosudarczej.** Warsaw: Mianowski, 1931, 680 p.
An exhaustive, scholarly treatment of the Far Eastern question from earliest times.

KRAUSE, FRIEDRICH ERNST AUGUST. **Geschichte Ostasiens.** Göttingen: Vandenhoek und Ruprecht, 1925, 3 v.
One of the most satisfactory scholarly histories of the Far East. Volume II deals entirely with the 19th and 20th centuries.

LE FAIVRE, PAUL. **Soleil Levant, Soleil Couchant.** Paris: Nouvelle Librairie Nationale, 1921.
England, the United States and Japan in the Far East.

McMAHON, THOMAS J. **The Orient I Found.** New York: Appleton, 1926, 223 p.
An Australian view of the future influence and power of the Oriental nations.

MILLARD, THOMAS FRANKLIN. **Democracy and the Eastern Question.** New York: Century, 1919, 446 p.
A review of Japanese policy, the Chinese problem and the Siberian question in the World War period, by a writer of confirmed Chinese sympathies.

MILLARD, THOMAS FRANKLIN. **Conflict of Policies in Asia.** New York: Century, 1924, 507 p.
A study of the rival imperialisms in Asia in the post-war period, with main emphasis on the part played by the United States.

MORLEY, FELIX. **Our Far Eastern Assignment.** New York: Doubleday, 1926, 185 p.
An analysis of the Far Eastern situation by a discerning American journalist. The book is intended as an introduction to the Far Eastern problem for American readers.

MORSE, HOSEA BALLOU and MACNAIR, HARLEY FARNSWORTH. **Far Eastern International Relations.** Boston: Houghton Mifflin, 1931, 846 p.
A valuable general text, supplemented with an extensive bibliography.

POWELL, EDWARD ALEXANDER. **Asia at the Crossroads.** New York: Century, 1922, 369 p.
A journalistic sketch of contemporary civilization and international problems in Japan, Korea, China and the Philippines. A good popular introductory treatment.

RĀDHĀKAMALA MUKHOPĀDHYĀYA. **Democracies of the East: A Study in Comparative Politics.** London: King, 1924, 402 p.
A comparative study of organic communal life in the Far East, especially in India and China.

ROHDE, HANS. **Der Kampf um Asien.** Stuttgart: Deutsche Verlagsanstalt, 1924-1926, 2 v.
One of the most attractively-presented studies of modern European imperialism and international rivalries. Volume I deals with the Near East, volume II with the Far East.

SARKAR, BENOY KUMAR. **The Futurism of Young Asia.** Berlin: Springer, 1922, 399 p.
A series of essays on the recent tendencies in Asiatic culture, and on the cultural interaction between East and West, by a young Hindu writer.

La Société des Missions-Étrangères. Paris: Letouzey, 1923, 150 p.
Excellent for a documentary description of the work of Catholic missionaries in the Far East.

SOYESHIMA, MICHIMASA and KUO PING WEN. **Oriental Interpretations of the Far Eastern Problem.** Chicago: Chicago University Press, 1925, 228 p.
Harris Lectures, to be read with "Occidental Interpretations of the Far Eastern Problem," listed below.

TREAT, PAYSON JACKSON. **The Far East.** New York: Harper, 1928, 560 p.
A reliable text on the history of China, Japan and the Far East generally in modern times. See also third volume of Howland's "Annual Survey of American Foreign Relations" (New Haven: Yale University Press, 1930).

TSUCHIDA, KYOSON. **Contemporary Thought of Japan and China.** New York: Knopf, 1927, 239 p.
A pioneer essay intended to introduce the western world to the present day philosophy of the Far East, and to explain the basis of this philosophy.

VINACKE, HAROLD MONK. **A History of the Far East in Modern Times.** New York: Knopf, 1928, 479 p.
A good systematic text, dealing primarily with the history of China and Japan, but noteworthy for the stress laid on social and economic aspects.

WHYTE, SIR ALEXANDER FREDERICK. **Asia in the Twentieth Century.** New York: Scribner, 1926, 184 p.
Four interesting lectures by the former president of the Indian Legislative Assembly.

WOODHEAD, HENRY GEORGE WANDESFORDE, ARNOLD, JULEAN HERBERT and NORTON, HENRY KITTREDGE. **Occidental Interpretations of the Far Eastern Problem.** Chicago: Chicago University Press, 1926, 261 p.
Harris Lectures, by authorities, dealing with extraterritoriality, China's international position, and Russian policy in the Far East.

CHINA
General

See also (Central Asia and India) Central Asia and Turkestan, p. 443, and Tibet, p. 445.

ABEND, HALLETT. **Tortured China.** New York: Ives Washburn, 1930, 318 p.
A far from optimistic survey of conditions and movements, by the correspondent of the *New York Times*.

ANDERSON, JOHAN GUNNAR. **The Dragon and the Foreign Devils.** Boston: Little, Brown, 1928, 352 p.
A noteworthy book on China, written by a Swedish scientist thoroughly acquainted with all parts of the country. The writer deals chiefly with Chinese culture, the foreign influences and current problems.

ARLINGTON, LEWIS CHARLES. **Through the Dragon's Eyes.** London: Constable, 1931, 347 p.
Reminiscences of fifty years spent in the Chinese navy, customs service and postal service.

AUXION DE RUFFÉ, R. D'. **Chine et Chinois d'Aujourd'hui.** Paris: Berger-Levrault, 1926, 496 p.
A Frenchman long resident in China decries the modern anti-foreign movement, the teachings of Sun Yat Sen, the extravagances of students, the connection with Moscow, etc.

BAKER, JOHN EARL. **Explaining China.** New York: Van Nostrand, 1927, 330 p.
A substantial and reliable account of various aspects of Chinese life, by one who was for years an adviser to the Chinese Government.

BRISSAUD-DESMAILLET, GENERAL. **L'Armée Chinoise.** Paris: Charles-Lavauzelle, 1927, 88 p.
An important contribution by the former military adviser of the Chinese Republic, dealing particularly with the question of excessive man power and inadequate equipment.

CHENG SIH GUNG. **Modern China.** Oxford: Clarendon Press, 1919, 380 p.
An interesting statement of Chinese conditions, problems and desiderata, by a member of the Chinese delegation at the Paris Peace Conference.

China Year Book. New York: Dutton. Annual since 1912.
The subjects treated embrace government, finance, communications, commerce, education, etc. A "Who's Who" is also included.

La Chine et le Monde. Paris: Presses Universitaires, 1925-1926, 2 v.
A valuable collection of essays, by former students of the École des Sciences Politiques, dealing with a large variety of Chinese problems—diplomatic, constitutional, economic and social.

CORDIER, HENRI. **Histoire Générale de la Chine.** Paris: Geuthner, 1921, 4 v.
The most comprehensive and reliable history of China in any language, written by the foremost French authority on Chinese history.

DOLSEN, JAMES H. **The Awakening of China.** Chicago: Daily Worker Publishing Company, 1926, 267 p.
A radical's account of the Chinese situation, with stress on industrialism, exploitation of the worker, the great strike of 1925, the communist party, etc.

DONOVAN, JOHN PATRICK. **Yesterday and Today in China.** London: Dranes, 1924, 237 p.
Essays and lectures on various aspects of Chinese life, by a former postal commissioner. Among the subjects treated are education, militarism, the press, religion, medicine and commerce.

DUBARBIER, GEORGES. **La Chine Contemporaine, Politique et Économique.** Paris: Geuthner, 1926, 373 p.
A survey of events since 1911, followed by a systematic analysis of finances, commerce, industry, agriculture and communications.

DUBOSCQ, ANDRÉ. **L'Évolution de la Chine.** Paris: Bossard, 1921, 194 p.
An excellent brief review of changes and tendencies in politics, culture and international relations from 1911 to 1921.

ERKES, EDUARD. **China.** Gotha: Perthes, 1919, 168 p.
An admirable German survey of the Chinese people, their industry, social organization and art. Excellent bibliographies.

ETHERTON, PERCY THOMAS. **The Crisis in China.** Boston: Little, Brown, 1927, 259 p.
A masterly survey of the main issues before China and the interested European Powers, by an experienced and moderate English official.

FRANCK, HARRY ALVERSON. **Wandering in Northern China.** New York: Century, 1923, 502 p.
Interesting descriptive material on Korea, Manchuria, Mongolia and North China.

GILBERT, RODNEY YONKERS. **What's Wrong with China?** New York: Stokes, 1932, 315 p.
A revised edition of a series of essays by a well-known journalist long resident in China, first published in the *North China Daily News*. The author criticizes, often very sharply, Chinese social traditions, history and standards. The last essays discuss foreign relations and influences.

GOODNOW, FRANK JOHNSON. **China.** Baltimore: Johns Hopkins Press, 1926, 279 p.
An analysis of economic, political and social aspects, based on Lowell Lectures.

GOWEN, HERBERT HENRY and CLOSE, UPTON, *pseud.* (JOSEF WASHINGTON HALL). **An Outline History of China.** New York: Appleton, 1926, 570 p.
A general text, stressing particularly the Republican period.

GROSE, GEORGE RICHMOND. **The New Soul in China.** New York: Abingdon, 1927, 152 p.
A Methodist bishop discusses the position of Christianity and the missions in the new China.

GULL, EDWARD MANICO. **Facets of the Chinese Question.** London: Benn, 1931, 198 p.
A series of studies of various phases of the Chinese situation, by a man long resident in China. Several of the essays deal with religious subjects, but others are devoted to political and international problems.

HIGH, STANLEY. **China's Place in the Sun.** New York: Macmillan, 1922, 212 p.
A summary of contemporary Chinese history and civilization and of Chinese-American relations.

Hsu Shih Chang. **China after the War.** Peiping: Bureau of Economic Information, 1920, 164 p.
    Written by the former President of the Republic. A general survey of the economic and educational problems confronting China after the great conflict.

Hu Shih and Lin Yu Tang. **China's Own Critics.** Peiping: China United Press, 1931, 166 p.
    Critical essays on various aspects of the Chinese scene, by two outstanding leaders of the Young China group.

Hülle, Hermann. **Neuerwerbungen Chinesischer und Manjurischer Bücher in den Jahren 1921-1930.** Leipzig: Hirsemann, 1931, 72 p.
    This bibliographical article describes in some detail most of the important books on politics, economics and history published in Chinese during the last decade. These it has seemed unnecessary to list in the present work.

King, Paul. **In the Chinese Customs Service.** London: Heath Cranton, 1930, 304 p.
    Reminiscences of a customs official, and an interesting commentary on the events of the recent period.

King, Paul. **Weighed in China's Balance.** London: Heath Cranton, 1928, 238 p.
    Written by a former commissioner of Chinese customs; a discussion of Chinese religions and missionary enterprise, together with a consideration of the effects of the war and revolution on the standing of Christianity.

Kotenev, Anatol M. **New Lamps for Old.** Shanghai: North China Daily News, 1931, 371 p.
    A documented narrative of events in China from 1911 to 1930, written by a Russian resident in the country.

Ku Hung Ming. **L'Esprit du Peuple Chinois.** Paris: Stock, 1927, 180 p.
    The writer, a Chinese of the old school who has lived in the west, bitterly condemns western civilization and its failure to enlist the individual in the service of the community. At the same time he gives an unusually clear evaluation of Chinese civilization. A notable book.

Kuo Shien Yen and Hinkel, Karl. **4600 Jahre China.** Göttingen: Oeffentliches Leben, 1930, 133 p.
    Most of the 4600 years are dealt with in summary fashion, and the book is devoted primarily to the current political, economic and cultural problems.

Latourette, Kenneth Scott. **The Development of China.** Boston: Houghton Mifflin, 1924, 309 p.
    This third edition of an excellent introductory history devotes considerable attention to events and problems since 1894.

Latourette, Kenneth Scott. **A History of Christian Missions in China.** New York: Macmillan, 1928, 942 p.
    The most complete and authoritative account.

Lee Teng Hwee. **Vital Factors in China's Problems.** New York: Stechert, 1927, 440 p.
    A useful selection and translation of current writings in Chinese.

Legendre, Aimé François. **Modern Chinese Civilization.** London: Cape, 1929, 295 p.
    A French scientist who has lived for years in China discusses the Chinese family, Chinese city life, the economic situation, etc. A good book.

Mänchen-Helfen, Otto. **China.** Dresden: Kaden, 1931, 232 p.
    A study of the social structure and the class struggle.

MONROE, PAUL. **China. A Nation in Evolution.** New York: Macmillan, 1928, 462 p.
An American educator, well-acquainted with China, surveys the scene. A good general
introduction to conditions and problems of modern China.

O Kitae. Moscow: Gosizdat, 1928, 219 p.
Soviet monographs dealing with the economic and political situation in China.

PEFFER, NATHANIEL. **China, the Collapse of a Civilization.** New York: Day, 1930,
306 p.
One of the best recent treatments of the Chinese problem and its causes.

RANSOME, ARTHUR. **The Chinese Puzzle.** Boston: Houghton Mifflin, 1927, 189 p.
A stimulating review of the Chinese difficulties, written by a keen English journalist
of advanced liberal tendencies.

RASMUSSEN, OTTO DURHAM. **What's Right with China.** New York: Stechert, 1927,
275 p.
A cogent reply to some of the criticisms most commonly made by foreigners of the
Chinese position, and an attack upon the treaty-port mentality.

RAWLINSON, FRANK, *ed.* **The China Christian Year Book, 1926.** Shanghai: Christian
Literature Society, 1926, 594 p.
Various chapters, written by many contributors, relate to the Christian movement
and national affairs, such as social and industrial problems, medical and health work,
education, missions and literature.

RODES, JEAN. **Les Chinois: Essai de Psychologie Ethnographique.** Paris: Alcan,
1923, 233 p.
An able French writer on China studies the characterizations given by early travellers
and then attempts to analyze the modern Chinese mind.

ROSTHORN, ARTHUR VON. **Geschichte Chinas.** Stuttgart: Perthes, 1923, 226 p.
This volume in Hartmann's "Weltgeschichte" gives a competent survey of Chinese
history for the educated layman.

RUSSELL, BERTRAND RUSSELL, EARL. **The Problem of China.** New York: Century,
1922, 276 p.
A survey of the development of China and Japan, followed by a sympathetic analysis
of the new forces.

SFORZA, CONTE CARLO. **L'Énigme Chinoise.** Paris: Payot, 1928, 208 p.
An able analysis of the Chinese situation, by a former Italian Minister to China. The
problems raised by the appearance of a popular press, the Bolshevik influence, the difficulties of the European administrations of the customs and posts, the crisis of the
Christian missions and the policies of the various European powers are all treated in
an original and stimulating way.

SMITH, JOHN NIND. **China's Hour.** London: Hopkinson, 1930, 176 p.
A study of the Chinese mind, of Chinese political ideas and of Chinese aspirations,
by a former professor at Hongkong.

SOOTHILL, WILLIAM EDWARD. **The Three Religions of China: A Study of Confucian-
ism, Buddhism, and Taoism.** New York: Oxford University Press, 2nd ed.,
1923, 271 p.
A good general introduction.

STRONG, ANNA LOUISE. **China's Millions.** New York: Coward-McCann, 1928, 413 p.
A fascinating picture of the social changes taking place in China as seen by a radical
observer during an extended journey in 1927.

T'ANG LEANG LI. **China in Revolt.** London: Douglas, 1927, 176 p.
One of the ablest nationalist publicists reviews China's enchainment—extraterritoriality, the missionary burden, the foreign loans—and then outlines the chief characteristics of the new national consciousness.

TOYNBEE, ARNOLD JOSEPH. **A Journey to China.** London: Constable, 1931, 346 p.
This travel book, like all that Professor Toynbee writes, is characterized by historical grasp, breadth of view, and keen observation.

TYLER, WILLIAM FERDINAND. **Pulling Strings in China.** London: Constable, 1929, 310 p.
Amusing memoirs of one who spent forty years in China as a customs official.

WEBSTER, JAMES BENJAMIN. **Christian Education and the National Consciousness in China.** New York: Dutton, 1923, 321 p.
An excellent study from the historical and sociological point of view.

WEGENER, GEORG. **China.** Leipzig: Teubner, 1930, 233 p.
A first rate introduction to the geography, resources, people and history of China.

WILHELM, RICHARD. **The Soul of China.** New York: Harcourt, 1928, 382 p.
The translation from the German of one of the best recent interpretations of Chinese psychology, by an admirer of China who has spent many years in the Far East.

WILLIAMS, EDWARD THOMAS. **China Yesterday and To-day.** New York: Crowell, rev. ed., 1927, 664 p.
An authoritative work on the civilization of present-day China, by one of the Americans who knows China best.

WILLIAMS, EDWARD THOMAS. **A Short History of China.** New York: Harper, 1928, 670 p.
One of the best general texts of Chinese history, with full treatment of the Manchu and Republican periods.

WOODHEAD, HENRY GEORGE WANDESFORDE. **The Yangtsze and Its Problems.** London: Simpkin, Marshall, 1931, 150 p.
A reprint of articles by the editor of the "China Year Book."

WU CHAO KWANG. **The International Aspect of the Missionary Movement in China.** Baltimore: Johns Hopkins Press, 1930, 294 p.
A Chinese professor examines the missionary problem with special reference to the legal position and political influence of the missionaries.

The Revolution and the Republic

General

See also (Russia: Foreign Policy) Relations with Specific Countries, p. 394.

AMANN, GUSTAV. **The Legacy of Sun Yat Sen.** New York: Carrier, 1929, 302 p.
The history of the Revolution, by an eyewitness.

BUKHARIN, NIKOLAĬ IVANOVICH. **Problemy Kitaĭskoĭ Revoliutsii.** Moscow: Pravda, 2nd ed., 1927, 63 p.
A valuable view of the Chinese Revolution by one of the chief Bolshevik theorists.

CHAPMAN, HERBERT OWEN. **The Chinese Revolution, 1926-27.** London: Constable, 1928, 328 p.
An important record of the communist period in 1926-1927 as seen at Hankow.

CHEN TSUNG HSI and others. **General Chiang Kai-shek: The Builder of New China**. Shanghai: Commercial Press, 1929, 107 p.
A usuable brief biography, enthusiastically written.

CLOSE, UPTON, *pseud*. (JOSEF WASHINGTON HALL). **In the Land of the Laughing Buddha**. New York: Putnam, 1924, 359 p.
The experiences and observations of an American correspondent recording developments after the death of Yuan Shih K'ai.

DALIN, S. **Ocherki Revoliutsii v Kitae**. Moscow: Moskovskiĭ Rabochiĭ, 1927, 282 p.
An outline history of the Chinese Revolution from the Soviet viewpoint.

GANNETT, LEWIS STILES. **Young China**. New York: The Nation, 1927, 51 p.
Penetrating observations on the situation in 1926, by one of the editors of the *Nation*.

HOLCOMBE, ARTHUR NORMAN. **The Chinese Revolution**. Cambridge: Harvard University Press, 1930, 400 p.
One of the best scholarly studies of the revolutionary movement and the Revolution, in its cultural as well as political and international aspects.

HOLCOMBE, ARTHUR NORMAN. **The Spirit of the Chinese Revolution**. New York: Knopf, 1930, 191 p.
Lowell Lectures, in which the author analyzes the leading tendencies in the Revolution and discusses the most representative leaders.

HUTCHINSON, PAUL. **What and Why in China**. Chicago: Willett, Clark and Colby, 1927, 131 p.
An introductory survey of the situation at a critical stage of the civil war.

IVIN, A. **Pis'ma iz Kitaia**. Moscow: Moskovskiĭ Rabochiĭ, 1927, 152 p.
Letters from China covering the period from 1919 to the Russian-Chinese Convention.

KING, LOUIS MAGRATH. **China in Turmoil**. London: Heath Cranton, 1927, 233 p.
Fascinating sketches of leading types in the China of today, by a former British consul.

KRARUP-NIELSEN, AAGE. **The Dragon Awakes**. New York: Dodd, 1928, 224 p.
One of the best books on the crisis of 1926-1927. The author, a Danish correspondent, was with both armies at one time or another, and gives a keen account of what he saw.

KREITNER, GUSTAV, RITTER VON. **Hinter China Steht Moskau**. Berlin: Mittler, 1932, 144 p.
A bitter indictment of the Kuomintang, described as a clique which is ruining China.

LINEBARGER, PAUL MYRON WENTWORTH. **Sun Yat Sen and the Chinese Republic**. New York: Century, 1925, 371 p.
A popular, uncritical biography, written by one of Sun's associates and supporters and based in part on information from Sun and his family.

LO REN YEN. **China's Revolution from the Inside**. New York: Abingdon, 1930, 307 p.
A discussion of the non-political aspects of the Chinese revival, by a well-informed student of Chinese affairs.

LOSOWSKY, ALEXANDER. **Revolution und Konterrevolution in China**. Berlin: Führer, 1928, 80 p.
A Bolshevik presentation.

MACNAIR, HARLEY FARNSWORTH. **China in Revolution**. Chicago: Chicago University Press, 1931, 244 p.
This general outline of the Chinese Revolution is intended for the non-specialist. It is readable and well-informed, and is one of the best brief accounts.

MADIAR, L. **Sovremennoe Sostoianie Kitaĭskoĭ Revoliutsii.** Moscow: Kommunis-ticheskaia Akademiia, 1929, 84 p.
The situation in China after the communist period, as viewed from Moscow.

MILLARD, THOMAS FRANKLIN. **China: Where It Is Today and Why.** New York: Har-court, 1928, 356 p.
One of the best-known American journalists in China surveys the events of the years 1925-1928 and attempts to analyze their causes. A useful summing up.

MITAREVSKIĬ, N. **World Wide Soviet Plots.** Tientsin: Tientsin Press, n. d., 203 p.
One of many editions and commentaries on the Bolshevik documents seized in the Russian Embassy at Peking. The author was associated with the commission appointed to examine the material.

NEARING, SCOTT. **Whither China?** New York: International Publishers, 1927, 225 p.
An economic interpretation of the recent troubles, based upon research and personal observation by a radical American. The writer distinguishes between the national struggle waged by native enterprise against foreign interests and the class struggle between the employers and the proletariat.

PARK NO YONG. **Making a New China.** Boston: Stratford, 1929, 315 p.
A good exposition of the Nationalist view of the Revolution, the Manchurian struggle, and the dominant economic and political problems of China.

RAFES, M. **Revoliutsiia v Kitae.** Moscow: Moskovskiĭ Rabochiĭ, 1927, 148 p.
The "betrayal" of Chiang Kai Shek.

RESTARICK, HENRY BOND. **Sun Yat Sen.** New Haven: Yale University Press, 1931, 167 p.
An important contribution. The author has collected much new material bearing on the formative years of the great Chinese leader.

RODES, JEAN. **La Chine Nationaliste, 1912-1930.** Paris: Alcan, 1931, 190 p.
A competent writer on Chinese affairs surveys the course of the Chinese Revolution from 1912 to 1930.

SHEN YI and STADELMANN, HEINRICH. **China und Sein Weltprogramm.** Dresden: Gutewort, 1925, 163 p.
An account of the origins and development and aims of Chinese nationalism, with a discussion of China's position in the modern world.

SOULIÉ, GEORGES. **Soun Iat-Sènn.** Paris: Nouvelle Revue Française, 1932, 217 p.
A general biography of the Chinese leader written by a leading French Sinologue.

SUN YAT SEN. **San Min Chu I: The Three Principles of the People.** Shanghai: China Committee, Institute of Pacific Relations, 1927, 514 p.
The lectures in full of Dr. Sun, the "Father of the Chinese Revolution," on the princi-ples of Nationalism, Democracy, and Livelihood. These lectures formulated the basic ideals and policies of the Revolution and have served as the guiding principles of the Nationalist Government. They have been translated into English by Frank W. Price and edited by L. T. Chen.

T'ANG LEANG LI. **The Foundations of Modern China.** London: Douglas, 1928, 290 p.
The author is concerned mainly with the background and history of the nationalist movement and the attitude of the Powers toward it. A good book.

T'ANG LEANG LI. **The Inner History of the Chinese Revolution.** New York: Dutton, 1930, 406 p.
In this interesting volume a representative of the Kuomintang reviews the develop-ment of the nationalist movement from the time of the Boxer Rebellion.

T'ANG LEANG LI. **Wang Ching Wei.** Peiping: China United Press, 1931, 223 p.
The career and teachings of Sun's most eminent successor.

Tsen Tson Ming. **La Chine Qui Lutte.** Paris: Nachbaur, 1931.
The author discusses recent developments within the Kuomintang.

Tyau Min Ch'ien Tuk Zung, *ed.* **Two Years of Nationalist China.** London: Simpkin, 1931, 523 p.
An elaborate record of two years of nationalist rule. Largely a collection of documents and statistics compiled by the director of publicity at the foreign office of the Nanking Government.

Valentin, Ferdinand. **L'Avènement d'une République.** Paris: Perrin, 1926, 316 p.
An account of Chinese domestic conflicts from 1911 to 1923, well-informed and impartial. Written by a Frenchman long resident in China.

Vandervelde, Émile. **À Travers la Révolution Chinoise.** Paris: Alcan, 1931, 240 p.
Thoughtful observations during a visit to China, by the well-known Belgian statesman. The discussion of the Bolshevik influence and the teachings of Sun Yat Sen are especially interesting.

Van Dorn, Harold Archer. **Twenty Years of the Chinese Republic.** New York: Knopf, 1932, 330 p.
Four of the five chapters are devoted to non-political aspects of Chinese life, and serve as a good introduction to recent educational, religious, social and economic changes.

Vilenskiĭ-Sibiriakov, V. **Sun Yat Sen.** Moscow: Gosizdat, 1924, 196 p.
The second edition of a popular Russian biography.

Wang Ching Wei and others. **The Chinese National Revolution.** Peiping: China United Press, 1931, 188 p.
A varied collection of essays by prominent Chinese leaders.

Weale, Putnam, *pseud.* (Bertram Lenox Simpson). **Why China Sees Red.** New York: Dodd, 1925, 349 p.
A competent survey of the situation in 1924 and 1925. The author stresses the new influence of students and people, the new press, etc.

Weale, Putnam, *pseud.* (Bertram Lenox Simpson). **The Vanished Empire.** New York: Macmillan, 1926, 388 p.
The larger part of the book is devoted to retelling the story of the fall of the Empire. The last part continues the author's chronicle of events and deals with 1925-1926.

William, Maurice. **Sun Yat Sen versus Communism.** Baltimore: Williams and Wilkins, 1932, 232 p.
An elaborate study of the relation between the writings of Sun and the author's "The Social Interpretation of History," which, it is claimed, led to a complete change in Sun's teaching, away from communism.

Woo, Thomas Tze Chung. **The Kuomintang and the Future of the Chinese Revolution.** London: Allen and Unwin, 1928, 278 p.
An important review of the whole history of the nationalist movement. The writer was head of the diplomatic department in the Hankow foreign office and relies largely upon documents.

Woodhead, Henry George Wandesforde. **The Truth about the Chinese Republic.** London: Hurst and Blackett, 1925, 287 p.
The editor of the "China Year Book" examines the history of the Republic and the main issues before the Powers. The viewpoint is rather pronouncedly that of foreign trade interests in China.

Wou Sao Fong. **Sun Yat Sen.** Paris: Presses Universitaires, 1930, 220 p.
A careful analysis of the historical, philosophical, political, economic and social teaching of the great Chinese leader.

Wu Chao Chu. **The Nationalist Program for China.** New Haven: Yale University Press, 1929, 116 p.
An authoritative presentation of the nationalist program, by a former Chinese Minister to the United States. Williamstown Lectures.

Constitutional Questions

Bau, Mingchien Joshua. **Modern Democracy in China.** Shanghai: Commercial Press, 1923, 467 p.
An able survey of China's constitutional development, followed by an extended study of fundamental problems such as the cabinet and the presidential systems, federalism and unitary government, local self-government, etc.

Chen Wan Li. **Les Développements des Institutions Politiques de la Chine depuis l'Établissement de la République.** Paris: Jouve, 1926, 185 p.
This dissertation (far from exhausting the subject) supplies a general outline of the evolution of the presidency, the cabinet, the parliament and local government from 1912 to 1924.

Chou Sie Ying. **Le Fédéralisme en Chine.** Paris: D'Arthez, 1924, 239 p.
This doctoral thesis is devoted chiefly to an analysis of some provincial constitutions with a view to the feasibility of a federal régime.

Hsieh Pao Chao. **The Government of China, 1644-1911.** Baltimore: Johns Hopkins Press, 1925, 414 p.
A valuable book for reference, containing material not otherwise available. The arrangement is topical, not chronological.

Kwang Eu Yang. **The Political Reconstruction of China.** Shanghai: St. John's University, 1922, 190 p.
A useful dissertation, analyzing the post-war organization, the party system, the judicature, military and foreign service, as well as the provincial and municipal governments.

Vinacke, Harold Monk. **Modern Constitutional Development in China.** Princeton: Princeton University Press, 1920, 280 p.
Reviews and analyzes all important documents from 1898 onwards. A careful, scholarly dissertation.

Woo, James. **Le Problème Constitutionnel Chinois.** Paris: Giard, 1925, 168 p.
Primarily an analysis of the constitution of 1923.

Wu, Friedrich C. **La Nouvelle Chine et le Gouvernement National.** Paris: Rivière, 1929, 216 p.
Another dissertation; the author analyzes the Organic Law of October 11, 1928.

Economic Problems

Anderson, Adelaide Mary. **Humanity and Labour in China.** London: S. C. M., 1927, 301 p.
The results of an investigation of industrial conditions by the Principal Lady Inspector of Factories in England. Full of important data, but not well presented.

Die Arbeiter Chinas im Kampf gegen die Imperialismus. Berlin: Führer, 1927, 72 p.
The report of the First Delegation of Soviet Trades Unions.

Arbeiterbewegung und Revolution in China. Berlin: Führer, 1925, 160 p.
Contains some significant essays by Radek and other communists.

ARNOLD, JULEAN HERBERT. **China: Commercial and Industrial Handbook.** Washington: Department of Commerce, 1926, 818 p.
An extremely useful and well-done handbook, prepared for the Bureau of Foreign and Domestic Commerce.

Bericht der China Studienkommission des Reichsverbandes der Deutschen Industrie. Leipzig: Volckmar, 1930, 191 p.
The report of the German industrial investigation.

COONS, ARTHUR GARDINER. **The Foreign Public Debt of China.** Philadelphia: University of Pennsylvania Press, 1930, 251 p.
A scholarly monograph, which deals not only with China's indebtedness, but also with her capacity to pay. The best book on the subject.

HALL, RAY OVID. **The Chinese National Banks.** Washington: Ballantyne, 1921, 291 p.
An American doctoral thesis covering the historical development and supplying a useful collection of documents.

KANN, EDUARD. **The Currencies of China.** Shanghai: Kelly and Walsh, 2nd ed., 1927, 562 p.
A fundamental historical treatment.

KING, FRANKLIN HIRAM. **Farmers of Forty Centuries.** New York: Harcourt, 1927, 379 p.
A new edition of the standard work on Chinese agriculture, edited by J. P. Bruce.

LEE, MABEL PING HUA. **The Economic History of China.** New York: Columbia University Press, 1921, 461 p.
This study deals primarily with agriculture. It is based on extensive use of Chinese material, much of which is given in translation.

LIEU, D. K. **China's Industries and Finance.** Shanghai: Chinese Government Bureau of Economic Information, 1928, 238 p.
A collection of essays on industrial and financial problems, with much statistical material. Written by the director of the Bureau of Economic Information.

MALLORY, WALTER HAMPTON. **China, Land of Famine.** New York: American Geographical Society, 1927, 199 p.
A substantial and scholarly book by the former Secretary of the International Famine Relief Commission. Indispensable for an understanding of geographical, economic and social problems.

MORSE, HOSEA BALLOU. **The Trade and Administration of China.** Shanghai: Kelly and Walsh, 3rd rev. ed., 1921, 505 p.
The latest edition of a standard descriptive and analytical work.

NORD, ADOLF. **Die Handelsverträge Chinas.** Leipzig: Köhler, 1920, 215 p.
A thorough, scholarly history of the Chinese commercial treaties.

OTTE, FRIEDRICH. W. K. **China.** Gotha: Perthes, 1927, 111 p.
The author, for many years a customs official in China, gives an excellent brief survey of the finances, trade, industry, banking and general resources.

OVERLACH, THEODORE WILLIAM. **Foreign Financial Control in China.** New York: Macmillan, 1919, 295 p.
An important study of the British, Russian, French, German, Japanese and American interests. A book useful for an understanding of the post-war situation.

PINNICK, ALFRED WILLIAM. **Silver and China.** London: King, 1931, 90 p.
An analysis of China's trade and prosperity as affected by the world silver situation.

REMER, CHARLES FREDERICK. **The Foreign Trade of China.** New York: Stechert, 1926, 269 p.
A scholarly historical study.

SCHOOTEN, JEAN ULLENS DE. **Les Chemins de Fer Chinois.** Brussels: Lamertin, 1928, 266 p.
An exhaustive study—historical, economic, financial.

SEE CHONG SU. **The Foreign Trade of China.** New York: Columbia University Press, 1919, 451 p.
The author reviews the entire history of China's trade relations in what is a really valuable contribution.

SHAW KINN WEI. **Democracy and Finance in China.** New York: Columbia University Press, 1926, 215 p.
A former professor at Hangchow shows the reaction of fiscal ideas upon the political evolution of the country.

SMITH, CADES ALFRED MIDDLETON. **The British in China.** London: Constable, 1920, 295 p.
A valuable study of British trade in China, its history, organization and location.

SMITH, WILFRED. **A Geographical Study of Coal and Iron in China.** Liverpool: University Press, 1926, 83 p.
Useful information on the distribution and exploitation of the coal reserves.

STRINGER, HAROLD. **China: A New Aspect.** London: Witherby, 1929, 240 p.
A former official of the Chinese railway service approaches the Chinese problem not from the standpoint of personal rivalries and antagonisms, but from the practical side of developing communications.

SUN YAT SEN. **The International Development of China.** New York: Putnam, 1922, 265 p.
Various programs of economic development outlined by the eminent nationalist leader who envisaged international development under a socialistic scheme.

TAYLER, JOHN BERNARD. **Farm and Factory in China.** London: Student Christian Movement, 1928, 105 p.
A competent introduction to the study of agricultural and industrial developments.

TSO, SHIH KAN SHELDON. **The Labor Movement in China.** Shanghai: 1928, 230 p.
An American dissertation giving a thoroughly documented analysis of conditions, organization and influence of the labor movement.

VINACKE, HAROLD MONK. **Problems of Industrial Development in China.** Princeton: Princeton University Press, 1926, 214 p.
An able study of Chinese industrial development, government finance, communications, etc.

WEN CHING YIN. **Le Système Fiscal de la Chine.** Paris: Éditions et Publications Contemporaines, 1930, 212 p.
An historical approach to the fiscal system, with a detailed exposition of the present organization.

WILHELM, RICHARD. **Chinesische Wirtschaftspsychologie.** Leipzig: Deutsche Wissenschaftliche Buchhandlung, 1930, 120 p.
A German economist studies the organization of Chinese economic life and the connection of industrialism and nationalism. An original and stimulating essay.

WITTFOGEL, KARL AUGUST. **Wirtschaft und Gesellschaft Chinas.** Leipzig: Hirschfeld,
1931, 768 p.
The first volume of a monumental economic and social study. The author here takes
up the productive forces and processes, and the distributing agencies.

International Relations and Status

General

*See also (Disarmament) Naval, p. 84; also (United States) Far Eastern Policy, p. 186; also
(Russia: Foreign Policy) Relations with Specific Countries, p. 394.*

ARIGA, NAGAO. **La Chine et la Grande Guerre Européenne.** Paris: Pedone, 1920,
342 p.
A scholarly documented study of China in international law and international affairs
during the war, by a Japanese Counsellor of the Chinese Government.

BASSI, UGO. **Italia e Cina.** Modena: Bassi, 1929, 104 p.
An historical sketch of Italian relations with China, commercial and diplomatic. Half
the volume is devoted to documents.

BAU, MINGCHIEN JOSHUA. **China and World Peace.** New York: Revell, 1928, 194 p.
The author, a professor at the University of Peiping, examines the chief points at
issue between China and the Powers, and suggests ways and means of a settlement.
Among the topics treated are extraterritoriality, the unequal treaties, the tariff, etc.

BAU, MINGCHIEN JOSHUA. **The Foreign Relations of China.** New York: Revell, 1922,
541 p.
A documented study of modern imperialism in China, differentiating somewhat the
policies of the several states. A useful volume, stressing particularly the problems
arising from the World War and the policy of Japan.

BAU, MINGCHIEN JOSHUA. **The Open Door Doctrine in Relation to China.** New York:
Macmillan, 1923, 245 p.
A well documented historical and analytical study.

DUBOSCQ, ANDRÉ. **La Chine et le Pacifique.** Paris: Fayard, 1931, 206 p.
An admirable popular survey by one of the leading writers of the *Temps*.

ESCARRA, JEAN. **La Chine et le Droit International.** Paris: Pedone, 1931, 419 p.
An elaborate treatise by a French professor long a counsellor of the Chinese Government.

HODGKIN, HENRY THEODORE. **China in the Family of Nations.** New York: Doran,
1923, 267 p.
An analysis of the country's international relations and of changes in Chinese society.

HSIA CHING LIN. **Studies in Chinese Diplomatic History.** New York: Stechert, 1924,
226 p.
The Chinese view on some much discussed questions, covering the period since 1895.

HSÜ SHUHSI. **China and Her Political Entity.** New York: Oxford University Press,
1926, 462 p.
A scholarly work, based in large part on Chinese sources, examining the international
relations of China with special reference to the Manchuria and Korea problems.

KIA YU TONG. **Relations Politiques de la France et de la Chine.** Paris: Jouve, 1920,
214 p.
This dissertation, while adding nothing, offers a convenient review of Franco-Chinese
relations since the 17th century. Despite the title the author discusses commercial,
missionary and cultural relations.

MacNair, Harley Farnsworth. **China's International Relations and Other Essays.** New York: Stechert, 1927, 326 p.
A collection of essays dealing with international relations, race problems, the position of the missionaries, etc.

MacNair, Harley Farnsworth. **Modern Chinese History; Selected Readings.** Shanghai: Commercial Press, 1927, 922 p.
An excellent selection of documents, correspondence, proclamations and statements to illustrate the history of Chinese international relations.

Norton, Henry Kittredge. **China and the Powers.** New York: Day, 1927, 275 p.
A dispassionate, sober examination of the situation in 1927, especially good for the account of Russian policy.

Reid, Gilbert. **China, Captive or Free?** New York: Dodd, 1921, 332 p.
A review of what happened to China during the World War, with sharp criticism of the policy not only of Japan, but of Great Britain and the United States.

Soothill, William Edward. **China and England.** New York: Oxford University Press, 1928, 238 p.
A series of lectures by an experienced observer, in which the history of Anglo-Chinese relations and the outstanding problems of the present are passed in review. The treatment of extraterritoriality is especially good.

Soothill, William Edward. **China and the West.** London: Milford, 1925, 224 p.
One of the best short accounts of the intercourse of the Chinese with the Western Powers, cultural and economic as well as political.

Sze, Sao Ke Alfred. **Addresses.** Baltimore: Johns Hopkins Press, 1926, 131 p.
These speeches, by one of the most eminent Chinese diplomats, deal with China's international position, the problem of extraterritoriality and the unequal treaties.

Tchen Ho Shien. **Étude sur les Relations Diplomatiques entre la Chine et le Japon de 1871 à Nos Jours.** Paris: Vie Universitaire, 1921, 328 p.
A dissertation of indifferent value, but useful because of the lack of other systematic treatments of the subject.

Wang Ching Wei. **China and the Nations.** New York: Stokes, 1927, 165 p.
A highly important document written by the Chairman of the governing committee of the People's Government and setting forth the principles of the foreign policy of the Kuomintang in its fight against "imperialism."

Weale, Putnam, *pseud.* (Bertram Lenox Simpson). **An Indiscreet Chronicle from the Pacific.** New York: Dodd, 1922, 310 p.
A British adviser of the Chinese foreign office discusses the background of the Washington Conference and the steps taken to bring about the abrogation of the Anglo-Japanese Alliance.

Weale, Putnam, *pseud.* (Bertram Lenox Simpson). **The Truth about China and Japan.** New York: Dodd, 1919, 248 p.
An outline and analysis of Japanese policy towards China, by a well-informed Englishman who writes prolifically on Chinese matters.

Weigh Ken Shen. **Russo-Chinese Diplomacy.** Shanghai: Commercial Press, 1928, 382 p.
A scholarly study, by an official of the Chinese foreign office. The most interesting part is that dealing with China and Soviet Russia.

Wheeler, William Reginald. **China and the World War.** New York: Macmillan, 1919, 263 p.
Primarily a study of China's international position and diplomacy during the war. A reliable survey, based on documents and press comment.

WHYTE, SIR ALEXANDER FREDERICK. **China and the Foreign Powers.** New York: Oxford University Press, 1928, 93 p.
A thoroughly revised edition of a brief outline which can be highly recommended. The important chapter on Chinese-Russian relations has been rewritten.

YEN EN TSUNG. **The Open Door Policy.** Boston: Stratford, 1923, 191 p.
An objective historical study of Chinese relations with foreign powers.

Unequal Treaties

See also (International Law) Intervention and Recognition, p. 36.

BONNINGUE, ALFRED. **La France à Kouang-Tchéou-Wan.** Paris: Berger-Levrault, 1931, 72 p.
A compact study of the history of the French leased territory.

BUSS, CLAUDE ALBERT. **The Relation of Tariff Autonomy to the Political Situation in China.** Philadelphia: University of Pennsylvania Press, 1927, 141 p.
A well-documented thesis reviewing the history of foreign trade in China and the political implications of the tariff and extraterritoriality.

CHAN CHUNG SING. **Les Concessions en Chine.** Paris: Presses Universitaires, 1925, 150 p.
A doctoral thesis. The author reviews briefly the historical development and then analyzes the concessions, chiefly from the legal standpoint.

ESCARRA, JEAN. **Droits et Intérêts Étrangers en Chine.** Paris: Sirey, 1928, 90 p.
A brief reliable statement, written by a counsellor of the Chinese Government.

GILBERT, RODNEY YONKERS. **The Unequal Treaties.** London: Murray, 1929, 248 p.
The author, who knows China well, reviews the contacts of China with the foreigner since the eighteenth century and examines with particular care the circumstances under which the various treaties were concluded. Their object, he points out, was not to put China into a position of subjection, but to enforce from the Chinese Government a recognition of the equality of the foreigner. Conditions have not changed materially, and the treaties are still "a feeble barrier between commerce and chaos."

HSIA CHING LIN. **The Status of Shanghai.** Shanghai: Kelly and Walsh, 1929, 202 p.
A general history of the international settlement and its government, with some discussion of desirable changes.

KEETON, GEORGE WILLIAMS. **The Development of Extraterritoriality in China.** New York: Longmans, 1928, 2 v.
An outstanding book. The author, a professor of law, makes a careful study of the theory and practice of extraterritoriality from the very beginning of European contact. The second volume is devoted to documents.

KOTENEV, ANATOL M. **Shanghai: Its Municipality and the Chinese.** New York: Stechert, 1927, 565 p.
An exhaustive treatise on the peculiar status of Shanghai and connected problems.

MAYBON, CHARLES B. and FREDET, JEAN. **Histoire de la Concession Française de Changhaï.** Paris: Plon, 1929, 458 p.
This is an authoritative history, written by two high French officials and published under the auspices of the French Foreign Office.

MILLARD, THOMAS FRANKLIN. **The End of Extraterritoriality in China.** Shanghai: The A. B. C. Press, 1931, 278 p.
The writer, a well-known journalist and adviser of the Chinese Government, approaches the problem from a thoroughly Chinese nationalist standpoint.

POTT, FRANCIS LISTER HAWKS. **A Short History of Shanghai.** Shanghai: Kelly and Walsh, 1928, 336 p.
A general sketch, for the layman.

SOULIÉ, GEORGES. **Exterritorialité et Intérêts Étrangers en Chine.** Paris: Geuthner, 1926, 508 p.
By a French consul and able Sinologue. A detailed examination of the theory of extraterritoriality, with an extended discussion of what the system has meant to China in practice.

TAO CHANG CHUNG. **Les Traités Inégaux de la Chine et l'Attitude des Puissances.** Paris: Rivière, 1929, 216 p.
The conventional nationalist view of the treaties.

WILLOUGHBY, WESTEL WOODBURY. **Foreign Rights and Interests in China.** Baltimore: Johns Hopkins Press, rev. and enl. ed., 1927, 2 v.
A fundamental monograph, by a former adviser of the Chinese Government. The standard treatment of the subject.

YANG LIEOU FONG. **Les Territoires à Bail en Chine.** Paris: Presses Universitaires, 1929, 215 p.
A thesis reviewing the diplomatic history of the leased territories and examining their legal status.

Manchuria

ADACHI, KINNOSUKÉ. **Manchuria, a Survey.** New York: McBride, 1925, 401 p.
An enthusiastic survey of Manchurian resources and development, by a Japanese journalist well-known in the United States.

Le Conflit Sino-Japonais. Paris: Nachbaur, 1931.
The anonymous author deals chiefly with Japanese railway policy in Manchuria and Mongolia.

EDDY, SHERWOOD. **The World's Danger Zone.** New York: Farrar and Rinehart, 1932, 125 p.
A brief review of the Manchurian question, based in part on the author's "Challenge of the East," supplemented by recent observations on the spot. The author formerly was head of the Y. M. C. A. in Asia.

ETHERTON, PERCY THOMAS and TILTMAN, HUBERT HESSELL. **Manchuria, the Cockpit of Asia.** New York: Stokes, 1932, 337 p.
A concise exposition of the political and economic rivalries in Manchuria, stressing the needs and claims of Japan.

HOSHINO, T. **Economic History of Manchuria.** Seoul: Bank of Chosen, 1920, 303 p.
A useful guide to the resources and industries of Manchuria.

HOUANG TCHANG SIN. **Le Problème du Chemin de Fer Chinois de l'Est.** Paris: Écrivains Réunis, 1927, 460 p.
A scholarly account of the history of the railway from the beginning to the present.

KAWAKAMI, KIYOSHI KARL. **Japan Speaks on the Sino-Japanese Crisis.** New York: Macmillan, 1932, 200 p.
A presentation of the Japanese case, written by an able newspaperman.

KINNEY, HENRY WALSWORTH. **Manchuria Today.** Dairen: South Manchuria Railway Co., 1930, 100 p.
The latest descriptive pamphlet brought out under the auspices of the South Manchuria Railway Company.

LATTIMORE, OWEN. **Manchuria, Cradle of Conflict.** New York: Macmillan, 1932, 327 p.
The author, who has travelled widely in China, Manchuria and Mongolia, deals at length with the fundamental factors in the conflict. His excellent book is based upon Chinese sources, as well as upon material in western languages and upon personal observations.

Manchuria Year Book. Tokyo: East-Asiatic Economic Investigation Bureau. Annual since 1930.
The only handbook of its sort in English.

MENG CHIH. **China Speaks.** New York: Macmillan, 1932, 211 p.
This is the Chinese counterpart of the Kawakami volume. The two books should be read together.

PARLETT, SIR HAROLD GEORGE. **A Brief Account of Diplomatic Events in Manchuria.** New York: Oxford University Press, 1929, 96 p.
The author brings to his task an unrivalled knowledge and a wide experience in Far Eastern affairs. His brief survey of the evolution of the question is succinct and accurate, and covers all the salient points of past negotiations. As an introduction and guide it can be highly recommended.

SOUTH MANCHURIA RAILWAY COMPANY. **Report on Progress in Manchuria.** Dairen: Author, 1929, 238 p.
A handsomely illustrated report covering the years 1907 to 1928 and setting forth the accomplishments of the railway company.

YOUNG, CARL WALTER. **The International Relations of Manchuria.** Chicago: Chicago University Press, 1929, 307 p.
This book, published under the auspices of the American Council of the Institute of Pacific Relations, is a basic work for all students of Far Eastern affairs. It analyzes and summarizes all the important agreements and negotiations between the Great Powers as they touched Manchuria for the period from 1895 to the present, and indicates their importance.

YOUNG, CARL WALTER. **Japan's Special Position in Manchuria. The International Legal Status of the Kwantung Leased Territory. Japanese Jurisdiction in the South Manchurian Railway Areas.** Baltimore: Johns Hopkins Press, 1931, 3 v.
These important volumes are from the pen of a man who has lived for a number of years in Manchuria and who has thus had direct access to valuable sources of information. The three volumes comprise a series under the general title "Japan's Jurisdiction and International Legal Position in Manchuria," although each separate book is itself a unified whole. The facts presented are intended for the student of politics, more than for the historian or the economist. Each volume is well documented and contains a good map as well as a bibliography.

Mongolia

See also (Russia) Foreign Policy, p. 393; also (Central Asia and India) Central Asia and Turkestan, p. 443.

CONSTEN, HERMANN. **Weideplätze der Mongolen im Reiche der Chalcha.** Berlin: Reimer, 1920, 2 v.
This scholarly work contains much interesting information on Mongolian relations with China and Russia.

KOROSTOVETS, IVAN IAKOVLEVICH. **Von Cinggis Khan zur Sowjetrepublik.** Berlin: De Gruyter, 1926, 351 p.

An excellent history of Mongolia, with emphasis on the more recent period. The best general account.

LARSON, FRANS AUGUST. **Larson, Duke of Mongolia.** Boston: Little, Brown, 1930, 296 p.
A useful descriptive study of the land and the people, by a Swedish missionary long resident there.

LATTIMORE, OWEN. **The Desert Road to Turkestan.** London: Methuen, 1928, 331 p.
A record of extensive travel in Mongolia, with valuable material on conditions and trade.

MAISKIĬ, I. **Sovremennaia Mongoliia.** Irkutsk: Gosizdat, 1921, 460 p.
A detailed descriptive work on contemporary Mongolia.

STRASSER, ROLAND. **The Mongolian Horde.** New York: Cape and Smith, 1930, 347 p.
An unusual study of Mongolia and the changes taking place there, by a German artist. The illustrations are noteworthy.

Shantung

GODSHALL, WILSON LEON. **The International Aspect of the Shantung Problem.** Philadelphia: University of Pennsylvania Press, 1923, 172 p.
An American dissertation, giving a thoroughly documented historical and analytical account of the problem.

GODSHALL, WILSON LEON. **Tsingtau under Three Flags.** New York: Stechert, 1929, 580 p.
An extensive study of the famous base under German, Japanese and Chinese adminis-tration.

WOOD GE ZAY. **The Shantung Question.** New York: Revell, 1922, 372 p.
A moderate work from the Chinese point of view, reprinting valuable documents. The best single treatment of the subject in its historical development.

JAPAN
General

ALLEN, GEORGE CYRIL. **Modern Japan and Its Problems.** London: Allen and Unwin, 1928, 226 p.
A survey of Japanese problems, understandingly written by one who for many years was a teacher in that country. Attention is concentrated on social and economic developments.

ASAMI, NOBORU. **Japanese Colonial Government.** New York: Columbia University Press, 1924, 83 p.
A well-documented study of colonial institutions and laws, and the actual organization of the various colonies. An American dissertation.

BALLARD, GEORGE ALEXANDER. **The Influence of the Sea on the Political History of Japan.** New York: Dutton, 1921, 311 p.
Written by an English admiral, this book traces the naval history of the Japanese through the war with Russia and discusses the importance of sea power in modern Japanese development.

BEARD, MIRIAM. **Realism in Romantic Japan.** New York: Macmillan, 1930, 531 p.
Keen observations of modern Japanese life, in part based on personal experience.

BIGELOW, POULTNEY. **Japan and Her Colonies.** New York: Longmans, 1923, 276 p.
Travel impressions of Formosa, Manchuria, Shantung, Korea and Saghalin in 1921,
by an American publicist.

BROWN, ARTHUR JUDSON. **The Mastery of the Far East.** New York: Scribner, rev.
ed., 1921, 671 p.
An admirable study of the evolution of Korea since 1895, with special reference to
Japanese policy, followed by an analysis of Japanese conditions and a discussion of
Christian missions in the Far East. A well-informed and instructive book.

BROWN, ARTHUR JUDSON. **Japan in the World of Today.** New York: Revell, 1928,
322 p.
This book is one of the best general surveys of Japanese life and conditions. Based in
part on the author's "The Mastery of the Far East."

BRYAN, JOHN INGRAM. **The Civilization of Japan.** New York: Holt, 1927, 256 p.
An admirable introductory survey along historical lines, in the Home University
Library.

CROCKER, WALTER RUSSELL. **The Japanese Population Problem.** New York: Macmillan, 1931, 240 p.
Though this is a technical book, it is to be recommended especially to the student
of foreign affairs, for the material is well presented and is put into the setting of
general international relations.

FRANCK, HARRY ALVERSON. **Glimpses of Japan and Formosa.** New York: Century,
1924, 235 p.
A fascinating descriptive volume by one of the best-known travellers in the East.

FUJISAWA, RIKITARO. **The Recent Aims and Political Development of Japan.** New
Haven: Yale University Press, 1923, 222 p.
Williamstown Lectures. The author reviews the recent political developments and
discusses briefly the aims of Japan.

GOWEN, HERBERT HENRY. **An Outline History of Japan.** New York: Appleton, 1927,
458 p.
One of the best general texts, with full treatment of the modern period.

GUBBINS, JOHN HARRINGTON. **The Making of Modern Japan.** Philadelphia: Lippincott, 1922, 316 p.
A comprehensive and reliable survey of the evolution of contemporary Japanese
civilization, based to a large extent on personal observation and original sources.

HARA, KATSURO. **Introduction to the History of Japan.** New York: Putnam, 1920,
411 p.
A masterly and highly original synthesis of Japanese history, by an eminent Japanese
historian.

HAUSHOFER, KARL. **Das Japanische Reich.** Vienna: Seidel, 1921, 171 p.
A competent and well-documented study of geographical factors in Japanese history
and of the forces working for and against expansion in the new Japan.

HERSHEY, AMOS SHARTLE and SUSANNE W. **Modern Japan.** Indianapolis: Bobbs, 1919,
382 p.
A well-balanced survey of social, religious and economic conditions, with some discussion of politics and foreign policies.

IWASAKI, UICHI. **The Working Forces in Japanese Politics.** New York: Longmans,
1921, 141 p.
A doctoral thesis which attempts a sociological interpretation of Japanese politics
between 1867 and 1920. The author studies the influence of the Elder Statesmen, the
officials, military men, political parties, capitalist class and workers.

Japan Year Book. Tokyo: Japan Year Book Office. Annual, since 1905.
A standard reference work.

JOFFE, A. A. **Iaponiia v Nashi Dni.** Moscow: Nauchnaia Assotsiatsiia Vostokovedeniia, 1926, 77 p.
A brief popular survey of the situation in Japan, by a special Soviet envoy to that country.

KAWABÉ, KISABURŌ. **The Press and Politics in Japan.** Chicago: Chicago University Press, 1921, 190 p.
An illuminating contribution to the study of Japanese politics.

KAWAKAMI, KIYOSHI KARL. **What Japan Thinks.** New York: Macmillan, 1921, 237 p.
An interesting collection of articles by Japanese writers originally published in China and Japan and reflecting the Japanese view on the most important constitutional and foreign problems.

KELIN, I. **Iaponiia.** Leningrad: Gosizdat, 1924, 167 p.
A general historical and economic survey of modern Japan.

KENNEDY, MALCOLM DUNCAN. **The Changing Fabric of Japan.** London: Constable, 1930, 282 p.
Interesting discussion of such problems as social unrest, the women's movement, growth of representative government, the press, religious forces, industrialism, etc.

KENNEDY, MALCOLM DUNCAN. **Some Aspects of Japan and Her Defence Forces.** London: Kegan Paul, 1929, 248 p.
A competent discussion of the Japanese war machine, which should take some of the wind out of the alarmists' sails.

KITAZAWA, NAOKICHI. **The Government of Japan.** Princeton: Princeton University Press, 1929, 130 p.
A scholarly introduction.

LATOURETTE, KENNETH SCOTT. **The Development of Japan.** New York: Macmillan, 1920, 237 p.
A brief introductory history, by an American authority on Far Eastern affairs.

McGOVERN, WILLIAM MONTGOMERY. **Modern Japan.** London: T. Fisher Unwin, 1920, 280 p.
The book is, in the main, a study of the governing oligarchy, from a sympathetic viewpoint.

MATSUNAMI, NIICHIRO. **The Constitution of Japan.** Tokyo: Maruzen, 1930, 358 p.
A scholarly treatment of the principles and practice of the constitution.

MONCHARVILLE, MAURICE. **Le Japon d'Outre-Mer.** Paris: Pedone, 1931, 238 p.
One of the few good descriptive political and economic studies of the Japanese possessions in Formosa, Korea, Kwantung and the Pacific.

NITOBÉ, INAZO OTA. **Japan.** New York: Scribner, 1931, 398 p.
One of the excellent volumes of the "Modern World" series, giving an historical background as well as a general survey of Japanese life and conditions. The author, formerly Under-Secretary General of the League of Nations, is a professor at the University of Tokyo.

NITOBÉ, INAZO OTA. **Japanese Traits and Foreign Influences.** London: Kegan Paul, 1927, 216 p.
A collection of essays and lectures delivered in Europe.

NITOBÉ, INAZO OTA and others. **Western Influences in Modern Japan.** Chicago: Chicago University Press, 1931, 544 p.
A coöperative survey of Japanese life, written by experts.

ODA, YOROZU. **Principes de Droit Administratif du Japon.** Paris: Sirey, 1928, 601 p.
An authoritative study, by a justice of the World Court.

OGAWA, GOTARO. **Conscription System in Japan.** New York: Oxford University Press, 1921, 245 p.
An excellent monograph in the Carnegie Series. The author examines the history of conscription in Japan and analyzes its effects on population, labor, productivity, etc.

OKAKURA, KAKUZO. **The Awakening of Japan.** New York: Japan Society, 1921, 225 p.
A most interesting and stimulating study of new Japan, with stress on the importance of national tradition in religion and art, as against foreign influences.

ROBERTSON-SCOTT, JOHN WILLIAM. **The Foundations of Japan.** New York: Appleton, 1922, 446 p.
An interesting impressionistic description of modern Japanese civilization. Particularly good on agrarian life and customs.

RUTTER, OWEN. **Through Formosa.** London: T. Fisher Unwin, 1923, 288 p.
An account of Formosan civilization and economic life by a well-known observer.

SANSOM, GEORGE BAILEY. **Japan: A Short Cultural History.** New York: Century, 1931, 553 p.
A book that fills a distinct need, by a member of the British Embassy at Tokyo.

TSURUMI, YUSUKE. **Present Day Japan.** New York: Columbia University Press, 1926, 119 p.
A series of stimulating lectures by a Japanese liberal publicist. The author deals primarily with new intellectual and literary currents, but discusses also the effect of American immigration laws on Japanese life.

WILDES, HARRY EMERSON. **Social Currents in Japan.** Chicago: Chicago University Press, 1927, 391 p.
An excellent study of the press and the movement of opinion in Japan.

YOUNG, ARTHUR MORGAN. **Japan in Recent Times.** New York: Morrow, 1929, 347 p.
A useful survey of the development of Japan from 1912 to 1926, by the editor of the *Japan Chronicle.*

ZAMORA, JUAN CLEMENTE. **Japón.** Havana: Sociedad Editorial Cuba Contemporánea, 1921, 140 p.
An analysis of the Japanese constitution and government.

Foreign Policy

See also (Disarmament) Naval, p. 84; also (United States) Far Eastern Policy, p. 186, and Immigration and Race Problems, p. 191; also (Russia) Foreign Policy, p. 393; also (China) Manchuria, p. 477; also (The Pacific Area) General Pacific Problems, p. 491.

CHALLAYE, FÉLICIEN. **La Chine et le Japon Politiques.** Paris: Alcan, 1921, 323 p.
This book, based upon extensive travels, is mainly concerned with the foreign policy of Japan.

DAVIS, WARREN JEFFERSON. **Japan: The Air Menace of the Pacific.** Boston: Christopher, 1928, 157 p.
A discussion of Japanese-American relations, with special reference to strategic considerations.

GÉRARD, AUGUSTE. **Ma Mission au Japon, 1907-1914.** Paris: Plon, 1919, 412 p.
The valuable reminiscences of the French Ambassador. An important source for the history of Far Eastern diplomacy.

KAWAKAMI, KIYOSHI KARL. **Japan and World Peace.** New York: Macmillan, 1919, 196 p.
An able journalistic review of Japan's aspirations, needs and policies, with stress on the pressure of population and need of raw materials.

KAWAKAMI, KIYOSHI KARL. **Japan's Pacific Policy.** New York: Dutton, 1922, 380 p.
A moderate apologia for Japanese policies at the Washington Conference, indicating their historic and diplomatic background. It reprints useful documents.

KUNO, YOSHI S. **What Japan Wants.** New York: Crowell, 1921, 154 p.
The book is devoted largely to an exposition of Japanese interests and policies with regard to the United States, the Pacific, China, Korea and Siberia.

ODATE, GYOJU. **Japan's Financial Relations with the United States.** New York: Columbia University Press, 1922, 136 p.
A doctoral dissertation containing the facts of the subject and analyzing them.

OSBORNE, SIDNEY. **The Isolation of Japan.** Amsterdam: Van Langenhuysen, 1919, 150 p.
Published anonymously. The contribution of a journalist, who foresees the isolation of Japan by an American-English-German combination which will liberate China.

OSBORNE, SIDNEY. **The New Japanese Peril.** London: Allen, 1921, 187 p.
The author continues the observations and speculations recorded in "The Isolation of Japan," and passes severe criticism on the Japanese policy in Shantung and China. The book contains an extended discussion of the Anglo-Japanese Alliance.

POOLEY, ANDREW MELVILLE. **Japan's Foreign Policies.** New York: Dodd, 1920, 202 p.
These chapters, written by a well-known publicist, deal chiefly with Japanese policy in China before and during the World War.

RIBAUD, MICHEL. **Le Japon pendant la Guerre Européenne.** Paris: Lethielleux, 1919, 264 p.
Interesting but rather disjointed notes and observations, dealing especially with Japan's relations to Russia, the United States and China.

STOKLITSKIĬ, A. **Iaponiia i Kitaĭ.** Moscow: Gosizdat, 1928, 103 p.
A typical communist indictment of Japanese imperialism in China.

TAFT, HENRY WATERS. **Japan and the Far East Conference.** New York: Macmillan, 1921, 75 p.
Expanded magazine and newspaper articles dealing with the Far Eastern situation in general, and with Japanese policy in particular on the eve of the Washington Conference.

TAFT, HENRY WATERS. **Japan and America.** New York: Macmillan, 1932, 359 p.
The record of a visit to Japan in 1920 and a detailed discussion of American-Japanese relations as well as of the 1931 crisis.

WOOD GE ZAY. **China, the United States and the Anglo-Japanese Alliance. The Chino-Japanese Treaties of May 25, 1915. The Twenty-one Demands.** New York: Revell, 1921, 2 v.
Three studies prepared by the former editor of *The Far Eastern Republic*, in anticipation of the Washington Conference. Each contains the important documentary material on the subject treated. Together they constitute a severe indictment of Japanese policy.

Financial and Economic Problems

ANDREADĒS, ANDREAS MICHAĒL. **Les Finances de l'Empire Japonais et Leur Évolution.** Paris: Alcan, 1932, 203 p.
A documented account of Japanese finances since 1868, by an expert in the field of government finance.

BRATTER, HERBERT M. **Japanese Banking.** Washington: Department of Commerce, 1931, 295 p.
A guide to Japanese methods of operation, the activities of foreign banks, and stock exchange operations; prepared for the Bureau of Foreign and Domestic Commerce.

INOUYE, JUNNOSUKE. **Problems of the Japanese Exchange, 1914-1926.** New York: Macmillan, 1931, 286 p.
A series of lectures, delivered in 1926, by a former Japanese Minister of Finance.

KOBAYASHI, USHISABURO. **War and Armament Loans of Japan.** New York: Oxford University Press, 1922, 221 p.
A companion volume to Ono's "War and Armament Expenditures."

KOBAYASHI, USHISABURO. **War and Armament Taxes of Japan.** New York: Oxford University Press, 1923, 255 p.
A continuation of the author's study of war loans of Japan.

MOULTON, HAROLD GLENN and KO, JUNICHI. **Japan.** Washington: Brookings Institution, 1931, 645 p.
A good monograph on Japan's economic development and present problems.

ONO, GIICHI. **War and Armament Expenditures of Japan.** New York: Oxford University Press, 1922, 314 p.
A detailed study of military expenditure since 1865, with an analysis of its economic and social effects. A volume in the Carnegie Series.

ORCHARD, JOHN EWING. **Japan's Economic Position.** New York: McGraw-Hill, 1930, 520 p.
This serious and scholarly investigation, based upon years of study, is probably the best thing on the subject.

PENROSE, E. F. **Food Supply and Raw Materials in Japan.** Chicago: Chicago University Press, 1930, 75 p.
A statistical work based on Japanese sources.

UYEHARA, SHIGERU. **The Industry and Trade of Japan.** London: King, 1926, 326 p.
An authoritative account of Japanese economic development in the last fifty years.

YAMAZAKI, KAKUJIRO and OGAWA, GOTARO. **The Effect of the World War upon the Commerce and Industry of Japan.** New Haven: Yale University Press, 1929, 345 p.
A volume in the Carnegie Series containing a wealth of statistical material.

Korea (Chosen)

CHUNG, HENRY. **The Case of Korea.** New York: Revell, 1921, 365 p.
A violent indictment of Japanese rule in Korea, with a warmly partisan account of the independence movement.

CYNN, HUGH HEUNG WO. **The Rebirth of Korea.** New York: Abingdon, 1920, 272 p.
A dispassionate statement of the aims of the independence movement, by a native Christian leader.

DRAKE, HENRY BURGESS. **Korea of the Japanese.** New York: Dodd, 1930, 225 p.
One of the best recent accounts, by a man well acquainted with the country.

HOSHINO, T., *comp.* **The Economic History of Chosen.** Seoul: Bank of Chosen, 1920, 266 p.
An illustrated survey, with special reference to the work of Japan.

IRELAND, ALLEYNE. **The New Korea.** New York: Dutton, 1926, 366 p.
About the best recent book on Japanese rule in Korea, its organization, working and achievement.

Kɪм, N. **Pod Gnetom Iaponskogo Imperializma.** Vladivostok: Knizhnoe Delo, n. d.,
152 p.
Modern Korea under the heel of Japan.

Mᴄᴋᴇɴᴢɪᴇ, Fʀᴇᴅᴇʀɪᴄᴋ Aʀᴛʜᴜʀ. **Korea's Fight for Freedom.** New York: Revell, 1920,
320 p
An account of the rising of the Koreans in 1919 and its repression, with stress on the
persecution and torture suffered by Christian Koreans.

Wᴀɢɴᴇʀ, Eʟʟᴀsᴜᴇ Cᴀɴᴛᴇʀ. **Korea, the Old and the New.** New York: Revell, 1931,
160 p.
The observations and reflections of a missionary.

SIBERIA

*See also (World War) Siberia, p. 139; also (Russia) Counter-Revolution and Intervention,
p. 367; also Polar Regions, p. 498.*

Aʀᴋʜɪᴘᴏᴠ, N. B. **Dal'nevostochnaia Oblast'.** Moscow: Gosizdat, 1926, 169 p.
A survey of industry and trade in the Russian Far East.

Aᴠɪɢᴅᴏʀ, D. and Wɪɴᴅsᴏʀ. **La Sibérie Orientale et le Japon.** Paris: Roger, 1922, 61 p.
A political and economic study of the situation in Eastern Siberia and of the Japanese
policy.

Bᴀɪᴇᴠsᴋʏ, Bᴏʀɪs. **Siberia: Its Resources and Possibilities.** Washington: Department
of Commerce, 1926, 69 p.
The resources, transportation facilities, industries and trade of Siberia are covered
in this handbook prepared for the Bureau of Foreign and Domestic Commerce.

Cʟᴇɪɴᴏᴡ, Gᴇᴏʀɢ. **Neu-Sibirien.** Berlin: Hobbing, 1928, 426 p.
A scholarly documented study of Russian activity in Siberia, of relations with China
in Mongolia, of economic developments, etc.

Hᴇʟʟᴇʀ, Oᴛᴛᴏ. **Sibirien: Ein Anderes Amerika.** Berlin: Neuer Deutscher Verlag, 1930,
256 p.
An enthusiastic account of the work done by the Bolsheviks in opening up Siberia.

Iᴀᴋᴜsʜᴇᴠ, Iᴠᴀɴ A. **Die Zukunft Sibiriens.** Prague: Legiografie, 1928, 217 p.
A thorough systematic study of the resources and trade of Siberia.

Mᴏᴏʀᴇ, Fʀᴇᴅᴇʀɪᴄᴋ Fᴇʀᴅɪɴᴀɴᴅ. **Siberia Today.** New York: Appleton, 1919, 334 p.
A frank record of impressions and conditions in Siberia, by an officer serving with the
American forces.

Nᴏʀᴛᴏɴ, Hᴇɴʀʏ Kɪᴛᴛʀᴇᴅɢᴇ. **The Far Eastern Republic of Siberia.** New York: Day,
1927, 316 p.
The best general account in English of this interesting experiment.

Revoliutsiia na Dal'nem Vostoke. Moscow: Gosizdat, 1923, 433 p.
An account of the Bolshevik revolution in the Far East, with a valuable collection of
reminiscences by participants.

Wᴏᴏᴅ, Jᴜɴɪᴜs Bᴏʏᴅ. **Incredible Siberia.** New York: Dial, 1928, 261 p.
A correspondent of the *Chicago Daily News* gives an unvarnished account of what he
saw in Siberia and does much to "de-bunk" some recent glowing stories.

INDO-CHINA, MALAY PENINSULA, EAST INDIES
General

BELL, SIR HESKETH JOUDOU. **Foreign Colonial Administration in the Far East.** London: Arnold, 1928, 320 p.
The former governor of Mauritius reviews the colonial system of France in Indo-China and of Holland in Java in a very competent and informing book.

BLEACKLEY, HORACE WILLIAM. **A Tour in Southern Asia.** London: Lane, 1928, 297 p.
Observations made in 1925-1926 in Indo-China, Malaya, Java, Sumatra and Ceylon.

HARRIS, WALTER BURTON. **East for Pleasure.** New York: Longmans, 1929, 399 p.
More than its title implies. The author gives a good comparative study of the working of the French, British and Dutch colonial administrations in Malaya and the East Indies.

POWELL, EDWARD ALEXANDER. **Where the Strange Trails Go Down.** New York: Scribner, 1921, 279 p.
An interesting American estimate of conditions and problems in the East Indies, Malaya and Indo-China.

Burma

See also (Centra. Asia and India) India, p. 446.

BROWN, GEORGE EUSTACE RIOU GRANT. **Burma as I Saw It.** New York: Stokes, 1926, 234 p.
A study of Burmese life, with a supplementary chapter on developments since 1917. Based on the observations of an official who was there for almost thirty years.

EDMONDS, PAUL. **Peacocks and Pagodas.** London: Routledge, 1924, 282 p.
One of the most vivid pictures of modern Burma and the Burmese.

SCOTT, SIR JAMES GEORGE. **Burma.** London: O'Connor, 1921, 536 p.
A general descriptive handbook, and the best survey of Burmese geography, government, economics and cultural life.

WARD, FRANCIS KINGDON. **In Farthest Burma.** London: Seeley, Service, 1921, 311 p.
A record of exploration and observation on the Chinese-Burmese frontier.

WHITE, SIR HERBERT THIRKELL. **Burma.** New York: Macmillan, 1923, 226 p.
An introductory survey, with emphasis on geography.

Indo-China

See also (France) Colonial Questions, p. 270.

AJALBERT, JEAN, *ed.* **L'Indochine par les Français.** Paris: Gallimard, 1931, 254 p.
The history and governmental system of Indo-China, in extracts from the best writers.

BAGOT, FERNAND. **La Situation Financière de l'Annam.** Paris: Larose, 1928, 222 p.
An historical and analytical study of the tax and budgetary system.

CAILLARD, GASTON. **L'Indochine.** Paris: Notre Domaine Colonial, 1922, 124 p.
A popular survey of the history and achievements of the French in Indo-China.

COLLARD, PAUL MARIE ALEXANDRE. **Cambodge et Cambodgiens.** Paris: Éditions Géographiques, Maritimes et Coloniales, 1925, 312 p.
An illustrated history of the French protectorate.

DANGUY, HENRI. **Le Nouveau Visage de la Cochinchine.** Paris: Larose, 1930, 200 p.
Journalistic studies of contemporary Indo-China, with stress on the native problem.

DAUSSE, MAURICE. **La Civilisation Annamite et le Protectorat Français.** Bordeaux:
Pech, 1919, 109 p.
A doctoral thesis describing the family, the commune, the mandarinat and the Emperor, and analyzing the native policy of the French administration.

DEVILAR, CAMILLE. **Comment On Perd une Colonie.** Paris: Ficker, 1931, 215 p.
A criticism of French policy in Indo-China, by the editor of one of the most important French papers in the country.

DUONG, VAN GIAO. **L'Indo-Chine pendant la Guerre de 1914-1918.** Paris: Budry,
1925, 450 p.
A substantial dissertation studying Indo-China's contribution to France, but dealing especially with the economic and political developments at home.

FRANCK, HARRY ALVERSON. **East of Siam.** New York: Century, 1926, 357 p.
One of the best and most discerning of recent travel books on Indo-China.

GALEMBERT, J. DE. **Les Administrations et les Services Publics Indochinois.** Hanoi:
Le-Van-Tan, 1931, 1023 p.
The second edition of an elaborate official publication, describing in detail the administrative system of the French possessions.

GOURDON, HENRI. **L'Indo-Chine.** Paris: Larousse, 1931, 224 p.
A general descriptive and historical work, written by a former director of education in Indo-China. Beautifully illustrated.

LECLERC, JEAN. **De l'Évolution et du Développement des Institutions Annamites
et Cambodgiennes sous l'Influence Française.** Rennes: Edoneur, 1923, 174 p.
A dissertation comparing institutions before and after the beginning of French rule, with an analysis of reforms for native representation.

LÉVI, SYLVAIN. **Indo-Chine.** Paris: Éditions Géographiques, 1931, 2 v.
One of the elaborate and competent surveys published for the Colonial Exposition.

MASPERO, GEORGES. **Un Empire Colonial Français: L'Indochine.** Paris: Van Oest,
1930, 2 v.
One of the most complete descriptive works, with articles by various authorities.

PERCHERON, M. and TESTON, EUGENE. **L'Indo-Chine Moderne.** Paris: Librairie de
France, 1932, 1060 p.
An elaborately illustrated encylopedic work, issued under government auspices.

RÉGISMANSET, CHARLES. **Le Miracle Française en Asie.** Paris: Duval, 1922, 358 p.
The French accomplishment in Indo-China.

ROUBAUD, LOUIS. **Viet Nam.** Paris: Valois, 1931, 320 p.
A somewhat emotional and impressionistic account of recent native troubles in Annam.

SIMONI, HENRI. **Le Rôle du Capital dans la Mise en Valeur de l'Indochine.** Paris:
Société Générale d'Imprimerie, 1929, 190 p.
A valuable contribution to the story of Indo-Chinese economic development. The author discusses banks, industries and public works.

Siam

BERJOAN, A. **Le Siam et les Accords Franco-Siamois.** Paris: Larose, 1927, 168 p.
A dissertation that does not go much beyond the obvious, but gives a convenient summary of the story to the Convention of August 1926.

DÖHRING, KARL. **Siam.** Darmstadt: Folkwang, 1923, 2 v.
A lavishly illustrated descriptive study.

GRAHAM, WALTER ARMSTRONG. **Siam.** London: Moring, 1924, 2 v.
The latest edition of an excellent illustrated handbook.

KORNERUP, EBBE ERLAND GUNNAR. **Friendly Siam.** New York: Putnam, 1929, 256 p.
A general description of the country, taking it up region by region, together with some personal reminiscences.

LE MAY, REGINALD STUART. **An Asian Arcady.** Boston: Houghton Mifflin, 1927, 274 p.
A beautiful and instructive historical, topographical and ethnological survey of Siam, by the Acting Adviser of the Siamese Government.

NATHABANJA, LUANG. **Extra-Territoriality in Siam.** Bangkok: Bangkok Daily Mail, 1924, 344 p.
A well-documented, scholarly study of the history and operation of extraterritoriality, by an American-trained Siamese judge.

Siam, Nature and Industry. Bangkok: Ministry of Commerce, 1930, 315 p.
A series of monographs dealing with geography, climate, resources, industry and communications.

ZEGGIO, VITTORIO. **Il Siam.** Florence: Vallecchi, 1923, 73 p.
Historical, descriptive and economic essays, by an Italian consul.

Malay States

GERMAN, RALPH LIONEL, *comp.* **Handbook of British Malaya.** London: Malayan Information Agency, 1930, 212 p.
The latest edition of the standard handbook.

GIBSON, ASHLEY. **The Malay Peninsula and Archipelago.** London: Dent, 1928, 236 p.
A handy descriptive manual, intended for the traveller.

MAKEPEACE, WALTER, *ed.* **One Hundred Years of Singapore.** London: Murray, 1921, 2 v.
A most elaborate study, by many authors, of Singapore's history, government, commerce, life, etc.

SIDNEY, RICHARD JOHN HAMILTON. **Malay Land.** London: Palmer, 1926, 300 p.
An interesting picture of many phases of life in Singapore and Malaya.

SIDNEY, RICHARD JOHN HAMILTON. **In British Malaya Today.** London: Hutchinson, n. d., 311 p.
Continues the author's sketches of Malayan life.

SWETTENHAM, SIR FRANK ATHELSTANE. **British Malaya.** London: Lane, 1929, 364 p.
The revised edition of the standard history of British rule.

WHEELER, LEONARD RICHMOND. **The Modern Malay.** London: Allen and Unwin, 1928, 300 p.
An excellent history of the Malay race, followed by a valuable survey and analysis of present conditions and problems.

WINSTEDT, RICHARD OLOF. **Malaya.** London: Constable, 1923, 280 p.
A general historical and descriptive handbook, by various authors.

East Indies

See also (Europe) Holland, p. 247.

ANGOULVANT, GABRIEL LOUIS. **Les Indes Néerlandaises.** Paris: Le Monde Nouveau, 1926, 2 v.
An extensive scholarly work, devoted chiefly to the economic history and position of the East Indies.

BLUMBERGER, PETRUS. **Le Communisme aux Indes Néerlandaises.** Paris: Éditions du Monde Nouveau, 1929, 190 p.
A Java official sets forth the serious labor problems in the Dutch colonies.

COLLET, OCTAVE. **L'Évolution de l'Esprit Indigène aux Indes Orientales Néerlandaises.** Brussels: Falck, 1921, 138 p.
A good brief account of the native problems in the Dutch possessions.

COUPERUS, LOUIS. **Eastward.** New York: Doran, 1924, 286 p.
Letters of a well-known Dutch writer from the East Indies in the years 1921 to 1923.

DE LEEUW, HENDRIK. **Crossroads of the Java Sea.** New York: Cape and Smith, 1931, 350 p.
A travel book of a superior kind, based not only on personal observation but on extensive study. It contains an excellent bibliography.

GERRITZEN, JOSEF. **De Welvaart van Indië.** Haarlem: Willink, 1926, 182 p.
A valuable series of lectures on the economic problems of the East Indies, by a former director of the Java Bank.

GONGGRIJP, G. **Schets eener Economische Geschiedenis van Nederlandsch-Indië.** Haarlem: Bohn, 1928, 251 p.
Intended for the general public, but nevertheless a competent sketch of the economic history of the Dutch East Indies.

Handbook of the Netherlands East Indies. Hague: Nijhoff, 1930, 424 p.
The latest edition of an excellent illustrated official handbook, published by the Department of Agriculture, Industry and Commerce.

HOSE, CHARLES. **Natural Man.** New York: Macmillan, 1926, 284 p.
A detailed study of tribal and village life, religion, etc., in Borneo, by a high official and well-known scientist.

METZ, THEODOR. **Java, Sumatra, Bali.** Leipzig: Wissenschaftliche Buchhandlung, 1932, 78 p.
An excellent study of the Dutch administration in the East Indies.

NOTO, SOCRATO. **Van Overheersching naar Zelfregeering.** Hague: Adi Poestaka, 1931, 160 p.
An Indonesian leader, educated in Holland, examines the basis for eventual self-government in the East Indies.

RUTTER, OWEN. **British North Borneo.** London: Constable, 1922, 404 p.
One of the best general books on Borneo, historical and descriptive.

SCHRIEKE, BERTRAM JOHANNES OTTO, *ed.* **The Effect of Western Influence on Native Civilizations in the Malay Archipelago.** Batavia: Kolff, 1929, 247 p.
A valuable collection of papers prepared for the Fourth Pacific Science Congress.

SCHRIEKE, J. J. **De Indische Politiek.** Amsterdam: De Bussy, 1929, 170 p.
A series of well-informed essays on Dutch East Indian policy.

STAPEL, FREDERIK WILLEM. **Geschiedenis van Nederlandsch-Indië.** Amsterdam: Meulenhoff, 1930, 361 p.
A general history of the East Indies, illustrated and with good bibliographical notes.

STIBBE, D. G., *ed.* **Neerlands Indië.** Amsterdam: Elsevier, 1929, 2 v.
A beautifully illustrated collaborative work, in which Dutch experts survey the history, conditions and problems of Holland's Asiatic possessions.

TORCHIANA, HENRY ALBERT VAN COENEN. **Tropical Holland.** Chicago: Chicago University Press, 1921, 317 p.
A collection of essays dealing with the historical title of the Dutch and with the general history of the islands. The author was a Dutch consul-general in the United States.

SEVENTH PART:

THE PACIFIC AREA

I. GENERAL PACIFIC PROBLEMS

See also (General International Relations) Civilizations and Race Conflicts, p. 4; also (League of Nations) Mandates, p. 58; also (United States) Far Eastern Policy, p. 186.

BLAKESLEE, GEORGE HUBBARD. **The Pacific Area.** Boston: World Peace Foundation, 1929, 230 p.
A leading American authority on questions of the Pacific has compressed into this short book a wealth of information dealing with the whole complex of international problems arising out of the changes in China and the conflicting imperialistic policies of the Great Powers. The volume is well-documented.

BROWN, JOHN MACMILLAN. **Peoples and Problems of the Pacific.** London: T. Fisher Unwin, 1927, 2 v.
A collection of papers by an authority, some of them dealing with present problems.

BYWATER, HECTOR CHARLES. **The Great Pacific War.** Boston: Houghton Mifflin, 1932, 321 p.
A reissue of a volume published seven years earlier, dealing with the American position in the Pacific war predicted by the author.

BYWATER, HECTOR CHARLES. **Sea-Power in the Pacific.** Boston: Houghton Mifflin, 1921, 334 p.
A general study of strategic factors, with special reference to Japanese-American naval rivalry.

DUBOSCQ, ANDRÉ. **La Pacifique et la Rencontre des Races.** Paris: Fayard, 1929, 125 p.
The author tells of the clash between the yellow races and American interests. A vividly written, somewhat sensational volume.

DUBOSCQ, ANDRÉ. **Le Problème du Pacifique.** Paris: Delagrave, 1927, 126 p.
A comprehensive and on the whole satisfactory survey of the present situation.

ETHERTON, PERCY THOMAS and TILTMAN, HUBERT HESSELL. **The Pacific: A Forecast.** Boston: Little, Brown, 1928, 261 p.
A very fair review of the problems of the Pacific and the policies of the Powers, though the writers seem to overemphasize the importance of the area.

FLETCHER, CHARLES BRUNSDON. **The Problem of the Pacific.** New York: Holt, 1919, 254 p.
A rather incoherent review of the policies and interests of the Powers. Much of the book is diatribe against German machinations.

FOX, SIR FRANK. **The Mastery of the Pacific.** New York: Sears, 1928, 285 p.
A plea for Anglo-American understanding to obviate a future clash in the Pacific.

GOLOVIN, NIKOLAÏ NIKOLAEVICH. **The Problem of the Pacific in the Twentieth Century.** London: Gyldendal, 1922, 256 p.
This volume treats of military and naval problems chiefly, assuming Japanese aggression as inevitable owing to the increase in population. Japan can be checked, the author believes, only by the United States in alliance with regenerated Russia and China.

GREENBIE, SYDNEY. **The Pacific Triangle.** New York: Century, 1922, 402 p.
A breezy survey of the geography, culture and problems of international relations in Australasia, China and Japan. The best section is that on Japan.

HAUSHOFER, KARL. **Geopolitik des Pazifischen Ozeans.** Berlin: Vowinckel, 1924, 453 p.
An admirable discussion of the Pacific as a geographical and political unit, by a leading German authority.

JACOMB, EDWARD. **The Future of the Kanaka.** London: King, 1919, 222 p.
The book discusses the native problem in the Pacific Islands, land questions, labor and administrative matters and the status of missionary work.

Problems of the Pacific. Chicago: Chicago University Press, 1925, 1927, 1929, 1931, 4 v.
The complete proceedings of the biennial Conferences of the Institute of Pacific Relations. An important and interesting record of the discussion of Pacific problems by unofficial representatives of the Pacific countries.

ROBERTS, STEPHEN HENRY. **Population Problems of the Pacific.** London: Routledge, 1927, 411 p.
A survey of conditions among the native races and of the problems arising from migrations, by a former professor at Melbourne.

ROOSEVELT, NICHOLAS. **The Restless Pacific.** New York: Scribner, 1928, 301 p.
The text of the book is Seward's famous dictum, which the author unreservedly accepts. Stressing geographical and economic aspects, he takes up the conflict of policies between Japan, Russia, England and the United States, and ends with a pungent discussion of the strategical importance of the Philippines and the necessity for a strong navy.

SCHOLEFIELD, GUY HARDY. **The Pacific, its Past and Future.** London: Murray, 1919, 346 p.
The best general historical survey, covering the policy of the powers from the 18th century to the present.

II. AUSTRALIA AND NEW ZEALAND

See also (Great Britain) Imperial Relations, p. 231.

ALLIN, CEPHAS DANIEL. **Australasian Preferential Tariffs and Imperial Free Trade.** Minneapolis: University of Minnesota Press, 1929, 228 p.
A scholarly study reviewing historically the whole problem of British free trade and the inclination of Australia for protective tariffs.

ATKINSON, MEREDITH, *ed.* **Australia: Economic and Political Studies.** London: Macmillan, 1920, 518 p.
Essays by Australian authorities, covering various aspects of present conditions.

CAMPBELL, PERSIA CRAWFORD, *ed.* **Studies in Australian Affairs.** New York: Macmillan, 1929, 270 p.
A survey of the most urgent problems, most of them economic, by a group of authoritative writers.

CANAWAY, ARTHUR PITCAIRN. **The Failure of Federalism in Australia.** New York: Oxford University Press, 1930, 221 p.
A scholarly examination of the Australian Commonwealth in its constitutional aspects.

CHIDELL, FLEETWOOD. **Australia—White or Yellow?** London: Heinemann, 1926, 255 p.
A detailed criticism of British and Australian policy in immigration, primarily because of the failure of the two countries to coöperate.

CONDLIFFE, JOHN BELL. **New Zealand in the Making.** Chicago: Chicago University Press, 1930, 524 p.
An excellent study of New Zealand and her problems, written by the former research secretary of the Institute of Pacific Relations. The chapter on imperialism and foreign affairs is particularly well done.

CONDLIFFE, JOHN BELL. **A Short History of New Zealand.** Christchurch: Isitt, 1925, 236 p.
The best introductory text, with good treatment of the later period, especially as regards economic and social problems.

CRIVELLI, GEORGES M. and LOUVET, PIERRE. **L'Australie et le Pacifique.** Paris: Crès, 1923, 245 p.
Primarily a survey of economic life, with some discussion of "White Australia" and French interests in the Pacific.

DUNBABIN, THOMAS. **The Making of Australasia.** New York: Macmillan, 1923, 218 p.
A general survey of British expansion in this area, devoting attention to social and economic history as well as to politics and international relations.

HANCOCK, WILLIAM KEITH. **Australia.** New York: Scribner, 1930, 326 p.
Like other volumes in the "Modern World" series, this book gives a brief historical introduction and then analyzes current conditions and problems.

HASSERT, KURT. **Australien und Neuseeland.** Gotha: Perthes, 1924, 178 p.
One of the excellent geographic and economic surveys in the Perthes series.

KERR, DONALD. **The Law of the Australian Constitution.** Sydney: Law Book Co., 1925, 382 p.
A technical treatise.

LATHAM, JOHN GREIG. **Australia and the British Commonwealth.** London: Macmillan, 1929, 150 p.
Like most Australians, the former Attorney-General of the Commonwealth rejects extreme interpretations and continues to stress the value of the connection with Britain. The present book consists of a series of lectures on the British Commonwealth, delivered at the University of Queensland.

New Zealand Affairs. Christchurch: Isitt, 1931, 241 p.
A series of essays published for the New Zealand branch of the Institute of Pacific Relations, in preparation for the Kyoto Conference of 1930.

PHILLIPS, PHILIP DAVID and WOOD, GORDON LESLIE, *eds.* **The Peopling of Australia.** Melbourne: Macmillan, 1928, 299 p.
A collection of studies, by Australian experts, to bolster up and justify the "White Australia" policy.

RUSSELL, GEORGE WARREN. **New Zealand Today.** Christchurch: Russell, 1919, 332 p.
A general survey intended to encourage immigration, compiled by the minister of internal affairs.

SHANN, EDWARD OWEN GIBLIN. **An Economic History of Australia.** New York: Macmillan, 1930, 456 p.
A competent monograph, interestingly written and presenting more especially the accomplishment of private initiative in the development of Australia. The author is Professor of History and Economics in the University of Western Australia.

SHANN, EDWARD OWEN GIBLIN and COPLAND, DOUGLAS BERRY. **The Battle of the Plans.** Sydney: Angus and Robertson, 1931, 169 p.
The battle between those who believed in budgetary stability and those who believed in monetary manipulation, told in memoranda and other documents.

SHANN, EDWARD OWEN GIBLIN and COPLAND, DOUGLAS BERRY. **The Crisis in Austra-lian Finance, 1929-1931.** London: Australian Book Company, 1931, 201 p.
A collection of documents bearing upon the budgetary problem.

THWING, CHARLES FRANKLIN. **Human Australasia.** New York: Macmillan, 1923, 270 p.
A sociological survey. The book contains chapters on White Australasia, the news-paper, education, etc.

TREGARTHEN, GREVILLE and BAYLEY, PERCY E. G. **The Australian Commonwealth.**
London: T. Fisher Unwin, 1924, 456 p.
A new edition of a standard work brought down to 1924.

WILKINSON, HAROLD LAUNCELOT. **The World's Population Problems and a White Australia.** London: King, 1930, 340 p.
A keen discussion of the Australian policy in its larger world setting.

WILLARD, MYRA. **History of the White Australia Policy.** Melbourne: Melbourne University Press, 1924, 217 p.
A reliable and important book on the exclusion of Orientals from Australia. The work is thoroughly documented and takes up the Kanaka system of labor as well as the Asiatic immigration.

III. PACIFIC ISLANDS

The Philippines

See also (United States) Far Eastern Policy, p. 186.

DIAMONON, VICTORIANO D. **The Development of Self-Government in the Philippine Islands.** Iowa City: University of Iowa, 1920, 162 p.
A scholarly dissertation stressing particularly the spirit of American administration and the attitude and aspirations of the Filipinos.

FORBES, WILLIAM CAMERON. **The Philippine Islands.** Boston: Houghton Mifflin, 1928, 2 v.
This complete survey by the former Governor-General is an authoritative work of reference. The first volume is devoted largely to a description of conditions and to the administrative régime since the American occupation began. The second is primarily political and traces the evolution of the attitude of the natives, the emergence of the independence movement and the history of the Philippine parties.

HARRISON, FRANCIS BURTON. **The Cornerstone of Philippine Independence.** New York: Century, 1922, 343 p.
A review of American achievements in the Philippines, particularly since 1913, urging an early grant of independence. Written by the American Governor-General from 1913 to 1921.

HART, ROBERT WATSON. **The Philippines Today.** New York: Dodd, 1928, 191 p.
Written by a surgeon in the public health service, this book is intended as a general historical and descriptive survey to enlighten the American public.

HAWES, HARRY BARTOW. **Philippine Uncertainty.** New York: Century, 1932, 377 p.
The impressions of an American senator after a six weeks' investigation.

JOHNSEN, JULIA EMILY, *comp.* **Independence for the Philippines.** New York: Wilson, 1924, 99 p.
Material for and against the independence movement.

KALAW, MAXIMO MANGUIAT. **Self-Government in the Philippines.** New York: Century, 1919, 210 p.
A forceful presentation of the extreme Filipino viewpoint, recounting the work accomplished si ce 1913 in the direction of establishing stable government. The author has since bec ne Dean of the University of the Philippines.

KALAW, MAXIMO MANGUIAT. **The Development of Philippine Politics, 1872-1920.** Manila: Orie al Commercial Company, n. d., 491 p.
An American dissertation, giving a documented account.

LAUBACH, FRANK CHARLES. **The People of the Philippines.** New York: Doran, 1925, 515 p.
A detailed account of the progress and achievements of Protestant Christianity since 1898.

MAYO, KATHERINE. **The Isles of Fear.** New York: Harcourt, 1925, 372 p.
A frank sociological study and survey of political conditions, in the style of Miss Mayo's more famous "Mother India."

QUEZON, MANUEL L. and OSIAS, CAMILO. **Governor-General Wood and the Filipino Cause.** Manila: Manila Book Company, 1924, 228 p.
Essentially a reply to the report of the Wood-Forbes mission, by two leaders of the independence party.

REYES, JOSÉ S. **Legislative History of America's Economic Policy toward the Philippines.** New York: Longmans, 1923, 205 p.
A survey of American economic policy in the Philippine area.

ROOSEVELT, NICHOLAS. **The Philippines.** New York: Sears, 1926, 315 p.
An eminently fair and broad-minded account of the Philippine problem in its political and economic aspects.

STOREY, MOORFIELD and LICHAUCO, MARCIAL PRIMITIVO. **The Conquest of the Philippines by the United States, 1898-1925.** New York: Putnam, 1926, 274 p.
A serious attempt to examine the history of the question in a scholarly way.

WILLIAMS, DANIEL RODERICK. **The United States and the Philippines.** New York: Doubleday, 1924, 335 p.
One of the important books on the subject. The author was secretary to the Taft Commission and has been resident in the Philippines for many years. He reviews the whole history of American rule, stressing the evolution of the independence movement.

WORCESTER, DEAN CONANT and HAYDEN, RALSTON. **The Philippines, Past and Present.** New York: Macmillan, 1930, 862 p.
This revised edition of a standard work contains a lengthy biographical sketch of Worcester and several additional chapters.

Hawaii

See also (United States) Far Eastern Policy, p. 186.

BUNKER, FRANK FOREST. **Hawaii and the Philippines.** Philadelphia: Lippincott, 1928, 207 p.
A good historical and descriptive introduction.

KINNEY, WILLIAM A. **Hawaii's Capacity for Self-Government All but Destroyed.** Salt Lake City: Jensen, 1927, 206 p.
An historical and analytical study of the Asiatic immigration, its effects on the Polynesians, and its results for American institutions.

KUYKENDALL, RALPH SIMPSON. **A History of Hawaii.** New York: Macmillan, 1926, 385 p.
A satisfactory handbook, prepared for the Historical Commission of Hawaii.

LITTLER, ROBERT MCDONALD CHARLES. **The Governance of Hawaii.** Stanford: Stanford University Press, 1929, 298 p.
The best general treatment of the American territorial administration.

PALMER, ALBERT WENTWORTH. **The Human Side of Hawaii.** Boston: Pilgrim Press, 1924, 144 p.
A series of lectures on the historical development of the islands, with special reference to the meeting of East and West and the grave race problem.

PORTEUS, STANLEY DAVID and BABCOCK, MARJORIE E. **Temperament and Race.** Boston: Badger, 1926, 364 p.
Historical and psychological material on the races in Hawaii, with some discussion of future problems.

WRISTON, ROSCOE C. **Hawaii Today.** New York: Doubleday, 1926, 147 p.
A well-written and rather fascinating survey of the island group, by an army air officer. The book contains some excellent air views.

Miscellaneous

See also (League of Nations) Mandates, p. 58.

ARCHIMBAUD, LÉON and SASPORTAS, DR. **Établissements Français de l'Océanie.** Paris: Société d'Éditions Géographiques, 1931, 128 + 80 p.
An excellent survey of conditions in the French possessions, prepared for the great Colonial Exposition.

BURTON, JOHN WEAR. **A Missionary Survey of the Pacific Islands.** New York: World Dominion Press, 1930, 124 p.
A review of the problems of the islands and a detailed survey of the mission work done and remaining to be done.

CHAPPLE, WILLIAM ALLAN. **Fiji—Its Problems and Resources.** Auckland: Whitcombe, 1921, 189 p.
A good introductory survey.

DEANE, WALLACE. **Fijian Society.** New York: Macmillan, 1921, 248 p.
A scholarly study of life and customs of the natives, by the former principal of the Teachers' Training College.

DOUGLAS, ARCHIBALD JOHN ANGUS and JOHNSON, PHILIP HENRY. **The South Seas of Today.** London: Cassell, 1926, 296 p.
The record of a scientific cruise to the lesser known islands. A frank account of conditions.

EGGLESTON, FREDERIC WILLIAM, *ed.* **The Australian Mandate for New Guinea.** Melbourne: Macmillan, 1928, 149 p.
A collection of papers from a Round Table discussion of mandate problems.

GREY, J. R. and MRS. BEATRICE BUCKLAND (TAYLOR). **South Sea Settlers.** London: Arrowsmith, 1927, 264 p.
An account of daily life and problems among white settlers.

GRIGNON-DUMOULIN, PHILIPPE. **Le Condominium et la Mise en Valeur des Nouvelles Hebrides.** Paris: Presses Universitaires, 1928, 190 p.
A doctoral thesis outlining the Anglo-French condominium established in 1906 and discussing the resources of the islands and their exploitation.

HENLEY, SIR THOMAS. **A Pacific Cruise.** Sydney: Sands, 1930, 176 p.
A stimulating discussion of current problems, especially in Tonga and Samoa. The author is a former New Zealand Cabinet Minister.

HOPKINS, ARTHUR INNES. **In the Isles of King Solomon.** London: Seeley Service, 1928, 269 p.
A study of native life, by a man who lived in the islands for twenty-five years.

KNIBBS, STANLEY GEORGE CURTHOYS. **The Savage Solomons.** Philadelphia: Lippincott, 1929, 282 p.
An account of the changes gradually taking place, by the British commissioner of lands.

LYNCH, BOHUN, *ed.* **Isles of Illusion.** London: Constable, 1928, 334 p.
A most unusual book, first published in 1923. The volume consists of letters written to the editor by an anonymous friend between 1912 and 1920. They give an extraordinarily frank and intimate picture of life in the South Sea Islands.

MURRAY, SIR HUBERT. **Papua of To-day.** London: King, 1925, 308 p.
A general study of conditions, with special attention to labor problems, European settlement and the native question. The author was British Lieutenant-Governor.

REGELSPERGER, GUSTAVE, PELLERAY, EMMANUEL and FROMENT-GUIEYSSE, GEORGES. **L'Océanie Française.** Paris: Notre Domaine Colonial, 1922, 158 p.
A popular descriptive survey of New Caledonia, the New Hebrides and lesser French possessions.

RIVERS, WILLIAM HALSE RIVERS, *ed.* **Essays on the Depopulation of Melanesia.** New York: Macmillan, 1922, 116 p.
A collection of essays by various authorities, and an important contribution to the study of Pacific problems.

ROLLIN, LOUIS. **Les Îles Marquises.** Paris: Société d'Éditions Géographiques, 1929, 334 p.
A general history and descriptive work of high merit, with a study of the impact of white civilization.

ST. JOHNSTON, THOMAS REGINALD. **South Sea Reminiscences.** London: T. Fisher Unwin, 1922, 213 p.
Easy-going but withal instructive sketches of conditions and problems, by the former district commissioner in Fiji.

WILLIAMSON, ROBERT WOOD. **The Social and Political Systems of Central Polynesia.** London: Cambridge University Press, 1924, 3 v.
A digest of ethnographical material collected by travellers, missionaries, officials, etc.; heavily-documented and scholarly.

EIGHTH PART:

POLAR REGIONS

See also (Northern Europe) Scandinavian States, p. 339; also (Finland) General, p. 345; also (Far East) Siberia, p. 485.

AMDRUP, GEORG CARL and others, *eds.* **Grønland i Tohundredaaret for Hans Egedes Landing.** Copenhagen: Reitzel, 1921, 2 v. and atlas.
A systematic account of the country and of its development under Danish supremacy. There are chapters devoted to trade, fishing and hunting, business and communications, administration and the legal system, and to the leading features in the history of Greenland and the scientific exploration of the island.

ANDREWS, CLARENCE LEROY. **Story of Alaska.** Seattle: Lowman and Hanford, 1931, 258 p.
Beginning with the Russian voyages of discovery, the author covers in concise form the entire history of Alaska to 1930, taking up government, industries, resources and general conditions.

BERLIN, KNUD. **Danmarks Ret Til Grønland.** Copenhagen: Busck, 1932, 160 p.
A Danish view of the East Greenland conflict.

BREITFUSS, LEV L'VOVICH. **Die Erforschung des Polargebietes Russisch-Eurasiens: See- und Landreisen während der Jahre 1912-24.** Gotha: Perthes, 1925, 113 p.
A volume of particular value as it presents to non-Russian readers a summary of Russian exploratory work in the Arctic during this period. There is an exhaustive bibliography of 400 titles.

BROWN, ROBERT NEAL RUDMOSE. **The Polar Regions: A Physical and Economic Geography of the Arctic and Antarctic.** New York: Dutton, 1927, 245 p.
Although the major part of the book deals with physical and biological geography, there are chapters on the Eskimo, whaling, political geography, trade routes and colonization.

BYRD, RICHARD EVELYN. **Little America.** New York: Putnam, 1930, 422 p.
The record of an aerial exploration in the Antarctic, throwing some light on national territorial claims.

CLARK, HENRY W. **History of Alaska.** New York: Macmillan, 1930, 208 p.
The author, a native of Alaska, surveys the development of the country since the middle of the 19th century, and discusses its frequent appearance in international affairs.

GANS, MARGARETE. **Das Hudsonmeer.** Hamburg: Hammerich und Lesser, 1926, 113 p.
The history of the exploration of the Hudson Bay region, with material on its physical and economic geography. There is an extensive bibliography.

GRAY, LOUIS HERBERT. **Spitsbergen and Bear Island.** Washington: Government Printing Office, 1919, 129 p.
An important memorandum giving the history of Spitsbergen, setting forth the official American view of the region's strategic importance, and discussing possible solutions of the problems arising out of conflicting national claims.

GREELY, ADOLPHUS WASHINGTON. **Handbook of Alaska: Its Resources, Products, and Attractions in 1924.** New York: Scribner, 1925, 330 p.
A new edition of a comprehensive work, with additional chapters on fisheries, fur-farming, gold-mining, petroleum, coal and railroads.

GREELY, ADOLPHUS WASHINGTON. **The Polar Regions in the Twentieth Century: Their Discovery and Industrial Evolution.** Boston: Little, Brown, 1928, 270 p.
The author writes of the "increased utilization of the material resources of the polar regions" in the present century.

Greenland. New York: Oxford University Press, 1928-1929, 3 v.
This monumental work deals with the discovery, exploration and nature of Greenland, the past and present population, colonization, and the history of the country to 1929. Published by the Commission for the Direction of the Geological and Geographical Investigations in Greenland.

HAYES, JAMES GORDON. **The Conquest of the South Pole.** London: Butterworth, 1932, 318 p.
A judicious and orderly summary of Antarctic exploration in the period 1906-31.

JOERG, WOLFGANG LOUIS GOTTFRIED. **Brief History of Polar Exploration since the Introduction of Flying.** New York: American Geographical Society, 2nd ed., 1930, 95 p.
A survey of polar exploration since 1925, with chapters on air navigation in the Polar regions, and political sovereignty in the Arctic and Antarctic.

KNOTHE, HERBERT. **Spitzbergen: Eine Landeskundliche Studie.** Gotha: Perthes, 1931, 109 p.
A detailed and comprehensive memoir which will long remain the standard work on the geography of the Spitsbergen archipelago. A section on man in Spitsbergen deals with the discovery of the country, and with whaling, hunting, coal and mineral exploitation, communications and political constitution.

LAKHTIN, VLADIMIR LEONT'EVICH. **Prava na Severnye Poliarnye Prostranstva.** Moscow: Commissariat of Foreign Affairs, 1928, 48 p.
An official exposition of the Russian claims to Arctic territory, in particular analyzing political, economic and legal questions connected with the development of aviation routes.

MARKHAM, SIR CLEMENTS ROBERT. **The Lands of Silence: A History of Arctic and Antarctic Exploration.** New York: Macmillan, 1921, 539 p.
This has been termed an "epic of Antarctic exploration." Particular stress is laid upon British naval endeavor, with a minimum of space devoted to scientific and non-British exploits.

NICHOLS, MRS. JEANNETTE (PADDOCK). **Alaska.** Cleveland: A. H. Clark, 1924, 456 p.
A history of the exploitation and industrial development of Alaska during its first half century as part of the United States.

NORDENSKJÖLD, OTTO and MECKING, LUDWIG. **The Geography of the Polar Regions.** New York: American Geographical Society, 1928, 359 p.
A systematic presentation of our knowledge of the Arctic and Antarctic, invaluable as a guide and book of reference. With many maps and photographs.

Problems of Polar Research. New York: American Geographical Society, 1928, 477 p.
A coöperative undertaking by thirty-one leaders in polar exploration, describing the problems awaiting solution and discussing methods of attack. There are chapters on the resources of the Arctic and political rights in Polar regions.

SKEIE, JON. **Greenland: The Dispute between Norway and Denmark.** New York: Dutton, 1932, 94 p.
A statement of the Norwegian claims in East Greenland, by the Deputy Judge of the Supreme Court of Norway. There is a foreword by G. M. Gathorne-Hardy.

SMEDAL, GUSTAV CATHRINUS HOFGAARD. **Acquisition of Sovereignty over Polar Areas.** Oslo: Dybwad, 1931, 143 p.
An English translation of an important Norwegian work. "Occupation" and "the Sector Principle" are dealt with, and almost one half of the book is devoted to the East Greenland controversy.

STAËL-HOLSTEIN, BARON LAGE VON. **Norway in Arcticum: From Spitsbergen to— Greenland?** London: Williams, 1932, 80 p.
The status of Spitsbergen considered in its historical, legal and economic setting by a Swedish authority who is critical of Norwegian rule.

STEFÁNSSON, VILHJÁLMUR and KNIGHT, JOHN IRVINE. **The Adventure of Wrangel Island.** New York: Macmillan, 1925, 424 p.
The story of the 1921 expedition, undertaken under "the strong conviction that the world is at the dawn of a revolution in transportation ideas," and that the Arctic offers a short-cut by air from one hemisphere to the other. Most of the book, however, is devoted to describing the tragedy which befell the expedition, and subsequent controversies.

STEFÁNSSON, VILHJÁLMUR. **The Friendly Arctic; the Story of Five Years in Polar Regions.** New York: Macmillan, 1927, 784 p.
This history of Stefánsson's Third Polar Expedition, 1913-1918, made under the auspices of the Canadian Government, records the general results attained, among them the addition of many thousands of square miles to the territory of Canada.

STEFÁNSSON, VILHJÁLMUR. **The Northward Course of Empire.** New York: Harcourt, 1922, 274 p.
"A brief summary of the history, the climate, and other conditions in the North, as they bear upon the problems of colonization." A chapter on transpolar commerce by air outlines the advantages of transpolar routes.

UNDERWOOD, JOHN JASPER. **Alaska, an Empire in the Making.** New York: Dodd, rev. ed., 1925, 440 p.
The author, a resident of Alaska for some years, gives a general description of the country and also deals briefly with its annexation to the United States and its present administration.

WEYER, EDWARD MOFFAT, JR. **The Eskimos: Their Environment and Folkways.** New Haven: Yale University Press, 1932, 491 p.
A study of the resources, customs and environment of the 35,000 people who inhabit the Arctic lands between East Cape, Siberia, and eastern Greenland.

NINTH PART:

AFRICA

I. GENERAL TREATISES; RACE PROBLEMS; MISSIONS

See also (Civilizations and Race Conflicts) General, p. 4; also (League of Nations) Mandates, p. 58; also (United States) Immigration and Race Problems, p. 191.

ANTONELLI, ÉTIENNE. **L'Afrique et la Paix de Versailles.** Paris: Grasset, 1921, 258 p.
A sketch of European colonial possessions in Africa in 1914, with a brief account of the war in Africa and the redisposition of African territory at the Peace Conference.

BOUNIOL, JOSEPH, *ed.* **The White Fathers and Their Missions.** London: Sands, 1929, 334 p.
A review and survey of the famous Catholic missions in Africa, based on the principal records.

BRIEY, RENAUD, COMTE DE. **Le Sphinx Noir.** Paris: Berger-Levrault, 1927, 360 p.
A Belgian official's study of economic, political and social problems in various parts of south and central Africa.

BUELL, RAYMOND LESLIE. **The Native Problem in Africa.** New York: Macmillan, 1928, 2 v.
An exhaustive study of the African native as he has been affected by the coming of the European. The author travelled through the larger part of Africa, interviewing government officials, collecting information and surveying the situation. He takes up in order all the territories under British, French or Belgian control, and the Republic of Liberia, discussing the domestic situation from every angle—administration, economics, health, education. The work is written in a scholarly manner and is equipped with imposing appendices.

BUXTON, CHARLES RODEN. **The Race Problem in Africa.** London: Hogarth, 1931, 60 p.
A vigorous plea for a broader policy toward the native, looking to eventual equality of rights, even in politics. The author has been a Labor M. P.

COOKSEY, JOSEPH JAMES and McLEISH, ALEXANDER. **Religion and Civilization in West Africa.** New York: World Dominion Press, 1931, 277 p.
A missionary survey of the British, French, Spanish and Portuguese possessions.

CRIPPS, ARTHUR SHEARLY. **An Africa for Africans.** New York: Longmans, 1927, 217 p.
A plea for extreme segregation and autonomy for the blacks.

DAVOL, RALPH. **Raw Products of the World.** Vol. I. Africa. Taunton, Mass.: Davol Publishing Co., 1923, 264 p.
A valuable compendium for those interested in foreign trade, though somewhat unscientifically compiled.

DELAFOSSE, MAURICE. **The Negroes of Africa.** Washington: Associated Publishers, 1931, 313 p.
A general, semi-popular historical and descriptive study, by a former French governor.

DIX, ARTHUR. **Was Geht Uns Afrika An?** Berlin: Stilke, 1931, 107 p.
The author stresses the economic importance of Africa in the modern world economy.

DU PLESSIS, JOHANNES. **The Evangelisation of Pagan Africa.** Capetown: Juta, 1930, 408 p.
A standard work on missionary and general European activity in Central Africa. Well-documented.

FRASER, DONALD. **The New Africa.** New York: Missionary Educational Movement, 1928, 221 p.
An optimistic view of European influence and missionary achievement in the Black Continent.

HAGEMANN, WALTER. **Die Revision der Kolonialmethoden in Afrika.** Münster: Aschendorff, 1929, 96 p.
The author foresees a great future for Black Africa, though he recognizes the continued necessity for white guidance and machinery.

HARDY, GEORGES. **Vue Générale de l'Histoire d'Afrique.** Paris: Colin, 1922, 200 p.
A masterly popular sketch, by one of the leading French authorities.

HARRIS, JOHN H. **Africa, Slave or Free?** London: Student Christian Movement, 1919, 244 p.
An analysis of modern problems such as the labor question, land tenure, racial contacts, education and missions.

HARRIS, NORMAN DWIGHT. **Europe and Africa.** Boston: Houghton Mifflin, 1927, 497 p.
The revised edition of the author's "Intervention and Colonization in Africa." A good historical study of European expansion and the partition of Africa.

JOHNSTON, SIR HARRY HAMILTON. **The Story of My Life.** Indianapolis: Bobbs, 1923, 536 p.
The autobiography of a famous explorer and administrator. Not as revealing as it might be.

JONES, THOMAS JESSE, ed. **Education in Africa.** New York: Phelps-Stokes Fund, 1922, 323 p.
A thorough study by American investigators of African needs in primary and secondary education, and in training in agriculture, trades, medicine and religion.

LEWIN, PERCY EVANS. **Africa.** Oxford: Clarendon Press, 1924, 224 p.
A popular survey of contemporary Africa, by an official of the Royal Colonial Institute.

LUCAS, SIR CHARLES PRESTWOOD. **The Partition and Colonization of Africa.** Oxford: Clarendon Press, 1922, 228 p.
A summary sketch in the form of lectures by a well-known authority.

OLDHAM, JOSEPH HOULDSWORTH and GIBSON, B. D. **The Remaking of Man in Africa.** New York: Oxford University Press, 1931, 185 p.
A stimulating discussion of the native problem. Dr. Oldham is Secretary of the National Missionary Council.

OLIVIER, SYDNEY HALDANE OLIVIER, BARON. **White Capital and Coloured Labour.** London: Hogarth, 1929, 348 p.
An entirely revised and modernized edition of a standard treatise published in 1906.

PLOMER, WILLIAM. **I Speak of Africa.** London: Hogarth, 1927, 260 p.
An able essay, forcefully presenting the urgency of current issues.

Report on African Affairs, 1929. London: Harrison, 1930, 368 p.
A valuable semi-official report, dealing with such matters as agriculture, education, immigration, labor, native policy, etc., in all the British possessions in Africa.

RICHTER, JULIUS. **Geschichte der Evangelischen Mission in Afrika.** Gütersloh: Bertelsmann, 1922, 813 p.
A monumental work.

SELIGMAN, CHARLES GABRIEL. **Races of Africa.** London: Thornton Butterworth, 1930, 256 p.
An introductory volume, in the Home University Library.

SMITH, EDWIN WILLIAM. **The Christian Mission in Africa.** London: Edinburgh House, 1926, 192 p.
A survey of the problem, based on the proceedings of the Le Zoute Conference of 1926, by an official of the British and Foreign Bible Society.

SMITH, EDWIN WILLIAM. **The Golden Stool.** New York: Doubleday, 1928, 328 p.
One of the notable post-war books on Africa. The author, a missionary and scholar, discusses many aspects of cultural conflict in Africa, and touches on numerous questions of religion, government, etc.

SMUTS, JAN CHRISTIAAN. **Africa and Some World Problems.** New York: Oxford University Press, 1930, 184 p.
A series of lectures by the eminent South African statesman on the problems of Africa and such questions as democracy, the League, and world peace.

SPANNAUS, GÜNTHER. **Züge aus der Politischen Organisation Afrikanischer Staaten und Voelker.** Leipzig: Werkgemeinschaft, 1929, 223 p.
A scientific study of native political organizations.

WEINTHAL, LEO, *ed.* **The Story of the Cape to Cairo Railway.** London: Pioneer Publishing Company, 1923, 3 v.
An immense and lavishly illustrated collection of articles, personal narratives and studies not only of the railway scheme, but of the countries through which the railway passes.

WEULERSSE, JACQUES. **Noirs et Blancs.** Paris: Colin, 1931, 242 p.
Observations on the color problem and difficulties of European colonization.

WIENER, LIONEL. **Les Chemins de Fer Coloniaux de l'Afrique.** Paris: Dunod, 1931, 574 p.
A standard work on an important aspect of African affairs.

WOOLF, LEONARD SIDNEY. **Empire and Commerce in Africa.** New York: Macmillan, 1919, 374 p.
Avowedly anti-imperialistic, but a thoroughly well informed and well written study of European expansion. One of the most interesting books on modern Africa.

II. INDEPENDENT STATES

EGYPT AND SUDAN

Egypt

ABBÂS II HILMI, PASHA. **A Few Words on the Anglo-Egyptian Settlement.** London: Allen, 1930, 105 p.
The former Khedive urges on his countrymen the acceptance of the draft treaty of 1929 as the first step to the full attainment of their ends.

ADAM, MME. JULIETTE. **L'Angleterre en Égypte.** Paris: Imprimerie du Center, 1922, 415 p.

An attack upon English domination of Egypt and a passionate plea for Egyptian independence. The book is a collection of more or less disjointed writings by a well-known journalist, all tending to recall Egypt's claims and England's evasion of them.

BEAMAN, ARDERN ARTHUR HULME. **The Dethronement of the Khedive.** London: Allen, 1929, 190 p.
This little book, by an Englishman with unrivalled experience of Egypt since 1879, is more than its title implies. It is a criticism of English policy under Cromer and Kitchener, of the treatment meted out to Abbas II, and of the whole post-war handling of the Anglo-Egyptian relationship.

BRINTON, JASPER YEATES. **The Mixed Courts of Egypt.** New Haven: Yale University Press, 1930, 416 p.
The standard treatment of a very interesting experiment in international administration. The author is an American justice of the Court of Appeals of the Mixed Courts of Egypt, and his book is full of valuable material.

CHAFIK, HASSAN. **Le Statut Juridique International de l'Égypte.** Paris: Éditions Internationales, 1928, 228 p.
A detailed analysis of Egypt's international status and the negotiations with England.

CHIROL, SIR VALENTINE. **The Egyptian Problem.** London: Macmillan, 1920, 331 p.
One of the most valuable analyses of the Egyptian problem since about 1900, and especially during the war and post-war period. The author takes a much fairer attitude towards the nationalist movement than most writers.

ELGOOD, PERCIVAL GEORGE. **Egypt and the Army.** New York: Oxford University Press, 1924, 382 p.
The development of the Egyptian independence movement during the World War period. A competent, detailed, critical account, by an English officer long in the service of the Egyptian Government.

ELGOOD, PERCIVAL GEORGE. **The Transit of Egypt.** New York: Longmans, 1928, 342 p.
One of the best general historical studies on modern Egypt, particularly competent on the history of the British occupation and the evolution of the nationalist movement.

GEORGES-GAULIS, BERTHE. **Le Nationalisme Égyptien.** Paris: Berger-Levrault, 1928, 204 p.
The authoress, well-known as a writer on Near Eastern affairs, here reviews the Egyptian situation from 1924 to 1928. The book is in the form of periodic reports on developments.

HANOTAUX, GABRIEL. **Regards sur l'Égypte et la Palestine.** Paris: Plon, 1929, 284 p.
The travel impressions of a well-known French historian.

HARRIS, MURRAY GEORGE. **Egypt under the Egyptians.** London: Chapman and Hall, 1925, 240 p.
A collection of articles on various phases of British rule, the nationalist movement, the economic situation, the Sudan problem, etc.

HASSAN, EL SAYED. **Essai sur une Orientation Nouvelle de l'Économie Égyptienne.** Toulouse: Vialelle, 1928, 267 p.
A useful dissertation, criticizing the overstress on cotton production and urging the need for a balanced industrial program.

HAYTER, SIR WILLIAM GOODENOUGH. **Recent Constitutional Developments in Egypt.** Cambridge: Cambridge University Press, 1924, 49 p.
A constitutional history of the attainment of Egyptian independence.

HOWELL, JOSEPH MORTON. **Egypt's Past, Present and Future.** Dayton: Service, 1929, 389 p.
A general, conventional account, by a former American Minister to Egypt.

HUSSEIN, I. SALEH. **Études Juridiques du Problème de l'Égypte.** Paris: Lac, 1931, 326 p.
A legal study of the position of Egypt in its relations with England.

KITAÏGORODSKIĬ, P. **Egipet v Bor'be za Nezavisimost'.** Moscow: no pub., 1925, 108 p.
The Egyptian question seen from a violently anti-British standpoint.

LAMBELIN, ROGER. **L'Égypte et l'Angleterre; Vers l'Indépendance.** Paris: Grasset, 1922, 259 p.
A valuable survey of the country's position in international relations during the last hundred years.

MAKRAM, HILMY. **Problèmes Soulevés par la Constitution Égyptienne.** Dijon: Bernigaud, 1927, 122 p.
A doctoral thesis. The author discusses the conflict of legislative and executive power, the inadequate guarantees, and especially the position of the monarchy.

MALACHE, MOHAMED KAMEL AMIN. **Les Instruments de Circulation et les Institutions de Crédit en Égypte.** Paris: Presses Universitaires, 1930, 448 p.
This scholarly dissertation, by an Egyptian professor, supplies an excellent history of the Egyptian currency and especially of the foreign and domestic banks operating there.

MARSHALL, JOHN EDWIN. **The Egyptian Enigma, 1890-1928.** London: Murray, 1928, 342 p.
A general survey of modern Egyptian history, based in large part on personal experience, by a high British official who writes in the orthodox Cromerian style.

MARTIN, PERCY FALCKE. **Egypt Old and New.** New York: Doran, 1923, 224 p.
A superior type of descriptive work, treating the geography, history and economic and political life of contemporary Egypt. The best single post-war survey.

MEYER, GEORGES. **L'Égypte Contemporaine et les Capitulations.** Paris: Presses Universitaires, 1930, 472 p.
A dissertation. Probably the best single historical and analytical study of the capitulatory régime, its connections with financial and commercial problems, various projects for reform, etc.

NEWMAN, EDWARD WILLIAM POLSON. **Great Britain in Egypt.** London: Cassell, 1928, 304 p.
One of the best single accounts of Britain's record in Egypt, giving a detailed account of war and post-war developments.

PASSARGE, SIEGFRIED. **Aegypten und der Arabische Orient.** Berlin: Zentralverlag, 1931, 70 p.
A popular introduction, with stress upon cultural and economic factors.

POLITIS, ATHANASE G. **L'Hellénisme et l'Égypte Moderne.** Paris: Alcan, 1929, 530 p.
A study of the important Greek element in Egypt during the later 18th, 19th and 20th centuries. An interesting contribution.

POLNAUER, ALEXANDRE. **Le Régime Douanier Égyptien.** Paris: Jouve, 1926, 134 p.
A dissertation reviewing Egypt's tariff treaties with European countries and analyzing the present situation. Useful, failing something better.

POWERS, HARRY HUNTINGTON. **Egypt.** New York: Macmillan, 1924, 327 p.
A general descriptive work of some merit.

SABRY, MOUSTAPHA. **Le Pouvoir Législatif et le Pouvoir Exécutif en Égypte.** Paris: Mechelinck, 1930, 421 p.
A very good study of the constitution, giving a detailed analysis of its provisions and of its operation between 1923 and 1930.

SABRY, MOUSTAPHA. **La Révolution Égyptienne.** Paris: Vrin, 1919-1921, 2 v.
Not serious history, but a documented, illustrated story of the nationalist movement, by an Egyptian historian.

SYMONS, M. TRAVERS. **Britain and Egypt. The Rise of Egyptian Nationalism.**
London: Palmer, 1925, 344 p.
A reliable history of the nationalist movement since the days of Arabi.

TAWWAF, *pseud.* **Egypt, 1919.** Oxford: Blackwell, 1925, 69 p.
A valuable diary of the revolution, by an eyewitness.

VAN DEN BOSCH, FIRMIN, BARON. **Vingt Années d'Égypte.** Paris: Perrin, 1931.
The experiences of an official, dealing primarily with the post-war period, and touching Syria and Palestine as well as Egypt.

YEGHEN, FOULAD. **Saad Zaghloul.** Paris: Cahiers de France, 1928.
A sympathetic appreciation of the late Egyptian statesman.

YOUNG, GEORGE. **Egypt.** New York: Scribner, 1927, 352 p.
A volume in the Modern World series, valuable as a review of the history of modern
Egypt since the time of Napoleon and Mehemet Ali. The viewpoint is that of a Labor-
ite, and the treatment of English policy is exceedingly critical throughout.

Suez Canal

See also (World War) Near and Middle Eastern Front, p. 137; also (Great Britain) Imperial
Relations, p. 231.

BENNO, I. J. **La Situation Internationale du Canal de Suez.** Lyon: Bosc and Riou,
1929, 183 p.
A mediocre dissertation, covering the entire history of the Canal.

BIRK, ALFRED and MÜLLER, KARL HERMANN. **Der Suezkanal.** Hamburg: Boysen und
Maasch, 1925, 144 p.
A short history of the Canal, with an able discussion of its present-day importance.

HALLBERG, CHARLES W. **The Suez Canal.** New York: Columbia University Press, 1931,
434 p.
A careful study of the history of the canal and the international problems connected
with it. On the whole the best brief account.

HUSNY, HUSSEIN. **Le Canal de Suez et la Politique Égyptienne.** Montpellier: Écono-
miste Méridionale, 1923, 331 p.
A general history of the building of the Canal, with some new material from the
Austrian archives.

REINHARD, ERNST. **Kampf um Suez.** Dresden: Kaden, 1930, 328 p.
A well-written and on the whole well-informed account of British imperial policy in
Egypt, the Red Sea and Arabia in the pre-war and post-war periods.

Sudan

DUGMORE, ARTHUR RADCLYFFE. **The Vast Sudan.** London: Arrowsmith, 1924, 312 p.
A travel book, with much interesting comment on recent changes.

MACMICHAEL, HAROLD ALFRED. **A History of the Arabs in the Sudan.** Cambridge:
Cambridge University Press, 1923, 2 v.
A thorough historical and ethnographic survey of a technical nature.

MARTIN, PERCY FALCKE. **The Sudan in Evolution.** London: Constable, 1921, 557 p.
A competent and reliable analysis of economic and governmental problems since the reconquest of the Sudan by Kitchener.

ROUARD DE CARD, EDGARD. **Situation Internationale du Soudan Égyptien.** Paris: Pedone, 1931, 80 p.
A compilation of facts and documents by a French authority on things African.

STIGAND, CHAUNCEY HIGH. **Equatoria: The Lado Enclave.** London: Constable, 1923, 253 p.
A study of the southern Sudan and its problems. The best general book on this area.

WINSHIP, NORTH. **Anglo-Egyptian Sudan: Commercial Handbook.** Washington: Department of Commerce, 1927, 80 p.
A handbook prepared for the Bureau of Foreign and Domestic Commerce, covering government activities in the Sudan, finance and banking conditions, communications, resources and industries.

ETHIOPIA

BAUM, JAMES EDWIN. **Savage Abyssinia.** New York: Sears, 1927, 357 p.
Essentially a travel book, with some account of present conditions.

BUDGE, SIR ERNEST ALFRED THOMPSON WALLIS. **A History of Ethiopia.** London: Methuen, 1928, 2 v.
The standard history in English, written by an eminent authority. Rather stronger on religious and cultural than on political or diplomatic history.

CERULLI, ENRICO. **Etiopia Occidentale.** Rome: Sindacato Italiano Arti Grafiche, 1929, 252 p.
A record of travel in the little-known western parts of Abyssinia.

CONTI-ROSSINI, CARLO. **L'Abissinia.** Rome: Cremonese, 1929, 172 p.
A brief popular survey written by the greatest living Italian authority on Abyssinian history.

DELATTE, M. **Politique Extérieure de l'Éthiopie.** Liège: Cobben-Marlot, 1926, 125 p.
A general study of Abyssinia's international status, relations to the Great Powers, the League of Nations, etc.

HODSON, ARNOLD WIENHOLT. **Seven Years in Southern Abyssinia.** London: T. Fisher Unwin, 1927, 277 p.
The British Consul for Southern Abyssinia gives a vivid account of his experiences during the years 1914 to 1927.

MACCREAGH, GORDON. **The Last of Free Africa.** New York: Century, 1928, 361 p.
An attractively written general descriptive work on Abyssinia.

NORDEN, HERMANN. **Africa's Last Empire.** London: Witherby, 1930, 240 p.
A well-written illustrated narrative of a journey across Abyssinia to Khartoum.

PIERRE-ALYPE, LOUIS MARIE. **Sous la Couronne de Salomon. L'Empire des Négus.** Paris: Plon, 1925, 312 p.
Abyssinia from earliest times, with emphasis on recent international complications.

POLLERA, ALBERTO. **Lo Stato Etiopico e la Sua Chiesa.** Rome: Società Editrice d'Arte Illustrata, 1926, 373 p.
A thorough study of the governmental and religious organization of Ethiopia.

POWELL, EDWARD ALEXANDER. **Beyond the Utmost Purple Rim.** New York: Century, 1925, 431 p.

Impressions and observations in Abyssinia, Somaliland, East Africa and Madagascar, by a well-known traveller.

REIN, G. K. **Abessinien.** Berlin: Reimer, 1919-1920, 3 v.
The greatest scientific survey ever made of Ethiopia. A complete and reliable account of the history, government, religion, culture, economic life, etc.

REY, CHARLES FERNAND. **Unconquered Abyssinia as It Is Today.** Philadelphia: Lippincott, 1924, 312 p.
The best short post-war survey of conditions, government, economic life, etc.

REY, CHARLES FERNAND. **In the Country of the Blue Nile.** London: Duckworth, 1927, 296 p.
Instructive and entertaining pictures of conditions and problems in modern Abyssinia.

ROUARD DE CARD, EDGARD. **L'Éthiopie au Point de Vue de Droit International.** Paris: Pedone, 1928, 100 p.
The best short account of the international status of Abyssinia at the present time, discussing encroachments of foreign powers, principally Great Britain and Italy, and her efforts to remain independent.

ZOLI, CORRADO. **Cronache Etiopiche.** Rome: Sindacato Italiano Arti Grafiche, 1931, 416 p.
This review of Abyssinian history gives a detailed account of contemporary problems.

LIBERIA

DURRANT, ROBERT ERNEST. **Liberia: A Report.** London: African International Corporation, 1925, 71 p.
A booklet describing the country from the trader's point of view.

MAUGHAM, REGINALD CHARLES FULKE. **The Republic of Liberia.** London: Allen, 1920, 299 p.
One of the best general historical and descriptive studies, by the British consul-general at Monrovia.

REEVE, HENRY FENWICK. **The Black Republic: Liberia; Its Political and Social Conditions of Today.** London: Witherby, 1923, 207 p.
A very critical account of conditions and government policy, with a plea for white intervention and tutelage.

SIBLEY, JAMES L. and WESTERMANN, DIEDRICH. **Liberia Old and New.** New York: Doubleday, 1928, 335 p.
An investigation conducted for the American Advisory Committee on Education. A complete survey of cultural and economic conditions and possibilities.

STRONG, RICHARD PEARSON, *ed.* **The African Republic of Liberia and the Belgian Congo.** Cambridge: Harvard University Press, 1930, 2 v.
An exhaustive study.

III. BRITISH POSSESSIONS

WEST AND CENTRAL AFRICA

See also (League of Nations) Mandates, p. 58.

BURNS, ALAN CUTHBERT. **History of Nigeria.** London: Allen and Unwin, 1929, 360 p.
The first complete history of this important province, written by an experienced English official. The book contains also a survey of present conditions and a selection of important documents.

CARDINALL, ALLAN WOLSEY. **In Ashanti and Beyond.** London: Seeley Service, 1927, 288 p.

A valuable descriptive study based on many years of experience, by a British district commissioner.

EVANS, IFOR LESLIE. **The British in Tropical Africa.** New York: Macmillan, 1929, 404 p.

A much-needed survey of the history of European penetration in Africa, followed by an account of the British rule in West and East Africa and the Sudan.

GEARY, SIR WILLIAM NEVILL MONTGOMERIE. **Nigeria under British Rule.** London: Methuen, 1927, 320 p.

The author traces the history of British rule from the beginning, using unpublished material for the period prior to 1900. The book is based in large part upon personal observation of developments and is well equipped with statistics.

GODDARD, THOMAS NELSON. **Handbook of Sierra Leone.** London: Grant Richards, 1925, 335 p.

A British official's account of the development of the colony and protectorate, and of economic life, population and administrative organization.

JOHNSON, J. W. DE GRAFT. **Towards Nationhood in West Africa.** London: Headley, 1928, 158 p.

A critique of the constitution of 1925 in the Gold Coast.

McPHEE, ALLAN. **The Economic Revolution in British West Africa.** London: Routledge, 1926, 322 p.

A heavily documented pioneer study of the economic life and problems in Nigeria and the other British West African colonies.

MEEK, CHARLES KINGSLEY. **The Northern Tribes of Nigeria.** New York: Oxford University Press, 1925, 2 v.

Scholarly scientific studies in history and ethnology.

MIGEOD, FREDERICK WILLIAM HUGH. **A View of Sierra Leone.** London: Kegan Paul, 1926, 351 p.

A fundamental historical and descriptive study, by a leading English authority on African affairs.

TALBOT, PERCY AMAURY. **The Peoples of Southern Nigeria.** New York: Oxford University Press, 1926, 4 v.

An extensive historical, ethnological and linguistic study, by one of the foremost authorities.

UTTING, F. A. J. **The Story of Sierra Leone.** London: Longmans, 1931, 178 p.

A convenient handbook of the area.

EAST AFRICA

See also (League of Nations) Mandates, p. 58.

CHURCH, ARCHIBALD GEORGE. **East Africa, a New Dominion.** London: Witherby, 1927, 315 p.

An excellent study of conditions, by a member of the Parliamentary Commission of 1924.

DRIBERG, JACK HERBERT. **The East African Problem.** London: Williams and Norgate, 1930, 96 p.

An eminently fair presentation of the race question, by a trained ethnologist.

HOBLEY, CHARLES WILLIAM. **Kenya. From Chartered Company to Crown Colony.**
London: Witherby, 1929, 256 p.
Reminiscences and observations of thirty years' experience in East Africa. The book has
some good discussion of British policy, the native question, etc.

HUXLEY, JULIAN SORELL. **Africa View.** New York: Harper, 1931, 464 p.
Though this is primarily the travel book of a biologist, the student of international
affairs will find occasional penetrating observations on East African problems.

INGRAMS, WILLIAM HAROLD. **Zanzibar.** London: Witherby, 1931, 527 p.
A good history and description. Written by a British official, this is probably the most
satisfactory modern book on the island.

JARDINE, DOUGLAS. **The Mad Mullah of Somaliland.** London: Jenkins, 1923, 336 p.
A detailed account of British activities in this area from 1899 to the final overthrow
of the Mad Mullah in 1919.

JOELSON, FERDINAND STEPHEN, *comp.* **Eastern Africa Today.** London: East Africa,
1928, 420 p.
A very complete handbook of the British possessions and mandates.

JOELSON, FERDINAND STEPHEN. **The Tanganyika Territory.** London: T. Fisher Unwin,
1920, 256 p.
A competent discussion of conditions and problems. One of the best recent books on
what was formerly German East Africa.

JONES, HERBERT GRESFORD. **Uganda in Transformation.** London: C. M. S., 1927, 270 p.
A missionary's account of the changes since 1876.

KOCH, LUDWIG. **Ostafrika in der Geschichte der Weltwirtschaft.** Berlin: Reimer,
1930, 194 p.
A valuable documented account of life and labor in East Africa before the coming of
the Whites, and of the great changes of the last half century, social as well as economic.

LEYS, NORMAN MACLEAN. **Kenya.** London: Hogarth, 3rd ed., 1926, 425 p.
A severe indictment of existing economic and social conditions in this British Crown
Colony, especially in regard to the exploitation of the natives.

LEYS, NORMAN MACLEAN. **A Last Chance in Kenya.** London: Hogarth, 1931, 173 p.
A new examination of the system of land and labor in Kenya, by a leading pleader
of native claims.

Light and Darkness in East Africa. London: World Dominion Press, 1928, 206 p.
A missionary survey of Uganda, the Sudan, Abyssinia, Eritrea and the Somalilands.

LUGARD, FREDERICK DEALTRY LUGARD, BARON. **The Dual Mandate in British Tropical Africa.** London: Blackwood, 2nd ed., 1923, 643 p.
This volume by a prominent British administrator is one of the most important books
on Africa. Dealing with the British possessions in West, Central and East Africa, the
author discusses in detail the problems of administering tropical lands, the relation
of colonial to home governments, taxation systems, land tenures, slavery and labor
problems, education, trade, justice, missionary work, and other matters.

MIGEOD, FREDERICK WILLIAM HUGH. **Across Equatorial Africa.** London: Heath Cranton, 1923, 397 p.
Economic and ethnographic material.

MITCHELL, NICHOLAS PENDLETON. **Land Problems and Policies in the African Man-
dates of the British Commonwealth.** Baton Rouge: Louisiana State University
Press, 1931, 155 p.
A documented study of an important phase of mandate administration.

PEARCE, FRANCIS BARROW. **Zanzibar.** London: T. Fisher Unwin, 1920, 431 p.
  Written by the British resident at Zanzibar, this is one of the best general surveys of
  the history and present status of the island.

ROSCOE, JOHN. **Twenty-five Years in East Africa.** New York: Macmillan, 1921, 288 p.
  The memoirs and observations of a missionary in East Africa and Uganda. Contains
  much interesting material on conditions and customs.

ROSS, WILLIAM McGREGOR. **Kenya from Within.** London: Allen and Unwin, 1927,
  486 p.
  A documented account of British rule by an official of more than twenty years experience. Very critical of the methods of early settlers and of government policy in the
  matter of native labor.

SHARPE, SIR ALFRED. **The Backbone of Africa.** London: Witherby, 1921, 232 p.
  The former governor of Nyasaland tells of his travels in the eastern parts of Africa
  during the war, and discusses desirable changes in administration.

WELLER, HENRY OWEN. **Kenya without Prejudice.** London: East Africa, 1931, 162 p.
  This volume has little to say about politics, but gives a fair and honest description
  of the country, its advantages and its drawbacks.

UNION OF SOUTH AFRICA

See also (Great Britain) Imperial Relations, p. 231.

ARNDT, ERNST HEINRICH DANIEL. **Banking and Currency Development in South
  Africa, 1652-1927.** Capetown: Juta, 1928, 542 p.
  An authoritative scholarly treatment, the best general work on the subject. Well-
  documented and equipped with an extensive bibliography.

BARNES, LEONARD. **Caliban in Africa.** London: Gollancz, 1930, 245 p.
  An able criticism of White policy and an indictment of "color madness."

BROOKES, EDGAR H. **The History of Native Policy in South Africa.** Pretoria: Van
  Schaik, 2nd ed., 1927, 524 p.
  A scholarly treatment covering the period since 1830. The best systematic account.

BROOKES, EDGAR H. **The Political Future of South Africa.** Pretoria: Van Schaik, 1927,
  99 p.
  A good brief presentation of current problems, written by a liberal professor.

BRUWER, ANDRIES JOHANNES. **Protection in South Africa.** Stellenbosch: Pro Ecclesia,
  1923, 203 p.
  An American dissertation, reviewing the South African tariff system from the earliest
  times to the end of the World War.

BUXTON, SYDNEY CHARLES BUXTON, EARL. **General Botha.** London: Murray, 1923,
  341 p.
  Written by the former Governor-General of South Africa. The book is chiefly a volume
  of personal reminiscences covering the years 1914 to 1919.

CAMACHO, BRITO. **Gente Bóer.** Lisbon: Guimarães, 1930, 233 p.
  A record of travel and observation in the areas inhabited by the Boers.

CAMPBELL, DUGALD. **In the Heart of Bantuland.** London: Seeley Service, 1922, 313 p.
  A study of life and customs based on twenty-nine years of residence among the Bantus.

COLQUHOUIN, MRS. ETHEL (COOKSON). **The Real Rhodesia.** London: Hutchinson, 1924,
  311 p.

An excellent book, by a woman active in South African politics. She recounts the struggle for self-government and surveys the economic and social situation in Rhodesia.

COTTON, WALTER AIDAN. **Racial Segregation in South Africa.** London: Sheldon, 1931, 158 p.
A suggestive though not altogether convincing essay by one who has lived among the natives for twenty years.

DAWSON, WILLIAM HARBUTT. **South Africa. People, Places and Problems.** New York: Longmans, 1926, 448 p.
A satisfactory general treatment.

EDGAR, JOHN. **A History of South Africa.** Oxford: Blackwell, 1923, 239 p.
One of the best introductory surveys of the history of South Africa.

ENGELENBURG, FRANS VREDENRIJK. **General Louis Botha.** London: Harrap, 1929, 352 p.
A somewhat too journalistic series of essays on various aspects of Botha's career.

GOODFELLOW, DAVID MARTIN. **A Modern Economic History of South Africa.** London: Routledge, 1931, 267 p.
The best general treatment of the period since 1892.

HARRIS, JOHN H. **The Chartered Millions.** London: Swarthmore, 1919, 320 p.
An unvarnished, documented account of the development and situation in Rhodesia from a pronouncedly anti-imperialistic standpoint.

HOFMEYR, JAN HENDRIK. **South Africa.** London: Benn, 1931, 331 p.
A volume in the Modern World series, giving an excellent historical survey and an analysis of post-war problems. The author is an educator and member of the Union House of Assembly for Johannesburg.

JABAVU, D. D. T. **The Black Problem.** Cape Province: Lovedale, 1921, 173 p.
A moderate statement of the political, educational, economic and social disabilities of the Blacks in South Africa, by a follower of Booker T. Washington.

JABAVU, D. D. T. **The Segregation Fallacy and Other Papers.** Cape Province: Lovedale, 1928, 137 p.
A defense of the threatened rights of the natives in the South African Union.

KIRK, JOHN. **The Economic Aspects of Native Segregation in South Africa.** London: King, 1929, 148 p.
A defense of what the author defines as "possessory segregation" in contrast to labor segregation.

KOCK, MICHIEL HENDRIK DE. **An Analysis of the Finances of the Union of South Africa.** Capetown: Juta, 1922, 238 p.
A thorough treatment, the outgrowth of an American doctoral dissertation.

LAURENCE, SIR PERCEVAL MAITLAND. **The Life of John Xavier Merriman.** London: Constable, 1930, 428 p.
The authorized biography of a prominent statesman and former prime minister. An important contribution to the recent history of South Africa.

LEHFELDT, ROBERT ALFRED. **The National Resources of South Africa.** London: Longmans, 1922, 79 p.
A brief but reliable survey of prices, industries, trade, etc., by a professor at the University of Johannesburg.

MACMILLAN, WILLIAM MILLER. **Complex South Africa.** London: Faber, 1930, 294 p.
A leading South African authority forcefully presents the economic futility of anti-race legislation. One of the most illuminating treatments of a vexed problem.

MILLIN, MRS. SARAH GERTRUDE. **The South Africans.** New York: Boni and Liveright, 1927, 287 p.
A vivid and sympathetic treatment, by a well-known South African writer. The author discusses the gold and diamond rushes and sketches the European and native types as they are now.

MOLEMA, S. M. **The Bantu, Past and Present.** Edinburgh: Green, 1920, 398 p.
This volume, written by a Bantu, is in part a discussion of contemporary problems, with added historical and ethnographical material on the South African natives.

NARATH, RUDOLF. **Die Union von Südafrika und Ihre Bevölkerung.** Leipzig: Teubner, 1930, 262 p.
A scientific history and analysis of the population of South Africa.

NATHAN, MANFRED. **South Africa from Within.** London: Murray, 1926, 324 p.
An historical survey followed by an analytic study of peoples, government and economic life of the Union.

NATHAN, MANFRED. **The South African Commonwealth.** Johannesburg: Specialty Press, 1919, 483 p.
A general discussion of the political and social problems of the Union; one of the best descriptive studies.

NEAME, LAWRENCE ELWIN. **General Hertzog.** London: Hurst, 1930, 288 p.
An eminently fair, though hardly sympathetic treatment of the Hertzog policies and the Boer viewpoint.

NIELSEN, PETER. **The Black Man's Place in South Africa.** Capetown: Juta, 1923, 149 p.
A discussion of the racial problem. The writer, well acquainted with the Blacks and their language, strongly favors segregation.

OLDHAM, JOSEPH HOULDSWORTH. **White and Black in Africa.** New York: Longmans, 1930, 79 p.
An effective criticism of Smuts's views on the native problem.

OLIVIER, SYDNEY HALDANE OLIVIER, BARON. **The Anatomy of African Misery.** London: Hogarth, 1927, 234 p.
A telling indictment of the racial labor legislation of the various South African states.

PHILLIPS, RAY EDMUND. **The Bantu Are Coming.** London: C. M. S., 1930, 239 p.
The author takes up various phases of the color problem.

SILBURN, PERCY ARTHUR BAXTER. **South Africa White and Black—or Brown?** London: Allen and Unwin, 1927, 192 p.
The author foresees the increase of degenerate Browns and a consequent danger to the development of South Africa; he therefore advocates segregation.

SMITH, EDWIN WILLIAM. **The Way of the White Fields in Rhodesia.** London: World Dominion Press, 1928, 172 p.
A missionary survey, giving a review of the situation in Northern and Southern Rhodesia.

VOIGT, BERNHARD. **Die Buren.** Berlin: Parey, 1930, 256 p.
Really a history of the conquest and colonization of South Africa, with special reference to the vicissitudes of the Boers.

WALKER, ERIC ANDERSON. **A History of South Africa.** New York: Longmans, 1928, 635 p.
A first rate general history. The point of view is commendably broad and the mastery of the material exceptional.

WILLOUGHBY, WILLIAM CHARLES. **Race Problems in the New Africa.** Oxford: Clarendon Press, 1923, 296 p.
A thoughtful and generally reliable work on various aspects of the relations between Whites and Bantus.

IV. FRENCH POSSESSIONS

MEDITERRANEAN AFRICA

General

See also (France) Colonial Questions, p. 270.

COOKSEY, JOSEPH JAMES. **The Land of the Vanished Church.** London: World Dominion Press, n. d., 107 p.
A review of the Christian history of North Africa and the present status of Christian missions.

COSNIER, HENRI CHARLES. **L'Afrique du Nord.** Paris: Larose, 1922, 356 p.
A detailed study of agrarian conditions and possibilities, by the former commissioner-general of agriculture.

CROS, LOUIS. **L'Afrique Française pour Tous.** Paris: Michel, 1928, 656 p.
A popular survey of the French African Empire.

DESLINIÈRES, LUCIEN. **La France Nord-Africaine.** Paris: Progrès Civique, 1920, 723 p.
A critical study of French colonization, followed by an elaborate program of systematic settlement.

FRIBOURG, ANDRÉ. **L'Afrique Latine: Maroc, Algérie, Tunisie.** Paris: Plon, 1922, 96 p.
A survey of the French colonial realm in northern Africa, with emphasis on French accomplishments and on the growing pains noticeable since the war.

GASSER, JULES. **Rôle Social de la France dans l'Afrique du Nord.** Paris: Crès, 1924, 270 p.
A thoroughgoing imperialistic sketch.

GERMAIN, JOSÉ, *pseud.* (JOSÉ GERMAIN DROUILLY) and FAYE, STÉPHANE. **Le Nouveau Monde Français: Maroc, Algérie, Tunisie.** Paris: Plon, 1924, 238 p.
Largely a descriptive survey.

JULIEN, CHARLES ANDRÉ. **Histoire de l'Afrique du Nord.** Paris: Payot, 1931, 866 p.
Beyond question the best history of North Africa yet published. It is scholarly, well-illustrated and equipped with an exhaustive bibliography.

JUNG, EUGÈNE. **L'Islam et les Musulmans dans l'Afrique du Nord.** Paris: La Jeune Parque, 1930, 100 p.
A stimulating essay on the new ferment among the Arabs, by one of the best writers on Islamic problems.

KITAĬGORODSKIĬ, P. and PURETSKIĬ, B. **Alzhir, Tunis, Marokko v Bor'be za Nezavisimost'.** Moscow: Gosizdat, 1925, 100 p.
A popular study of the capitalist oppression of backward populations in North Africa.

MANGIN, JOSEPH ÉMILE. **Regards sur la France d'Afrique.** Paris: Plon, 1924, 308 p.
A collection of speeches and essays by the well-known French general and administrator.

POWELL, EDWARD ALEXANDER. **In Barbary.** New York: Century, 1926, 505 p.
An indefatigable traveller's appreciative if sometimes uncritical survey of conditions in French North Africa.

SICARD, J. **Le Monde Musulman dans les Possessions Françaises.** Paris: Larose, 1928, 240 p.
An important contribution to the understanding of France's colonial problems. Primarily a survey of the present status of Mohammedanism.

SLOANE, WILLIAM MILLIGAN. **Greater France in Africa.** New York: Scribner, 1924, 293 p.
Appreciative observations after an officially-conducted trip through Morocco and Algeria.

STEEG, THÉODORE. **La Paix Française en Afrique du Nord.** Paris: Alcan, 1926, 288 p.
A collection of speeches touching on most contemporary problems of Algeria and Morocco, by the French resident-general.

Algeria and Tunis

See also (Italy) Policy in the Mediterranean and the Levant, p. 285.

ABBAS, FERHAT. **Le Jeune Algérien.** Paris: La Jeune Parque, 1931, 149 p.
A Moslem native outlines a program for the future designed to secure fraternity and social equality for the inhabitants.

BERNARD, AUGUSTIN. **L'Algérie.** Paris: Larousse, 1931, 224 p.
The best historical and descriptive work on Algeria, comparable to the author's splendid survey of Morocco.

BODLEY, R. V. C. **Algeria from Within.** London: Hutchinson, 1927, 320 p.
Probably the most satisfactory general study in English of Algeria, written by a man long resident there.

BONURA, FRANCESCO. **Gli Italiani in Tunisia ed il Problema della Naturalizzazione.** Rome: Tiber, 1929, 176 p.
One of the few good systematic treatments of the serious Franco-Italian problem involved in the nationality conflict in Tunis.

CASSERLY, GORDON. **Algeria To-day.** London: Laurie, 1923, 262 p.
An interesting survey of the development of Algeria under French domination, by a very sympathetic observer.

Collection du Centenaire de l'Algérie. Paris: Alcan, 1928-1931, 18 v.
An excellent series of scholarly studies published in celebration of the centenary of the French occupation. The volumes thus far published, by many different authors, deal with a large variety of topics—natural history, economic life, the history and organization of French rule, colonization, etc.

COMMON, JACQUES. **Le Budget et le Fisc Algériens.** Paris: Presses Modernes, 1929, 252 p.
A good dissertation; the most up-to-date scholarly treatment of Algerian finance and taxation.

DEPONT, OCTAVE. **L'Algérie du Centenaire.** Paris: Sirey, 1928, 214 p.
A centenary volume stressing the accomplishments of the French and the evolution of the native population.

DESFEUILLES, PAUL. **L'Algérie.** Paris: Roger, 1931, 96 p.
Primarily a review of Algerian economic resources and possibilities. Contains an excellent bibliography.

DUMÉNIL, GUY. **La Banque de l'Algérie.** Paris: Boccard, 1927, 322 p.
A doctoral thesis, dealing mainly with the farm credit operations of the Bank.

DUNBAR, IANTHE M. **The Edge of the Desert.** London: Allen, 1923, 148 p.
An interesting description of the manners and customs of Tunis under French rule.

FALCK, FELIX. **Guide Économique de l'Algérie.** Paris: Michel, 1922, 191 p.
A brief popular account, dealing chiefly with agriculture and mining.

FITOUSSI, ÉLIE and BÉNAZET, ARISTIDE. **L'État Tunisien et le Protectorat Français.**
Paris: Rousseau, 1931, 2 v.
A standard study of the historical evolution of Tunis before 1881 and of the organiza-
tion and working of the French protectorate.

GALLICO, AUGUSTO. **Tunisi, i Berberi e l'Italia nei Secoli.** Ancona: La Lucerna, 1928,
274 p.
A well-informed brief survey of Italian relations and interests in Tunis from earliest
times to the present.

GAUTIER, ÉMILE FÉLIX. **L'Algérie et la Métropole.** Paris: Payot, 1920, 254 p.
Studies of the conquest and the evolution of European rule, with an extended discussion of the native question.

GSELL, STÉPHANE, MARÇAIS, GEORGES and YVER, GEORGES. **Histoire d'Algérie.** Paris:
Boivin, 1927, 328 p.
A general historical account from the earliest times, by competent French writers. The
best brief treatment.

HUC, PAUL. **L'Œuvre Politique et Économique du Protectorat Français en Tunisie.**
Toulouse: Imprimerie Régionale, 1924, 368 p.
A substantial doctoral thesis reviewing the financial and judicial reforms and especially
the background of the political reforms of 1922.

MESSERSCHMITT, RAOUL ELISÉE. **Le Régime Douanier et le Commerce Extérieur
de l'Algérie.** Algiers: Imprimerie Algérienne, 1927, 172 p.
A dissertation giving an outline of Algerian trade since earliest times, examining the
present trade system and analyzing French commercial activity since 1900.

MORI, ATTILIO. **La Tunisia.** Rome: Cremonese, 1930, 172 p.
A general historical and descriptive work, useful for the discussion of the position of
the Italians in Tunis.

PIQUET, VICTOR. **L'Algérie Française.** Paris: Colin, 1930, 432 p.
A general review of the century of French rule since the conquest, with special attention to colonization and administration.

PIQUET, VICTOR. **Les Réformes en Algérie.** Paris: Larose, 1919, 207 p.
Primarily a study of the evolution of French native policy and the administration of
the communes.

SAINT GERMÈS, JOSEPH JEAN VIVIEN. **La Banque de l'Algérie et le Crédit pendant
et après la Guerre.** Algiers: Typo-Litho, 1925, 230 p.
A doctoral thesis devoted to a study of the stabilization of the franc and the various
types of credit operations of the Bank.

SARFATTI, MARGHERITA GRASSINI. **Tunisiaca.** Milan: Mondadori, 1924, 109 p.
Essays on Tunisian topics, the most important being those on the Italian colony and
on the Franco-Italian nationality dispute.

SCHMITTHENNER, HEINRICH. **Tunesien und Algerien.** Stuttgart: Strecker, 1924, 174 p.
A competent geographical and ethnographical survey, by a German geographer.

TUMEDEI, CESARE. **La Questione Tunisina e l'Italia.** Bologna: Zanichelli, 1922, 277 p.
A documented study of the dispute from 1896 to 1920, with the texts of most important documents.

VIOLLETTE, MAURICE GABRIEL. **L'Algérie Vivra-t-elle?** Paris: Alcan, 1931, 498 p.
An intensive study of Algerian life and the possibilities of the future, written by a former governor-general.

WINKLER, PIERRE. **Essai sur la Nationalité dans les Protectorats de Tunisie et du Maroc.** Paris: Jouve, 1926, 264 p.
A well-documented dissertation on the vexed problem of nationality in Tunis.

WORSFOLD, WILLIAM BASIL. **France in Tunis and Algeria.** New York: Brentano, 1930, 256 p.
A lively, accurate guide book and descriptive study of the French administrative system. One of the best books in English.

Morocco

General

See also (Spain) Colonial Policy, the War in Morocco, p. 297.

ANCEY, CÉSAR. **Nos Intérêts Économiques au Maroc.** Paris: La Prime, 1920, 157 p.
A good popular survey of organization, resources and developments.

BARTELS, ALBERT. **Auf Eigene Faust.** Leipzig: Koehler, 1925, 191 p.
The thrilling adventures of a German who escaped from French captivity during the war and joined the Arabs in their resistance to French power.

BARTHOU, LOUIS. **La Bataille du Maroc.** Paris: Champion, 1919, 124 p.
A brief popular survey of French action in Morocco, with more than enough emphasis on German machinations.

BARTHOU, LOUIS. **Lyautey et le Maroc.** Paris: Le Petit Parisien, 1931.
A tribute to the labors of the great French administrator.

BECKER, GEORGES. **D'Algésiras au Maroc d'Aujourd'hui.** Paris: Berger-Levrault, 1929, 128 p.
The political, economic and social evolution of Morocco under French rule.

BÈGUE, LÉON. **Le Secret d'une Conquête.** Paris: Tallandier, 1929, 224 p.
The *dessous* of the French action by an author who knows the country well and was associated with Lyautey. Journalistic and impressionistic.

BERNARD, AUGUSTIN. **Le Maroc.** Paris: Alcan, 1931, 481 p.
The seventh edition of what is unquestionably the best general historical and descriptive work on Morocco.

BONNET-DEVILLIERS, RENÉ. **La Guerre du Riff.** Paris: Occitania, 1926, 142 p.
Observations made with the French troops in Morocco.

BRITSCH, AMÉDÉE. **Le Maréchal Lyautey.** Paris: Renaissance du Livre, 1921, 262 p.
A warmly eulogistic review of the Marshal's military and political career, with a detailed bibliography.

CÉLÉRIER, JEAN. **Le Maroc.** Paris: Colin, 1931, 220 p.
A popular descriptive work by a professor at the institute at Rabat.

CHAVAGNES, RENÉ DE. **Le Feu d'Artifice Marocain.** Paris: Delpeuch, 1929, 162 p.
The reverse side of the Moroccan medal. Not a very edifying picture of events.

CLÉRISSE, HENRY. **Album de la Guerre du Rif.** Paris: Desgrandchamps, 1927, 132 p.
Richly illustrated and supplemented with the text of important documents.

COISSAC DE CHAVREBIÈRE. **Histoire du Maroc.** Paris: Payot, 1931, 540 p.
One of the best general surveys of Moroccan history, based upon profound knowledge
of native as well as European sources. Unfortunately it is not documented.

COLLIEZ, ANDRÉ. **Notre Protectorat Marocain.** Paris: Rivière, 1930, 630 p.
An exhaustive study of the French in Morocco, covering the story from 1912 onward,
with much emphasis on economic development.

COLMEL, GÉNÉRAL. **Le Trans-Mauritanien.** Paris: Larose, 1921.
A general discussion of the Moroccan railway problem.

DAMIDAUX, C. **Combats au Maroc.** Paris: Berger-Levrault, 1928, 144 p.
A technical military account of the war in Morocco, covering the period 1925-1926, by a
staff officer.

DESFEUILLES, PAUL. **Le Maroc.** Paris: Roger, 1932.
A popular review of the economic life and resources of present-day Morocco.

DONON, JEAN. **Le Régime Douanier du Maroc et le Développement du Commerce
Marocain.** Paris: Larose, 1920, 177 p.
An excellent documented study. The author, a French official, analyzes the develop-
ment of Moroccan trade and shows the effect of internal as well as foreign customs.

DUBLY, HENRY LOUIS. **Lyautey, le Magicien.** Lille: Bresle, 1931, 479 p.
A detailed account of Lyautey's whole career, with emphasis on his accomplishments
in Morocco.

DU TAILLIS, JEAN. **Le Nouveau Maroc.** Paris: Challamel, 1923, 341 p.
Primarily a study of the organization of the French protectorate, the work of Lyautey
and the pacification.

FORBES, MRS. ROSITA (TORR). **El Raisuni.** London: Butterworth, 1924, 322 p.
The story of the most picturesque of modern Moroccan leaders, as told by himself
to the writer.

GEORGES-GAULIS, BERTHE. **La France au Maroc (L'Œuvre du Général Lyautey).**
Paris: Colin, 1919, 311 p.
An appreciation of the work of Lyautey, by a well-known writer on Moslem countries.

GOULVEN, JOSEPH. **Le Maroc.** Paris: Larose, 2nd ed., 1920, 282 p.
An admirable survey of resources and economic developments in Morocco, by a high
French official.

GOULVEN, JOSEPH. **Traité d'Économie et de Législation Marocaines.** Paris: Rivière,
1921, 2 v.
A standard treatise on the governmental system and policies in Morocco.

GRAUX, LUCIEN. **Le Maroc Économique.** Paris: Champion, 1928, 600 p.
An immense, documented survey, with much statistical material, submitted to the
Ministry of Commerce and Industry.

HARDY, GEORGES and AURÈS, PAUL. **Les Grandes Étapes de l'Histoire du Maroc.**
Paris: Larose, 1921, 134 p.
A popular survey.

HARDY, GEORGES and CÉLÉRIER, JEAN. **Les Grandes Lignes de la Géographie du
Maroc.** Paris: Larose, 1922, 213 p.
The best introductory handbook of Moroccan geography.

HARDY, GEORGES. **Le Maroc.** Paris: Renouard, 1930, 252 p.
A survey of Moroccan history and life, followed by an anthology of extracts from many writers.

HARRIS, WALTER BURTON. **France, Spain and the Rif.** New York: Longmans, 1927, 350 p.
A splendid book on events in Morocco, written by the experienced correspondent of the London *Times*. Easily the best account available in English.

HOWE, MRS. SONIA ELIZABETH. **Lyautey of Morocco.** London: Hodder and Stoughton, 1931, 338 p.
An authorized study which gives a reliable account of Lyautey's career, but lacks the charm of the Maurois biography.

HUBERT-JACQUES, ——. **L'Aventure Riffaine et Ses Dessous Politiques.** Paris: Bossard, 1927, 375 p.
A well-informed, critical account of events and operations from 1922 to 1925, by one long associated with Moroccan affairs.

IAKOVLEV, V. I. **Bor'ba za Marokko.** Leningrad: Gosizdat, 1926, 72 p.
A brief propagandist account of capitalist conflict in Morocco.

KANN, RÉGINALD. **Le Protectorat Marocain.** Paris: Berger-Levrault, 1920, 280 p.
A general popular survey of the pacification of Morocco and the French system, by a journalist and officer well acquainted with conditions.

LADREIT DE LACHARRIÈRE, JACQUES. **La Rêve d'Abd-el-Kerim.** Paris: Peyronnet, 1925, 272 p.
A useful account of post-war events in Morocco, with a consideration of the international aspects of Adb-el-Krim's activities.

LAURE, AUGUSTE MARIE ÉMILE. **La Victoire Franco-Espagnol dans le Rif.** Paris: Plon, 1927, 272 p.
The campaign journal of one of Pétain's staff officers; a valuable military study of the operations of 1925-1926.

LECLERC, MAX. **Au Maroc avec Lyautey.** Paris: Colin, 1927, 134 p.
A history of the critical period in 1921, by one of Lyautey's close friends.

LÓPEZ RIENDA, RAFAEL. **Marruecos, Abd-el Krim contra Francia.** Madrid: Talleres, 1925, 366 p.
Impressions of a Spanish journalist.

LYAUTEY, LOUIS HUBERT GONZALVE. **Paroles d'Action.** Paris: Colin, 1927, 480 p.
Interesting and instructive papers of a famous administrator, covering his work in Madagascar, Oran and Morocco.

MAESTRACCI, NOËL. **Le Maroc Contemporaine.** Paris: Charles-Lavauzelle, 1928, 227 p.
A brief handbook and guide designed for the use of French officers.

MAGRINI, LUCIANO. **Marocco.** Milan: La Promotrice, 1926, 236 p.
A leading Italian journalist's letters from Morocco in the summer of 1925, with a study of the situation in the Rif.

MARTIN, ALFRED GEORGES PAUL. **Le Maroc et l'Europe.** Paris: Leroux, 1928, 146 p.
A splendid survey covering the past twenty-five years and stressing the international negotiations of 1927-1928 between France and Spain.

MARTIN, ALFRED GEORGES PAUL. **Quatre Siècles d'Histoire Marocaine.** Paris: Alcan, 1923, 591 p.
Covers the period 1504-1902 in the Sahara, but only the years 1894 to 1912 in Morocco. An important account, based in part on native sources.

MARTINOT, A. **Les Délires de l'Impérialisme et les Folies Marocaines.** Paris: Figuière, 1925, 219 p.
A collection of material calculated to deflate the extravagant accounts of French achievement in Morocco.

MAUROIS, ANDRÉ. **Lyautey.** New York: Appleton, 1931, 369 p.
The career of the great French administrator, interestingly pictured by a popular biographer. Based in part on unpublished material made available to the author by Lyautey.

NAHON, MOÏSE. **Propos d'un Vieux Marocain.** Paris: Larose, 1930, 264 p.
A collection of stimulating and original articles dealing with the Moroccan mentality, problems of colonization, administration and adjustment.

NATAF, F. **Le Crédit et la Banque au Maroc.** Paris: Geuthner, 1929, 217 p.
A substantial dissertation on the position and credit operations of the Bank.

NEUMANN, KURT. **Die Internationalität Marokkos.** Berlin: Der Neue Orient, 1919, 291 p.
A careful, documented history of Morocco with emphasis on its international status and relations with foreign powers.

O'CONNOR, VINCENT CLARENCE SCOTT. **A Vision of Morocco.** London: Butterworth, 1923, 377 p.
A travel book that has much to say of the political and military situation, the Tangier question, etc.

ODINOT, PAUL. **Le Monde Marocain.** Paris: Rivière, 1926, 258 p.
A semi-popular sociological and descriptive study.

PIQUET, VICTOR. **Le Maroc.** Paris: Colin, 1920, 484 p.
Another good general book. The emphasis is on geography, history and the French administrative organization.

PIQUET, VICTOR. **Le Peuple Marocain; Le Bloc Berbère.** Paris: Larose, 1925, 320 p.
An important ethnographical contribution.

La Renaissance du Maroc. Rabat: Résidence Générale, 1922, 495 p.
A collection of articles on many aspects of the first decade of the French protectorate.

ROGER-MATHIEU, J., *ed.* **Mémoires d'Abd-el-Krim.** Paris: Librairie des Champs Élysées, 1927, 243 p.
The Riffian leader's autobiography, as told to the editor on the eve of his exile.

ROUX, PIERRE DE. **La Réforme Monétaire au Maroc.** Paris: Presses Universitaires, 1928, 201 p.
A scholarly dissertation reviewing the monetary and banking history of Morocco, with special reference to the reforms of 1920 and the introduction of the franc.

SHEEAN, VINCENT. **An American among the Riffi.** New York: Century, 1926, 345 p.
A visit to Abd-el-Krim and the Rif at the height of the war with the Spaniards and French.

TARDE, ALFRED DE. **Le Maroc École d'Énergie.** Paris: Plon, 1923, 127 p.
A sympathetic study of the results of the French occupation for both Morocco and France.

TERHORST, BERND. **With the Riff Kabyles.** London: Arrowsmith, 1926, 237 p.
Descriptive studies of Northern Africa and the Rif, by a sympathizer with the Arabs.

TERRIER, AUGUSTE. **Le Maroc.** Paris: Larousse, 1931, 224 p.
A beautifully illustrated descriptive work, written by a French colonial authority.

VAULANDE, RENÉ. **Au Maroc. Sous les Ordres de Lyautey.** Paris: Peyronnet, 1926, 224 p.
Chiefly personal reminiscences.

WIRTH, ALBRECHT. **Der Kampf um Marokko.** Munich: Einhorn, 1925, 204 p.
A useful recapitulation of the Moroccan question in its international and diplomatic aspects.

Tangier Problem

BALDONI, C. **La Zona di Tangeri nel Diritto Internazionale e nel Diritto Marocchino.** Padua: C. E. D. A. M., 1931, 55 p.
A technical legal study of the status of Tangier.

BRAGADIN, LIVIO. **Tangeri.** Rome: Porta, 1927, 86 p.
An Italian analysis, with particular reference to recent agreements.

GRAEVENITZ, KURT FRITZ HERMANN ALFRED RICHARD. **Die Tanger Frage.** Berlin: Dümmler, 1925, 85 p.
An able examination.

RAYMOND, CHARLES. **Le Statut de Tanger; Son Passé, Son Avenir.** Algiers, Typo-Litho, 1927, 193 p.
A thoroughly documented dissertation, giving the historical background of the agreement of 1923 and examining its terms and working.

ROUARD DE CARD, EDGARD. **Le Statut de Tanger.** Paris: Pedone, 1925, 90 p.
An historical outline, followed by a competent analysis of the settlement of December 1923.

RUIZ ALBÉNIZ, VICTOR. **Tánger y la Colaboración Franco-Española en Marruecos.** Madrid: Sáez, 1927, 150 p.
A review of Spanish relations with France, together with an able defense of Spanish action and claims, especially as regards Tangier.

STUART, GRAHAM HENRY. **The International City of Tangier.** Stanford: Stanford University Press, 1931, 323 p.
An up-to-date treatment of one of the oldest and most difficult problems of international administration. This is easily the best scholarly study of the history of the Tangier question and of the existing arrangement.

Tanger et Sa Zone. Paris: Leroux, 1921, 463 p.
A complete survey of the ethnography, history, religions, resources, etc., of the Tangier area. This is Volume VII of the series "Villes et Tribus du Maroc," published by the French administration in Morocco.

WEST AND CENTRAL AFRICA

See also (League of Nations) Mandates, p. 58.

ABADIE, MAURICE. **La Colonie du Niger.** Paris: Société d'Éditions Géographiques, 1927, 466 p.
An exhaustive scholarly survey of Upper Nigeria—the land, the people, the government, economic possibilities, etc.

ABADIE, MAURICE. **Nos Richesses Soudanaises et le Chemin de Fer Transsaharien.** Paris: Société d'Éditions Géographiques, 1928, 78 p.
A plea for a railway across the Sahara.

L'Afrique Équatoriale Française. Paris: La Vie Technique, 1927, 120 p.
A general survey, published under the auspices of the colonial government.

BECKER, GEORGES. **La Pénétration Française au Sahara.** Paris: Berger-Levrault, 1928, 88 p.
The author is concerned chiefly with the possibility of a Trans-Saharan railway, which he considers highly desirable.

BOUCHET, M. A. **Le Commerce de l'Afrique Occidentale Française.** Villefranche: Réveil du Beaujolais, 1921, 184 p.
A thin and rather unsatisfactory dissertation, but useful for want of something better.

BRUEL, GEORGES. **L'Afrique Équatoriale Française.** Paris: Larose, 1930, 256 p.
A descriptive work, by a French administrator. The book has good chapters on administration and resources.

BUCHANAN, ANGUS. **Out of the World North of Nigeria.** London: Murray, 1921, 258 p.
Adventures and observations during the exploration of Aïr.

CAMERON, DONALD ROBERT GRANT. **A Saharan Venture.** London: Arnold, 1928, 314 p.
Observations and records of a journey through the Central Sahara.

CHAZELAS, VICTOR. **Territoires Africains sous Mandat de la France: Cameroun et Togo.** Paris: Société d'Éditions Géographiques, 1931, 240 p.
A general survey of the Cameroons and Togo, prepared with the aid of official documents for the great Colonial Exposition.

COSNIER, HENRI CHARLES. **L'Ouest Africain Français.** Paris: Larose, 1921, 253 p.
A valuable study of the economic possibilities of West Africa, and especially of agrarian conditions.

COSTEDOAT, RENÉ. **Le Mandat Français et la Réorganisation des Territoires du Cameroun.** Besançon: Jacques, 1930, 288 p.
The most extensive treatment of the French mandate. A dissertation dealing largely with the social and economic policy of the mandatory power.

DELAVIGNETTE, ROBERT. **Afrique Occidentale Française.** Paris: Société d'Éditions Géographiques, 1931, 244 p.
A beautifully illustrated descriptive survey, published by the commission of the Colonial Exposition in Paris.

FERJUS, SAMUEL. **La Mise en Valeur du Togo sous Mandat Français.** Paris: Presses Modernes, 1926, 119 p.
A slight dissertation, devoted chiefly to a study of the land problem and the question of native labor.

FERRANDI, JEAN. **Le Centre-Africain Français: Tchad, Borkou, Ennedi.** Paris: Lavauzelle, 1930, 251 p.
The story of the exploration and pacification of the Lake Chad and Eastern Saharan areas.

FOCK, ANDREAS. **Le Chemin de Fer Transsaharien.** Paris: Société d'Éditions Géographiques, 1929, 188 p.
A complete historical and analytical study, with full consideration of routes, expense, probable returns, etc.

FRANCESCHI, ROGER. **Le Mandat Français au Cameroun.** Paris: Sirey, 1929, 285 p.
This dissertation reviews the conditions in the Cameroons under German rule, the history of the colony during the war, the mandatory administration, and the French achievement.

GAUTIER, ÉMILE FELIX. **Le Sahara.** Paris: Payot, 1923, 172 p.
A brief, popular description by the foremost French authority.

GILLIER, L. **La Pénétration en Mauritanie.** Paris: Geuthner, 1926, 359 p.
A history of the exploration and pacification of the western Saharan tribes, by a French officer.

GUEYE, LAMINE. **De la Situation Politique des Sénégalais.** Paris: La Vie Universitaire, 1922, 105 p.
An historical sketch of French native policy in Senegal, and especially of the laws of 1915-1916.

Guide de la Colonisation au Cameroun. Paris: Larose, 1923, 170 p.
An official handbook which gives a reliable survey of administration, transport, agriculture, trade and general conditions of life.

HAARDT, GEORGES MARIE and AUDOUIN-DUBREUIL, LOUIS. **La Première Traversée du Sahara en Automobile.** Paris: Plon, 1923, 307 p.
A well-illustrated record of the famous Citroën expedition.

HILAIRE, JEAN. **Du Congo au Nil.** Paris: Ficker, 1931, 350 p.
The account of a five years' stay in the Wadai region.

MAIGRET, JULIEN. **Afrique Équatoriale Française.** Paris: Société d'Éditions Géographiques, 1931, 220 p.
One of the admirable descriptive studies prepared for the Colonial Exposition.

MAXWELL, J. LOWRY. **Nigeria. The Land, the People and Christian Progress.** New York: World Dominion Press, n. d., 164 p.
One of the excellent missionary surveys published in the World Dominion series.

MOULY, J. **L'Afrique Équatoriale Française.** Toulouse: 1921, 98 p.
A slight doctoral thesis reviewing the history, administration and economic life of the French Congo.

NIEGER, J. **Mission du Transafricain.** Paris: Société d'Éditions Géographiques, 1924-1925, 2 v.
The elaborate technical reports of the mission sent out by the Société d'Études du Chemin de Fer Transafricain to investigate the feasibility of a railroad.

PAULIN, HONORÉ. **Le Domaine Extérieur de la France; Afrique Équatoriale Française.** Paris: Eyrolles, 1923, 101 p.
A brief popular survey of the French Congo.

PELLERAY, EMMANUEL. **L'Afrique Occidentale Française.** Paris: Notre Domaine Colonial, 1923, 132 p.
A good sketch of economic and administrative problems and achievements.

PROUST, LOUIS. **Visions d'Afrique.** Paris: Quillet, 1924, 266 p.
A survey of the French possessions in West Africa, of the native races, of economic possibilities, etc.

RODD, FRANCIS JAMES RENNELL. **People of the Veil.** New York: Macmillan, 1926, 504 p.
A valuable detailed study of the organization and customs of the Tuareg tribes of the Central Sahara.

ROUARD DE CARD, EDGARD. **Les Mandats Français sur le Togoland, et le Cameroun.** Paris: Pedone, 1924, 76 p.
A concise, competent statement of the French position and organization in the mandated territories.

SABATIÉ, ALEXANDRE CAMILLE. **Le Sénégal, Sa Conquête et Son Organisation, 1364-1925.** Saint-Louis: Imprimerie du Gouvernement, 1925, 435 p.
The best general history of one of the oldest French establishments.

Salvati, Cesare. **Italia e Francia nel Sahara Orientale.** Milan: Libreria d'Italia, 1929, 190 p.
The growing rivalry between the two countries in the hinterland of Tripoli.

Vermale, Paul. **Au Sahara pendant la Guerre Européenne.** Paris: Larose, 1926, 221 p.
The notes and letters of a French commander who travelled through much of the Sahara.

EAST AFRICA AND MADAGASCAR

Catat, Paul. **L'Activité Bancaire à Madagascar.** Paris: Jouve, 1928, 152 p.
An undocumented dissertation describing the four chief banks of Madagascar and their operations, as well as their general rôle in the development of the island.

Dandouau, A. **Géographie de Madagascar.** Paris: Larose, 1922, 243 p.
An economic as well as a physical and political geography. A scholarly survey of the island.

Delélée-Desloges, Jules Gaston. **Madagascar et Dépendances.** Paris: Société d'Éditions Géographiques, 1931, 240 p.
One of the beautiful descriptive studies published for the Colonial Exposition.

Foucque, Hippolyte, Barquissau, Raphaël and others. **L'Île de la Réunion.** Paris: Larose, 1925, 242 p.
An authoritative general survey, historical and descriptive.

Grandidier, Guillaume. **Gallieni.** Paris: Plon, 1931, 264 p.
This study of Gallieni deals primarily with his work in colonial administration.

Grandidier, Guillaume. **Le Myre de Vilers, Duchesne, Gallieni. Quarante Années de l'Histoire de Madagascar, 1880-1920.** Paris: Société d'Éditions Géographiques, 1923, 252 p.
A scholarly study of the establishment of French rule, by the leading authority on Madagascan history.

Guilloteaux, Erique. **Madagascar et la Côte des Somalis, Sainte-Marie et les Seychelles; Leur Rôle et Leur Avenir.** Paris: Perrin, 1922, 294 p.
Enthusiastic travel impressions.

Guy, Canulle. **L'Afrique Orientale Française.** Paris: Larose, 1929, 208 p.
A general descriptive account, by a former French governor.

Hachette, René and Ginestou, J. **Djibouti; et, Les Possessions Françaises de l'Inde.** Paris: Redier, 1930, 159 p.
A popular, well-illustrated descriptive work on French Somaliland and the Indian posts.

Nemours, Charles Philippe, Duc de. **Madagascar et Ses Richesses.** Paris: Roger, 1930, 294 p.
A useful, semi-popular survey.

Olivier, Marcel. **Six Ans de Politique Sociale à Madagascar.** Paris: Grasset, 1931, 279 p.
Written by a former governor-general; a study primarily of the problems of agricultural and native labor.

Osborn, Chase Salmon. **Madagascar.** New York: Republic Publishing Company, 1924, 443 p.
One of the best books in English, both historical and descriptive in scope. The author is critical of French policy and administration.

PAULIN, HONORÉ. **Madagascar.** Paris: Eyrolles, 1925, 119 p.
A survey of the island; largely a technical review of geographic factors and economic resources.

SIBREE, JAMES. **Fifty Years in Madagascar.** London: Allen, 1924, 359 p.
In a sense the book is a history of Protestant missionary enterprise in the last half century. Written by one of the leading authorities on Madagascar.

THOREL, JEAN. **La Mise en Valeur des Richesses Économiques de Madagascar.** Paris: Presses Modernes, 1927, 228 p.
The best parts of this dissertation are those surveying the resources of the island, and the railroad, port and other facilities.

YOU, ANDRÉ. **Madagascar.** Paris: Société d'Éditions Géographiques, 1931, 556 p.
The author, a high French colonial official, describes the country and discusses in detail the system and problems of administration. The best French handbook.

V. ITALIAN POSSESSIONS

See also (Italy) Foreign and Colonial Policies, p. 283.

AGOSTINO ORSINI, PAOLO D'. **La Nostra Economia Coloniale.** Salerno: Manzoni, 1923, 313 p.
A study of the possibilities and conditions of economic exploitation in Eritrea, Tripoli and Somaliland.

AGOSTINO ORSINI, PAOLO D'. **L'Italia nella Politica Affricana.** Bologna: Cappelli, 1926, 225 p.
A reconsideration of Italy's past policy and present position.

BARTOLOTTI, DOMENICO. **Il Passato e l'Avvenire de la Tripolitania.** Turin: Lattes, 1919, 205 p.
A general outline of Tripoli's past, with emphasis on the Italian conquest.

BATTISTELLI, V. **Affrica Italiana.** Florence: Bemporad, 1930, 261 p.
A general descriptive account, with many good photographic illustrations.

CANTALUPO, ROBERTO. **L'Italia Musulmana.** Rome: La Voce, 1928, 434 p.
A general discussion of Italian expansion, of conditions in Eritrea and Libya, of the general problem of Christianity and Islam in Africa and the Near East, and of the desirability of revising the mandates. The author was formerly Italian Under-Secretary for the Colonies.

CAROSELLI, FRANCESCO SAVERIO. **Ferro e Fuoco in Somalia.** Rome: Sindacato Italiano Arti Grafiche, 1931, 333 p.
The story of the long-drawn struggle of the British and Italians against the Mad Mullah of Somaliland.

CIARLANTINI, FRANCO and CUESTA, UGO. **Antologia Coloniale.** Rome: Augustea, 1929, 302 p.
The Italian colonial movement, colonial campaigns, and the colonies themselves, described in numerous short extracts from authoritative writers.

GIACCONE, EDGARDO. **Le Colonie d'Italia.** Turin: Bocca, 1930, 220 p.
A brief, semi-popular historical account, with a discussion of the geography of the different colonies.

Il Governo Fascista nelle Colonie. Milan: Ghidoni, 1925, 43 p.
A severe criticism of the Fascist government in Somaliland, Eritrea and Libya.

LAURO, RAFFAELE DI. **Tripolitania.** Naples: Chiurazzi, 1932, 250 p.
An up-to-date descriptive work.

MANDOSIO, M. **La Tripolitania d'Oggi.** Milan: Ceschina, 1929, 300 p.
A good descriptive work, stressing the recent changes and the pacification.

Oltre Giuba. Rome: Sindacato Italiano Arti Grafiche, n. d., 370 p.
Published by the Italian Ministry for Colonies. A detailed description of the territory ceded by Great Britain in 1924, and its inhabitants.

Per le Nostre Colonie. Florence: Vallecchi, 1927, 284 p.
A collection of essays by Italian authorities, dealing primarily with agricultural and colonization problems in the African possessions.

PETRAGNANI, ENRICO **Il Sahara Tripolitano.** Rome: Sindacato Italiano Arti Grafiche, 1928, 516 p.
A detailed description of the Tripolitan Sahara, its peoples, customs, etc., together with a narrative of the author's imprisonment by the natives.

RAVIZZA, ADALGISO. **La Libia nel Suo Ordinamento Giuridico.** Padua: Milani, 1931, 377 p.
An authoritative scholarly treatment of the organization and functioning of the Italian administration in all its aspects.

La Rinascita della Tripolitania. Milan: Mondadori, 1926, 586 p.
An elaborately illustrated review of Count Volpi's governorship. Various contributors discuss in detail the country and people, the Italian operations of 1921-1925, the new organization and reforms, the economic possibilities, etc.

STEFANINI, GIUSEPPE. **I Possedimenti Italiani in Affrica.** Florence: Bemporad, 1929, 276 p.
The revised edition of a convenient handbook on Libya, Eritrea and Somaliland.

TERUZZI, ATTILIO. **Cirenaica Verde.** Milan: Mondadori, 1931, 372 p.
A record of Fascist accomplishment during the years 1927-1928.

Il Valore Economica delle Colonie Italiane. Trieste: La Vedetta Italiana, 1928, 213 p.
A series of authoritative lectures delivered at the Associazione Coloniale Triestina in 1926.

VIRGILII, FILIPPO. **Le Colonie Italiane.** Milan: Hoepli, 1927, 242 p.
A popular survey of the history and present status of Italy's colonial possessions.

WIGHTWICK HAYWOOD, CECIL WALTER INGLEFIELD. **To the Mysterious Lorian Swamp.** London: Seeley Service, 1927, 275 p.
A record of travel and exploration in unknown parts of Jubaland.

VI. BELGIAN POSSESSIONS

See also (League of Nations) Mandates, p. 58.

BARNS, THOMAS ALEXANDER. **An African Eldorado.** London: Methuen, 1926, 245 p.
A superior travel book, containing much of interest on contemporary conditions in the Congo.

DAYE, PIERRE. **L'Empire Colonial Belge.** Brussels: Éditions du Soir, 1923, 669 p.
One of the most extensive surveys of conditions, accomplishments and problems under Belgian rule.

DAYE, PIERRE. **Congo et Angola.** Brussels: Renaissance du Livre, 1929.
Further records of travel and investigation.

DELCOMMUNE, ALEXANDRE. **L'Avenir du Congo Belge Menacé.** Brussels: Lebègue,
2nd ed., 1921, 2 v.
A detailed critical review of the first ten years of direct Belgian administration, with
special reference to land and labor problems.

FRANCK, LOUIS. **Le Congo Belge.** Brussels: Renaissance du Livre, 1928, 2 v.
A beautiful, lavishly illustrated work by a former Belgian Minister for Colonies. The
book contains historical, descriptive and analytical articles on all phases of Congo
problems, mostly by men directly connected with the building and administration of
the state.

FRANCK, LOUIS. **Congo. Land en Volk.** Bruges: Centrale Boekhandel, 1926, 344 p.
An authoritative general survey, by a former Belgian Minister of Colonies.

HABRAN, LOUIS. **Coup d'Oeil sur le Problème Politique et Militaire du Congo
Belge.** Brussels: De Wit, 1925, 173 p.
An authoritative sketch of the international aspects of the Belgian possessions.

HABRAN, LOUIS. **La Politique Extérieure du Congo Belge.** Brussels: Weverbergh, 1928.
A concise history of the Congo question from the beginning to the present time.

JADOT, J. M. **Blancs et Noirs au Congo Belge.** Brussels: Revue Sincère, 1930, 271 p.
A competent discussion of the color problem, by a Congo magistrate.

KEITH, ARTHUR BERRIEDALE. **The Belgian Congo and the Berlin Act.** Oxford: Clarendon Press, 1919, 344 p.
A dispassionate, scholarly account of the evolution of the Congo problem in its domestic and international aspects. The author, a leading Orientalist, has often been sent
on missions by the British Colonial Office, and has written extensively on philosophical,
legal and constitutional matters.

LÉGER, L. TH. **Du Tanganika à l'Atlantique.** Brussels: De Wit, 1921, 156 p.
Travel impressions in the Congo, with much discussion of Belgian efforts at development.

MICHIELS, A. and LANDE, N. **Notre Colonie.** Brussels: De Wit, 1923.
The sixth edition of one of the best general historic and geographic surveys.

PIRENNE, JACQUES. **Coup d'Oeil sur l'Histoire du Congo.** Brussels: Lamertin, 1921,
73 p.
A very brief but well-informed sketch of Congo history.

ROBERT, MAURICE. **Le Centre Africain.** Brussels: Lamertin, 1932, 262 p.
A valuable compendium of information on the Congo basin, treating mineral resources
fully, especially copper, also agricultural and forestry resources and communications.

SALKIN, PAUL. **Études Africaines.** Paris: Challamel, 1920, 413 p.
A series of studies by a Belgian judge, dealing chiefly with the fundamental problems
of colonization, the native question, and the governmental system of the Congo.

VERLAINE, LOUIS. **Notre Colonie; Contribution à la Recherche de la Méthode de
Colonisation.** Brussels: Denis, 1923, 2 v.
A general study of problems of educating the native, based more especially on in-
vestigations in the Belgian Congo.

WAUTERS, JOSEPH. **Le Congo au Travail.** Brussels: L'Eglantine, 1926, 221 p.
The second edition of a book by one of the great authorities on the history and problems of the Congo. An admirable review of contemporary conditions in the colony.

VII. PORTUGUESE POSSESSIONS

See also Portugal, p. 299.

BARNS, THOMAS ALEXANDER. **Angolan Sketches.** London: Methuen, 1928, 206 p.
    The book consists largely of travel narrative but contains much of interest regarding present conditions.

FERREIRA PINTO, JÚLIO. **Angola.** Lisbon: Rodrigues, 1926, 558 p.
    The best detailed up-to-date handbook of Angola, with full discussion of land and labor problems, native policy, administrative organization, etc.

MARQUARDSEN, HUGO. **Angola.** Berlin: Reimer, 1920, 134 p.
    A scholarly, documented review of the land and the people.

MATOS, NORTON DE. **Á Província de Angola.** Lisbon: Maranus, 1926, 391 p.
    A history of the colony, with extended discussion of present problems, especially economic.

RATES, J. CARLOS. **Angola, Moçambique, S. Tomé.** Lisbon: Didot, 1929, 226 p.
    A good, well-illustrated descriptive survey of the Portuguese possessions in Africa.

STATHAM, JOHN CHARLES BARRON. **Through Angola.** London: Blackwood, 1922, 388 p.
    Travel observations, followed by a detailed historical and descriptive study of the colony, and some discussion of its economic potentialities.

INDEX TO AUTHORS